The Art and Science of Logic

Daniel Bonevac
UNIVERSITY OF TEXAS AT AUSTIN

Mayfield Publishing Company
MOUNTAIN VIEW, CALIFORNIA

Library of Congress Cataloging-in-Publication Data

Bonevac, Daniel A., 1955–
    The art and science of logic/Daniel Bonevac.
        p.   cm.
    Bibliography: p.
    Includes index.
    ISBN 0-87484-805-9
    1. Logic.   I. Title.
BC71.B59   1990   89-35191
160—dc20   CIP

Quotations from Berton Roueche, "A Pinch of Dust," appeared in *Eleven Blue Men* (Boston: Little, Brown and Company, 1953), and in *Medical Detectives II* (New York: Washington Square Press, 1986), pp. 61, 66–67. Reprinted by permission of Harold Ober Associates, Incorporated. Copyright 1951, 1979 by Berton Roueche. First published in *The New Yorker*.

Manufactured in the United States of America
10 9 8 7 6 5 4 3 2 1

Mayfield Publishing Company
1240 Villa Street
Mountain View, California 94041

Sponsoring editor, James Bull; managing editor, Linda Toy; copy editor, Antonio Padial; text designer, Joe di Chiarro; cover designer, Jeanne M. Schreiber; cover art, *Ocean Park No. 140* by Richard Diebenkorn, from the Collection of Douglas S. Cramer. The text was set in 10/12 Times Roman by Syntax International and printed on 50# Finch Opaque by R. R. Donnelley & Sons.

DEDUCTION RULES (Chapters 8 and 13)

SENTENTIAL RULES

BASIC RULES

RULES APPLYING ONLY TO ENTIRE FORMULAS

Assumption

n. $\mathcal{A}$ A

Simplification (S)

n. $\underline{\mathcal{A}\ \&\ \mathcal{B}}$

n + m. $\mathcal{A}$ (or $\mathcal{B}$)   S, n

Conjunction (C)

n. $\mathcal{A}$

m. $\underline{\mathcal{B}}$

p. $\mathcal{A}\ \&\ \mathcal{B}$ C, n, m

Consequent Conjunction (CC)

n. $\mathcal{A} \rightarrow \mathcal{B}$

m. $\underline{\mathcal{A} \rightarrow \mathcal{C}}$

p. $\mathcal{A} \rightarrow (\mathcal{B}\ \&\ \mathcal{C})$ CC, n, m

Modus Ponens (MP)

n. $\mathcal{A} \rightarrow \mathcal{B}$

m. $\underline{\mathcal{A}}$

p. $\mathcal{B}$ MP, n, m

Self Implication (SI)

n. $\mathcal{A} \rightarrow \mathcal{A}$ SI

Addition (Ad)

n. $\underline{\mathcal{A}}$ (or $\mathcal{B}$)

n + p. $\mathcal{A} \lor \mathcal{B}$ Ad, n

Constructive Dilemma (CD)

n. $\mathcal{A} \lor \mathcal{B}$

m. $\mathcal{A} \rightarrow \mathcal{C}$

p. $\underline{\mathcal{B} \rightarrow \mathcal{D}}$

q. $\mathcal{C} \lor \mathcal{D}$ CD, n, m, p

INVERTIBLE RULES

Double Negation (DN)

n. $\underline{\underline{\mathcal{A}}}$ DN, m

m. $\neg\neg\mathcal{A}$ DN, n

Biconditional (B)

n. $\underline{\underline{\mathcal{A} \leftrightarrow \mathcal{B}}}$ B, m

m. $(\mathcal{A} \rightarrow \mathcal{B})\ \&\ (\mathcal{B} \rightarrow \mathcal{A})$ B, n

Commutativity of Disjunction (Cm)

n. $\underline{\underline{\mathcal{A} \lor \mathcal{B}}}$ Cm, m

m. $\mathcal{B} \lor \mathcal{A}$ Cm, n

Associativity of Disjunction (As)

n. $\underline{(\mathcal{A} \lor \mathcal{B}) \lor \mathcal{C}}$ As, m

m. $\mathcal{A} \lor (\mathcal{B} \lor \mathcal{C})$ As, n

DeMorgan's Law #1 (DM)

n. $\underline{\neg(\mathcal{A}\ \&\ \mathcal{B})}$ DM, m

m. $\neg\mathcal{A} \lor \neg\mathcal{B}$ DM, n

DeMorgan's Law #2 (DM)

n. $\underline{\neg(\mathcal{A} \lor \mathcal{B})}$ DM, m

m. $\neg\mathcal{A}\ \&\ \neg\mathcal{B}$ DM, n

Material Conditional (MC)

n. $\underline{\underline{\mathcal{A} \rightarrow \mathcal{B}}}$ MC, m

m. $\neg\mathcal{A} \lor \mathcal{B}$ MC, n

CONTENTS

Preface ix

PART I REASONING AND LANGUAGE 1

1. Truth and Validity 2

1.1 Arguments 3
1.2 Recognizing Arguments 6
1.3 Good Arguments 17
1.4 Reliability 20
1.5 Implication and Equivalence 24
1.6 Logical Properties of Sentences 29

2. Evidence and Relevance 37

2.1 Begging the Question 38
2.2 Complex Questions 43
2.3 Relevance: Refutations 46
2.4 Relevance: Confusing the Issue 56

3. Grounding 62

3.1 Appeals to Emotion 64
3.2 Practical Fallacies 69
3.3 Superficiality 78

4. Meaning 90

4.1 Equivocation 90
4.2 Amphiboly 93
4.3 Accent 99
4.4 Composition and Division 101
4.5 Traditional Criteria for Definitions 104

PART II SENTENTIAL LOGIC 113

5. Sentences 114

5.1 Sentence Connectives 114
5.2 A Sentential Language 117
5.3 Truth Functions 121
5.4 Symbolization 125
5.5 Validity 133

6. Truth Tables 139

6.1 Truth Tables for Formulas 139
6.2 Other Uses of Truth Tables 145

7. Semantic Tableaux 155

7.1 Rules for Negation, Conjunction, and Disjunction 160
7.2 Rules for the Conditional and Biconditional 167
7.3 Decision Procedures 172

8. Deduction 186

8.1 Proofs 186
8.2 Conjunction and Negation Rules 188
8.3 Conditional and Biconditional Rules 193
8.4 Disjunction Rules 197
8.5 Rules of Definition 201
8.6 Derived Rules 208
8.7 Indirect Proof 225

PART III PREDICATE LOGIC 229

9. Syllogisms 230

9.1 Categorical Sentences 231
9.2 Diagramming Categorical Sentence Forms 236
9.3 Immediate Inference 242
9.4 Syllogisms 253
9.5 Rules for Validity 263
9.6 Expanding the Aristotelian Language 276

10. Quantifiers 289

10.1 Constants and Quantifiers 290
10.2 Categorical Sentence Forms 294
10.3 Polyadic Predicates 298
10.4 The Language QL 303

11. Symbolization 311

11.1 Noun Phrases **311**
11.2 Verb Phrases **322**
11.3 Definitions **331**

12. Quantified Tableaux 340

12.1 Quantifier Tableau Rules **340**
12.2 Strategies **344**

13. Quantified Deduction 358

13.1 Deduction Rules for Quantifiers **358**
13.2 Universal Generalization **366**
13.3 Formulas with Overlapping Quantifiers **372**
13.4 Quantifiers and Connectives **376**

PART IV INDUCTIVE REASONING 393

14. Generalizations 394

14.1 Inductive Reliability **395**
14.2 Enumeration **398**
14.3 Evaluating Enumerations **400**
14.4 Statistical Generalizations **403**
14.5 Analogies **412**

15. Causes 425

15.1 Kinds of Causes **425**
15.2 Agreement and Difference **431**
15.3 Residues and Concomitant Variation **440**
15.4 Causal Fallacies **447**

16. Explanations 450

16.1 Explanations and Hypothetical Reasoning **450**
16.2 Scientific Theories **458**
16.3 Evaluating Explanations **464**

APPENDIX I DEDUCTION: STYLE TWO 472

A: Sentential Logic 472

A.1 Proofs **472**
A.2 Conjunction and Negation Rules **475**

A.3 Conditional and Biconditional Rules **481**
A.4 Disjunction Rules **484**
A.5 Derived Rules **486**

B. Adding Quantifiers 501

B.1 Deduction Rules for Quantifiers **501**
B.2 Universal Generalization **506**
B.3 Formulas with Overlapping Quantifiers **508**
B.4 Derived Rules for Quantifiers **512**

APPENDIX **II** DEDUCTION: STYLE THREE **518**

A: Sentential Logic 518

A.1 Proofs **518**
A.2 Conjunction and Negation Rules **522**
A.3 Conditional and Biconditional Rules **529**
A.4 Disjunction Rules **533**
A.5 Derived Rules **535**

B: Adding Quantifiers 551

B.1 Deduction Rules for Quantifiers **551**
B.2 Universal Proof **556**
B.3 Derived Rules for Quantifiers **557**

Bibliography 563

Answers to Selected Problems 565

Index 699

PREFACE

This book is a comprehensive introduction to logic. Logic continues to occupy an important position in contemporary university curriculums for much the same reason it occupied such a position in ancient academies, medieval centers of learning, and Enlightenment universities: Its object of study, reasoning, is fundamental to all intellectual activity and to most other human endeavors. My aim in this book is to introduce readers to the traditional areas of logic: (1) "informal logic," concerned with language, communication, and fallacies; (2) "formal logic," including the theory of the syllogism and modern symbolic techniques; and (3) "inductive logic," the study of empirical reasoning.

In its structure, therefore, this book follows the now common pattern for introductory logic texts established by John Stuart Mill, Morris Cohen, Ernest Nagel, and others. Part I introduces two of the basic concepts of logic, truth and validity, in the context of a general theory of argument. It proceeds to discuss other criteria of good reasoning—evidence, relevance, and grounding—and ways of recognizing violations of them. Part I concludes with a discussion of meaning and definition. Part II covers sentential logic, developing three methods for evaluating sentential arguments: truth tables, semantic tableaux, and natural deduction. Part III covers predicate logic. It presents syllogistic logic and the modern theory of quantification, extending semantic tableau and natural deduction methods to the latter. Part IV covers inductive logic, discussing generalizations, analogies, causal inferences, and explanations. Finally, two appendixes present alternative deduction systems for sentential and quantificational logic.

As Richard Whately observed in his 1826 book, *Elements of Logic*, logic is both an art and a science. Logic is concerned with constructing a theory of correct reasoning, making it a science. Indeed, modern symbolic developments have led to sophisticated mathematical theories of reasoning. But logic is also concerned with applying theory to practice, making it an art. Most people study logic to improve their ability to reason: to argue, to analyze, and to think critically about issues that concern them. This book, therefore, concentrates on the art of logic. It focuses on applying logical concepts and theories to reasoning in everyday language in a wide variety of contexts. But it's important to remember that without theories of reasoning, there would be nothing to apply. The art of logic depends crucially on the science of logic.

Organization and New Features

Despite its traditional structure, this book contains a number of new features. The first is a novel treatment of fallacies as aspects of a general theory of argumentation and communication. Part I of the book concerns the art of logic. Much of it is devoted to a discussion of fallacies. Too often, such discussions read like mere lists of mistakes. As a chorus of authors has pointed out, there has been no theory of fallacy to give these discussions structure. Moreover, if fallacies are invalid forms of argument, as many authors have taken them to be, then there can be no theory of fallacy. Part I locates the discussion of fallacies in the context of a theory of conditions for good argument. The theory derives from a general theory of communication that Robert Stalnaker, Hans Kamp, and Irene Heim, among others, have developed over the past ten to fifteen years. From this approach, fallacies emerge not as kinds of invalidity but as violations of other conditions of good argumentation.

Part I begins with a chapter developing this general theory. It presents fundamental logical concepts—argument, validity, truth, implication, equivalence, logical truth, and contradictoriness—defining these concepts rigorously while concentrating on their usefulness in understanding natural-language inference. Truth and validity emerge as two of the conditions good arguments ought to meet. Chapter 2 discusses two other conditions for good arguments: evidence and relevance. Violating these conditions leads to fallacies such as begging the question and *ignoratio elenchi*. Chapter 3 discusses the grounding condition for good arguments: An argument should take for granted only the set of beliefs and assumptions that occupies the common ground of the conversation in which it occurs. Violations of this condition lead to fallacies such as appeals to authority, emotion, force, and pity, as well as accident and misapplication. Chapter 4 concerns problems arising from miscommunication: equivocation, amphiboly, accent, composition, and division. The chapter also presents the traditional theory of definition as a way of clarifying meaning and avoiding such problems.

A second novelty of this book is its treatment of semantic tableaux. Based on E. W. Beth's tableaux, the method bears much similarity to Richard Jeffrey's truth trees. It is very easy to teach and to learn; it directly mirrors the semantics of the logical operators. Tableaux provide a ready test for validity and other logical properties in both sentential and predicate logic. (Of course, in full predicate logic, the method is not a decision procedure.) Semantic tableaux are even simpler than truth trees, for tableaux have the subformula property: On a tableau, formulas are decomposed into their subformulas.

A third novelty of this book is its presentation of three deduction systems, each of which has some special characteristics. The system in the text itself descends from the systems presented in Irving Copi's *Introduction to Logic*. It uses only simple rules, that is, rules stating that formulas of certain kinds can be deduced from formulas of other kinds. There are, consequently, no subordinate proofs. The system of this book goes beyond Copi's system, however, in three respects. First, it doesn't require premises; categorical as well as hypothetical proofs are possible. Second, the rules divide into basic and derived rules. The derived rules make proofs much easier, but they aren't required. The distinction allows instructors to omit some rules if they choose while maintaining the completeness of the deduction system. Also, a limited, indirect proof method can be added to simplify proofs further. Third, the system extends to encompass all of predicate logic. Many instructors, of course, will not want to cover polyadic predicates and multiply quantified formulas. They can avoid these topics without encountering unnecessary complications simply by omitting parts of Chapter 13. For those who want to cover full predicate logic, however, the extension of the system is presented there.

Appendix I presents a second deduction system, in the style of E. J. Lemmon and of Copi's *Symbolic Logic*. Appendix II presents a third deduction system, based on one developed by Donald Kalish and Richard Montague and presented in my earlier book, *Deduction*. Both systems use conditional and indirect proof, thus making use of subordinate proofs, and mark a distinction between basic and derived rules. The pattern of rules is easy to understand: Most connectives come with introduction and exploitation rules. The former introduce formulas with a given connective as main connective into proofs, while the latter exploit the presence of such formulas to deduce others. (In Appendix I, the rules retain their traditional names; in Appendix II, they have explicit introduction/exploitation labels.) The system used in Appendix II has an unusual form that greatly simplifies deductive rules and strategies.

The treatment of quantification in this book is slightly unorthodox. Neither the tableau system nor the deduction systems use free variables; instantiation always involves a constant. Indeed, in this book, formulas never contain free variables; quantifiers on the same variable never overlap in scope. There are no vacuous quantifiers. The need for distinguishing free from bound variables arises only in the final section of Chapter 13, in order to achieve a complete system of rules for full predicate logic without resorting to subordinate proofs. These unusual features of the language of predicate logic reflect the semantics and intended use of the language and simplify quantificational tableau and deduction rules.

Part IV discusses induction. Chapter 14 concerns generalization, both enumerative and statistical, and analogy. It analyzes the forms such arguments take and the means of evaluating them. Chapter 15 discusses the structure and evaluation of causal reasoning by considering Mill's methods.

Unlike most textbooks, this book does not maintain that the word 'cause' is ambiguous. The context-sensitive approach to language developed in Part I allows for a uniform analysis of the concept of causation. Chapter 16 discusses explanation. Here, too, taking context into account allows for a treatment simpler but richer than the usual.

Throughout, I have tried to present logical theories and their applications as simply and elegantly as possible. I have kept the focus on natural language: on constructing English arguments, analyzing their structure, and evaluating them. Natural language, after all, makes use of far richer resources than any introductory logic text can explicate. I hope that by equipping readers with a refined set of logical tools and making them aware of the issues that arise in using them, this book will enable its readers to go beyond its own limited realm.

Acknowledgments

I thank everyone at Mayfield Publishing Company for making the task of an author as pleasant as possible. I am especially grateful to Jim Bull, who gave me the idea of writing this book and encouraged me throughout. I am also grateful to Antonio Padial, whose editing helped me to say things more clearly and elegantly, and to Linda Toy, who shepherded the manuscript through production.

I owe a special debt of thanks to Bill Keith of the University of Louisville, who convinced me that a theory of fallacy was possible and, consequently, that this book was worth writing. Many of the ideas in Part I of this book stem from his work. Bill also developed many of the exercises in Part I and gave me valuable criticisms and advice on the entire manuscript.

I am also indebted to the other reviewers whose comments did much to improve the book: Richard Behling, University of Wisconsin—Eau Claire; Winfred Phillips, Trinity University; Nelson Pole, Cleveland, State University; and Frank E. Wilson, Bucknell University.

I would like to thank Gerald Massey, who formulated the version of Beth's semantic tableaux used in this book, instilled in me a deep (but, he will surely think, insufficient) skepticism toward informal logic, and, more than anyone else, taught me what logic is all about. I also owe a great deal to my other logic teachers: Nuel Belnap, Ermanno Bencivenga, Kenneth Manders, Charles Parsons, and Carl Posy. Finally, what understanding of induction I have I owe to Carl Hempel, who used the case of the eleven blue men to introduce undergraduates to the philosophy of science.

I want to thank my colleagues Nicholas Asher and Hans Kamp, who used earlier versions of some chapters to teach introductory logic courses and suggested many improvements. Many ideas in this book arose from listening to them and to my former colleagues Stanley Peters and Irene Heim. I am also grateful to former colleagues Maria Slowiaczek and Richard Larson for their comments on drafts of various chapters.

I would like to thank all those who have made suggestions concerning my previous book, *Deduction*, especially William Wisdom of Temple University, Wayne Davis of Georgetown University, Edmund Gettier of the University of Massachusetts at Amherst, Christopher Hill of the University of Arkansas, and Ruth Manor of San Jose State University. Many of the suggested changes appear here in the portions that overlap the content of that book.

I am grateful to all the teaching assistants and students at the University of Texas who have used versions of this book and helped to improve it. I owe special thanks to Sally Ferguson-Ramzy and Andy Schwartz, who caught some mistakes and helped write the answers that appear in the back.

Finally, I want to thank my wife Beverly, who was essential in helping me with the chapter on generalizations and in countless other ways, and my daughter Molly, during whose naps most of what follows was written.

PART

I

REASONING
AND
LANGUAGE

1

TRUTH

AND

VALIDITY

Logic is the study of correct reasoning. Aristotle (384–322 B.C.) founded the discipline of logic as a system of principles on which all other knowledge rests. Indeed, logic pertains to all subjects, since people can reason about anything they can think about. Politics, the arts, literature, business, the sciences, and everyday problems are all subjects open to reasoning. Sometimes the reasoning is good; sometimes, not so good. People use logic to tell the difference.

Reasoning well is more than an academic exercise. Gathering information, making decisions, and carrying out plans all require reasoning. Good reasoning tends to lead to accurate information, good decisions, and appropriate plans, whereas bad reasoning tends to lead to inaccuracies, bad decisions, and misguided plans. The consequences of reasoning well or poorly also reach beyond the life of any one person. The twentieth century has witnessed remarkable advances in science and technology that have improved the lives of vast numbers of people. These applications of scientific method required a great deal of good and highly sophisticated reasoning. But the twentieth century has also suffered the results of reasoning gone astray. There were arguments—seriously flawed arguments, to be sure—that led to Gallipoli and Stalingrad, Dresden and Hiroshima, Auschwitz and Kolyma.

Part I of this book discusses both the fundamental features of good reasoning and common sources of bad reasoning. Parts II and III present the core of modern symbolic logic: a rigorous theory of inference. Part IV presents the fundamentals of the theory of induction, the kind of reasoning used frequently in the sciences.

Using logic, we can evaluate bits of reasoning as proper or improper, good or bad. Logic is not the study of how people do reason, but how they should reason. We might put this point differently by saying that logic does not describe the psychology of reasoning, with its flashes of insight and oversight; it prescribes methods for justifying reasoning, that is, for showing that a given bit of reasoning is proper. Just as arithmetic describes the rules for addition rather than the psychological process of addition, logic describes the rules for correct reasoning, not the process of reasoning. Logic thus describes an ideal that actual reasoning strives for but often fails to reach.

Logic, however, involves not only constructing abstract theories of reasoning but also applying them to arguments in natural languages such as English, French, Arabic, or Japanese. Logic can help in devising and evaluating arguments. In this sense, logic is an art as well as a science; it comprises both developing principles of correct reasoning and putting them into practice.

1.1 Arguments

Arguments are bits of reasoning in language. Frequently, we think of arguments as altercations or conflicts. Sometimes, however, we speak of a politician arguing for the passage of a bill, a lawyer arguing a case, or a reader of spy novels arguing that *Tinker, Tailor, Soldier, Spy* is the pinnacle of that genre. In this latter sense, an argument starts with some assertions and tries to justify a particular thesis. Arguments are attempts to establish a conclusion.

Arguments in natural language can be complicated. A lawyer arguing for the innocence of a client, for instance, offers many specific arguments in presenting the case. The lawyer may argue that a piece of evidence is inadmissible, that results from a lab test are ambiguous, that the client could not have reached the scene of the crime by the time it was committed, and so on. All these smaller arguments form part of the larger argument for the client's innocence.

We can divide arguments, then, into two groups: *extended* arguments, which contain other arguments, and *simple* arguments, which don't. A simple argument, like an extended argument, starts with some assertions trying to justify a thesis. The initial assertions of the argument are its *premises;* the thesis the argument tries to justify is its *conclusion.* Because extended arguments are good only if the simple arguments within them are good, we'll usually analyze simple arguments. In fact, we'll be so often concerned with simple arguments that we'll drop the adjective *simple* and speak simply of *arguments.*

> **Definition**   An *argument* consists of a finite sequence of sentences, called *premises,* together with another sentence, the *conclusion,* which the premises are taken to support.

An argument is a string or sequence of sentences.[1] The sentences that make up the argument are in a particular order, whether the argument is spoken, written, or encoded in a computer language. For our purposes in this text, the order in which an argument presents its premises rarely makes a difference. So, we generally won't worry about order of presentation. But it's important that the string of premises be finite. If the premises never end, the conclusion is never established.

The word 'sentence' has two uses relevant to logic. According to the first, a sentence is any grammatical string of words that ends with a period (or exclamation point, or question mark). Winston Churchill once said that no one who could write an English sentence would long be out of a job; he probably had this sense of the word in mind. Computer programs for counting the number of sentences in a text count sentences in this sense; they count the strings between the above punctuation marks (generally, by counting those marks themselves).

Logicians and linguists use 'sentence' in a second, slightly different way. Consider this variant of the traditional aphorism, "When the going gets tough, the tough get going," called Lynch's Law.

(1) When the going gets tough, everyone leaves.

How many sentences are there in (1)? In the first sense of 'sentence', the answer is one. But, in another sense, it would be reasonable to answer three. Lynch's law itself is a sentence. Within it, furthermore, are two other sentences: 'The going gets tough' and 'Everyone leaves'. The aphorism (1) results from combining these two shorter sentences. Logicians use 'sentence' in this second sense, roughly equivalent to 'independent clause', in which one sentence may be a part or component of another. The number of premises in an argument, therefore, is not always one less than the number of periods, exclamation points, and so on. Indeed, an entire argument, with premises and conclusion, can appear within a single sentence (in the first sense of 'sentence').

This example of a simple argument is Abraham Lincoln's explanation of why he did not expect to marry:

(2) I have come to the conclusion never again to think of marrying, and for this reason: I can never be satisfied with anyone who would be blockhead enough to marry me.

We can represent Lincoln's argument as

(3) I can never be satisfied with anyone who would be blockhead enough to marry me.
∴ I shall never again think of marrying.

When we write an argument "officially," in what we'll call *standard form,* we'll list the premises in the order in which they are given and then list the conclusion. In addition, we'll preface the conclusion with the symbol $\therefore$, which means "therefore." So, in our official representations, conclusions will always come last. This isn't true in natural language, as Lincoln's argument shows. Conclusions may appear at the beginning, in the middle, or at the end of arguments, if they are stated at all.

Another simple argument is from French essayist Joseph Joubert (1754–1824):

> (4) Nothing that is proved is obvious; for what is obvious shows itself and cannot be proved.

This argument, too, starts with its conclusion and then introduces premises to justify it. In standard form, the argument becomes:

> (5) What is obvious shows itself and cannot be proved.
> $\therefore$ Nothing that is proved is obvious.

Unlike simple arguments, extended arguments contain not only premises and conclusion but also other arguments. Extended arguments may consist of several simple arguments in sequence. They may contain other extended arguments. And they may consist of a list of premises, followed by several conclusions stated at once. Typically, the conclusion of one part of an extended argument serves as a premise for another part.

Consider an extended argument that the ancient skeptic Sextus Empiricus (*circa* A.D. 150–225) offered to challenge our usual notion of change:

> (6) If Socrates died, he died either when he was living or when he was dead. But he did not die while living; for assuredly he was living, and as living he had not died. Nor when he was dead; for then he would be twice dead. Therefore Socrates did not die.

The argument as a whole tries to establish the startling conclusion that Socrates did not die. Moreover, it includes two subarguments. Signaling them is the word 'for', which, as in the argument from Joubert above, tends to follow a conclusion and introduce a premise supporting it. In this argument, the first 'for' introduces premises supporting the intermediate conclusion that Socrates did not die while living:

> (7) Assuredly, Socrates was living.
> As living, he had not yet died.
> $\therefore$ Socrates did not die while living.

The second 'for' introduces premises to support the conclusion that Socrates didn't die while he was dead:

> (8) If Socrates died while he was dead, he would be twice dead.
> $\therefore$ Socrates did not die while he was dead.

The conclusions of these subarguments act as premises in the larger argument that Socrates never died:

(9) If Socrates died, he died either when he was living or when he was
dead.
He did not die while living.
He did not die while he was dead.
∴ Socrates did not die.

Premises and conclusions are sentences. In this text, we'll be interested only in sentences that can be true or false. Many ordinary sentences, including almost every one in this book, fall into this category. Grammatically, they are declarative, in the indicative mood. They say something about the way the world is, and they might be correct or incorrect in so describing it. But commands, for example, are different. 'Shut the door' can be appropriate or inappropriate, irritating or conciliatory, friendly or hostile, but it cannot be true or false. Questions, too, are neither true nor false: consider 'What time is it?' or 'What is the population of Mozambique?' Interjections— 'Ouch!', 'All right!', 'Alas!', and most curses—are likewise neither true nor false.

A sentence is true or false in a particular context: as used on a particular occasion, by a particular speaker, to a particular audience, in a given circumstance, as part of a given discourse. Without all this contextual information, we can't tell whether sentences such as these are true or false:

(10) a. I love you.
b. We're going to Houston tomorrow.
c. They don't understand what they're supposed to do.
d. Jill then ran down the stairs and called the police.

Whether (10)a is true, for example, clearly depends on who you and I are, when the sentence is spoken, and so on. Sentences have truth values only relative to a context of use.

Nevertheless, only in Chapters 2 and 3 will we be concerned with context directly. We'll continue, throughout the other parts of this book, to speak of sentences as having truth values, trusting ourselves to remember that these values are relative to context.

1.2 RECOGNIZING ARGUMENTS

Language serves many purposes. People use language to express emotion, to describe the world around them, to speak their minds, to persuade others to act in certain ways, and to perform actions themselves. Sometimes people use language to advance arguments. How do arguments differ from other uses of language?

First, it's helpful to ask what these uses of language have in common. All linguistic acts aim to bring about a change. A description, for example, may be intended to inform others about a particular topic or event. An expression of emotion may be designed, not to convey information, but to "let off steam." A marriage vow, properly made, transforms a single person into a married one. In each case, people use language to alter a situation; to inform others, to release emotion, or to enter into a marriage.

What circumstance results from a given linguistic act depends on the context in which it occurs as well as on the content of the language used. If, in response to the minister's question, "Do you take this woman . . . as long as you both shall live?" the groom responds with "Omnis Gallia divisa est in partes tres," he does not succeed in marrying the bride. Similarly, if he responds "I do" to a Latin examination question, "What is the first sentence of Caesar's *Gallic Wars*?" he neither answers the question correctly nor marries his intended. To achieve the desired result, both context and content must be appropriate.

How, then, do arguments change circumstances? Arguments have a special purpose: They are primarily intended to *persuade,* that is, to change beliefs. A person may construct an argument to persuade others—to change their beliefs—or to persuade himself or herself—to change his or her own beliefs. Arguments correspondingly differ from descriptions, expressions of emotion, marriage vows, and other uses of language. The premises of an argument are meant to support the conclusion. The relation of intended support distinguishes arguments from other uses of language.

You can recognize arguments, then, by recognizing when some sentences are offered in support of others. You can do this most easily, in turn, if you can distinguish premises from conclusions. But how can you pick out the conclusion of an argument? In the earlier examples from Joubert and Sextus, the word 'for' indicated that a premise was being introduced. In English, various words and phrases can signal the premises or the conclusion of an argument.

Conclusion Indicators	**Premise Indicators**
therefore	because
thus	as
hence	for
so	since
consequently	
it follows that	
in conclusion	
as a result	
then	
must	

These words and phrases have other uses; they are not always premise or conclusion indicators.

> (11) John has been depressed since Mary left him.

is not an argument; 'since' here expresses not a logical relation but a relation in time. But these expressions can, and often do, serve as indicators because they can attest to relations of support among the sentences of an argument. The single English sentence

> (12) Since state legislatures will reapportion voting districts after the next census, control of those legislatures will be hotly contested.

presents a simple argument. The word 'since' indicates that we should take what follows it,

> (13) State legislatures will reapportion voting districts after the next census,

as a premise, supporting the conclusion

> (14) Control of those legislatures will be hotly contested.

Premise indicators often signal not only that one or more sentences are premises but also that a certain sentence is a conclusion. 'Since', for example, exhibits a relation of support between the sentences it links. The occurrence of 'since' in (12) points out not only that the sentence immediately following it is a premise but also that (14) is a conclusion. As you saw earlier, 'for' usually indicates that the sentences following it are premises and that the sentence preceding it is the conclusion.

Indicators provide important clues to the structure of arguments. Often, however, no explicit indicators appear. Sometimes the conclusion isn't even stated. In such cases, you must consider the point of the argument. What is the author trying to establish? In some arguments, the conclusions are quite clear, but others are very hard to analyze. Consider, for example, this argument from the French essayist Voltaire (1694–1778):

> (15) If it were permitted to reason consistently in religious matters, it is clear that we all ought to become Jews, because Jesus Christ was born a Jew, lived a Jew, and died a Jew, and because he said that he was accomplishing and fulfilling the Jewish religion.

Voltaire seems to be arguing for the conclusion that we all ought to become Jews. The word 'because' indicates that the rest of the argument consists of a list of premises. But Voltaire, a satirist, is really aiming not at this conclusion but at another. Everything he says is supposed to follow from the hypothetical, 'if it were permitted to reason consistently in religious matters'. This is a clue that the simple argument that we ought to become Jews is part of an extended argument. Voltaire does not state the conclusion of the larger argument. But it's easy to see that he is trying to show that it is not permitted to reason consistently in religious matters. The conclusion of the smaller argument—'we all ought to become Jews'—is an observation few among his intended audience of Christians would accept, even though, according to Voltaire, their own doctrine commits them to it.

Problems

Which of the following passages contain arguments? Label each argument you find as simple or extended, and identify its premises and conclusions.

▶ 1. It is absurd to bring back a runaway slave. If a slave can survive without a master, is it not awful to admit that the master cannot live without the slave? (Diogenes of Sinope)

▶ 2. Children make the most desirable opponents in Scrabble as they are both easy to beat and fun to cheat. (Fran Lebowitz)

▶ 3. It is possible to own too much. A man with one watch knows what time it is; a man with two watches is never quite sure. (Lee Segall)

▶ 4. Do not love your neighbor as yourself. If you are on good terms with yourself, it is an impertinence; if on bad, an injury. (George Bernard Shaw)

▶ 5. The idea of strictly minding our own business is moldy rubbish. Who could be so selfish? (Myrtie Barker)

▶ 6. If there hadn't been women we'd still be squatting in a cave eating raw meat, because we made civilization in order to impress our girlfriends. (Orson Welles)

7. If I agreed with you, I'd have to chew me out. I don't, so I won't. (Malcolm S. Forbes)

8. When all is summed up, a man never speaks of himself without loss; his accusations of himself are always believed; his praises never. (Montaigne)

9. Every luxury must be paid for, and everything is a luxury.... (Cesare Pavese)

10. Life does not agree with philosophy: there is no happiness that is not idleness, and only what is useless is pleasurable. (Anton Chekhov)

11. I should take little comfort in a world without books, but reality is not to be found in them because it is not there whole. (Marguerite Yourcenar)

▶ 12. I am right and therefore shall not give up the contest. (Rutherford B. Hayes)

13. We owe a lot to Thomas Edison—if it wasn't for him, we'd be watching television by candlelight. (Milton Berle)

14. Cats are smarter than dogs. You can't get eight cats to pull a sled through snow. (Jeff Valdez)

15. Since we take an average of 45,000 car trips over the course of a lifetime, say statisticians, the chance of being in a serious accident is nearly one in two. (Jane Stein)

16. One has to belong to the intelligentsia to believe things like that; no ordinary man could be such a fool. (George Orwell)

17. Ireland set out to crack down on alcohol-related traffic accidents. A spokesman for the Automobile Association in Dublin said it's time to stop blaming accidents on motorists: "In many cases the pedestrian is to blame. Often, he is lying prone in the roadway." (*Esquire*)

▶ **18.** Man being a reasonable, and so a thinking creature, there is nothing more worthy of his being than the right direction and employment of his thoughts; since upon this depends both his usefulness to the public, and his own present and future benefits in all respects. (William Penn)

19. It's fun politically to attack the rich on behalf of the poor—the Robin Hood syndrome. But if you're serious about helping the poor, you'd better give economic security to those in the middle, so they're paying the necessary taxes. You're just not going to be able to finance all social programs from tax collections from the rich. (Gary Hart)

20. Stunned by his defeat, Dewey later said he felt like the man who woke up to find himself inside a coffin with a lily in his hand and thought: "If I'm alive, what am I doing here? And if I'm dead, why do I have to go to the bathroom?" (Paul F. Boller, Jr.)

21. Everything is new. And we are living among events so singular that old people have no more knowledge of them, are no more habituated to them, and have no more experience of them than young people. We are all novices, because everything is new. (Joseph Joubert)

22. An Iron Curtain is being drawn down over their front. We do not know what lies behind it. It is vital, therefore, that we reach an understanding with Russia now before we have mortally reduced our armies and before we have withdrawn into our zones of occupation. (Winston Churchill)

23. ... astrology was progressive. Astrology differed in asserting the continuous, regular force of a power at a distance. The influences of heavenly bodies on the events on earth it described as periodic, repetitious, *invisible* forces like those that would rule the scientific mind. (Daniel J. Boorstin)

▶ **24.** If we take in hand any volume; of divinity or school metaphysics, for instance; let us ask, *Does it contain any abstract reasoning concerning quantity or number?* No. *Does it contain any experimental reasoning concerning matter of fact and existence?* No. Commit it then to the flames; for it can contain nothing but sophistry and illusion. (David Hume)

25. The pure sciences express results of comparison exclusively; comparison is not a conceivable effect of the order in which outer impressions are experienced—it is one of the house-born portions of our mental structure; therefore, the pure sciences form a body of propositions with whose genesis experience has nothing to do. (William James)

26. Since happiness consists in peace of mind, and since durable peace of mind depends on the confidence we have in the future, and since that confidence is based on the science we should have of the nature of God and the soul, it follows that science is necessary for true happiness. (Gottfried Leibniz)

27. Science demands an uncompromising approach to reality—measurement and experiment surrounded by theory, yielding careful definition of degrees of certainty. Science also demands independent investigator initiative, diversity, dialogue, and, above all, *freedom* of debate and discussion. Our culture does endeavor to cherish such values in the humanities and in politics as well, despite . . . frustration with scientific hedging. And that is, of course, my point. The manifest power of science to explain and predict phenomena has made science appear to dominate *all* values, and even the human condition. Nevertheless, the opposite more clearly describes the condition. Culture dominates science. (E. E. David, Jr.)

Write each of the following arguments in standard form. If there are several arguments in a passage, write each separately.

28. When you negotiate with people who take hostages you are obliged, in the negotiation, to give something. It may be just a little, it may be a lot, but you have to give something. Once you have given something, the kidnapper gains from his action. So what is his normal and spontaneous reaction? He does it again, thinking that it is a way of obtaining what he cannot obtain by other means.

So you get caught in a process. Naturally you can get maybe two, three or four hostages freed. But you immediately give the kidnapper an inducement to seize another three, four, five or six. So it is an extraordinarily dangerous and irresponsible process. That is why I don't negotiate. (Jacques Chirac)

29. But we are convinced that the American national purpose must at some point be fixed. If it is redefined—or even subject to redefinition—with every change of administration in Washington, the United States risks becoming a factor of inconstancy in the world. The national tendency to oscillate between exaggerated belligerence and unrealistic expectation will be magnified. Other nations—friends or adversaries—unable to gear their policies to American steadiness will go their own way, dooming the United States to growing irrelevance. (Henry Kissinger and Cyrus Vance)

▶ **30.** The "housing crisis" agitating Mayor Koch and Governor Cuomo is actually a product of local attempts to suspend economic law. Everybody who isn't a tenant admits how destructive the city's World War II rent controls have been, but tenants have the most votes. An extralegal free market in abandoned factory-loft conversions compensated somewhat, but City Hall's first instinct was to prohibit most conversions. Anyone fool enough to want to build new apartments has to pay double the standard price for concrete because of a Mafia stranglehold on the commodity. Vast areas of New York City are a wasteland of abandoned housing and rubble. (*Wall Street Journal*)

31. It is absurd to call Pope John Paul II a traditionalist. Seldom has there been a more future-oriented pope, such a visionary activist. It would also be wrong to call him a "progress"; the "progressives" hate him. The Pope criticizes both traditionalists and progressives.

True, the progressives call everybody to their right "conservative." If by a "neoconservative" we mean a nontraditionalist who criticizes the illusions of progressives, then the Pope is a neoconservative. (Michael Novak)

32. ... Mars would be the next logical niche for human expansion in the universe. Why Mars? Clearly, Mars will have priority in any manned solar system exploration program because it offers the least severe environment for humans. Due to its atmosphere, its accessible surface, its probable availability of water and its relatively moderate temperatures ... it is the most hospitable of all the planets other than earth.

Moreover, Mars resources include materials that could be adapted to support human life, including air, fuels, fertilizers, building materials and an environment that could grow food. ... (James M. Beggs)

33. Computer makers must recognize that the old marketing rule is still golden: Listen to your customers. What corporate computer customers say they want is hardware and software that will allow them to tie their entire organization together in a true information network. Before the industry can give them that, individual manufacturers must agree on the uniform standards under which computers will "talk" to one another. This will be a complex effort. But as long as makers delay, customer frustration rises. (*Business Week*)

34. At this critical point in history, American immigration policies are in a shambles.

Our borders are totally out of control. Our border patrol apprehends 3,000 illegal immigrants per day, 1.2 million per year. And two get in for every one caught; those caught just try again. There has been a 3,000 percent increase in apprehensions since 1965 with only a 50 percent increase in manpower.

> Not just our borders, but our whole immigration apparatus is out of control: 400,000 more people fly into the U.S. than fly out every year. INS believes that 30 percent of the persons granted permanent residence each year on the basis of family ties are making fraudulent claims. (Richard D. Lamm)

35. The specific case against business schools is that they have neglected certain skills and outlooks that are essential to America's commercial renaissance while inculcating values that can do harm. The traditional strength of business education has been to provide students with a broad view of many varied business functions—marketing, finance, production, and so forth. But like sociology and political science, business training has gotten all wrapped up in mathematical models and such ideas as can be boiled down to numbers. This shift has led schools to play down two fundamental but hard-to-quantify business imperatives: creating the conditions that will permit the design and production of high-quality goods, and waging the constant struggle to inspire, cajole, discipline, lead and in general persuade employees to work in a common cause. (James Fallows)

▸ 36. In 1983 government agents in South Florida seized some six tons of cocaine and 850 tons of marijuana (which tends to come by the boatload). In 1985 the figures were twenty-five and 750 tons respectively. In other words, seizures of cocaine, a potentially lethal drug, have quadrupled while seizures of marijuana, a substance that looks benign in comparison, have fallen off. It is generally believed that the amounts of drugs seized reflect the amounts coming in. Thus, almost certainly, more cocaine is being imported now than ever before. . . .

 Why the sudden abundance of cocaine? The government's strategy in the war on drugs may be partly to blame. The heightened risk of interdiction has prompted smugglers to favor drugs that are compact and expensive, like cocaine, over drugs that are bulky and relatively cheap, like marijuana. (*Atlantic Monthly*)

37. Being good liberals themselves, they had no ground in principle by which to justify indefinite Israeli rule over a rebellious Palestinian population. Nor could they answer the contention that continued Israeli occupation of the territories would ultimately erode the Jewishness of the state or transform it from a democracy into another South Africa. The only argument they could rely on was security: the argument that Israeli withdrawal in favor of a Palestinian state run by the PLO posed so great a danger to the "body" of Israel that, for the time being and for the foreseeable future, it had to take precedence over the danger to Israel's "soul" admittedly posed by continued occupation. (Norman Podhoretz)

38. He does not want to overturn the Soviet system; he wants to strengthen it. To paraphrase Churchill from another context, Gorbachev did not

become general secretary to preside over the demise of the Communist Party. We have an interest in the success of his reforms only to the extent that they change the system to make it less threatening to our security and interests. We should applaud glasnost and perestroika but not pay for them, for if his reforms do not irrevocably alter Soviet foreign policy we will be subsidizing the threat of our own destruction. (Richard Nixon)

39. Those of a more conservative bent, in contrast, believe that the recent changes are little more than a public relations campaign aimed at getting naive Americans to make unilateral concessions that will allow Castro to weather Cuba's current crisis. They argue that U.S. policy toward Cuba had worked and continues to work. Castro is no longer seen abroad as a charismatic revolutionary hero, but rather as a ruthless dictator and an abuser of human rights who has ruined Cuba. . . .

In either case, the United States cannot lose. If Cuba becomes more open economically and politically, that is good for the United States. And if the Soviets have to keep bankrolling Cuba, that is better than what they believe the more liberal policy would lead to—the American subsidy of a Cuba that remains under Castro's control and militarily allied with the Soviet Union. (Susan Kaufman Purcell)

40. A struggle for existence inevitably follows from the high rate at which all organic beings tend to increase. Every being, which during its natural lifetime produces several eggs or seeds, must suffer destruction during some period of its life, and during some season or occasional year; otherwise on the principle of geometric increase, its numbers would quickly become so inordinately great that no country could support the product. Hence, as more individuals are produced than can possibly survive, there must in every case be a struggle for existence, either one individual with another of the same species, or with the individuals of distinct species, or with the physical conditions of life. It is the doctrine of Malthus applied with manifold force to the whole animal and vegetable kingdoms; for in this case there can be no artificial increase in food, and no prudential restraint from marriage. Although some species may now be increasing, more or less rapidly, in numbers, all cannot do so, for the whole world would not hold them. (Charles Darwin)

Philosophers have advanced these arguments to try to prove that there is a God. The first three are from Saint Anselm of Canterbury (1033–1109); the others, from Thomas Aquinas (1225–1274).[2] The proofs from Aquinas are presented out of order, from simplest to most complicated, rather than in the order in which he presented them. Write the arguments in standard form. If a passage contains several arguments, write each separately.

41. Even the fool . . . is forced to agree to the existence, in the intellect, of something so great that a greater cannot be conceived, since he understands this when he hears it, and whatever is understood is in the intellect. And surely that greatest conceivable thing cannot exist in the intellect alone. For even if it exists solely in the intellect, it can be thought to exist in reality, which is greater than existence merely in the intellect. If, then, that greatest conceivable thing exists in the intellect alone, then it is possible to conceive of something greater than the greatest conceivable being. But surely this is impossible. Therefore, there can be absolutely no doubt that something so great that a greater cannot be conceived exists both in the intellect and in reality.

▶ **42.** Certainly, this being exists so truly that one cannot even think that it does not exist. For whatever must be thought to exist is greater than whatever can be thought not to exist. Hence, if that greatest conceivable being can be thought not to exist, then it is not the greatest conceivable being, which is absurd. Therefore, something so great that a greater cannot be conceived exists so truly that it cannot even be thought not to exist.

43. You exist so truly, Lord my God, that You cannot even be thought not to exist. And this is as it should be. For, if a mind could think of something better than You, the creature would rise above its creator and judge its creator, and that is completely absurd. In fact, everything else, except You alone, can be thought not to exist. You alone, then, of all things most truly exist, and therefore of all things possess existence to the highest degree; for nothing else exists as truly, and everything else possesses existence to a lesser degree.

44. The fifth way is based on the rule-governed character of nature. The ordering of actions toward an end is observed in all bodies obeying natural laws, even when they lack awareness. For their behavior hardly ever varies and will practically always turn out well; this shows that they truly tend toward a goal and do not merely hit it by accident. Nothing, however, that lacks awareness tends toward a goal, except under the direction of someone aware and intelligent. The arrow, for example, requires an archer. All things in nature, therefore, are directed toward a goal by someone intelligent, and this we call 'God'.

45. The second way is based on the nature of causation. In the observable world causes are to be found ordered in series; we never observe, or even could observe, something causing itself, for this would mean it preceded itself, and this is impossible. Such a series of causes, however, must stop somewhere. For in all series of causes, an earlier member causes an intermediate, and the intermediate a last (whether the intermediate be one or many). If you eliminate a cause, you also eliminate its effects. Therefore, there can be neither a last nor an intermediate cause unless there is a first. But if the series of causes goes on to infinity, and there is no first cause, there would be neither intermediate causes nor a final effect, which is patently false. It is therefore necessary to posit a first cause, which all call 'God'.

46. The fourth way is based on the gradation observed in things. For some things are found to be more good, true, and noble, and other things less. But 'more' and 'less' describe varying degrees of approximating the maximum; for example, things are hotter and hotter the more nearly they approach the hottest. Something, therefore, is the best and truest and noblest of things, and consequently exists to the highest degree; for Aristotle says that the truest things exist to the highest degree. Now when many things have a common property, the one having it most fully causes the others to have it. Fire, the hottest of all things, causes the heat in all other things, to use Aristotle's example. Therefore, something causes all other things to be, to be good, and to have any other perfections, and this we call 'God'.

47. The third way depends on what is possible and necessary, and goes like this. We observe in things something that can be, and can fail to be, for we observe them springing up and dying away, and consequently being and not being. Now not everything can be like this, for whatever can fail to be, once was not. If all things could not be, therefore, at one time there was nothing. But if that were true there would be nothing even now, because something that does not exist can be brought into being only by something that already exists. So, if there had been nothing, it would have been impossible for anything to come into being, and there would be nothing now, which is patently false. Not all things, therefore, are possible but not necessary; something is necessary. Now what is necessary may or may not have its necessity caused by something else. It is impossible to go on to infinity in a series of necessary things having a cause of their necessity, just as with any series of causes. It is therefore necessary to posit something which is itself necessary, having no other cause of its necessity, but causing necessity in everything else.

▶ **48.** The first and most obvious way is based on change. Certainly, our senses show us that some things in the world are changing. Now anything changing is changed by something else. For nothing changes except what can but does not yet have some actuality; something that causes change has that actuality already. For to cause change is to bring into being what was before only potential, and only something that already is can do this. Thus, fire, which is actually hot, causes wood, which can be hot, to become actually hot, and so causes change in the wood. Now it is impossible for the same thing to be simultaneously actually F and potentially F, though it can be actually F and potentially G: The actually hot cannot at the same time be potentially hot, though it can be potentially cold. It is therefore impossible for something undergoing a change to cause itself to undergo that very change. It follows that anything changing must be changed by something else. If this other thing is also changing, it is being changed by another thing, and that by another. Now this does not go on to infinity, or else there would be no first cause of the change and, consequently, no other changes. The intermediate causes will not produce change unless they are affected by the first change, just as a stick does not move unless moved by a hand. Therefore, it is necessary to arrive at some first cause of change, itself changed by nothing, and this all understand to be God.

1.3 Good Arguments

Some arguments are good; others aren't. According to the definition of 'argument' given before, any collection of sentences counts as an argument if it's possible to single out one sentence as the conclusion, purportedly supported by the others. What distinguishes good from bad arguments? What makes a good argument good?

People typically demand many things of an argument. Arguments are meant to change circumstances in particular ways. People use arguments to convince themselves or others of some conclusion, or to get themselves or others to do something. Primarily, arguments aim to persuade—to bring about a change of belief. Such a change requires communication. Communication, in turn, requires a set of shared beliefs, at least about language. The beliefs, assumptions, and items of knowledge that the participants in a conversation share are the *common ground* of that conversation.

> **Definition** The *common ground* of a conversation is the set of beliefs, items of knowledge, and assumptions that its participants share.

People advance arguments to change beliefs, that is, to alter the common ground. Successful arguments do change the common ground.

Arguments succeed, or fail to succeed, for many reasons. The audience may be especially gullible or hostile. The arguer may be especially eloquent or obnoxious. Success in persuasion thus depends on both the rhetorical character of an argument and the psychological state of the audience. Because the psychological process of reasoning falls outside the scope of logic, success and persuasion do, too.

Logic can't specify what makes arguments succeed in changing beliefs. But it can specify what makes arguments deserve to succeed. Let's call arguments that deserve to succeed *good*. To return to the question: What makes a good argument good?

Imagine an idealized situation in which somebody advances an argument to convince someone else of a conclusion. Suppose that John asks Mary whether he should major in philosophy. Mary responds that he should and articulates certain premises in support of this conclusion. She points out that John has really liked his philosophy courses; that philosophy trains people to think carefully and, so, helps them in whatever field they enter; and that, five years after graduation, salaries of liberal arts majors are on average higher than those of business majors. Additionally, she may rely on the common ground between herself and John: the set of assumptions, items of knowledge, and background beliefs that she shares with John. For example, her premises rely on background beliefs that it's good to major in a subject you enjoy, that thinking carefully helps people in their careers, that John wants to do well in whatever field he enters, and that John would like to earn a good salary. If the argument is successful, then Mary convinces John that he should major in philosophy. Mary and John now share at least one additional belief, so the argument expands their common ground.

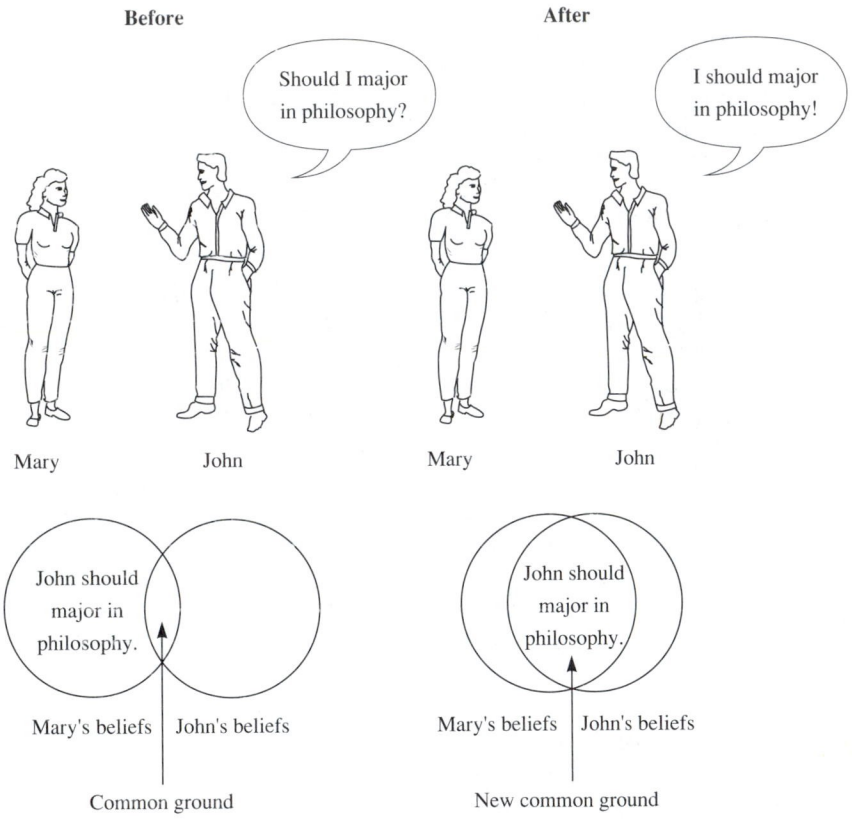

This portrait of success in argumentation shows that good arguments have several important features. First, in a good argument, the premises offer evidence for the conclusion. The premises provide information that the audience can interpret as leading toward the conclusion. Second, a good argument tries to establish the point at issue. Mary's argument has 'John should major in philosophy' as its conclusion. If it didn't, it might well be irrelevant to answering John's question. Third, the argument must assume only what is available in the common ground. Most arguments in natural language rely on unstated assumptions; these must be legitimately shared between advocate and audience for the argument to succeed. John must want to do well in the profession he eventually choses, to earn a good salary, and so on, for Mary's premises to lead him to the conclusion that he should be a philosophy major. Fourth, the premises and unstated assumptions must be true. Mary might convince John by giving him false information, but there would still be something wrong with her argument. Fifth, a good argument uses reliable forms of inference in moving from the premises to the conclusion. The conclusion, that is, must follow from the premises together with the common ground.

This analysis leads us to five conditions that good arguments must fulfill:

1. *Evidence.* The premises of the argument must offer evidence in support of the conclusion.

2. *Relevance.* The argument must be relevant to the proper issue.

3. *Grounding.* The argument must employ, as unstated assumptions, only things in the common ground between advocate and audience.

4. *Truth.* The premises and unstated assumptions used in the argument must be true.

5. *Reliability.* The inference from the premises and unstated assumptions to the conclusion must be reliable.

Good arguments meet all five conditions.

Two cautions about these conditions deserve mention. First, being good is relative to context. We can judge whether a sequence of sentences meets these requirements only by taking circumstances into account. An argument may deserve to succeed with one audience, for example, without deserving to succeed with another. The difference between the groups may involve what they are willing to take as evidence or what they share as common ground.

Second, arguments can succeed without fulfilling every requirement. Consider, for example, the relevance condition. Sometimes, we construct an argument not to reach a preordained conclusion but to see what follows from certain facts or hypotheses. In such cases, we have no definite end point in mind, so we cannot judge relevance in relation to it. Consider a more extreme case, a demagogue devising an argument as propaganda. The demagogue may have no interest at all in relevance, evidence, grounding, truth or validity; the argument, however fallacious, may simply be a tool for persuasion. Unfortunately, history indicates that arguments may succeed in persuading an audience without deserving to succeed at all.

Problems

1. For each argument in the problems at the end of section 1.2, (a) identify premises and conclusions and (b) evaluate, to whatever extent possible, whether it meets the five criteria for a good argument.

2. Choose a topic currently in the newspaper, and, for each of the five criteria of a good argument, construct an argument that fails to meet the criterion. Start with a conclusion and build by adding premises. Explain why the argument fails and say what changes might make it work.

3. Which of the five criteria is most important? Why?

1.4 RELIABILITY

This chapter focuses on two of the conditions for success in argument: truth and reliability. The condition of reliability requires that a good argument link its premises to its conclusion in the right way. There should be some special connection between the premises and the conclusion. To see what this special connection is, consider an argument that has true premises and a true conclusion but is nevertheless bad:

> (16) The U.S. entered World War II in 1941.
>   Dayton is to the west of Columbus.
>   ∴ The Red Sox lost the World Series in 1986.

What's wrong with this argument? Basically, the facts cited in the premises have little to do with the conclusion. The Red Sox could have won the 1986 World Series if a few players had made plays they in fact failed to make. They might have done so even if the facts of American involvement in the Second World War or Ohio geography were unchanged. That is, the conclusion of this argument could have turned out false even when the premises were true. The truth of the premises does nothing to guarantee the truth of the conclusion. This is the mark of a *deductively invalid* argument: its premises could all be true even when its conclusion is false. In fact, the truth of the premises lends no support to the conclusion at all. This marks the argument as altogether unreliable.

In a *deductively valid* argument, the truth of the premises does guarantee the truth of the conclusion. If the premises are all true, then the conclusion has to be true. Consider, for example, this argument:

> (17) All Canadians are North Americans.
>   Jeff is a Canadian.
>   ∴ Jeff is a North American.

In any circumstance in which the premises of this argument are true, the conclusion must be true as well. It's impossible to conceive of a state of affairs in which, while all Canadians are North Americans, Jeff is a Canadian but not a North American. To put this differently, the only way to imagine Jeff being a Canadian without being a North American is to imagine a case where some Canadians, at least, are not North Americans. In a deductively valid argument, the truth of the premises guarantees the truth of the conclusion. Or, to say the same thing, if the conclusion of a deductively valid argument is false, at least one premise must also be false.

> **DEFINITION** An argument is *deductively valid* if and only if it's impossible for its premises all to be true while its conclusion is false.

It's possible, then, for a deductively valid argument to have true premises and a true conclusion, (some or all) false premises and a false conclusion, or false premises and a true conclusion. But no deductively valid argument has true premises and a false conclusion.

Some Deductively Valid Arguments

True Premises, True Conclusion	False Premises, False Conclusion	False Premises, True Conclusion
Daniel Bonevac is an author.	Daniel Bonevac is a spaniel.	Daniel Bonevac is a spaniel.
All authors are mortal.	All spaniels eat mice.	All spaniels like baseball.
∴ Daniel Bonevac is mortal.	∴ Daniel Bonevac eats mice.	∴ Daniel Bonevac likes baseball.

Each of these arguments is deductively valid: in each case, there is no possible circumstance in which the premises are all true but the conclusion is false. How could it be true that Daniel Bonevac is a spaniel, and true that all spaniels eat mice, but false that Daniel Bonevac eats mice? Whether the premises and conclusion are actually true or false makes little difference to the validity of the argument. We evaluate deductive validity as if the premises were true. What matters is that the conclusion cannot be false if the premises are true.

Not every argument with true premises and a true conclusion is deductively valid. Similarly, many arguments with false premises and a true conclusion are deductively invalid. The same is true for arguments with false premises and a false conclusion. So, although valid arguments can have any of these three combinations of truth and falsity, not every argument with those combinations is valid. An argument is deductively invalid if it's *possible* for the premises to be true while the conclusion is false. Similarly, an argument is deductively valid if and only if its conclusion *has* to be true if its premises are all true.

Deductively valid arguments are only one species of reliable argument. Others are *inductively reliable*. Although the truth of the premises of such an argument does not guarantee the truth of its conclusion, it does make the truth of the conclusion probable. Consider, for example, this argument:

(18) Every crow that has been observed is black.
∴ All crows are black.

It's possible for the premise to be true while the conclusion is false. Perhaps there are white crows, but nobody has seen them yet. Thus, the argument is deductively invalid. Nevertheless, the premise lends some support to the conclusion. Inductively reliable arguments are extremely important in both scientific and everyday reasoning. They are the subject of Part IV of this book. Until then, we'll focus on deductive reliability, that is, validity.

Next, consider the condition of truth, the requirement that a good argument have true premises. In most circumstances, people want to learn or say true things; they want to come to true conclusions. So, arguments with false premises tend to lack interest. Using premises we know to be false, we may be able to convince many people, but this is sophistry, not an ideal of argumentative success.

A *sound* argument meets the conditions of both truth and validity. It has true premises, and it is valid. Furthermore, since, in any valid argument, the truth of the premises guarantees the truth of the conclusion, it also has a true conclusion.

> **DEFINITION**   An argument is *sound* if and only if (a) it is valid and (b) all its premises are true.

Most of this book focuses not on soundness but on validity. This focus is easy to understand. First, validity is obviously a crucial component of soundness. We can't evaluate whether an argument is sound without first determining whether it's valid. Second, evaluating soundness requires judging the actual truth or falsehood of premises. This is not the business of a logician: determining truth or falsehood requires a knowledge of the subject matter of the argument. Consider some of the premises of the arguments in this chapter:

(19) a. I (Lincoln) can never be satisfied with anyone who would be blockhead enough to marry me.
b. What is obvious shows itself and cannot be proved.
c. If Socrates died, he died either when he was living or when he was dead.
d. Five years after graduation, salaries of liberal arts majors are, on average, higher than those of business majors.

Whether these are true or false determines whether the arguments containing them are sound or unsound. But logicians as such have no expertise concerning Lincoln's psychology or salaries of college graduates with various majors.

Third, although we usually want to argue from true premises, many useful arguments start from false ones. The purpose of some arguments is to show that a certain sentence is false because it can be used to reach an outrageous or absurd conclusion. Logicians sometimes adopt a premise purely as a hypothesis, to see what would follow if it were true. Aristotle first realized how important such arguments are; he characterized them as having *dialectical*, rather than *demonstrative*, premises.

Problems

Evaluate these arguments as valid or invalid. If the argument is invalid, describe a circumstance in which the premises would be true but the conclusion would be false.

▶ **1.** If Socrates died, he died either while he was living or while he was dead. But he did not die while living; moreover, he surely did not die while he was already dead. Hence, Socrates did not die. (Sextus Empiricus)

▶ **2.** A man cannot serve both God and Mammon. But if a man does not serve Mammon, he starves; if he starves, he can't serve God. Therefore, a man cannot serve God.

▶ **3.** Modern physics asserts that there is no such thing as absolute motion. If this is correct, then there is no such thing as absolute time, and our ordinary notions of time are wrong. So, either our ordinary ideas about time or modern physics is mistaken.

▶ **4.** Either we ought to philosophize or we ought not. If we ought, then we ought. If we ought not, then also we ought (to justify this view). Hence in any case we ought to philosophize. (Aristotle)

▶ **5.** Most logic problems are easy. Nothing easy gives me a headache. Therefore, most things that give me a headache aren't logic problems.

▶ **6.** All flying horses are quick and clever; all flying horses live forever. And sad but true, all horses die. It follows that no horses fly.

7. Some illegal acts go unpunished. All blatantly wrong acts are punished. Therefore, some illegal acts are not blatantly wrong.

8. All who do not remember the past are condemned to repeat it. No one condemned to repeat the past looks forward to the future with eagerness. So, everyone who eagerly looks forward to the future remembers the past.

9. John respects no one who insults him. Everyone who dislikes John insults him. Thus, John respects everyone who likes him.

10. I like any bread that isn't too sweet. I dislike some breads that don't contain rye flour. So, some breads that don't contain rye flour are too sweet.

11. Lori is unhappy with some people who didn't write thank-you notes. Lori will send presents next year to everyone with whom she's happy. Therefore, some people who didn't write thank-you notes won't get presents from Lori next year.

▶ 12. Anyone who is not an idiot can see that Jake is lying. Some people in this room can't tell that Jake is lying. Hence, some people in this room are idiots.

13. Genevieve befriends anyone who has been treated unfairly. But she doesn't befriend some really obnoxious people. So, some really obnoxious people receive fair treatment.

14. The President is willing to appoint anyone who didn't work for opposing candidates. Not only people who worked for opposing candidates will accept the job. So, it's not true that nobody the President is willing to appoint will take the job.

15. No mammals but bats can fly. Every commonly kept house pet is a mammal, but none are bats. So nothing that can fly is a commonly kept house pet.

16. Nothing stupid is difficult. Everything you can do is stupid; anything that isn't difficult, I can do better than you. So anything you can do, I can do better.

17. A person is famous if and only if everyone has heard of him or her. So all famous people have heard of each other.

▶ 18. Popeye and Olive Oyl like each other, since Popeye likes everyone who likes Olive Oyl, and Olive Oyl likes everyone.

19. I like everyone who likes everyone I like. So, I don't dislike everyone.

20. A person is humble if and only if he or she doesn't admire himself or herself. It follows that nobody who admires all humble people is humble.

1.5 IMPLICATION AND EQUIVALENCE

A concept closely related to validity is *implication*. The verb 'imply' has various uses in English. Here we'll discuss just one, highly specialized use. We can express the idea that an argument is valid by saying that its conclusion *follows from* its premises. Equivalently, we can say that its premises *imply* or *entail* its conclusion. At least part of what we mean, in either case, is that the truth of the premises guarantees the truth of the conclusion. If the premises are true, the conclusion has to be true, too. Implication, then, is very similar to validity. But validity is a property of arguments; implication is a relation between sentences and sets of sentences.

A set of sentences implies a given sentence just in case the truth of that sentence is guaranteed by the truth of all the members of the set.

> **Definition** A set of sentences *implies* a sentence if and only if it's impossible for every member of the set to be true while that sentence is false.

If an argument is valid, the set consisting of its premises implies its conclusion.

We can also speak of a single sentence implying another sentence.

> **Definition** One sentence *implies* another if and only if it's impossible for the former to be true while the latter is false.

One sentence implies another, that is, if and only if the truth of the former guarantees the truth of the latter. In every circumstance in which the first is true, the second must be true as well.

Consider these two pairs of sentences:

(20) a. Alice was born in New York but now lives in Texas.
     b. Alice was born in New York.

(21) a. Bill will spend his vacation skiing or sailing.
     b. Bill will spend his vacation sailing.

Sentence (20)a implies (20)b. It's impossible to conceive of a situation in which it's true that Alice was born in New York but now lives in Texas, and false that Alice was born in New York. In such a circumstance, Alice would have to have been born, and not been born, in New York; the sentence 'Alice was born in New York' would have to be both true and false at the same time. There are no such circumstances; no sentence can be both true and false at the same time. So, the truth of (20)a guarantees the truth of (20)b. Does the truth of (21)a similarly guarantee the truth of (21)b? Obviously not. Imagine that Bill spends his vacation in Sun Valley, never going near the water. In this situation, (21)a is true, but (21)b is false. So, (21)a does not imply (21)b.

If two sentences imply each other, they must be true in exactly the same circumstances. In such a case, we say that they are *equivalent*.

> **Definition** One sentence is *equivalent* to another if and only if it's impossible for them to disagree in truth value.

Equivalent sentences must be true in the same circumstances, and false in the same circumstances. There could be no situation in which one would be true while the other would be false. Thus, equivalence amounts to implication in both directions. A is equivalent to B if and only if A implies B and B implies A.

Consider these more concrete examples:

(22) a. No dollar bills are purple.
     b. Nothing purple is a dollar bill.

(23) a. All bears are animals.
     b. All animals are bears.

The sentences in (22) are equivalent. Any circumstance in which no dollar bills are purple is one in which nothing purple is a dollar bill, and vice versa. Both sentences say that nothing is both purple and a dollar bill. In (23), however, the sentences are obviously not equivalent. All bears are animals, so (23)a is true. But not all animals are bears, so (23)b is false. The real world is a case in which these sentences disagree in truth value.

Problems

Consider the sentences in each pair: are they equivalent? If not, does either sentence imply the other?

▸ **1.** (a) I'll help with the dishes. (b) Frank and I will help with the dishes.

▸ **2.** (a) Geraldine went to Jamaica this year. (b) Geraldine went to Jamaica or Trinidad this year.

▸ **3.** (a) Paul and Kate are both from Cleveland. (b) Paul is from Cleveland, and so is Kate.

▸ **4.** (a) Donna and Miguel won't both win reelection. (b) Neither Donna nor Miguel will win reelection.

▸ **5.** (a) Dr. Jones or Dr. Smith will see you. (b) If Dr. Jones sees you, Dr. Smith won't.

▸ **6.** (a) If a fetus is a human being, then abortion is wrong. (b) If a fetus isn't a human being, then abortion is permissible.

7. (a) Xenia will graduate only if she improves her GPA. (b) If Xenia doesn't improve her GPA, she won't graduate.

8. (a) If Orrin retires next year, we will promote Edna. (b) We won't promote Edna unless Orrin retires next year.

9. (a) If either Barry or Jane drops out of the race, Yvonne will reap a huge windfall. (b) If Barry drops out of the race, Yvonne will reap a huge windfall.

10. (a) If Sandra and Harold leave by 11:00, I'll be amazed. (b) If Harold leaves by 11:00, I'll be amazed.

11. (a) Irma knows that Carl has been seeing Nina. (b) Carl has been seeing Nina, and Irma knows it.

▶ 12. (a) Quincy and Lou will join only if you do. (b) Quincy will join only if you do; the same holds for Lou.

13. (a) Fred will drop the suit if you settle for at least $50,000. (b) Fred will drop the suit only if you settle for $50,000.

14. (a) Everyone who can answer this question is clever. (b) Everyone who is clever can answer this question.

15. (a) No French wines are inexpensive. (b) No inexpensive wines are French.

16. (a) Several cabinet ministers are Socialists. (b) Several Socialists are cabinet ministers.

17. (a) All linebackers are strong and agile. (b) All linebackers are strong, and all are agile.

▶ 18. (a) No Communists favor both a free market and individual liberties. (b) No Communists favor a free market, and no Communists favor individual liberties.

19. (a) Few students have found jobs with metals or utility companies. (b) Few students have found jobs with utility companies, and few have found jobs with metals companies.

20. (a) Tracy ran up the stairs. (b) Tracy ran.

21. (a) You didn't have to leave the ring. (b) You could have stayed in the ring.

22. (a) Julian ate. (b) Julian ate something.

23. (a) Sam and Bob are brothers. (b) Bob is Sam's brother.

▶ 24. (a) Sam and Bob are brothers. (b) Sam is a brother, and so is Bob.

25. (a) Andy and Roxanne gave me a blow-by-blow description. (b) Andy gave me a blow-by-blow description, and so did Roxanne.

26. (a) Most cats like fish. (b) Few cats don't like fish.

27. (a) It's not true that at most two people can identify Pat. (b) At least three people can identify Pat.

28. (a) Karen knows Alice if anyone does. (b) Either Karen knows Alice, or nobody does.

29. (a) None but the brave deserve the fair. (b) All the brave deserve the fair.

▶ 30. (a) Only the good die young. (b) All who die young are good.

Consider the statement: 'If Ralph fails the final exam, he will fail the course'. What follows from this, together with the information listed?

31. Ralph will fail the final exam.   **32.** Ralph will fail the course.

33. Ralph won't fail the final exam.   **34.** Ralph won't fail the course.

Consider the statement: 'The patient will die unless we operate immediately'. What follows from this, together with the information listed?

35. The patient will die.   ▶ **36.** The patient will not die.

37. We will operate immediately.   **38.** We won't operate immediately.

Consider the statement: 'You may have soup or eggroll'. What follows from this?

39. You may have soup.

40. You may have both soup and eggroll.

Consider the statement: 'If a fetus is a person, it has a right to life'. Which of the following sentences follow from this? Which imply it?

41. A fetus is a person.

▶ **42.** If a fetus has a right to life, then it's a person.

43. A fetus has a right to life only if it's a person.

44. A fetus is a person only if it has a right to life.

45. If a fetus isn't a person, it doesn't have a right to life.

46. If a fetus doesn't have a right to life, it isn't a person.

47. A fetus has a right to life.

▶ **48.** A fetus isn't a person only if it doesn't have a right to life.

49. A fetus doesn't have a right to life only if it isn't a person.

50. A fetus doesn't have a right to life unless it's a person.

51. A fetus isn't a person unless it has a right to life.

52. A fetus is a person unless it doesn't have a right to life.

53. A fetus has a right to life unless it isn't a person.

Consider this statement from IRS publication 17, *Your Federal Income Tax:* 'If you are single, you must file a return if you had gross income of $3560 or more for the year'. What follows from this, together with the information listed?

▶ **54.** You are single with an income of $2500.

55. You are married with an income of $2500.

56. You are single with an income of $25,000.

57. You are married with an income of $25,000.

58. You are single but do not have to file a return.

59. You are married but do not have to file a return.

▶ **60.** You have an income of $4500 but do not have to file a return.

61. An old joke: Mutt says, "See you later"; Jeff answers, "Not if I see you first." Suppose that both statements are true. What follows?

62. Lao-Tzu said, "Real words are not vain, vain words not real." Are these two sentences equivalent? If not, in what circumstances could one be true while the other is false?

1.6 LOGICAL PROPERTIES OF SENTENCES

We use logic primarily to investigate logical connections among sentences. Nevertheless, we can also use it to classify individual sentences. The following sentences could be either true or false, depending on what the facts are. It's possible to conceive of cases in which they would be true and other cases in which they would be false.

(24) The next president will be a Democrat.

(25) Nicholas is flying to Santa Fe this weekend.

Such sentences are *contingent*.

> **DEFINITION** A sentence is *contingent* if and only if it's possible for it to be true and possible for it to be false.

Contingent sentences could be true, given the right set of circumstances. Of course, they could also be false, depending on the facts.

Some sentences, in contrast, cannot help being true. It's simply impossible for them to be false. Such sentences are called *tautologies* (or *tautologous, valid,* or *logically true*).

> **DEFINITION** A sentence is a *tautology* (or *tautologous, valid,* or *logically true*) if and only if it's impossible for it to be false.

If you doubt that there are any sentences that cannot be false, no matter what the facts may be, then try to imagine circumstances in which these sentences are false:

(26) A rose is a rose.

(27) When you're hot, you're hot.

These sentences are true in every possible circumstance. They also seem to say very little. But not all tautologies are so straightforward; (28), for example, is logically true:

(28) If everyone loves a lover, and Sam doesn't love Jeanne, then Jeanne doesn't love Greg.

Tautologies can be useful. They often set up the structure of an argument.

Tautologies and contingent sentences are *satisfiable*: They could be true. Some sentences could never be true. They are false, regardless of the facts. These sentences are *contradictory* (or *contradictions*).

> **DEFINITION**   A sentence is *contradictory* if and only if it's impossible for it to be true. (Otherwise, the sentence is *satisfiable*.)

Here are some examples of contradictions:

(29) The number 17 is both odd and even.

(30) Nobody's seen the trouble I've seen.

In no conceivable circumstance could these sentences be literally true. Try, for example, to imagine a situation in which 17 is both odd and even. And, since I've seen the trouble I've seen, somebody (namely, me) has indeed seen the trouble I've seen. Contradictions tend to signal that we should interpret some terms generously, since we assume that our colleagues in communication are trying to say something that could be true. Hearing (30), then, we tend to read 'nobody' as 'nobody else'. Contradictions often fulfill important functions in arguments. In fact, as you'll see in later chapters, one rule of logical deduction involves contradictions.

Since every sentence is either tautologous, contingent, or contradictory, the terms introduced in this section divide sentences into three groups, as shown in the accompanying diagram.

Sentences		
Tautologous	**Contingent**	**Contradictory**
True in every circumstance	True in some circumstances, false in others	False in every circumstance
	Satisfiable	
	True in some circumstances	

Problems

Classify these sentences as tautologous, contradictory, or contingent.

▸ **1.** Austin is in Texas.

▸ **2.** Every Texas city is in Texas.

▸ **3.** Some cats are calicos.

▸ **4.** All calicos are calicos.

▸ **5.** Some calicos are not calicos.

▸ **6.** I know what I know.

7. Some cats eat fish, and some don't.

8. Some cats eat fish and do not eat fish.

9. Most cats eat fish, and most don't.

10. There are many trees in Cibola National Forest.

11. All trees in Cibola National Forest are trees.

▸ **12.** I'll see you when I see you.

13. Some people respect everyone.

14. Some people respect no one.

15. Nobody respects nobody.

16. Anyone who respects everyone respects himself or herself.

17. Some bachelors are unhappy.

▸ **18.** All bachelors are unmarried.

19. Some bachelors are female.

20. ... what we are, we are.... (Alfred, Lord Tennyson)

21. The market may move in any direction.... (*USA Today*)

22. A lie is a lie, no matter how ancient; a truth is a truth, though it was born yesterday. (American proverb)

23. Nothing in business is so valuable as time. (John H. Patterson)

▸ **24.** Nay, Sir, argument is argument. (Samuel Johnson)

25. We are on an irreversible trend toward more freedom and democracy— but that could change. (Dan Quayle)

26. Nobody goes there any more—it's too crowded. (Yogi Berra)

27. He is audibly tan. (Fran Lebowitz)

28. ... if it doesn't work, it doesn't work. (Prince Charles)

29. Just because everything is different doesn't mean anything has changed. (Irene Peter)

▸ **30.** I've been healthy my whole career, except for nagging injuries the last few years. (Cincinnati farm system pitcher Mike Smith, at age 25)

31. It is a foolish man that hears all he hears. (Austin O'Malley)

32. Bigness is bigness in spite of a hundred mistakes. (Jawaharlal Nehru)

33. If you are a dog and your owner suggests that you wear a sweater ... suggest that he wear a tail. (Fran Lebowitz)

34. All babies are young. (Benjamin Spock)

35. If there's one major cause for the spread of mass illiteracy, it's the fact that everybody can read and write. (Peter de Vries)

▸ **36.** When people are out of work, unemployment results. (Calvin Coolidge)

37. All-out agitators, to be successful, must be moving with history. (Eric Goldman)

38. Our past has gone into history. (William McKinley)

39. The nobles are to be considered in two different manners; that is, they are either to be ruled so as to make them entirely dependent on your fortunes, or else not. (Niccolo Machiavelli)

40. There are two kinds of people in the world: those who divide the world into two kinds of people, and those who don't. (H. L. Mencken)

41. Suppose sentence A implies another sentence, B. What can we conclude about B, if A is (a) a tautology? (b) contingent? (c) satisfiable? (d) contradictory?

▸ **42.** Suppose sentence A implies another sentence, B. What can we conclude about A, if B is (a) a tautology? (b) contingent? (c) satisfiable? (d) contradictory?

43. Suppose sentence A is equivalent to sentence B. What can we conclude about A, if B is (a) a tautology? (b) contingent? (c) satisfiable? (d) contradictory?

The Englishman William of Ockham (*circa* 1285–1349), perhaps the most influential philosopher and logician of the fourteenth century, recorded eleven rules of logic in a chapter of his *Summa Totius Logicae*. Eight of these use concepts we've already developed. Say whether each is true, given the definitions of this chapter, and explain why.

44. The false never follows from the true.

45. The true may follow from the false.

46. Whatever follows from the conclusion of a valid argument follows from its premises.

47. The conclusion of a valid argument follows from anything that implies the argument's premises.

▶ **48.** The contingent does not follow from the valid.

49. The contradictory does not follow from the satisfiable.

50. Anything whatsoever follows from the contradictory.

51. The valid follows from anything whatsoever.

True or false? Explain your answer.

52. All tautologies are equivalent.

53. All contingent sentences are equivalent.

▶ **54.** All contradictions are equivalent.

55. All arguments with tautologies as conclusions are valid.

The following problems illustrate concepts from this chapter and raise some further puzzles:

You receive this party invitation: "Please come to a party this Friday at the Ashers' house at 8:00 P.M. Respond only if you can't come." Do you abide by this request if you:

56. Respond and don't come?   **57.** Respond and come?

58. Don't respond and come?   **59.** Don't respond and don't come?

▶ **60.** A road sign outside Donora, Pennsylvania, greeted visitors with this message: "Donora. The nicest town on earth, next to yours." Could this be true for every visitor? If so, what does that imply about Donora?

Discuss the following, and explain what's odd about them:

61. I exist.   **62.** It is I.

63. Stock up and save. Limit 1. (Advertisement in the Akron *Beacon-Journal*)

64. ... there is nothing to indicate the child is actually lost, other than the fact that she is missing. (Policeman, quoted in the Washington *Spotlight*)

65. Illiterate? Write Today for Free Help. (Sign in San Francisco buses)

These puzzles concern a land of knights and knaves. Knights always say true things; knaves always utter falsehoods. You are a traveler in this strange land and must try to identify the people you meet as either knights or knaves.[3] You encounter two people, Punch and Judy, one or both of whom speak to you. What can you deduce in each case about whether they are knights or knaves?

▸ **66.** *Judy:* Either I'm a knight, or I'm not.

67. *Judy:* If Punch is a knave, so am I.

68. *Punch:* If I'm a knight, Judy's a knave.

69. *Judy:* Neither of us is a knight.

70. *Punch:* We're not both knights.

71. *Judy:* Punch is a knight, and I'm a knave.

▸ **72.** *Judy:* If either of us is a knight, Punch is.

73. *Punch:* If either of us is a knave, I am.

74. *Punch:* Judy's a knave.
    Judy: We're not both knaves.

75. *Punch:* Judy's a knight.
    Judy: At least one of us is a knave.

76. *Punch:* Judy's a knight if and only if her sister is.
    Judy: Unfortunately, my sister's a knave.

77. *Punch:* Judy and her brother are both knights.
    Judy: Well, I'm a knight, but my brother isn't.

At this point, you meet three people in the land of knights and knaves. What can you deduce about their status?

▸ **78.** *Curly:* Larry's a knave.
    Moe: Either Curly or Larry is a knave.
    Larry: If I'm a knave, they are too.

79. *Curly:* Moe's a knight.
    Moe: We're all knaves.
    Larry: Curly, Moe, and their cousins are all knaves.

80. *Curly:* We're not all knaves.
    Moe: Curly is.
    Larry: If Curly is, Moe is too.

Some of the following paradoxes are ancient, some are medieval, and some are modern. Many still provoke debate among philosophers and logicians.

81. In an ancient paradox, the liar says: "This sentence is false." Is the sentence true or false?

82. The paradox of the heap: "Every man with no hair on his head is bald. But if we add just one hair to a bald man's head, he remains bald. Therefore, every man is bald, no matter how many hairs he has on his head." Where does the argument go wrong?

83. The paradox of the horned man: "What you have not lost you still have. But you haven't lost horns. Therefore, you still have horns." Where does the argument go wrong?

▶ 84. The paradox of the hooded man: "You know your brother. But that man who just walked in with a hood over his head is your brother, and you didn't know him." How is this possible?[4]

85. The paradox of the court: "Protagoras taught a student, Euathlus, the law; they agreed that the student would pay Protagoras a fee when he won his first case. After a time Euathlus had engaged no cases, and Protagoras sued for his fee. He argued, 'If I win this case, you must pay me the fee, by the court's decision. If you win, you must pay me the fee by our agreement. Therefore, in either case, you must pay me the fee'. The student answered, 'If I win, then I need not pay, by the court's decision. If you win, I need not pay, by our agreement. So, in either case, I need not pay'." Surely Protagoras and Euathlus can't both be right. But where does the reasoning of either go astray?

86. A medieval puzzle: "Every part of Socrates is smaller than Socrates. But, if all of Socrates is smaller than Socrates, Socrates is smaller than himself." What went wrong?

87. Another medieval puzzle: "Suppose one cat, Tibbles, is sitting on a mat. Let's say Tibbles has 1000 hairs. If any hair (say h) were missing, what would be left (Tibbles $- h$) would still be a cat. But Tibbles is not the same as Tibbles $- h$. Moreover, pulling a hair from a cat does not generate a cat. Therefore, there are at least 1001 cats on the mat." What went wrong?[5]

88. A variant on the liar, called the strong liar: "This sentence is not true." Is the sentence true, false, or neither?

89. A paradox of fulfillment: "Don't obey this command." Can the command be obeyed? Disobeyed?

▶ 90. Another paradox of fulfillment: "I promise not to keep this promise." Can the promise be kept?

91. The paradox of the knower: "This sentence can't be known." Is the sentence true or false?

92. The barber paradox: "In a certain village is a barber who shaves all and only those who do not shave themselves. Who shaves the barber?"[6]

93. Russell's paradox: "Consider the set of all sets that are not members of themselves. Is it a member of itself?"

94. Grelling's paradox: "Say that a term is *heterological* if and only if it doesn't apply to itself. 'Dog' is heterological, for the word is not itself

a dog. 'Word', 'short', and 'multisyllabic', however, are not heterological. Is 'heterological' heterological?"

95. The surprise examination paradox: The professor announces that the final exam will be next week at 9:00 A.M. but that the students won't know on which day (Monday, Tuesday, Wednesday, Thursday, or Friday) the exam will occur until the day of the exam. A student reasons: "The exam won't be given on Friday; if it hasn't occurred by Thursday at 9:01 A.M., we'll all know then—before the day of the exam—that it will be on Friday. But then it won't be given on Thursday; if it hasn't occurred by 9:01 A.M. Wednesday, we'll know that it must be Thursday, since it can't of course be on Friday. By the same reasoning, it can't be given on any day next week." Confident of this reasoning, the student doesn't bother to study, and leaves for home. Much to the student's surprise, the exam is given on Thursday, and the student fails the course. What was the error in the student's reasoning?

Notes

[1] There are arguments without any premises. They consist of an empty sequence of premises and a conclusion.

[2] See Anselm, *Proslogion* II, III; Aquinas, *Summa Theologiae*, Ia. 2, 3. (The translations are my own.)

[3] These examples are based on puzzles developed by Raymond Smullyan in *What Is the Name of this Book?* (Englewood Cliffs, N.J.: Prentice-Hall, 1978).

[4] This and the preceding three paradoxes were discovered by Eubulides, a Megarian logician of the fourth century B.C.

[5] This puzzle, from William of Sherwood (1200/1210–1266/1271), is discussed by Peter Geach in *Reference and Generality* (Ithaca, N.Y.: Cornell University Press, 1962, 1980), pp. 215–16.

[6] This and the following paradox were posed by Bertrand Russell.

2

EVIDENCE

AND

RELEVANCE

ruth and reliability are important components of good arguments. But, as we saw in Chapter 1, good arguments must meet other conditions. A good argument generally presents premises to provide evidence for a conclusion that follows from those premises and to which the premises are relevant. The definitions of validity and soundness, however, mention neither evidence nor relevance. A variety of sound arguments therefore appear, from an intuitive point of view, peculiar and unsuccessful.

Some violate our ordinary notion of evidence. Suppose that the earth will be invaded by purple people eaters next year, but that we possess no evidence now to support this. Then the argument

(1) The earth will be invaded by purple people eaters next year.
∴ The earth will be invaded by purple people eaters next year.

is sound. Given our supposition, the premise is true, and the conclusion is surely true whenever the premise is, since they are the same sentence. But this argument won't convince anyone that we ought to be building defenses; it doesn't establish its conclusion in the usual, evidence-related sense of 'establish'.

Some arguments also count as sound even though they violate our usual notion of relevance. The argument

(2) Queens is the largest borough in New York City.
∴ Every Buick is a Buick.

is sound. The premise is true, and the conclusion can never be false while the premise is true, simply because the conclusion can never be false. Yet this argument, too, seems bizarre. The premise is irrelevant to the conclusion. Thus, an adequate theory of argument must take evidence and relevance into account.

2.1 BEGGING THE QUESTION

The condition of evidence requires that the premises of an argument offer evidence for its conclusion. We can think of the common ground as the starting point of an argument, and the desired conclusion—or, better, a new common ground incorporating that conclusion—as its endpoint. A successful argument changes the common ground; the premises move the audience from the starting point to the end point.

The requirement of evidence presupposes that people can think of sentences, relative to a given common ground, as more evident or less evident. That is, from some particular point of view, some sentences may be well known; others may be known, but not very widely. Some may be easily justifiable, whereas others would require extensive justification to be accepted. Some may be regarded as dubious; some may be known to be false.

Aristotle spoke of some sentences as coming before others "in the order of knowledge." If we can think of some sentences having priority over others in this way (relative to some common ground), then we can express the condition of evidence differently: The premises of a successful argument should be more evident than the conclusion. In the words of the influential seventeenth-century Port Royal *Logic*, "what serves as proof must be clearer and better known than what we seek to prove."[1]

More evident

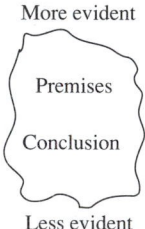

Premises

Conclusion

Less evident

The condition of evidence becomes clear when we consider the effects of violating it. What fallacies result from violations of the condition of evidence? Consider the argument about the future invasion of the earth:

(1) The earth will be invaded by purple people eaters next year.
∴ The earth will be invaded by purple people eaters next year.

The premise doesn't provide evidence for the conclusion; it *is* the conclusion. Unless we already accepted the conclusion, we would have no reason to accept the premise. The premise and conclusion, being the same sentence, are evident to the same degree no matter what information the common ground contains.

The situation is no better if premises are added to the argument. Consider this more expanded version:

(2) The earth will be invaded by purple people eaters next year.
I've told several people about it.
Gary thought I was crazy, but Penelope was quite upset.
∴ The earth will be invaded by purple people eaters next year.

So long as any premise needed to derive the conclusion is no more evident than the conclusion itself, the argument is unsuccessful because it violates the condition of evidence.

Any argument in which the conclusion appears explicitly as a premise exemplifies a fallacy called *begging the question*. Other sorts of argument also exemplify this fallacy. For example, the conclusion may appear among the premises, not verbatim, but substantially rephrased. The phrasing makes no difference; the conclusion will still depend on a premise no more evident than the conclusion itself.

(3) Next year, violet, human-devouring creatures will invade this planet.
∴ The earth will be invaded by purple people eaters next year.

This argument should convince no one. Nobody who doesn't already believe the conclusion would subscribe to the premise.

A more interesting begging of the question occurs when the conclusion does not appear in the premises directly but is *presupposed* by the premises.

Definition   A set of sentences S *presupposes* a sentence A if and only if anyone felicitously asserting S must take A for granted.[2]

A felicitous assertion is apt or appropriate in the circumstances, whether it happens to be true or false. If Jorge asks what time it is, and you respond, "12:15," your response is felicitous. It's the right *kind* of response, even if the time is really 3:30. If, in contrast, you say, "Yes," or "Central Standard," or "Rain," you have answered inappropriately. Your response is infelicitous.

Some philosophers have held that infelicitous assertions are false; others, that they are neither true nor false. Some have held that felicity and truth are completely independent, so that a sentence may be both infelicitous and true. We won't worry about that question here. What matters is that infelicitous assertions are in some way deviant. Recognizing a statement as infelicitous, people tend to react, not with an expression of assent or dissent, but one of puzzlement: "What?" "Wait a minute." "Huh?" "I don't understand." "What do you mean?" "But . . ." We assume that there is a problem of communication, not of reasoning.

Some examples may make the definition of presupposition clearer. Suppose that Kim enters the room and exclaims,

(4) The king of Connecticut has been assassinated!

This sentence presupposes that Connecticut has a king. Someone can felicitously assert the sentence only if there is a king of Connecticut. Since, in fact, Connecticut has no king, we would regard Kim's statement as infelicitous— as a joke, perhaps, or as revealing some serious deficiencies in Kim's education.

Here is another example. Suppose we read in the newspaper,

(5) Ursula now regrets having married her accountant.

This presupposes that Ursula did marry her accountant. If she didn't, then the newspaper's assertion is infelicitous.

Finally, suppose Ming declares,

(6) Denise's husband is an idiot.

This assertion presupposes that Denise is married. Someone can felicitously call Denise's husband an idiot only if Denise's husband exists, that is, only if Denise has a husband. And she can have a husband only if she is married.

Presupposition plays a role in questions of evidence because the presuppositions of a felicitous statement are at least as evident as the statement itself. An assertion may be no more evident than what it presupposes. Consider the above examples. The sentence 'The king of Connecticut has been assassinated' cannot be more evident than 'Connecticut has a king': Any evidence for the former would by its very nature constitute evidence for the latter. And any evidence against the latter would constitute evidence for the infelicity, if not the outright falsehood, of the former. For the same reason, 'Ursula regrets having married her accountant' cannot be more evident than 'Ursula married her accountant', and 'Denise's husband is an idiot' cannot be more evident than 'Denise is married'.

We may now define begging the question in general terms:

> **DEFINITION** An argument *begs the question* if and only if the premises include or presuppose the conclusion.[3]

A classic instance of an argument whose premises presuppose its conclusion is this:

(7) The Bible says that God exists.
The Bible was inspired by God.
Any writing inspired by God is true.
∴ God exists.

The second premise, 'The Bible was inspired by God', presupposes the conclusion. One can't felicitously assert 'The Bible was inspired by God' without taking it for granted that God exists. Consequently, any evidence for the second premise would automatically be evidence for the conclusion, and any evidence against the conclusion would tell against that premise. The premise cannot be any more evident than the conclusion. The argument, therefore, violates the condition of evidence.

Problems

What are the presuppositions of each of these sentences?

▶ **1.** Quincy likes Wanda.

▶ **2.** Ellen knows where Rick and Ted were last night.

▶ **3.** Irma has stopped complaining about the price.

▶ **4.** Polly's cat is asleep.

▶ **5.** All of Alan's friends hope he succeeds.

▶ **6.** Even Saul was angry.

7. Danielle managed to finish the story.

8. Federico left Del Rio just after midnight.

9. Genevieve didn't realize that Hawaii is farther south than Miami.

10. Hank's dog barked at her own reflection.

11. It's odd that nobody recognized Jerry.

▶ **12.** The present king of France is bald.

13. Lois says that the present king of France is bald.

14. If France now has a king, he's bald.

15. France now has a king, and he's bald.

16. Either the present king of France is bald, or there is no king of France.

17. Zoe hopes to marry the present king of France.

▸ **18.** Carla knows the present king of France, and Violet is dating him.

19. If Ben realizes that we've absconded, the police will be after us.

20. If Ben had realized that we'd absconded, the police would have been after us.

Which of these arguments beg the question? Explain.

21. It's disloyal to be a communist, for communism is a traitorous doctrine.

22. Adultery is immoral, since sexual relations outside marriage violate ethical principles.

23. Certainly there is life after death. The proof may be found in the ouija board, since the messages the board transmits are from departed souls.

▸ **24.** Abortion is wrong, because it's tantamount to murder.

25. Of course there's an Earl of Kent. I've seen his house.

26. Nick knows that Mindy is married, since he's met her husband.

27. Abortion is wrong, because it involves the killing of innocent human life.

28. Matt is unemployed; so, he's out of work.

29. Terrorism is bad, because it encourages further acts of terrorism.

▸ **30.** Many people have argued about the existence of mind reading, and, although they've reached no clear consensus, it's hard to doubt that some form of mind reading exists.

Using each of the five following sentences as a conclusion, construct an argument that begs the question. The premises should presuppose, not merely contain, the conclusion. Explain what's wrong with the argument.

31. The sea meets the shore.

32. Water is wet.

33. $2 + 2 = 4$.

34. Triangles have three angles.

35. Things equal to the same thing are equal to each other.

36. Begging the question has sometimes been called the most serious fallacy, on the grounds that an argument committing it has a fatal flaw and can't easily be repaired. Do you agree? Why, or why not?

2.2 Complex Questions

Sometimes questions have presuppositions: we can't felicitously ask them without taking certain things for granted. Since questions aren't assertions, however, and can't act as premises of arguments, this in itself poses no logical difficulties. But questions with presuppositions have a further feature: they can't be answered unless what they presuppose is true. Any answer to them presupposes what they presuppose. The classic case is,

(8) Have you stopped beating your wife?

You can't answer yes or no without, in effect, admitting your former wife-beating. If you respond, "Yes, I have," your answer presupposes that you've beaten your wife in the past. If you respond, "No, I haven't," it's even worse: You not only have beaten your wife in the past but are also still doing it! The only way to respond without admitting prior wife-beating is to challenge the presupposition: "What? I've never beaten my wife." This amounts to rejecting the question rather than answering it. If you answer, you've admitted the presupposition into the common ground, where it can be used against you, without its having been justified.

Questions like (9) are called *complex questions.*

> **Definition**   A question *presupposes* a sentence if and only if the question can't be answered unless the sentence is true.

> **Definition**   A question is *complex* if and only if it has presuppositions.

Such questions are ubiquitous. Most are harmless. The question

(9) What's the capital of Pennsylvania?

presupposes that Pennsylvania exists and has a capital. It's unlikely that anyone would object to these assumptions. So, complex questions are a problem only when their answers have dubious presuppositions. Asking a question with a presupposition, or drawing a conclusion from such a question, involves no fallacy unless the presupposition isn't part of, and shouldn't be accepted into, the common ground.

Even in such circumstances, complex questions would rarely lead to inappropriate conclusions if it were not for an important and pervasive linguistic phenomenon involving presupposition. This phenomenon is known as *accommodation.* Presuppositions required by a statement enter the common ground unless someone objects to them.[4] Perhaps nobody reading the article on Ursula's love life knows that Ursula married her accountant. That information is not included in the common ground. Nevertheless, as soon as the newspaper says that she regrets having married her accountant, the presupposition springs into existence and is accepted into the common ground.

Similarly, when we hear Ming decry the idiocy of Denise's husband, we adopt as part of our shared assumptions that Denise is married and has a husband, even if we knew nothing about this before.

Of course, accommodation is not automatic. An objection can prevent it. Suppose you are in the room when Kim exclaims that the king of Connecticut has been assassinated. You can prevent the assimilation of the presupposition that Connecticut has a king by objecting, perhaps by saying, "What are you talking about? States don't have kings." Accommodation, therefore, is not inevitable, but it is the default option: We admit presuppositions into the common ground unless someone challenges them.

This explains the power, and the danger, of complex questions. A complex question makes a presupposition that, if not challenged, becomes part of the common ground. Once in that body of shared assumptions, it may serve as a conclusion and play a role in additional arguments, leading to further and possibly illegitimate conclusions. Unless you effectively deny the presupposition that you've beaten your wife, for example, the audience may well base further conclusions on the assumption that you are a wife beater. It's important, therefore, to recognize presuppositions and be prepared to challenge them. Precisely because accommodation is the norm, however, challenging them is difficult. We are in the habit of trying to cooperate with our partners in conversation. We are so accustomed to accommodating their presuppositions that we have a hard time casting a critical eye upon them.

An excellent example of a complex question occurs in a rhetorical question at the beginning of Cicero's most famous oration against Cataline: "How much longer will you abuse us, O Cataline? How much longer will your unbridled boldness thrash itself about?" These questions presuppose that Cataline has been abusing us with reckless audacity. They don't, however, present any evidence for this presupposition. Cicero is in danger, therefore, of committing the fallacy of complex question. His oration avoids that fallacy by going on to present evidence of Cataline's abuses.

Other cases of complex questions involve compound questions that, in effect, pose two questions and presuppose that a single answer suffices for both. "Will you be kind and let me have an extension on that paper?" suggests that kindness and agreeing to the extension go together. "Are we going to sign and be cheated by them again?" presupposes that they've cheated us in the past and that our signing will let them cheat us again. To respond to these questions without assenting to their presuppositions, we can split them into their components and insist on giving different answers to each. For example, we might respond, "I'll be kind, but you can't have the extension," or, "We're going to sign, but the contract is solid; they won't be able to cheat us again." In parliamentary procedure, a motion to divide the question—to split a question into two or more component questions—takes precedence over other motions, precisely because of the danger of fallacy that complex questions involve.

Why do complex questions sometimes lead to a violation of the condition of evidence? The condition requires that the premises be more evident to the audience than the conclusion. But the presuppositions of a felicitous statement are at least as evident as the statement itself. Nothing is more evident than what it presupposes. In an argument relying on a complex question, the conclusion is presupposed by the way the issue has been framed. So, again, the conclusion is at least as evident as a premise. A question, though it may frame the issue, rarely offers evidence for anything.

Problems

What are the presuppositions, if any, of the following questions?

▶ **1.** How long have you been poisoning people?

▶ **2.** When did you start seeing roaches in your apartment?

▶ **3.** What time is it?

▶ **4.** When did you stop embezzling money from the bank?

▶ **5.** Did you realize it was wrong to take the money?

▶ **6.** Are you sorry that you cheated on the test?

7. Don't you want to go to the movies?

8. When will you stop stealing candy from babies?

9. Why don't you like your family?

10. Would you like another beer?

11. Are you proud of cheating on your taxes?

▶ **12.** How can anyone govern a nation that has 246 different kinds of cheese? (Charles de Gaulle)

13. Why was American slavery the most awful the world has ever known? (Nathan Glazer)

14. How is it that little children are so intelligent and men so stupid? (Alexandre Dumas, fils)

15. Why does not the pope, whose riches are at this day more ample than those of Croesus, build the basilica of St. Peter with his own money rather than with that of poor believers? (Martin Luther, 1517)

16. (a) Why aren't American goods competitive abroad?
   (b) Why do things break?
   (c) Why don't they work anymore?
   (d) Whatever happened to good old American workmanship and quality? (James Brady)

17. (a) Was Reconstruction shamefully harsh or surprisingly lenient?
   (b) Could Lincoln have succeeded where Johnson failed?
   (c) Was the latter a miserable bungler or a heroic victim?
   (d) How well did the freedman meet his new responsibilities?
   (e) When did racial segregation harden into its elaborate mold? (Don E. Fehrenbacher)

18. Ezra is accused of murdering his rich uncle Elias by running him over with a car. You are a prosecutor with no real case but with a desire to trap Ezra into admitting that he had a motive, had opportunity, and actually committed the crime. (a) Write a set of complex questions designed to presuppose and lead Ezra into admitting these things. (b) Swap the answers to (a) with others, and state the presuppositions of their questions.

2.3 RELEVANCE: REFUTATIONS

The condition of relevance requires that an argument be directed at the point at issue. This demand seems both straightforward and easy to meet. Straightforward it may be, but people have devised various ways of frustrating it. Sometimes a person advances an irrelevant argument as an intentional bit of sophistry to avoid a tough issue. Sometimes the parties to the conversation are confused about what the issue really is; sometimes they are arguing at cross purposes. And sometimes people agree about what the issue is at the outset but change the issue during the course of the conversation because of fatigue, inattention, confusion, or retreat.

As with the condition of evidence, it's easiest to understand the criterion of relevance by witnessing its violation. In this section, therefore, we'll consider several fallacies based on violations of the relevance condition. All are attempted refutations: They try to refute another argument. What they actually accomplish, however, is something else.

Ad hominem (or *ad personam*) arguments—arguments "to the man (or person)"—attempt to refute positions by attacking those who hold or argue for them. The attack may consist of an assault on a person's integrity, moral character, psychological health, or intellectual ability. If so, the *ad hominem* is termed *abusive*. Or, the attack may consist of a charge of inconsistency or unreliability due to a person's special circumstances. In such cases, the *ad hominem* is termed *circumstantial*. Both may violate the condition of relevance, for they are directed, not at the issue at hand, but at the people holding some view of that issue.

Abusive *Ad Hominem*

Abusive *ad hominem* arguments try to discredit an argument by insulting the arguer.

> **DEFINITION**   An argument is an *abusive ad hominem* argument if and only if it purports to discredit a position by insulting those who hold it.

The insult may assail a person's integrity or moral character. The political opponents of Edward Kennedy, for example, have occasionally raised the issue of his accident at Chappaquiddick. This may be relevant to the senator's character, which in turn may be relevant to his qualifications for office. When used to argue against a position he holds, however, the charge is *ad hominem*. Whether or not the senator is personally irresponsible has no bearing on the truth of his beliefs on whether the government should provide universal health insurance, raise the minimum wage, or have an activist judiciary.

The insult may strike at a person's mental health. Franklin Roosevelt, while in office, was derided as insane, suffering from an Oedipus complex and a "silver cord complex"; his next-door neighbor termed him "a swollen-headed nitwit with a Messiah complex and the brain of a boy scout."[5] These insults aren't arguments, let alone fallacious arguments. To use them against Roosevelt's positions or policies, however, is fallacious. Some writers have argued that Bishop Berkeley's philosophy, according to which all "material" objects are really just complexes of ideas, stems from an obsessive-compulsive neurosis (that is, bad toilet training). This psychological hypothesis is not itself a fallacy. But to use it to discredit Berkeley's philosophy, to argue that it is false, is to commit an *ad hominem* fallacy. Other writers have condemned the German philosopher Friedrich Nietzsche's works as the ravings of a lunatic. Nietzsche did spend the last years of his life in a mental institution; this does not show, however, that what he wrote is false. Neurotics and even madmen may speak the truth.

Finally, an *ad hominem* argument may insult the intellectual capacities of an opponent. Some people believe that only a stupid person would disagree with them. American journalist H. L. Mencken abused American presidents fiercely, for intellectual as well as other failings. He referred to Warren Harding as a "stonehead," but most of his attacks concerned moral character. He called Theodore Roosevelt "blatant, crude, overly confidential, devious, tyrannical, vainglorious and sometimes quite childish." Coolidge was "petty, sordid and dull," "a cheap and trashy fellow . . . almost devoid of any notion of honour . . . a dreadful little cad." Mencken attributed to Herbert Hoover "a natural instinct for low, disingenuous, fraudulent manipulators" but saved his best abuse for Franklin Roosevelt, calling him "the Führer" and "the quack," and terming his administration "an astounding rabble of impudent nobodies," "a gang of half-educated pedagogues, non-constitutional lawyers, starry-eyed uplifters and other such sorry wizards."[6]

Ad Lincoln

Abraham Lincoln, one of our greatest presidents, was widely abused in both the northern and southern press while in office. In the South, he was called "a drunk" and "a cross between a sandhill crane and an Andalusian jackass," among other things. Northern newspapers used these terms to assault Lincoln's character between 1861 and 1865:[7]

Abraham Africanus I
an awful, woeful ass
baboon
blackguard
craftiest and most dishonest politician that ever disgraced an office
   in America
empty skull
filthy story-teller
gorilla
half-witted usurper
head ghoul at Washington
Illinois beast
mole-eyed monster with a soul of leather
obscene clown
orangutan
original gorilla
pitiable
political coward
shattered, dazed and utterly foolish
slang-wanging stump speaker
timid and ignorant
too slow
turtle at the head of the government
Tyrant
unmentionably diseased
woodenhead at Washington

Beware of drawing conclusions even from widespread and extreme abuse.

Circumstantial *Ad Hominem*

Circumstantial *ad hominem* arguments try to discredit an argument by appealing to the situation, motives, beliefs, or other characteristics of the arguer. They attempt to refute a person's position by claiming that he or she "has an ax to grind."

DEFINITION   An argument is a *circumstantial ad hominem* argument if and only if it purports to discredit a position by appealing to the circumstances or characteristics of those who hold it.

Usually, circumstantial *ad hominem* arguments charge a person or group with holding a position solely because it serves their own interests. People tend to advance arguments of this sort against lobbying groups. The Tobacco Institute, for example, frequently releases reports raising questions about the link between smoking and disease and routinely denounces reports claiming to establish such links. Critics of the institute often dismiss its statements on the grounds that the tobacco industry funds its research. This is a circumstantial *ad hominem*: The critics charge that the motives of those who pay for the institute's work suffice to discredit it. Of course, to point out this fallacy is not to recommend the institute's research or its conclusions. Rather, to determine the health effects of smoking, we must evaluate the content of research on both sides of the question. To reject a position because of the motives or sources of financial support behind it is to advance a circumstantial *ad hominem* argument.

Although such arguments violate the relevance condition and fail to establish the point in question, they are often very persuasive. As William Paley once remarked, "Who can refute a sneer?" Consider the inference from the Tobacco Institute's funding sources to the worthlessness of its reports. The inference is fallacious, but the tobacco industry's funding of the institute does show that it may be biased and, so, not a reliable source of information.

Evaluating the reliability of an argument is very different from evaluating the reliability of a person. We decide whether to accept what someone else says, in part, on the basis of how reliable we judge that person to be. This is as it should be. If we find out that someone is biased, we will probably judge that person less reliable. When a person advances an argument, however, giving reasons for a conclusion, then reliability is no longer so important. The reliability of others bears on whether we should accept any premises they introduce, but not on whether their arguments are good and deserve to convince us. In the words of Samuel Johnson,

> Nay, Sir, argument is argument. You cannot help paying regard to their arguments if they are good. If it were testimony, you might disregard it.... Testimony is like an arrow shot from a long bow; the force of it depends on the strength of the hand that draws it. Argument is like an arrow shot from a cross bow, which has equal force though shot by a child.[8]

Circumstantial *ad hominem* arguments, then, may establish something about the reliability of an opponent but do not establish the incorrectness of that person's position.

The same holds for abusive *ad hominem* arguments. A crook, madman, or idiot may provide accurate information, but it's reasonable not to bet on it. If the crook, madman, or idiot advances an argument, we are obliged to evaluate the argument on its own. But we may—indeed, should—consider the person's reliability when deciding whether to believe the premises. Of course, abusive *ad hominem* arguments are suspect for another reason: The abuse heaped on an opponent is rarely deserved. Many more people are called fools, cowards, and imbeciles than actually deserve those insults. So, abuse should affect our judgment of someone's reliability only if there is some basis for it.

Neither sort of *ad hominem* gives us any right, however, to believe the opposite of what someone says. We may refuse to accept the premises of an opponent's argument because we judge that person to be unreliable. But we may not, on the strength of that, assume that the premises or the conclusion are false. Just because a corrupt, crazy, silly, stupid, or biased person believes something is no justification for thinking the opposite.

Of course, sometimes the reliability of a person is the issue at hand. Suppose that Jones is testifying in court about Hanlon's racketeering. The opposing lawyer may introduce evidence to show that Jones himself is an ex-convict who still associates with shady characters; that his initial statement to the police conflicts with his current testimony; that he is a known liar and confidence artist; and that he owed Hanlon money, giving him a motive to help send Hanlon to prison. Some of these charges may seem to be abusive *ad hominem* arguments; others, circumstantial. They do not, however, make the lawyer's argument fallacious. Jones's reliability is precisely the issue. Therefore, his character and situation are highly relevant.

Tu Quoque

A special sort of circumstantial *ad hominem* argument appeals to the situation, motives, beliefs, or other characteristics of the audience to charge them with inconsistency or hypocrisy unless they accept the conclusion.

> **Definition** An argument is *tu quoque* if and only if it purports to discredit a position by charging those who hold it with inconsistency or hypocrisy.

Tu quoque (pronounced too-KWOH-kway), literally, means "you, too." *Tu quoque* arguments based on a charge of inconsistency point out that an opponent does not believe his or her own argument: If the opponent doesn't believe it, then surely the rest of us don't need to take it seriously. Those based on a charge of hypocrisy point out that an opponent is not practicing what he or she is preaching: If the opponent doesn't act on the basis of his or her own argument, then the rest of us may ignore it also.

A classic case of this fallacy involves a confrontation between a hunter and a person who eats meat but objects to hunting. The latter denounces shooting animals; the hunter responds by saying, "If you think killing animals is wrong, why do you eat meat?" The hunter is charging the meat eater with inconsistency or hypocrisy, depending on whether that person believes that his or her own meat eating is justifiable or not.

Inconsistent or hypocritical people may advance successful arguments and utter true sentences. The fallacy, then, consists in arguing from someone's inconsistency or hypocrisy to the falsity of one of his or her beliefs. Like other forms of circumstantial *ad hominem* arguments, *tu quoque* arguments often persuade. Nobody likes to be inconsistent or hypocritical. If the argument convinces the hearers that they exhibit one of these failings, they will naturally try to revise their beliefs or practices. For this reason, *tu quoque* arguments may succeed in persuading despite violating the condition of relevance.

Tu quoque arguments may demonstrate someone's inconsistency or hypocrisy. They may even be convincing. But do they establish anything about the issue at hand? Some do, and some don't. We need to distinguish those based on a charge of inconsistency from those based on allegations of hypocrisy.

Consider first a case of alleged hypocrisy. Suppose that Gus has just received an unexplained credit of $100 on his MasterCard bill. Pepe tells him that he should write to the bank explaining the error. Gus argues that Pepe would keep the money if it had been credited to his account; he concludes that he should keep the money. Gus's argument has this form:

(10) If the bank had credited the money to your account, you'd keep it.
The money was credited to my account.
∴ I should keep it.

Clearly, the premises show something irrelevant to the desired conclusion. Pepe may be a hypocrite, but that shows nothing about whether Gus should keep the money. The argument thus violates the condition of relevance. Nevertheless, it has some point: It challenges Pepe to explain why he would keep the money, even if he believes it to be wrong. Perhaps he doesn't really believe it's wrong. (This is what Gus would like him to admit.) Perhaps, however, he is weak-willed. "Do as I say, not as I do," goes the old saying. That someone doesn't do as he or she says proves nothing about the correctness or incorrectness of what that person says.

Consider, in contrast, a case of alleged inconsistency. Candidate Jack observes that the incumbent, Jill, is surrounded by underlings accused of serious wrongdoing, and assaults her ethical standards. Jack proclaims that anyone who exhibits even an appearance of impropriety should be fired. During the campaign, Jack's campaign manager and several officials of Jack's party are charged with criminal activities. Jack, however, defends these officials and allows them to retain their posts. Jill seizes upon this as a campaign issue, refuting Jack's charges of ethical laxity by accusing him of inconsistency.

In effect, Jill advances this argument:

> (11) Jack says that anyone exhibiting an appearance of impropriety should be fired, and that failure to fire such a person is itself an ethical offense.
>
> Jack now says that, although several staff members and party officials appear to have committed improprieties, they should be kept on.
>
> ∴ There's nothing wrong with my ethical standards.

On its face, this appears to be a terrible argument. What Jack does or says is irrelevant to the issue of whether Jill's ethical standards are sufficiently rigorous.

Yet the argument has real power, for three reasons. First, it does establish Jack's inconsistency. It shows that there is something wrong with his position. Second, a basic principle of moral philosophy holds that similar situations should be judged similarly: that differences in ethical judgment or treatment can be justified only by morally relevant differences between the cases involved. Supplemented by this principle, Jill's argument seems to show that the two candidates are on a par. Jack's behavior is acceptable if and only if Jill's is; either both are guilty of ethical laxity or neither is. This is not the conclusion Jill is trying to reach, but it is a legitimate and perhaps illuminating conclusion nonetheless. Third, the voters must choose between Jill and Jack. The moral laxity of one would seem to be a reason to vote for the other. But, if they are equally lax (or equally rigorous), then the ethical issue provides no reason for voting for one over the other at all. Jill's argument, therefore, may justifiably succeed in neutralizing Jack's rhetorical attack, even though it fails to establish its conclusion.

The problem with *tu quoque* arguments, then, is that "the conclusion which is actually established is not the *absolute* and *general* one in question, but *relative* and particular; viz., not that 'such and such is the fact,' but that '*this man* is bound to admit it' . . . ," on pain of inconsistency or hypocrisy.[9] Gus shows, not that keeping the money is permissible, but that, if Pepe doesn't admit it, he's a hypocrite. Similarly, Jill's argument fails to demonstrate her ethical solidity but does show that Jack must admit it or stand so charged as well.

Consequently, *tu quoque* arguments, although they fail to establish the desired conclusion, can be effective. If the opponent really is inconsistent or hypocritical, then there is a problem with his or her position. A *tu quoque* argument is thus a kind of counterattack. It defends the person using it only by forcing the opponent to take the defensive.

As the above examples suggest, however, charges of inconsistency are more effective than allegations of hypocrisy. The opponent may admit to hypocrisy or weakness of will but cannot blunt the attack by similarly admitting to inconsistency. To return to our original dispute between the hunter and the critic, the meat eater could respond to the hunter's charge of hypocrisy by granting his or her hypocrisy. Meat eaters could say that they believe that eating meat is wrong but can't give it up. There's no analogue with inconsistency. The meat eaters could say that they haven't the strength to act as they believe but not that they haven't the strength to believe as they believe.

Problems

Do the following contain any *ad hominem* fallacies? Explain. Some attribute *ad hominem* fallacies to others. Do you agree with these attributions? Why, or why not?

▶ **1.** Of course I don't believe that grades are all that important. Only a nerd like you would think they are.

▶ **2.** People who smoke can hardly tell others not to.

▶ **3.** Surely this proposal isn't in the best interests of the students. It was passed by an all-faculty committee.

▶ **4.** How can the wealthy bureaucrats and technocrats on Capitol Hill be expected to create good laws for the common people?

▶ **5.** Nijinsky's theories about dance are probably not very worthwhile, since, after all, he spent the last 25 years of his life in an asylum.

▶ **6.** Few issues this year have generated more hysteria than the problems of American agriculture. You can be sure that common sense has departed when a congressional panel reverentially takes testimony on the farm crisis from actresses who recently played farm wives in the movies. Tears flowed copiously from the lovely eyes of Jessica Lange, Sissy Spacek, and Jane Fonda as they described their feelings for beleaguered farmers. Miss Fonda's testimony was especially credible—after all, she is the second generation of Fonda thespians to play a farmer. (Henry Hyde)

7. The danger of [political and media] consultants is not the money they spend but the power they assume. Recently, the *Wall Street Journal* exposed the fact that the Republican team of Black, Manafort and Stone and their Democratic associate, Peter Kelly, had raised money for both Democratic Senate candidate John Breaux and his Republican opponent, Henson Moore of Louisiana. When one firm works for both candidates, it's not hard to guess who wins on election night. (Raymond Struther)

8. ... in last spring's House debate over a bill to send ... aid to the Nicaraguan rebels ... a Democratic congressman rose, said that he was for the aid, and urged his fellow Democrats to vote for it too. Otherwise, he said, they would be vulnerable to attack in the next election for being "soft on communism." Reporters later cited the argument as swaying many other Democrats to support the bill, which passed 248–184. ...

[This] motive was a base one. It is plainly contemptible to vote for the killing of men, women and children so that your political career may be prolonged. (Jack Beatty)

9. If we consider, by whom this practice of Promiscuous Dancing was first invented, by whom patronized, and by whom witnessed against, we may well conclude that the admitting of it, in such a place as *New England,* will be a thing highly pleasing to the Devil, but provoking to the Holy God. Who were the inventors of Petulant Dancings? They had not their origin amongst the people of God, but amongst the heathen. By whom have the Promiscuous Dances been patronized? Truly, by the worst of the heathen. *Caligula, Nero,* and such like atheists and Epicures were delighted in them. *Lucius* (that infamous apostate) hath written an oration in defence of profane and promiscuous dancings. (Increase Mather, in a Puritan tract against dancing between men and women)

10. Striped bass may be endangered by the Westway's dredging and landfill. Rita Thompson, a Westway supporter, questioned both the moral character of the bass and the wisdom of those who eat them. "Bass eat sewage and garbage; I wouldn't think of eating bass," she said. "A study should be made of people who eat bass." (*New York Times*)

11. If a stockbroker were so smart, he would not be making his riches by selling stock tips to widows and orphans. In the style of the chain letter, the tipster divulges inside information for his gain and your loss. The rhetorical pose of stockbrokers and racetrack tipsters to be offering prudent advice is contradicted by their circumstances, a contradiction catalogued in rhetoric as the "circumstantial *ad hominem.*" That is to say, "Being so smart, why don't you do it yourself, if it's such good advice?" (Donald N. McCloskey)

▶ 12. Hitherto I had stuck to my resolution of not eating animal food, and on this occasion, I consider'd, with my master Tryon, the taking every fish as a kind of unprovoked murder, since none of them had, or ever could do us any injury that might justify the slaughter. All this seemed very reasonable. But I had formerly been a great lover of fish, and, when this came hot out of the frying-pan, it smelt admirably well. I balanc'd some time between principle and inclination, till I recollected that, when the fish were opened, I saw smaller fish taken out of their stomachs; then thought I, "If you eat one another, I don't see why we mayn't eat you." So I din'd upon cod very heartily, and continued to eat with other people, returning only now and then occasionally to a vegetable diet. (Benjamin Franklin)

13. Our Dec. 29 cover story, "Are we spending too much on education?" simply suggested that spending more money wasn't necessarily the best way to deal with the decline in educational standards, but from some of

the furious reactions you would have thought we were defending ignorance and illiteracy. I mean some of those educational types really got nasty in criticizing our article. One college president went so far as to make ethnic slurs against the writer. Can it be that a certain kind of educator has a guilty conscience about the quality of the product his kind is delivering? (James W. Michaels, *Forbes*)

14. If the Senate is entitled to pass judgment on John Tower's personal history, then the public is also entitled to know salient facts about those who judge Mr. Tower. . . . The point here is not merely "you're another," but that the essence of the Tower debate cannot be understood without first understanding its total hypocrisy. If the Senate wanted to improve ethical standards in Washington it could start in its own backyard, particularly by outlawing honorariums. But it has no such intention; about drinking and conflicts of interest it is utterly cynical. These are not ethical concerns, but weapons in a political battle. (*Wall Street Journal*)

15. Indeed, of all the millions of square miles of territory conquered through aggression by various nations since 1945 alone, only those taken by Israel in a war of self-defense were expected to be returned. "It is natural enough," said J. William Fulbright, who was Chairman of the Senate Foreign Relations Committee at the time of the Six-Day War, "for Israel to resist the honor of being the first modern military victor to be obliged by the principles of the United Nations Charter, especially when the greater powers who dominate the Security Council have set such a wretched example. Be that as it may, the principle is too important to be cast away because of the hypocrisy or self-interest of its proponents." In other words, as one commentator sardonically remarked, "all the self-interested hypocrites have a right to ask of Israel what they would not dream of doing themselves." (Norman Podhoretz)

16. "Why should freedom of speech and freedom of the press be allowed? Why should a government which is doing what it believes to be right allow itself to be criticized? It would not allow opposition by lethal weapons. Ideas are much more fatal things than guns. Why should any man be allowed to buy a printing press and disseminate pernicious opinions calculated to embarrass the government?" asked Nikolai Lenin.
   Oh, him. (Liz Smith)

17. Sir:
Your letter of the 12th is before me.
In a moment it will be behind me.
Very truly yours,
Morris Goldsmith

▶ **18.** Mr. Fast . . . says, "I have been active in one part and another of the peace movement over the past 40 years." 1989 minus 40 equals 1949. In

1949, Howard Fast was everyday defending Josef Stalin. Fast was the true Stalinist Stakhanovite. . . . (William F. Buckley, Jr.)

19. Suppose that Sammy So-so is running for mayor. Construct some arguments against him that are relevant to the election and don't commit an *ad hominem* fallacy.

20. Construct other arguments against Mr. So-so that do commit the fallacy.

21. In 1984, a bumper sticker favoring the Democratic candidate for President over then-President Ronald Reagan read, "No Mo' Ron for President." What argument is implicit in the bumper sticker's message? Does this commit an *ad hominem* fallacy? Why or why not?

2.4 Relevance: Confusing the Issue

In the previous section we examined several fallacious kinds of refutation. All violate the condition of relevance: All establish something other than what is at issue. The same problem may befall arguments other than refutations. Traditionally, a positive argument for a conclusion that violates the condition of relevance is called an *ignoratio elenchi*—an argument ignorant of its own goal or purpose—and is therefore fallacious. Such violations of the condition of relevance confuse the issue. They in effect slip one conclusion in place of another, hoping that the audience will not notice the difference.

This is, in effect, playing games with the common ground. A conversation can progress only if its participants are talking about the same thing at the same time. In cases of argument, the common ground should contain a mutual understanding of what issue is at stake. Because of accommodation, however, the issue often becomes established without any explicit discussion, creating an opportunity for participants to introduce new issues.

Of course, people can argue about whatever they want. The participants of a conversation can agree to change the issue under discussion. An argument that deviates from the participants' understanding of the issue, however, can't contribute to any progress on that issue. Sometimes arguers shift to a similar but irrelevant issue because they can't or won't argue about what's really at stake. Suppose that Bob and Carol are arguing about abortion, specifically, about Carol's pro-choice stance. Bob, having trouble arguing against her position, describes her as being "pro-abortion," that is, in favor of abortions, and proceeds to argue that abortions are bad. This, however, is not the issue; Carol might agree that abortions are bad but might nevertheless contend that outlawing abortion is worse. Because Bob has deviated from the original issue in the common ground without making the change explicit or negotiating it with Carol, he makes no progress on the original issue. Moreover, Bob and Carol may now be arguing at cross purposes, since Carol may have failed to recognize the shift from one issue to another.

Red Herrings

A *red herring* is an irrelevant point introduced into an argument or debate, so called because hunters sometimes drag a red herring, a particularly smelly fish, to obscure their own scent. It proves nothing concerning the point at issue. But a red herring is usually introduced as if it were pertinent to the question and may succeed in convincing an audience in spite of its irrelevance. It may show something resembling the desired conclusion, or it may wield great emotional power. In either case, however, it confuses the issue. What it proves is not the conclusion or even a weaker version of it, but something quite beside the point.

> **DEFINITION** An argument is a *red herring* if and only if it tries to justify a conclusion irrelevant to the issue at hand.

Consider, for example, a debate on the morality of extravagant expenditures. Don says that buying a Mercedes, or an airplane, or a mink coat is immoral, because many people are homeless and hungry; the money could, and should, be put to far better use in helping them. Michelle disagrees. Among other things, she argues that spending money on expensive toys is perfectly legal. Warming to the subject, she continues by asking Don, "What would you do? Throw Mercedes owners and private pilots in jail?" But the legality of extravagance is a red herring. The debate is about whether extravagant expenditure is moral or immoral, not about whether it's legal or illegal or even whether it ought to be legal or illegal.

Whether something is truly a red herring may be controversial. Occasionally the parties to a dispute go beyond disagreeing about the issue and disagree even about what the issue is. In such cases, one side may regard as a red herring what the other treats as central to the problem. In 1988, the United States Senate debated the Intermediate Nuclear Forces Treaty between the United States and the Soviet Union. Senator Jesse Helms argued against ratification of the treaty, pointing out that, while it required dismantling European intermediate-range missiles, the treaty did not mandate the destruction of any nuclear warheads, the part of the missiles designed to explode. Senator Dan Evans responded by calling Helms's charge "more than a red herring; I'd call it a crimson whale." Is Helms's argument a red herring? Is the failure of an arms control treaty to eliminate warheads irrelevant to the decision of whether to ratify it? The answer depends on what the treaty is supposed to accomplish. If the two sides in the debate can't agree about the proper purposes of the treaty and of arms control in general, then they're unlikely to agree about what's relevant to the issue of ratification. What is or is not a red herring can thus itself become a matter of dispute. Agreement on the issues to be argued is thus a condition for an argument that makes progress. *Ignoratio elenchi* arguments reflect confusions about what the issues are and, so, can't make progress on resolving them.

Straw Man

A particular form of the red herring fallacy is the exaggeration of an op-ponent's position to make it seem ridiculous. An opponent's stance is easier to refute, of course, if you attack an exaggerated, distorted, misrepresented, or particularly problem-riddled form of it. You may therefore set up a "straw man"—a feeble version of your opponent's convictions—and then knock it down. This exercise can succeed in demonstrating the inadequacy of the tottery view you set up for assault but fails to show the inadequacy of your opponent's actual belief.

This description of the straw man fallacy suggests that it afflicts primarily refutations. But it can afflict positive arguments, since they often proceed by trying to show the inadequacy of alternative positions. In general, an argu-ment erects a straw man when it claims to refute an assertion by assailing another, less defensible assertion.

> **DEFINITION** An argument erects a *straw man* if and only if it tries to justify the rejection of a position by an attack on a different, and usually weaker, position.

This fallacy is extremely common. It pervades political discussion especially. Suppose that a senator is arguing in favor of a trade bill. He or she may adduce examples of unfair trade practices by foreign competitors, point to a large trade deficit with certain nations, and cite examples of domestic in-dustries losing markets to overseas corporations. These arguments may indicate that there are important problems about trade, but they do not prove that the trade bill should be enacted. To establish that conclusion, one would have to show not only that there are problems but also (a) that the proposed legislation can solve them and (b) that it is better, on balance, than any feasible alternative. Of course, it's difficult to show these things. This is why straw man arguments are so widespread: It's easy to substantiate that certain problems need a solution but much harder to show that a par-ticular plan will solve them and, furthermore, that it is the best plan.

Problems

Do the following contain red herrings or straw men? Explain.

▶ 1. *Joshua:* We need federal legislation banning the sale of semiautomatic weapons to civilians. Such weapons have no use other than killing people.
   Tad: We don't need any such thing. There are already laws requiring people to register those guns, and murder is already illegal.

▶ 2. *Penny:* It's important to work for equal rights and opportunities for the disabled. Too often, they've been excluded, from prejudice or just thought-lessness.

Enid: Don't you think we're all disabled in some way or another? My uncle, for example, walks with a limp. My grandfather has a bad back. My grandmother has arthritis. But your programs aren't set up to help them. In fact, they don't need help.

▸ **3.** If children's writing skills are as bad as everyone says, we ought to take another look at standardized tests. If these tests don't measure writing ability, it's no wonder that students never develop it.

▸ **4.** It's just wrong to change the rules, raising the academic standards for athletic scholarships. It's going to keep these kids out of the college of their choice, and that's not the American way. That's not what the American Constitution is all about.

▸ **5.** *Jane:* We shouldn't be sending aid to that country. I've seen several anti-American demonstrations from their capital on the news. There are allegations of human rights abuses.
Ned: All foreign capitals have anti-American demonstrations from time to time. I see them on the news all the time, from all parts of the world. I guess people like to blame problems on some powerful factor they can't control.

▸ **6.** It's important that we place restrictions on foreign investment in this country. Almost 75% of the commercial real estate in Los Angeles is owned by the Japanese. More and more American companies are being bought by foreign firms.

7. We are wrong if we suppose that man alone is gifted with esthetic feeling. Many animals are more beautiful than the featherless biped that transiently rules the earth. . . . (Will Durant)

8. Man walks because things in nature move. . . . Similarly, man digests because nature is chemical. . . . Man predicts because nature is mechanical. . . . Once more man is free because nature is contingent. (Sterling P. Lamprecht)

9. *Howard Fast* (Arguing that anti-abortion advocates can't be sincere, because their concern for life stops at birth): I have never heard a right-to-life voice raised in protest against the 60,000 innocents murdered by the death squads of El Salvador.
William F. Buckley, Jr.: The lifers are, by Mr. Fast and others who think as he does, encumbered by the responsibility for everything that happens to the fetus after it materializes into a human being in the eyes of the law. And if you aren't around to see to it that at age 14 the kid is receiving the right education, ingesting the right foods, leading a happy, prosperous life, why, you had no business bringing him into this world. You are a hypocrite to the extent that you support life for everyone who suffers in life. It is only left for Mr. Fast to close the logic of his own

argument, which would involve him in a syllogistic attempt along the lines of:

> Everyone alive suffers.
> No one not living suffers.
> Therefore, no one should live.

10. The current campaign introduces a new variation on an old theme: If women buy designer clothes and play along, they can "go places" in a man's world. The will to succeed is presented as the ticket to power, though in reality, it is the system itself that locks women out.

    Consider the retail industry. In 1983, it employed more than fifteen million workers, three-quarters of them women. But the decision-makers are mostly men. Though the work force at J. C. Penney's is 77 percent female, just three women serve among the corporation's top sixty-one officers.... Behind the glitter and hype for professional women, real wages for retail workers have declined since 1966, and the giant department stores are eager to roll back wages even further. (Richard Moore and Elizabeth Marsis)

11. In the following passage, accounting firms claim that their critics are committing a fallacy. Do you think their claim is correct? Do you find any fallacies in the response of the accounting firms?

    > Some critics aren't surprised at the recent strains at major accounting firms because they have long believed that consulting and auditing, like oil and water, don't mix.
    >
    > That's because accounting firms serving as outside auditors are supposed to judge objectively whether their client companies are making proper business decisions. But auditors are likely to be less critical of decisions in which they themselves have been deeply involved, critics say.
    >
    > Some consultants and legislators call this a potential conflict of interest. And some independent consulting firms complain that consultants at accounting firms gain an unfair competitive advantage by pushing their services to clients that their firms may also audit.
    >
    > In response, accounting firms call the problem of a seeming conflict of interest a red herring. They contend that the experience gained as auditors makes them better consultants and that criticism of their gains in the consulting field comes simply from competitors irked by their own loss of business. (*Wall Street Journal*)

12. Suppose you are arguing about changing the grading system at your school from letter grades to pass/fail. (a) Pick a side of the issue, and construct an argument for your position. (b) Evaluate your argument critically. Does it contain any red herrings or straw men? (c) If so, can you add something to your arguments to relate them to the issue? (d) If not, devise a red herring, and explain why it is one.

13. Suppose you wish to argue that television has an extremely negative effect on its viewers, but you don't quite know how to proceed. What red herrings or straw men could you use instead of a valid argument? Make a list, and, for each, explain why it doesn't address the original issue.

Notes

[1] Antoine Arnauld (1611–1694), *Logic, or, The Art of Thinking* (Indianapolis: Bobbs-Merrill, 1964; originally published in 1662), p. 247, following Aristotle: "demonstration is from things more creditable and prior" (*Prior Analytics* ii, 16).

[2] This is Robert Stalnaker's definition of speaker presupposition, adapted to apply to sentences. See "Assertion," in Peter Cole (ed.) *Syntax and Semantics 9: Pragmatics* (New York: Academic Press, 1978), pp. 321, 326. The definition is a variant of that originally proposed by Lauri Karttunen for pragmatic presupposition. See "Presupposition and Linguistic Context," *Theoretical Linguistics* 1 (1974): 182–194.

[3] This definition is Whately's. See his *Elements of Logic* (New York: Sheldon and Company, 1869), p. 179: An argument begs the question "when one of the Premisses (whether true or false) is either plainly equivalent to the conclusion, or depends on that for its own reception." See also p. 220: In a question-begging argument, "one of the Premisses either is manifestly the same in sense with the Conclusion, or is actually proved from it or is such as the persons you are addressing are not likely to know, or admit, except as an inference from the Conclusion. . . ." Compare Aristotle's definition, which relates even more directly to the evidence condition: "Whether a person does not conclude at all, or whether he does so through things more unknown, or equally unknown, or whether he concludes what is prior through what is posterior" (*Prior Analytics* ii, 16).

[4] See David Lewis, "Scorekeeping in a Language Game," *Journal of Philosophical Logic* 8 (1979): 339–59, pp. 340, 347.

[5] See George Wolfskill and John Hudson, *All But the People: Franklin D. Roosevelt and His Critics* (New York: Macmillan, 1969), pp. 5–16.

[6] Paul Johnson, *Modern Times* (New York: Harper and Row, 1983), p. 258.

[7] Thomas Keiser, "'The Illinois Beast': One of Our Greatest Presidents," *Wall Street Journal*, February 11, 1988.

[8] Samuel Johnson, quoted in David Hackett Fischer, *Historians' Fallacies* (New York: Harper and Row, 1970), p. 282.

[9] Whately, p. 237. (Emphasis in original.)

3

GROUNDING

In logic textbooks, arguments tend to have the flavor of the traditional syllogism:

(1) Socrates is human.
All humans are mortal.
∴ Socrates is mortal.

The premises of the argument contain everything needed to derive its conclusion. But such aptness rarely occurs except in textbook examples. Arguments in natural language rely on the set of beliefs and assumptions shared, at least temporarily, by the participants in a conversation. We've called this set of background beliefs and assumptions the *common ground* of the conversation. An argument tries to justify adding its conclusion to the common ground. Ordinarily, arguments rely extensively on the common ground; many assertions needed to derive the conclusion are not stated but assumed as part of this background. Thus, argument (1) might be stated more naturally as

(2) Socrates is human.
∴ He's mortal.

or

(3) All humans are mortal.
∴ Socrates is mortal.

There is no need to say what the advocate and audience both already accept. In fact, there's a strong presumption in favor of not saying it. We expect our conversational partners to inform us. Statements reiterating what is already in the common ground, under normal circumstances, don't convey any new information.

The condition of grounding requires that, to be successful, an argument must assume only what's available in the common ground. The unstated assumptions required to derive the conclusion must be shared between advocate and audience if the argument is to succeed. If the argument employs, as an unstated assumption, anything outside the common ground of the conversation, its conclusion is groundless: The premises, together with the shared background assumptions of the participants, don't justify it.

Arguments with unfounded conclusions might not pose a significant threat in reasoning were it not for accommodation. But presuppositions required by an assertion pop into existence if nobody objects. Similarly, we tend to accommodate our partners in discourse by admitting into the common ground assumptions required by their arguments. This tendency is so strong that it requires great conscious effort to recognize and evaluate assumptions underlying arguments.

The task becomes especially difficult when an argument assumes something very close to, or misapplies, what is available in the common ground. Such arguments, in effect, try to pass counterfeit assumptions as legitimate common ground currency. In this chapter, we'll examine some arguments that violate the grounding condition by assuming things similar to, but not equivalent to, suppositions in the common ground.

Of course, any argument making an assumption that's illegitimate in its context violates the grounding condition. There are consequently as many kinds of grounding fallacies as there are false or unfounded assertions. But all the fallacies presented in this chapter have a common structure: They single out one factor present in the common ground and treat it as the only relevant factor. Many of the following fallacies are more specific: They are fallacies of *misapplication*.

> **Definition**   An argument exhibits a fallacy of *misapplication* if and only if it tries to justify its conclusion about a particular case by appealing to a rule that is generally sound but inapplicable or outweighed by other considerations in that case.

The common ground typically includes rules about what to do in various circumstances. Together these rules make up much of what we ordinarily call "common sense." Commonsense rules, however, are fairly rough guidelines; they don't hold in every possible circumstance. In computer terminology, they're *default* rules: They say what to do under normal circumstances. They specify a default course of action. But, in unusual cases, the default can be overridden. Rules such as "Follow your emotions," "Do what's best for you," "Help others," and "Listen to the experts" are valuable, but they have exceptions. Failing to recognize exceptions involves a fallacy of misapplication.

Philosophers have tended to think of these rules as containing the clause "other things being equal." You should think of them, for example, as "Follow your emotions, other things being equal," "Do what's best for you, other things being equal," and so on. In effect, these rules say what to do if nothing else indicates otherwise. Ignoring the cautionary clause leads to misapplication fallacies.

In the *Republic*, Plato discusses a classic example of misapplication. Suppose that a friend (let's call him Rip) has lent you a knife. You've promised to return it when he needs it. One day Rip knocks on your door and demands the knife back. A neighbor's insult has infuriated him, it turns out, and he wants to stab his neighbor. You've promised to return the knife when he asks for it, and, other things being equal, you ought to keep your promises. Nevertheless, Plato says, you shouldn't return the knife. To apply the rule "You ought to keep your promises" would be, in this case, to misapply it. Other things are not equal. Your obligations to prevent harm to the neighbor, and to keep your friend from doing something he'd regret, outweigh your obligation to keep your promise.

For other examples of misapplication fallacies, we can turn to the history of the United States Supreme Court, which has not only declared many lower-court decisions to be misapplications of law but has also reversed its own earlier decisions on a number of occasions. The *Dred Scott* decision (1857), for example, held that Congress did not have the authority to exclude slavery from the territories. After the Civil War, the court held that this had been a misapplication of constitutional principles. In a series of cases early in the twentieth century, the Court applied a principle of freedom of contract to strike down laws regulating working hours, working conditions, and wages, on the grounds that employees should be free to contract for extra working hours, poor conditions, or subminimum wages if they chose. After Franklin Roosevelt threatened to pack the Court, it reversed itself and declared its earlier reasoning a misapplication of the freedoms guaranteed by the Constitution.

The condition of grounding has intimate connections with the condition of relevance. Relevance requires that we appeal to relevant factors to establish our conclusion. Grounding requires that we take account of *all* relevant factors in doing so. There is another link as well. In interpreting an argument that seems to establish something other than what is at issue, we may judge it guilty of a fallacy of relevance. Alternatively, we may construe the arguer as assuming a connection between what the argument actually proves and what is at issue, thus committing, if the assumption is incorrect, a fallacy of grounding.

3.1 APPEALS TO EMOTION

This chapter examines violations of the grounding condition that treat a legitimate and important factor in obtaining information or reaching a decision as if it were the only factor. Those violations consist in treating one kind of consideration as if it always overrode other considerations. The common ground typically contains assumptions about the role of emotions in reaching conclusions and making decisions. In particular, the common ground usually contains a rule like "Follow your emotions, other things being equal." This commonsense rule has been expressed in many ways. "Trust your feelings," Obiwan Kenobe tells Luke Skywalker in *Star Wars*. "Have the convictions of your passions," urges a character in *The Hot L Baltimore*.[1] "Listen to your gut," advises real estate tycoon Donald Trump.[2] These versions omit the clause "other things being equal." Without it, they have more force. But they also encourage misapplication.

Appeal to the People (or Gallery)

Franklin Delano Roosevelt and Ronald Reagan owed some of their success as presidents to their ability to communicate ideas clearly and persuasively. Faced with recalcitrant Congresses, they tended to appeal directly to the people, in fireside radio chats or television addresses, to achieve their legislative goals. Nothing in this procedure itself involves a fallacy. Some politicians, however, have made reputations for using nonrational, emotional appeals to win support for their positions. Any argument based not on rational considerations but on emotional appeals counts as an appeal to the people.[3] (Such arguments are sometimes called "appeals to the gallery," an allusion to politicians' practice of directing arguments to the observers in the gallery rather than fellow legislators.)

> **DEFINITION** An argument is an *appeal to the people* (or *to the gallery*) if and only if it tries to justify its conclusion by appealing to the emotions of the audience.

Cicero employed appeals to the people brilliantly. Consider this portion of his argument to the Roman Senate in favor of the death penalty for Cataline, with its emotional description of the terror wrought by Cataline's plots:

> Yet I am not a man so iron-hearted to be unaffected by the grief of my most dear and loving brother, present here, nor by the tears of all these friends you see seated around me. Nor can I prevent my thoughts being often recalled to my own home by my despondent wife, my terrified daughter and my infant son (whom I think the state is cherishing as a sort of pledge for my loyalty as consul), or by my son-in-law who stands within my view awaiting anxiously the result of this day.[4]

Appeals to the people are not confined to the ancients. Almost every modern politician uses them, often with the aid of a team of "media consultants" to maximize their effect. Here, for example, is a classic from Richard Nixon's "Checkers" speech:

> My family was one of modest circumstances, and most of my early life was spent in a store out in East Whittier. It was a grocery store—one of those family enterprises. I worked my way through college and, to a great extent, through law school.

> The only reason we were able to make it go was because my mother and dad have five boys and we all worked in the store.
> Why do I feel so deeply? Why do I feel that, in spite of the smears, the misunderstanding, the necessity for a man to come up here and bare his soul as I have? And I want to tell you why. Because, you see, I love my country.[5]

Often appeals to the people take the form of slanted language that conveys a certain attitude toward what is being said without support for that language. Examples, unfortunately, are extremely easy to find. In 1977, Leonid Brezhnev defended the persecution of political protestors in the Soviet Union:

> In our country it is not forbidden "to think differently" from the majority. . . . It is quite another matter if a few individuals who have . . . actively come out against the socialist system, embark on the road of anti-Soviet activity, violate laws and, finding no support inside their own country, turn for support abroad, to imperialist subversive centres. . . . Our people demand that such . . . activists be treated as opponents of socialism, as persons acting against their own motherland, as accomplices if not actual agents of imperialism. . . . We have taken and will continue to take against them measures envisaged by our law.[6]

Emotional or slanted language may lead the audience to overestimate the evidence in favor of certain conclusions, or overemphasize their importance in the common ground. Notice the emotionally packed words and phrases Brezhnev used: 'come out against the socialist system', 'anti-Soviet', 'imperialist subversive centres', 'motherland', 'accomplices', and 'agents of imperialism'. They try to lead the listener to think of protestors as enemies rather than fellow citizens.

Nevertheless, the use of slanted terms does not always mark an argument as unacceptable. What matters is whether the argument relies on slanting to lead the audience toward its conclusion, and whether the slanting is part of the common ground. Political magazines with a definite and strongly expressed perspective tend to use much language that would strike an uncommitted observer as slanted. A right-wing magazine may speak of a conflict between Communists and anti-Communists as a fight between Marxist-Leninist thugs and freedom fighters. A left-wing magazine may speak of the same conflict as a battle between socialist revolutionaries and reactionary totalitarians. Is a fallacy lurking here? Perhaps, but not necessarily. We need to answer two questions: (a) Are the slanted terms essential to deriving the conclusion of the argument? and (b) What is the intended audience? The right-wing magazine addresses itself largely to an audience that opposes Communist governments. Similarly, the left-wing magazine addresses itself largely to an audience with some sympathy for Marxist revolutions. The slantings, if this is correct, reflect assumptions in the common grounds of the two very different conversations taking place between these magazines and their readers. Many publications are mostly preaching to the converted. Their use of slanted language, therefore, is not fallacious but does have a negative consequence. Their arguments, to the extent that they rely on slanting, deserve to succeed only with a limited audience.

Problems

First (a) identify the slanted words and phrases in the following. Rewrite each, (b) substituting emotionally neutral words and phrases for those that are slanted, and then (c) substituting words and phrases that are equally emotionally charged, but in the other direction. For (c), imagine that you hold an opposing view and would like to convey essentially the same information, but in terms favorable to your position.

▶ **1.** William Jennings Bryan, a 36-year-old Congressman from Nebraska, gave the silver forces their war cry at the Democratic convention in July [1896]. "You shall not crucify mankind upon a cross of gold!" were the words that made Bryan the Democratic nominee for President. (*Wall Street Journal*)

▶ **2.** The finest historians will not be those who succumb to the dehumanizing methods of social science, whatever their uses and values, which I hasten to acknowledge. Nor will the historian worship at the shrine of the Bitch-Goddess QUANTIFICATION. (Carl Bridenbaugh)

▶ **3.** To a great extent, right-wing ideologies are modes of thought designed not to spur action or to enhance collective responsibility, but to provide a moral justification for egocentricity. . . . Insofar as political commitment requires qualities of self-sacrifice or a capacity to find personal fulfillment through social participation, such personal qualities do not resonate well with right-wing ideological perspectives. (Richard Flacks)

▶ **4.** We repudiate all morality taken apart from human society and classes. We say that it is a deception, a fraud, a befogging of the minds of the workers and peasants by the landlords and capitalists. (V. I. Lenin)

▶ **5.** On Wednesday 22 March 1933, the first concentration camp will be opened near Dachau. It will accommodate 5,000 prisoners. Planning on such a scale, we refuse to be influenced by any petty objection, since we are convinced this will reassure all those who have regard for the nation and serve their interests. (Heinrich Himmler)

▶ **6.** The Reverend Jesse Jackson has been rotating around the world, broadcasting over Radio Havana to add his bit to the South African mess and comparing Botha to Adolf Hitler, among other insults to human intelligence.

　　Americans have indulged this demagogue too long. Official Democrats do not dare anathematize him because he allegedly speaks for blacks, who vote Democratic. If that is so, at least non-Democrats can make the point that needs making, namely that if Mr. Jackson were white, he'd be run out of town. (William F. Buckley, Jr.)

7. The judiciary has thus reached into the Constitution's spirit and structure, and has elaborated from the spare text an idea of the "human" and a conception of "being" not merely contemplated but required. (Laurence Tribe)

8. Henry, king not by usurpation, but by the holy ordination of God, to Hildebrand, not pope, but false monk.

    This is the salutation which you deserve, for you have never held any office in the Church without making it a source of confusion and a curse to Christian men, instead of an honor and a blessing. To mention only the most obvious cases out of many, you have not only dared to lay hands on the Lord's anointed, the archbishops, bishops, and priests, but you have scorned them and abused them, as if they were ignorant servants not fit to know what their master was doing. This you have done to gain favor with the vulgar crowd. (Henry IV, 1076)

9. The distress and misery that oppress all the Christian estates, more especially in Germany, have led not only myself, but every one else, to cry aloud and to ask for help, and have now forced me, too, to cry out and to ask if God would give His Spirit to any one to reach a hand to His wretched people. Councils have often put forward some remedy, but it has adroitly been frustrated, and the evils have become worse, through the cunning of certain men. Their malice and wickedness I will now, by the help of God, expose. . . . (Martin Luther)

10. The bourgeoisie, wherever it has got the upper hand, has put an end to all feudal, patriarchal, idyllic relations. It has pitilessly torn asunder the motley feudal ties that bound man to his "natural superiors," and has left remaining no other nexus between man and man than naked self-interest, than callous "cash payment." (Karl Marx and Friedrich Engels)

11. This is a sad day for all of us, and to none is it sadder than to me. Everything that I have worked for, everything that I have hoped for, everything that I have believed in during my public life, has crashed into ruins. There is only one thing left for me to do; that is, to devote what strength and powers I have to forwarding the victory of the cause for which we have to sacrifice so much. (Neville Chamberlin, 1940)

▸ 12. . . . the National Socialist movement began its work of unifying the German people and thereby initiating resurgence of the Reich. This rise of our people from distress, misery and shameful disregard bore all the signs of a purely internal renaissance. . . . Nevertheless, a new policy of encirclement against Germany, born as it was of hatred, recommenced immediately. Internally and externally there resulted that plot familiar to us all . . . with the sole aim of inhibiting the establishment of the German people's State, and of plunging the Reich anew into impotence and misery. (Adolf Hitler)

If a speaker is faced with an audience of college students and the issue of whether or not the following (13–29) should be legal, what mistakes could he or she make in appealing to the emotions of the audience? Make a list, and explain why each emotional appeal is logically irrelevant.

13. Sport hunting

14. Animal trapping

15. Boxing

16. Marijuana use

17. Marijuana dealing

18. Cocaine use

19. Cocaine dealing

20. Cigarette smoking

21. Cigarette smoking in public places

22. Prostitution

23. Pornography involving consenting adults only

24. Child pornography

25. Prayer in schools

26. Christmas or Hanukkah displays on public property

27. Use of experimental drugs by terminally ill patients

28. Allowing young workers to labor for less than minimum wage

29. Clubs admitting members of only one sex

30. You are a political consultant charged with convincing voters in your state or country (a) to raise taxes; (b) not to raise taxes. What emotional appeals can you use in your campaign? Write a TV commercial using them, and explain whether, and why, they are or aren't logically relevant.

3.2 PRACTICAL FALLACIES

Some fallacies pertain solely to *practical reasoning*, reasoning aimed at a conclusion about what ought to be done. Whereas arguments, in general, may have any sort of sentence as conclusion, practical arguments always conclude with a sentence evaluating an action or kind of action:

(4) I ought to return the money.

(5) It's acceptable for John to send the contracts to Fran.

(6) Nobody should deny the obvious.

What a person ought to do depends, in general, on many factors, for instance on the situation, on the probable consequences of the actions the person might perform, and on the applicability of moral or religious norms. Successful practical reasoning weighs these factors to decide what, on balance, is the best thing to do. Sometimes, however, an argument bases a conclusion on just a single factor, treating it as if it were the only factor relevant to making the decision. Such arguments violate the grounding condition by ignoring the "other things being equal" clauses of commonsense practical rules. They ignore countervailing factors in the common ground and thereby commit fallacies of practical reasoning.

Appeal to Common Practice

"When in Rome, do as the Romans do." This might be the slogan of appeals to common practice. Virtually everyone can recall, as a child, using an argument of this kind. You and your friends, perhaps, were playing outside on a warm summer evening. Someone said, "Let's go to the park!" Some of the children readily assented; you and a few others decided to ask permission. Your mother, it turned out, didn't like the idea at all. "But everyone else is going!" you cried. If you were particularly sophisticated, you bent the truth a bit and added, "All the other mothers said it was OK!"

This kind of argument is called an *appeal to common practice* (or *steamrolling*). The conclusion asserts that a certain kind of action is acceptable, permissible, or even obligatory. The premises indicate that the kind of action is common practice: that everyone, most people, or at least many people are doing it.

> **DEFINITION** An argument *appeals to common practice* if and only if it tries to justify an action by appealing to the common practice of the community.

Appeals to common practice have the form

> (7) X is common practice. (All, or most, or many people do X.)
> ∴ X is acceptable (or obligatory).

What's wrong with such arguments?

Sometimes, nothing. Suppose you travel to Europe and observe people holding their forks in their left hands as they eat. You may infer, quite properly, that holding your fork in your left hand is acceptable behavior there. Or, suppose you visit Central America and note that, when introduced, people say "Mucho gusto" to each other. You may legitimately conclude that in that part of the world saying "Mucho gusto" is not only acceptable but obligatory when meeting someone. In general, what people do is a good guide to what a community counts as acceptable. So, there's nothing wrong with appealing to common practice to support a conclusion about what a certain community's standards allow.

Appeals to common practice are fallacious, however, when the conclusion involves a stronger and more serious sense of acceptability or obligation. Consider your argument, directed to your mother, that you should be allowed to go to the park with your friends. That everyone else's mother has granted permission may show that community standards allow her to grant permission. She won't be a social pariah if she says you may go. But this, of course, is not what you want to establish. You are trying to show that she ought to let you go. She might indicate the problem with appeals to common practice with a question: "Would you jump off a bridge if all your friends were doing it?"

The unstated assumption behind an appeal to common practice is that anything commonly done is right. Occasionally advertisers make this assumption explicit: "Fifty million Americans can't be wrong!" But, of course, this isn't true. Fifty million Americans *can* be wrong. The assumption that whatever many, or most, or all people do is right at least requires an "other things being equal" clause to indicate the limitations of drawing conclusions from common practice. Perhaps the assumption doesn't deserve any place in the common ground at all in normal circumstances. Common practices in many societies, at many different times, appear to later observers wrong-headed and even barbaric.

Why, then, do these arguments persuade anyone? Perhaps they gain some force from a confusion between what is morally right and what is socially acceptable. But their power stems from another source as well. We all compare our own beliefs and actions to those of other people. We want to "fit in"; we also want to be reasonable. In evaluating our own behavior we look to other people for guidance. We shape our own identities, in part, on the models that others provide for us. Faced with a difficult decision, we turn to others for advice. If a belief or action receives positive reinforcement from others, we tend to assume its legitimacy; we reserve our most careful scrutiny for those beliefs and actions that run counter to community norms. Moreover, we have no choice but to rely extensively on other people's information, decisions, and good will. All these factors incline us to believe what others believe and act as others act. Consequently, the fact that a practice is common inclines us to accept it.

Furthermore, we tend to learn what is morally right and wrong from other people. Eventually, we develop our own standards, but we base those standards on what we've learned from others. The fact that everyone behaves in a certain way is therefore evidence that the behavior is acceptable, not merely socially, but morally as well.

The fallacy of appealing to common practice, then, is again relying on a single factor—what others do—to decide an issue affected by many different factors. We all obtain information, attitudes, and standards from other people. But to rely solely on other people for our standards is, in individual cases, to follow the crowd; throughout a lifetime, to be shallow. Although the beliefs and behaviors of others, then, provide some evidence about what we ought to do, there are many other pertinent sources of evidence. An appeal to common practice is good if and only if its conclusion concerns the community's common practice, or there are no countervailing considerations. That everyone does something doesn't in itself make it right. We learn about standards of behavior from others, but those standards themselves are independent of what others do and say.

Appeal to Force (or Fear)

A rather different sort of fallacy occurs when someone uses a threat. The threat may be physical: A thief with a .357 Magnum may suggest that you should turn over your wallet; a loan shark may warn you that you will take a vacation in the hospital if you don't pay up; a mobster may make you an offer you can't refuse. Or, the threat may be financial: An employer may tell workers that they'll be fired if they reveal secrets; a law may penalize speeding or littering with a hefty fine. Or, the threat may involve embarrassment: A lobbyist may intimidate a legislator by threatening to expose sordid details of past business dealings. These are not arguments. They are nonrational attempts at persuasion or, more accurately, coercion.

Usually, appeals to force seek to coerce more subtly. Most people want to be liked. They want other people to think well of them. This makes them manipulable. Threats of disapproval are far more frequent than threats of physical violence or economic harm. Suppose someone begins to disparage a public figure you respect. Do you voice your disagreement? Perhaps, but it's tempting to remain silent, especially if you respect and want the approval of the person doing the disparaging. Suppose an acquaintance, in a meeting, argues for a course of action you sharply disapprove. The rest of the group seems ready to adopt the plan. Do you explain your objections? Strength of character, it may seem, is incompatible with acquiescence stemming from a fear of disapproval. But many people give in to pressure from their peers or from authorities. The desire to accommodate others, not only by accepting the presuppositions of their statements and arguments but by acting in ways they approve, is very strong. Pollsters, for example, find that their results are very easily biased by people's desire to please the person asking the question.

Again, threats, peer pressure, desires to conform, and so on, aren't arguments. But arguments may try to engender feelings of fear or insecurity. An appeal to force is an argument relying on a threat.

> **Definition**   An argument *appeals to force* if and only if it tries to justify a kind of action by threatening the audience.

Although the appeal to force has been counted among logical fallacies since ancient times, it's not very clear when threats should count as arguments rather than nonargumentative attempts at persuasion. Brainwashing and subliminal suggestion are attempts at persuasion, but nobody would consider them kinds of argument. Furthermore, when an argument contains a threat, what's wrong with it? A thief with a .357 Magnum argues very effectively.

To answer these questions, we first need to ask, What do all appeals to force have in common? How do they violate the grounding condition? In essence, appeals to force have the form:

(8) If A does X, A will suffer.
    $\therefore$ A shouldn't do X.

Consider this case: A lobbyist threatens a congressman with defeat in the next election if he doesn't support subsidies for the lobbyist's industry. The lobbyist may have large sums to spend on political activity, and the congressman's margin of victory in the last election may have been slim. So, suppose that the lobbyist can make good on the threat. In effect, the lobbyist argues

(9) If you don't vote for subsidies, you won't be reelected.
    $\therefore$ You should vote for subsidies.

What assumptions underlie this argument? Two rather different sets of assumptions would make the argument succeed. One is based on what the congressman wants; the other, on what is best for him. These may not be the same thing. He may covet a committee chairmanship that, in fact, would so overwhelm him with work that he would suffer a heart attack. And it may be best for him to retire to his farm in the country, when that is the last thing he wants to do.

First, let's analyze the argument in terms of what the congressman wants. What does the argument assume? Certainly it assumes that the congressman wants reelection; if he doesn't, then the argument seems pointless. Second, it assumes that he should do what is required to get what he wants. The argument depends on an unstated premise that a person should do what's necessary to achieve his or her goals.

Before reflecting further on this assumption, analyze the argument in terms of what's best for the congressman. The argument assumes that it's best for him to be reelected, and, furthermore, that he should do whatever is best for him. "Do whatever's best for you" is the maxim underlying the lobbyist's appeal.

Appeals to force thus rest on one of two assumptions: (a) you should do what you have to do to get what you want; or (b) you should do what's best for you. These assumptions have great force. The first is a basic principle of practical reasoning. We often use arguments of the form

(10) A wants X.
     To get X, A must do Y.
     $\therefore$ A should do Y.

We rely on arguments of this form very frequently when planning our own actions or evaluating the actions of others. Consider these examples:

(11) I want to wake up at 6:00 A.M.
     To do that, I need to set the alarm.
     $\therefore$ I should set the alarm.

(12) Rudy wants to eat lunch.
       To do that, he must walk to the cafeteria.
       ∴ He should walk to the cafeteria.

(13) Donna wants to become a lawyer.
       To do that, she must go to law school.
       ∴ She should go to law school.

These arguments are as convincing as they are commonplace. What we want, and what we must do to obtain it, are important factors in determining what we should do. So, the rule "Do what's necessary to get what you want" is almost always in the common ground.

Like other rules in the common ground, however, it contains the clause "other things being equal." When other things aren't equal—when there are countervailing considerations—arguments of this form fail. Consider the horribly defective but historically significant argument:

(14) Hitler wants a racially pure Germany.
       He can achieve that only by eliminating all non-Aryans.
       ∴ Hitler should eliminate all non-Aryans.

What Hitler wants is itself morally wrong. Furthermore, his goal seems paltry in comparison with the tremendous human suffering required to achieve it. The countervailing factors far outweigh Hitler's desire.

So, arguments of this nature presuppose (a) that the person's desires are themselves morally acceptable and (b) that no other factors outweigh their desires. The argument concerning Hitler falls short on both counts. Usually, however, these requirements are met. Rudy's desire to eat lunch does not, of itself, pose moral difficulties, nor is his going to the cafeteria likely to involve anything pernicious. There's nothing wrong with waking up at 6:00 A.M. nor does setting the alarm raise any other moral problems. Appeals to force may thus treat one important factor—a person's desires, together with what is necessary to fulfill them—as the only factor relevant to making a decision.

Consider the other assumption often underlying appeals to force: that you should do what's best for you. This is a maxim of prudence on which we rely constantly. Thinking about how to invest money, we naturally think about what will be best for us financially. Contemplating a change in careers, we think carefully about the benefits and costs. Reaching almost any personal decision, we try to determine what will make us happiest. In most circumstances, there's nothing wrong with this. So, the principle "Do what's best for you" is usually in the common ground.

Again, this rule presupposes the clause "other things being equal." What's best for us is a very important factor, and, often, the only very important factor, in determining what we ought to do. Sometimes, however, other factors are also significant. Suppose that Mischa is drafted in wartime. Fighting may not be best for him, but perhaps he should do it anyway for the good of his country. Suppose that Evelyn can profit handsomely by accepting a payoff and failing to report some defects in materials that could result in serious injuries to users of some machinery. It may be best *for her* to accept the payoff and remain silent, but surely that's not what she ought to do. So, what's best for you is only one consideration in reaching a decision. Appeals to force tend to treat that consideration as if it were the only one. They are therefore guilty of misapplication.

We can now appreciate the difference between the thief's and the lobbyist's appeals to force. The thief argues, persuasively, that it will be best for you to part with your money. And, as many police officers would counsel, you should probably do it. The threat to your life clearly outweighs the harm of losing the money. So, the thief commits no fallacy, unless the conclusion is supposed to be that it's morally right for the thief to get the money. Whether or not there's anything logically wrong with the thief's argument, of course, there is certainly something morally wrong with it. The lobbyist, in contrast, argues that it will be best for the congressman if he votes in favor of subsidies. If subsidies are a bad idea, however—if they impose significant costs on consumers, say, or if they harm our allies economically—then those costs almost certainly outweigh the harm to the congressman of not being reelected. Appeals to force point to a possible harm or frustrated desire and treat it as overriding all other considerations. If, in a particular circumstance, that harm is not overriding, the appeal is fallacious.

Appeal to Pity

Just as an appeal to force assumes that you should do what's best for yourself, an appeal to pity assumes that you should do what's best for me, or for some other person. The argument tries to arouse pity for someone and exploit it to persuade the listener to act for that person's benefit.

In general, an appeal to pity is an argument relying on arousing feelings of sympathy or pity among the listeners.

> **Definition** An argument *appeals to pity* if and only if it tries to justify an action by arousing sympathy or pity in the audience.

A classic example, close to college professors' hearts, is an argument used by a student seeking a higher grade. "I'm pre-med. I really want to go to medical school and become a doctor. But my grades, so far, are just borderline. If this C stays on my record, I'll never make it. All these years of hard work will be wasted."

Like other grounding fallacies, appeals to pity treat a factor relevant to reaching a conclusion as if it were the only relevant factor. We generally assume, in the common ground, that we should take the feelings and welfare of others into account when we make decisions. All other things being equal, we try to help others. Appeals to pity try to play on our altruism by presenting an argument having one of these forms:

(15) *A*'s doing *X* will harm *B*.
∴ *A* shouldn't do *X*.

(16) *A*'s doing *Y* will help *B*.
∴ *A* should do *Y*.

Some such arguments succeed. If doing *Y* will help someone, and there's no reason not to do it, then you probably should do *Y*. If, by giving to charity, you can help save lives without producing any harm to yourself or others, then you should.

But the condition 'there's no reason not to do it' is very important. The rule "Help others" holds only when other things are equal. Suppose that giving the pre-med student a C really will harm that student. Before concluding anything about the grade, it's necessary to consider the effect on others of raising the grade, as well as any general principles of fairness involved. If changing the grade to a B would help the student get into a medical school, the change would help that particular student but would cost some other student a place. So, the consequences are not unambiguously positive; one student would benefit, another would suffer. Further, another C student performing as well as or perhaps even better than the pre-med student would receive a lower grade. This seems unfair: It violates a general principle of justice, that similar cases should be judged similarly. If the professor yields to appeals to pity, this will no longer be true.

A particularly sophisticated student may argue explicitly that there's no reason not to change the grade by pointing out not only how much a grade change would help him or her but also how little it would affect anyone else. "Whom will it hurt?" the student may ask. The student, in effect, is arguing both that the action would have some benefit and that there is no reason not to do it. If both theses were true, then the argument would be good. But we need to balance a proper sympathy for the individual against the needs of all. Small harms add up, and groups of actions, none of which seems harmful, may collectively be quite harmful.

Problems

Discuss whether the following contain appeals to common practice, force, or pity. Are the arguments good? Some passages accuse others of these fallacies; are the accusations correct?

▸ **1.** I can't stand this proliferation of paperwork. It's useless to fight the forms. You've got to kill the people producing them. (Vladimir P. Kubaidze)

▸ **2.** No man will take counsel, but every man will take money; therefore money is better than counsel. (Jonathan Swift)

▶ **3.** "You tell me. Your kids go to bed crying at night because they're hungry. Is 'off the books' going to bother you?" asks a former steelworker. (Clare Ansberry)

▶ **4.** Good sense is, of all things among men, the most evenly distributed; for everyone thinks himself so abundantly provided with it, that even those who are the most difficult to satisfy in everything else, do not usually desire a larger measure of this quality than they already possess. (René Descartes)

▶ **5.** Gentlemen: You have undertaken to cheat me. I won't sue you, for the law is too slow. I'll ruin you. Yours truly, Cornelius Vanderbilt

▶ **6.** No [college football] team that's ever appeared in your Top Twenty over the past 100 years is guiltless of cheating in one way or another. (Dan Jenkins)

7. While the role of dope in damping social unrest in early industrial England has not been extensively investigated, every historian of the period knows that it was common practice at the time for working mothers to start the habit in the cradle by dosing their hungry babies on laudanum ("mother's blessing," it was called). (Theodore Roszak)

8. Mrs. Harris has serious heart problems, and clearly she has suffered over the last eight years. Just as it is unlikely that she poses a threat to society, so it is certain that she could do more good as a sensible prison reformer on the outside than as a lifetime prisoner on the inside. According to Mrs. Harris, Bedford's correctional officers always refer to the inmates as "ladies." It is time to release the lady who wrote this book. (John J. DiIulio, Jr.)

9. Plea 4. *Such dancing is now become customary among Christians. Ans:* Which cannot be thought on without horror. A great and Learned Divine takes notice of it as a very sad thing, that all the profane Dances in use amongst the Lascivious Greeks of Old, have of late years been revived in the Christian World; yea, and in places where the Reformed Religion has taught men better. But shall [a] Christian follow the course of the World? They ought to swim against the stream, and to keep themselves pure from the sins of the Times of which this of *mixed dancing* is none the least. (Increase Mather)

10. Plea 5. *Some Good men think it is lawful! Ans:* We are not to walk by the opinion of this or that good Man, but by the Scriptures. *To the Law and to the Testimony, if they speak not according to that there is no light in them.* Fearful Judgments have befallen a Professing People for doing such things as some good Men through error of judgment have approved of. (Increase Mather)

11. *Son.*   What is a traitor?
    Wife.   Why, one that swears, and lies.
    Son.   And be all traitors that do so?
    Wife.   Everyone that does so is a traitor and must be hanged.
    Son.   And must they all be hanged that swear and lie?
    Wife.   Every one.
    Son.   Who must hang them?
    Wife.   Why, the honest men.
    Son.   Then the liars and swearers are fools; for there are liars and swearers enow to beat the honest men and hang them up. (William Shakespeare)

12. Make a list of appeals to force that parents typically use to make their children do things. Make another list of appeals to pity that children typically use to avoid doing those things. In each case, explain why the appeal does or doesn't constitute a good argument.

13. Devise an argument justifying some potentially controversial everyday action or habit—for example, eating meat, using disposable plastic utensils, driving a car, or buying records when there are starving people—without appealing to common practice. (a) Why is this difficult? Explain. (b) What must be done to avoid appealing to common practice in these cases?

14. List some appeals to pity that students might make when asking for a grade change. In each case, do they constitute good arguments? Why, or why not?

3.3 SUPERFICIALITY

We've considered fallacies resulting from misapplications of rules concerning emotion and practical reasoning. Other grounding fallacies stem from *superficiality*: from seizing upon one fairly obvious feature of a thing or circumstance and drawing sweeping conclusions about it, while overlooking other fundamental features that might point to a different conclusion.

Appeal to Ignorance

Most arguments try to establish a conclusion by relying on what is known. Some, however, rely on what is unknown. This is not always fallacious. For example, suppose that a year-long investigation into Ben's activities has produced no evidence that he has committed any crime. We might argue Ben's innocence from the lack of evidence of wrongdoing. The argument, furthermore, may be good. The lack of evidence of criminal activity may itself be evidence of innocence.

Nevertheless, arguments on the basis of a lack of knowledge easily go awry. Consider what we need to know about the investigation before we can justifiably conclude that Ben is innocent. First, the investigation must have been extensive and thorough. If the entire process lasted two hours, or if the investigation encompassed only one limited aspect of Ben's dealings, then an argument for Ben's overall innocence appears weak. Second, the investigators must have been competent. If they were not well qualified—if the team consisted of, say, two stand-up comics and a plumber—then the absence of evidence could stem from their incompetence rather than Ben's innocence. Third, the investigators must have been in a position to turn up evidence, if there were any. If the investigators received inadequate funding or could not examine relevant documents, or if several key witnesses met sudden, unnatural deaths just before being questioned, a conclusion of innocence based on the results of the investigation would be hasty.

Appeals to ignorance rely on the unknown to support their conclusions.

> **Definition**   An argument *appeals to ignorance* if and only if it
> tries to justify its conclusion by appealing to what is not known.

Such appeals succeed only under certain conditions. As we've seen, a lack of knowledge shows something only if there has been a competent, thorough, unfrustrated attempt to secure that knowledge. Otherwise, pointing toward a lack of knowledge is an unfair attempt to shift the burden of proof onto one's opponents.

Some dramatic examples of this kind of fallacy arose in the context of Senator Joseph McCarthy's crusade against Communists in government. Presenting a list of alleged Communists in the State Department, he said about one official, "I do not have much information on this except the general statement of the agency that there is nothing in the files to disprove his Communist connections."[7] Lack of disproof, clearly, is not tantamount to proof.

Other examples concern parapsychic phenomena (such as ESP) or controversial but unproven hypotheses (such as the existence of UFOs). On one side, people tend to argue that there's no scientific evidence that anyone has extrasensory perception or that UFOs are anything but natural phenomena. Sometimes, they conclude that there are no such things. But this is an appeal to ignorance. We can't infer the nonexistence of these happenings from a lack of evidence for them. On the other side, people tend to argue that nobody has proven that ESP doesn't exist, or that all unidentified flying objects are merely natural phenomena. Sometimes, they conclude that ESP or UFOs are real. This, too, is an appeal to ignorance. We can draw conclusions from a lack of evidence only if we know a great deal about attempts to find such evidence.

Appeal to Authority

A second kind of fallacy involving superficiality is the *appeal to authority*. Appealing to authorities to establish facts or conclusions isn't in itself a fallacy. Modern life is so complex that we all rely extensively on other people for information. You probably know that Bismarck is the capital of North Dakota. But how do you know? Have you been there, seen the legislature meet there, seen the official documents declaring it the state capital? Most people haven't. They've obtained their information from geography books, maps, or teachers. Those sources, in turn, have usually relied on other geography books, maps, or teachers. Between you and Bismarck may be a long chain of people, each relying on the authority of another.

This is fine, of course, provided that the people relied on are trustworthy and knowledgeable about the matter at hand. There are degrees of trustworthiness and knowledge; accordingly, there are degrees of reliability. A recent map is probably more reliable about the capital of North Dakota, for example, than a second-grader, and a second-grader may be more reliable than a telephone salesperson asking you to buy part of a timeshare resort in beautiful Pick City. It's one thing to believe that Romania is bulldozing most of its villages because you've read it in the *New York Times* or the *Wall Street Journal,* and quite another to believe it because you learned it from a supermarket tabloid or a TV comedy skit.

Consequently, although we often justifiably and unavoidably base our opinions on the opinions of others, we must be careful to assess the reliability of our sources. The views of a rightful authority on a particular subject are relevant evidence concerning that subject. In the common ground of a conversation, typically, is a principle that the opinions of authorities carry weight in their fields of expertise. Like other legitimate principles, however, this one has limitations. Opinions of authorities count, for example, only in their areas of expertise. If such limitations are ignored, the principle is susceptible to abuse. Sometimes people cite the opinions of authorities outside their fields of expertise. Sometimes people treat expert opinions as if they were the only evidence relevant to the point at issue, when, even at best, expert testimony is only part of the story.

Consider the first sort of fallacy. If an argument relying on authority is to succeed, the opinions it cites must fall within the expertise of the authority. To quote Albert Einstein on physics, Henry Kissinger on foreign policy, and Bill James on baseball is perfectly acceptable. (It's acceptable, that is, unless the arguer is also an expert in the same field. Physicists don't quote other physicists to each other; they appeal to facts, experiments, and theoretical principles.) To quote Einstein on foreign policy, Kissinger on baseball, and James on physics, however, yields no convincing evidence, although it might have some biographical interest.

Now consider the second sort of fallacy: Suppose that you are arguing with a friend about foreign policy. You advance various arguments directed against, let's say, an arms control treaty; your friend responds simply by saying, "Henry Kissinger supports the treaty. Cyrus Vance supports the treaty." Now Henry Kissinger and Cyrus Vance are foreign policy experts; they certainly have the credentials to be taken seriously. But their opinions are not so weighty that any other facts and arguments are irrelevant. Although pertinent to the debate, their views aren't decisive. Other experts may disagree with them. Furthermore, even if all the experts agree, they may all be wrong. Most European statesmen in the 1930s believed that Hitler could be appeased through territorial accession; the invasion of Poland in 1939 proved them wrong. Most American foreign policy experts in the early 1960s believed that American intervention in Southeast Asia would quickly lead to victory over North Vietnam; they, too, were proven wrong.

> **DEFINITION** An argument *appeals to authority* if and only if it tries to justify its conclusion by citing the opinions of authorities.

Appeals to authority thus have the form

(17) *A* says *P*.
∴ *P*.

We might advance, for example, these arguments:

(18) According to Einstein, the idea of absolute motion is incoherent.
∴ The idea of absolute motion is incoherent.

(19) According to Kissinger, the president should proceed cautiously.
∴ The president should proceed cautiously.

(20) According to Bill James, Lefty Grove was the greatest pitcher who ever lived.
∴ Lefty Grove was the greatest pitcher who ever lived.

All are appeals to authority.

When is it appropriate to base a conclusion on the opinions of authorities? First, the subject must be one on which there can be authorities. Some philosophers have held that there are no authorities on moral questions. Very likely nobody can be an authority on whether God exists or on what the one true religion is. For very different reasons, probably nobody can be an authority on what the stock market will do next week or next year. Second, the opinions cited in the argument must fall within the authority's area of expertise. Third, the authority must be trustworthy; there must be no additional factors that might make the expert misrepresent matters. (If the authority is a pathological liar or a comedian, or has strong political reasons for being on a particular side of an issue, or is in danger of persecution from the Spanish Inquisition or a congressional committee, the testimony is not very reliable.)

A special problem arises when legitimate experts disagree. Frequently, the testimony of one authority conflicts with that of another. At times, the preponderance of expert opinion is on one side of a question; in the mid-1980s, labor union leaders were able to find only one economist in the United States willing to speak out in favor of protectionism. Even such an overwhelming majority could be wrong, although the weight of such opinion provides substantial evidence in favor of the majority's view. In many circumstances, however, opinion is more evenly divided, and the nonexpert cannot easily judge who is correct. Whenever legitimate experts disagree, appeals to authority lose much of their force. It becomes necessary to look at the arguments in detail.

Incomplete Enumeration

Another sort of fallacy of superficiality is called *incomplete enumeration, false dilemma,* or *false disjunction.* Sometimes we seem to face dilemmas: your money or your life, truth or consequences, trick or treat. These dilemmas may be real. At times, however, they are only apparent; there are other possibilities. The thief who challenges Dirty Harry with "Your money or your life" is likely to find that his own life is in jeopardy. And an explanation that you've just run out of candy usually provides an alternative to trick or treat. Whenever your argument passes over possibilities you ought to recognize, you are guilty of the fallacy of incomplete enumeration.

> **DEFINITION** An argument exhibits the fallacy of *incomplete enumeration* if and only if it presupposes a disjunction that does not include all available possibilities.

An argument may exhibit this fallacy by "failing to make an exhaustive enumeration of alternatives, that is, not sufficiently considering all the ways in which something may exist or happen."[8]

Historian David Hackett Fischer has compiled a list of titles, of actual works by reputable historians, published by reputable presses, that exhibit this fallacy. Among them are the following:

> *Napoleon III: Enlightened Statesman or Proto-Fascist?*
> *The Causes of the War of 1812: National Honor or National Interest?*
> *The Abolitionists: Reformers or Fanatics?*
> *Jacksonian Democracy: Myth or Reality?*
> *Plato: Totalitarian or Democrat?*
> *The Dred Scott Decision: Law or Politics?*
> *John D. Rockefeller—Robber Baron or Industrial Statesman?*
> *The Robber Barons—Pirates or Pioneers?*
> *The New Deal—Revolution or Evolution?*
> *Ancient Science—Metaphysical or Observational?*
> *Feudalism—Cause or Cure of Anarchy?*
> *The Medieval Mind—Faith or Reason?*
> *Renaissance Man—Medieval or Modern?*
> *The Origins of Nazi Germany—German History or Charismatic Leadership?*
> *What Is History—Fact or Fancy?*

It should be obvious that there's something wrong with these titles. Perhaps Napoleon III was neither an enlightened statesman nor a proto-fascist. Perhaps the War of 1812 was fought for national honor as well as national interest, and for other reasons as well. Perhaps some abolitionists were both reformers and fanatics, some were one and not the other, and some were neither. It's clear that every title illustrates a spurious dichotomy because each presents an incomplete enumeration of the possibilities.

Accident

A final kind of grounding fallacy is the fallacy of *accident*. Writers on logic have described this fallacy in two quite different ways. First, and as we'll use the term, the fallacy of accident has been described as making "an unqualified judgment of a thing on the basis of an accidental characteristic."[9] Philosophers have traditionally held that some attributes of a thing are essential to it in the sense that, without them, the thing would not be what it is, whereas others are accidental in the sense that the thing could retain its identity without them. Your mind, for example, is essential to you; without it, you wouldn't be the person you are. But reading this book is accidental to you; you could stop reading it without ceasing to be you. Arguments that mistake accidental for essential attributes commit the fallacy of accident.

A famous and humorous example occurs in Shakespeare's *Henry V*, in which Fluellen argues that King Henry of Monmouth is the equal of Alexander the Great of Macedon:

> I tell you, captain, if you look in the maps of the 'orld, I warrant you sall find, in the comparisons between Macedon and Monmouth, that the situations, look you, is both alike. There is a river in Macedon, and there is also moreover a river at Monmouth. It is call'd Wye at Monmouth; but it is out of my prains what is the name of the other river; but 'tis all one; 'tis alike as my fingers is to my fingers, and there is salmons in both.

Ruling a kingdom with a river containing salmon is accidental to being a great king; Fluellen's argument mistakes it for an essential feature of greatness. Literary critic Richard Levin has correspondingly called the logic of arguments committing the fallacy of accident "Fluellenism."[10]

In its second sense, the fallacy of accident has been characterized as "applying a general rule to a particular case whose 'accidental' circumstances render the rule inapplicable."[11] This is precisely what we've called misapplication. Suppose, for example, that you've promised to meet a friend at seven o'clock. Driving to the meeting, you're involved in a collision, and the other driver is injured. You can meet your friend on time only if you leave the scene before the police arrive. Despite the general rule that you should keep your promises, it would be foolish to leave the scene. To apply the rule in such a contrary case is to commit a fallacy of misapplication, or of accident in this second sense.

Do we have one fallacy here or two? That is, are these two definitions of the fallacy of accident equivalent? Are accident and misapplication the same? Evidently not. We can perhaps think of Fluellen as applying the rule, "Recognize as great any king ruling a territory with a salmon-filled river," but this rule is foolish. The problem is not with the accidental circumstances of this particular case, but with the rule itself. So, Fluellen commits the fallacy of accident in the first sense, but not in the second. Conversely, it is misleading to say that, in leaving the scene of the collision, you are mistaking an accidental feature of the circumstance (your having promised to meet your friend at seven) for an essential feature. The promise is an important part of the situation; it has some moral force. But it's not as important as remaining on the scene. If you justify leaving the scene by the rule that promises ought to be kept, therefore, you commit the fallacy of accident only in the second sense.

Here, we reserve the term *accident* for fallacies in the first sense and retain the term *misapplication* for fallacies in the second.

> **Definition** An argument exhibits the fallacy of *accident* if and only if it tries to justify its conclusion by treating as essential an accidental feature of something.

We've already seen a humorous instance of the fallacy of accident. A far grimmer example is from M. Y. Latsis, a high official in Lenin's secret police, the Cheka:

> We are not looking for evidence or witnesses to reveal deeds or words against the Soviet power. . . . The first question we ask is—to what class does he belong, what are his origins, upbringing, education or profession? These questions define the fate of the accused. This is the essence of the Red Terror.[12]

In just two and a half years, the Cheka executed over 50,000 people, condemned not because of any crime but because of their parentage, education, or occupation. Yet surely these factors are accidental; they are irrelevant to whether someone deserves punishment, let alone death. Lenin didn't think so, of course. But Lenin was wrong.

Similar fallacies have been part of other revolutions. In 1959, Fidel Castro tried to justify invalidating "innocent" verdicts and sentencing forty-four political opponents to long prison terms by declaring, "Revolutionary Justice is based not on legal precepts but on moral conviction."[13] But someone else's moral indignation hardly justifies punishment.

Problems

Do the following passages contain examples of fallacies of superficiality? Explain. If a passage accuses someone else of such a fallacy, evaluate the allegation.

► **1.** "Shoes! Frivolity! Marie Antoinette!" In the Philippines I built houses for 30,000 slum dwellers. I planted 80 million trees around Manila . . . and they talk only about shoes! (Imelda Marcos)

► **2.** Most of the people who are supposed to be powerful really aren't. They may be powerful in their company—but they still can't get a cab in the rain. (Ed Kosner)

► **3.** Nelson would have been afraid of ten thousand fleas, but a flea wouldn't have been afraid of ten thousand Nelsons. (Mark Twain)

► **4.** The thing that appalls me about the newspaper business is the number of trees it consumes. (Prince Charles)

► **5.** If we think to regulate printing, thereby to rectify manners, we must regulate all recreations and pastimes, all that is delightful to man. No music must be heard, no song be set or sung, but what is grave and Doric. There must be licensing dancers, that no gesture, motion, or deportment be taught our youth but what by their allowance shall be thought honest. . . . (John Milton)

► **6.** Mr. Muravchik is troubled by my characterization of IPS angel Samuel Rubin as a Communist party member, when the evidence suggests only that Rubin was registered as a Communist party voter and that therefore he was not under party discipline. Let me just say that no one on the Left has denied Rubin's CP membership, and I am hardly the first to have made the charge. . . . (Scott Steven Powell)

7. . . . an historian's professed inability to discern any plot, rhythm, or predetermined pattern is no evidence that blind Samson has actually won his boasted freedom from the bondage of "Laws of Nature." The presumption is indeed the opposite; for, when bonds are imperceptible to the wearer of them, they are likely to prove more difficult to shake off than when they betray their presence and reveal something of their shape and texture by clanking and galling. (Arnold Toynbee)

8. Attorney General Earl Warren testified at the congressional Tolan Committee hearings in San Francisco that "because we have had no sabotage and no fifth column activities in this State," therefore "the sabotage we are to get" has been carefully concealed and precisely timed, as at Pearl Harbor and as in occupied Europe. (Eric J. Sundquist)

9. In Saudi Arabia, yes, they cut off the hands of a thief. So, every year, they cut off—what, six, seven people's hands? And what is the population of Saudi Arabia? Seven million? In Saudi Arabia, people do not steal. Is that worse than in America, where there are not these "brutal" punishments, and 15 people get killed or banged on the head or something every week on Park Avenue? Which is the more important? The lives of the people who get murdered there? Or the hands of the people they punish in Saudi Arabia? The one is the price you pay to avoid the other. I do not know. Perhaps you prefer to see the dead men on the streets in New York? Perhaps that is not so offensive to you? (Mohammed Mannei)

10. There is an incredible amount of empty space in the universe. The distance from the sun to the nearest star is about 4.2 light years, or 25 followed by 12 noughts miles. . . . And as to mass: the sun weighs about 2 followed by 27 noughts tons, the Milky Way weighs about 160,000 times as much as the sun and is one of a collection of galaxies of which, as I said before, about 30 million are known. It is not very easy to retain a belief in one's own cosmic importance in view of such overwhelming statistics. (Bertrand Russell)

11. A young woman, a smartly outfitted executive type, was talking about the counterman in the deli in her office building. He had presented her with a stuffed lion and a stocking filled with chocolates. In a little more than a year, he had proposed to her four times. The woman insisted that she had no romantic interest in the man.

"So what do I do?" she asked her companion-possibly-mother.

There was a thoughtful pause. Finally, the older woman spoke. "I have one question. Does he own the deli?" (Dale Boorstein)

▶ 12. Two battleships assigned to the training squadron had been at sea on maneuvers in heavy weather for several days. I was serving on the lead battleship and was on watch on the bridge as night fell. The visibility was poor with patchy fog, so the captain remained on the bridge keeping an eye on all activities.

Shortly after dark, the lookout on the wing of the bridge reported, "Light, bearing on the starboard bow."

"Is it steady or moving astern?" the captain called out.

Lookout replied, "Steady, captain," which meant we were on a dangerous collision course with that ship.

The captain then called to the signalman, "Signal that ship: We are on a collision course, advise you to change course 20°."

Back came a signal, "Advisable for you to change course 20°."

In reply, the captain said, "Send: I'm a captain, change course 20°."

"I am a seaman second class," came the reply. "You had better change course 20°."

By that time, the captain was furious. He spit out, "Send: I'm a battleship, change course 20°."

Back came the flashing light, "I'm a lighthouse!"

We changed course. (Frank Koch)

13. For each of the book titles listed at the end of the section "Incomplete Enumeration," give at least three alternatives not enumerated in the title.

14. Using the front page of a recent newspaper, identify five authorities used by newswriters in their stories. Given the information you have, is the appeal to authority justified? Explain.

For each of the following proverbs, create two arguments: one that represents a proper application of the proverb, and one that represents a misapplication of the proverb.

15. A stitch in time saves nine.

16. Haste makes waste.

17. A penny saved is a penny earned.

▶ **18.** Look before you leap.

19. He who hesitates is lost.

20. Absence makes the heart grow fonder.

21. Out of sight, out of mind.

22. More is less.

23. Less is more.

▶ **24.** Honey catches more flies than vinegar.

25. The apple never falls far from the tree.

26. A bird in the hand is worth two in the bush.

27. There are two sides to every question.

28. The early bird gets the worm.

In each pair below, both sentences could be argued by appeals to ignorance. Construct such an appeal for each sentence.

29. (a) God exists.
(b) God doesn't exist.

▶ **30.** (a) There is intelligent life elsewhere in the universe.
(b) There's no intelligent life elsewhere in the universe.

31. (a) Humans are smarter than dolphins.
(b) Dolphins are smarter than humans.

Each of the following are fundamental rights or freedoms. Consider the cases below each, and explain why they are correct applications, or misapplications, of that right or freedom. Some are controversial: In those cases, choose one side, and give reasons.

Freedom of speech:

32. Publishing a newspaper critical of the government

33. Producing a controversial film on political subjects

34. Publishing an article claiming, without evidence, that a public figure is a criminal

35. Publishing an article claiming, without evidence, that an ordinary citizen is a criminal

36. Producing a highly pornographic movie

37. Showing a highly pornographic movie in your theater

38. Shouting "Fire!" in a crowded theater

39. Burning the American flag in public

40. Barricading a public building to protest government policy

Freedom of religion:

41. Holding a worship service in a private building

42. Holding a worship service in a public park

43. Holding a worship service in the middle of a busy public roadway

44. Privately displaying religious articles or symbols

45. Publicly displaying religious articles or symbols

46. Refusing medical help on religious grounds

47. Refusing medical help for one's children on religious grounds

48. Using illegal drugs as part of a religious ceremony

49. Conducting a religious ceremony involving the handling of poisonous snakes

50. Handing out religious pamphlets in a public airport

Freedom to keep and bear arms:

51. Keeping sharp knives in the kitchen

52. Keeping a baseball bat under the bed

53. Keeping a pistol in a desk drawer

54. Keeping a hunting rifle in the basement

55. Keeping a semiautomatic rifle in the closet

56. Keeping a submachine gun in the nightstand

57. Carrying a stickpin in a purse

58. Carrying a switchblade in a pocket

59. Carrying a pistol in a shoulder holster under a jacket

60. Carrying a rifle over a shoulder

Notes

[1] Lanford Wilson, *The Hot L Baltimore* (New York: Hill and Wang, 1973), pp. 140, 142.

[2] *Trump: The Art of the Deal,* quoted in *Forbes* (June 27, 1988), p. 36.

[3] Some writers use this term differently, for what appears later as "appeal to common practice."

[4] Cicero, fourth oration against Cataline, 1.

[5] Richard Nixon, "Checkers" speech.

[6] *Reprints from the Soviet Press,* April 30, 1977, pp. 22–23.

[7] Richard H. Rovere, *Senator Joe McCarthy* (New York: Harper and Row, 1959), p. 132.

[8] Antoine Arnauld, *Logic, or The Art of Thinking* (Indianapolis: Bobbs-Merrill, 1964; originally published in 1662), p. 255.

[9] Arnauld, p. 259.

[10] See Richard Levin, *New Readings v. Old Plays* (Chicago: University of Chicago Press, 1979).

[11] Copi, *Introduction to Logic* (New York: Macmillan, 1978), p. 95.

[12] M. Y. Latsis quoted in Harrison Salisbury, *Black Night, White Snow: Russia's Revolutions, 1905–1917* (Garden City, N.J.: Doubleday, 1978), p. 565.

[13] Fidel Castro quoted in Hugh Thomas, *Cuba, or the Pursuit of Freedom* (New York: Harper and Row, 1971), pp. 1202–3.

4

MEANING

M any problems in reasoning
arise, not from violations of the criteria for good arguments, but from making
mistakes about meaning. These errors often lead to other errors in reasoning.
Someone who misunderstands a term, for example, is likely to address arguments to the wrong issue. Someone who misinterprets an opponent is likely
to misconstrue the opponent's position and arguments for it. So, confusing
the issue, attacking a straw man, and other fallacies of relevance often stem
from mistakes about meaning.

Mistakes about meaning are not simply errors of reasoning; they are
also instances of miscommunication. The communication may be an argument, but it may also be a description, a piece of advice, or an invoice. In
this chapter, we'll examine the illness: We'll consider some of the most important mistakes people commonly make about meanings. We'll also search
for a cure: We'll develop rules for definition.

4.1 EQUIVOCATION

Perhaps the simplest mistake about meaning involves misconstruing a word
or phrase. Most words have more than one meaning. The common ground,
in some circumstances, doesn't determine which meaning is intended. If the
listener attaches to a word a meaning that the speaker didn't intend, then
miscommunication takes place; what the listener understands is not what
the speaker meant to convey.

Some words have meanings that differ greatly from one another. Mistaking one meaning for another in these cases is possible, but difficult; context usually makes the speaker's intention clear. When a listener does choose
the wrong meaning, the result seems like a joke:

(1) *A*: We ran our boat right into the bank.
    B: Were you trying to rob it?

(2) *A*: I keep my pet rabbit in a pen.
    B: It must be a very small rabbit.

(3) *A*: It's a free country.
    B: Seems pretty expensive to me.

Gross confusions of meaning, therefore, are usually easy to correct, if, of course, they are identified in time. Evelyn Waugh, in East Africa in 1959, wrote of a tragic misunderstanding based on an ambiguous word:

> I spent one day with the Masai.... They had a lovely time during the Mau Mau rising. They were enlisted and told to bring in all the Kikuyu's arms. Back they proudly came with baskets of severed limbs.[1]

Much harder to recognize and correct are confusions between the meanings of terms with several closely related meanings. Consider, for example, the political terms 'liberal' and 'conservative'. Each has several different meanings relevant to politics:

Liberal

(a) Giving freely; generous
(b) Not restricted to the literal meaning; not strict
(c) Tolerant of views different from one's own
(d) Of democratic or republican forms of government
(e) Favoring reform

Conservative

(a) Conserving, or tending to conserve
(b) Tending to preserve established traditions
(c) Moderate; cautious; safe

The English philosophers John Locke (1632–1704) and John Stuart Mill (1806–1873) are often called liberals; they advocated tolerance and democracy, and, so, are liberals in senses (c) and (d). In their own time, they also favored reform, and, so, were liberals in sense (e) as well. Franklin Delano Roosevelt (1882–1945) was called a liberal for instituting the New Deal. Because that collection of programs involved government spending on programs directed at helping people, Roosevelt was liberal in sense (a), an economic rather than social sense of 'liberal'. Most people who now consider themselves liberals mean the term in sense (e); they favor reform and social change.

An argument can easily go astray when these senses of the word are confused. Thus, someone who deduces that a candidate will try to help the poor from the fact that the candidate is a liberal—when that term is used in any of senses (b)–(e)—equivocates. Similarly, someone who argues that a candidate would promote tolerance simply because that candidate is a liberal in the sense of favoring social change commits a fallacy of *equivocation*.

The ambiguity of the term 'conservative' can also promote equivocation. A voter who chooses the conservative as a safe or moderate choice may be making a mistake, if that candidate is conservative in the sense of favoring established traditions. After all, one might use extreme measures to defend established tradition. Conversely, a candidate who favors moderation does not necessarily seek to preserve the establishment.

In general, an argument exhibits the fallacy of equivocation if it confuses meanings of a word or phrase:

> **DEFINITION**   An argument exhibits *equivocation* if and only if it tries to justify its conclusion by relying on an ambiguity in a word or phrase.

Equivocation may involve phrases containing more than one word as well as individual words. Consider these exchanges (the ambiguous phrases are in italics):

(4) *A*: The painter got so angry he *kicked the bucket*.
     B: You mean he died right there?

(5) *A*: Do you *believe in* infant baptism?
     B: Yes—I've seen it done!

A particularly interesting case of an inference based on equivocation concerns J. Edgar Hoover, former director of the Federal Bureau of Investigation. "One of [J. Edgar] Hoover's many quirks was his demand that no memo should exceed one page, with wide margins. An agent ran into trouble getting his reports onto one page, so he encroached on the prescribed margin width. Hoover wrote back, 'Good analysis, but watch the borders'. Since no subordinate was willing to question 'The Chief,' the FBI dispatched agents to the Canadian and Mexican borders, to 'watch'. Nobody knew what they were looking for, but for a while, these borders were watched as never before."[2]

Problems

Discuss the confusions in meaning, intentional or unintentional, involved in the following passages.

▶ **1.** "The Louis XV bed is too small," a client once told the legendary decorator, Ruby Ross Wood. "I think I'd better get a Louis XVI." (Gerald Clarke)

▶ **2.** At a time of grave crisis during the Civil War, Abe Lincoln was awakened by an opportunist who reported that the head of customs had just died.

"Mr. President, would it be all right if I took his place?" "Well," said Lincoln, "if it's all right with the undertaker, it's all right with me." (Morris Udall)

▶ 3. There was a time when you were an imperialist if you invaded an alien territory and imposed on independent peoples an authority they rejected. Today, you are an imperialist if you oppose such aggression. (Jean-François Revel)

▶ 4. T. J. was one of those linebackers who didn't need pharmaceuticals to get ready to play. One day a sportswriter asked him how he always managed to get "up" for the games. T. J. said, "Aw, Coach just comes by and knocks on the door." (Dan Jenkins)

▶ 5. [I remember] the 1930s story about a policeman in New York's Union Square wielding a billy club to break up a Communist rally. "But I'm an *anti*-Communist," one demonstrator protested, to which the policeman—stepping up his blows—replied, "I don't care what kind of a communist you are!" (Allen Weinstein)

▶ 6. Adele F. Weiss telephones the Whitney Museum of American Art to find out if her husband should bring along his camera.

"Hello," she says. "Is picture-taking permitted at the Sargent exhibit?"

"Would you repeat that, please?"

Mrs. Weiss asks the question a second time.

"No. You have to look at the pictures on the wall. You can't take them off the wall." (Ron Alexander)

Give at least two meanings for each of the following words.

7. art	**8.** bass	**9.** carriage	**10.** dance
11. escalator	▶ **12.** funny	**13.** go	**14.** ham
15. interest	**16.** jog	**17.** key	▶ **18.** lump
19. mind	**20.** narrow	**21.** out	**22.** pin
23. quick	▶ **24.** run	**25.** sign	**26.** tip
27. usher	**28.** view	**29.** well	▶ **30.** yoke
31. zero			

32. Can you think of any words that aren't ambiguous? List three.

4.2 Amphiboly

Some sentences are ambiguous, not because they contain ambiguous words or phrases, but because of their grammatical construction. Such sentences are *syntactically ambiguous;* they can be read in two different ways, because they have two different syntactic or grammatical structures. The grammar of a language tells how to combine words of different categories, according to rules, to construct sentences. Two very different paths may lead to the same sentence. In some cases, the results of the two paths of construction coincide in meaning. In other cases, they don't; the sentence is syntactically ambiguous.

David Hackett Fischer devised these hypothetical sentences to illustrate amphiboly:

(6) Richly carved Chippendale furniture was produced by colonial craftsmen with curved legs and claw feet.

(7) The measures of the New Deal were understandably popular, for many men received jobs, and women also.[3]

Frequently, amphiboly results from misplacement of a clause or phrase in a sentence. We can rewrite the amphibolous sentences so that they are unambiguous:

(8) Richly carved Chippendale furniture with curved legs and claw feet was produced by colonial craftsmen.

(9) The measures of the New Deal were understandably popular, for many men, and women also, received jobs.

Sometimes amphiboly results from an elliptical construction. The classic example is a wartime poster urging citizens to "Save soap and waste paper." Another is the topic of a debate between some well-known conservatives and liberals in 1988: "Resolved, that the Right is better able to deal with the Soviets than the Left."

In general, an argument exhibits the fallacy of amphiboly if it confuses sentence structure in a way that affects the meaning of the sentence.

> **DEFINITION** An argument exhibits *amphiboly* if and only if it tries to justify its conclusion by relying on an ambiguity in sentence structure.

A special kind of ambiguity results from the indeterminacy of the reference of pronouns or other anaphoric devices. A pronoun (for instance, I, me, my, you, your, he, him, his, she, her, it, they, them, or their) derives its reference from context. First- and second-person pronouns derive their reference from extralinguistic features of the context: primarily, from who is speaking or writing to whom. Third-person pronouns may derive their reference in this way but may also derive their reference from linguistic features of the context. Often, the context does not determine a single referent; the pronoun may refer to any of several objects. This, too, can produce ambiguity.

A funny and unintended example of this ambiguity occurs in the King James version of the Old Testament:

(10) "Saddle me the ass," he said unto his sons. And they saddled him. (II Samuel)

Here is an example from Yankee sportscaster Jerry Coleman:

> (11) The ball's hit deep to center. Winfield's going back, back. He slams his head into the wall! It's rolling toward second base!

Another example is in Shakespeare:

> (12) The Duke yet lives that Henry shall depose
> But him outlive, and die a violent death.

Who is 'him'? Henry or the duke? Sometimes, as in this example, the ambiguity is intentional. Most often, however, it is a sign of bad writing.

How can referential ambiguity be avoided? Sentences in which a pronoun may plausibly be interpreted as referring to several different objects should be rewritten to remove the ambiguity. Rephrasing sometimes is enough. Sometimes, a definite description—'my donkey', 'the duke'—clarifies the reference without introducing awkwardness. Replacing 'him' with 'the duke' or 'the king' resolves the ambiguity of who will outlive whom.

Problems

Explain the equivocation or amphiboly, if any, that creates confusion in these passages. Rewrite to remove the ambiguity or amphiboly.

▶ **1.** Bob is a pest. The exterminator will kill pests. So, the exterminator will kill Bob.

▶ **2.** Sue carries a comb. Bees keep honey in combs. So, Sue carries honey.

▶ **3.** Xavier is running in a race for governor. Jorge is running in a race for charity. So, Xavier and Jorge may be running against each other.

▶ **4.** Hard work is the key to success. A key can be put on a chain. So, hard work can be put on a chain.

▶ **5.** Cheryl is pro-choice. Scott is a golf pro. So, Cheryl and Scott are both pros.

▶ **6.** You can avoid the potholes by driving in the middle of the road. But, if cars are coming the other way, you have to hit them.

7. Listening to the blues music, Chad went into a state of depression. Going into another state involves traveling and crossing the border. So, Chad traveled and crossed the border.

8. Nothing is better than liberty. Prison life is better than nothing. So, prison life is better than liberty.

9. The meat I bought yesterday was raw. We're eating the meat I bought yesterday. So, we're eating raw meat.

10. Not to give to charity is selfish. To pay the rent is not to give to charity. So, to pay the rent is selfish.

11. No cat has nine tails. Every cat has one more tail than no cat. So, every cat has ten tails.

▶ 12. Man is studied by psychology. Robert is a man. So, Robert is studied by psychology.

13. All that glitters is not gold. Gold glitters. So, gold is not gold.

14. Food is necessary to life. Sauerkraut is food. So, sauerkraut is necessary to life.

15. Humans are the only animals that laugh. Brenda is human. So, Brenda is the only animal that laughs.

16. The animal is the one type of sentient being. The wolf is an animal. So, the wolf is the one type of sentient being.

17. Gather the dough and knead for at least five minutes. You cannot knead too much.

▶ 18. *A*: "We must distribute the money fairly, so we'll give everyone equal shares." *B*: "That means I get more, since I'm starting out with less."

19. At Wednesday's meeting both mothers and fathers of twins will meet for the first time. (Bloomington, Illinois, *Pantagraph*)

20. As in previous years, the evening concluded with a toast to the new president on champagne provided by the retiring president, drunk as usual at midnight. (Bangkok *Post*)

21. Mrs. Samuel Calcotte entertained at luncheon Monday, honoring Mrs. Dale McIntyre, who was again celebrating her 29th birthday. (Drayton Plains, Michigan, *Lakeland Tribune*)

22. Workmen swept the snow from the seats of 20,000 spectators. (Cincinnati *Post and Times-Star*)

23. They enjoyed a most delicious dinner, but also put in a good time on quilts. (Salem, Oregon, *Keizer News*)

▶ 24. Strong westerly winds blew down the Rockies in Wyoming. (Kansas City *Times*)

25. Mrs. Pike C. Ross left today for Le Harpe and the Brookfield Zoo in Chicago to visit relatives. (Lewistown, Illinois, *Evening Record*)

26. Columbia, Tenn., which calls itself the largest outdoor mule market in the world, held a mule parade yesterday, headed by the governor. (Jefferson City, Missouri, paper)

27. Local police are puzzled over the finding of a car parked outside the Methodist Church containing a full case of Scotch whisky. So far they

have found no trace of the owner, but Captain Casey is diligently working on the case. (Muscatine, Iowa, *Journal and News-Tribune*)

28. Miss Roberta Ford was injured while driving a car near the city yesterday. The area in which Miss Ford was injured is spectacularly scenic. (Monterey, California, *Peninsula Herald*)

29. She declines to give her name, but says she's been something for the birds for more than 40 years. (Milwaukee *Journal*)

▸ 30. Mr. Okun lives with his wife, his high-school sweetheart, and three sons. (Leo Rosten, quoting Okun)

31. Class Q allotments are based upon the number of dependents up to a maximum of three, so, if the birth of a child will mean your husband is entitled to more quarters allowance, notify him to take the necessary action. (Form enclosed with soldiers' allotment checks, 1955)

32. Otto von Hapsburg, heir apparent to the defunct Austro-Hungarian throne, in 1988 was asked if he was going to see the Austria-Hungary soccer match. "No," replied the head Hapsburg, "But how interesting. Tell me, whom are we playing?" (Malcolm S. Forbes)

33. If liberated ladies would start lighting up cigars, maybe we who love 'em could use them more often in more places. (Malcolm S. Forbes)

34. Like if I'd said, "In the future everyone will be famous for 15 minutes," it could come out, "In 15 minutes everybody will be famous." (Andy Warhol)

35. When Sargent's painting of Belle Steward Gardner in a low-cut dress was exhibited at a Boston club, a member was heard to remark crudely (in a reference understood by anyone familiar with the White Mountains) that she was naked "all the way down to Crawford's Notch." Belle was unperturbed, although she did remark, when asked for a contribution to the Charitable Eye and Ear Infirmary, that she did not know there was a charitable eye or ear in Boston. (Joseph J. Thorndike, Jr.)

Explain and correct the equivocation or amphiboly in these newspaper headlines.

▸ 36. Joe Bananas with Bunch in North Africa. (Utica, New York, *Observer-Dispatch*)

37. Rubberized Roads Springing Up, Says Goodyear Executive. (Los Angeles *Times*)

38. British Virgins Get Set for Tourist Boom. (Charlotte Amalie, Virgin Islands, *News*)

39. Parks Will Not Issue Parking Permits to Fish. (Highland Park, Illinois, *Advertiser*)

40. Jury Gets Drunk Driving Case Here. (Austin, Texas)

41. Night School to Hear Pest Talk. (Oakland, California)

► 42. County Officials to Talk Rubbish. (Los Angeles, California)

43. High School Girls Learn to Fill Out Their Forms. (New York, New York)

44. Pocatello Mattress Factory Plays Important Role in City's Growth. (Pocatello, Idaho)

45. Young Democrats Elect Bone Head. (Selma, Alabama, *Times-Journal*)

46. Father of 11 Fined $200 for Failing to Stop. (Lancaster, Pennsylvania, *New Era*)

47. Rev. Key Resigns; Attendance Doubles. (LaGrange, Georgia, *News*)

► 48. Antique Stripper to Demonstrate Wares at Store. (Hartford *Courant*)

49. Continuing Education for Women Mushrooms. (Washington *Star*)

50. Zoo: Open Unless Wildcat Strike Resumes. (Philadelphia *Inquirer*)

51. Pardon Me. (McAlester, Oklahoma, Penitentiary *Eye Opener*)

Explain and correct these examples of equivocation or amphiboly in advertisements.

52. Hear . . . the Weatherman. The complete dope on the weather! (Rochester *Times-Union*)

53. Wanted—Old piano for child in fairly good condition. (Westfield, Massachusetts, *Wallace Pennysaver*)

► 54. Now is your chance to have your ears pierced and get an extra pair to take home too! (Auburn, New York, *Citizen-Advertiser*)

55. Four-poster bed 101 years old with springs. Perfect for antique lover. (Ann Arbor, Michigan, *News*)

56. Girl for photo-finishing plant, to develop prints, and experienced to handle three oversize printers. (Denver *Post*)

57. *Everybody's* buying our turkeys, geese and fowl because they know no better. (Belfast, Ireland, *Telegraph*)

58. First run if you haven't seen it. (Tulsa, Oklahoma, movie ad)

59. If you have two grave cemetery lots you are not dying to use, contact *Times-Union,* stating location and price. (Jacksonville, Florida, *Times-Union*)

60. Wildlife Museum and Taxidermy Studio. Come and see—
Mounted Wildlife in Natural Habitat

Fish Mounted in Under Water Scenes
Special Mountings for Children. (Eagle River, Wisconsin, *Vilas County News-Review*)

4.3 Accent

Sentences, as you have seen, often have presuppositions. Accenting or stressing a word in a sentence can change those presuppositions. Most frequently, emphasis on a particular word adds presuppositions to those of the unstressed sentence. Consider this fairly straightforward, unambiguous sentence:

(13) John shouldn't berate his employees in public.

This presupposes only that John has employees. But, if you stress certain words in the sentence, additional presuppositions arise. Stressing the subject of the sentence, for example, suggests that (13) is true because of something special about John:

(14) **John** shouldn't berate his employees in public.

This presupposes that it may be acceptable for others to berate their employees publicly. Stressing the verb suggests a contrast between berating and some other activity:

(15) John shouldn't **berate** his employees in public.

This presupposes that he should instead do something else.

(16) John shouldn't berate **his** employees in public.

This seems to presuppose that it's acceptable to berate other people's employees.

(17) John shouldn't berate his **employees** in public.

This suggests that it's alright for him to berate others. Finally,

(18) John shouldn't berate his employees in **public.**

presupposes that it's acceptable for him to berate them in private.
  In each case, emphasis on a particular word or phrase suggests that there is an important contrast between what that word or phrase conveys and some alternative. Another example illustrates how such contrasts give rise to presuppositions:

(19) The **pastor** didn't father an illegitimate child this year.

This contrasts the pastor with someone else; it presupposes that someone else did.

(20) The pastor didn't **father** an illegitimate child this year.

This draws a contrast between fathering and having some other relation to an illegitimate child. It presupposes that the pastor had some other relation to an illegitimate child—adopted it, perhaps, or found it a home.

(21) The pastor didn't father an **illegitimate** child this year.

The contrast here is between legitimacy and illegitimacy; it presupposes that the pastor's child is legitimate.

(22) The pastor didn't father an illegitimate child **this** year.

This emphasis contrasts this year with other years. It presupposes that the pastor has fathered an illegitimate child in at least one other year.

To put this in the context of argument, suppose that a historian of an old New England town finds a letter containing the sentence "The pastor didn't father an illegitimate child this year." Why did the author write these words? There are many possibilities. Perhaps someone had accused the pastor of doing so. Perhaps someone else had fathered an illegitimate child. Perhaps the pastor became a father, but legitimately, or perhaps the sentence indicates that this year was unusual. The historian will doubtless seek further evidence concerning these possibilities. But to jump to a conclusion, in the absence of additional information, is to commit the fallacy of accent.

In general, an argument exemplifies the fallacy of accent if, by misplacing emphasis, it relies on presuppositions not justified originally by the premises:

> **DEFINITION**   An argument exemplifies the fallacy of *accent* if and only if it tries to justify its conclusion by relying on presuppositions arising from a change in stress in a premise.

Guarding against this fallacy requires making emphasis clear in one's own writing and reporting fairly the use of emphasis in the writings of others. Quotations with italics or other emphatic devices should be accompanied by a note saying whether the emphasis is in the original.

A striking example of the accent fallacy occurred during Richard Nixon's presidency. Shortly after the highly publicized Tate-LaBianca murders, for which Charles Manson and his followers were arrested, Nixon gave a speech. In an aside, he mentioned Manson's crime. Apparently by oversight, Nixon said, "Manson murdered," rather than "Manson allegedly murdered." Though the reference to Manson was a minor illustration of a point in the speech, at least one big-city newspaper the next day carried the headline "Manson Guilty, Nixon Declares." The headline plainly encouraged readers to think that Nixon had tried to prejudice the outcome of a criminal trial. To draw such an inference, however, is to commit the fallacy of accent.

Problems

Explain the differences between the following by indicating what each stressed sentence presupposes that the unstressed sentence doesn't.

▶ **1.** a. **John** hasn't killed Tom.
  b. John hasn't **killed** Tom.
  c. John hasn't killed **Tom.**

▶ **2.** a. **I** never see any roaches around here.
  b. I never **see** any roaches around here.
  c. I never see any **roaches** around here.
  d. I never see any roaches around **here.**

3. a. **Senator** Pristine hasn't taken any bribes while in office.
  b. Senator **Pristine** hasn't taken any bribes while in office.
  c. Senator Pristine hasn't **taken** any bribes while in office.
  d. Senator Pristine hasn't taken any **bribes** while in office.
  e. Senator Pristine hasn't taken any bribes **while in office.**

4. a. **Larry** bet on the Seahawks this time.
  b. Larry **bet** on the Seahawks this time.
  c. Larry bet on the **Seahawks** this time.
  d. Larry bet on the Seahawks **this time.**

5. a. **Boris** certainly hasn't been acting crazy around me.
  b. Boris certainly hasn't been **acting** crazy around me.
  c. Boris certainly hasn't been acting **crazy** around me.
  d. Boris certainly hasn't been acting crazy around **me.**

4.4 Composition and Division

The fallacy of *composition* consists of attributing something to a whole or group because it can be attributed to the parts or members. An individual pin dropping makes no perceptible sound, but it isn't reasonable to conclude that dropping a boxful of pins would make no perceptible sound. Similarly, each book in a library collection may be good, without the collection as a whole being good.

We've already seen, in Chapter 3, a case of the fallacy of composition. Appeals to pity, if they are sophisticated, involve an assertion that someone can be helped without significant harm to anyone else. But a large number of acts, each of which causes only tiny, imperceptible harms, may collectively cause great harm. Raising one student's grade harms others only a small amount, but a general policy of grade inflation harms students, employers, and universities substantially. To argue that the overall effects will be minor because the effect in each case is minor is to commit the fallacy of composition.

The fallacy of *division* is the inverse of the fallacy of composition. It involves arguing from the properties of a group or whole to the properties of members or parts. That a forest is verdant and dense does not imply that all, or even most, trees in it are verdant and dense. That a group tends toward violent behavior doesn't establish that the individual members tend toward violent behavior. A comical example of this fallacy is the argument

(23) Whales are in danger of extinction.
This is a whale.
∴ This is in danger of extinction.

The fallacies of composition and division are more common than these examples may suggest. Academics, for example, frequently rate academic departments by rating the individual faculty members in those departments. In turn, they rate universities on the basis of the quality of their departments. Performed carelessly, this rating involves two fallacies of composition. The excellence of the members of a department does not guarantee the excellence of the department itself; it may be sharply divided, or extremely narrow, or unbalanced, or simply not organized into an effective unit. Similarly, the excellence of most or all departments of a university does not establish the excellence of the university in educating its students effectively. A university may be more or less than the sum of its parts. The parts may function well or poorly together, and that has a large effect on the quality of the university as a whole. Conversely, the excellence of a college or university does not entail the excellence of its departments taken individually, much less the excellence of its individual faculty members. Obviously, the quality of the whole and the quality of the parts are not unrelated. But to argue, without further support, from the quality of one to the quality of the other is to commit a fallacy of composition or division.

Problems

Do these arguments commit a fallacy of composition or division? Explain.

▶ **1.** Modern societies have many conflicts; the people in a modern society, therefore, have many conflicts.

▶ **2.** Our team is particularly strong this year. Joe is on our team; so, he must be particularly strong this year.

▶ **3.** The changes that television makes in any of us are small and barely noticeable. So, the changes television makes in society are small and barely noticeable.

▶ **4.** Each part of Socrates is smaller than Socrates. All of Socrates, therefore, is smaller than Socrates.

▶ **5.** I'll bet Jane has a big, beautiful room. I've seen a picture of her house, and it's very big and very beautiful.

▶ **6.** The company has performed badly this year. We can only conclude that the employees have performed badly this year.

7. All employees are entitled to health benefits. John is an employee. John is thus entitled to health benefits.

8. The Libertarians I know aren't extreme in their views. That shows that the Libertarian party isn't extreme in its views.

9. Linguists have published many books on Romance languages. Tony is a linguist. Therefore Tony has published many books on Romance languages.

10. Linguists are usually clever. Tony is a linguist. Tony, therefore, is usually clever.

11. Linguists know more than one language. Tony is a linguist. Tony, therefore, knows more than one language.

► 12. Lawrence is a member of a wealthy family. Lawrence, therefore, is wealthy.

13. Uruguay is a poor country. Felipe lives in Uruguay. So, Felipe is poor.

14. India's citizens are mostly poor. Therefore, India is a poor country.

15. Karen teaches at Oxford, which is an outstanding university. So, Karen must be an outstanding scholar.

16. The Ford Foundation is generous. Hence, the people who work for the Ford Foundation are generous.

17. The American Civil Liberties Union supports legalizing all pornography. Mort belongs to the ACLU. So, Mort supports legalizing all pornography.

► 18. The party got wild and completely out of hand. Geoffrey was there; it follows that Geoffrey got wild and completely out of hand.

19. Everyone at the party got wild and completely out of hand. Geoffrey was there; it follows that Geoffrey got wild and completely out of hand.

20. Everyone at the party got wild and completely out of hand. The party, therefore, got wild and completely out of hand.

Some sentences are very difficult to decipher, for various reasons. They may be ambiguous, poorly constructed, obscure, unclear, overly complicated, or just incoherent. What do the following sentences mean? What did their authors probably intend them to mean? Why are they hard to understand?

21. Nobody said it would be easy, and nobody was right. (George Bush)

22. Line up alphabetically according to height. (Yogi Berra)

23. Sudden death, though fortunately it is rare, is frequent. (*British Medical Journal*)

► 24. All seven of the patients who died never completely recovered. (*Medicine*)

25. Scientific papers are sometimes written in a complementary part-object relationship between the paper-dictating function of the writer's ego and the dictation-taking function of a scribe or secretary. (*American Journal of Psychotherapy*)

4.5 TRADITIONAL CRITERIA FOR DEFINITIONS

One way to combat fallacies arising from ambiguities is to define terms. Many disputes arise more from unclear use of language than from disagreement over substantive issues. It's important, therefore, to make sure that speaker and audience have the same understanding of the terms of a discussion.

There are various ways of clarifying meaning. Correspondingly, there are various kinds of definitions. We may classify definitions according to their goal or purpose and also according to how they try to achieve it.

Goals of Definition

First, consider the goals a definition might have:

1. *Description.* Most definitions try to describe the meaning of a term as it is commonly used. Descriptive definitions are called *lexical,* because they are the kind of definition given in dictionaries or lexicons. Such definitions attempt to characterize the actual usage of an expression in natural language.

2. *Stipulation.* Some definitions try to introduce new terms into discourse. *Stipulative* definitions assign meanings to terms without regard to their ordinary use. The baseball rule book, for example, defines 'out', 'hit', 'home run', 'sacrifice', and so on, for the purposes of the game. It makes no attempt to use these terms as they are used outside baseball.

3. *Precision.* Some definitions try to remain close to the meaning of a term in natural language but also to make that meaning more precise or more useful for a particular purpose. Suppose that you hire someone to remove rocks from your yard. You need to agree on what the job entails. So, you may suggest that a rock, for this purpose, is any stone weighing more than a pound; anything weighing less is a pebble. This is a "precising," or clarifying, definition of 'rock' and 'pebble'. The ordinary concepts of rock and pebble aren't very precise. To make sure you both have in mind the same task, you may need to sharpen those terms.

These definitions are helpful in resolving two kinds of problems. The first, which the 'rock' and 'pebble' definitions solve, is a problem of *vagueness.* Many terms in natural language have fuzzy boundaries. How many hairs can a man have on his head, for example, before he stops being bald? How high an IQ score must someone have to count as intelligent? How hard does it have to rain for a drizzle to become a rain, and a rain to become a storm? These questions have no definite answers. In most circumstances, that's not a problem. Setting up the terms of a contract, however, or developing a scientific theory, may demand more precision. Then, a clarifying definition can help.

The second sort of problem a clarifying definition can solve is ambiguity. As we've seen, most words have more than one meaning. The context of an utterance usually makes clear which meaning the speaker intends. Sometimes context fails to remove ambiguity; fortunately, this is fairly uncommon. But, in scientific or legal language, for instance, ambiguity can cause so much trouble that precautions must be taken against it. Again, clarifying definitions can help. A definition may make it clear that, for the purposes of a contract, article, or discussion, a term is to have only one meaning. A food processing company that buys chickens, for example, should probably specify in a clarifying definition exactly what they expect to receive. An actual court case arose out of a company's failure to do just that; it expected fryers but received old hens, and it lost when it sued the supplier.

4. *Persuasion. Persuasive* definitions explain the meaning of a term, but contentiously; they try to convey not only the meaning but also a certain attitude. These definitions can be extremely effective in persuading and in exposing another's misuse of a term. Consider Alben Barkley's definition of 'bureaucrat':

(24) A bureaucrat is a Democrat who holds some office that a Republican wants.

Or, Frank Vanderlip's definition of 'conservative':

(25) A conservative is a man who does not believe that anything should be done for the first time.

On the other side of the political spectrum, Thomas Sowell offers a glossary of some political terms:

(26) A matter of principle: A political controversy involving the convictions of liberals.

An emotional issue: A political controversy involving the convictions of conservatives.

Antiwar movement: Disarmament advocates who know the idea won't fly under its own name.

Compassion: The use of tax money to buy votes.

Insensitivity: Objection to the use of tax money to buy votes.

Constitutional interpretation: Judges reading their own political views into the Constitution.

Politicizing the courts: Criticizing judges for reading their own political views into the Constitution.

Public-interest group: Politically organized liberals.

Special-interest lobby: Politically organized conservatives.

Persuasive definitions can provide important insights into the way words are used. Nevertheless, it's important to recognize them as persuasive and to distinguish the information they convey from the attitude they try to communicate. Persuasive definitions can expose appeals to the people by exposing slanted uses of language, but they can also perpetrate such appeals by slanting language themselves.

Means of Definition

Second, consider how a definition might try to achieve its goal:

1. *Ostension. Ostensive* definitions clarify the meaning of a term by citing examples to which it applies. In most circumstances, the easiest and practically most useful way of defining 'mango', for example, is to display a mango. The simplest way to explain the meaning of 'laugh' is to point to people laughing.

2. *Listing.* Some definitions specify the meanings of a word by listing things to which the word applies. The list may be complete or incomplete. To define 'House of Congress', for example, we might say 'Senate or House of Representatives', a complete list; to define 'fruit', we might say, 'things like apples, bananas, oranges, and pears'. Definitions by ostension and by listing are *denotative* definitions: They explain the meanings of terms by listing or pointing to part or all of their denotations.

3. *Synonymy.* Some definitions simply give a synonym for the word being defined: 'detective' for 'gumshoe', for example, or 'freedom' for 'liberty'. These are sometimes called *synonymous* definitions.

4. *Analysis.* Other definitions try to explain the meaning of a term by indicating what the things to which it applies have in common. Such definitions are often called *analytical.* Plato's dialogues revolve around usually unsuccessful attempts to devise analytical definitions of such terms as 'courage', 'piety', 'friendship', 'knowledge', and 'justice'.

Aristotelian logicians refer to such definitions as definitions *per genus et differentiae,* definitions "by genus and difference." The idea behind this terminology is that we can define a species or kind of thing by indicating, first, what genus, or more general classification of thing, it falls under, and second, what distinguishes the species from others of the same genus. Thus, we might define a bachelor as a male adult who has never been married; 'adult' here specifies the genus, while 'male' and 'who has never been married' specify the differences, or distinguishing features, of bachelors.

The accompanying table summarizes the kinds of definition.

Kinds of Definition

		Methods			
		Ostension	Listing	Synonymy	Analysis
Goals	Description				
	Stipulation				
	Precision				
	Persuasion				

We can classify any definition according to its goal and the method it uses to achieve it. There are, therefore, at least sixteen kinds of definition.

Rules

Logicians have traditionally used four rules to evaluate definitions:

1. A definition must state the essential attributes of the kind.

2. A definition must not be circular.

3. A definition must not be negative when it can be positive.

4. A definition must not use ambiguous, obscure, or figurative language.

Let's examine these rules in turn.

1. *A definition must state the essential attributes of the kind.* We can express much of the content of this rule by saying that a definition must be neither too broad nor too narrow. The term being defined, the *definiendum,* should apply to exactly those things to which the defining expression, the *definiens,* applies. A definition is *too narrow* if the defining expression applies to too little, and *too broad* if it applies to too much. Consider, for example, a dictionary definition of 'chair': "a seat, esp. for one person, having four legs for support and a rest for the back and often having rests for the arms."[4] To determine whether the definition is too narrow, you can ask, could there be a chair that was not a seat for one person, having four legs? Arguably, the answer is yes: A bean-bag chair has no legs. This definition, therefore, may be too narrow. Is it also too broad? Could there be a seat for one person, having four legs, that was not a chair? Probably not. So, the definition is too narrow, but not too broad.

A traditional philosophical definition of 'human being' is 'rational animal'. This definition is probably both too broad and too narrow. It is too broad, because extraterrestrial beings could be rational animals without counting as humans. It is too narrow, because there are irrational humans.

In logical terms, rule 1 requires that the definiens and definiendum be equivalent. The sentence asserting that something satisfies the definiens always agrees in truth value with the sentence asserting that it satisfies the definiendum.

Specifying the essential attributes of the kind being defined is only a small step beyond giving an equivalent for the term being defined. A definition that is neither too broad nor too narrow gives necessary and sufficient conditions for applying the term it defines. There may, however, be various ways of stating such conditions. Rule 1 decrees that the conditions must state the essential attributes of the kind being defined. Suppose, for example, that we are trying to define 'sphere'. The following definitions meet rule 1:

Set of points in three dimensions equidistant from a single point
Three-dimensional figure having a maximum ratio of volume to surface
    area

Three-dimensional figure whose intersection with any plane is either null or a circle

Three-dimensional figure preserved under any rotation about any of its axes

How should we choose among these definitions? None is to broad or too narrow. Nevertheless, they aren't equally appealing. The first definition is what we usually mean in speaking of spheres; the others are equivalent characterizations, but their equivalence isn't obvious. Rule 1, then, says that we should try, as much as possible, to articulate the usual meaning of the term in a definition.

2. *A definition must not be circular.* An expression should not be defined in terms of itself. If the definiendum appears anywhere in the definiens, the definition can't fulfill its purpose of clarifying meaning. Nobody who didn't understand the term already could understand the definition. Gertrude Stein's "A rose is a rose is a rose" hence fails to count as an adequate definition. (Of course, she didn't intend it as such.)

Rarely is a proposed definition directly circular. But, in systems of definitions, indirect circularity is not unusual. Indeed, dictionaries are condemned to it. A dictionary tries to give a definition of every word in a language. But, as Aristotle first realized, trying to define everything leads to a dilemma. Either the chain of definitions must be infinite, or it must loop back on itself. Dictionaries have only a finite number of pages, so they must be circular. Usually a dictionary's circles are so large that few users ever recognize them.

Consider a definition of 'friendly': "characteristic of or befitting a friend."[5] Is this circular? Certainly it explains the meaning of an expression in terms of another very closely related to it. But whether it is circular depends on the system of definitions of which this forms a part. How is 'friend' defined? If the answer is, 'person who acts friendly', then the system of definitions is circular. If the definition of 'friend' is independent, however—for instance, 'a person whom one knows well and is fond of'—then there is no circle.

Sometimes this rule is taken to ban from the defining expression not only the term being defined but any of its synonyms. Defining 'fib' as 'lie' is not directly or indirectly circular, so long as there is an independent definition of 'lie,' but it isn't analytical either. Synonymous definitions, in general, may clarify meaning, but do little to explain the meaning of a term; they aren't definitions by genus and difference. Whether rule 2 prohibits the use of synonyms, therefore, depends on whether the synonymous expressions are defined in a circle—'fib' as 'lie', 'lie' as 'prevaricate', 'prevaricate' as 'dissimulate', and 'dissimulate' as 'lie', for example—or whether some link is explained analytically.

3. *A definition must not be negative when it can be positive.* We could try to define 'white' as 'a color that is neither black, red, orange, yellow, green,

blue, or purple', but that's not very informative; it's a poor definition of 'white'. Similarly, defining 'claret' as 'wine that is not sweet and is neither white nor rose', seems perverse, even though it's equivalent to the acceptable definition 'dry red wine'. In general, positive definitions are preferable to negative ones.

Sometimes, however, negative definitons are unavoidable. 'Dark' may be defined as 'wholly or partly without light'; 'bald' as 'without hair'; 'poor' as 'lacking material possessions'; and 'amorphous' as 'without shape or form'. These definitions have no obvious positive equivalents.

4. *A definition must not use ambiguous, obscure, or figurative language.* Definitions are tools for clarifying meaning. A definition using ambiguous, obscure, or figurative language is flawed; it cannot fulfill its chief purpose because it tries to clarify the meaning of an expression by equating it with another expression whose meaning is unclear. Kahlil Gibran gives the figurative definition "Beauty is eternity gazing at itself in a minor"; this hardly helps to explain the meaning of the term 'beauty'. Samuel Johnson obscurely defined 'net' as "anything made with interstitial vacuities," and Martin Heidegger similarly defined 'truth' as "the dissimulation of the dissimulated." To explain the meaning of a term in terms more obscure than the term itself is, usually, to explain nothing.

This is not to say, however, that all definitions using figurative or obscure language are worthless. Samuel Johnson defined 'language' as "the dress of thought." That is metaphorical, but also rich in insight. Bertrand Russell called a series *continuous* when it is Dedekindian and contains a median class having $\aleph_0$ terms.[6] To most of us, this definition is obscure. But, to anyone who has worked through Russell's discussion of continuity, it is perfectly clear. Obscurity is, to some extent, in the eye of the beholder. That is, obscurity is relative to the common ground. One audience may find obscure what another finds intelligible. Whether a definition satisfies rule 4, consequently, may depend the audience to whom it's addressed and the common ground of the conversation of which it forms a part.

Problems

1. Give an example of each of the sixteen kinds of definition.

2. Find the definitions in the "Problems" section at the end of Chapter 11. For each, (a) identify its goal; (b) identify the method it uses to achieve it; and (c) evaluate it according to the four rules of definition.

The following are definitions from Samuel Johnson's ground-breaking dictionary, first published in 1755. (a) Identify the goal and method of each. (b) Have the meanings of these terms changed since the eighteenth century? To answer this question, say whether these definitions are now too broad or too narrow, and, if so, explain why.

▸ **3.** Anecdote: Something yet unpublished; secret history.

▸ **4.** To belch: To throw out from the stomach; to eject from any hollow place. It is a word implying coarseness; hatefulness; or horrour.

▸ **5.** Blockhead: A stupid fellow; a dolt; a man without parts.

▸ **6.** Bug: A stinking insect bred in old household stuff.

7. Chitchat: Prattle; idle prate; idle talk. A word used only in ludicrous conversation.

8. Compliment: An act, or expression of civility, usually understood to include some hypocrisy, and to mean less than it declares.

9. Diploma: A letter or writing conferring some privilege, so called because they used formerly to be written on waxed tables, and folded together.

10. Excise: A hateful tax levied upon commodities, and adjudged not by the common judges of property, but wretches hired by those to whom excise is paid.

11. Fastidious: Disdainful; squeamish; delicate to a vice; insolently nice.

▸ **12.** Funk: A stink. A low word.

13. Glee: Joy; merriment; gayety. It anciently signified musick played at feasts. It is not now used, except in ludicrous writing, or with some mixture of irony or contempt.

14. Horseplay: Coarse, rough, rugged play.

15. Informal: Offering an information; accusing. A word not used.

16. Jargon: Unintelligible talk; gabble; gibberish.

17. Jogger: One who moves heavily and dully.

▸ **18.** Lizard: An animal resembling a serpent, with legs added to it ... In America they eat *lizards*. . . .

19. Lunch, luncheon: As much food as one's hand can hold.

20. To marvel: To wonder; to be astonished. Disused.

21. Nincompoop: A fool; a trifler.

22. Occult: Secret; hidden; unknown; undiscoverable.

23. To pamper: To glut; to fill with food; to saginate; to feed luxuriously.

▸ **24.** Ruse: Cunning; artifice; little stratagem; trick; wile; fraud; deceit.

25. Rug: (1) A coarse, nappy, woollen cloath. (2) A coarse nappy coverlet used for mean beds. (3) A rough woolly dog.

26. Scalp: The scull; the cranium; the bone that encloses the brain.

27. Tarantula: An insect whose bite is only cured by musick.

28. Unkempt: Not combed. Obsolete.

29. Vegetable: Anything that has grown without sensation, as plants.

▶ **30.** Vermicelli: A paste rolled and broken in the form of worms.

31. Warren: A kind of park for rabits.

32. Zealous: Ardently passionate in any cause.

Notes

[1] Mark Amory (ed.), *Letters of Evelyn Waugh* (London: Weidenfeld and Nicolson, 1980), p. 517.

[2] Mortimer R. Feinberg, "When to Engender Fear . . . or at Least a High Degree of Anxiety," *Wall Street Journal,* October 24, 1988, p. A14.

[3] David Hackett Fischer, *Historians' Fallacies* (New York: Harper and Row, 1970), p. 267.

[4] *The Random House Dictionary of the English Language,* 2nd edition, unabridged (New York: Random House, 1987), p. 341.

[5] *The Random House Dictionary of the English Language,* 2nd edition, unabridged (New York: Random House, 1987), p. 768.

[6] Bertrand Russell, *Introduction to Mathematical Philosophy* (New York: Simon and Schuster, 1919), p. 104.

SENTENTIAL LOGIC

5

SENTENCES

Every successful theory explains some things in terms of others. A theory treats certain phenomena as problematic, requiring explanation. It explains them, ultimately, in terms of things taken as basic to the theory. These basic units remain unanalyzed within the theory; they may receive an explanation within another, supplementary theory. In *sentential logic* (sometimes called *propositional logic*) simple, declarative sentences are the basic units. Its aim is to examine relationships, as they pertain to reasoning, between the sentences. This chapter therefore focuses on connections between sentences. We'll develop a theory of connections that involve just the truth values of sentences. The truth values of compound sentences formed with certain words and phrases—called *truth-functional connectives*—depend entirely on the truth values of the smaller sentences they connect.

5.1 SENTENCE CONNECTIVES

Recall that logicians use 'sentence' in a special sense, in which one sentence may be a part of another. Within the single sentence

(1) When the going gets tough, the tough get going.

are two other sentences.

(2) a. The going gets tough.
    b. The tough get going.

Sentence (1) results from combining these two shorter sentences. Sentence (1) is therefore a *compound;* (2)a and (2)b are its *components*. Words such as 'when', which link sentences to form compounds, are *sentence connectives*.

Expressions that convert single sentences into other sentences are *singular* or *unary* connectives. Those that combine two sentences into a single sentence are *binary* connectives. In general, where *n* is any number:

> **Definition** An *n-ary sentence connective* is a word or phrase that forms a single, compound sentence from *n* component sentences.

Here are some singular connectives:　　Here are some binary connectives:

not	and
maybe	but
of course	however
possibly	although
necessarily	if
may	or
can	unless
could	though
might	before
must	because
should	

The *truth value* of a sentence is *truth,* if it is true, or *falsehood,* if it is false. Some connectives form compound sentences whose truth values are a function of the truth values of their components. These connectives are *truth-functional*.

> **Definition** An *n*-ary sentence connective is *truth-functional* if and only if the truth values of the *n* component sentences always completely determine the truth value of the compound sentence formed by the connective.

If a connective is truth-functional, then two compounds formed from it have the same truth value whenever their corresponding components match in truth value. To determine the truth value of the compound, we need to know only whether the component sentences are true or false.

Consider the sentence

(3) John hasn't met Mary.

which contains the component

(4) John has met Mary.

If the component is true, the compound is false: If it's true that John hasn't met Mary, it's false that he has met her. If the component is false, the compound is true: If it's false that John has met Mary, then it's true that he hasn't met her. The truth value of (4), in other words, completely determines the truth value of (3). This does not depend on any special feature of the sentence 'John has met Mary'. Any sentence would behave similarly. 'Not' is thus a truth-functional sentence connective.

In contrast, consider

(5) Surprisingly, John has met Mary.

If the component, (4), is false—if John hasn't met Mary—then this sentence, too, is false. But the truth of the component sentence doesn't determine the truth or falsehood of the sentence as a whole. That John has met Mary does not guarantee that this fact is surprising. Nor does it guarantee that it's not.

We can summarize these examples in a small table. We consider the possible truth values (T stands for true and F for false) of the sentences and see whether, in every case, they determine the truth value of the compound.

John has met Mary	John hasn't met Mary	Surprisingly, John has met Mary
T	F	T or F
F	T	F

Because 'Surprisingly, John has met Mary' could be either true or false if John has met Mary, 'surprisingly' is not truth-functional.

We can draw the same contrast with binary connectives. Consider the two connectives 'and' and 'after'. The sentences

(6) George arrived, and Joan left.

and

(7) George arrived after Joan left.

for example, both contain the components 'George arrived' and 'Joan left'. If both these components are true, then it's true that George arrived and Joan left. But the truth of both components doesn't similarly fix a truth value for (7). George may have arrived before or after Joan left. So, 'after' is not truth-functional.

The sufficiency of the components' truth values to determine the compound's truth value in some cases isn't enough to guarantee truth-functionality. They must suffice in *every* case if the connective is truth-functional. The truth value of the components sometimes fixes the value of the compound formed from them by 'after': if George didn't arrive at all, he certainly didn't arrive after Joan left. 'After', nevertheless, is not truth-functional.

George arrived	Joan left	George arrived and Joan left	George arrived after Joan left
T	T	T	T or F
T	F	F	F(?)
F	T	F	F
F	F	F	F

A connective is truth-functional if and only if it's possible to fill in every entry under the compound sentence with a determinate truth value. If, as with 'after', there is any row that can't be filled in with just a single truth value, then the connective is not truth-functional.

Problems

Classify the following connectives as singular or binary. Are these connectives truth-functional? Why or why not?

▶ **1.** or   ▶ **2.** because   ▶ **3.** before

▶ **4.** not   ▶ **5.** it is true that   ▶ **6.** it's obvious that

   7. John believes that   **8.** may   **9.** can

  10. could   **11.** should   ▶ **12.** in order that

  13. it's not known whether   **14.** allegedly

  15. however   **16.** when

  17. definitely   ▶ **18.** whether or not

  19. it's probable that   **20.** it's necessarily true that

  21. maybe   **22.** in spite of

  23. regardless whether   ▶ **24.** nevertheless

  25. insofar as

5.2 A SENTENTIAL LANGUAGE

A central strategy of logic is constructing symbolic or artificial languages.[1] Armed with such a language, we can evaluate arguments as valid or invalid by symbolizing them—by translating them into the symbolic language—and then testing the resulting *argument form* for validity.

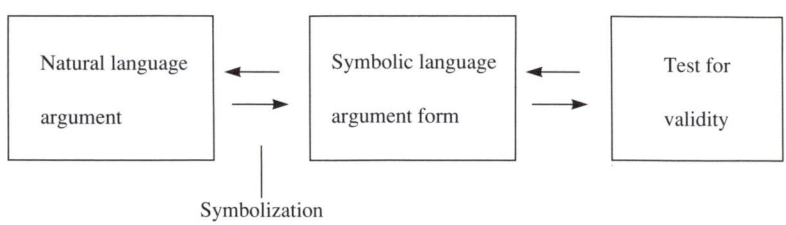

In this section, we'll develop a symbolic language, SL, that allows us to evaluate arguments depending on truth-functional sentence connectives.

To use any language, natural or symbolic, we need to understand its *syntax* and its *semantics*. The *syntax* of a language consists of its vocabulary and grammar. The vocabulary consists of the meaningful signs of the language. In a natural language, it's a collection of words and idioms. The grammar of a language specifies how to put the meaningful signs of the language together to form sentences. (In symbolic languages, we'll refer to these as *formulas* rather than sentences.) The *semantics* of a language is its theory of meaning. It indicates what the signs in the vocabulary mean and also how the meanings of sentences depend on the meanings of those signs.

The syntax of SL is simple. Vocabulary items fall into three basic categories: *sentence letters, connectives,* and *grouping indicators.*

Vocabulary

Sentence letters:	Lowercase letters, with or without numerical subscripts
Connectives:	¬ & ∨ → ↔
Grouping indicators:	( )

The symbol ¬ has no name in the literature; we'll call it the hook or the hoe. The other connectives have standard names: & is the ampersand; ∨, the wedge; →, the arrow; and ↔, the double arrow.

The grammar of SL allows us to combine these vocabulary elements to form formulas. In presenting the rules, we must distinguish carefully between the symbolic language, SL, that we're defining, and the language, English, that we're using to define it. We'll call the artificial language we're defining the *object language;* the language we're using to discuss it is the *metalanguage.* In the metalanguage, we'll use script variables, such as $\mathcal{A}$, $\mathcal{B}$, x, y, p, and q, to range over items in the object language. The script variables are in the metalanguage but stand for items in the object language. In particular, we'll assume that $\mathcal{A}$ and $\mathcal{B}$ stand for formulas of SL.

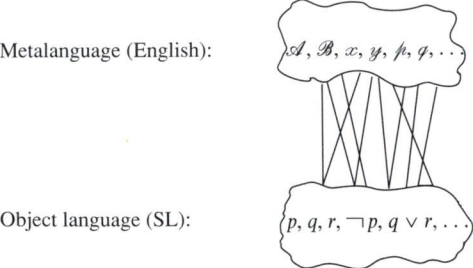

Metalanguage (English): $\{\mathcal{A}, \mathcal{B}, x, y, p, q, \ldots\}$

Object language (SL): $\{p, q, r, \neg p, q \vee r, \ldots\}$

A string of symbols containing a script variable is not a formula of SL; script letters aren't sentence letters. Strings containing script letters are part of the metalanguage. We'll call capitals such as $\mathscr{A}$ and $\mathscr{B}$ *schematic letters* and strings such as $(\mathscr{A} \to \mathscr{B})$ *schemata*.[2]

Formation Rules

1. Any sentence letter is a formula.
2. If $\mathscr{A}$ is a formula, then $\neg\mathscr{A}$ is a formula.
3. If $\mathscr{A}$ and $\mathscr{B}$ are formulas, then $(\mathscr{A} \& \mathscr{B})$, $(\mathscr{A} \lor \mathscr{B})$, $(\mathscr{A} \to \mathscr{B})$, and $(\mathscr{A} \leftrightarrow \mathscr{B})$ are formulas.
4. Every formula can be constructed by a finite number of applications of these rules.

A formula is *atomic* if and only if it contains no connectives. Atomic formulas of SL are sentence letters. We'll adopt a convention so that we can use SL more easily. We'll allow ourselves to drop the outside parentheses of a formula, since they do no further work.

The definition of a formula allows us to tell how a formula can be built from sentence letters. We can record this information in a tree, in which the formula appears at the top and the sentence letters appear at the bottom. These trees chart the construction of $\neg p$, $(p \& q)$, $p \lor \neg(q \to r)$, and $\neg(p \leftrightarrow \neg p)$ from the vocabulary items of SL.

At each node of each tree is a formula. The tree always ends with atomic formulas, that is, sentence letters. Each transition from a higher node to one or more lower nodes reflects a rule used in building the formula. Any formula appearing at any node of a tree is a *subformula* of the formula at the top of the tree.

There is an important theoretical difference between the syntax of SL and the syntax of a natural language. As we saw in Chapter 4, some English sentences, such as 'They watched the fireworks explode on the porch', can be constructed in more than one way. As a result, they are ambiguous. No such ambiguities arise in our symbolic language. Every formula is associated with one and only one tree.

Two additional concepts, *scope* and *main connective,* will prove extremely useful.

> **DEFINITION**   The *scope* of a connective occurrence in a formula is the connective occurrence itself, together with the subformulas (and any grouping indicators) it links.

Specifically, the scope of $\neg$ in a formula or subformula of the form $\neg \mathscr{A}$ is $\neg \mathscr{A}$; the scope of & in a formula or subformula of the form $(\mathscr{A}\ \&\ \mathscr{B})$ is $(\mathscr{A}\ \&\ \mathscr{B})$; and similarly for the other binary connectives.

> **DEFINITION**   The *main connective* of a formula is the connective occurrence in the formula with the largest scope.

The main connective is always the connective occurrence having the entire formula as its scope. In a phrase structure tree for the formula, a rule for that connective occurrence is applied in descending from the top node. This rule is the first to be applied in decomposing the formula into its component parts and the last to be applied in building it up from those parts.

Connective Occurrence	Formula	Scope	Main Connective
$\neg$	$(p \to \neg q)$:	$\neg q$	$\to$
$\neg$	$\neg(p \to q)$:	$\neg(p \to q)$	$\neg$
$\vee$	$(p \vee (q\ \&\ r))$:	$(p \vee (q\ \&\ r))$	$\vee$
&	$(p \vee (q\ \&\ r))$:	$(q\ \&\ r)$	$\vee$

Problems

Classify each of these as (a) a formula, according to the official formation rules, (b) a formula, given our convention about dropping outside parentheses, or (c) neither. If you answer a or b, identify the main connective.

▶ **1.** $\neg p$ ▶ **2.** $p\ \&\ q$ ▶ **3.** $(p \vee q)$

▶ **4.** $\neg a \vee \neg b$ ▶ **5.** $\neg(c\ \&\ \neg d)$ ▶ **6.** $\neg(g)$

7. $(\neg p)$ **8.** $(\neg f \vee \neg e)$ **9.** $(\&h \vee \&j)$

10. $(k \vee m) \to r$ **11.** $p \vee (n \to r)$ ▶ **12.** $(s \vee (q \to r))$

13. $t \vee q \to u$ **14.** $(v \vee q \to w)$ **15.** $x \vee (q \to z)$

16. $(p \vee y) \to r)$ **17.** $((P \vee Q) \to D)$

▶ **18.** $\neg((p \vee (q \vee r))\ \&\ q$ **19.** $\neg[x \to (y \to \neg z) \leftrightarrow \neg p]$

20. $a \to (b \leftrightarrow (c \vee d)$ **21.** $\neg((f \to (g \to h)) \vee \neg g$

22. $\neg p \vee (a \to q) \to (p \to b)$ **23.** $q \vee (p \to (r \to (s \vee \neg q)))$

▶ **24.** $\neg(((p \rightarrow \neg(q \leftrightarrow r)) \,\&\, \neg(r \rightarrow (s \lor a))) \leftrightarrow (p \leftrightarrow \neg(q \lor \neg c)))$

25. The rules for forming formulas of sentential logic admit no ambiguity. How could these rules be altered to admit ambiguity? (a) Give an example of a set of rules allowing ambiguity. (b) Specify an ambiguous formula together with at least two trees showing its construction according to those revised rules.*

5.3 TRUTH FUNCTIONS

Truth-functional connectives, in English or in SL, yield compounds whose truth values depend solely on the truth values of their components. To understand the meanings of formulas of SL, we need to specify the meanings of those connectives. Each truth-functional connective represents a corresponding function from truth values into truth values.[3] Such a function takes as inputs the truth values of the component sentences and yields the truth value of the compound sentence. These functions are *truth functions*.

> **DEFINITION** An *n-ary truth function* is a function taking n truth values as inputs and producing a truth value as output.

There are four singulary truth functions. These take a single truth value as input and produce a truth value as output. Only two inputs—truth and falsehood—are possible. These are also the only two possible outputs.

Function 1		Function 2		Function 3		Function 4	
Input	Output	Input	Output	Input	Output	Input	Output
T	T	T	F	T	T	T	F
F	T	F	F	F	F	F	T

There are infinitely many truth functions all together. How can we formulate a theory to describe this infinite array of functions? Luckily, it's not very difficult. This chapter presents a few commonly used truth functions. Any truth function at all can be defined in terms of them alone. In fact, a single binary truth function suffices to define every truth function in this infinite collection.

The first function we'll define is singulary. Appearing before as function 4, it's called *negation,* and we'll use the symbol $\neg$ to represent it. In this definition, $\mathscr{A}$ is any formula.

$\mathscr{A}$	$\neg \mathscr{A}$
T	F
F	T

Negation transforms the truth value of the component sentence into its opposite.

An English connective that has this effect is the logical particle 'not'. Other English expressions having much the same effect are 'it is not the case that', 'it's false that', and, often, the prefixes 'un-', 'dis-', 'a-', 'im-', and so on.

The second function is binary. Called *conjunction,* we'll represent it with the ampersand.

$\mathcal{A}$	$\mathcal{B}$	$(\mathcal{A}\ \&\ \mathcal{B})$
T	T	T
T	F	F
F	T	F
F	F	F

A conjunction is true if and only if both its components—called *conjuncts*—are true.

Functioning in this way are most grammatical conjunctions: 'and', 'both ... and', 'but', 'though', and 'although'. These don't all have the same meaning, but they affect truth values in the same way. They are very faithful to the truth table definition of conjunction, except that 'and' sometimes seems to express a temporal ordering. 'Heidi fell down and got up' and 'Heidi got up and fell down' seem to differ in meaning, although the definition of conjunction indicates that these should be true in exactly the same circumstances. Also, English treats conjunction as a *multigrade* connective, one that can take two, three, or more sentences and combine them into a single compound sentence. The logical & always links two sentence letters, but in English we can say 'John brought the mustard, Sally brought the pickles, and I brought the hot dogs'. We'll simulate this in SL by allowing continued, ungrouped conjunctions. For example, we'll allow $p\ \&\ q\ \&\ r$ as an abbreviation for either $((p\ \&\ q)\ \&\ r)$ or $(p\ \&\ (q\ \&\ r))$. These last two formulas are equivalent; grouping, within a conjunction, makes no difference to truth value.

The third function is also binary. Represented by $\lor$, it's called *disjunction.*

$\mathcal{A}$	$\mathcal{B}$	$(\mathcal{A}\ \lor\ \mathcal{B})$
T	T	T
T	F	T
F	T	T
F	F	F

A disjunction is true just in case one or both of its components—called *disjuncts*—is true.

Corresponding to this function in English are 'or' and 'either ... or'. The correlates to disjunction are also quite close to the logical definition, although 'or', like 'and', is multigrade in English. Consequently, we'll allow continued, ungrouped disjunctions. We'll use $p \vee q \vee r$, for instance, as an abbreviation for either $((p \vee q) \vee r)$ or $(p \vee (q \vee r))$, which are equivalent. Grouping, within a disjunction, makes no difference to the truth value of the formula.

The fourth function, again binary, is represented by $\rightarrow$, and is called the *conditional:*

$\mathscr{A}$	$\mathscr{B}$	$(\mathscr{A} \rightarrow \mathscr{B})$
T	T	T
T	F	F
F	T	T
F	F	T

Here, for the first time, the order of the components makes a difference. The first component of a conditional is its *antecedent;* the second is its *consequent.* A conditional is true just in case it doesn't have a true antecedent and false consequent.

English expressions having roughly the force of the conditional truth function are:

$\mathscr{B}$ if $\mathscr{A}$
if $\mathscr{A}$ then $\mathscr{B}$
$\mathscr{A}$ only if $\mathscr{B}$
$\mathscr{A}$ so long as $\mathscr{A}$
$\mathscr{B}$ provided that $\mathscr{A}$
$\mathscr{B}$ assuming that $\mathscr{A}$
$\mathscr{B}$ on the condition that $\mathscr{A}$

Because the direction of the conditional matters, symbolizing expressions of these forms requires care. In English, it's easy to confuse the antecedent with the consequent.

At first it may seem surprising that '$\mathscr{A}$ only if $\mathscr{B}$' and 'If $\mathscr{A}$, then $\mathscr{B}$' are both correlates of the conditional $(\mathscr{A} \rightarrow \mathscr{B})$. But these sentences are equivalent:

(8) a. If a number is even, it is divisible by 2.
    b. A number is even only if it is divisible by 2.

We can symbolize both in the same way because they are true in exactly the same circumstances.

The conditional truth function matches the English correlates of the conditional in many respects. Nevertheless, it omits some features of English conditionals. Consider these sentences, all of which, according to our definitions of negation and the conditional, we would symbolize as equivalent formulas:

(9) a. If we don't operate, the patient will die.
 b. The patient will survive only if we operate.
 c. If the patient survives, we'll operate.
 d. We won't operate only if the patient dies.

The first two are plainly equivalent. The third and fourth, however, sound bizarre. The third suggests that we'll operate only when the patient is out of danger, and the fourth suggests that we'll operate as long as we have a live body to operate on. The conditional doesn't capture these differences. Whatever follows the English word 'if' imposes a condition on the other component. Often, this condition is causal: What follows 'if' is a cause or causal factor, and the other component is the effect.[4] The truth-functional rendering of the conditional can't capture the causal meaning of the English conditional.

The English connective 'unless' raises similar issues. Consider the sentences:

(10) a. The patient will die unless we operate.
 b. If we don't operate, the patient will die.

These are equivalent to each other and to (9)a and b. In general, we can interpret '$\mathscr{A}$ unless $\mathscr{B}$' as '$\mathscr{A}$, if not $\mathscr{B}$'. This, as we'll see below, is equivalent to '$\mathscr{A}$ or $\mathscr{B}$' according to our definitions of the connectives. So, we can symbolize 'unless' as a disjunction.

But, as with 'if' and 'only if', we can't express causal aspects of the meaning of 'unless' in SL. Sentences (10)a and b seem to assert that there is a causal connection between the operation and the patient's chances for survival. Our logical symbolism doesn't capture this. $\mathscr{A} \vee \mathscr{B}$ is true if either $\mathscr{A}$ or $\mathscr{B}$ is true. But we wouldn't normally count (10)a as true just because the operation was performed or just because the patient died.[5]

Finally, the *biconditional* is a binary truth function, symbolized by ↔.

$\mathscr{A}$	$\mathscr{B}$	$(\mathscr{A} \leftrightarrow \mathscr{B})$
T	T	T
T	F	F
F	T	F
F	F	T

Biconditionals are true just in case their components agree in truth value. English expressions such as 'if and only if', 'when and only when', and (in one of its uses) 'just in case' correspond to the biconditional.

The symbols ¬, &, ∨, →, and ↔ are in common use. Unfortunately, however, no logical notation is standard. This table shows other symbols that have been used as logical connectives. The last in each case is so-called Polish notation, which requires no parentheses.

Truth Function	Our Symbol	Other Symbols
Negation	$\neg p$	$-p, \sim p, p', \bar{p}, \mathrm{N}p$
Conjunction	$p \;\&\; q$	$p \wedge q, pq, p \cdot q, \mathrm{K}pq$
Disjunction	$p \vee q$	$p \veebar q, \mathrm{A}pq$
Conditional	$p \rightarrow q$	$p \supset q, \mathrm{C}pq$
Biconditional	$p \leftrightarrow q$	$p \equiv q, p \sim q, \mathrm{E}pq$

Every truth function can be defined in terms of these five truth functions alone. Indeed, not even all five are necessary. Negation and conjunction alone suffice; so do negation and disjunction, or negation and the conditional. Any set of truth functions that allows us to define every other truth function is *functionally complete*.

Problems

Explain how a connective in each of these sentences deviates somewhat from the truth function with which it is generally correlated.

▶ **1.** John and Sam are brothers.

▶ **2.** Kate becomes angry if someone insults her.

▶ **3.** Only if I have thirty days can I finish the work.

▶ **4.** Give me thirty undergraduates and I'll give you thirty-five opinions. (Neil Rudenstine, Princeton Provost, 1984)

▶ **5.** Make three correct guesses consecutively and you will establish a reputation as an expert. (Laurence Peter)

▶ **6.** Discourse on virtue and they pass by in droves, whistle and dance the shimmy, and you've got an audience. (Diogenes of Sinope)

7. Why, if 'tis dancing you would be, there's brisker pipes than poetry. (A. E. Housman)

8. If a man sits down to think, he is immediately asked if he has a headache. (Ralph Waldo Emerson)

9. Show me a good loser, and I'll show you an idiot. (Leo Durocher)

10. Lajoie chews Red Devil tobacco/Ask him if he don't (Queen City Tobacco Co. advertisement, circa 1900)

5.4 Symbolization

We've constructed our symbolic language so that we can use it to evaluate arguments. We can determine whether English arguments are valid by translating them into SL and then judging the validity of the translations. To use SL, therefore, we must develop a way to translate arguments into it.

To symbolize a discourse in SL:

1. Identify sentence connectives; replace them with symbolic connectives.

2. Identify the smallest sentential components of the sentences, and replace each distinct component with a distinct sentence letter. (A record of which sentence letter symbolizes which sentence component is called a *dictionary*.)

3. Use the structure of the sentence to determine grouping.

The goal of symbolization is to devise a formula that is true exactly when the corresponding sentence is true, and false exactly when that sentence is false. In the process, we want to represent, in our symbolism, as much of the logical structure of the corresponding sentence as possible.

Several factors complicate these steps. The first step—identify and replace sentence connectives—relies on the correlation between truth functions and certain English sentence connectives. Because English connectives don't always match their closest symbolic counterparts exactly, this step can produce distortions in meaning.

Consider, for example, the paradoxical extended argument given by the ancient skeptic Sextus Empiricus, discussed in Chapter 1:

(11) If Socrates died, he died either when he was living or when he was dead.
But he did not die while living; for assuredly he was living, and as living he had not died.
Nor when he died; for then he would be twice dead.
∴ Socrates did not die.

The second and third premises contain arguments that support them. Omitting those, we obtain this argument:

(12) If Socrates died, he died either when he was living or when he was dead.
But he did not die while living.
Nor when he died.
∴ Socrates did not die.

It's easy to identify truth-functional sentence connectives:

(13) *If* Socrates died, he died *either* when he was living *or* when he was dead.
But he did *not* die while living.
Nor when he died.
∴ Socrates did *not* die.

We may replace these with corresponding connectives of SL:

(14) Socrates died → he died when he was living ∨ when he was dead.
& he did ¬ die while living.
¬ when he died.
∴ Socrates did ¬ die.

The 'but' that begins the second premise corresponds to a conjunction. But it doesn't link components of the same sentence; it links the entire second premise to the sentence before it. So, there's no need to symbolize it. Conjunctions between distinct premises add no content to an argument. Ignoring that conjunction, then, we obtain the structure

> (15) Socrates died $\rightarrow$ he died when he was living $\vee$ when he was dead.
>   he did $\neg$ die while living.
> $\neg$ when he died.
> $\therefore$ Socrates did $\neg$ die.

Step 2—identify and replace atomic sentences—is complicated because English arguments try not to be repetitive or dull. Rarely will an author use even a component sentence twice in the same passage. Even if the meaning is the same, the wording may vary. To allow for this, we'll judge atomic sentences to be the same if they clearly have the same meaning.

For example, in the argument from Sextus, we find these sentences:

> (16) a. Socrates died.
>   b. He died when he was living.
>   c. (He died) when he was dead.
>   d. He did die while living.
>   e. (He did die) when he died.
>   f. Socrates did die.

How many sentences should we distinguish? (16)a and f differ in wording but plainly have the same meaning. The same is true of (16)b and d and of (16)c and e. So, it seems reasonable to count three atomic sentences. Replacing them according to the dictionary

> *s*: Socrates died.
> *l*: Socrates died while he was living.
> *d*: Socrates died while he was dead.

we obtain

> (17) $s \rightarrow l \vee d$
> $\neg l$
> $\neg d$
> $\therefore \neg s$

This is not yet an argument form, since the first premise isn't a formula.

The third step—determining the grouping—is trickiest of all. SL avoids ambiguity by using parentheses as grouping indicators. English doesn't, and so natural language sentences are sometimes ambiguous. But English has some devices for making grouping clear.

One is the use of commas. The English sentence

> (18) John will come and Fred will leave only if you sign.

has no very clear grouping. Using the dictionary

> p: John will come.
> q: Fred will leave.
> r: You sign.

we can symbolize this sentence as either $(p \& q) \rightarrow r$ or $p \& (q \rightarrow r)$. But a comma can make it clear that 'and' is the main connective:

(19) John will come, and Fred will leave only if you sign.

should be symbolized as $p \& (q \rightarrow r)$. A comma emphasizes a break in the sentence, marking the combination of two different phrases. Commas, therefore, tend to suggest that the nearest connective has some priority.

English also has coordinate phrases such as 'either . . . or', 'both . . . and', and 'if . . . then'. The coordinate phrase in

(20) Either Bill brought Mary and Susan brought Sam, or Susan brought Bob.

makes the intended grouping clear. Using the dictionary

> p: Bill brought Mary.
> q: Susan brought Sam.
> r: Susan brought Bob.

we can symbolize it as $(p \& q) \vee r$. The coordinated connective takes priority over any connective appearing within the coordinated sections.

Finally, English allows a device that logicians call "telescoping" and linguists call "conjunction reduction." The sentence

(21) Susan brought Sam, or Susan brought Bob.

for example, "reduces" to the shorter sentence

(22) Susan brought Sam or Bob.

Similarly,

(23) Fred likes Wanda, and Kim likes Wanda.

reduces to

(24) Fred and Kim like Wanda.

This, too, can clarify grouping: We could group (20) in another way by saying 'Bill brought Mary, and Susan brought Sam or Bob'.

These techniques are combined in the example from Sextus Empiricus. The first premise of the argument is

(25) If Socrates died, he died either when he was living or when he was dead.

The comma after 'died' emphasizes the break between 'If Socrates died' and the rest of the sentence. The coordinate phrase 'either . . . or' acts to group 'when he was living or when he was dead' as a unit, as does the telescoping of 'he died when he was living or he died when he was dead' to 'he died when he was living or when he was dead'. All these cues suggest that the proper grouping is $s \rightarrow (l \vee d)$.

The three steps thus lead us to symbolize Sextus's skeptical argument as

(26) $s \rightarrow (l \vee d)$
$\neg l$
$\neg d$
$\therefore \neg s$

To see a more complex example, consider this passage from the *Magna Carta,* which limits inheritance taxes:

(27) If any of our earls, or barons, or others who hold of us in chief by military service, shall die, and at the time of his death his heir shall be of full age, and owe a relief, he shall have his inheritance by the ancient relief. . . .

First, we identify English connectives and replace them with their symbolic correlates:

(28) any of our earls $\vee$ barons $\vee$ others who hold of us in chief by military service, shall die, & at the time of his death his heir shall be of full age, & owe a relief, $\rightarrow$ he shall have his inheritance by the ancient relief. . . .

The only problem is determining where the $\rightarrow$ should go. Here, it's in the only position where the English word 'then' would make sense.

Second, we identify atomic sentence components and replace distinct components with distinct sentence letters. Here is the dictionary:

e: An earl dies.
b: A baron dies.
m: Another who holds of us in chief by military service dies.
f: At the time of death the heir is of full age.
r: At the time of death the heir owes a relief.
h: The heir has his inheritance by the ancient relief.

(29) $e \vee b \vee m, \& f, \& r, \rightarrow h$

Third, we determine grouping. The telescoping of disjuncts in 'If any of our earls, or barons, or others who hold of us in chief by military service, shall die' tells us that they should be grouped together:

(30) $(e \vee b \vee m) \& f, \& r, \rightarrow h$

Our placement of the arrow tells us that it must be the main connective:

(31) $((e \lor b \lor m) \& f, \& r) \to h$

Finally, the comma after 'of full age' suggests that we should group f with the disjunction

(32) $(((e \lor b \lor m) \& f) \& r) \to h$

although the symbolization

(33) $((e \lor b \lor m) \& (f \& r)) \to h$

is equivalent.

Problems

Symbolize each of these sentences in SL.

▶ **1.** Life is either daring adventure or nothing. (Helen Keller)

▶ **2.** God is, and all is well. (John Greenleaf Whittier)

▶ **3.** Excellence cannot be bought, but it must be paid for. (Val L. Fitch)

▶ **4.** Wealth serves a wise man, but commands a fool. (Thomas Fuller)

▶ **5.** Money is a terrible master, but an excellent servant. (P. T. Barnum)

▶ **6.** Activity conquers cold, but stillness conquers heat. (Lao-Tzu)

7. . . . if there is no love, nothing is possible. (Erich Fromm)

8. Life is not a spectacle or a feast; it is a predicament. (George Santayana)

9. Money is a stupid measure of achievement, but unfortunately, it is the only universal measure we have. (Charles Steinmetz)

10. Ideas pull the trigger, but instinct loads the gun. (Don Marquis)

11. Life is a misery if you don't get more than you deserve. (Harry Oppenheimer)

▶ **12.** Wealth does not bring excellence, but that wealth comes from excellence. (Plato)

13. If you ain't got no boots, it's tough to lift yourself up by your bootstraps. (Jack Kemp)

14. You can't expect to win unless you know why you lose. (Benjamin Lipson)

15. If you never assume importance, you never lose it. (Lao-Tzu)

16. Anger is never without a reason, but seldom with a good one. (Benjamin Franklin)

17. This is a world of action, and not of moping and droning in. (Charles Dickens)

▶ **18.** Opposition enflames the enthusiast, never converts him. (Johann Schiller)

19. And if you have been thoroughly prepared, you will not be afraid. (Dale Carnegie)

20. Loyalty to petrified opinion never yet broke a chain or freed a human soul. (Mark Twain)

21. Though he treads upon the tiger's tail, it does not bite him. (*I Ching*)

22. It is the contest that delights us, not the victory. (Blaise Pascal)

23. If you do not know how to spend money, you are not rich. (Mohammed Mannei)

▶ **24.** Progress might have been all right once but it has gone on too long. (Ogden Nash)

25. A man may be a fool and not know it, but not if he is married. (H. L. Mencken)

26. If one tells the truth, one is sure, sooner or later, to be found out. (Oscar Wilde)

27. One either meets or one works. One cannot do both at the same time. (Peter Drucker)

28. I never give them hell. I just tell the truth and they think it's hell. (Harry Truman)

29. If the wise erred not it would go hard with fools. (George Herbert)

▶ **30.** God cannot alter the past, but historians can. (Samuel Butler)

31. It doesn't depend on size, or a cow would catch a rabbit. (Pennsylvania German proverb)

32. I know well what I am fleeing from, but not what I am in search of. (Michel de Montaigne)

33. I have failed to take advantage of many opportunities, but the world has not failed in offering them. (Edgar W. Howe)

34. If you neglect your work, you will dislike it; if you do it well, you will enjoy it. (Sidney Smith)

35. The United States has become great not because of things but because of ideas. (James Michener)

▶ **36.** I am opposed to millionaires, but it would be dangerous to offer me the position. (Mark Twain)

37. If you ask too many people their views and you consider them carefully, you end up doing nothing. (Prince Charles)

38. Man is not the creature of circumstances, circumstances are the creature of man. (Benjamin Disraeli)

39. The trouble ain't that there is too many fools, but that the lightning ain't distributed right. (Mark Twain)

40. Democracy means government by discussion, but it is only effective if you can stop people talking. (Clement Richard Attlee)

41. Thrift is care and scruple in the spending of one's means. It is not a virtue, and it requires neither skill nor talent. (Immanuel Kant)

► 42. The idea that all wealth is acquired through stealing is popular in prisons and at Harvard. (George Gilder)

43. Those who are in reality superior in intelligence can be accepted only if they pretend they are not. (Marya Mannes)

44. One will not go too far wrong if one attributes extreme actions to vanity, average ones to habit, and petty ones to fear. (Friedrich Nietzsche)

45. Doing is overrated, and success undesirable, but the bitterness of failure even more so. (Cyril Connolly)

46. Ambition has its disappointments to sour us, but never the good fortune to satisfy us. (Benjamin Franklin)

47. If we cannot be powerful and happy and prey on others, we invent conscience and prey on ourselves. (Elbert Hubbard)

► 48. The hard fact was, circumstances rarely misled, and appearances were always full of truth. (James Gould Cozzens)

49. The only way to keep your health is to eat what you don't want, drink what you don't like, and do what you'd rather not. (Mark Twain)

50. If you do not know where you are going, every road will get you nowhere. (Henry Kissinger)

51. If you say yes too quickly you may have to say no, if you think things are done too easily you may find them hard to do; if you face trouble sanely it cannot trouble you. (Lao-Tzu)

52. Though men pride themselves on their great actions, often they are not the result of any great design but of chance. (La Rochefoucauld)

53. The race is not always to the swift, nor the battle to the strong—but that's the way to bet. (Damon Runyan)

► 54. If other people are going to talk, conversation becomes impossible. (James McNeill Whistler)

55. The Christian ideal has not been tried and found wanting. It has been found difficult and left untried. (G. K. Chesterton)

56. Imagining is good, provided you do not believe you see what can only be imagined. (Joseph Joubert)

57. If all the year was playing holidays, to sport would be as tedious as to work. (Shakespeare)

58. I am not sure just what the unpardonable sin is, but I believe it is a disposition to evade the payment of small bills. (Kin Hubbard)

59. If a man has rendered himself correct, he will have no trouble governing. If he cannot render himself correct, how can he correct others? (Confucius)*

▶ 60. The lion and the calf shall lie down together but the calf won't get much sleep. (Woody Allen)*

5.5 VALIDITY

Our symbolic language allows us to evaluate arguments as valid or invalid by symbolizing them—by translating them into SL—and then testing the resulting *argument form* for validity. Recall the diagram presented earlier in this chapter:

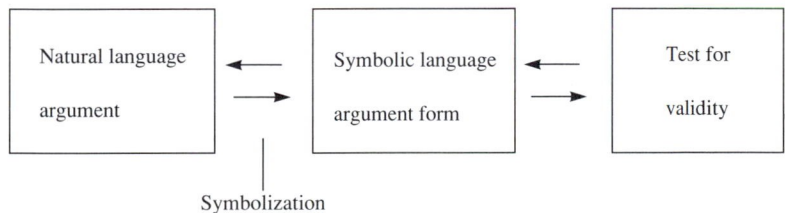

This suggests that our tactic for analyzing English arguments and sentences should be twofold. First, we should symbolize the sentences or arguments in SL. Second, we should evaluate the results for validity or other logical properties.

Sequences of sentences, when symbolized in SL, become sequences of formulas, or *argument forms*.

DEFINITION An *argument form* consists of a finite sequence of formulas, called its *premise formulas,* together with another formula, its *conclusion formula.*

For instance, we symbolized the argument from Sextus Empiricus as

(34) $s \rightarrow (l \vee d)$
$\quad \neg l$
$\quad \neg d$
$\therefore \neg s$

This is an argument form. We'll say that it's a *form of,* or *corresponds to,* Sextus's argument.

Under what circumstances is an argument form valid? An argument is valid if its conclusion is true in every circumstance in which its premises are true. An argument form is a symbolized argument. It's tempting to say, then, that an argument form is valid if its conclusion formula is true in every circumstance in which its premise formulas are true.

Unfortunately, as it stands this makes no sense. Consider the form of Sextus's argument. Under what circumstances is $\neg s$ true? The question is absurd; formulas such as $\neg s$, $s \rightarrow (l \vee d)$, and so on, are not themselves true or false. They have truth values only when they are interpreted. Before we can talk about the validity of argument forms, therefore, we must say how formulas can be interpreted.

One way to interpret formulas is to link them to the sentences they symbolize. This allows us to talk about $\neg s$ as true or false, for example, since we can think of that formula as abbreviating 'Socrates did not die'. But this technique gives us no simple way of surveying all the possible circumstances under which the sentence and corresponding formula might be true or false. And we need to do that to evaluate validity.

In SL, there's a more direct and useful way of interpreting formulas. SL is a language of truth functions. All its connectives are truth-functional. For this reason, SL uses nothing about a sentence beyond its truth value. So, in SL, we can interpret formulas by assigning them truth values. To survey all possible circumstances within truth-functional sentential logic, we just need to survey all possible combinations of truth and falsehood.

In analyzing formulas and argument forms for validity, therefore, we'll speak about possible combinations of truth values. We can interpret a formula of SL by saying whether the sentence letters it contains are true or false.

> **DEFINITION** (a) An *interpretation* of a sentence letter is an assignment of a truth value to it. (b) An *interpretation* of a formula of SL is an assignment of truth values to its sentence letters. (c) An *interpretation* of an argument form or set of formulas in SL is an assignment of truth values to all the sentence letters in the argument form or set.

We can use the concept of an interpretation as an easy way to formulate definitions of validity and other logical properties of formulas and argument forms.

A formula is *valid* if and only if it's true on every interpretation of it.
    contradictory if and only if it's false on every
        interpretation of it.
    satisfiable if and only if it's true on at least one
        interpretation of it.
    contingent if and only if it's neither valid nor
        contradictory.
An argument form is *valid* if and only if there is no interpretation of
    it making its premise formulas all true and its conclusion
    formula false.
A set of formulas $\mathscr{S}$ *implies* a formula $\mathscr{A}$ if and only if there is no
    interpretation of $\mathscr{S}$ together with $\mathscr{A}$ making every member of
    $\mathscr{S}$ true but $\mathscr{A}$ false.
Two formulas are *equivalent* if and only if they agree in truth value
    on every interpretation of them.

The definitions of the logical connectives specify the truth values of complex formulas on the basis of the values of their components. This allows us to compute the truth value of a formula of any length, given the values of the atomic formulas—that is, sentence letters—appearing in the formula.

For example, suppose that p and q are true but r is false. What is the truth value of the formula $((p \rightarrow q) \rightarrow r)$? Its main connective is the second arrow. The antecedent of the conditional is another conditional, both of whose components are true; the definition of the conditional indicates that this smaller conditional, $p \rightarrow q$, is true. The larger conditional, then, has a true antecedent, but its consequent, r, is false. The definition of the conditional tells us that the larger conditional is false.

Approaching this problem more systematically, we might list the values of the sentence letters first and then proceed to generate the values of subformulas until we reach the formula as a whole. We might, in other words, work our way up the tree for the formula at hand. The tree on the left would lead us to the table on the right, and, perhaps, to the more compressed table below it:

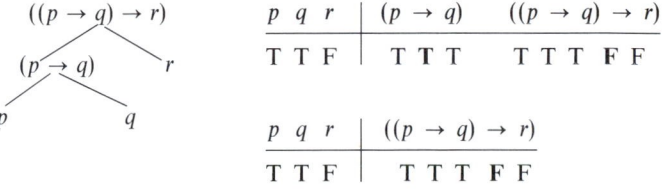

A boldface letter in the tables represents the truth value of the entire formula above it.

In constructing these tables, we begin with the sentence letters, which appear at the bottom of any tree that charts the construction of a formula. We then assign values to items one level up from the lowest sentence letters in the tree and work our way, gradually, to the top level, where the formula itself appears. In other words, we work from inside parentheses out. Whenever two subformulas are nested equally deeply inside parentheses—whenever, alternatively, they occupy the same level of the tree—it makes no difference which we attack first. Our definitions thus allow us to compute the value of a formula, given some interpretation assigning values to its sentence letters. This is the central idea behind the method of *truth tables,* which we'll develop in the next chapter.

Problems

Classify these sentences as correct or incorrect about SL, and explain why.

▸ **1.** Valid argument forms having valid conclusion formulas are valid.

▸ **2.** Some argument forms with contradictory premise formulas aren't valid.

▸ **3.** There is a formula that implies every other formula.

▸ **4.** There is a formula that is equivalent to every other formula.

▸ **5.** Any formula that follows from a satisfiable formula is satisfiable.

▸ **6.** Any formula that implies a contingent formula is not valid.

7. Any formula that follows from a contingent formula is contingent.

8. Any formula that follows from a valid formula is valid.

9. Any formula that implies a valid formula is valid.

10. All contradictory formulas imply one another.

11. All contingent formulas imply one another.

▸ **12.** All valid formulas imply one another.

13. Some argument forms with contradictory formulas as conclusion formulas are valid.

14. No formula implies its own negation.

15. Any formula that implies its own negation is contradictory.

16. Any formula implied by its own negation is valid.

Calculate the truth values of these formulas on the interpretations listed.

17. $(p \vee q) \mathbin{\&} (p \vee \neg r)$ $\qquad\qquad$ (p and q false; r true)

▶ **18.** $(p \to (q \leftrightarrow r)) \to (q \leftrightarrow \neg r)$ (p and r true; q false)

19. $((r \to q) \& \neg p) \leftrightarrow (\neg q \& p)$ (p true; q and r false)

20. $\neg((p \& \neg q) \vee (q \to \neg r))$ (p false; q and r true)

21. $(p \leftrightarrow \neg r) \leftrightarrow (r \leftrightarrow q)$ (p, q, and r true)

22. $\neg(p \vee q) \to \neg(p \& r)$ (p, q, and r false)

23. $(p \leftrightarrow (q \& r)) \vee (p \to q)$ (p and q true; r false)

▶ **24.** $(\neg p \leftrightarrow \neg q) \leftrightarrow \neg r$ (p and r true; q false)

25. $\neg(\neg(\neg p \to \neg q) \vee \neg r)$ (p true; q and r false)

26. $\neg((\neg q \vee \neg p) \to \neg r)$ (p false; q and r true)

27. $(p \leftrightarrow \neg(q \vee r)) \leftrightarrow \neg p$ (p and q false; r true)

28. $(p \& \neg q) \leftrightarrow (p \to \neg r)$ (p and r false; q true)

29. $(\neg(p \vee r) \leftrightarrow \neg q) \to \neg q$ (p, q, and r false)

▶ **30.** $\neg((p \leftrightarrow \neg q) \leftrightarrow \neg r)$ (p, q, and r true)

31. Suppose that $\mathscr{A}$ is a tautology. What can we conclude about the logical properties of (a) $\neg \mathscr{A}$; (b) $\mathscr{A} \vee \mathscr{B}$; (c) $\mathscr{A} \& \mathscr{B}$; (d) $\mathscr{A} \to \mathscr{B}$; (e) $\mathscr{B} \to \mathscr{A}$; (f) $\mathscr{A} \leftrightarrow \mathscr{B}$?

32. Suppose that $\mathscr{A}$ is contradictory. What can we conclude about the logical properties of (a) $\neg \mathscr{A}$; (b) $\mathscr{A} \vee \mathscr{B}$; (c) $\mathscr{A} \& \mathscr{B}$; (d) $\mathscr{A} \to \mathscr{B}$; (e) $\mathscr{B} \to \mathscr{A}$; (f) $\mathscr{A} \leftrightarrow \mathscr{B}$?

33. Suppose that $\mathscr{A}$ is contingent. What can we conclude about the logical properties of (a) $\neg \mathscr{A}$; (b) $\mathscr{A} \vee \mathscr{B}$; (c) $\mathscr{A} \& \mathscr{B}$; (d) $\mathscr{A} \to \mathscr{B}$; (e) $\mathscr{B} \to \mathscr{A}$; (f) $\mathscr{A} \leftrightarrow \mathscr{B}$?

34. Suppose that $\mathscr{A}$ and $\mathscr{B}$ are both tautologies. What can we conclude about the logical properties of (a) $\neg \mathscr{A}$; (b) $\mathscr{A} \vee \mathscr{B}$; (c) $\mathscr{A} \& \mathscr{B}$; (d) $\mathscr{A} \to \mathscr{B}$; (e) $\mathscr{B} \to \mathscr{A}$; (f) $\mathscr{A} \leftrightarrow \mathscr{B}$?

35. Suppose that $\mathscr{A}$ and $\mathscr{B}$ are both contradictory. What can we conclude about the logical properties of (a) $\neg \mathscr{A}$; (b) $\mathscr{A} \vee \mathscr{B}$; (c) $\mathscr{A} \& \mathscr{B}$; (d) $\mathscr{A} \to \mathscr{B}$; (e) $\mathscr{B} \to \mathscr{A}$; (f) $\mathscr{A} \leftrightarrow \mathscr{B}$?

▶ **36.** Suppose that $\mathscr{A}$ and $\mathscr{B}$ are both contingent. What can we conclude about the logical properties of (a) $\neg \mathscr{A}$; (b) $\mathscr{A} \vee \mathscr{B}$; (c) $\mathscr{A} \& \mathscr{B}$; (d) $\mathscr{A} \to \mathscr{B}$; (e) $\mathscr{B} \to \mathscr{A}$; (f) $\mathscr{A} \leftrightarrow \mathscr{B}$?

37. What can we infer about the logical properties of $\mathscr{A}$ and $\mathscr{B}$ if $\mathscr{A} \& \mathscr{B}$ is (a) a tautology; (b) contradictory; (c) contingent?

38. What can we infer about the logical properties of $\mathscr{A}$ and $\mathscr{B}$ if $\mathscr{A} \vee \mathscr{B}$ is (a) a tautology; (b) contradictory; (c) contingent?

39. What can we infer about the logical properties of $\mathcal{A}$ and $\mathcal{B}$ if $\mathcal{A} \rightarrow \mathcal{B}$ is (a) a tautology; (b) contradictory; (c) contingent?

40. What can we infer about the logical properties of $\mathcal{A}$ and $\mathcal{B}$ if $\mathcal{A} \leftrightarrow \mathcal{B}$ is (a) a tautology; (b) contradictory; (c) contingent?

Notes

[1] Aristotle was also the first logician to use symbols. The Stoics made the practice common, using numbers to stand for sentences. Nevertheless, no one developed a fully symbolic logical language until the nineteenth century, when Englishman George Boole (1815–1864) saw that logic could profit from mathematical analysis.

[2] The singular form of 'schemata' is 'schema'. We'll assume that sentence connectives and other vocabulary items of our symbolic language are names of themselves. '$(\mathcal{A} \rightarrow \mathcal{B})$' thus refers to the *formula* resulting from concatenating a left parenthesis, the formula $\mathcal{A}$, an occurrence of the conditional connective, the formula $\mathcal{B}$, and a right parenthesis. We can't refer to this formula by using ordinary quotation: '$(\mathcal{A} \rightarrow \mathcal{B})$' signifies the *string* of symbols quoted, that is, a left parenthesis, followed by the letter '$\mathcal{A}$', followed by an occurrence of the conditional, followed by the letter '$\mathcal{B}$', followed by a right parenthesis.

[3] Where n is any number, an n-ary function relates n inputs to a unique output. The inputs are called *arguments* of the function; the outputs are its *values*.

[4] For further discussion of the notion of causation, see Chapter 15.

[5] These problems with the truth-functional rendering of the conditional have been recognized since the third century B.C., when the Greek logician Philo of Megara—a classmate of Zeno (336–264 B.C.), the founder of Stoicism—first proposed the analysis reflected in our table above. Diodorus, Philo's teacher, held that conditionals involve necessity, and Chrysippus (279–206 B.C.), the third head of the Stoic school and widely acclaimed as the greatest logician of his time, held that the sort of necessity involved is specifically logical, as opposed, for instance, to causal necessity. The controversy among their followers became so intense that Callimachus wrote that "even the crows on the roofs caw about the nature of conditionals."

CHAPTER

6

TRUTH
TABLES

Because SL contains only truth-functional connectives, we can determine the truth value of a compound sentence by examining the truth values of its components. The method of *truth tables* exploits this fact to provide a general technique for evaluating formulas and argument forms.

6.1 TRUTH TABLES FOR FORMULAS

Given an interpretation, we can compute the truth value of a formula on that interpretation. This is interesting only if we have reason to single out a particular interpretation, for instance, because we think it corresponds to circumstances as they actually are. But a formula is a tautology if and only if it is true on every interpretation of it. Surveying the set of all possible interpretations thus gives us a way of determining the logical properties of formulas.

A *truth table* is a computation of the truth value of a formula or set of formulas under each of its possible interpretations.[1] If a formula is a tautology, then the main column of its truth table will contain a string of Ts. If it's contradictory, the main column will contain a string of Fs. If it's contingent, finally, the main column will contain both Ts and Fs. Truth tables amount simply to several simple tables, of the kind we saw in section 5.5, done at once. But they allow us to evaluate any formula of sentential logic as tautologous, contradictory, or contingent.

A truth table for a formula consists of four elements:

1. A list of the sentence letters of the formula

2. The formula itself

139

3. A list of the possible interpretations of the formula

4. A computation of the truth value of the formula on each interpretation

Truth tables have this form:

Sentence letters	Formula
List of interpretations	Computation

The top of a table lists the formula to be evaluated, preceded by the sentence letters in the formula.

To see how this works, consider an example.

(1) Either Paul is behind the movement, or Jorge will join only if Paul is.

Is the formula $(p \lor (q \to p))$ valid, contradictory, or contingent? We can set up column heads of the table by listing the sentence letters in the formula, followed by the formula.

$$p \quad q \qquad (p \lor (q \to p))$$

Under the sentence letters, we list their possible interpretations in tabular form. If there's one sentence letter, there are only two interpretations: one assigning truth and one assigning falsehood. Two letters have four possible interpretations, three letters have eight possible interpretations, and so on. (In general, n sentence letters can be given 2^n interpretations.) One way to list all these possibilities in a standard order is to imagine an array of the following kind. The second letter, for instance, could be either true or false, no matter what the truth value of the first letter happens to be.

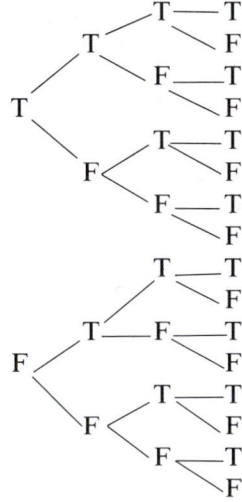

As long as all interpretations are included, their order makes no difference. To make truth tables easy to read and compare, however, let's agree that the lists of possible interpretations, for cases involving one, two, three, or four sentence letters, should look like this:

T	T T	T T T		T T T T			
F	T F	T T F		T T T F			
	F T	T F T		T T F T			
	F F	T F F		T T F F			
		F T T		T F T T			
		F T F		T F T F			
		F F T		T F F T			
		F F F		T F F F			
				F T T T			
				F T T F			
				F T F T			
				F T F F			
				F F T T			
				F F T F			
				F F F T			
				F F F F			

If a formula contains more than four sentence letters, its table will have 32 or more rows, one for each possible interpretation of the formula. In such cases, the method works, but awkwardly.

Our example has only two sentence letters. We begin by listing the four possible interpretations:

p	q	$(p \lor (q \to p))$
T	T	
T	F	
F	T	
F	F	

Now, we copy the interpretations for each letter under its occurrences in the formula. This gives us values for the bottom nodes of the tree charting the formula's construction.

p	q	$(p$	$\lor$	$(q$	$\to$	$p))$
T	T	T		T		T
T	F	T		F		T
F	T	F		T		F
F	F	F		F		F

Then, begin searching for subformulas one level up from the bottom of the tree. Look for subformulas as far inside parentheses as possible. Negations of single sentence letters are always safe, since the value of the negated letter depends on nothing but the value of the letter itself. As a rule, compute values for negations of single sentence letters first. Then, compute values for subformulas, working from inside parentheses out.

In the example, we begin with the conditional:

p *q*	$(p \vee (q \rightarrow p))$
T T	T · T T T
T F	T · F T T
F T	F · T F F
F F	F · F T F

We thus work our way up the tree charting the formula's construction until, finally, we reach the formula itself at the top. The last computation should be for the main connective of the entire formula.

So, we can conclude the truth table by computing the value of the larger disjunction. Since the ∨ is the formula's main connective, we are now computing the truth value of the entire formula on each interpretation.

p *q*	$(p \vee (q \rightarrow p))$
T T	T **T** T T T
T F	T **T** F T T
F T	F **F** T F F
F F	F **T** F T F

Truth tables follow a "bottom-up" strategy; we begin with the letters at the bottom of the tree charting the formula's construction and work up the tree to compute values for more complex units.

In summary, to compute the truth value of a formula under each interpretation of it:

1. Copy the interpretations of each sentence letter under its occurrences in the formula.

2. Compute the values of negations of single sentence letters.

3. Compute values of subformulas, working from inside parentheses out.

Under each sentence letter and connective of the formula, a completed table will have a column of Ts and Fs. These represent the truth value of the formula or subformula under each interpretation of it. The column for the entire formula itself—the last to be filled in—is the table's *main column*. It specifies the truth value of the formula on each interpretation. In the preceding table, and throughout this chapter, the main column is in boldface.

> **DEFINITION** The *main column* of a truth table is the column under the main connective of the formula at the top of the table.

We can use truth tables to evaluate formulas for logical truth, contradiction, and so on. A tautology is true on all its interpretations; the main column of a table for a tautology, therefore, should contain all Ts. A contradictory formula is false on all its interpretations; the main column of a table for it, therefore, should contain all Fs. The main columns of tables for contingent formulas, finally, contain both Ts and Fs. The main column in the table for $(p \lor (q \to p))$ does contain both Ts and Fs, so $(p \lor (q \to p))$ is contingent. To summarize:

Main Column	Formula
All Ts	Tautologous (logically true)
All Fs	Contradictory
Ts and Fs	Contingent

Consider another, more complex example:

(2) It is true neither that the Soviets will withdraw from Eastern Europe if we so encourage them, nor that the Eastern European nations will remain firmly socialist if the Soviets do withdraw.

We might symbolize (2) as $\neg((p \to q) \lor (q \to r))$. To evaluate it, we begin a truth table, writing the three sentence letters in the formula, followed by the formula itself. We then list all possible interpretations, copying them under the occurrences of the sentence letters in the formula:

p q r	$\neg((p$	$\to$	$q) \lor (q$	$\to$	$r))$
T T T	T	T	T	T	
T T F	T	T	T	F	
T F T	T	F	F	T	
T F F	T	F	F	F	
F T T	F	T	T	T	
F T F	F	T	T	F	
F F T	F	F	F	T	
F F F	F	F	F	F	

Now, we compute the values of subformulas, working our way up the tree charting the construction of the formula. There are no negations of single sentence letters—the negation here is the main connective—so we begin as far inside parentheses as possible. We can do the conditionals in either order, ending up with the table:

p q r	$\neg((p$	$\to$	$q) \lor (q$	$\to$	$r))$
T T T	T	T T	T	T T	
T T F	T	T T	T	F F	
T F T	T	F F	F	T T	
T F F	T	F F	F	T F	
F T T	F	T T	T	T T	
F T F	F	T T	T	F F	
F F T	F	T F	F	T T	
F F F	F	T F	F	T F	

Now, we can calculate the values of the disjunction:

p q r	$\neg((p \rightarrow q) \vee (q \rightarrow r))$
T T T	T T T T T T T
T T F	T T T T T F F
T F T	T F F T F T T
T F F	T F F T F T F
F T T	F T T T T T T
F T F	F T T T T F F
F F T	F T F T F T T
F F F	F T F T F T F

The disjunction is valid; it's true on every interpretation. Finally, then, we use the definition of negation to calculate the values of the entire formula:

p q r	$\neg((p \rightarrow q) \vee (q \rightarrow r))$
T T T	F T T T T T T T
T T F	F T T T T T F F
T F T	F T F F T F T T
T F F	F T F F T F T F
F T T	F F T T T T T T
F T F	F F T T T T F F
F F T	F F T F T F T T
F F F	F F T F T F T F

Since the formula is false on every row—that is, on every interpretation of it—it's contradictory. Notice that (2), the English sentence the formula symbolizes, doesn't seem contradictory, because of the discrepancies between English and SL conditionals discussed in Chapter 5.

Problems

Construct truth tables for these formulas and determine whether they are tautologous, contradictory, or contingent.

▸ **1.** p ▸ **2.** $p \rightarrow p$ ▸ **3.** $p \rightarrow \neg p$ ▸ **4.** $p \vee \neg p$

▸ **5.** $p \leftrightarrow \neg p$ ▸ **6.** $p \& \neg p$ **7.** $\neg(\neg p \rightarrow p)$ **8.** $\neg(\neg p \rightarrow q)$

9. $p \rightarrow (q \rightarrow p)$ **10.** $q \rightarrow (q \rightarrow p)$ **11.** $(q \rightarrow p) \rightarrow p$ ▸ **12.** $(q \rightarrow p) \rightarrow q$

13. $(\neg p \rightarrow p) \leftrightarrow p$ **14.** $(\neg p \rightarrow p) \leftrightarrow \neg p$ **15.** $\neg p \rightarrow (p \rightarrow q)$

16. $\neg p \rightarrow (q \rightarrow p)$ **17.** $(p \rightarrow q) \rightarrow \neg p$ ▸ **18.** $p \rightarrow (q \& p)$

19. $(p \& q) \rightarrow q$ **20.** $(p \rightarrow q) \vee (q \rightarrow p)$ **21.** $(p \rightarrow q) \& (q \rightarrow p)$

22. $(p \rightarrow q) \& \neg(q \rightarrow p)$ **23.** $(p \rightarrow q) \rightarrow (q \rightarrow p)$ ▸ **24.** $(p \rightarrow q) \leftrightarrow (q \rightarrow p)$

25. $(p \& q) \rightarrow (p \rightarrow q)$ **26.** $(p \rightarrow q) \rightarrow (p \& q)$ **27.** $(p \vee q) \rightarrow (p \leftrightarrow q)$

28. $(p \mathbin{\&} q) \to (p \lor q)$ **29.** $\neg(p \to q) \to (q \to p)$

▸ **30.** $\neg(p \to q) \to \neg(q \to p)$ **31.** $\neg(p \to q) \leftrightarrow \neg(q \to p)$

32. $((p \mathbin{\&} \neg q) \to q) \to \neg p$ **33.** $\neg((p \to q) \to \neg(q \to p))$

34. $(p \lor q) \leftrightarrow \neg(\neg p \mathbin{\&} \neg q)$ **35.** $(p \mathbin{\&} \neg(q \lor r)) \leftrightarrow \neg(p \to q)$

▸ **36.** $(p \lor ((p \leftrightarrow q) \mathbin{\&} (p \leftrightarrow \neg q)))$ **37.** $(p \mathbin{\&} ((p \to q) \mathbin{\&} (p \to \lor \neg q)))$

38. $(p \leftrightarrow ((p \to \neg q) \mathbin{\&} (p \to \neg\neg q)))$

39. $(q \lor r) \to ((r \to p) \lor (q \to p))$

40. $(q \lor r) \to ((p \to q) \lor (p \to r))$

41. $(q \to r) \to ((p \to q) \mathbin{\&} (p \to r))$

▸ **42.** $(q \mathbin{\&} r) \leftrightarrow ((p \leftrightarrow q) \lor (p \leftrightarrow r))$

43. $(p \lor (q \to r)) \leftrightarrow ((p \lor q) \to (p \lor r))$

44. $(p \mathbin{\&} (q \lor r)) \leftrightarrow ((p \mathbin{\&} q) \lor (p \mathbin{\&} r))$

45. $(p \lor (q \mathbin{\&} r)) \leftrightarrow ((p \lor q) \mathbin{\&} (p \mathbin{\&} r))$

46. $(p \to (q \lor r)) \leftrightarrow ((p \to q) \lor (p \to r))$

47. $(p \leftrightarrow (q \to r)) \leftrightarrow ((p \leftrightarrow q) \to (p \leftrightarrow r))$

▸ **48.** $(p \leftrightarrow (q \to r)) \leftrightarrow ((p \leftrightarrow q) \to (p \leftrightarrow r))$

49. $(p \to (q \leftrightarrow r)) \leftrightarrow ((p \leftrightarrow q) \leftrightarrow (p \leftrightarrow r))$

50. $\neg(p \leftrightarrow \neg(q \to r)) \leftrightarrow \neg(\neg(p \leftrightarrow q) \to \neg(p \leftrightarrow r))$

6.2 Other Uses of Truth Tables

Argument Forms

An argument form is valid if and only if each interpretation making its premise formulas true also makes its conclusion formula true. Truth tables let us calculate the truth values of formulas under each of their interpretations. So, a truth table can give us the information we need to evaluate an argument form.

We can set up a single table that computes values for each of the premise formulas, and the conclusion formula, separately. We can then interpret these tables as evaluating argument forms. To do so:

1. List the sentence letters appearing in the argument form.

2. Beneath them, list all possible interpretations of them.

3. List each premise formula, and then the conclusion formula, as column heads.

4. Compute the value of each formula.

The computation produces a main column for each formula. An argument form is valid just in case no interpretation makes the premise formulas all true but the conclusion formula false. We can determine whether this is so by examining the columns.

Here are some sample argument forms of simple English arguments:

(3) People will buy the product if the advertising reaches them. The advertising will reach them; so, people will buy the product.

(4) $p \rightarrow q$
p
$\therefore q$

(5) The cost of insurance will go down only if damage awards decrease. Those awards will decrease if and only if legislation to limit them passes. Hence, the cost of insurance will go down if legislation to limit damage awards passes and those awards decrease.

(6) $p \rightarrow q$
$q \leftrightarrow r$
$\therefore (r \mathbin{\&} q) \rightarrow p$

(7) If Houston or Cincinnati makes the playoffs, then not both Cincinnati and Cleveland will make it. Cincinnati will make the playoffs. So, Cleveland won't.

(8) $(p \vee q) \rightarrow \neg(q \mathbin{\&} r)$
q
$\therefore \neg r$

It's easy to evaluate them for validity. Argument form (4) is valid; on no row are the premises all true while the conclusion is false.

p q	p	$(p \rightarrow q)$	q
T T	T	T **T** T	T
T F	T	T **F** F	F
F T	F	F **T** T	T
F F	F	F **T** F	F

Argument form (6) is invalid.

p q r	$(p \to q)$	$(q \leftrightarrow r)$	$((r \; \& \; q) \to p)$
T T T	T T T	T T T	T T T T T
T T F	T T T	T F F	F F T T T
T F T	T F F	F F T	T F F T T
T F F	T F F	F T F	F F F T T
F T T	F T T	T T T	T T T F F
F T F	F T T	T F F	F F T T F
F F T	F T F	F F T	T F F T F
F F F	F T F	F T F	F F F T F

The interpretation

p	q	r
F	T	T

makes the conclusion formula false but the premise formulas all true. Transferring this information to the English argument (5): even given the truth of the premises, it could happen that legislation to limit damage awards passes, that those awards decrease, but that nevertheless the cost of insurance doesn't go down.

Argument form (8) is valid. On every row making the premises all true, the conclusion is true as well.

p q r	$((p \lor q) \to \neg(q \; \& \; r))$	q	$\neg r$
T T T	T T T F F T T T	T	F T
T T F	T T T T T T F F	T	T F
T F T	T T F T T F F T	F	F T
T F F	T T F T T F F F	F	T F
F T T	F T T F F T T T	T	F T
F T F	F T T T T T F F	T	T F
F F T	F F F T T F F T	F	F T
F F F	F F F T T F F F	F	T F

When a truth table shows an argument form to be invalid, it specifies an interpretation making the premise formulas true and the conclusion formula false. The table indicates that there is such an interpretation and, moreover, tells us what it is. One such row is enough to show the argument form to be invalid. But if there are several, it specifies them all. To see under what circumstances the premise formulas would be true but the conclusion formula false, check those rows of the table that have F in the final column.

Implication

In a valid argument form, the premise formulas imply the conclusion formula. A set of formulas implies a given formula just in case every interpretation making every member of the set true makes the given formula true as well. This is exactly the relation that holds between the premise formulas of an argument form and the conclusion formula. Consequently, truth tables can evaluate implication. To find out whether a set of formulas $\{\mathscr{A}_1, \ldots, \mathscr{A}_n\}$ implies a formula $\mathscr{B}$, we can construct a table for the argument form

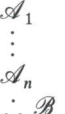

$\mathscr{A}_1$
$\vdots$
$\mathscr{A}_n$
$\therefore \mathscr{B}$

To determine whether

(9) Either the filmmakers had a very low opinion of their audience, or they were just incompetent.

implies

(10) If the filmmakers had a very low opinion of their audience, they weren't incompetent.

for example, we can ask whether $p \lor q$ implies $p \to \neg q$. We list the letters p and q, write the four possible combinations of truth values between them, and write the two formulas as column heads.

p	q	$p \lor q$	$p \to \neg q$
T	T	T T T	T **F** FT
T	F	T T F	T **T** TF
F	T	F T T	F **T** FT
F	F	F **F** F	F **T** TF

On the first row, $p \lor q$ comes out true, but $p \to \neg q$ is false. Thus, $p \lor q$ does not imply $p \to \neg q$. The interpretation assigning truth to both p and q makes $p \lor q$ true but $p \to \neg q$ false. The implication between the English sentences doesn't hold, then, because the filmmakers might have had a very low opinion of their audience and been incompetent as well.

Equivalence

Equivalence is implication in both directions. $\mathscr{A}$ and $\mathscr{B}$ are equivalent just in case they have the same truth value on each of their interpretations.

To show that p is equivalent to $\neg\neg p$, for example, we can construct the table:

p	p	$\neg\neg p$
T	T	T FT
F	F	F TF

The table shows that p and $\neg\,\neg\,p$ agree in truth value on every interpretation of them; they are equivalent.

Strengths and Limitations

Truth tables are simple but remarkably powerful tools for solving problems in sentential logic. They can evaluate argument form validity, the logical properties of formulas, implication, and equivalence. They achieve all this, furthermore, in a clear and easily understandable way. A truth table surveys all possible interpretations of a formula, argument form, or set of formulas and computes truth values on each interpretation.

Truth tables constitute a *decision procedure* for validity in SL.

> **DEFINITION** A *decision procedure* for a property is a mechanical method for determining, within a finite time, whether any given thing has or doesn't have that property.

Decision procedures are completely mechanical; using them involves no more than following rules. They require no ingenuity or creativity. A decision procedure, applied to an object, always gives a *yes* or *no* answer after a finite time. Truth tables, clearly, are decision procedures for validity, equivalence, and other logical properties. We can construct tables by following rules; the tables always have a finite size. If there is a decision procedure for a property, the property is *decidable*. In SL, formula and argument form validity, formula and set satisfiability, implication, and equivalence are all decidable.

The clarity of the truth table technique comes at a price. When a formula or argument form is very complex, the number of possible interpretations may be very large. Using the truth table method, we don't always reach a decision within a reasonable amount of time. The size of a truth table grows exponentially with the number of sentence letters involved; someone who began a truth table for a problem with 139 sentence letters at the moment of the big bang would still not be finished.[2] In the next chapter, therefore, we'll develop a method of searching for an interpretation to answer a question about validity, implication, and so on, without examining every possible way of assigning truth values to sentence letters.

Truth tables are decision procedures for formula and argument form validity in SL. How does the validity of its symbolization in SL, however, bear on the validity of an argument in natural language? Recall that our strategy is twofold:

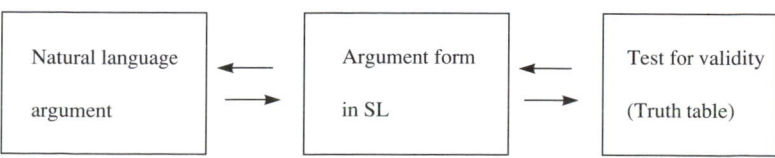

Truth tables can tell us whether any given argument form is valid or invalid in SL. What can we infer from this verdict about the validity of the original English argument?

In Chapter 5, and again in this chapter, we saw that the connectives of SL don't match English connectives in every respect. The symbolic connectives approximate their natural language counterparts closely, but the fit isn't exact. So, especially when an argument contains conditionals, we need to check whether its premises and conclusion would be true under the same conditions as the formulas symbolizing them.

Suppose that there's no problem about the match between English and symbolic connectives. Then, if an argument form resulting from the process of symbolization is valid in SL, then the original argument it symbolizes is valid. But an invalid argument form doesn't show that the original argument was invalid. The symbolic languages logicians use are only partial theories of logical relations. Logic aims at a comprehensive theory that would take account of all such relations, but no such theory yet exists. So, in particular, SL accounts for only some cases of validity. Many English arguments depend on logical relationships that sentential logic doesn't capture. Consider, for example, this argument:

(11) All captains are officers.
      Some of the troops caught behind enemy lines are captains.
      ∴ Some of the troops caught behind enemy lines are officers.

This argument contains no sentence connectives: we can symbolize it in SL, at best, as

(12) p
      q
      ∴ r

This is a paradigm of an invalid SL argument form. We can conclude, not that the English argument is invalid, but that it's *invalid in* (or *relative to*) *SL*. A form for the argument showing as much logical structure as possible within SL is invalid, even though the argument is valid.

Therefore, in drawing conclusions about natural language arguments, valid truth table verdicts merit more trust than invalid verdicts. The same holds of other concepts. Contradictory verdicts merit more trust than satisfiable verdicts, and "implies" and "are equivalent" verdicts merit more trust than their opposites. It's always possible that, to establish the validity of an argument, the equivalence of two sentences, and so on, we would have to use more machinery than the logical theory we're working in provides.

Problems

Symbolize these arguments in SL and evaluate the corresponding argument forms as valid or invalid.

▶ **1.** Larry is either a knave or a fool. Larry is a knave; so, he's no fool.

▶ **2.** The President is either at Camp David or in Maine. He is not in Maine; therefore, he is at Camp David.

▶ **3.** If I'm right, then I'm a fool. But if I'm a fool, I'm not right. Therefore, I'm no fool.

▶ **4.** If I'm right, then I'm a fool. But if I'm a fool, I'm not right. Therefore, I'm not right.

▶ **5.** Unless I'm mistaken, I'm a fool. But if I am a fool, I must be mistaken. So, I'm mistaken.

▶ **6.** If I'm right, then you're a fool. If I'm a fool, I'm not right. If you're a fool, I am right. Therefore, one or the other of us is a fool.

7. If I'm right, then you're a fool. If I'm a fool, I'm not right. If you're a fool, I am right. Therefore, we're not both fools.

8. Hank will believe you only if he's incredibly gullible. Hank won't believe you. Therefore, he isn't incredibly gullible.

9. Airports in majors cities have been suffering congestion problems. So, airports in major cities have been either suffering congestion problems or closing down altogether.

10. If Kim scores over 1500 on her GREs, she'll get into Yale. She will score over 1500 on her GREs. It follows that she'll get into Yale.

11. If Kim scores over 1500 on her GREs, she'll get into Yale. She will get into Yale. It follows that she'll score over 1500 on her GREs.

▶ **12.** The members of this department agree when and only when the issue at hand is of no significance. This issue is significant, but the members nevertheless agree. Therefore, the end of the earth is at hand.

13. If you have a cake, just looking at it will make you hungry; if looking at it makes you hungry, you will eat it. So, you can't both have your cake and fail to eat it.

14. A man cannot serve both God and Mammon. But if a man does not serve Mammon, he starves; if he starves, he can't serve God. Therefore, a man cannot serve God.

15. Modern physics asserts that there is no such thing as absolute motion. If this is correct, then there is no such thing as absolute time, and our ordinary notions of time are wrong. So, either our ordinary ideas about time or modern physics is mistaken.

16. Sarah knows that the company is unlikely to promote her. She will look for another job if and only if she's unhappy. She's bound to be unhappy if she knows that she's unlikely to be promoted. So, unless she has some other reason for staying, Sarah will look for another job.

17. If nobody catches on to Rudy's scam, he'll make a lot of money, but other people will lose a lot of cash. Rudy won't make a lot of money. It follows that somebody will figure out Rudy's scam.

▸ **18.** If Socrates died, he died either while he was living or while he was dead. But he did not die while living; moreover, he surely did not die while he was already dead. Hence, Socrates did not die. (Sextus Empiricus)

19. Nothing can be conceived as greater than God. If God existed in our imaginations, but not in reality, then something would be conceivable as greater than God (namely, the same thing, except conceived as existing in reality). Therefore, if God exists in our imaginations, He exists in reality. (Anselm)

20. Either we ought to philosophize or we ought not. If we ought, then we ought. If we ought not, then also we ought (to justify this view). Hence, in any case, we ought to philosophize. (Aristotle)

Chrysippus (279–206 B.C.) regarded the following argument forms as basic to sentential logic. In some cases, however, he thought of connectives as having meanings different from those we've associated with them. Which of these are valid in SL?

21. $p \rightarrow q$; p; $\therefore q$.

22. $p \rightarrow q$; $\neg q$; $\therefore \neg p$.

23. $\neg(p \,\&\, q)$; p; $\therefore \neg q$.

▸ **24.** $p \lor q$; p; $\therefore \neg q$.

25. $p \lor q$; $\neg q$; $\therefore p$.

26. Cicero (106–43 B.C.), the famous Roman orator, summarized Stoic logic by citing seven principles: the five of Chrysippus (21–25), a repeat of the third (23), and $\neg(p \,\&\, q)$; $\neg p$; $\therefore q$. Is this valid in SL?

Sextus Empiricus, a Greek skeptic who wrote in the third century A.D., preserved some argument forms, the validity of which the Stoics thought followed from their basic principles. Which of these are valid in SL?

27. $p \rightarrow (p \rightarrow q)$; p; $\therefore q$.

28. $(p \,\&\, q) \rightarrow r$; $\neg r$; p; $\therefore \neg q$.

29. $p \rightarrow q$; $p \rightarrow \neg q$; $\therefore \neg p$.

▸ **30.** $p \rightarrow p$; $\neg p \rightarrow p$; $\therefore p$.

Use truth tables to determine whether the formulas in each pair are equivalent in SL. If they are not, say whether either formula implies the other.

31. $q \rightarrow p$ and $q \leftrightarrow (q \,\&\, p)$

32. $\neg(q \lor p)$ and $\neg q \lor \neg p$

33. $\neg(q \,\&\, p)$ and $\neg q \,\&\, \neg p$

34. $\neg(q \rightarrow p)$ and $\neg q \rightarrow \neg p$

35. $\neg(q \leftrightarrow p)$ and $\neg q \leftrightarrow \neg p$

▸ **36.** $\neg(q \leftrightarrow p)$ and $\neg q \leftrightarrow p$

37. $\neg(q \rightarrow p)$ and $q \,\&\, \neg p$

38. $\neg(q \,\&\, p)$ and $\neg q \lor \neg p$

39. $\neg(q \lor p)$ and $\neg q \,\&\, \neg p$

40. $q \,\&\, p$ and $(q \lor p) \,\&\, (q \leftrightarrow p)$

41. $q \& p$ and $(q \vee p) \& (q \to p)$ ▸ 42. $q \& p$ and $(q \vee p) \& (p \to q)$

43. $q \vee p$ and $\neg q \to p$ 44. $q \vee p$ and $\neg p \to q$

45. $q \to p$ and $q \leftrightarrow (q \vee p)$ 46. $q \to p$ and $p \leftrightarrow (q \vee p)$

47. $q \leftrightarrow p$ and $(q \to p) \& (p \to q)$ ▸ 48. $q \leftrightarrow p$ and $(q \& p) \& (\neg q \& \neg p)$

49. $q \leftrightarrow p$ and $\neg q \leftrightarrow \neg p$ 50. $q \leftrightarrow p$ and $(q \leftrightarrow p) \leftrightarrow q$

Use truth tables to determine whether each formula in the left column implies the corresponding formula in the right column.

51. $r, p \to \neg q$ $\neg q$

52. $\neg(r \to p)$ $r \to \neg p$

53. $r, (r \vee p) \to p$ $r \& p$

▸ 54. $r \to (\neg \neg p \to q)$ $(r \& \neg q) \to \neg p$

55. $r \to (p \vee q), r \to \neg p$ $\neg(r \to \neg q)$

56. $p \leftrightarrow (r \to (p \vee \neg q)), \neg(r \to (p \vee q))$ $\neg q$

57. $r \to \neg p, (q \& r) \to p$ $\neg((q \& \neg r) \to r)$

58. $\neg(r \to (p \& \neg q)), r \vee (p \& \neg q)$ $q \& \neg(r \vee p)$

59. $(r \vee \neg p) \leftrightarrow (r \to q), r \leftrightarrow (p \& (q \to \neg r))$ $\neg p$

▸ 60. $\neg(r \leftrightarrow \neg p), r \leftrightarrow (q \leftrightarrow p)$ $\neg(p \to (r \leftrightarrow q))$

61. $r, (p \vee q) \to (r \vee \neg p)$ $\neg r \leftrightarrow (p \leftrightarrow \neg q)$

62. $p \to (r \vee q), r \to (q \& \neg p)$ $\neg q \to \neg(p \& r)$

63. $(q \& p) \to \neg(p \& r), (r \vee p) \leftrightarrow (p \vee q)$ $\neg((r \leftrightarrow q) \to (p \leftrightarrow \neg r))$

64. $r \vee (p \vee (\neg r \& q)), \neg((r \& \neg p) \to (q \vee r))$ $\neg(\neg r \leftrightarrow \neg q)$

65. $((r \to p) \to r) \to q, ((q \to r) \to q) \to p$ $((p \to q) \to p) \to r$

Consider the following formulas: $p \vee q$, $p \& q$, $p \to q$, $p \leftrightarrow q$, $\neg p$, and $\neg q$. Where A and B are different formulas from among this collection, there are 30 possible statements of the form "A implies B." Of these, only five are true. Show that these are the five.

▸ 66. $p \& q$ implies $p \vee q$ 67. $p \& q$ implies $p \to q$

68. $p \& q$ implies $p \leftrightarrow q$ 69. $p \leftrightarrow q$ implies $p \to q$

70. $\neg p$ implies $p \to q$

Chrysippus held as a basic valid argument form $p \vee q$; p; $\therefore$ $\neg q$, which indicates that he did not think of $\vee$ as having the truth table we've associated with it. Subsequent logicians advanced a number of principles, some of which we would consider invalid in SL. Do any of these follow from $\neg(p \,\&\, q)$, a premise that, if added to $p \vee q$; p; $\therefore \neg q$, would produce a valid argument form?

71. $((p \to \neg q) \,\&\, p) \to \neg(p \to q)$ (Stoics)

▸ **72.** $((\neg p \to q) \,\&\, \neg q) \to \neg(p \to q)$ (Stoics)

73. $(\neg(p \,\&\, q) \,\&\, \neg p) \to q$ (Cicero)

74. $(p \to \neg q) \leftrightarrow \neg(p \to q)$ (Boethius)

75. $((p \to (q \to r)) \,\&\, (q \to \neg r)) \to \neg p$ (Boethius)

Notes

[1] The American logician Emil Post and the Austrian philosopher Ludwig Wittgenstein (1889–1951) developed the truth table method independently in 1921.

[2] Christopher Cherniak, *Minimal Rationality* (Cambridge, Mass.: Bradford Books, 1986), p. 89.

7

SEMANTIC TABLEAUX

The method of truth tables constitutes a decision procedure for the validity of both formulas and argument forms, for implication and equivalence, and for the satisfiability of formulas and sets of formulas. But truth tables can be very large: To evaluate an argument form containing six distinct sentence letters we need a table with 64 rows. To evaluate an argument form with ten distinct sentence letters we need a table with 1024 rows. Englishman Charles Dodgson (1832–1898), a mathematician, logician, and photographer, better known under his pen name *Lewis Carroll,* devised "Froggy's Problem." The puzzle is an argument with eighteen distinct letters, requiring a table of 262,144 rows. The table would contain over 31 million Ts and Fs. A person filling in a symbol per second and working nonstop would take almost a year to complete it! Furthermore, although truth tables serve as a decision procedure for sentential logic, they don't extend easily to other, more comprehensive logical systems. Once a symbolic language becomes powerful enough to symbolize the English words 'some' and 'all', the truth table method breaks down.

In this chapter, we'll develop another decision procedure for sentential logic that offers many practical advantages. It approximates intuitive ways of thinking about arguments more closely than truth tables do. It evaluates arguments more efficiently. And it extends readily to more comprehensive logical systems.

The method is that of *semantic tableaux:* treelike diagrams that serve as tests for validity, implication, contradiction, and so on.[1] Semantic tableaux are semantic because they concern truth and falsehood. They test for validity and other logical relations by searching for interpretations.

Tableaux are trees with labels. At the top of each is its *root;* at the bottom are its *tips,* or *leaves.* A path going directly from the root to a leaf is a *branch.*

Trees with more than one branch *split* where the paths diverge. A tableau has exactly as many branches as leaves. The portion of a tree above any splitting is its *trunk*.

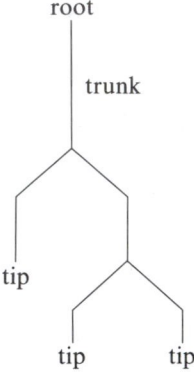

A *semantic tableau* is a tree with formulas. A formula may appear on either the left side or the right side of a branch. Any formula on the trunk of a tableau appears on every branch. Some formulas, furthermore, may be marked with a *dispatch mark,* ✓, to indicate that rules have been applied to them. The dispatch mark signals that we've used the information in the formula to extend the tableau; we can safely ignore dispatched formulas, because we've already taken account of the information they provide. Dispatched formulas are *dead;* undispatched formulas are *live.*

Branches that have the same formula appearing live on both sides are *closed.* Tableaux with all their branches closed are also *closed.*

> **DEFINITION**   A *tableau branch is closed* if and only if the same formula appears live on both sides of it. Otherwise, the branch is *open.*

> **DEFINITION**   A *tableau is closed* if and only if every branch of it is closed. Otherwise, it is *open.*

Closure is important because it signals the end of the tableau process.

> **DEFINITION**   A tableau is *finished* if and only if (a) it is closed, or (b) only atomic formulas are live on it.

In constructing a tableau, we continue until it is finished, that is, until all branches close or we run out of formulas to apply rules to, having only atomic formulas left.

All the tableaux in this text have special features. We'll construct them by using certain explicit rules. The tableaux will be finite. And they will be *binary* in the sense that, whenever they split, one path will divide only into two. These are examples of semantic tableaux:

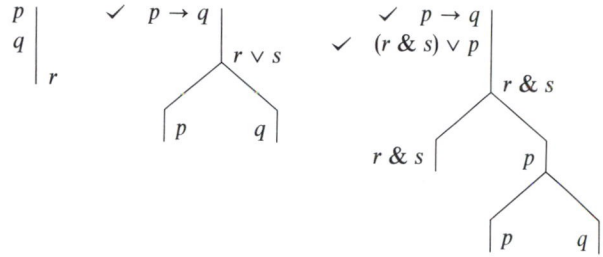

Notice that formulas never appear as tips or as other nodes on a branch; they are always on the left or right of a branch.

The left side of a tableau branch is the *truth* side; we assume that formulas on the left are true. The right side is the *falsehood* side. The leftmost tableau above, then, embodies the assumption that p and q are true, while r is false. It has only one branch, which is open. We can record the information on the tableau by writing

True: p, q False: r

The center tableau has two branches: the left branch has $p \rightarrow q$ on its left and $r \lor s$ and p on its right. The right branch has $p \rightarrow q$ and q on its left, and $r \lor s$ on its right. The formula $r \lor s$ is live, but not atomic, so this tableau is unfinished. Both branches are open. We can record the information on this tableau by writing

(Branch 1) True: False: $p, r \lor s$
(Branch 2) True: q False: $r \lor s$

The rightmost tableau has three branches. The formula $r \& s$, on the right, is live but not atomic, and so this tableau is unfinished. The left branch has $p \rightarrow q, (r \& s) \lor p$, and $r \& s$ on its left, and $r \& s$ on its right. This branch is closed; $r \& s$ appears on both sides. The center branch has $p \rightarrow q, (r \& s) \lor p$, and p on its left, and $r \& s$ and p on its right. The branch is also closed, because p appears on both sides. The right branch has $p \rightarrow q, (r \& s) \lor p, p$, and q on its left, and $r \& s$ on its right. So far, this branch is open. The tableau as a whole is therefore open. We can record the tableau information by writing

(Branch 1) True: $r \& s$ False: $r \& s$
(Branch 2) True: p False: $r \& s, p$
(Branch 3) True: p, q False: $r \& s$

Branches 1 and 2 are closed. Only branch 3, then, can specify an interpretation making $p \rightarrow q$ true, $(r \& s) \lor p$ true, and $r \& s$ false.

Problems

Begin by (a) recording the information on each branch of each of the following tableaux; then (b) say whether each branch, and each tableau, is open or closed; and (c) say whether each tableau is finished.

▶ **1.**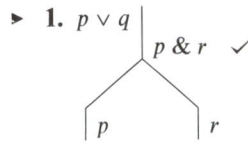

▶ **2.**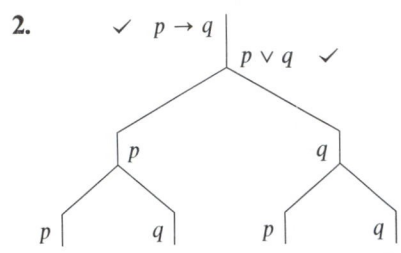

▶ **3.**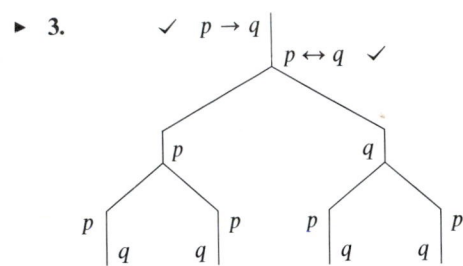

▶ **4.**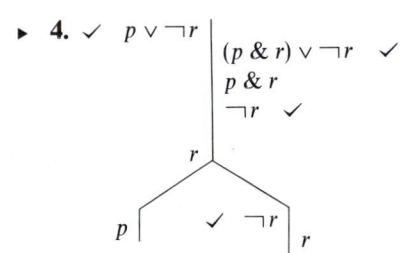

▶ **5.**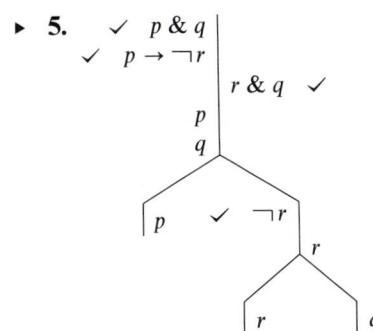

▸ **6.**

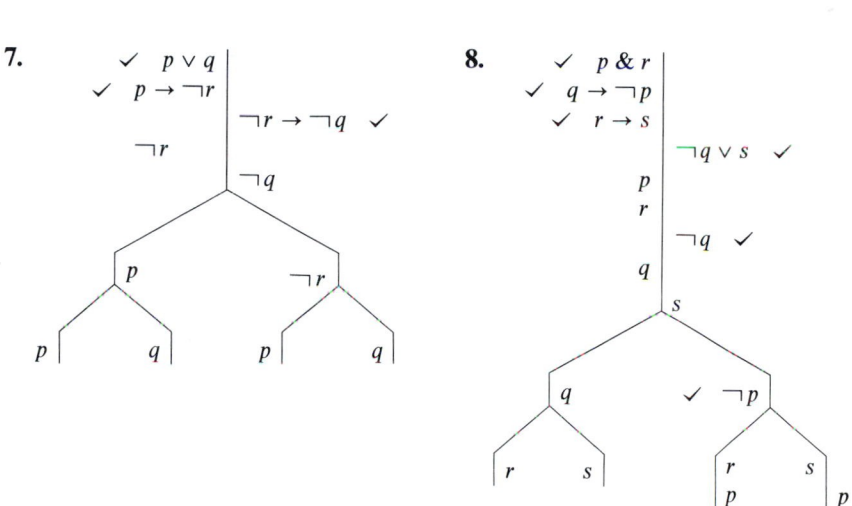

7.

8.

9.

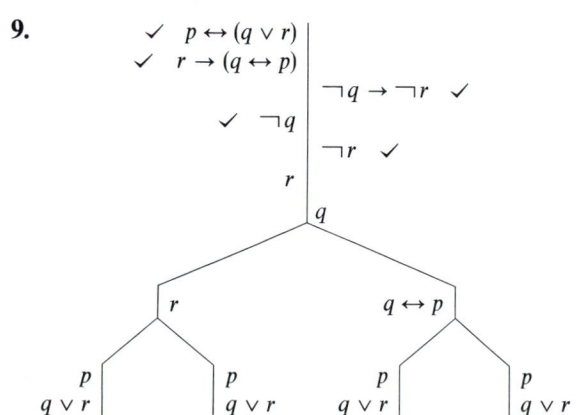

10.

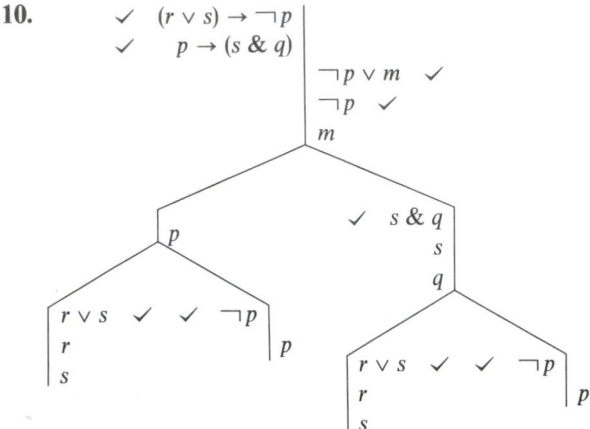

7.1 RULES FOR NEGATION, CONJUNCTION, AND DISJUNCTION

Before we develop rules for the connectives, we should note two aspects of the general strategy underlying the use of semantic tableaux. First, a tableau branch represents an interpretation or a possible circumstance. It corresponds to a row of a truth table. A tableau begins with a set of assumptions about the truth or falsehood of certain formulas. We represent these assumptions by placing formulas on the left or right side of the tableau. By way of the rules, we generate other formulas, which extend the branches. We use the tableau to build a picture of how the world could be, given the initial assumptions. We try, in other words, to describe some possible circumstances—that is, some interpretations—under which the initial assumptions would hold. When a branch closes—when the same formula appears live on both sides— our attempt ends in a contradiction; the rules have forced us to assign some formula both truth and falsehood. When all branches close, then every attempt ends in contradiction. When this happens, we can conclude that under no possible circumstances would the initial assumptions hold. If some branches remain open, they reveal interpretations that would meet the initial assumptions.

Second, once we place some formulas on the tableau, we try to generate pictures of possible circumstances by inferring the truth values of the sentence letters they contain. The strategy is the opposite of the one used in constructing truth tables. A truth table begins with a set of assignments of truth values to sentence letters; the table generates values for entire formulas. Truth tables follow a "bottom-up" strategy. The table assigns values to sentence letters, which appear at the bottom of trees charting formula construction, and gradually assigns values to more complex parts of the formula. The table ends with the formula's main connective. A tableau, in contrast, starts with an assignment of truth values to formulas and tries to find corresponding assignments to sentence letters. Semantic tableaux follow a "top-down" strategy. They begin with a value for an entire formula (or set of formulas) and, starting with the formula's main connective, assign values to parts of formulas until the tableau closes or reaches the bottom level of sentence letters.

Tableau rules come in pairs. Since we follow a "top-down" strategy, we are interested in decomposing formulas. We always begin, therefore, by applying a rule to the main connective of a formula. The formula could be on the left or right side of a branch. We need, then, two rules for each connective: one to handle formulas appearing on the left and having that connective as a main connective, the other to handle similar formulas on the right. In this section, we'll develop six rules: ¬L (Negation Left), ¬R (Negation Right), &L (Conjunction Left), &R (Conjunction Right), ∨L (Disjunction Left), and ∨R (Disjunction Right).

Negation

The rules reflect the definitions of the truth functions in Chapter 5. We can see this more clearly, in the case of negation, by expressing the tabular definition differently.

> $\neg \mathscr{A}$ is true on an interpretation if and only if (iff) $\mathscr{A}$ is false on that interpretation.

¬L (Negation Left)

This rule applies to formulas with a negation sign as main connective, appearing on the left side of a tableau branch. The left side represents truth. So, the question becomes: If a formula $\neg \mathscr{A}$ is true, what is the truth value of $\mathscr{A}$? The answer, clearly, is falsehood. So this rule takes the form:

$$\checkmark \ \neg \mathscr{A} \ \Big| \ \mathscr{A}$$

Since $\mathscr{A}$ must be false, we check $\neg \mathscr{A}$ and, extending the branch, write $\mathscr{A}$ on the right side of it. In our statement of the rule, what is in regular type must be present for the rule to be applied; applying the rule consists in writing what is in boldface. The checkmark beside the decomposed formula on the left signals that a rule has been applied to this formula. Formulas dispatched with a check may be ignored for the rest of the tableau.

¬R (Negation Right)

This rule applies to negated formulas appearing on the right side of a branch, which represents falsehood. If a formula $\neg \mathscr{A}$ is false, then $\mathscr{A}$ must be true, so we write $\mathscr{A}$ on the left side of the tableau branch:

$$\mathscr{A} \quad \Big| \quad \neg \mathscr{A} \quad \checkmark$$

Conjunction

Rules for conjunction are also derived from the definition of that truth function. We can express the tabular definition of Chapter 5 in a different form:

> $\mathscr{A}$ & $\mathscr{B}$ is true on an interpretation iff $\mathscr{A}$ is true on that interpretation, and $\mathscr{B}$ is true as well.

The rules mirror this definition directly.

&L (Conjunction Left)

This rule applies to formulas appearing on the left of a branch, with conjunctions as their main connectives. Under what circumstances is a formula $(\mathscr{A}$ & $\mathscr{B})$ true? Obviously, circumstances in which $\mathscr{A}$ and $\mathscr{B}$ are both true. So we can write both $\mathscr{A}$ and $\mathscr{B}$ on the left side of the branch:

$$\checkmark \quad \mathscr{A} \text{ \& } \mathscr{B} \quad \Big| \\ \mathscr{A} \\ \mathscr{B}$$

&R (Conjunction Right)

This rule applies to formulas appearing on the right of a branch, with conjunctions as their main connectives. Under what circumstances is $(\mathscr{A}$ & $\mathscr{B})$ false? There are two possibilities: Either $\mathscr{A}$ or $\mathscr{B}$ is false. To reflect the two options, we split the branch. On one, we reflect the possibility that $\mathscr{A}$ is false by writing $\mathscr{A}$ on the right. On the other, we write $\mathscr{B}$ on the right to reflect the possibility that $\mathscr{B}$ is false. The rule thus takes the form:

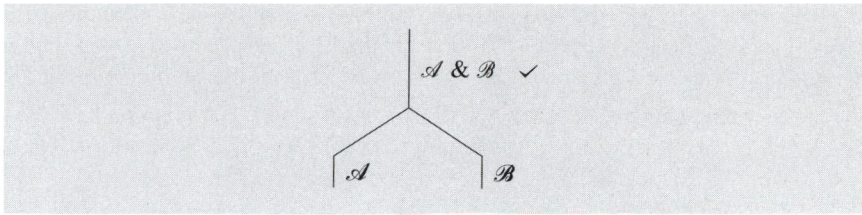

We don't need a third branch to reflect the possibility that both $\mathscr{A}$ and $\mathscr{B}$ might be false; these branches already take care of that possibility. Consider the left branch, which says that $\mathscr{A}$ is false. It says nothing about $\mathscr{B}$; $\mathscr{B}$ could be either true or false. This branch alone, then, really captures two possibilities, when we consider the truth value of $\mathscr{B}$. It reflects the possibility that $\mathscr{A}$ is false and $\mathscr{B}$ is true as well as the possibility that $\mathscr{A}$ and $\mathscr{B}$ are both false.

Disjunction

The rules for disjunction reflect its definition. We can express the content of our tabular definition in Chapter 5 in somewhat different form:

> $\mathscr{A} \vee \mathscr{B}$ is true on an interpretation iff either $\mathscr{A}$ is true on that interpretation, or $\mathscr{B}$ is true on it.

Given this formulation, it's easy to see what the rules should be.

∨L (Disjunction Left)

This rule, for formulas on the left with disjunctions as main connectives, tells when formulas of the form $(\mathscr{A} \vee \mathscr{B})$ are true: whenever either $\mathscr{A}$ or $\mathscr{B}$ is true. Again we must split the branch to reflect these two possibilities:

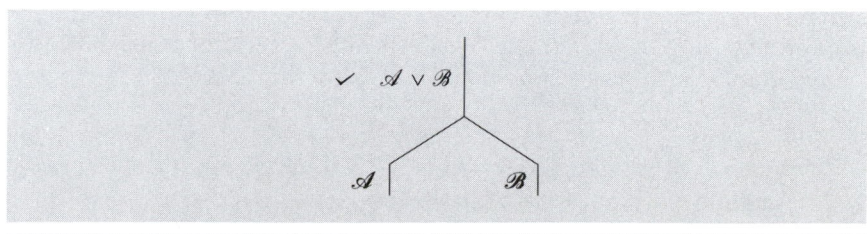

∨R (Disjunction Right)

This rule applies to formulas on the right with disjunctions as main connectives. When is $(\mathscr{A} \lor \mathscr{B})$ false? When both $\mathscr{A}$ and $\mathscr{B}$ are false. Dispatching the disjunction, we write both disjuncts on the right side of the branch:

$$
\begin{array}{l}
\mathscr{A} \lor \mathscr{B} \quad \checkmark \\
\mathscr{A} \\
\mathscr{B}
\end{array}
$$

Policies

In applying these rules, several questions arise. First, when a rule directs us to enter a formula on a given side of a branch, where do we put it? After all, there may already be formulas under the one to which we're applying the rule. We'll adopt this policy:

> 1. Always write the new formula at the bottom of the branch, underneath all the formulas already appearing there.

For example, we may want to apply &L to the second formula in the following tableau on the left. The rule says to enter two new formulas (the conjuncts of the conjunction) on the left. We write these below the other formulas, as in the tableau on the right.

$$
\begin{array}{c|c}
\begin{array}{l}
p \lor q \\
q \& r \\
r \to s
\end{array}
&
\begin{array}{l}
p \lor q \\
\checkmark \quad q \& r \\
r \to s \\
q \\
r
\end{array}
\end{array}
$$

Second, what happens when the tableau splits? Suppose we want to apply a rule to a formula above a split in the tableau. The rule says to enter a new formula on the branch. But which branch? What was one branch before is now two (or four, or eight, and so on). To capture the meaning of the formula on every branch on which it appears, we must make the required entries on every such branch. We'll adopt this policy:

> 2. When applying a rule to a formula, make the entries it calls for on every branch on which that formula appears.

Normally, this means that we must make the entries on each branch that extends the one on which the formula appeared. The progress on a tableau beginning with $(p \& q)$ on the right and $(q \vee r)$ on the left might take this form:

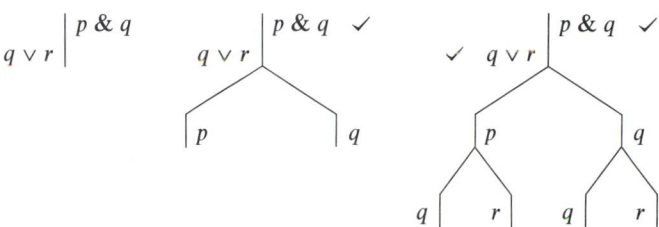

Applying the rule &R to $(p \& q)$ results in the middle tableau. Applying $\vee$L to $(q \vee r)$ results in the rightmost tableau. Notice that we had to make the entries—and perform the required split—on both branches that resulted from applying &R.

We'll follow two other policies in applying rules. The order of application of rules, within the bounds of sentential logic, makes no difference in results. But it does make a difference in efficiency. To create as few branches as possible, we'll adopt this policy:

> 3. Apply rules that don't require any splitting before those that do.

So, we'll apply $\neg$L, $\neg$R, &L, and $\vee$R before &R and $\vee$L.

In addition, closed branches merit no further interest, since they contain a contradiction. No matter what rules are applied to them, they will remain closed; they cannot depict any possible circumstance. We'll therefore adopt this policy:

> 4. Abandon branches as soon as they close, marking them with the notation 'Cl' to indicate why.

This, too, adds to efficiency.

To see why these rules are worth following, compare two tableaux for the following argument:

(1) The nations of Europe will not be able to coordinate policies unless they cede authority to some international body. Unless public opinion in Europe shifts markedly, they won't give up authority to such a

body. Economics, however, is a powerful persuader, and the European nations will manage to coordinate policy. Therefore, either public opinion in Europe will shift markedly, or the governments involved will simply have no choice.

Symbolizing (1) produces this argument form:

(2) $\neg p \vee q$
$r \vee \neg q$
$p \,\&\, s$
$\therefore r \vee t$

As we'll see later, to test an argument form for validity, we place its premise formulas on the left and its conclusion formula on the right. The tableaux begin with the same formulas and contain the same logical information, but one is much simpler than the other. (The numbers indicate in which order the rules were applied in constructing the tableaux.)

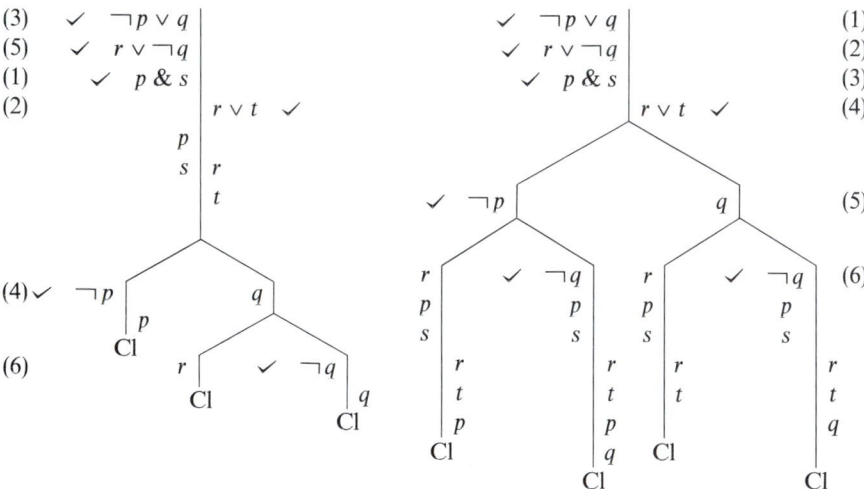

Both show that the argument form is valid. Although the more complicated tableau yields the same result as its more elegant cousin, it's far more cumbersome.

Problems

Write and apply the relevant rules to the tableau with these initial formula placements. Identify each branch as either open or closed.

▶ **1.** Right: $q \vee \neg q$.

▶ **2.** Left: $q \vee \neg q$.

▶ **3.** Left: $\neg q$. Right: $q \vee (\neg p \,\&\, q)$.

▶ **4.** Left: $q \vee (\neg p \,\&\, q)$. Right: $\neg q$.

▶ **5.** Left: q & p. Right: $s \lor q$.   ▶ **6.** Left: $s \lor q$. Right: q & p.

7. Left: $(q \lor s)$ & p. Right: $q \lor p$.

8. Left: $(q \lor p)$ & s. Right: $(q \lor s)$ & p.

9. Left: $q \lor p$. Right: $\neg(\neg q$ & $\neg p)$.

10. Left: q & $\neg s, r \lor \neg q$. Right: r & $\neg s$.

11. Left: q & $\neg s, r \lor s$. Right: $r \lor \neg q$.

▶ **12.** Left: $\neg(q$ & $s), s \lor p$. Right: q & p.

13. Left: $\neg(q$ & $s), q$ & p. Right: $s \lor p$.

14. Left: $\neg(\neg q \lor \neg s)$. Right: q & s.

15. Left: $\neg q \lor \neg s$. Right: $\neg(q$ & $s)$.

16. Left: $q, \neg q \lor p, (p$ & $r) \lor \neg p$. Right: $\neg q$.

17. Left: $q, \neg q \lor p, (p \lor r)$ & $\neg p$. Right: $\neg q$.

▶ **18.** Left: $(q$ & $\neg p) \lor (p$ & $\neg q), \neg q \lor r$. Right: $\neg(\neg p$ & $\neg r)$.

19. Left: $(q$ & $\neg p) \lor (p$ & $\neg q), \neg(\neg p$ & $\neg r)$. Right: $\neg q \lor r$.

20. Left: $(q$ & $\neg p) \lor (p$ & $\neg q), \neg q$ & r. Right: $\neg(\neg p$ & $\neg r) \lor q$.

7.2 Rules for the Conditional and Biconditional

So far we've developed rules for three of our five connectives. Rules for the conditional and biconditional are similar, though slightly less intuitive. Like the rules for negation, conjunction, and disjunction, they come in pairs. Also, like those rules, they mirror the definitions of the conditional and biconditional truth functions. We can express the definition of the conditional in this form:

> $\mathscr{A} \to \mathscr{B}$ is true on an interpretation iff either $\mathscr{A}$ is false on that interpretation or $\mathscr{B}$ is true on it.

→L (Conditional Left)

This rule applies to conditional formulas appearing on the left of a branch. Under what circumstances is a conditional formula true? The truth table definition of the conditional indicates that $(\mathscr{A} \to \mathscr{B})$ is false only when $\mathscr{A}$ is true and $\mathscr{B}$ is false. So $(\mathscr{A} \to \mathscr{B})$ is true whenever $\mathscr{A}$ is false or $\mathscr{B}$ is true. These two possibilities force us to split the branch.

$$\checkmark \ (\mathscr{A} \rightarrow \mathscr{B})$$

$$\mathscr{A} \qquad \mathscr{B}$$

→R (Conditional Right)

This rule applies to conditionals on the right. These formulas, according to the tableau branch, are false. $(\mathscr{A} \rightarrow \mathscr{B})$ is false just in case $\mathscr{A}$ is true and $\mathscr{B}$ is false, as we've seen, so the rule asks us to enter $\mathscr{A}$ on the left and $\mathscr{B}$ on the right:

$$\mathscr{A} \ \Big| \ \begin{array}{c} (\mathscr{A} \rightarrow \mathscr{B}) \ \checkmark \\ \mathscr{B} \end{array}$$

The rules for the biconditional also reflect its definition:

$\mathscr{A} \leftrightarrow \mathscr{B}$ is true on an interpretation iff $\mathscr{A}$ and $\mathscr{B}$ agree in truth value on that interpretation.

↔L (Biconditional Left)

This rule applies to biconditionals on the left side of a branch. If $(\mathscr{A} \leftrightarrow \mathscr{B})$ is true, $\mathscr{A}$ and $\mathscr{B}$ must have the same truth value. Both must be true, or both must be false. Since there are two possibilities, the rule splits the branch:

$$\checkmark \ (\mathscr{A} \leftrightarrow \mathscr{B})$$

$$\begin{array}{ccc} \mathscr{A} & & \mathscr{A} \\ \mathscr{B} & & \mathscr{B} \end{array}$$

↔R (Biconditional Right)

This rule applies to biconditionals on the right. If $(\mathscr{A} \leftrightarrow \mathscr{B})$ is false, then $\mathscr{A}$ and $\mathscr{B}$ must have opposite truth values. That is, either $\mathscr{A}$ is true and $\mathscr{B}$ is false, or $\mathscr{B}$ is true and $\mathscr{A}$ is false. Again, the rule forces splitting to reflect these two possibilities.

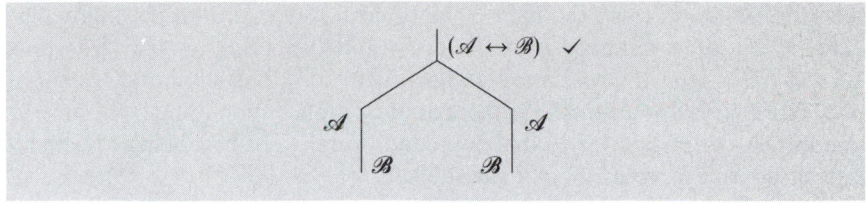

To see how the rules function, consider two examples. Suppose that

(3) Rocky will win the fight only if he keeps moving.

is true, but that

(4) Rocky will win the fight if and only if he keeps moving.

is false. In the first tableau, we assume that $p \rightarrow q$ is true but that $p \leftrightarrow q$ is false. We decompose these formulas to find out what these mean about the truth values of p and q alone. The order in which we apply the rules makes no difference, even to efficiency, since both conditional left and biconditional right split the tableau. We end up, therefore, with four branches: two closed and two open.

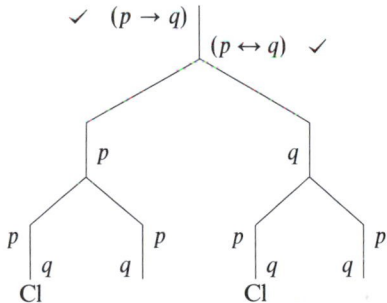

Starting with the initial conditions that $(p \rightarrow q)$ is true but $(p \leftrightarrow q)$ is false, this tableau considers a variety of possibilities for assignments to p and q. The tableau, in effect, is trying to describe a circumstance in which these formulas would have this particular combination of truth values. The two branches that close don't describe possible circumstances that would make $(p \rightarrow q)$ true and $(p \leftrightarrow q)$ false, but the open branches do. As it happens, the open branches describe the same interpretation: one in which q is true and p false. To see this, look at each open branch, and record the atomic formulas appearing on each side:

Left open branch: True: q False: p, p
Right open branch: True: q, q False: p

The duplication of appearances makes no difference. These branches, therefore, describe the same interpretation. Both branches describe a circumstance in which q is true and p is false. (In which, that is, Rocky keeps moving but nevertheless doesn't win the fight.) The tableau, then, tells us the following. There is an interpretation of the letters p and q making $(p \to q)$ true and $(p \leftrightarrow q)$ false. That interpretation assigns truth to q and falsehood to p.

Here is a second example: Is there an interpretation making $(p \leftrightarrow q) \leftrightarrow p$ true but $(p \to q)$ false? Here, applying conditional right first helps efficiency, since it doesn't force us to split the tableau:

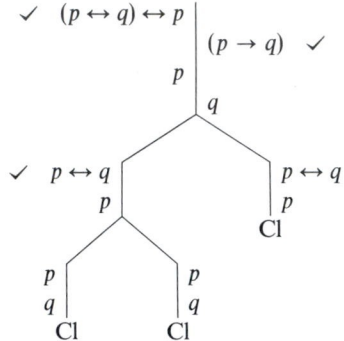

Every branch is closed, so the tableau itself is closed. Thus, there is no interpretation meeting the initial conditions; no interpretation makes $(p \leftrightarrow q) \leftrightarrow p$ true but $(p \to q)$ false. No matter which way the tableau turns in trying to describe a possible circumstance meeting these conditions, it runs into a contradiction.

A special problem arises when a branch doesn't contain every sentence letter involved in the tableau. Suppose that we want to evaluate the argument

(5) The theft will shock the art world unless the painting is returned unharmed, and quickly. If it does shock the art world, the painting will be returned unharmed. Thus, the painting will be returned unharmed, and museums will review their security measures carefully.

Symbolizing, we obtain the argument form

(6) $p \lor (q \& s)$
$p \to q$
$\therefore q \& r$

We need to know whether any interpretation makes $p \lor (q \& s)$ and $p \to q$ true but $q \& r$ false. We can place the first two formulas on the left, and the last on the right, and apply rules:

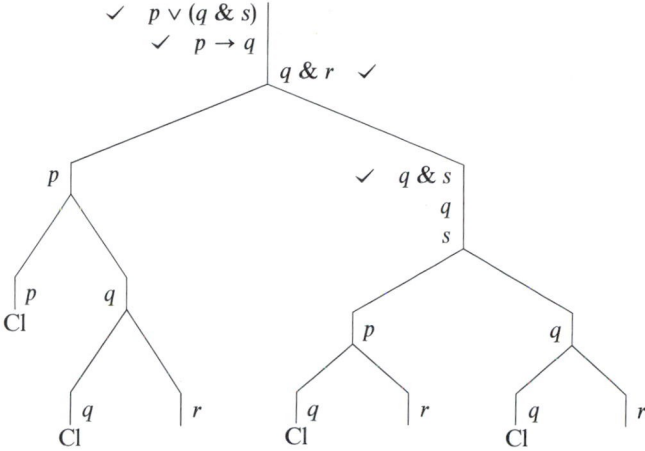

There are three open branches, signaling that there is such an interpretation. On the leftmost open branch, p and q both appear on the left, indicating that both p and q must be true. Moreover, r appears on the right, and so it must be false. But the branch says nothing about s. Thus, any interpretation making p and q true and r false meets the initial conditions, no matter what truth value is assigned to s. In terms of the English argument: the theft could shock the art world, and the painting could be returned unharmed, without museums carefully reviewing their security measures. The argument is invalid; the conclusion does not follow, whether the painting is returned quickly or not. The leftmost branch thus reveals two interpretations making $p \lor (q \& s)$ and $p \to q$ true but $q \& r$ false. One makes p true, q true, r false, and s true. The other makes p true, q true, r false, and s false.

Problems

Use tableaux to determine whether any interpretation meets these sets of conditions. If such an interpretation does exist, specify it.

▶ **1.** True: $\neg(p \to r)$. False: $\neg p \to \neg r$.

▶ **2.** True: $\neg(p \leftrightarrow r)$. False: $\neg p \leftrightarrow r$.

▶ **3.** True: $\neg p \leftrightarrow r$. False: $\neg(p \leftrightarrow r)$.

▶ **4.** True: $\neg p \leftrightarrow \neg r$. False: $\neg(p \leftrightarrow r)$.

▶ **5.** True: $p \to r$. False: $p \leftrightarrow (p \& r)$.

▶ **6.** True: $p \leftrightarrow (p \& r)$. False: $p \to r$.

7. True: $p \lor r$. False: $\neg p \to r$.

8. True: $r \lor q$, $p \to \neg r$. False: $p \to q$.

9. True: $r \vee q$, $p \to q$. False: $p \to \neg r$.

10. True: $p \vee (r \to q)$. False: $r \to (p \vee q)$.

11. True: $r \to (p \vee q)$. False: $p \vee (r \to q)$.

▸ **12.** True: $(p \vee r) \to r$, $\neg(p \,\&\, r)$. False: $\neg p$.

13. True: $p \to (r \to q)$, $\neg((p \,\&\, \neg q) \to \neg r)$.

14. True: $p \vee (r \to q)$, $\neg((p \vee \neg q) \leftrightarrow \neg r)$.

15. True: $p \leftrightarrow (r \to q)$, $\neg((p \leftrightarrow \neg q) \,\&\, \neg r)$.

16. False: $((p \to r) \to p) \to p$.

17. False: $(\neg(p \to r) \to p) \to p$.

▸ **18.** True: $(p \to r) \to \neg q$. False: $(p \vee q) \to r$.

19. True: $(p \vee r) \to \neg q$. False: $(p \leftrightarrow q) \to r$.

20. True: $\neg((p \leftrightarrow \neg r) \to q)$. False: $(p \leftrightarrow q) \to q$.

21. True: $\neg((p \to \neg r) \leftrightarrow q)$. False: $(p \to q) \leftrightarrow q$.

22. True: $p \vee (r \vee (q \to p))$. False: $\neg p \vee (r \to q)$.

23. True: $p \vee (\neg r \to (\neg q \to p))$. False: $\neg p \to (\neg r \to \neg q)$.

▸ **24.** True: $\neg(p \to (r \vee q))$. False: $p \leftrightarrow (r \,\&\, \neg q)$.

25. True: $\neg(p \leftrightarrow (r \vee q))$. False: $p \leftrightarrow (r \to \neg q)$.

26. True: $(p \leftrightarrow r) \leftrightarrow (p \leftrightarrow q)$. False: $r \leftrightarrow q$.

27. True: $r \leftrightarrow q$. False: $(p \to q) \leftrightarrow (p \to r)$.

28. True: $q \to (p \to r)$. False: $p \to (r \to q)$.

29. True: $q \leftrightarrow (p \to r)$. False: $p \leftrightarrow (r \to q)$.

▸ **30.** True: $p \to q$. False: $(r \to p) \to (r \to q)$.

31. True: $p \leftrightarrow q$. False: $(r \leftrightarrow p) \to (r \leftrightarrow q)$.

32. True: $(r \to p) \to (r \to q)$. False: $p \to q$.

33. True: $(\neg r \to \neg p) \to (\neg r \to \neg q)$. False: $\neg p \to \neg q$.

34. True: $(p \to r) \vee (p \to q)$. False: $p \to (r \vee (r \to q))$.

7.3 DECISION PROCEDURES

A semantic tableau is a treelike search for an interpretation meeting certain initial conditions. Closed branches represent contradictions; they correspond to blind alleys in the search. A branch having the same formula on both sides indicates that the formula is both true and false, an absurdity. If all branches of a tableau close, then, no matter what choices we might make in our search, we reach contradictions. In a closed tableaux, all paths lead to absurdity. A closed tableau hence demonstrates that the initial conditions can't be met. No interpretation will produce the truth value assignment that began the tableau.

The usefulness of tableaux in searching for interpretations makes them ideal for evaluating argument forms. An argument form is valid, after all, just in case there is no interpretation making its premise formulas true but its conclusion formula false. This suggests an easy method: Search for such an interpretation. If the tableau produces one, then the argument form is invalid; some truth value assignment does indeed make the premise formulas all true but the conclusion formula false. If the tableau closes, however, there's no such interpretation, and so the argument form is valid.

Tableaux force us to think backward about argument form validity. We begin by assuming that an argument form is invalid and see what develops from this assumption. If the tableau closes, we have reached contradictions; the argument form is valid. If the tableau remains open, we have reached an interpretation showing that the argument form is invalid.

Since the validity of argument forms is a kind of implication, furthermore, the same test is a decision procedure for implication. To see whether a set of formulas implies a given formula, assume that every formula in the set is true but that the given formula is false. The tableau will then search for an interpretation with this effect. If there is one, a branch will remain open and specify it. If not, the tableau will close.

The tableau test for validity (and implication), then, is this. Suppose that your argument form has premise formulas $\mathscr{A}_1, \ldots, \mathscr{A}_n$ and conclusion formula $\mathscr{B}$. We list the premise formulas on the left, and place the conclusion formula on the right. If the tableau closes, the argument form is valid:

Test for Argument Form Validity (and Implication)

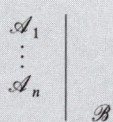

Closes: Valid (Argument Form); Implied (Implication)
Open: Invalid (Argument Form); Not Implied (Implication)

For example, consider the argument

(7) If Nancy passes the course, she'll get her degree. If she doesn't, she'll quit school. She won't quit school. So, Nancy will get her degree.

and the corresponding argument form

(8) $p \rightarrow q$
$\quad \neg p \rightarrow r$
$\quad \neg r$
$\quad \therefore q$

We begin by writing the premise formulas on the left and the conclusion formula on the right. At this point, we have three choices, but only one—using $\neg$L—doesn't force us to split the tableau. So, we begin by applying $\neg$L and then move to $\rightarrow$L. It makes no difference which conditional we take first. Suppose we apply the rule to the first premise to obtain this tableau:

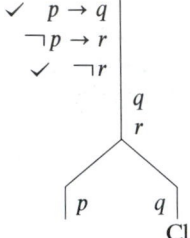

The right branch has already closed; q appears on both sides. (It doesn't matter that q appears on different levels of the tableau. What does matter is that it appears on both sides of the same branch.) We can finish the tableau by applying conditional left again, to the second premise, and then applying $\neg$R to the leftmost branch, to get this tableau:

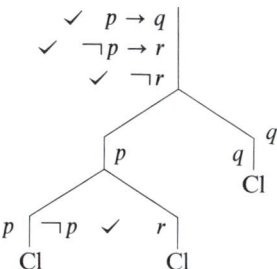

All three branches close, so the tableau closes. Our assumption that the premise formulas were true but the conclusion formula false thus leads to absurdity at every turn; the argument form is valid.

Since semantic tableaux constitute a decision procedure for implication, they also amount to a test for equivalence. Equivalence, after all, is just implication in two directions. Equivalent formulas have the same truth value on every interpretation of them. This means that there should be no interpretation making one true but the other false. To test for this, we can construct two tableaux. Say that the two formulas are $\mathcal{A}$ and $\mathcal{B}$. One tableau starts with the assumption that $\mathcal{A}$ is true and $\mathcal{B}$ is false; the other, with the assumption that $\mathcal{B}$ is true and $\mathcal{A}$ is false. If both close, no interpretations assign the formulas different truth values. If at least one tableau remains open, however, it specifies an interpretation making one formula true and the other false.

The test, then, is this:

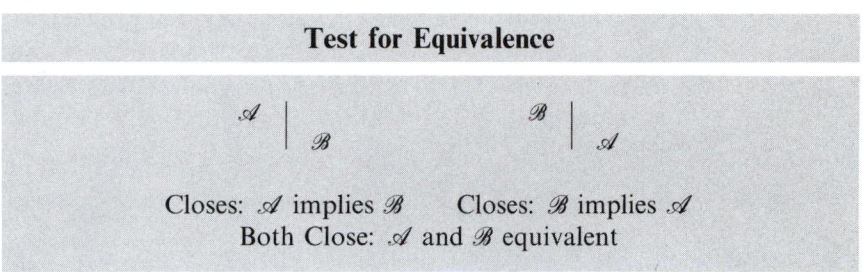

Test for Equivalence

Closes: $\mathcal{A}$ implies $\mathcal{B}$ Closes: $\mathcal{B}$ implies $\mathcal{A}$
Both Close: $\mathcal{A}$ and $\mathcal{B}$ equivalent

For example, we can use tableaux to show that

(9) Bartering can help to reduce taxes, but it's best hidden from the IRS.

is equivalent to

(10) It's true neither that bartering can't reduce taxes nor that it shouldn't be hidden from the IRS.

by showing that $p \,\&\, q$ is equivalent to $\neg(\neg p \vee \neg q)$.

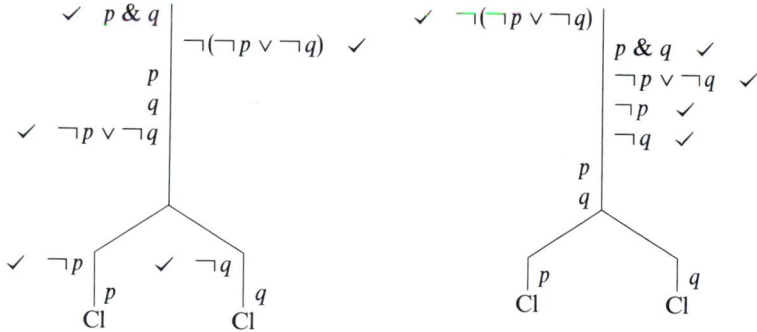

Tableaux also offer an elegant test for the logical truth of formulas. A tautology is true on every interpretation of it. No assignment of truth values makes a tautology false. To determine whether a formula $\mathcal{A}$ is a tautology, therefore, we can search for an interpretation making it false. If the search succeeds—if, that is, the tableau we construct remains open—then we have found an interpretation that makes the formula false. If the search fails, the tableau closes, and the formula is a tautology.

Test for Logical Truth

$$| \; \mathscr{A}$$

Closes: Tautology
Open: Contingent or Contradictory

For example, this tableau shows that $((p \to q) \to p) \to p$ ("Peirce's law") is a tautology:

Similarly, tableaux present a method for testing formulas for contradiction or satisfiability. A satisfiable formula has an interpretation that makes it true; a contradictory formula doesn't. To test for contradiction, then, simply search for an interpretation that makes the formula in question true. An open branch specifies such an interpretation, establishing satisfiability; a closed tableau establishes contradiction.

Test for Contradiction or Satisfiability

$$\mathscr{A} \; |$$

Closes: Contradictory
Open: Satisfiable

Together, these tests allow us to classify any formula as tautologous, contingent, or contradictory. One test does not always determine the status of a formula: if it is contingent, then testing it for validity will result in an open tableau. This means that the formula has an interpretation making it false, and so it must be either contradictory or contingent. To determine which, we need the other test.

For example, consider the formula $\neg(p \to \neg p)$. To test it for logical truth, we would place this formula on the right of a tableau. We would then apply ¬R, →L, and ¬R (in that order) to produce:

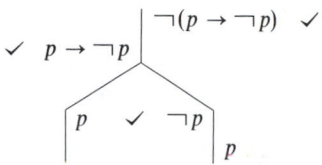

Both branches are open, with p on the right. So, the formula does have an interpretation that makes it false, namely, that of assigning falsehood to p. But, to find out whether $\neg(p \rightarrow \neg p)$ is contradictory or contingent, we need to apply the other test, beginning a tableau with $\neg(p \rightarrow \neg p)$ on the left:

$$
\begin{array}{c|c}
\checkmark \;\; \neg(p \rightarrow \neg p) & \\
& p \rightarrow \neg p \;\; \checkmark \\
p & \\
& \neg p \;\;\;\;\; \checkmark \\
p &
\end{array}
$$

This tableau, too, is open, so the formula is satisfiable. Since it is neither contradictory nor tautologous, it must be contingent. Indeed, the tableau provides an interpretation making the formula true: that of assigning truth to p. Surprisingly, then, the formula $\neg(p \rightarrow \neg p)$ always has the same truth value as p; $\neg(p \rightarrow \neg p)$ and p are equivalent.

Semantic tableaux, then, provide a simple and efficient way of testing argument forms for validity; formulas for validity or contradictoriness; pairs of formulas for equivalence; and sets of formulas, paired with formulas, for implication. Tableaux always terminate after a finite number of steps. Their construction, furthermore, requires no ingenuity, but the mechanical following of rules. Tableaux are thus decision procedures for the logical properties and relations we've discussed. As later chapters will demonstrate, the tableau technique extends readily to more complex and comprehensive logical languages.

Problems

By using tableaux, determine whether the formula on the left implies the formula on the right.

► **1.** p $\neg\neg p$ ► **2.** $\neg\neg p$ p

► **3.** p $p \vee q$ ► **4.** p $p \,\&\, q$

► **5.** $p \vee q$ q ► **6.** $p \,\&\, q$ p

    7. p $p \rightarrow q$ **8.** q $p \rightarrow q$

    9. $p \rightarrow q$ p **10.** $p \rightarrow q$ q

11. $p \mathbin{\&} q$ $\qquad$ $p \vee q$ $\qquad\qquad$ ▶ **12.** $p \mathbin{\&} q$ $\qquad$ $p \rightarrow q$

13. $p \mathbin{\&} q$ $\qquad$ $p \leftrightarrow q$ $\qquad\qquad$ **14.** $p \vee q$ $\qquad$ $\neg p \rightarrow q$

15. $p \vee q$ $\qquad$ $p \leftrightarrow q$ $\qquad\qquad$ **16.** $p \vee q$ $\qquad$ $p \mathbin{\&} q$

17. $p \rightarrow q$ $\qquad$ $p \vee q$ $\qquad\qquad$ ▶ **18.** $p \rightarrow q$ $\qquad$ $\neg p \vee q$

19. $p \leftrightarrow q$ $\qquad$ $p \rightarrow q$ $\qquad\qquad$ **20.** $p \leftrightarrow q$ $\qquad$ $\neg p \vee \neg q$

21. $\neg(p \mathbin{\&} q)$ $\qquad$ $\neg p$ $\qquad\qquad$ **22.** $\neg(p \rightarrow q)$ $\qquad$ $\neg p$

23. $\neg(p \rightarrow q)$ $\qquad$ $\neg q$ $\qquad\qquad$ ▶ **24.** $\neg(p \mathbin{\&} q)$ $\qquad$ $\neg p \mathbin{\&} \neg q$

25. $\neg(p \mathbin{\&} q)$ $\qquad$ $\neg p \vee \neg q$ $\qquad\qquad$ **26.** $\neg(p \vee q)$ $\qquad$ $\neg p \vee \neg q$

27. $\neg(p \vee q)$ $\qquad$ $\neg p \mathbin{\&} \neg q$ $\qquad\qquad$ **28.** $\neg(p \vee q)$ $\qquad$ $p \leftrightarrow q$

29. $\neg(p \mathbin{\&} q)$ $\qquad$ $\neg p \leftrightarrow q$ $\qquad\qquad$ ▶ **30.** $\neg(p \rightarrow q)$ $\qquad$ $\neg p \rightarrow \neg q$

31. $\neg(p \leftrightarrow q)$ $\qquad$ $\neg(p \rightarrow q)$ $\qquad\qquad$ **32.** $\neg(p \leftrightarrow q)$ $\qquad$ $\neg p \leftrightarrow \neg q$

33. $\neg(p \leftrightarrow q)$ $\qquad$ $p \leftrightarrow \neg q$ $\qquad\qquad$ **34.** $p \rightarrow (q \rightarrow r)$ $\quad$ $q \rightarrow (p \rightarrow r)$

35. $p \rightarrow (q \rightarrow r)$ $\quad$ $(p \mathbin{\&} q) \rightarrow r$ $\qquad$ ▶ **36.** $p \rightarrow (q \vee r)$ $\quad$ $(p \rightarrow q) \vee (p \rightarrow r)$

37. $p \vee (q \mathbin{\&} r)$ $\quad$ $(p \vee q) \mathbin{\&} (p \vee r)$ $\quad$ **38.** $p \mathbin{\&} (q \vee r)$ $\quad$ $(p \mathbin{\&} q) \vee (p \mathbin{\&} r)$

Use tableaux to determine whether these argument forms are valid in SL.

39. p; q; $\therefore p \mathbin{\&} q$ $\qquad\qquad\qquad$ **40.** p; $p \rightarrow r$; $\therefore r$

41. p; $p \rightarrow q$; $\therefore p \mathbin{\&} q$ $\qquad\qquad$ ▶ **42.** $p \rightarrow q$; $\neg q$; $\therefore \neg p$

43. $p \rightarrow q$; $p \rightarrow \neg q$; $\therefore \neg p$ $\qquad\qquad$ **44.** $\neg p \rightarrow \neg q$; $p \rightarrow \neg q$; $\therefore \neg q$

45. $p \rightarrow q$; $\neg p \rightarrow q$; $\therefore \neg \neg q$ $\qquad\qquad$ **46.** $p \rightarrow q$; $\neg p \rightarrow q$; $\neg q$; $\therefore r$

47. $\neg p \vee q$; $\neg q$; $\neg p \leftrightarrow r$; $\therefore \neg r \leftrightarrow q$

▶ **48.** $\neg p \vee q$; $\neg q$; $\neg p \rightarrow r$; $\therefore \neg r \rightarrow q$

49. $(p \vee \neg q) \rightarrow r$; $p \leftrightarrow \neg r$; $\therefore \neg((q \mathbin{\&} r) \vee p)$

50. $(p \mathbin{\&} \neg q) \rightarrow r$; $p \leftrightarrow \neg r$; $\therefore (q \mathbin{\&} r) \vee p$

51. $(p \vee \neg q) \rightarrow r$; $p \leftrightarrow \neg r$; $\therefore (q \mathbin{\&} \neg r) \mathbin{\&} p$

52. $(\neg q \mathbin{\&} r) \rightarrow \neg p$; $p \rightarrow r$; $\therefore \neg(q \leftrightarrow (\neg r \mathbin{\&} p))$

53. $(\neg q \vee r) \leftrightarrow \neg p$; $p \leftrightarrow \neg r$; $\therefore \neg p \mathbin{\&} (\neg q \rightarrow r)$

54. $r \rightarrow (p \leftrightarrow s)$; $\neg q \vee (\neg r \leftrightarrow \neg p)$; $\neg((s \mathbin{\&} t) \leftrightarrow (p \rightarrow r))$; $\therefore t \mathbin{\&} \neg q^*$

55. $p \rightarrow (q \rightarrow (r \mathbin{\&} \neg p))$; $\neg p \rightarrow \neg(s \vee k)$; $(m \mathbin{\&} t) \leftrightarrow q$; $\therefore s \rightarrow (m \rightarrow \neg t)^*$

56. $(p \leftrightarrow \neg q) \leftrightarrow \neg r$; $r \vee (p \mathbin{\&} s)$; $s \rightarrow (p \mathbin{\&} (q \mathbin{\&} t))$; $\therefore (s \mathbin{\&} k) \rightarrow (r \mathbin{\&} q)^*$

57. $\neg(p \vee q) \rightarrow r$; $(s \vee t) \rightarrow (m \mathbin{\&} k)$; $\neg r \leftrightarrow s$; $\therefore (s \vee n) \rightarrow ((p \mathbin{\&} m) \vee (k \mathbin{\&} q))^*$

Symbolize these arguments in SL, and evaluate the resulting argument forms for validity. If the argument form is invalid, describe the interpretations under which the premises would be true but the conclusion false.

58. If Nathan publishes several more papers, he'll get tenure. He won't get tenure. Hence, he won't publish several more papers.

59. If Nathan publishes several more papers, he'll get tenure. He won't publish several more papers. Thus, he won't get tenure.

▶ **60.** It's not true that, if Nathan publishes several more papers, he'll get tenure. So, Nathan won't get tenure.

61. If 4 is odd, then 2 is odd. But 2 is even. Since nothing can be both odd and even, it's false that 4 is odd.

62. If 4 is odd, then 2 is odd. If 2 is odd, every even number is odd. But, if so, then 100 is odd. 4 isn't odd; neither, therefore, is 100.

63. If God is all powerful, then He can make a rock so heavy that He can't lift it. But if God is omnipotent, then He can lift any rock that He can make. Therefore, God isn't all powerful.

64. If Geraldine signs the contract, she'll lose money. If she loses money, we'll lose money too. Geraldine will sign the contract. So, we'll lose money.

65. If the United States doesn't agree to arms limitation talks, tensions with the Soviets will remain high. But even if the U.S. agrees to such talks, tensions between the U.S.S.R. and the U.S. will remain high. Thus, tensions between the United States and the Soviets will remain high.

▶ **66.** If God is all powerful, He is able to prevent evil. If He is all good, He is willing to prevent evil. Evil does not exist unless God is either unwilling or unable to prevent it. If God exists, He is both all good and all powerful. Therefore, if evil exists, God doesn't.

67. God is all powerful only if He is able to prevent evil. He is all good only if He is willing to prevent evil. If evil exists, then God must be either unwilling or unable to prevent it. Therefore, either there is no evil, or God is not both all good and all powerful.

68. Interest rates will rise unless Congress enacts a tax increase. But rates will rise even if Congress raises taxes. If interest rates rise, the unemployment level will rise. Either unemployment won't increase, or the budget deficit will. It follows that there will be an increase in the budget deficit.

69. If nobody objects, the council will adopt Holly's plan. Somebody will object if those affected by the plan believe it harms their interests. Thus, the council will adopt Holly's plan if those it affects don't think it will harm their interests.

70. If Kelly refuses the operation, she'll never regain full use of her arm. But if Kelly doesn't regain full use of the arm, she'll regret not having the operation. So, either Kelly will agree to the operation, or she'll regret not doing so.

71. If Pittsburgh beats Cleveland, then either Cincinnati or Houston will make the playoffs. If Houston wins, then Houston will make it; but, if Cleveland beats Pittsburgh, Cleveland will be in the playoffs. So, either Houston or Cleveland will be in the playoffs.

▶ 72. If you want to maximize your job opportunities after graduation, you'll major in business. But you'll succeed in the top ranks of industry only if you can write effectively; you'll be able to write effectively, however, only if you major in the liberal arts. Hence, you'll succeed in the top ranks of industry only if you don't want to maximize your job opportunities after graduation.

73. Money either serves you or dominates you; never both. If it serves you, and you handle it wisely, then it can help you to attain happiness. If it dominates you, you will gain much of it but never be satisfied with your lot. Therefore, you'll be satisfied with your lot if and only if money can't help you attain happiness.

74. There will be scorpions in the house this week if there's any building going on in the neighborhood. There will be building only if the depression in the housing market ends. If there are scorpions in the house, the cats will kill them and bring them to me as trophies. Therefore, if the housing depression ends, my cats will bring me scorpions as trophies.

75. My cat will not sing opera unless all the lights are out. If I am very insistent, then my cat will sing opera; and if I either turn all the lights out or howl at the moon, you can be sure that I am very insistent indeed. I always howl at the moon if I am not very insistent. Therefore, my lights are never turned on, my cat is singing opera, and I am perpetually very insistent.

76. If the president retaliates against Libya with military force, the public will be ambivalent. But if Libya directs terrorist attacks toward Americans on American soil, then the American public will not be ambivalent at all. So, Libya will not engage in terrorism against Americans on U.S. soil unless the president doesn't retaliate militarily.

77. If mainstream churches continue to lose membership, then they'll have less influence on even the religious affairs of the nation. But these churches will lose influence if they appear outdated to the public at large.

Mainstream churches don't appear outdated; so, they'll continue to lose membership only if they do nothing to halt their current decline.

▶ **78.** If people don't conserve energy, or tolerate much greater despoiling of the environment, utilities will have no choice but to rely on nuclear power. They'll avoid relying on atomic energy, moreover, just in case it's prohibitively expensive and risky. Nuclear power will remain expensive. If it also remains risky, therefore, the environment will suffer unless people conserve energy.

79. If happiness can't be defined, there's no way to measure it. If we can't measure happiness, we can say whether someone is happy only if we take that person's word for it. Determining whether someone is happy is a necessary condition for testing the psychological effects of jobs of various kinds. So, we can't test the psychological effects of various jobs if happiness can't be defined.

80. Georgia Tech won't make the finals unless they beat Villanova and St. John's loses. St. John's will make the finals if they win or if both Georgia Tech and Maryland lose. If Maryland wins, either Georgia Tech or Indiana will make the finals. Hence, if Villanova and Maryland win, either St. John's or Indiana will make the finals.

81. If John attends the meeting, he'll be able to convince at least a few people to vote against the development proposal. If we can get most of the neighborhood to sign a petition, then the developers will change their proposal. Either we'll get most of the neighborhood to sign a petition, or John will attend the meeting. So, John will be able to convince at least a few people to vote against the development proposal, unless the developers change their proposal.

82. If Congress erects trade barriers and grants further subsidies to American farmers, then other countries will retaliate. If that happens, however, the economy will slow down; if there is a slowdown, then Congress won't give farmers additional subsidies unless it finds new sources of revenue. If Congress doesn't erect trade barriers, it won't give farmers added subsidies, but at least other countries won't retaliate. Therefore, unless Congress finds new revenue sources, farmers will get no additional subsidies from Congress.

83. If changes in baseball over the past decade continue, then power pitching will gradually drive out power hitting. This will happen just in case managers select players with speed over players with home run power. But they won't unless runs become very difficult to score. Finally, if power pitching doesn't drive out power hitting, power hitting will drive out power pitching. Consequently, either the changes in baseball over the past decade will continue, or power hitting will drive out power pitching.

► **84.** If advertisers continue to use Saturday morning cartoons to peddle toys by creating shows about them, pressure will build for regulation, and ratings will decline if parents understand what's going on. If ratings decline, then advertisers will stop using cartoons to sell toys by having toys as their main characters. If pressure builds for regulation, then either advertisers will stop, or Congress will act. If Congress acts, then advertisers will stop. Hence, if advertisers continue, parents won't know what's going on, children will become obsessed with material goods, and American culture will irrevocably decline.

85. If the Soviet economy is restructured, decision making will have to be decentralized, and bureaucracies in charge of economic planning will have to become smaller and less powerful. The bureaucracies, of course, won't become smaller if the bureaucrats can help it. Decision making will be decentralized only if the party hierarchy is willing to cede power to a wide group it can't easily control. Unless the bureaucracies become less powerful, decision making will remain centralized, and central planning will continue to dominate the economy. Hence, the Soviet economy won't be restructured if central planning continues to dominate the economy.

86. If the earth has been visited recently by extraterrestrial beings, then the government will have kept the information silent although the visits occurred. If some reported UFO sightings have been authentic, then the earth has been visited recently by extraterrestrials. But if those sightings have been authentic, then our current understanding of our place in the universe is seriously mistaken. Therefore, either our understanding of our place in the universe is seriously mistaken, or, even if there have been recent extraterrestrial visits to the earth and the government has kept information about them silent, no reported UFO sightings are authentic.

87. If Jill has to pay more than $400 to repair her car, she'll be better off getting a new one. But if Jill has to pay more than $400 to get her car fixed, somebody will be cheating her. If someone cheats Jill, she'll be better off with a new car. But, even if Jill will be better off with a new car, she might not buy one. So, unless it's true that, if someone cheats her, Jill might not buy a new car, Jill will be better off with a new car although she won't have to pay more than $400 to repair her old one.

88. The central administration won't increase the department's budget if it doesn't improve its performance. But the department won't perform better if the administration doesn't increase its budget allocation. If the department fails to improve, then its chairman will be replaced. If the central administration refuses to increase the department's budget, it will begin to lose some good people. If the department's chairman is replaced, however, it won't lose any good people. So, the central administration will increase the department's budget if the chairman is replaced.

89. If the party maintains its current economic policy, there will be a flight of capital to other countries. But the party won't change its economic policy if it tightens its control over the economy. If the party maintains its policy, and capital flees to other countries, then it will tighten its grip on the economy. If the party maintains its current policy, however, the nation will have to pay large amounts of foreign debt in hard currency, and this it won't do. So, the party won't tighten its grip on the economy.

Use semantic tableaux to solve these problems.

90. A brutal ax murder has been committed and is being investigated by none other than Sherlock Holmes. Holmes feels that he has evidence to support each of these contentions concerning the case: (a) If Mr. Perry committed the murder, Ms. Jackson is innocent. (b) Ms. Jackson is guilty unless the butler's testimony hasn't been delivered with a clear conscience. (c) If Mr. Perry committed the murder and Ms. Jackson is innocent, then the butler's testimony hasn't been delivered with a clear conscience. (d) If the butler isn't guilty of the murder, then neither is Mr. Perry. Holmes, stumped by the situation, calls you in as a logical consultant. To get your share of the reward, you must answer these questions: (i) Is any one of Holmes's contentions implied by the other three? (ii) Does Holmes's theory imply anything about the guilt or innocence of Mr. Perry? (iii) Does Holmes's theory imply anything about the guilt or innocence of Ms. Jackson?

91. You have been diagnosed as having a rare psychological disorder manifesting itself in intense bouts of fear and loathing whenever you are faced with a logic problem. Your psychiatrist tells you that (a) if you don't undergo psychoanalysis, you won't recover. But you know, given his rates, that (b) if you do undergo psychoanalysis, you'll be poverty stricken. Unknown to both of you, the reasoning involved in undergoing psychoanalytic treatment will make your condition worse; if you improve at all, it will be for reasons unrelated to your treatment. So (c) if you undergo psychoanalysis, then you will recover only if you improve spontaneously. Do these facts imply that you will recover only if you improve spontaneously? That you will recover only if you become poverty stricken? That if you become poverty stricken, you'll recover?

92. Roger, a hapless accounting major, works on a takehome final exam in a course on U.S. tax law. He attempts to analyze a problem concerning the tax liability of a corporation involved in overseas shipping. Some of the fleet counts as American for tax purposes, but some doesn't. Roger thinks that the definition of 'American vessel' goes something like this: "A ship is an American vessel if and only if (a) it is either numbered or registered in the United States, or (b), if it is neither numbered nor registered in the U.S. and is not registered in any foreign country, then its crew members are all U.S. citizens or all employees of corporations based in the U.S." Unfortunately for Roger, this is not the right definition. Show that Roger's version implies that, if a ship is registered in a foreign country, it's an American vessel.*

These puzzles concern a land of knights and knaves. Knights always say true things; knaves always utter falsehoods. You are a traveler in this strange land and must try to identify those you meet as knights or knaves.[2] You encounter two people, Punch and Judy, one or both of whom speak to you. What can you deduce in each case, using semantic tableaux, about whether they are knights or knaves? (Hint: a person is a knight if and only if what he or she says is true.)

93. *Punch:* I'm a knight.

94. *Judy:* Punch is a knight.

95. *Punch:* Judy's a knave.

▸ **96.** *Judy:* Either I'm a knight, or I'm not.

97. *Punch:* I'm a knight, and, then again, I'm not.

98. *Judy:* If Punch is a knave, so am I.

99. *Judy:* Neither of us is a knight.

100. *Punch:* We're not both knights.

101. *Punch:* I'm a knave if and only if Judy's a knight.

▸ **102.** *Judy:* Punch is a knight, and I'm a knave.

103. *Punch:* I'm a knave unless Judy's a knight.

104. *Punch:* If either of us is a knave, I am.

105. *Punch:* Judy's a knave.
   Judy: We're not both knaves.

106. *Punch:* I'm a knight if and only if Judy's a knave.
   Judy: Punch is a knave.

107. *Punch:* Judy's a knight.
   Judy: At least one of us is a knave.

▸ **108.** *Punch:* I'm a knight if and only if Judy is.
   Judy: Punch is a knight.

109. *Punch:* If I'm a knave, we both are.
   Judy: Either he's a knight, or I'm a knave.

110. *Punch:* Judy's a knight if and only if her sister is.
   Judy: Unfortunately, my sister's a knave.

111. *Punch:* Judy and her brother are both knights.
   Judy: Well, I'm a knight, but my brother isn't.

At this point, you meet three people in the land of knights and knaves. What can you deduce about their status?

112. *Curly:* Larry's a knave.
   Moe: Either Curly or Larry is a knave.
   Larry: If I'm a knave, they are too.

113. *Curly:* We're all knights.
   Moe: I'm a knight, but Larry's a knave.
   Larry: The other two are both knaves.

▶ **114.** *Curly:* Moe's a knight.
   Moe: We're all knaves.
   Larry: Curly, Moe, and their cousins are all knaves.

115. *Curly:* We're not all knaves.
   Moe: Curly is.
   Larry: If Curly is, Moe is too.

116. *Curly:* If Moe's a knight, Larry is too.
   Moe: Larry's a knave if Curly is.
   Larry: Curly and Moe aren't both knaves.

117. *Curly:* If any of us are knights, Larry is.
   Moe: Larry's a knave.
   Larry: I'm a knave if and only if Moe is.

118. *Curly:* If Moe's a knave, Larry is too.
   Moe: If Larry's a knave, Curly is too.
   Larry: If Moe's a knight, we all are.

Notes

[1] 'Tableaux' is the plural of 'tableau'. (Both are pronounced tab-LOH.) The Dutch logician E. W. Beth and the Finnish-American logician Jaakko Hintikka independently developed this technique in 1955 by simplifying a logical system that the German logician Gerhard Gentzen (1909–1945) devised in the 1930s. See Beth, "Semantic Entailment and Formal Derivability," in Hintikka (ed.) *Philosophy of Mathematics* (Oxford: Oxford University Press, 1969), pp. 9–41; Hintikka, "Form and Content in Quantification Theory," *Acta Philosophica Fennica* 8 (1955): 7–55; Gentzen, "An Investigation into Logical Deduction," in M. Szabo (ed.), *The Collected Papers of Gerhard Gentzen* (Amsterdam: North-Holland, 1969). The method of this chapter is very close to Gentzen's original system, although Gentzen thought of the technique as purely syntactic.

[2] These examples are based on puzzles developed by Raymond Smullyan in *What Is the Name of this Book?* (Englewood Cliffs, N. J.: Prentice-Hall, 1978).

8

DEDUCTION

Truth tables and semantic tableaux can evaluate arguments clearly and efficiently. But they say almost nothing about how to *construct* arguments. In this chapter, we'll develop a system designed to simulate people's construction of arguments. The deduction system is *natural* in the sense that it is meant to reflect the way people construct arguments in legal, scientific, philosophical, and mathematical contexts.

8.1 PROOFS

A *natural deduction system* is a set of rules: specifically, *rules of inference* that allow us to deduce formulas from other formulas.[1] Central to the concept of a natural deduction system is the idea of *proof*. Proofs are extended arguments. There are two kinds of proofs. *Hypothetical* proofs begin with *assumptions* (or *hypotheses*). The assumptions act as premises; the proof's conclusion follows from them. Such proofs show that the conclusion is true, not unconditionally, but if the assumptions are true. These proofs are the most direct way of showing the validity of an argument form. *Categorical* proofs, by contrast, contain no assumptions. They show that their conclusions are true outright. Categorical proofs are the most direct way to show that a certain formula is a tautology.

A *proof* in a natural deduction system is a series of *lines*. On each line appears a formula. Each formula in a proof (a) is an assumption or (b) derives, by a rule of inference, from formulas on previously established lines. In the system presented in this chapter, the last line of a proof is its *conclusion;* the proof *proves* that formula *from* the assumptions. Conclusions proved from no assumptions at all are *theorems* of the system.

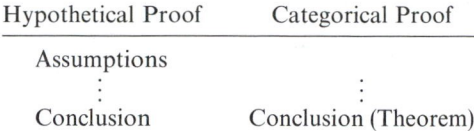

Hypothetical Proof	Categorical Proof
Assumptions	
⋮	⋮
Conclusion	Conclusion (Theorem)

Rules of Inference

All rules of inference in this chapter allow us to derive formulas of certain kinds in a proof if other formulas of certain kinds occupy lines already established there. For example, our system has a rule letting us write $\mathscr{A}$ or $\mathscr{B}$, whichever we choose, if we've already established $\mathscr{A}$ & $\mathscr{B}$.

Our deduction system has at least two rules for most connectives. One rule indicates how to derive a formula with a certain connective as main connective. In short, it specifies how to *introduce* formulas of that form into proofs. Another rule indicates how to use information encoded in a formula having that connective as main connective. That is, it specifies how to *exploit* formulas of that kind in proofs. Other rules may show how to exploit and introduce the connective in one step. Still other rules show how to define some connectives in terms of others. The basic rules of the system, therefore, will fall into four groups: *introduction, exploitation, combination,* and *definition.*

Proof Format

Here is an example of a simple hypothetical proof:

1. p A
2. $p \to q$ A
3. q MP, 1, 2

All proofs are series of lines structured in certain ways. As this example shows, proofs have three columns. The middle column consists of a sequence of formulas. The left column numbers these formulas; the right column provides justifications for them. Thus, if a formula derives from previously established formulas by a rule of inference, the right column specifies what rule of inference and what earlier lines were used. If the formula is an assumption, the right column so indicates. The 'A' in the justification column on lines 1 and 2 signals that p and $p \to q$ are assumptions. The 'MP, 1, 2' in line 3 indicates that q follows from the formulas on lines 1 and 2 by the rule MP (*modus ponens,* one of the most important rules of our system). The example is a successful, completed proof of q from the assumptions p and $p \to q$.

Proof Lines

Number	Formula	Justification

A hypothetical proof begins with assumptions and proceeds to its conclusion. A successful, completed proof of $\mathscr{B}$ from the assumptions $\mathscr{A}_1, \ldots, \mathscr{A}_n$ thus looks like this:

Proof

$$1. \qquad \mathscr{A}_1 \qquad A$$
$$\vdots$$
$$n. \qquad \mathscr{A}_n \qquad A$$
$$\vdots$$
$$n + m. \quad \mathscr{B}$$

Obtaining $\mathscr{B}$ completes the proof.

Central to the idea of a hypothetical proof is the *assumption rule,* which allows a proof to begin with a list of assumptions. At any point in a proof, we may write assumptions. Any conclusion we derive, of course, may depend on these assumptions. Therefore, when we use natural deduction to demonstrate the validity of an argument form, we'll begin by writing its premise formulas as assumptions and make no other assumptions during the proof.

Assumption

$$n. \ \mathscr{A} \qquad A$$

To prove q hypothetically from $p \to q$ and $p \vee q$, for example, we write the premises, hoping to obtain the conclusion:

1. $p \to q$ A
2. $p \vee q$ A
$\vdots$
n. q

In every hypothetical proof, we list the assumptions of the proof at the beginning.

8.2 CONJUNCTION AND NEGATION RULES

Conjunction

The rule of *simplification* shows how we can use the information encoded in a conjunction. It reflects the reasoning manifested in the argument:

  (1) Jonas dropped out of college and found work as a gravedigger.
     ∴ Jonas dropped out of college.

What follows from the truth of a conjunction? The truth of both conjuncts. If $\mathscr{A}$ & $\mathscr{B}$ is true, both $\mathscr{A}$ and $\mathscr{B}$ must be true. The rule allowing us to exploit conjunctions thus takes two forms:

Simplification (S)		

n.	$\mathscr{A}$ & $\mathscr{B}$	
n + m.	$\mathscr{A}$	S, n
n.	$\mathscr{A}$ & $\mathscr{B}$	
n + m.	$\mathscr{B}$	S, n

Hereafter, we'll abbreviate rules having two forms by using parentheses. We can write S as

n.	$\mathscr{A}$ & $\mathscr{B}$	
n + m.	$\mathscr{A}$ (or $\mathscr{B}$)	S, n

This rule asserts that, from a conjunction, we can derive each conjunct. The conjuncts may be written on any later line. When applying this rule, we write a conjunct together with the explanation that the line comes by application of S—simplification—to the formula on line n. (The line just above the formula that results from applying this rule separates the formula deduced from its required antecedents; it won't appear in actual proofs.)

To apply S to a formula, the conjunction must be its main connective. We can move from p & $(q \rightarrow r)$ to $q \rightarrow r$, but not from $(p$ & $q) \rightarrow r$ to $p \rightarrow r$. The latter inference isn't valid; the simplification rule doesn't, and shouldn't, allow it.

To demonstrate the use of the simplification rule, let's show the validity of the following argument:

(2) Fran and Gloria both attended, but Hilary did not introduce them.
∴ Gloria attended.

To apply this rule, we assume $(p$ & $q)$ & $\neg r$ and prove q. We begin with an assumption.

1. $(p$ & $q)$ & $\neg r$ A

Now, we can exploit the conjunction to derive a smaller conjunction, $(p$ & $q)$. Note that we can't derive q directly: The connective to which we apply the rule must be the main connective of the formula.

```
1. (p & q) & ¬r    A
2. (p & q)         S, 1
```

The right column tells us that the formula on line 2 comes from line 1 by applying S. We can easily apply that same rule again to obtain q, thereby finishing the proof.

```
1. (p & q) & ¬r    A
2. (p & q)         S, 1
3. q               S, 2
```

The rule of *conjunction* indicates how to introduce conjunctions. It reflects the form of the reasoning in this argument:

(3) Jack knows where the money is.
    Kendall knows where the money is.
    ∴ Jack and Kendall both know where the money is.

It's a very simple rule; to prove a conjunction, prove each conjunct. If $\mathscr{A}$ is true, and $\mathscr{B}$ is true also, then $\mathscr{A}$ & $\mathscr{B}$ is true. So, from the two formulas $\mathscr{A}$ and $\mathscr{B}$ we can derive $\mathscr{A}$ & $\mathscr{B}$:

Conjunction (C)

```
n. 𝒜
m. ℬ
p. 𝒜 & ℬ      C, n, m
```

The right column indicates that $\mathscr{A}$ & $\mathscr{B}$ comes from conjoining the formulas on lines n and m. The order in which $\mathscr{A}$ and $\mathscr{B}$ occur in the proof does not matter. We could just as easily have concluded $\mathscr{B}$ & $\mathscr{A}$.

To see how we might use C in a proof, let's show that p & q allows us to derive q & p. Again, we begin by using the assumption rule:

```
1. p & q    A
```

To show q & p, we need to separate the two conjuncts. We can derive them separately, using S, and put them back together in the other order, using C:

```
1. p & q    A
2. p        S, 1
3. q        S, 1
4. q & p    C, 3, 2
```

The conjunction rule allows us to conjoin two formulas on previous lines. Like most of our rules, it operates on entire formulas. From $p \rightarrow q$ and r, we can derive $(p \rightarrow q)$ & r, but not p & r or q & r.

An additional rule allows us to introduce conjunctions in a special context: within the consequent of a conditional. It reflects the form of the argument:

(4) If the president vetoes, then the House will vote to override.
 If the president vetoes, then the Senate will uphold the veto.
 ∴ If the president vetoes, then the House will vote to override, but the Senate will uphold the veto.

If two conditionals have the same antecedent, we can deduce another conditional, whose consequent conjoins their consequents.

Consequent Conjunction (CC)

$$n. \quad \mathcal{A} \rightarrow \mathcal{B}$$
$$m. \quad \mathcal{A} \rightarrow \mathcal{C}$$
$$p. \quad \mathcal{A} \rightarrow (\mathcal{B} \mathbin{\&} \mathcal{C}) \qquad \text{CC, n, m}$$

We can use this rule to demonstrate the validity of

(5) Percy will testify only if Quincy agrees to testify.
 Although there is little danger, if Percy testifies, then Smythe or Triton will refuse to testify.
 ∴ If Percy testifies, Quincy will agree to testify, and, moreover, Smythe or Triton will refuse to testify.

which we can symbolize as $p \rightarrow q$; $r \mathbin{\&} (p \rightarrow (\neg s \vee \neg t))$;
∴ $p \rightarrow (q \mathbin{\&} (\neg s \vee \neg t))$.

1. $p \rightarrow q$ — A
2. $r \mathbin{\&} (p \rightarrow (\neg s \vee \neg t))$ — A
3. $p \rightarrow (\neg s \vee \neg t)$ — S, 2
4. $p \rightarrow (q \mathbin{\&} (\neg s \vee \neg t))$ — CC, 1, 3

Notice that although this rule allows us to conjoin the consequents of conditionals having the same antecedent, it too applies only to entire formulas. Those formulas must have conditionals as their main connectives.

Negation

One negation rule acts as both an introduction and an exploitation rule. It always introduces or exploits two negation symbols at once. We'll therefore refer to it as DN, the *double negation* rule. This rule asserts that we can add or delete two consecutive negation signs without affecting truth values.

Double Negation (DN)

n. $\mathcal{A}$
n + p. $\neg\,\neg\mathcal{A}$ DN, n

n. $\neg\,\neg\mathcal{A}$
n + p. $\mathcal{A}$ DN, n

We can express this rule more concisely by writing a double line between $\mathcal{A}$ and $\neg\,\neg\mathcal{A}$ to indicate that the rule *inverts*—that we can go from what is above the lines to what is below them, or from what is below the lines to what is above them. The rule works in both directions.

n. $\overline{\overline{\mathcal{A}}}$ DN, m

m. $\neg\,\neg\mathcal{A}$ DN, n

To illustrate this rule, let's show that we can derive $\neg\,\neg p\, \&\, \neg q$ from $\neg\,\neg(p\, \&\, \neg\,\neg\,\neg q)$.

1. $\neg\,\neg(p\, \&\, \neg\,\neg\,\neg q)$ A
2. $p\, \&\, \neg\,\neg\,\neg q$ DN, 1
3. p S, 2
4. $\neg\,\neg p$ DN, 3
5. $\neg\,\neg\,\neg q$ S, 2
6. $\neg q$ DN, 5
7. $\neg\,\neg p\, \&\, \neg q$ C, 4, 6

Replacement

In general, we can apply rules only to formulas with the appropriate main connectives. For instance, we can apply S only to conjunctions—formulas with '&' as their main connectives. Invertible rules, however, have a special and important feature: They apply to parts of formulas—more precisely, subformulas—as well as to entire formulas. Invertible rules are justified by the equivalence of the formulas they link. If, in any formula, we replace a subformula with an equivalent subformula, we obtain a formula equivalent to the original. If p and $\neg\,\neg p$ are equivalent, for instance, then so are $p \to q$ and $\neg\,\neg p \to q$. In addition to our derivable rules, therefore, we'll adopt a principle of *Replacement*, allowing us to apply invertible rules to subformulas as well as entire formulas. So we can use DN to move from $\neg\,\neg p$ to p, but also from $\neg\,\neg p \to q$ to $p \to q$.

We can therefore streamline the previous proof in this way:

1. $\neg\neg(p \& \neg\neg\neg q)$ A
2. $p \& \neg\neg\neg q$ DN, 1
3. $p \& \neg q$ DN, 2
4. $\neg\neg p \& \neg q$ DN, 3

Problems

Show that the conclusion of each argument form is provable from the premises.

▶ **1.** $p \& q; \therefore q$ ▶ **2.** $p \& (q \& r); \therefore r$

▶ **3.** $p \& \neg\neg q; \therefore q$ ▶ **4.** $\neg\neg p \& \neg q; \therefore \neg\neg\neg q \& p$

▶ **5.** $p \& \neg q; \neg r \& s; \therefore s \& p$ ▶ **6.** $(p \& q) \& r; \therefore p \& (q \& r)$

7. $p \& \neg q; \neg r \& s; \therefore s \& p$

8. $\neg p \& \neg q; r \& \neg s; \therefore \neg\neg r \& \neg s$

9. $\neg p \& (\neg q \vee r); q; \therefore \neg p \& \neg\neg q$

10. $\neg p \rightarrow \neg q; \neg p \rightarrow q; \therefore \neg p \rightarrow (q \& \neg q)$

11. $p \& (q \& (r \rightarrow s)); \therefore (p \& q) \& (r \rightarrow s)$

▶ **12.** $p \rightarrow q; (p \rightarrow \neg r) \& s; \therefore \neg\neg p \rightarrow (q \& \neg r)$

13. $p \& \neg q; r \& (s \vee \neg t); \therefore \neg q \& (\neg\neg s \vee \neg t)$

14. $(p \leftrightarrow \neg r) \& (q \& \neg s); \therefore \neg s \& (q \& (p \leftrightarrow \neg r))$

15. $p; q \rightarrow \neg p; \neg\neg q \rightarrow r; \therefore (q \rightarrow (r \& \neg p)) \& \neg\neg p$

16. $p; q \rightarrow r; \neg r; \neg\neg q \rightarrow s; \therefore (q \rightarrow (r \& s)) \& (\neg r \& p)$

17. $p \rightarrow (\neg\neg q \& r); \neg\neg q \vee \neg s; p \rightarrow s; \therefore (p \rightarrow (s \& (q \& r))) \& (q \vee \neg s)$

▶ **18.** $\neg q \rightarrow r; \neg(p \& q) \& \neg p; \neg q \rightarrow (r \rightarrow s); \therefore \neg p \& (\neg q \rightarrow ((r \rightarrow s) \& r))$

19. $\neg\neg p \& (q \rightarrow \neg r); q \& (p \rightarrow t); (q \rightarrow s) \& t; \therefore (p \& q) \& (q \rightarrow (\neg r \& s))$

20. $(\neg p \rightarrow q) \& (q \rightarrow \neg\neg r); (\neg p \rightarrow s) \& (q \rightarrow \neg t);$
    $\therefore (\neg p \rightarrow (q \& s)) \& (q \rightarrow (r \& \neg t))$

8.3 CONDITIONAL AND BICONDITIONAL RULES

The Conditional

Some axiom systems have only one rule of inference: the rule for exploiting conditionals. Called *modus ponens,* it sanctions the inference from p and

$p \rightarrow q$ to q. It stands behind arguments such as

(6) If Socrates is human, then Socrates is mortal.
Socrates is human.
∴ Socrates is mortal.

Modus Ponens (MP)

> n. $\mathscr{A} \rightarrow \mathscr{B}$
> m. $\underline{\mathscr{A}}$
> p. $\mathscr{B}$ MP, n, m

This rule, for example, lets us show that

(7) If Wendy understands the situation, she'll tread carefully.
She does understand, and everything will be alright.
∴ Wendy will tread carefully, and everything will be alright.

is valid, because it lets us derive $p \,\&\, q$ from the premises $r \rightarrow q$ and $r \,\&\, p$.

1. $r \rightarrow q$ A
2. $r \,\&\, p$ A
3. r S, 2
4. p S, 2
5. q MP, 1, 3
6. $p \,\&\, q$ C, 4, 5

A rule allowing us to introduce conditionals has an extremely simple form. Every formula of the form $\mathscr{A} \rightarrow \mathscr{A}$ is a tautology. English sentences such as

(8) a. If you're wrong, you're wrong.
     b. If this is Tuesday, this is Tuesday.

are logical truths. At any point in an argument, therefore, we may write down a conditional whose antecedent is the same as its consequent:

Self Implication (SI)

> n. $\mathscr{A} \rightarrow \mathscr{A}$ SI

This rule is unusual, since it has no premises, and refers to no previous lines. No matter what has happened earlier in the proof, $\mathscr{A} \rightarrow \mathscr{A}$ must be true. Therefore, we can write such a formula at any point.

We can use self-implication to show that the formula $\neg \neg p \rightarrow p$ is a tautology.

1. $p \rightarrow p$ SI
2. $\neg \neg p \rightarrow p$ DN, 1

This is a categorical proof; it has no assumptions. It shows that $\neg \neg p \rightarrow p$ is a theorem of our system.

The Biconditional

When may we introduce a biconditional into a proof? What does it take to establish the truth of a biconditional? A biconditional is so-called because it amounts to two conditionals. Mathematicians, for example, often prove biconditionals in two steps. They prove the "left-to-right" and "right-to-left" directions separately. In other words, they prove two conditionals. To exploit biconditionals, we can simply reverse this procedure. If we've established a biconditional, we can deduce either or both conditionals. Our rule for the biconditional serves as an introduction and exploitation rule, equating a biconditional with two conditionals:

Biconditional (B)

     n. $\mathscr{A} \leftrightarrow \mathscr{B}$

n + m. $(\mathscr{A} \rightarrow \mathscr{B})\ \&\ (\mathscr{B} \rightarrow \mathscr{A})$ B, n

---

This rule inverts. It applies to subformulas as well as formulas. We can use the biconditional rule to show that (9)a and (9)b imply (9)c:

(9) a. Ed will run if and only if he thinks he can win.
     b. Ed thinks he can win.
     c. Ed will run.

by showing that $p \leftrightarrow q$ and q imply p.

1. $p \leftrightarrow q$ A
2. q A
3. $(p \rightarrow q)\ \&\ (q \rightarrow p)$ B, 1
4. $q \rightarrow p$ S, 3
5. p MP, 4, 2

Problems

Show that the conclusions of these argument forms are provable from their premises.

▶ **1.** $p \rightarrow q;\ p;\ \therefore q$ ▶ **2.** $p \leftrightarrow q;\ p;\ \therefore q$

▶ **3.** $p \leftrightarrow q;\ q;\ \therefore p$ ▶ **4.** $(p \rightarrow p) \rightarrow p;\ \therefore p$

▶ **5.** $p \leftrightarrow \neg q; \neg \neg p; \therefore \neg q$ ▶ **6.** $p \rightarrow q; p \& r; \therefore r \& q$

7. $p \rightarrow q; \therefore p \rightarrow (p \& q)$ **8.** $p \rightarrow q; p \rightarrow r; p; \therefore q \& r$

9. $\neg p \leftrightarrow q; \neg \neg q \& \neg \neg s; \therefore \neg p$

10. $p \leftrightarrow q; p \rightarrow r; \therefore p \rightarrow (q \& r)$

11. $p \rightarrow q; p \& r; \therefore p \& (q \& r)$

▶ **12.** $\neg q \& (r \rightarrow p); \neg \neg r; \therefore p \& \neg q$

13. $p \rightarrow (q \rightarrow \neg r); q \& r; p; \therefore r \& \neg r$

14. $p \& \neg t; p \rightarrow (r \& q); r \rightarrow s; \therefore s \& q$

15. $\neg p \rightarrow (q \& (r \rightarrow \neg s)); \neg p \& r; \therefore \neg s \& q$

16. $p \& q; \neg \neg p \rightarrow r; q \rightarrow s; p \rightarrow t; \therefore (r \& t) \& s$

17. $(p \rightarrow (p \& q)) \rightarrow (r \rightarrow s); r \& m; p \leftrightarrow q; \therefore s \& m$

▶ **18.** $\neg p \leftrightarrow \neg q; \neg q \rightarrow \neg r; \neg p \rightarrow \neg s; \neg p \& t; \therefore \neg s \& \neg r$

19. $p \rightarrow (q \rightarrow \neg r); \neg \neg q \rightarrow \neg p; r \& p; \therefore q \rightarrow (\neg p \& \neg r)$

20. $p \leftrightarrow q; p \leftrightarrow r; r \rightarrow q; \therefore (p \rightarrow (q \& r)) \& (r \rightarrow (p \& q))$

21. $(p \rightarrow (q \& p)) \leftrightarrow (p \leftrightarrow r); p \rightarrow q; r \& s; \therefore p \& (q \& (r \& s))$

22. $s \rightarrow (q \& t); \neg m \rightarrow p; (p \rightarrow r) \& \neg k; p \& s; (q \& r) \rightarrow \neg m;$
$\therefore \neg m \& (q \& r)$

23. $q \& k; (s \& \neg r) \rightarrow \neg p; (q \rightarrow \neg t) \leftrightarrow \neg p; q \rightarrow s; (q \& s) \rightarrow \neg r;$
$\therefore k \& \neg t$

Show that these formulas are theorems of our natural deduction system.

▶ **24.** $p \leftrightarrow \neg \neg p$ **25.** $(p \& q) \leftrightarrow (p \& q)$

Show that these arguments are valid by using deduction.

26. If the Democrats obstruct the president's legislative program, the market will lose confidence. The Democrats will obstruct that program only if they can gain politically by so doing. The Democrats will obstruct the president's legislative initiatives. Therefore, the Democrats will gain politically, but the market will lose confidence.

27. Assuming that the coach doesn't throw Matt off the team, we'll do well in the tournament. The team's morale will remain high if and only if the coach doesn't throw him off. Thus, if the coach doesn't throw Matt off the team, team morale will stay high, and we'll do well in the tournament.

28. Georgia will lose the case if and only if the Court decides to base its decision on *Davis*. Although the composition of the Court is more conservative than it was a few years ago, it will base its decision on *Davis*. So, Georgia will lose.

29. If many students come to the party, they'll eat lots of food and the party will be rowdy. If students eat lots of food, the party will be expensive. Many students will come to the party, although only a few have been invited. Thus, the party will be rowdy and expensive.

▶ 30. This product will fail if and only if it isn't given adequate advertising support. If it fails, then the company won't show a profit for the year. It won't be advertised adequately only if the vice-president believes that another product has more potential. The product is great, but it will not succeed. It follows that the vice president thinks another product has more potential, and the company won't show a profit this year.

8.4 Disjunction Rules

Like most connectives, disjunction has introduction and exploitation rules. The introduction rule asserts that we may introduce a disjunction into a proof if we've already obtained either disjunct. It underlies arguments such as

(10) Rachel is in London.
∴ Rachel is in London or East Grinstead.

Addition (Ad)		
n.	$\mathcal{A}$ (or $\mathcal{B}$)	
n + p.	$\mathcal{A} \vee \mathcal{B}$	Ad, n

We can use this rule to show that the following argument is valid:

(11) Terry is a cautious investor.
   If she turns the account over to a professional manager, or invests cautiously herself, then the funds will be secure.
∴ The funds will be secure.

Symbolizing the argument as p; $(q \vee p) \to r$; ∴ r, we begin by stating the premises as assumptions. We then obtain the antecedent of the conditional by addition and apply modus ponens to get the conclusion.

1. p A
2. $(q \vee p) \to r$ A
3. $q \vee p$ Ad, 1
4. r MP, 2, 3

How can we exploit the information encoded in a disjunction? How can we use a disjunction to derive a conclusion? The answer lies in two rules. The first rule of disjunction exploitation amounts to "proof by cases." It underlies arguments such as:

(12)   Paul will win the event unless Ann scores perfectly in the final round.
     If Paul wins, Ann will get the silver medal.
     If Ann scores perfectly in the final round, she'll get the gold medal.
     ∴ Ann will win the silver or the gold medal.

Constructive Dilemma (CD)

n. $\mathscr{A} \lor \mathscr{B}$
m. $\mathscr{A} \to \mathscr{C}$
p. $\mathscr{B} \to \mathscr{D}$
q. $\mathscr{C} \lor \mathscr{D}$ CD, n, m, p

To see how CD works, let's demonstrate the validity of

(13)   Serge will write on the Russian revolution or on the Versailles conference.
     If he writes on the Russian revolution, he'll do very well.
     ∴ Serge will do very well unless he writes on the Versailles conference.

by deriving $r \lor q$ from $p \lor q$ and $p \to r$.

1. $p \lor q$ A
2. $p \to r$ A
3. $q \to q$ SI
4. $r \lor q$ CD, 1, 2, 3

The next rule allows us to transform disjunctions into conditionals, and vice versa. It reflects the equivalence, noted in Chapter 5, of the following statements:

(14) a. The patient will die unless we operate.
     b. If we don't operate, the patient will die.

'If $\mathscr{A}$ then $\mathscr{B}$' is equivalent to '$\mathscr{B}$ unless not $\mathscr{A}$'.

Material Conditional (MC)

n. $\mathscr{A} \to \mathscr{B}$ MC, m
m. $\neg\mathscr{A} \lor \mathscr{B}$ MC, n

This rule allows a very simple proof of 'the law of the excluded middle', $p \vee \neg p$.

1. $\neg p \rightarrow \neg p$ SI
2. $\neg \neg p \vee \neg p$ MC, 1
3. $p \vee \neg p$ DN, 2

It also allows a proof of the validity of this argument:

(15) If Ned accepts the job, he'll be thrown into a nearly impossible situation.
   If his company doesn't counter the offer, Ned will accept the job.
   $\therefore$ Unless his company counters the offer, Ned will be thrown into a nearly impossible situation.

We can symbolize the argument as $r \rightarrow q; \neg p \rightarrow r; \therefore p \vee q$.

1. $r \rightarrow q$ A
2. $\neg p \rightarrow r$ A
3. $\neg \neg p \vee r$ MC, 2
4. $p \vee r$ DN, 3
5. $p \rightarrow p$ SI
6. $p \vee q$ CD, 4, 5, 1

A fourth disjunction rule says that disjunctions are *commutative:* that order, within a disjunction, makes no difference. It underlies the equivalence of sentences such as

(16) a. Either Joe will call, or Kate will write you a letter.
   b. Either Kate will write you a letter, or Joe will call.

Commutativity of Disjunction (Cm)

n. $\mathcal{A} \vee \mathcal{B}$ Cm, m
m. $\mathcal{B} \vee \mathcal{A}$ Cm, n

A final rule for disjunction says that grouping, within a disjunction, makes no difference.

Associativity of Disjunction (As)

n. $(\mathcal{A} \vee \mathcal{B}) \vee \mathcal{C}$ As, m
m. $\mathcal{A} \vee (\mathcal{B} \vee \mathcal{C})$ As, n

We already assumed in Chapter 5 that this principle holds, when we allowed $p \lor q \lor r$, for example, as an abbreviation for either $(p \lor q) \lor r$ or $p \lor (q \lor r)$.

Problems

Show that these argument forms are valid.

▶ **1.** p; $\therefore$ $p \lor q$ ▶ **2.** p & q; $\therefore$ $p \lor q$

▶ **3.** $p \lor q$; $\lnot q$; $\therefore$ p ▶ **4.** $\lnot p \lor q$; p; $\therefore$ q

▶ **5.** $q \to r$; $p \lor q$; $p \to s$; $\therefore$ $r \lor s$ ▶ **6.** $p \lor q$; $\lnot r$; $p \to r$; $\therefore$ q

   7. $p \lor q$; $r \leftrightarrow q$; $\therefore$ $r \lor p$

   8. $p \leftrightarrow \lnot q$; $\lnot p \lor q$; r; $\therefore$ $\lnot p \lor (p \to s)$

   9. $p \to r$; $\lnot s$; $p \lor \lnot q$; $\lnot q \to s$; $\therefore$ r

  10. $p \leftrightarrow s$; $q \lor p$; $q \to r$; $\therefore$ $s \lor r$

  11. $(p \lor q) \to r$; $s \to p$; $(r \to t)$ & s; $\therefore$ t

▶ **12.** $(p$ & $q) \lor (r \lor s)$; $\therefore$ $((p$ & $q) \lor r) \lor s$

  13. $p \to q$; $\lnot r$ & s; $p \lor r$; $\therefore$ s & q

  14. $p \lor r$; $\lnot p \lor \lnot q$; p; $\lnot r \lor q$; $\therefore$ $\lnot r$

  15. p & s; $q \lor r$; $p \leftrightarrow \lnot q$; $\therefore$ r & s

  16. $p \lor q$; $r \lor s$; $\lnot p$ & $\lnot s$; $\therefore$ $(q$ & $r) \lor t$

  17. p; $\lnot s \lor \lnot p$; $p \to r$; $\therefore$ $\lnot s$ & r ▶ **18.** $\lnot p \lor q$; $\lnot q \lor r$; $\lnot r$; $\therefore$ $\lnot p$

  19. p & s; $p \to (\lnot s \lor r)$; $\therefore$ r **20.** $\lnot p \lor q$; $\lnot q$; $\lnot p \to r$; $\therefore$ r

  21. p & $\lnot s$; $r \to s$; $p \to (q \lor r)$; $\therefore$ q

  22. p & q; r & $\lnot s$; $q \to (p \to k)$; $k \to (r \to (s \lor m))$; $\therefore$ m

  23. $p \lor (r \lor q)$; $(r \to m)$ & $(q \to n)$; $(m \lor n) \to (p \lor q)$; $\lnot p$; $\therefore$ q

▶ **24.** p & $(q \to r)$; $q \lor \lnot p$; $(r \lor s) \to t$; $\therefore$ $t \lor m$

  25. $\lnot r \leftrightarrow \lnot q$; $p \lor \lnot q$; $p \leftrightarrow s$; $\therefore$ $s \lor \lnot r$

  26. p & q; $p \to \lnot \lnot r$; $q \to s$; $\lnot r \lor m$; $p \to t$; $\therefore$ $(m$ & $s)$ & t

Show that these formulas are theorems of our system.

  27. $((p \lor q) \lor \lnot r) \to \lnot \lnot (p \lor (\lnot \lnot q \lor \lnot r))$

  28. $(p \lor (q \lor r)) \leftrightarrow ((p \lor q) \lor r)$ **29.** $(p \to p) \lor (p \to q)$

Use deduction to show that these arguments are valid.

▶ **30.** No one knows where Rick was last night. Unless he has an alibi, he's the prime suspect in the murder. He has an alibi only if somebody knows where he was last night. Therefore, unless new evidence points to someone else, Rick is the prime murder suspect.

31. Peter won't believe me unless you come along and explain things to him. Margaret won't tell him anything about our idea. If you explain things to him, he'll understand. Margaret will tell him about our idea if he doesn't believe me, but what she tells him will just make him angry. Therefore, Peter will understand unless you chicken out.

32. The dollar will fall if foreign banks sterilize their intervention in the currency markets or if the Fed does nothing to defend it. Germany and Japan are eager to keep their currencies strong, but they'll intervene in the markets if the dollar drops. If Germany and Japan want to maintain strong currencies, foreign banks will sterilize their interventions. It follows that they will intervene in the markets.

33. The house contains either a fireplace or a deck; it contains either a fourth bedroom or a den. Evidently it doesn't have a fourth bedroom and doesn't have a deck. Hence, it has a den and a fireplace.

34. Patricia is clever but won't work very hard. If she's clever, the boss will like her and either promote her or give her a bonus. If Patricia is promoted, she'll work hard. Therefore, the boss will give Patricia a bonus.

8.5 RULES OF DEFINITION

The final two rules of our basic system show how to define certain connectives in terms of others. As we saw in Chapter 5, we don't need all five of our basic connectives to express every truth function. Several pairs of connectives—negation and conjunction, negation and disjunction, and negation and the conditional—are functionally complete by themselves. The two basic rules of definition are called *DeMorgan's laws.*[2] As definitions, they invert; they work in either direction.

DeMorgan's laws are extremely useful. Without them, negations would be difficult to exploit; we could eliminate negations only in pairs. To help simplify formulas beginning with a negation, these rules give equivalents for negated formulas. The first asserts that the negation of a conjunction is equivalent to a disjunction. It reflects the form of the following inferences:

(17) Don's mother and father won't both go to the wedding.
∴ Either Don's mother or his father won't go to the wedding.

(18) Either Israel or Syria will disapprove of the plan.
∴ Not both Israel and Syria will approve of the plan.

DeMorgan's Law #1 (DM)

n.	$\neg(\mathscr{A}\ \&\ \mathscr{B})$	DM, m
m.	$\neg\mathscr{A} \vee \neg\mathscr{B}$	DM, n

If not both $\mathscr{A}$ and $\mathscr{B}$ are true, then either $\mathscr{A}$ is false or $\mathscr{B}$ is false. This rule lets us show the validity of

(19) Zelda and Carl can't both be on the affirmative team.
If Zelda isn't on the affirmative team, Ralph won't be.
∴ Ralph and Carl won't both be on the affirmative team.

which we can symbolize as $\neg(p\ \&\ q)$; $\neg p \rightarrow \neg r$; ∴ $\neg(r\ \&\ q)$

1.	$\neg(p\ \&\ q)$	A
2.	$\neg p \rightarrow \neg r$	A
3.	$\neg q \rightarrow \neg q$	SI
4.	$\neg p \vee \neg q$	DM, 1
5.	$\neg r \vee \neg q$	CD, 4, 3, 2
6.	$\neg(r\ \&\ q)$	DM, 5

It lets us prove "the law of noncontradiction," $\neg(p\ \&\ \neg p)$.

1.	$p \rightarrow p$	SI
2.	$\neg p \vee p$	MC, 1
3.	$\neg p \vee \neg\neg\neg p$	DN, 2
4.	$\neg(p\ \&\ \neg p)$	DM, 3

The second rule asserts that the negation of a disjunction is equivalent to a conjunction. It underlies the following inferences:

(20) Neither Brazil nor Argentina has nuclear weapons.
∴ Brazil doesn't have nuclear weapons, and Argentina doesn't either.

(21) Kermit doesn't live in a garbage can, and Miss Piggy doesn't live in a garbage can.
∴ Neither Kermit nor Miss Piggy lives in a garbage can.

DeMorgan's Law #2 (DM)

n.	$\neg(\mathscr{A} \vee \mathscr{B})$	DM, m
m.	$\neg\mathscr{A}\ \&\ \neg\mathscr{B}$	DM, n

If neither $\mathscr{A}$ nor $\mathscr{B}$ is true, then $\mathscr{A}$ and $\mathscr{B}$ are both false. This rule allows us to show the validity of

(22) Neither Vinnie nor Barbara took home a trophy.
∴ Either Vinnie or Juan didn't take home a trophy.

by constructing a proof of $\neg(p \vee q)$; ∴ $\neg p \vee \neg r$.

1. $\neg(p \vee q)$ A
2. $\neg p \mathbin{\&} \neg q$ DM, 1
3. $\neg p$ S, 2
4. $\neg p \vee \neg r$ Ad, 3

Note that the last three rules—Associativity of Disjunction and DeMorgan's rules—invert. The principle of replacement allows them to operate on sub-formulas as well as entire formulas.

To summarize our basic rules:

RULES APPLYING ONLY TO ENTIRE FORMULAS

Assumption

n. $\mathscr{A}$ A

Simplification (S)

n. $\mathscr{A} \mathbin{\&} \mathscr{B}$
n + m. $\mathscr{A}$ (or $\mathscr{B}$)   S, n

Conjunction (C)

n. $\mathscr{A}$
m. $\mathscr{B}$
p. $\mathscr{A} \mathbin{\&} \mathscr{B}$ C, n, m

Consequent Conjunction (CC)

n. $\mathscr{A} \rightarrow \mathscr{B}$
m. $\mathscr{A} \rightarrow \mathscr{C}$
p. $\mathscr{A} \rightarrow (\mathscr{B} \mathbin{\&} \mathscr{C})$ CC, n, m

Modus Ponens (MP)

n. $\mathcal{A} \to \mathcal{B}$
m. $\underline{\mathcal{A}}$
p. $\mathcal{B}$ MP, n, m

Self Implication (SI)

n. $\mathcal{A} \to \mathcal{A}$ SI

Addition (Ad)

n. $\underline{\mathcal{A}}$ (or $\mathcal{B}$)
n + p. $\mathcal{A} \vee \mathcal{B}$ Ad, n

Constructive Dilemma (CD)

n. $\mathcal{A} \vee \mathcal{B}$
m. $\mathcal{A} \to \mathcal{C}$
p. $\underline{\mathcal{B} \to \mathcal{D}}$
q. $\mathcal{C} \vee \mathcal{D}$ CD, n, m, p

Invertible Rules

Double Negation (DN)

n. $\underline{\underline{\mathcal{A}}}$ DN, m
m. $\neg \neg \mathcal{A}$ DN, n

Biconditional (B)

n. $\underline{\mathcal{A} \leftrightarrow \mathcal{B}}$
n + m. $(\mathcal{A} \to \mathcal{B}) \, \& \, (\mathcal{B} \to \mathcal{A})$ B, n

Commutativity of Disjunction (Cm)

$$\text{n.} \quad \underline{\mathscr{A} \vee \mathscr{B}} \qquad \text{Cm, n}$$
$$\text{m.} \quad \mathscr{B} \vee \mathscr{A} \qquad \text{Cm, n}$$

Associativity of Disjunction (As)

$$\text{n.} \quad \underline{(\mathscr{A} \vee \mathscr{B}) \vee \mathscr{C}} \qquad \text{As, m}$$
$$\text{m.} \quad \mathscr{A} \vee (\mathscr{B} \vee \mathscr{C}) \qquad \text{As, n}$$

DeMorgan's Law #1 (DM)

$$\text{n.} \quad \underline{\neg(\mathscr{A} \mathbin{\&} \mathscr{B})} \qquad \text{DM, m}$$
$$\text{m.} \quad \neg\mathscr{A} \vee \neg\mathscr{B} \qquad \text{DM, n}$$

DeMorgan's Law #2 (DM)

$$\text{n.} \quad \underline{\neg(\mathscr{A} \vee \mathscr{B})} \qquad \text{DM, m}$$
$$\text{m.} \quad \neg\mathscr{A} \mathbin{\&} \neg\mathscr{B} \qquad \text{DM, n}$$

Material Conditional (MC)

$$\text{n.} \quad \underline{\mathscr{A} \to \mathscr{B}} \qquad \text{MC, m}$$
$$\text{m.} \quad \neg\mathscr{A} \vee \mathscr{B} \qquad \text{MC, n}$$

Problems

Theophrastus (371–286 B.C.), a pupil of Aristotle, cited these principles as hypothetical syllogisms. Show that their conclusions are provable from their premises.

▸ **1.** $r \to p; p \to q; \therefore r \to q$ ▸ **2.** $r \to p; p \to q; \therefore \neg q \to \neg r$

▸ **3.** $r \to p; \neg r \to q; \therefore \neg p \to q$ ▸ **4.** $r \to p; \neg r \to q; \therefore \neg q \to p$

  5. $r \to q; p \to \neg q; \therefore r \to \neg p$

Show that the conclusion formulas of these argument forms can be proved from the premise formulas. (Starred problems are very difficult.)

▶ **6.** $\neg r \vee \neg p$; $\therefore p \rightarrow \neg r$ ▶ **7.** $r \rightarrow p$; $\therefore r \leftrightarrow (r \& p)$

▶ **8.** $r \leftrightarrow (r \& p)$; $\therefore r \rightarrow p$ ▶ **9.** $r \vee p$; $\neg r \& s$; $\therefore p \vee q$

▶ **10.** $r \rightarrow p$; $q \rightarrow r$; $\therefore \neg q \vee p$ ▶ **11.** $\neg r \vee \neg q$; $\therefore \neg (r \& \neg \neg q)$

▶ **12.** $\neg (r \& \neg p) \vee \neg r$; $\therefore r \rightarrow p$ **13.** $r \vee p$; $\neg r \vee \neg p$; $\therefore r \leftrightarrow \neg p$

14. $r \rightarrow (p \vee q)$; $\therefore (r \rightarrow p) \vee q$ **15.** $r \vee p$; $r \rightarrow q$; $p \rightarrow s$; $\therefore \neg q \rightarrow s$

16. $\neg s \vee (s \& r)$; $(s \rightarrow r) \rightarrow q$; $\therefore q$

17. $r \rightarrow (\neg q \vee s)$; $r \rightarrow \neg s$; $\therefore r \rightarrow \neg q$*

▶ **18.** $(r \& \neg p) \rightarrow \neg q$; q; $\therefore \neg r \vee (r \& p)$

19. $(q \& \neg r) \vee (p \& q)$; $\therefore (r \rightarrow p) \& q$*

20. $r \rightarrow \neg p$; q; $q \rightarrow (p \vee \neg s)$; $\therefore s \rightarrow \neg r$

21. $r \rightarrow \neg p$; $\neg r \vee q$; p; $(p \& q) \rightarrow r$; $\therefore \neg q$

22. $r \rightarrow \neg p$; $\neg r \rightarrow \neg q$; $q \vee \neg s$; $\therefore \neg p \vee \neg s$

23. $s \rightarrow (q \& r)$; $p \rightarrow (\neg q \& \neg t)$; $\therefore (p \& s) \rightarrow u$*

▶ **24.** $r \leftrightarrow p$; $\therefore \neg r \leftrightarrow \neg p$*

25. $(r \& p) \vee (p \& q)$; $\therefore \neg p \rightarrow s$*

26. $r \& p$; $r \rightarrow (s \vee q)$; $\neg (q \& p)$; $\therefore s$

27. $(r \vee p) \& q$; $p \rightarrow s$; $\therefore \neg r \rightarrow (q \rightarrow s)$

28. $s \rightarrow r$; $(s \& r) \rightarrow p$; $q \rightarrow t$; $q \vee s$; $\therefore p \vee t$

29. $r \rightarrow (s \& q)$; $(q \vee \neg s) \rightarrow (p \& m)$; $m \leftrightarrow n$; $\therefore r \rightarrow n$*

▶ **30.** $(s \& \neg q) \rightarrow \neg r$; $(p \rightarrow \neg s) \leftrightarrow \neg r$; $\therefore r \leftrightarrow (q \& (s \& p))$*

31. $(r \leftrightarrow p) \leftrightarrow (r \leftrightarrow q)$; $\neg ((\neg r \& \neg p) \& \neg q)$; $\therefore r \leftrightarrow (p \leftrightarrow q)$*

32. $r \& (\neg p \& \neg t)$; $r \rightarrow (s \rightarrow q)$; $s \rightarrow (q \leftrightarrow (t \vee p))$; $\therefore \neg s$*

33. $r \vee (p \vee s)$; $t \& \neg k$; $\neg (\neg t \vee k) \rightarrow \neg r$; $(s \rightarrow q) \& \neg q$; $\therefore p$

34. $\neg (p \vee \neg s)$; $\neg p \rightarrow (q \vee r)$; $\neg r \vee \neg s$; $(q \vee t) \rightarrow (m \& (k \rightarrow \neg s))$; $\therefore \neg (m \rightarrow k)$

These argument forms and formulas are useful in showing that each of the derived rules in the next section can be derived from the basic rules of this section.

35. $\neg (p \rightarrow q)$; $\therefore p \& \neg q$ ▶ **36.** $p \& \neg q$; $\therefore \neg (p \rightarrow q)$

37. $p \rightarrow q; \neg q; \therefore \neg p$

38. $p; \neg p; \therefore q$

39. $(p \vee q) \& (p \vee r); \therefore p \vee (q \& r)$

40. $p \& (q \vee r); \therefore (p \& q) \vee (p \& r)$

41. $p \vee p; \therefore p^*$

▶ **42.** $(p \& q) \rightarrow p^*$

43. $p \rightarrow (p \vee q)^*$

44. $p \leftrightarrow \neg q; \therefore \neg (p \leftrightarrow q)^*$

45. $\neg (p \leftrightarrow q); \therefore p \leftrightarrow \neg q^*$

46. $(p \& q) \vee (p \& r); \therefore p \& (q \vee r)^*$

47. $p \vee (q \& r); \therefore (p \vee q) \& (p \vee r)^*$

▶ **48.** $(p \& q) \vee r; \therefore (q \& p) \vee r^*$

49. $p \rightarrow q; \therefore \neg q \rightarrow \neg p$

Use deduction to show that the following arguments are valid.

50. If I'm right, then I'm a fool. But if I'm a fool, I'm not right. Therefore, I'm not right.

51. If I'm right, then you're a fool. If I'm a fool, I'm not right. If you're a fool, I am right. Therefore, we're not both fools.

52. If Socrates died, he died either while he was living or while he was dead. But he did not die while living; moreover, he surely did not die while he was already dead. Hence, Socrates did not die. (Sextus Empiricus)

53. If you have a cake, just looking at it will make you hungry; if looking at it makes you hungry, you will eat it. So you can't both have your cake and fail to eat it.

▶ **54.** A man cannot serve both God and Mammon. But if a man does not serve Mammon, he starves; if he starves, he can't serve God. Therefore, a man cannot serve God.

55. Sarah knows that the company is unlikely to promote her. She will look for another job if and only if she's unhappy. She's bound to be unhappy if she knows that she's unlikely to be promoted. So, unless she has some other reason for staying, Sarah will look for another job.

56. If the United States doesn't agree to arms limitation talks, tensions with the Soviets will remain high. But even if the U.S. agrees to such talks, tensions between the U.S.S.R. and the U.S. will remain high. Thus, tensions between the United States and the Soviets will remain high.

57. Nothing can be conceived as greater than God. If God existed in our imaginations, but not in reality, then something would be conceivable as greater than God (namely, the same thing, except conceived as existing in reality). Therefore, if God exists in our imaginations, He exists in reality. (Saint Anselm)

58. If God is all powerful, He is able to prevent evil. If He is all good, He is willing to prevent evil. Evil does not exist unless God is either unwilling or unable to prevent it. If God exists, He is both all good and all powerful. Therefore, if evil exists, God doesn't.

8.6 DERIVED RULES

The series of proof methods and rules we've adopted allow us to prove the validity of any valid argument form in sentential logic. Our system is *complete*—every valid argument form can be proved valid in the system. This guarantees that we have enough rules. Our system is also *sound*—we can derive a conclusion from given premises only if the argument form is valid. Our rules never lead us astray. Our system thus can serve as a method for demonstrating validity. To speak in terms of formulas rather than argument forms: All tautologies—and only tautologies—are provable. Our system's completeness guarantees that every tautology is a theorem; its soundness guarantees that every theorem is a tautology. Thus, we can use our system of natural deduction to show that formulas are tautologies. Establishing the soundness and completeness of this chapter's natural deduction system requires a sophisticated proof that goes beyond the scope of this book.

To encompass sentential logic, therefore, we need no further rules. Nevertheless, this section develops some additional, commonly used rules. Everything we can prove with them is still valid. Indeed, they are all *derived* rules; they abbreviate series of proof lines that we could write in terms of our basic rules. They are short cuts that force us to accept nothing new about the logical connectives.

Negations of Complex Formulas

As we noted in the discussion of DeMorgan's laws, negations of formulas are hard to handle in our basic system. DeMorgan's laws give us a way of exploiting negations of conjunctions and disjunctions. The following two rules allow us to exploit negations of conditionals and biconditionals as well.

The first rule, *negated conditional,* rests on the truth table definition of the conditional:

$\mathscr{A}$	$\mathscr{B}$	$\mathscr{A} \rightarrow \mathscr{B}$
T	T	T
T	F	F
F	T	T
F	F	T

$\mathscr{A} \rightarrow \mathscr{B}$ comes out false only on the row on which $\mathscr{A}$ is true and $\mathscr{B}$ is false.

Negated Conditional (NC)

$$
\begin{array}{lll}
\text{n.} & \underline{\neg(\mathscr{A} \to \mathscr{B})} & \text{NC, m} \\
\text{m.} & \mathscr{A} \,\&\, \neg\mathscr{B} & \text{NC, n}
\end{array}
$$

If $\mathscr{A} \to \mathscr{B}$ is false, then $\mathscr{A}$ must be true and $\mathscr{B}$ must be false. This rule lets us show more easily the validity of

(23) If Max was carrying a gun, he was guilty of a felony.
It's not true that if Max carried a gun, he'll serve time in prison.
∴ It's not true that if Max committed a felony, he'll serve time.

by allowing a shortened proof of $p \to r;\ \neg(p \to q);\ \therefore\ \neg(r \to q)$.

$$
\begin{array}{lll}
1. & p \to r & \text{A} \\
2. & \neg(p \to q) & \text{A} \\
3. & p \,\&\, \neg q & \text{NC, 2} \\
4. & p & \text{S, 3} \\
5. & r & \text{MP, 1, 4} \\
6. & \neg q & \text{S, 3} \\
7. & r \,\&\, \neg q & \text{C, 5, 6} \\
8. & \neg(r \to q) & \text{NC, 7}
\end{array}
$$

This proof uses NC to go from a negation to a conjunction on line 3; the proof then uses the rule in the opposite direction to derive a negation on line 8 from a conjunction.

The second rule rests on the truth table definition of the biconditional:

Negated Biconditional (NB)

$$
\begin{array}{lll}
\text{n.} & \underline{\neg(\mathscr{A} \leftrightarrow \mathscr{B})} & \text{NB, m} \\
\text{m.} & \neg\mathscr{A} \leftrightarrow \mathscr{B}\ (\text{or } \mathscr{A} \leftrightarrow \neg\mathscr{B}) & \text{NB, n}
\end{array}
$$

If $\mathscr{A} \leftrightarrow \mathscr{B}$ is false, then $\mathscr{A}$ and $\mathscr{B}$ must have opposite truth values. $\mathscr{A}$ is false if and only if $\mathscr{B}$ is true. Equivalently, $\mathscr{A}$ is true if and only if $\mathscr{B}$ is false. This rule allows a shortened proof of $\neg(p \leftrightarrow q);\ r \,\&\, \neg q;\ \therefore\ p \,\&\, r$.

$$
\begin{array}{lll}
1. & \neg(p \leftrightarrow q) & \text{A} \\
2. & r \,\&\, \neg q & \text{A} \\
3. & p \leftrightarrow \neg q & \text{NB, 1} \\
4. & \neg q & \text{S, 2} \\
5. & (p \to \neg q) \,\&\, (\neg q \to p) & \text{B, 3} \\
6. & \neg q \to p & \text{S, 5}
\end{array}
$$

7. *p*   MP, 6, 4
8. *r*   S, 2
9. *p* & *r*   C, 7, 8

Order and Grouping

Several derived rules illustrate important algebraic properties of conjunction and disjunction. The rules for the commutativity and associativity of disjunction in our basic system assert that order and grouping, in a continued disjunction, make no difference. Two additional rules extend this idea. Together they affirm that the order and grouping of subformulas in continued conjunctions make no difference. The first indicates that the order of conjuncts doesn't matter: *𝒜* & *ℬ* is equivalent to *ℬ* & *𝒜*. It thus states that conjunction is *commutative*.

Commutativity of Conjunction (Cm)		
n.	<u>*𝒜* & *ℬ*</u>	Cm, m
m.	*ℬ* & *𝒜*	Cm, n

It underlies the equivalence of sentences such as

(24) a. Both Sandra and Dave worked on the project.
     b. Both Dave and Sandra worked on the project.

The second rule asserts that the grouping of conjuncts makes no difference; conjunction is *associative*. It underlies the equivalence of sentences such as

(25) a. France and Germany have sent representatives, and
        Hungary has, too.
     b. France has sent representatives, and Germany and Hungary
        have, too.

Associativity of Conjunction (As)		
n.	<u>(*𝒜* & *ℬ*) & *𝒞*</u>	As, m
m.	*𝒜* & (*ℬ* & *𝒞*)	As, n

A final derived rule allows us to assert that a disjunction with identical disjuncts is redundant; we can collapse the disjuncts. From *𝒜* ∨ *𝒜*, we can deduce $\mathscr{A}$. The rule underlies reasoning such as that from (26)a to (26)b:

(26) a. Either the new part will work, or the new part will work.
     b. The new part will work.

Because we can also deduce $\mathscr{A} \vee \mathscr{A}$ from $\mathscr{A}$ by addition, we can express this as an invertible rule.

Idempotence (I)

$$
\begin{array}{lll}
\text{n.} & \underline{\mathscr{A} \vee \mathscr{A}} & \text{I, m} \\
\text{m.} & \mathscr{A} & \text{I, n}
\end{array}
$$

This rule is surprisingly useful. It permits, for example, a simple proof of a special form of constructive dilemma:

$$
\begin{array}{lll}
1. & p \vee q & \text{A} \\
2. & p \rightarrow r & \text{A} \\
3. & q \rightarrow r & \text{A} \\
4. & r \vee r & \text{CD, 1, 2, 3} \\
5. & r & \text{I, 4}
\end{array}
$$

Abbreviations

Finally, eight rules abbreviate commonly used proof steps. The first four provide alternative techniques for exploiting conditionals and biconditionals. The fifth allows negated formulas to interact with disjunctions. The sixth relates conjunctions and disjunctions, whereas the seventh generalizes the rule of self-implication. The eighth expresses the principle that anything follows from a contradiction.

The first rule allows negations to function readily, without detours, in exploiting conditionals. In some ways, it is similar to *modus ponens,* but it allows us to use negated formulas. Suppose we've established that if the butler committed the crime, it must have occurred before dark. Suppose we also establish that the crime did not occur before dark. We can infer that the butler is innocent. The rule sanctioning this inference is called *modus tollens.*

Modus Tollens (MT)

$$
\begin{array}{lll}
\text{n.} & \mathscr{A} \rightarrow \mathscr{B} & \\
\text{m.} & \neg \mathscr{B} & \\
\text{p.} & \neg \mathscr{A} & \text{MT, n, m}
\end{array}
$$

If $\mathcal{A}$ is true only if $\mathcal{B}$ is true, and $\mathcal{B}$ is false, then $\mathcal{A}$ must also be false. We can use this rule to show that (27) is valid:

> (27) Laura will agree only if Patrick raises no objections.
> If Oliver doesn't file his report, Patrick will raise objections.
> Oliver is away on vacation, and won't file his report.
> ∴ Laura will not agree.

We prove the arguments validity by showing that $p \rightarrow \neg q$, $\neg r \rightarrow q$ and $s \,\&\, \neg r$ imply $\neg p$.

$$
\begin{array}{lll}
1. & p \rightarrow \neg q & \text{A} \\
2. & \neg r \rightarrow q & \text{A} \\
3. & s \,\&\, \neg r & \text{A} \\
4. & \neg r & \text{S, 3} \\
5. & q & \text{MP, 2, 4} \\
6. & \neg\,\neg q & \text{DN, 5} \\
7. & \neg p & \text{MT, 1, 6}
\end{array}
$$

This rule also allows a shortened proof of the validity of

> (28) If Ireland advances to the semifinals, so will Tunisia.
> Neither Tunisia nor Uruguay will make the semifinals.
> ∴ Neither Uruguay nor Ireland will advance to the semifinals.

or, symbolized, of $p \rightarrow q$; $\neg(r \lor q)$; ∴ $\neg(r \lor p)$. (Notice the use of both directions of DM.)

$$
\begin{array}{lll}
1. & p \rightarrow q & \text{A} \\
2. & \neg(r \lor q) & \text{A} \\
3. & \neg r \,\&\, \neg q & \text{DM, 2} \\
4. & \neg r & \text{S, 3} \\
5. & \neg q & \text{S, 3} \\
6. & \neg p & \text{MT, 1, 5} \\
7. & \neg r \,\&\, \neg p & \text{C, 4, 6} \\
8. & \neg(r \lor p) & \text{DM, 7}
\end{array}
$$

The second abbreviation rule is an argument form traditionally called *hypothetical syllogism*. It allows conditionals to act together to form chains of reasoning. It underlies arguments such as

> (29) If your baby cries, my baby will wake up.
> If my baby wakes up, she'll cry.
> ∴ If your baby cries, my baby will too.

> ### Hypothetical Syllogism (HS)
>
> n. $\mathscr{A} \rightarrow \mathscr{B}$
> m. $\mathscr{B} \rightarrow \mathscr{C}$
> p. $\mathscr{A} \rightarrow \mathscr{C}$ HS, n, m

This rule permits a straightforward proof of the validity of

(30) Rhonda will play unless Ernest quits.
    If Ernest quits, Walt will replace him.
    If Walt does, Margaret is sure to win.
    If Walt replaces Ernest, moreover, the game will take longer.
    ∴ Either Rhonda will play, or Margaret will win and the game will take longer.

by allowing a simplified proof of $p \vee q; q \rightarrow r; r \rightarrow s; r \rightarrow t; \therefore p \vee (s \,\&\, t)$.

1. $p \vee q$ A
2. $q \rightarrow r$ A
3. $r \rightarrow s$ A
4. $r \rightarrow t$ A
5. $r \rightarrow (s \,\&\, t)$ CC, 3, 4
6. $q \rightarrow (s \,\&\, t)$ HS, 2, 5
7. $p \rightarrow p$ SI
8. $p \vee (s \,\&\, t)$ HS, 1, 7, 6

The third rule relates two equivalent conditionals. 'If $\mathscr{A}$, then $\mathscr{B}$' is equivalent to 'If $\neg\mathscr{B}$, then $\neg\mathscr{A}$'. For example,

(31) a. If noboby called to tell him not to come, Ned will be here soon.
    b. If Ned isn't here soon, then somebody called to tell him not to come.

are equivalent.

> ### Transposition (Tr)
>
> n. $\underline{\mathscr{A} \rightarrow \mathscr{B}}$ Tr, m
> m. $\neg\mathscr{B} \rightarrow \neg\mathscr{A}$ Tr, n

This rule allows a simple proof of

(32) The United States will negotiate with Libya only if Libya renounces terrorism.

Libya won't do so unless Qadhafy is no longer its leader.

∴ The U.S. won't negotiate with Libya unless Qadhafy is no longer its leader.

which we may symbolize as $p \to q; \neg q \lor \neg r; \therefore \neg r \lor \neg p$.

1. $p \to q$ A
2. $\neg q \lor \neg r$ A
3. $\neg q \to \neg p$ Tr, 1
4. $\neg r \to \neg r$ SI
5. $\neg r \lor \neg p$ HS, 2, 4, 3

The fourth rule makes it easier to exploit biconditionals. Our basic biconditional rule equates a biconditional with a conjunction of two conditionals. By applying simplification and then *modus ponens* and *modus tollens* to those conditionals, we can derive the following rule, which underlies arguments such as

(33) a. Connie will follow the rules if and only if she's watched carefully.
Connie will be watched carefully.
∴ Connie will follow the rules.
b. Romania's economy will grow next year if and only if Bulgaria's does.
Romania's economy won't grow next year.
∴ Bulgaria's economy won't grow next year.

Biconditional Exploitation (BE)

n. $\mathscr{A} \leftrightarrow \mathscr{B}$
m. $\mathscr{A}$ (or $\mathscr{B}$)
p. $\mathscr{B}$ (or $\mathscr{A}$)   BE, n, m

n. $\mathscr{A} \leftrightarrow \mathscr{B}$
m. $\neg \mathscr{A}$ (or $\neg \mathscr{B}$)
p. $\neg \mathscr{B}$ (or $\neg \mathscr{A}$)   BE, n, m

Given a biconditional and one component of it, we can obtain the other component. Given a biconditional and the negation of one component, we can obtain the negation of the other component.

The next abbreviation rule concerns disjunction. It reflects the reasoning in this argument:

(34) Either Yvonne or Ursula arrived in town last night.
Yvonne didn't arrive last night.
∴ Ursula did.

If at least one of $\mathscr{A}$ or $\mathscr{B}$ is true, and $\mathscr{A}$ is false, $\mathscr{B}$ must be true. Similarly, if $\mathscr{A}$ or $\mathscr{B}$ is true, $\mathscr{A}$ must be true if $\mathscr{B}$ is false.

Disjunctive Syllogism (DS)

> n. $\mathscr{A} \vee \mathscr{B}$
> m. $\neg \mathscr{A}$ (or $\neg \mathscr{B}$)
> p. $\mathscr{B}$ (or $\mathscr{A}$)   DS, n, m

To illustrate this rule, let's show that the following argument is valid:

(35) Iggy got the letter unless someone intercepted it.
If our agents supervised the delivery, then nobody intercepted it.
I've checked with Orrin; our agents did supervise.
∴ Iggy got the letter.

Symbolizing, we obtain $p \vee q; r \to \neg q; s \& r; \therefore p$.

1. $p \vee q$ A
2. $r \to \neg q$ A
3. $s \& r$ A
4. r S, 3
5. $\neg q$ MP, 2, 4
6. p DS, 1, 5

The sixth abbreviation rule asserts that conjunctions of disjunctions are equivalent to disjunctions of conjunctions. It has two forms. The first underlies the equivalence of

(36) a. Bob and either Vanna or Carol will star in the series.
b. Either Bob and Vanna or Bob and Carol will star in the series.

while the second underlies the equivalence of

(37) a. Either Zeke or Al and Sam rode the horse.
b. Zeke or Al rode the horse, and Zeke or Sam rode the horse.

Distribution (D)

> n. $\mathscr{A} \& (\mathscr{B} \vee \mathscr{C})$ D, m
>
> m. $(\mathscr{A} \& \mathscr{B}) \vee (\mathscr{A} \& \mathscr{C})$ D, n
>
> n. $\mathscr{A} \vee (\mathscr{B} \& \mathscr{C})$ D, m
>
> m. $(\mathscr{A} \vee \mathscr{B}) \& (\mathscr{A} \vee \mathscr{C})$ D, n

The seventh abbreviation rule generalizes the self-implication rule. Like that rule, it requires no premises. Called *weakening* (or *thinning*), it has two forms. The first allows us to write, on any line, a conditional with a conjunction as antecedent and one of the conjuncts as consequent. The second lets us write, on any line, a conditional with a disjunction as consequent and one of the disjuncts as antecedent. The weakening rule reflects the fact that sentences such as these are tautologies:

(38) a. If Dan and Fran ran, Dan ran.
b. If Gary knows Harry, Gary knows Harry or Jerry.

Weakening (W)

n. $(\mathscr{A} \& \mathscr{B}) \rightarrow \mathscr{A}$ (or $(\mathscr{A} \& \mathscr{B}) \rightarrow \mathscr{B})$ W
n. $\mathscr{A} \rightarrow (\mathscr{A} \vee \mathscr{B})$ (or $\mathscr{B} \rightarrow (\mathscr{A} \vee \mathscr{B}))$ W

The last derived rule asserts that a contradiction implies anything.

Contradiction (!)

n. $\mathscr{A}$
m. $\neg \mathscr{A}$
p. $\mathscr{B}$!, n, m

If $\mathscr{A}$ is both true and false, then anything follows. This is our most surprising derived rule. But it follows from basic rules. This is the original medieval deduction of the contradiction rule, which uses disjunctive syllogism.[3]

1. p A
2. $\neg p$ A
3. $p \vee q$ Ad, 1
4. q DS, 3, 2

The contradiction rule allows us to count a proof complete whenever we obtain a contradiction within it: We may write the desired conclusion on the next line.

This summarizes our derived rules:

RULES APPLYING ONLY TO ENTIRE FORMULAS

Modus Tollens (MT)

n. $\mathscr{A} \rightarrow \mathscr{B}$
m. $\neg \mathscr{B}$
p. $\neg \mathscr{A}$ MT, n, m

Hypothetical Syllogism (HS)

n. $\mathscr{A} \to \mathscr{B}$
m. $\mathscr{B} \to \mathscr{C}$
p. $\mathscr{A} \to \mathscr{C}$ HS, n, m

Biconditional Exploitation (BE)

n. $\mathscr{A} \leftrightarrow \mathscr{B}$
m. $\mathscr{A}$ (or $\mathscr{B}$)
p. $\mathscr{B}$ (or $\mathscr{A}$)   BE, n, m

n. $\mathscr{A} \leftrightarrow \mathscr{B}$
m. $\neg \mathscr{A}$ (or $\neg \mathscr{B}$)
p. $\neg \mathscr{B}$ (or $\neg \mathscr{A}$)   BE, n, m

Disjunctive Syllogism

n. $\mathscr{A} \vee \mathscr{B}$
m. $\neg \mathscr{A}$ (or $\neg \mathscr{B}$)
p. $\mathscr{B}$ (or $\mathscr{A}$)   DS, n, m

Weakening (W)

n. $(\mathscr{A} \& \mathscr{B}) \to \mathscr{A}$ (or $(\mathscr{A} \& \mathscr{B}) \to \mathscr{B}$)   W
n. $\mathscr{A} \to (\mathscr{A} \vee \mathscr{B})$ (or $\mathscr{B} \to (\mathscr{A} \vee \mathscr{B})$)   W

Contradiction (!)

n. $\mathscr{A}$
m. $\neg \mathscr{A}$
p. $\mathscr{B}$!, n, m

INVERTIBLE RULES

Negated Conditional (NC)

n. $\neg(\mathcal{A} \rightarrow \mathcal{B})$ NC, m
m. $\mathcal{A} \,\&\, \neg \mathcal{B}$ NC, n

Negated Biconditional (NB)

n. $\neg(\mathcal{A} \leftrightarrow \mathcal{B})$ NB, m
m. $\neg \mathcal{A} \leftrightarrow \mathcal{B}$ (or $\mathcal{A} \leftrightarrow \neg \mathcal{B}$)   NB, n

Commutativity of Conjunction (Cm)

n. $\mathcal{A} \,\&\, \mathcal{B}$ Cm, m
m. $\mathcal{B} \,\&\, \mathcal{A}$ Cm, n

Associativity of Conjunction (As)

n. $(\mathcal{A} \,\&\, \mathcal{B}) \,\&\, \mathcal{C}$ As, m
m. $\mathcal{A} \,\&\, (\mathcal{B} \,\&\, \mathcal{C})$ As, n

Idempotence (I)

n. $\mathcal{A} \vee \mathcal{A}$ I, m
m. $\mathcal{A}$ I, n

Transposition (Tr)

n. $\mathcal{A} \rightarrow \mathcal{B}$ Tr, m
m. $\neg \mathcal{B} \rightarrow \neg \mathcal{A}$ Tr, n

Distribution (D)

n.	$\mathscr{A}$ & $(\mathscr{B} \vee \mathscr{C})$	D, m
m.	$(\mathscr{A}$ & $\mathscr{B}) \vee (\mathscr{A}$ & $\mathscr{C})$	D, n
n.	$\mathscr{A} \vee (\mathscr{B}$ & $\mathscr{C})$	D, m
m.	$(\mathscr{A} \vee \mathscr{B})$ & $(\mathscr{A} \vee \mathscr{C})$	D, n

Strategy

Overall proof strategies derive, primarily, from what we're trying to prove and, secondarily, from what we already have. To prove a formula with a given main connective, try (a) using an introduction rule for that connective, (b) using a rule combining that connective with another, or (c) using a rule defining that connective in terms of others. To use a formula with a given main connective, try (a) using an exploitation rule for that connective, (b) using a rule combining that connective with another, or (c) using a rule defining that connective in terms of others. The following table contains some of the most important strategies.

Proof Strategies

To get	Try to
$\neg\mathscr{A}$	use double negation, DeMorgan's laws, or *modus tollens*.
$\mathscr{A}$ & $\mathscr{B}$	prove $\mathscr{A}$ and $\mathscr{B}$ separately.
$\mathscr{A} \vee \mathscr{B}$	(a) use constructive dilemma or material conditional, or (b) prove $\mathscr{A}$ or $\mathscr{B}$ separately.
$\mathscr{A} \to \mathscr{B}$	use material conditional, consequent conjunction, hypothetical syllogism, self-implication, weakening, or transposition.
$\mathscr{A} \leftrightarrow \mathscr{B}$	prove the two conditionals $\mathscr{A} \to \mathscr{B}$ and $\mathscr{B} \to \mathscr{A}$.

To exploit	Try to
$\neg\mathscr{A}$	(a) use it with other lines that have $\mathscr{A}$ as a part, or (b) use DeMorgan's laws or negated (bi)conditional.
$\mathscr{A}$ & $\mathscr{B}$	use simplification to get $\mathscr{A}$ and $\mathscr{B}$ individually.
$\mathscr{A} \vee \mathscr{B}$	(a) get the negation of one disjunct, and use disjunctive syllogism to get the other, or (b) use constructive dilemma by taking each case separately, or (c) use material conditional.
$\mathscr{A} \to \mathscr{B}$	(a) get $\mathscr{A}$ and then reach $\mathscr{B}$ by *modus ponens,* or (b) use hypothetical syllogism, consequent conjunction, or material conditional, or (c) get $\neg\mathscr{B}$ and then reach $\neg\mathscr{A}$ by *modus tollens*.
$\mathscr{A} \leftrightarrow \mathscr{B}$	use biconditional to obtain a conjunction of conditionals, or use biconditional exploitation.

Problems

Construct a deduction to show that each of these arguments is valid.

▶ **1.** If you are ambitious, you'll never achieve all your goals. But life has meaning only if you have ambition. Thus, if you achieve all your goals, life has no meaning.

▶ **2.** If Adam comes to the party, then Barbara will come, too. Furthermore, if Barbara comes to the party, so will Adam. So, Carlos will be happy if Adam comes only if Carlos will be happy if Barbara comes.

▶ **3.** Interest rates will rise unless Congress enacts a tax increase. But rates will rise even if Congress raises taxes. If interest rates rise, the unemployment level will rise. Either unemployment won't increase, or the budget deficit will. It follows that there will be an increase in the budget deficit.

▶ **4.** God is omnipotent if and only if He can do everything. If He can't make a stone so heavy that He can't lift it, then He can't do everything. But if He can make a stone so heavy that He can't lift it, He can't do everything. Therefore, either God is not omnipotent, or God does not exist.

▶ **5.** If the president pursues arms limitations talks, then, if he gets the foreign policy mechanism working more harmoniously, the European left will acquiesce to the placement of additional nuclear weapons in Europe. But the European left will never acquiesce to that. So, either the president won't get the foreign policy mechanism working more harmoniously, or he won't pursue arms limitations talks.

▶ **6.** If we either introduce a new product line or give an existing line a new advertising image, then we'll be taking a risk, and we may lose market share. If we don't introduce a new product line, we won't have to make large expenditures on advertising. So, if we don't take risks, we won't have to make large expenditures on advertising.

7. If we can avoid terrorism only by taking strong retaliatory measures, then we have no choice but to risk innocent lives. But if we don't take strong retaliatory measures, we'll certainly fall prey to attacks by terrorists. Nevertheless, we refuse to risk innocent lives. Consequently, terrorists will find us, more and more, an appealing target.

8. My cat does not sing opera unless all the lights are out. If I am very insistent, then my cat sings opera; but if I either turn out all the lights or howl at the moon, I am very insistent indeed. I always howl at the moon if I am not very insistent. Therefore, my lights are out, I am very insistent, and my cat is singing opera.

9. If we continue to run a large trade deficit, then the government will yield to calls for protectionism. We won't continue to run a large deficit only if our economy slows down or foreign economies recover. So, if foreign economies don't recover, then the government will resist calls for protectionism only if our economy slows down.

10. Money either serves you or dominates you; never both. If it serves you, and you handle it wisely, then it can help you to attain happiness. If it dominates you, you will gain much of it, but never be satisfied with your lot. Moreover, you'll be satisfied with your lot if and only if money can't help you attain happiness. So, money can help you attain happiness if you handle it wisely.

11. There will be scorpions in the house this week if there's any building going on in the neighborhood. There will be building if and only if the depression in the housing market ends. If there are scorpions in the house, the cats will kill them and bring them to me as trophies. Therefore, if the housing depression ends, my cats will bring me scorpions as trophies.

▶ 12. If the president retaliates against Libya with military force, the public will be ambivalent. But if Libya directs terrorist attacks toward Americans on American soil, then the American public will not be ambivalent at all. So, Libya will not engage in terrorism against Americans on American soil unless the president doesn't retaliate militarily.

13. If people don't either conserve energy or tolerate much greater despoiling of the environment, utilities will have no choice but to rely on nuclear power. They'll avoid relying on atomic energy, moreover, just in case it's prohibitively expensive and risky. Nuclear power will remain expensive. If it also remains risky, therefore, the environment will suffer unless people conserve energy.

14. If happiness can't be defined, there's no way to measure it. If we can't measure happiness, we can say whether someone is happy only if we take that person's word for it. Determining whether someone is happy is a necessary condition for testing the psychological effects of jobs of various kinds. We can't take a person's word concerning his or her own happiness. So, we can't test the psychological effects of various jobs if happiness can't be defined.

15. If the objects of mathematics are material things, then mathematics can't consist entirely of necessary truths. Mathematical objects are immaterial only if the mind has access to a realm beyond the reach of the senses. Mathematics does consist of necessary truths, although the mind has no access to any realm beyond the reach of the senses. Therefore the objects of mathematics are neither material nor immaterial.

16. We cannot both maintain high educational standards and accept almost every high school graduate unless we fail large numbers of students when (and only when) many students do poorly. We will continue to maintain

high standards; furthermore, we will placate the legislature and admit almost all high school graduates. Of course, we can't both placate the legislature and fail large numbers of students. Therefore, not many students will do poorly.

17. If management remains resolute, it can stop the hostile takeover attempt. But unless the company can improve its cash flow position, there will be no way to stop the takeover. Management will remain resolute only if it understands the consequences of the acquisition for its own position. Management understands the consequences, but the company can't improve its cash flow position. Therefore, management will not stop the hostile takeover.

▶ 18. If Congress erects trade barriers and grants further subsidies to American farmers, then other countries will retaliate. If that happens, however, the economy will slow down; if there is a slowdown, then Congress won't give farmers additional subsidies unless it finds new sources of revenue. If Congress doesn't erect trade barriers, it won't give farmers added subsidies, but at least other countries won't retaliate. Therefore, unless Congress finds new revenue sources, farmers will get no additional subsidies from Congress.

19. If advertisers continue to use Saturday morning cartoons to peddle toys by creating shows about them, pressure for regulation will build, and ratings will decline if parents understand what's going on. If ratings decline, then advertisers will stop using cartoons to sell toys by having toys as their main characters. If pressure for regulation builds, then either advertisers will stop, or Congress will act. If Congress acts, then advertisers will stop. Hence, if advertisers continue, parents won't know what's going on, children will become obsessed with material goods, and American culture will irrevocably decline.

20. If the Soviet economy is restructured, decision making will have to be decentralized, and bureaucracies in charge of economic planning will have to become smaller and less powerful. The bureaucracies, of course, won't become smaller if the bureaucrats can help it. Decision making will be decentralized only if the party hierarchy is willing to cede power to a wide group it can't easily control. Unless the bureaucracies become less powerful, decision making will remain centralized, and central planning will continue to dominate the economy. Hence, the Soviet economy won't be restructured if the hierarchy won't cede power or the bureaucrats can help it.

21. If the earth has been visited recently by extraterrestrial beings, then the government has withheld the information although the visits occurred. If some reported UFO sightings have been authentic, then the earth has

been visited recently by extraterrestrials. But if those sightings have been authentic, then our current understanding of our place in the universe is seriously mistaken. Therefore, either our understanding of our place in the universe is seriously mistaken, and the government has withheld information, or no reported UFO sightings are authentic.

22. If the party maintains its current economic policy, there will be a flight of capital to other countries. But the party won't improve its image abroad if the party tightens its control over the economy. If the party maintains its policy, and capital flees to other countries, then the party will tighten its grip on the economy. If the party maintains its current image, however, the nation will have to pay large amounts of foreign debt in hard currency, and the nation won't do this. So, the party won't maintain its current policy.

Construct deductions to demonstrate the validity of these argument forms.

23. $p \vee (q \vee r)$; $\neg q$; $\therefore$ $p \vee r$ ▶ 24. p; $\neg (p \vee r)$; $\therefore$ q

25. $p \rightarrow q$; $\neg (q \ \& \ p)$; $\therefore$ $\neg p$ 26. $p \leftrightarrow q$; $\neg (m \rightarrow q)$; $\therefore$ $\neg p$

27. $p \leftrightarrow q$; $\therefore$ $\neg (\neg p \vee \neg r) \rightarrow q$ 28. $p \ \& \ q$; $\therefore$ $\neg (\neg q \ \& \ \neg r) \ \& \ p$

29. $((p \ \& \ q) \ \& \ r) \ \& \ \neg s$; $\therefore$ $p \ \& \ (q \ \& \ \neg s)$

▶ 30. $(\neg p \rightarrow q) \vee r$; $\therefore$ $\neg p \rightarrow (q \vee r)$

Other authors have adopted rules for sentential logic that correspond to these argument forms. Show that each argument form is valid in our system.

31. $p \rightarrow q$; $\therefore$ $p \rightarrow (p \ \& \ q)$ (Absorption)

32. $(p \ \& \ q) \rightarrow r$; $\therefore$ $p \rightarrow (q \rightarrow r)$ (Exportation)

33. $p \rightarrow (q \rightarrow r)$; $\therefore$ $(p \ \& \ q) \rightarrow r$ (Exportation)

34. $p \leftrightarrow q$; $\therefore$ $(p \ \& \ q) \vee (\neg p \ \& \ \neg q)$ (Material Equivalence)

35. $(p \ \& \ q) \vee (\neg p \ \& \ \neg q)$; $\therefore$ $p \leftrightarrow q$ (Material Equivalence)

▶ 36. $p \leftrightarrow q$; $\therefore$ $\neg q \leftrightarrow \neg p$ (Biconditional Contraposition)

37. $\neg q \leftrightarrow \neg p$; $\therefore$ $p \leftrightarrow q$ (Biconditional Contraposition)

38. $p \leftrightarrow q$; $\therefore$ $q \leftrightarrow p$ (Biconditional Commutation)

39. $p \rightarrow q$; $r \rightarrow s$; $\neg q \vee \neg s$; $\therefore$ $\neg p \vee \neg r$ (Destructive Dilemma)

40. $p \rightarrow q$; $p \rightarrow r$; $\neg q \vee \neg r$; $\therefore$ $\neg p$ (Destructive Dilemma)

41. $\neg (p \ \& \ q)$; p; $\therefore$ $\neg q$ (Conjunctive Argument)

▶ 42. $p \vee q$; $\neg q \vee r$; $\therefore$ $p \vee r$ (Disjunctive Transitivity)

Use deduction to solve each of these problems.

43. Roger, a hapless accounting major, is trying to analyze a problem on an accounting exam. He needs to figure the tax liability of a corporation engaged in overseas shipping. Some of the fleet counts as American for tax purposes, and some does not. Poor Roger recalls the definition in the tax code of an American vessel as running like this: "A ship counts as an American vessel if and only if (a) it is either numbered or registered in the U.S., or (b) if it is neither registered nor numbered in the U.S. and is not registered in any foreign country, then either its crew members are all U.S. citizens, or they are all employees of U.S. corporations." Show that this is the wrong definition, by showing that it implies that if a ship is registered in a foreign country, it counts as an American vessel.

44. On the way to the barber shop (adapted from Lewis Carroll), you are trying to decide which of three barbers—Allen, Baker, and Carr—will be in today. You know Allen has been sick and so reason that (a) if Allen is out of the shop, his good friend Baker must be out with him. But, since they never leave the shop untended, (b) if Carr is out of the shop, then, if Allen is out with him, Baker must be in. Show that (a) and (b) imply (c) that not all three are out; (d) that Allen and Carr are not both out; (e) that, if Carr and Baker are in, so is Allen.

Show that the following argument forms are valid by using deduction.

45. $\neg(\neg p \mathbin{\&} q)$; $(p \vee r) \to \neg(m \mathbin{\&} s)$; $q \leftrightarrow s$; $\therefore\ m \to \neg(q \vee s)$*

46. $p \to (q \vee r)$; $(\neg q \mathbin{\&} m) \vee (s \to \neg p)$; $\neg(\neg r \to \neg p)$; $\therefore\ \neg s \mathbin{\&} q$*

47. $p \to (q \to \neg r)$; $(\neg q \leftrightarrow s) \to \neg p$; $p \vee m$; $\therefore\ (r \mathbin{\&} s) \to m$*

▶ **48.** $\neg s \to \neg k$; $(s \mathbin{\&} t) \to (p \leftrightarrow q)$; $\neg(\neg p \vee q)$; $\therefore\ t \to \neg k$*

49. $(q \leftrightarrow \neg p) \to \neg r$; $(\neg q \mathbin{\&} s) \vee (p \mathbin{\&} m)$; $(s \vee m) \to r$; $\therefore\ p \to q$*

50. $(p \mathbin{\&} \neg r) \leftrightarrow (s \vee \neg q)$; $t \mathbin{\&} ((\neg s \mathbin{\&} \neg r) \to p)$; $(t \to q) \vee (t \to r)$; $(p \mathbin{\&} s) \to r$; $\therefore\ q \mathbin{\&} r$*

Each of the following has been adopted as an axiom for sentential logic by the logician listed. Show that each is a theorem of our system of deduction.

Jan Lukasiewicz:

51. $(\neg p \to p) \to p$ **52.** $p \to (\neg p \to q)$

53. $(p \to q) \to ((q \to r) \to (p \to r))$*

Gottlob Frege:

▶ **54.** $(p \to q) \to (\neg q \to \neg p)$ **55.** $p \to (q \to p)$

56. $(p \to (q \to r)) \to ((p \to q) \to (p \to r))$*

57. $(p \to (q \to r)) \to (q \to (p \to r))$

Bertrand Russell and Alfred North Whitehead:

58. $(p \vee p) \rightarrow p$ **59.** $(p \vee q) \rightarrow (q \vee p)$

▶ **60.** $(p \vee (q \vee r)) \rightarrow (q \vee (p \vee r))$ **61.** $q \rightarrow (p \vee q)$

62. $(q \rightarrow r) \rightarrow ((p \vee q) \rightarrow (p \vee r))$*

David Hilbert and Paul Bernays:

63. $(p \rightarrow (p \rightarrow q)) \rightarrow (p \rightarrow q)$*

64. $(p \rightarrow q) \rightarrow ((p \rightarrow r) \rightarrow (p \rightarrow (q \ \& \ r)))$*

65. $(p \rightarrow r) \rightarrow ((q \rightarrow r) \rightarrow ((p \vee q) \rightarrow r))$*

8.7 INDIRECT PROOF

Although our basic rules allow us to establish the validity of every valid argument form of SL, the derived rules make proofs easier. This section concerns another way to simplify proofs: the method of *indirect proof*.

Consider a simple derived rule, idempotence, which asserts that $\mathscr{A} \vee \mathscr{A}$ may be deduced from $\mathscr{A}$ and vice versa. Justifying this rule in just one direction requires that we perform, among other things, a somewhat tricky proof of the argument form $p \vee p$; $\therefore$ p from basic rules alone:

1. $p \vee p$	A
2. $p \rightarrow p$	SI
3. $\neg p \vee p$	MC, 2
4. $\neg \neg p \vee p$	DN, 1
5. $\neg p \rightarrow p$	MC, 4
6. $\neg p \rightarrow \neg p$	SI
7. $\neg p \rightarrow (p \ \& \ \neg p)$	CC, 5, 6
8. $\neg p \vee \neg \neg p$	DN, 3
9. $\neg (p \ \& \ \neg p)$	DM, 8
10. $\neg \neg p \vee (p \ \& \ \neg p)$	MC, 7
11. $p \vee (p \ \& \ \neg p)$	DN, 10
12. $(p \ \& \ \neg p) \vee p$	Cm, 11
13. $\neg \neg (p \ \& \ \neg p) \vee p$	DN, 12
14. $\neg (p \ \& \ \neg p) \rightarrow p$	MC, 13
15. p	MP, 14, 9

This proof isn't very natural at all. It would be much more straightforward to reason in the following way. 'Suppose $p \vee p$ is true. Then p must be true as well; for, if it were false, then $\neg p$ and $p \vee p$ would both be true. But then, by disjunctive syllogism, p would be true. So, p would have to be both true and false, an absurdity'. This is an indirect proof. It begins by assuming the premises or assumptions, then also assuming the negation of the conclusion. The proof ends with a contradiction.

We could prove $p \lor p$; $\therefore$ p valid, indirectly, by writing out this reasoning:

1. $p \lor p$ A
2. $\neg p$ AIP (assumption for indirect proof)
3. p DS, 1, 2
4. $p \,\&\, \neg p$ C, 3, 2

This proof is far easier to construct and understand than our earlier, direct proof derived from basic rules alone.

In general, hypothetical indirect proofs trying to derive $\mathscr{B}$ from the assumptions $\mathscr{A}_1, \ldots, \mathscr{A}_n$ will have the form:

Indirect Proof (Hypothetical)

$$
\begin{array}{lll}
1. & \mathscr{A}_1 & \text{A} \\
& \vdots & \\
\text{n.} & \mathscr{A}_n & \text{A} \\
\text{n} + 1. & \neg\mathscr{B} & \text{AIP} \\
& \vdots & \\
\text{m.} & \mathscr{C} \,\&\, \neg\mathscr{C} &
\end{array}
$$

Every indirect proof begins with assumptions: first, the assumptions corresponding to premises, on which the conclusion depends; and second, the assumption for indirect proof, which is the negation of the desired conclusion. The proof succeeds when we reach a contradiction of the form $\mathscr{C} \,\&\, \neg\mathscr{C}$, for any formula $\mathscr{C}$.

If the proof is categorical, we begin with the assumption for indirect proof:

Indirect Proof (Categorical)

$$
\begin{array}{lll}
1. & \neg\mathscr{B} & \text{AIP} \\
& \vdots & \\
\text{m.} & \mathscr{C} \,\&\, \neg\mathscr{C} &
\end{array}
$$

The assumption for indirect proof is, again, the negation of what we want to prove. A categorical proof of this form, therefore, shows that $\mathscr{B}$ is a theorem.

An indirect proof is sometimes called a *reductio ad absurdum*—a reduction to absurdity. It takes an assumption and shows that it leads to an absurdity, thereby proving the opposite of the assumption. If the assumption is shown to be false, then its negation must be true.

Why do indirect proofs work? Why, that is, do they show arguments to be valid? Recall that an argument is valid if the truth of its premises guarantees the truth of its conclusion—if, equivalently, its premises can never be true while its conclusion is false. An indirect proof begins with the assumption that the premises are true and the conclusion is false and shows that this assumption leads to a contradiction. In effect, then, indirect proofs begin with an assumption that an argument is invalid, and show that the assumption is absurd.

Let's consider an example of a hypothetical indirect proof:

(39) Rob is taking chemistry, but Pat and Terry aren't.
     If Rob takes chemistry, he'll pass only if he gets help.
     If Rob is to pass, he'll get help if and only if Terry or Pat
     takes chemistry, too.
     ∴ Rob won't pass chemistry.

This proof shows that the argument is valid by establishing the validity of the corresponding argument form r & $(\neg p$ & $\neg t)$; $r \rightarrow (s \rightarrow q)$; $s \rightarrow (q \leftrightarrow (t \vee p))$; $\therefore \neg s$.

1.	r & $(\neg p$ & $\neg t)$	A
2.	$r \rightarrow (s \rightarrow q)$	A
3.	$s \rightarrow (q \leftrightarrow (t \vee p))$	A
4.	$\neg\neg s$	AIP
5.	s	DN, 4
6.	$q \leftrightarrow (t \vee p)$	MP, 3, 5
7.	$\neg p$ & $\neg t$	S, 1
8.	r	S, 1
9.	$s \rightarrow q$	MP, 2, 8
10.	q	MP, 9, 5
11.	$t \vee p$	BE, 6, 10
12.	$p \vee t$	Cm, 11
13.	$\neg(\neg p$ & $\neg t)$	DM, 12
14.	$(\neg p$ & $\neg t)$ & $\neg(\neg p$ & $\neg t)$	C, 7, 13

Indirect proof is especially useful in proving theorems. Directly deducing a tautology such as $((p \rightarrow q) \rightarrow p) \rightarrow p$ is quite difficult, even with the help of derived rules. An indirect proof of this formula, however, is easy.

1.	$\neg(((p \rightarrow q) \rightarrow p) \rightarrow p)$	AIP
2.	$((p \rightarrow q) \rightarrow p)$ & $\neg p$	NC, 1
3.	$(p \rightarrow q) \rightarrow p$	S, 2
4.	$\neg p$	S, 2
5.	$\neg(p \rightarrow q)$	MT, 3, 4
6.	p & $\neg q$	NC, 5
7.	p	S, 6
8.	p & $\neg p$	C, 7, 4

For another example, consider Frege's axiom
$(p \rightarrow (q \rightarrow r)) \rightarrow ((p \rightarrow q) \rightarrow (p \rightarrow r))$:

1.	$\neg((p \rightarrow (q \rightarrow r)) \rightarrow ((p \rightarrow q) \rightarrow (p \rightarrow r)))$	AIP
2.	$(p \rightarrow (q \rightarrow r)) \,\&\, \neg((p \rightarrow q) \rightarrow (p \rightarrow r))$	NC, 1
3.	$p \rightarrow (q \rightarrow r)$	S, 2
4.	$\neg((p \rightarrow q) \rightarrow (p \rightarrow r))$	S, 2
5.	$(p \rightarrow q) \,\&\, \neg(p \rightarrow r)$	NC, 4
6.	$p \rightarrow q$	S, 5
7.	$\neg(p \rightarrow r)$	S, 5
8.	$p \,\&\, \neg r$	NC, 7
9.	p	S, 8
10.	$\neg r$	S, 8
11.	$q \rightarrow r$	MP, 3, 9
12.	q	MP, 6, 9
13.	r	MP, 11, 12
14.	$r \,\&\, \neg r$	C, 13, 11

Indirect proof thus allows for simpler proofs of theorems. It also allows easier proofs of the validity of arguments, especially those with negated or disjunctive conclusions.

Problems

Using indirect proof, do the problems at the end of sections 8.5 and 8.6.

Notes

[1] Gerhard Gentzen, a German logician, and Stanislaw Jaskowski, a Polish logician, independently devised the first natural deduction systems in 1934. The system of this chapter owes a great deal to them, to the German logician and mathematician David Hilbert (1862–1943), to the Swiss mathematician Paul Bernays, and to the American logician Irving Copi.

[2] These rules are named after the British logician Augustus DeMorgan (1806–1871). They are first known to appear in the works of William of Ockham (1285–1349), an English philosopher, about 500 years before DeMorgan rediscovered them.

[3] The contradiction rule was first derived, independently and in this fashion, by the fourteenth-century logicians Walter Burleigh and Psuedo-Scot (so called because his writings were for a time attributed to the better-known medieval philosopher John Duns Scotus). Most of our other rules, incidentally, have been known since medieval times. Robert Kilwardby, Archbishop of Canterbury from 1272 to 1277, developed the addition rule. Ockham's works contain DeMorgan's laws, simplification, *modus ponens, modus tollens,* and disjunctive syllogism, as well. The double negation rule and the idea of developing logic axiomatically originated with the Stoics, a group of Greek philosophers who wrote in the third century B.C.

III

PREDICATE LOGIC

9

SYLLOGISMS

Aristotle invented the discipline of logic. He also developed a theory of logic that survived as the discipline's core for more than two thousand years. This theory differs sharply from the sentential logic discussed in Part II. Sentential logic is so called because it takes sentences as its basic units of analysis. Aristotle developed the theory of *categorical syllogisms,* which takes *general terms* or *predicates* as its basic units. For this reason, the theory of syllogisms forms a part of *predicate logic.* Because we won't discuss other kinds of syllogisms, we'll drop the adjective 'categorical' and speak simply of *syllogisms.*

To understand the theory of syllogisms, we need to study general terms.

> **DEFINITION**   A *general term* is an expression that is true or false of individual objects.

General terms occupy different grammatical categories:

- Adjectives: red, noble, clever, logical, friendly, fair

- Adjective phrases: somewhat strange, extremely nice, very friendly

- Common nouns: man, woman, cat, dog, chair, molecule, number

- Common noun phrases: tall tree, very affectionate kitten, well-written answer, man who left, child I saw last Thursday

- Participles: excited, exciting, made, understanding, disturbed

- Participial phrases: made in Costa Rica, disturbed by his friend's comment, interested in pursuing the deal

- Verb phrases: eats, makes money, gave Fred the key, will see Kim on Tuesday, knows everybody who is anybody

All general terms are true or false of individual objects. Pick any object: It will either be a cat or not be a cat. It will either make money or not make money. Alone, general terms are not true or false. But they yield a truth value when combined with the name of an object. Objects of which a general term are true *satisfy* it; the general term *applies to* them.

Each general term sorts objects into two groups: those of which it's true, and those of which it's false. The set of objects of which a general term is true is called the *extension* of the term.[1] 'Red', for example, applies to all red things but is false of everything else. The set of red things, then, is the extension of 'red'.

9.1 CATEGORICAL SENTENCES

General terms become parts of sentences in two ways. First, they can be predicated of an object by being attached to a proper name or pronoun. (The vertical lines divide singular from general terms.)

(1) a. Alice | is extremely clever.
 b. That | 's a very tall tree.
 c. This | is not a well-written answer.
 d. Socrates | is a man.
 e. He | 's friendly.
 f. Ninja | was a very affectionate kitten.

Sentences combining a proper name or singular pronoun with a general term are *singular;* they purport to say something about a single object.

Second, a *determiner* such as 'all', 'every', 'any', 'each', 'most', 'many', 'few', 'no', 'some', 'several', 'a', or 'an' may relate two general terms. (Vertical lines separate these units.)

(2) a. Some | court decisions | are unfair.
 b. Every | one I know | likes chocolate.
 c. A | policeman called by the airline | walked down the aisle.
 d. Several | disturbed students | were committed.
 e. Each | day | presents new difficulties.
 f. Few | philosophers | read Mill's logical works.

Sentences combining a determiner with a pair of general terms are *general* sentences.

General sentences may contain many determiners. General terms such as 'knew many scientists' or 'was admired by several influential critics' themselves contain determiners. We'll call the determiner that forms a sentence by linking two general terms the sentence's *main determiner*. Singular and general sentences together comprise the class of *categorical sentences* (so called because they contain no sentential connectives except, perhaps, negation).

Some individual words contain both a determiner and a general term. 'Everything' and 'something' contain both the determiners 'every' and 'some', respectively, and the general term 'thing'. 'Everybody', 'everyone', 'nobody', 'anybody', 'anyone', 'somebody', and 'someone' all contain a determiner together with the general terms 'body' or 'one', which are equivalent to 'person'.

It's important to recognize that there is an asymmetry between the grammatical subject and the grammatical predicate of a general sentence. Determiners must combine with nominal expressions, that is, expressions that act as nouns. The combination of determiner and nominal that forms the grammatical subject, however, must combine with a verb phrase to form a sentence. A general term that is a nominal, such as 'cat', must become the verb phrase 'is a cat' to function as the grammatical predicate, and a general term that is a verb phrase, such as 'climbs trees', must become a nominal such as 'thing that climbs trees', 'climber of trees', 'treeclimber', and so on, to function as part of the grammatical subject.

Aristotelian logic treats a limited class of general sentences. It focuses on general sentences with main determiners of the following kinds:

- Universal: Affirmative: all, each, every, any*, only**, none but**
  Negative: no, there is (are), no, none

- Existential: some, a*, an*, there is (are), at least one

The starred determiners, 'any', 'a', and 'an', have several uses. 'Any' is usually universal. Sometimes it functions more like an existential, but this is rare in the realm of the syllogism. The indefinite articles 'a' and 'an', in contrast, are usually existential. 'I saw a man who was running from the store', for example, implies that there was a man running from the store. Sometimes, however, they act as *generics,* which are similar to universals. Consider the difference between the sentences in the following pairs. In the first member of each pair, 'a' seems to introduce a particular object. In the second, the sentence seems to speak about the typical instances of a kind.

(3) a. A whale followed the boat into the harbor.
    b. A whale is a mammal.

(4) a. A tree was struck by lightning.
    b. A tree needs an ample supply of water.

The semantic rules governing the meaning of the indefinite article are complex. But there are two simple tests. The first way to tell whether 'a' or 'an' is acting as an existential or a generic is to substitute 'some' for it. If the meaning of the sentence doesn't change, 'a(n)' is acting as an existential. If the meaning of the sentence does change, 'a(n)' is generic. The second way is to drop the article and make the noun plural. If the meaning changes, 'a(n)' is acting as existential. If it doesn't, 'a(n)' is generic.

The expressions with a double star, 'only' and 'none but', are not really determiners. But, within the limited context of the theory of syllogisms and in some of their uses, they act like determiners. They have the odd semantic feature, however, that they "reverse" a sentence's general terms. 'Only PhDs will be considered' does not mean that every PhD will be considered but, rather, that nobody without a PhD will be considered. This is equivalent to saying that everyone who will be considered will have a PhD.

For the moment, we will limit our investigation to categorical sentences with universal or existential main determiners linking their general terms. A categorical sentence is *universal* if its main determiner is universal, and *particular* if its main determiner is existential. (This is the sentence's *quantity*.) Thus, 'all frogs swim' and 'no frogs fly' are universal; 'some frogs croak' and 'some frogs don't climb trees' are particular. Further, a categorical sentence is *affirmative* if it affirms that a general term applies to some objects, and *negative* if it denies that some general term applies. (This is the sentence's *quality*.) 'All frogs swim' and 'some frogs croak' are affirmative; 'no frogs fly' and 'some frogs don't climb trees' are negative.

Categorical sentences thus fall into four groups. This table summarizes the forms of categorical sentences, together with the letters *A*, *E*, *I*, and *O*, which medieval logicians used to abbreviate them. (*A* and *I* are the first two vowels of *affirmo*, Latin for "I affirm"; *E* and *O*, of *nego*, "I deny.")

	Affirmative	Negative
Universal	*A*: All *F* are *G*	*E*: No *F* are *G*
Particular	*I*: Some *F* are *G*	*O*: Some *F* are not *G*

Universal Affirmative Sentences

These categorical sentences are both universal and affirmative. Their main determiners are universal, and they affirm that the things they talk about satisfy some general term. Each of these sentences is universal affirmative:

(5) a. All men are mortal.
    b. Each student picked up a copy of the exam.
    c. Every stock with an initially low price/earnings ratio outperformed the market.
    d. Anybody who would believe that story is a fool.

Throughout this chapter we'll symbolize general terms with uppercase letters, usually drawn from the middle of the alphabet, with or without numerical subscripts. We'll furthermore select 'all' to represent any universal determiner. We'll symbolize universal affirmative sentences such as those in (5) by writing

All *F* are *G*,

which we'll call a *categorical sentence form*. 'All *F* are *G*' is, in particular, a universal affirmative categorical sentence form. 'All' represents a sentence's main determiner; F and G represent the general terms it relates, expressed in nominal form (for example, as 'cat lovers' or 'people who love cats' rather than 'love cats').

Universal Negative Sentences

These sentences are universal, but they deny that some general term applies to certain objects. Typically, their main determiners are negative. These sentences are universal negative:

(6) a. Nobody knows the trouble I've seen.
　　 b. No Philadelphia team won a pennant between 1950 and 1980.
　　 c. There are no even prime numbers greater than 2.

We'll select 'no' to represent negative determiners and symbolize universal negative sentences such as those in (6) by writing

　　No F are G,

a universal negative categorical sentence form.

Particular Affirmative Sentences

These sentences have an existential main determiner and affirm that some general term applies to certain objects. The following sentences are particular affirmative:

(7) a. Some quarterbacks call their own plays.
　　 b. A research team announced the development of a new drug.
　　 c. There's an outrageously funny comedian appearing at the Warehouse tonight.

We'll select 'some' to represent existential determiners and symbolize particular affirmative sentences by writing

　　Some F are G,

a particular affirmative categorical sentence form.

Particular Negative Sentences

These sentences have an existential main determiner but deny that some general term applies to certain objects. Each of the following is particular negative:

(8) a. Some roaches aren't affected by common insecticides.
　　 b. A new approach Jane has developed doesn't fall prey to these difficulties.

    c. There's a new work of art on display at the Whitney that Manuela didn't mention in her article.

We'll symbolize these sentences by writing

    Some F are not G,

a particular negative categorical sentence form.

Problems

Which of the following are general terms?

▶ **1.** Juanita   ▶ **2.** admire   ▶ **3.** admirer   ▶ **4.** Odessa

▶ **5.** friendly   ▶ **6.** wisely   **7.** kennel   **8.** many

   9. but   **10.** ridiculous   **11.** alas   ▶ **12.** sleep

   13. admit   **14.** the   **15.** people   **16.** most people

   17. people who watch "Geraldo"

▶ **18.** people Manny knows who watch "Geraldo"

   19. water

   20. ice cube

Which of the following sentences are categorical? Classify each categorical sentence as universal or particular, affirmative or negative.

   21. Some cats chase mice.

   22. Some cats don't chase mice.

   23. Most cats chase mice.

▶ **24.** All cats chase mice.

   25. No students listen to graduation speeches.

   26. Few students listen to graduation speeches.

   27. John is a student.

   28. John didn't listen to the speech at his graduation.

   29. The king planned the feast carefully.

▶ **30.** Every king plans feasts carefully.

   31. The king plans every feast carefully.

   32. A dean was late for the meeting.

   33. The dean was late for the meeting.

34. At least two deans were late for the meeting.

35. All but one of my friends showed up.

▸ **36.** Every one of my friends showed up.

37. Nobody was even there to bluff.

38. A few people were there to bluff.

39. Olga thinks that someone is following her.*

40. Thor is seeking a unicorn.*

9.2 DIAGRAMMING CATEGORICAL SENTENCE FORMS

The language of Aristotelian logic, AL, is thus extremely simple:

Vocabulary

Predicates: uppercase letters, with or without numerical subscripts
Determiners: all, no, some
Particle: not

Formation Rules

1. If X and Y are predicates, then 'All X are Y', 'No X are Y', 'Some X are Y', and 'Some X are not Y' are formulas.
2. There are no other formulas.

To develop a semantics for this language, we need a way of representing the meanings of categorical sentence forms.

Universal Affirmative Sentence Forms

The Swiss mathematician Leonhard Euler (1707–1783) and the British mathematician John Venn (1834–1923) devised systems for representing the meanings of categorical sentence forms in diagrams.[2] Here we'll consider just Venn's method. Consider first a universal affirmative sentence:

(9) All cats like tuna.

This appears to say that everything that is a cat is also a thing that likes tuna; that is, that the extension of 'cat' is included in the extension of 'likes tuna'. Using circles to represent the extensions of *F* and *G*, therefore, we can represent the meaning of 'All *F* are *G*' in this diagram:

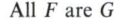

All *F* are *G*

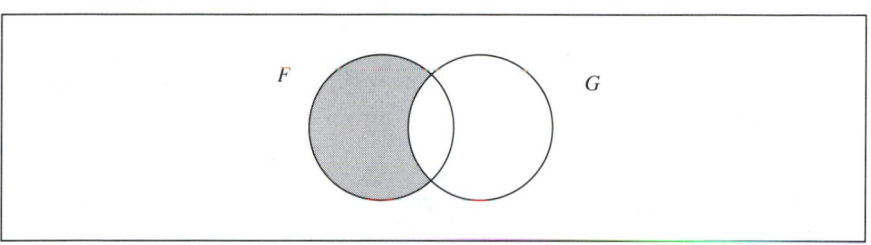

The diagram shows that the *F*s are a subset of the *G*s by the shading of a part of the *F* circle. The box in the background represents the *universe of discourse,* the domain of objects under discussion in the discourse.

> Shading a portion of a diagram indicates that it is empty, that is, that nothing occupies that portion.

So, shading the portion of the *F* circle outside the *G* circle indicates that nothing is an *F* without being a *G* or, in other words, that all *F* are *G*.

The *converse* of a categorical sentence form is the sentence form that results from switching its predicates. Thus, 'All *G* are *F*' is the converse of 'All *F* are *G*', and 'Some *G* are *F*' is the converse of 'Some *F* are *G*'. This method of representing the meanings of universal affirmative sentence forms shows that universal affirmative sentence forms are not in general equivalent to their converses.

(10) Everyone in this room is a musician.

is not equivalent to

(11) Every musician is in this room.

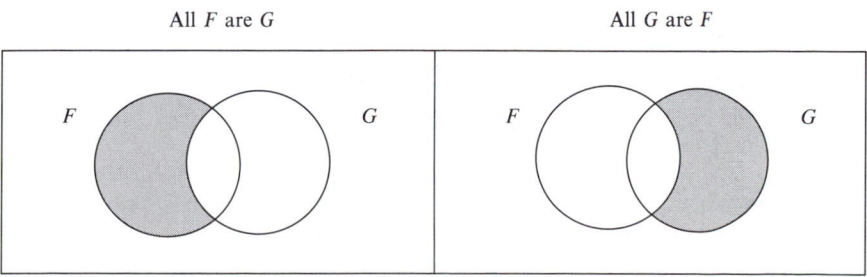

Universal Negative Sentence Forms

The universal negative sentence

(12) No Republicans are communists.

says that the set of Republicans and the set of communists have no members in common. It says that the extensions of the general terms 'Republican' and 'communist' are disjoint. Accordingly, we can represent the meaning of 'No F are G' by shading out the intersection of the F and G circles.

No F are G

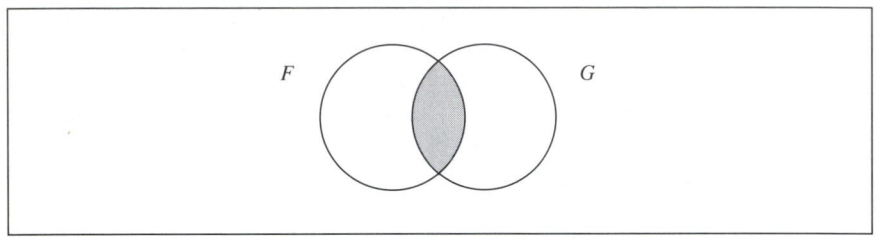

Venn's method reveals that universal negative sentence forms are equivalent to their converses. That is, 'No F are G' is equivalent to 'No G are F'. Both assert that nothing is both an F and a G.

(13) No foods that are high in fat are low in calories.

for example, is equivalent to

(14) No foods that are low in calories are high in fat.

Particular Affirmative Sentence Forms

A particular affirmative sentence such as

(15) Some professors enjoy giving exams.

asserts that the set of professors has at least one member in common with the set of those who enjoy giving exams: The extension of 'professor' overlaps the extension of 'enjoys giving exams'. We may represent a particular affirmative 'Some F are G' as follows.

> A plus sign indicates that the region it occupies is nonempty, that is, that there is at least one thing in that region.

If a region is shaded, we know that it's empty. If it contains a plus sign, we know that it's nonempty. If it's unshaded but contains no plus sign, we have no information; there may or may not be anything in the region.

Some *F* are *G*

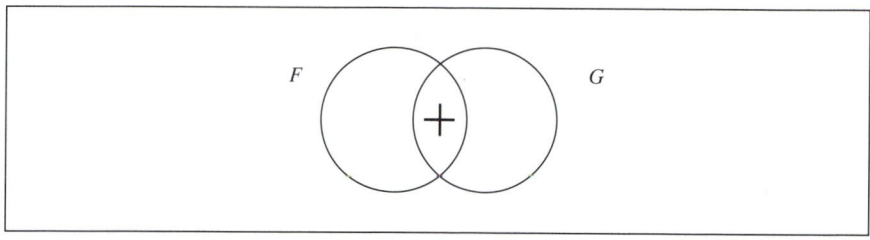

The plus sign in the intersection of the circles indicates that something is both an *F* and a *G*.

This method of diagramming the meaning of a particular affirmative sentence form demonstrates that such sentence forms are equivalent to their converses. 'Some *F* are *G*' and 'Some *G* are *F*' both assert that something is both an *F* and a *G*. Thus, the following are equivalent:

(16) a. Some of her ancestors came to this country on the *Mayflower*.
b. Some who came to this country on the *Mayflower* were her ancestors.

Particular Negative Sentence Forms

Finally, a particular negative sentence such as

(17) Some steel factories are not used any longer.

asserts that there are things that are steel factories but that are not used any longer. To represent a particular negative sentence form 'Some *F* are not *G*', we can draw diagrams of this sort:

Some *F* are not *G*

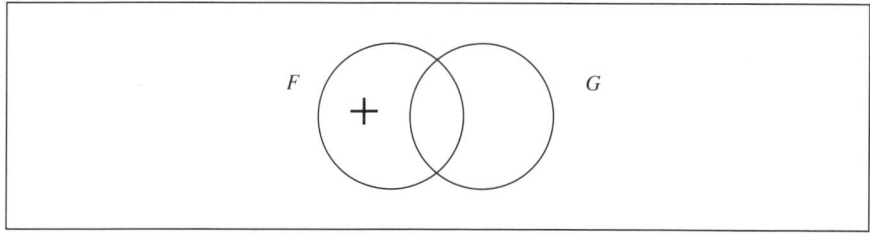

Here the plus sign appears in the portion of the *F* circle outside the *G* circle. This indicates that something is an *F* but not a *G*.

From this method of representing the meanings of particular negative sentence forms, we can see that particular negatives are not equivalent to their converses.

(18) Some people are not my relatives.

is not equivalent to

(19) Some of my relatives are not people.

In general, 'Some F are not G' asserts that something is an F without being a G, while 'Some G are not F' asserts that something is a G without being an F.

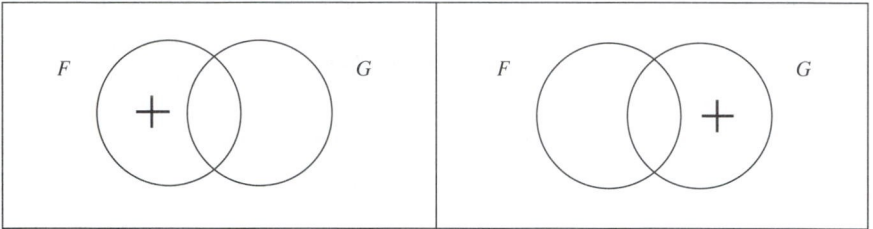

Some F are not G · Some G are not F

Problems

Diagram the following sentences.

▸ **1.** Nothing is more useful than silence. (Menander)

▸ **2.** No one is exempt from talking nonsense. (Michel de Montaigne)

▸ **3.** It is always the adventurers who accomplish great things. (Montesquieu)

▸ **4.** No guest ever left too soon for me. (Ms. Stuyvesant Fish, to a guest)

▸ **5.** No victor believes in chance. (Friedrich Nietzsche)

▸ **6.** What the heart knows today the head will understand tomorrow. (James Stephens)

7. The absent are always in the wrong. (Philippe Destouches)

8. Who does not know the value of words will never come to understand his fellow men. (Confucius)

9. He who feels punctured must once have been a bubble. (Lao-Tzu)

10. All good things which exist are the fruits of originality. (John Stuart Mill)

11. Art never expresses anything but itself. (Oscar Wilde)

▸ **12.** Every science has been an outcast. (Ralph W. Ingersoll)

13. All men are weak. (William Landor)

14. Everything is new. (Joseph Joubert)

15. No man is a hero to his valet. (Madame de Cornuel)

16. Every principle contains within itself the germs of prophecy. (Samuel Taylor Coleridge)

17. All prejudices may be traced to the intestines. (Friedrich Nietzsche)

▸ 18. He who complains, sins. (Saint Francis de Sales)

19. There is no location in Britain more than 65 miles from the sea. (John McKinney)

20. There are men who are happy without knowing it. (Vauvenargues)

21. All intelligent thoughts have already been thought. (Goethe)

22. The only biography that is really possible is autobiography. (G. K. Chesterton)

23. Who has the fame to be an early riser may sleep till noon. (James Howell)

▸ 24. All that time is lost which might be better employed. (Jean-Jacques Rousseau)

25. Nothing endures but personal qualities. (Walt Whitman)

26. Those who know do not tell; those who tell do not know. (Lao-Tzu)

27. Only an optimist can win in playing the game of business. (J. P. Morgan)

28. There is no excellence without difficulty. (Ovid)

29. It is all over for the man of forty who is held in aversion. (Confucius)

▸ 30. . . . nobody has money who ought to have it. (Benjamin Disraeli)

31. There is nothing good or evil save in the will. (Epictetus)

32. Whatever men aspire to, they deem best. (Petronius)

33. The trees that are slow to grow bear the best fruit. (Molière)

34. It is only shallow people who do not judge by appearances. (Oscar Wilde)

35. No man was ever wise by chance. (Seneca)

▸ 36. No facts are to me sacred; none are profane. . . . (Ralph Waldo Emerson)

37. He who acts, spoils; he who grasps, lets slip. (Lao-Tzu)

38. A lucky man always ends as a fool. (German proverb)

39. Fidelity bought with money is overcome by money. (Seneca)

40. Success is the child of audacity. (Benjamin Disraeli)

9.3 IMMEDIATE INFERENCE

Before applying Venn diagrams to syllogisms, we can see that there are logical relations among the four types of categorical sentence forms. First, as we've already seen, 'Some *F* are *G*' and its converse, 'Some *G* are *F*', receive the same diagram. They are equivalent. The same is true of 'No *F* are *G*' and its converse, 'No *G* are *F*'. These sentence forms are true under exactly the same interpretations of *G* and *F*. The principle of conversion summarizes this:

Conversion

E and I sentence forms are equivalent to their converses. Thus, (a) 'Some *F* are *G*' and 'Some *G* are *F*' are equivalent, and (b) 'No *F* are *G*' and 'No *G* are *F*' are equivalent.

Not all sentence forms are equivalent to their converses. 'All *F* are *G*', for example, isn't equivalent to 'All *G* are *F*'. (Compare 'All dogs are animals' and 'All animals are dogs'.) Similarly, 'Some *F* are not *G*' isn't equivalent to 'Some *G* are not *F*'. (Compare 'Some humans are not professors' and 'Some professors are not human'.)

Second, our diagrams indicate that particular affirmative and universal negative sentence forms are closely related. When we diagram 'Some *F* are *G*', we place a plus sign in the region we shade in diagramming 'No *F* are *G*'. 'Some *F* are *G*' asserts that there's something in the intersection of the extensions of *F* and *G*; 'No *F* are *G*' asserts that the intersection is empty. These sentence forms, therefore, directly contradict each other. We'll call them *contradictories*.

> **DEFINITION** Two sentences (or sentence forms) are *contradictories* if and only if they always disagree in truth value.

'Some pigs chew coal' and 'No pigs chew coal', for instance, always have opposite truth values. Any circumstance making one true makes the other false.

The same holds of 'All *F* are *G*' and 'Some *F* are not *G*'. These, too, always disagree in truth value. If 'All *F* are *G*' is true, then 'Some *F* are not *G*' must be false, and vice versa. 'All ducks swim' and 'Some ducks don't swim', for example, are contradictories. If one is true, the other must be false. Universal affirmative and particular negative sentences, then, are also contradictories.

Contradictories

'Some *F* are *G*' and 'No *F* are *G*' are contradictories. So are 'All *F* are *G*' and 'Some *F* are not *G*'.

The Square of Opposition

Aristotle encoded this and other logical relations among categorical sentence forms in what is traditionally called *the square of opposition*. The square summarizes the relations between *A*, *E*, *I*, and *O* sentence forms with the same subject and predicate terms:

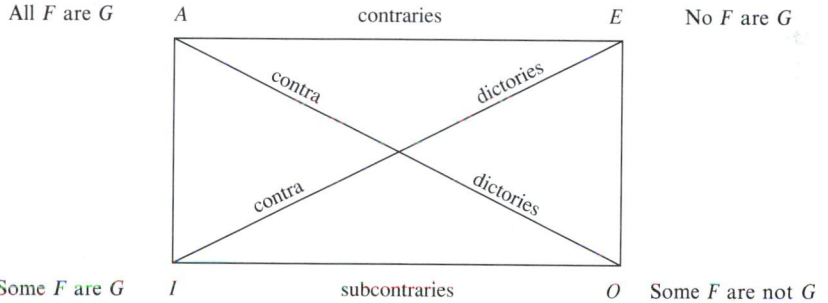

Contradictories, as we've seen, always disagree in truth value. *Contraries* are never both true, and *subcontraries* are never both false.

> **Definition** Two sentences (or sentence forms) are *contraries* if and only if they can never both be true, but can both be false.

> **Definition** Two sentences (or sentence forms) are *subcontraries* if and only if they can never both be false, but can both be true.

Thus, 'Socrates is alive and kicking' and 'Socrates is alive, but not kicking' are contraries. They can never both be true, but can both be false (if Socrates isn't alive). 'Anne is either hungry or grumpy' and 'Anne is either hungry or not grumpy' are subcontraries. They can never both be false because Anne, at any given time, must be either grumpy or not grumpy; either case makes one of the sentences true. Of course, if Anne is hungry, both are true.

Aristotle called particular sentence forms *subalterns* of universal forms of the same quality. The relation he had in mind, in our terminology, is implication. Aristotle held that 'All *F* are *G*' implies 'Some *F* are *G*', and that 'No *F* are *G*' implies 'Some *F* are not *G*'.

Using the square of opposition, we can use the truth value of one categorical sentence form to determine the truth values of some of the other forms. Suppose that 'All *F* are *G*' is true. What can we conclude about the corresponding *E*, *I*, and *O* forms? *A* and *O* forms are contradictories; so, if 'All *F* are *G*' is true, then 'Some *F* are not *G*' must be false. *A* and *E* forms are contraries; they can't both be true. So, 'No *F* are *G*' must also be false. Finally, *A* forms imply *I* forms; thus, if 'All *F* are *G*' is true, then 'Some *F* are *G*' is also true.

To take an English example: Suppose that 'All professors are human' is true. Then 'Some professors are human' must also be true, but 'No professors are human' and 'Some professors are not human' must be false.

The square doesn't allow us to infer truth values for all the other sentence forms in every case. Suppose that 'No *F* are *G*' is false. Its contradictory, 'Some *F* are *G*', must consequently be true. But we can conclude nothing about the corresponding *A* and *O* forms; they could be either true or false. If it's false that no pigs eat milo, then it's true that some pigs do. But we can't infer whether or not all do.

Existential Import

Aristotle's square concisely expresses a variety of logical relations. But, does it do so correctly? Do the relations the square posits really hold?

Certainly, *A* and *O* sentence forms are contradictories. Under no circumstances can 'All *F* are *G*' and 'Some *F* are not *G*' have the same truth value. Similarly, *E* and *I* sentence forms are contradictories: 'No *F* are *G*' and 'Some *F* are *G*' always disagree in truth value. This much is uncontroversial.

Every other relation in the square of opposition, however, is questionable. In fact, our Venn diagram representations of sentence forms indicate that none of the others hold. Consider first the contention that 'All *F* are *G*' implies 'Some *F* are *G*'. At first glance, this seems plausible. But consider the diagrams:

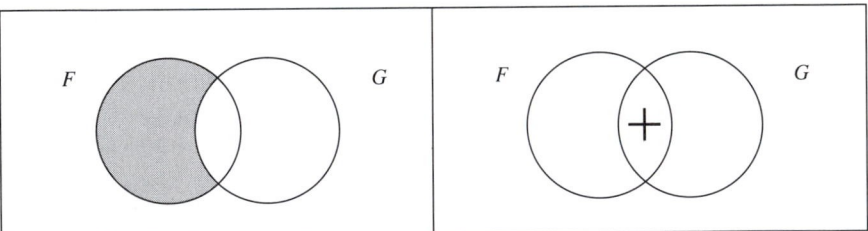

All *F* are *G*   Some *F* are *G*

Clearly, the diagram for 'All *F* are *G*' doesn't guarantee the truth of 'Some *F* are *G*'. Nothing there indicates whether there is anything in the intersection of the *F* and *G* circles.

The same is true of the alleged implication between 'No *F* are *G*' and 'Some *F* are not *G*'. The diagrams don't support the square of opposition's claim that *E* sentence forms entail *O* sentence forms.

No F are G   Some F are not G

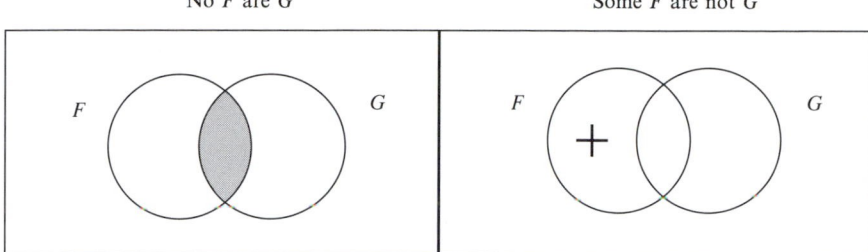

The diagram on the left, 'No F are G', doesn't specify whether anything is in the portion of the F circle outside the G circle. Thus, it doesn't guarantee the truth of 'Some F are not G'. If our diagrams represent the meanings of categorical sentence forms faithfully, then the implication relations in the square of opposition don't hold.

The same is true of the contrary and subcontrary relations. We can try to diagram 'All F are G' and 'No F are G' together, for example, to see whether they can both be true:

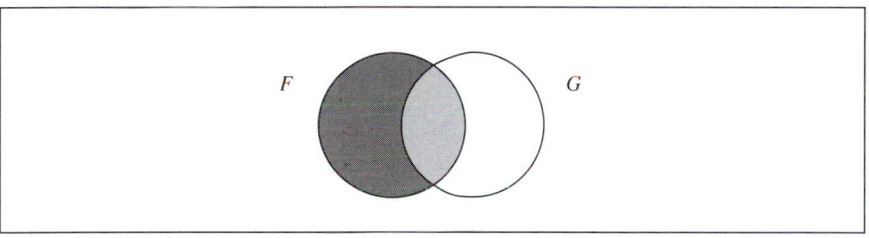

Diagramming A and E sentence forms together leads to no contradiction. Never are we forced to shade and mark with a plus sign the same region. So, 'All F are G' and 'No F are G' can be true at the same time. The diagram, moreover, indicates when: Both sentence forms are true if there are no Fs. The diagram also shows that 'Some F are G' and 'Some F are not G' can both be false. Indeed, both are false if the extension of F is empty.

It may seem bizarre to maintain that 'All F are G' doesn't imply 'Some F are G', and that 'All F are G' and 'No F are G' might both be true. But consider some examples of English sentences with subjects that could have empty extensions.

(20) a. All shoplifters will be prosecuted.
     b. Some shoplifters will be prosecuted.
     c. No shoplifters will be prosecuted.

Because (20)b and (20)c are contradictories, the question whether (20)a implies (20)b is the same as the question whether (20)a and (20)c can both be true. Venn diagrams say that (20)a and (20)c are true, and (20)b is false, if there are no shoplifters. This seems right. If a store posts a sign saying that all shoplifters will be prosecuted, and the sign works to deter shoplifters, then nobody will be prosecuted for shoplifting. This doesn't contradict what the sign says. In such a case, (20)a and (20)c are true, while (20)b is false.

Here is another example: Suppose that a teacher announces that all students who fail to do the homework fail the course. This frightens the students; everyone does the homework, and everyone passes. What the teacher said remains true; but, since nobody failed the course, nobody who failed to do the homework failed the course. So, (21)a and (21)c are true, while (21)b is false:

(21) a. All students who failed to do the homework failed the course.
b. Some students who failed to do the homework didn't fail the course.
c. No students who failed to do the homework failed the course.

A final example: The theory of relativity states that accelerating a body to the speed of light would require an infinite amount of energy. So, 'All accelerations of a body to the speed of light require an infinite amount of energy' is true. But this doesn't imply that there are, or even could be, such accelerations. In fact, it implies that accelerating a body to the speed of light is impossible.

The square of opposition poses another problem as well. If A sentence forms imply I sentence forms, then how can A and O sentence forms be contradictories? As we've seen, 'All F are G', if it's to imply 'Some F are G', must imply that there are Fs. But 'Some F are not G' also seems to imply that there are Fs. So, if there are no Fs, both 'All F are G' and 'Some F are not G' must be false. This, however, means that they aren't contradictories, for there are circumstances in which they have the same truth value. The same difficulty arises for E and I sentence forms.

These problems leave a defender of Aristotle's square with two options. First, it's possible to say that the relations that the square alleges hold, but only when all terms have instances. That is, we can see Aristotle's square as describing the relations of categorical sentence forms having terms with non-empty extensions. This would lead us to say that 'All F are G' and 'No F are G', for example, aren't strictly contraries, but they can't both be true if there are Fs. Similarly, we could say that 'Some F are G' and 'Some F are not G' aren't strictly subcontraries, but they can't both be false if there are Fs. We might even go further and claim that A and E sentence forms presuppose the existence of things satisfying their subject terms. This would make the square hold in all cases in which the presupposition is accommodated into the common ground.

Second, we could try to alter our understanding of the meanings of categorical sentence forms so that the relations alleged by the square do hold absolutely. We could interpret 'All F are G' as asserting that every F is G and, moreover, that there are Fs. Because 'Some F are not G' is this sentence form's contradictory, we must interpret it as asserting that either some Fs aren't Gs or that there are no Fs. Analogously, we could interpret 'No F are G' as carrying existential import—as implying that there are Fs—and interpret 'Some F are G' as asserting that either there are Fs that are Gs or that there are no Fs. This preserves the relations of the square of opposition. But it has some bizarre consequences. There are no unicorns; there are no golden mountains. This strategy would force us to call the following sentences true:

(22) a. Some unicorns are eating my computer as I write this.
   b. Some unicorns are not pleased with their depiction in the tapestries.
   c. Some golden mountains have been found in New Mexico.
   d. Some golden mountains aren't popular with skiers.

It also runs into difficulties with further relations among categorical sentence forms.

Other Immediate Inferences

Aristotle discussed two other relations among categorical sentence forms. They go beyond the framework we've developed so far. In particular, they involve the notion of the *complement* of a general term.

The *complement nonF* of a predicate F is true of exactly those things of which F is false. Many general terms in English are formed from other general terms by adding 'not' or a prefix such as 'a-', 'in-', 'im-', 'un-', 'ab-', 'non-', 'il-', and so on. Consider, for example, the pairs of terms in this list:

F	Non$F$
mortal	immortal
legal	illegal
normal	abnormal
legitimate	illegitimate
able	unable
complete	incomplete
adequate	inadequate
fair	unfair
entity	nonentity

Of course, many terms whose meanings are similarly opposed contain no prefix that signals the opposition. Note that the complement of the complement of a term applies just to objects in the extension of the original term. For this reason, we can cancel (or add) pairs of 'non's: *nonnonF* and F are interchangeable.

The negations or complements of more complex general terms are trickier to form because we must be careful to negate the entire content of the term. The negation of 'fair and complete hearing' is not 'unfair and incomplete hearing', or 'unfair and incomplete nonhearing'; rather, the negation is a concept such as 'not a fair and complete hearing', or 'something other than a fair and complete hearing'.

The first relation involving complements is *contraposition*. We say that the *contrapositive* of a categorical sentence form is the form that results from (a) switching the order of the terms and (b) replacing each term with its complement. The following table gives contrapositives for each of the four categorical sentence forms.

Sentence Form	Contrapositive
All F are G	All non$G$ are non$F$
No F are G	No non$G$ are non$F$
Some F are G	Some non$G$ are non$F$
Some F are not G	Some non$G$ are not non$F$

Of these, only universal affirmatives and particular negatives are equivalent to their contrapositives. The following pairs are equivalent:

(23) a. All horses are animals.
  b. Anything that isn't an animal isn't a horse.

(24) a. Some mortals are not careful.
  b. Some who aren't careful are not immortal.

Thus, we can state a principle of contraposition:

Contraposition

A and O sentence forms are equivalent to their contrapositives. Thus, (a) 'All F are G' is equivalent to 'All non$G$ are non$F$', and (b) 'Some F are not G' is equivalent to 'Some non$G$ are not non$F$'.

To see that this principle doesn't extend to E and I sentence forms, consider the following pairs of sentences, which are not equivalent:

(25) a. No humans are vegetables.
  b. Nothing that isn't a vegetable is nonhuman.

(26) a. Some people are nondrivers.
  b. Some drivers are nonpeople.

The second relation involving complements is *obversion*. The *obverse* of a categorical sentence form is the sentence form that results from (a) changing its quality (from affirmative to negative, or vice versa) and (b) replacing its predicate term with its complement. The following table gives obverses for each sentence form.

Categorical Sentence Form	Obverse
All *F* are *G*	No *F* are non*G*
No *F* are *G*	All *F* are non*G*
Some *F* are *G*	Some *F* are not non*G*
Some *F* are not *G*	Some *F* are non*G*

Obversion always yields an equivalent sentence form. Consider, for example, the following pairs of sentences, which illustrate obversion for each sentence form:

(27) a. All humans are mortal.
  b. No humans are immortal.

(28) a. No administrators are helpful.
  b. All administrators are unhelpful.

(29) a. Some kinds of killing are legal.
  b. Some kinds of killing are not illegal.

(30) a. Some laws passed by Congress are not constitutional.
  b. Some laws passed by Congress are unconstitutional.

This allows us to state a principle of obversion:

Obversion

Any categorical sentence form is equivalent to its obverse. Thus,
  (a) 'All *F* are *G*' is equivalent to 'No *F* are non*G*';
  (b) 'No *F* are *G*' is equivalent to 'All *F* are non*G*';
  (c) 'Some *F* are *G*' is equivalent to 'Some *F* are not non*G*';
  (d) 'Some *F* are not *G*' is equivalent to 'Some *F* are non*G*'.

The principles of contraposition and obversion are uncontroversial. As we'll see in section 9.6, we can use Venn diagrams to demonstrate their validity. Accepting these principles, however, leads to further difficulties for Aristotle's square of opposition. The square alleges that 'All *F* are *G*' implies 'Some *F* are *G*' and that 'No *F* are *G*' implies 'Some *F* are not *G*'. But, with the help of conversion, contraposition, and obversion, we can show that 'All *F* are *G*' and 'No *F* are *G*' imply not only that there are *F*s but also that there are *G*s, non*F*s, and non*G*s. Consider the following derivations:

(31) All *F* are *G*.
  Some *F* are *G*.   Square
  ∴ There are *G*s.

(32) All *F* are *G*.
     All non*G* are non*F*.   Contraposition
     Some non*G* are non*F*.   Square
     ∴ There are non*G*s and non*F*s.

(33) No *F* are *G*.
     Some *F* are not *G*.   Square
     ∴ There are *F*s and non*G*s.

(34) No *F* are *G*.
     No *G* are *F*.   Conversion
     Some *G* are not *F*.   Square
     ∴ There are *G*s and non*F*s.

Thus, in Aristotle's logic, no terms may have empty extensions; furthermore, no terms may have the entire universe of discourse as extensions. If we adopt the first strategy—of limiting the application of Aristotle's square—we must limit ourselves to categorical sentence forms with terms that apply to some, but not all, things. We must banish not only terms such as 'shoplifter', 'student who fails to do the homework', 'unicorn', and 'acceleration to the speed of light', which can or do have empty extensions, but also terms such as 'thing' and 'object', which can or do have the universe as their extension. This is a severe limitation on the theory.

If we adopt the second strategy—of reformulating the meanings of the categorical sentence forms—we must reformulate them more radically. To see why, consider 'All *F* are *G*' and 'All non*G* are non*F*'. By contraposition, these sentence forms are equivalent. But, if we construe the first as meaning 'Every *F* is *G*, and there are *F*s' and the second as 'Every non*G* is non*F*, and there are non*G*s', the two sentence forms aren't equivalent at all. To preserve contraposition and obversion, we would have to interpret 'All *F* are *G*' to mean that 'Every *F* is *G*, and there are *F*s, *G*s, non*F*s, and non*G*s'. 'Some *F* are *G*' would have to mean that 'Either there is an *F* that is also a *G*, or there are no *F*s, or there are no *G*s, or there are no non*F*s, or there are no non*G*s'. This is extremely implausible. No one would assert the truth of 'Some things are both round and square' on the grounds that there are no nonthings.

For reasons such as these, logicians since the nineteenth century have almost invariably rejected Aristotle's thesis that universal sentence forms have existential import, implying the corresponding particular sentence forms. They have therefore rejected the relations posited in the square of opposition, with the exception of contradictoriness. To summarize: Modern logic accepts the principles of contradictoriness, conversion, contraposition, and obversion; however, modern logic rejects the idea that *A* and *E* sentence forms are contraries, that *I* and *O* forms are subcontraries, that *A* forms imply *I* forms, and that *E* forms imply *O* forms.

Problems

For each of the following sentences, give (a) its converse, (b) its obverse, (c) its contrapositive, and (d) its contradictory. Which are equivalent to the original sentence?

▸ **1.** A bird in the hand is worth two in the bush.

▸ **2.** Blessed are the peacemakers.

▸ **3.** Some books are worth reading twice.

▸ **4.** A stitch in time saves nine.

▸ **5.** He jests at scars who never felt a wound.

▸ **6.** Not one of the Greeks at Thermopylae escaped.

7. Whatever you say, I shall not believe you.

8. Only the good die young.

9. Among those who voted against the motion were some Republicans.

10. None but the brave deserve the fair.

11. No man was ever wise by chance. (Seneca)

▸ **12.** There are men who are happy without knowing it. (Vauvenargues)

13. He who feels punctured must once have been a bubble. (Lao-Tzu)

14. Art never expresses anything but itself. (Oscar Wilde)

15. None deserves praise for being good who has not spirit enough to be bad. (La Rochefoucauld)

16. All who remember, doubt. (Theodore Roethke)

17. All that I know, I learned after I was thirty. (Georges Clemenceau)

▸ **18.** There is no detail that is too small. (George Allen)

19. Only the shallow know themselves. (Oscar Wilde)

20. ... And now nothing will be restrained from them, which they have imagined to do. (Genesis 11:6)

The terms 'contradictory', 'contrary', and 'subcontrary' apply to all sentences, not just those of categorical form. For each of the following, wherever possible, give (a) a contradictory, (b) a contrary, and (c) a subcontrary.

21. It's raining.

22. Jesse is sick today.

23. Verne doesn't like Clarence.

▸ **24.** Somebody saw us.

25. Everyone left hours ago.

26. Albania and Bulgaria are both Balkan countries.

27. Rhoda or her assistant sent us the forms.

28. If you argue with me, I won't listen to you.

29. All that glitters is not gold.

▸ **30.** Some, but not all of us, got away.

31. If 'All roads lead to Rome' is true, what may we deduce about the truth values of the following?
 (a) Some roads lead to Rome.
 (b) No roads lead to Rome.
 (c) Some roads don't lead to Rome.
 (d) Anything that leads to Rome is a road.
 (e) Nothing that leads to Rome is not a road.
 (f) No road fails to lead to Rome.
 (g) Anything that doesn't lead to Rome is no road.
 (h) Some things that don't lead to Rome aren't roads.
 (i) Only roads lead to Rome.

32. What may we deduce about these sentences if 'All roads lead to Rome' is false?

33. If 'Nobody knows the trouble I've seen' is true, what can we deduce about the truth values of the following?
 (a) Everyone knows the trouble I've seen.
 (b) Somebody knows the trouble I've seen.
 (c) Somebody doesn't know the trouble I've seen.
 (d) Everybody is ignorant of the trouble I've seen.

34. What may we deduce about the preceding sentences if 'Nobody knows the trouble I've seen' is false?

35. If 'Some actors aren't vain' is true, what can we deduce about the truth values of the following?
 (a) All actors are vain.
 (b) Some actors are vain.
 (c) No actors are vain.
 (d) Some who aren't vain are actors.
 (e) Some who are vain aren't actors.
 (f) Only actors are vain.
 (g) Only vain people are actors.
 (h) Nobody who isn't an actor is vain.
 (i) Nobody who isn't vain is an actor.

▶ **36.** What can we deduce about these sentences if 'Some actors aren't vain' is false?

37. If 'Some beasts eat their young' is true, what can we deduce about the truth values of these sentences?
(a) No beasts eat their young.
(b) All beasts eat their young.
(c) Some beasts don't eat their young.
(d) Some that eat their young are beasts.
(e) None that eat their young are beasts.
(f) Some that don't eat their young aren't beasts.
(g) Some that aren't beasts don't eat their young.
(h) All beasts avoid eating their young.
(i) All that eat their young are beasts.
(j) Only those that eat their young are beasts.

38. What can we deduce about these sentences if 'Some beasts eat their young' is false?

9.4 SYLLOGISMS

Aristotle defined *syllogism* very broadly, so that virtually any argument counted as a syllogism. His theory, however, treats arguments of a much more restricted form. We define the term as follows:

> **DEFINITION**   A *syllogism* is an argument form containing three categorical sentence forms and three predicates, where each predicate appears in two sentence forms.

Each of the following is a syllogism:

(35) a. All *F* are *G*.   b. Some *H* are *F*.
  No *G* are *H*.   No *G* are *F*.
  ∴ No *H* are *F*.   ∴ Some *G* are not *H*.
 c. All *F* are *G*.   d. Some *F* are not *H*.
  Some *F* are not *H*.   No *H* are *G*.
  ∴ Some *G* are not *H*.   ∴ Some *G* are *F*.

Some syllogisms are valid, but others aren't. In this section we'll develop a method for determining the validity of a syllogism.

As we've seen, Venn devised a way to represent the meanings of categorical sentence forms. It extends easily to a procedure for evaluating syllogisms. Every syllogism contains three predicates. Consequently, we begin evaluating a syllogism by constructing a diagram showing a circle for each term:

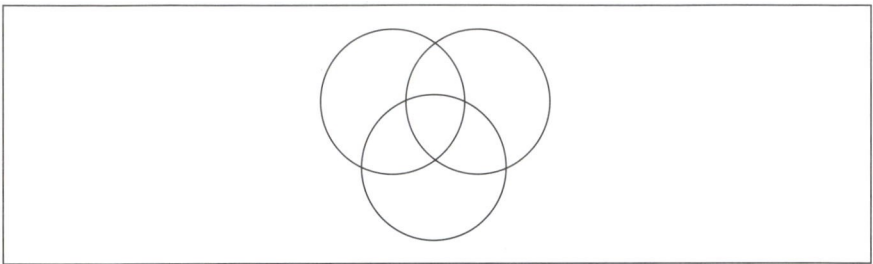

It's important that these circles overlap. Otherwise, the diagram would not reflect all possible relationships between the extensions of the syllogism's predicates.

Second, we label each circle with a predicate. Third, we diagram the syllogism's premises. Diagramming universal sentence forms is unaffected by the presence of three circles instead of two. We simply ignore the circle for the term uninvolved in the sentence form.

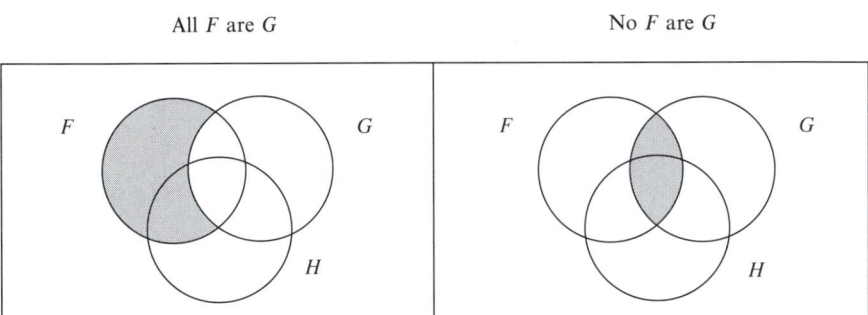

The situation for particular sentence forms, however, is more com-plicated. Consider a particular affirmative, 'Some F are G'. When two circles are involved, we put a plus sign in the intersection of the circles labeled F and G.

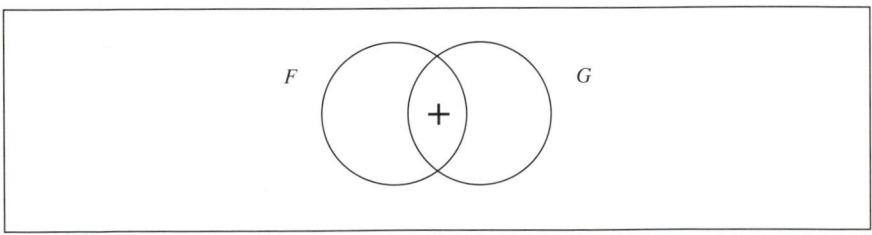

When three circles are considered, however, this region is divided by the circle for the uninvolved term (*H*). Placing the plus sign outside the uninvolved *H* circle indicates that something is an *F*, a *G*, and not an *H*.

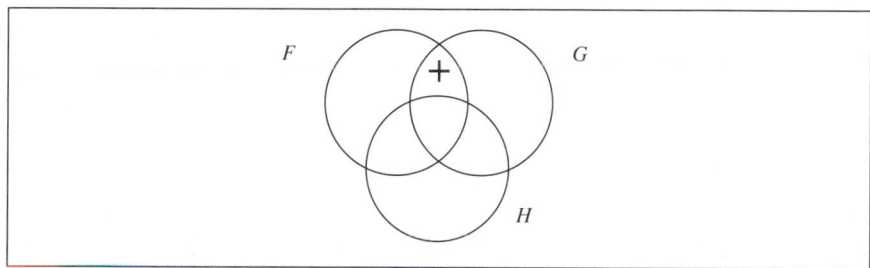

But 'Some *F* are *G*' doesn't assert anything about *H*; so, this diagram is wrong. Alternatively, putting the plus sign inside the *H* circle indicates that something is an *F*, a *G*, and an *H*.

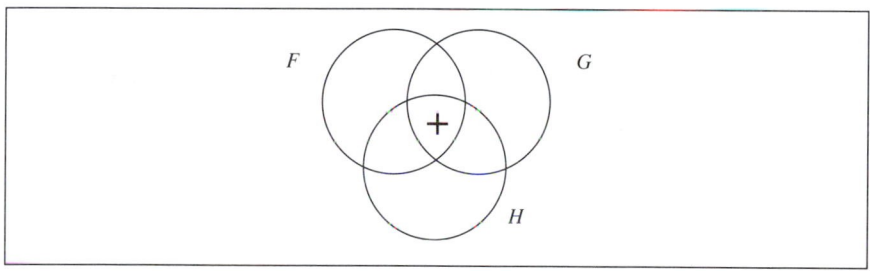

Again, this diagram presumes too much; the sentence form makes no commitment regarding *H*. To remain uncommitted about whether the thing that is both *F* and *G* is also *H*, we can "straddle the fence": We can place a bar through the line that divides the intersection of the *F* and *G* circles. A bar indicates that something is on one side or the other of the line it crosses.

We can represent 'Some *F* are *G*' on a diagram with three circles, in this fashion:

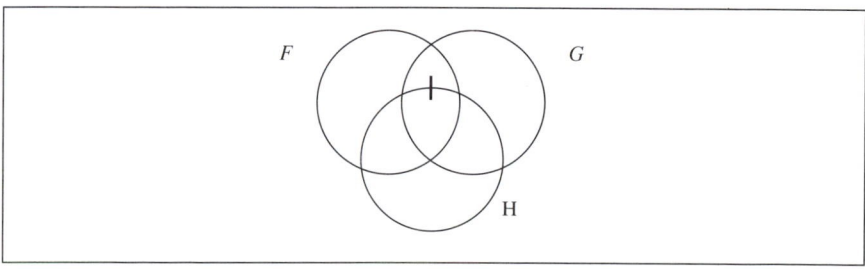

Similarly, we can represent 'Some *F* are not *G*' as follows.

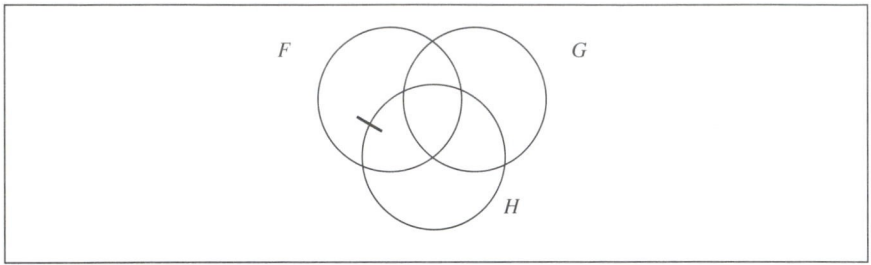

The bar indicates that we don't know whether any *F*s are *H*. We know only that some *F*s aren't *G*. In both cases, the bar crosses the circle for the term not present in the sentence form being represented. The bar indicates that something is in the larger region made up of both areas into which it extends.

After diagramming both premises, we check to see whether the diagram guarantees the truth of the conclusion. If the diagram does, the syllogism is valid. If the diagram doesn't, the argument form is not valid. The diagram, at this point, provides an interpretation of the syllogism in which the premises are true. If the conclusion must also be true, on this interpretation, the syllogism is valid.

Consider the examples of syllogisms from the beginning of this section. The first,

(35) a. All *F* are *G*.
     No *G* are *H*.
     ∴ No *H* are *F*.

is a form of an argument such as

(36) Every student in this class wants an A.
     Nobody who wants an A neglects homework assignments.
     ∴ No one who neglects homework assignments is a student in this class.

To test the argument form for validity, we construct a diagram with three intersecting circles, labeling them *F*, *G*, and *H*, and begin to diagram the premises. The first premise, a universal affirmative sentence form, results in the following diagram:

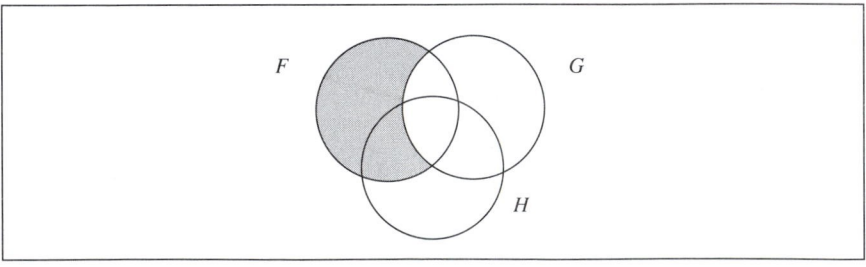

After diagramming the second, we obtain:

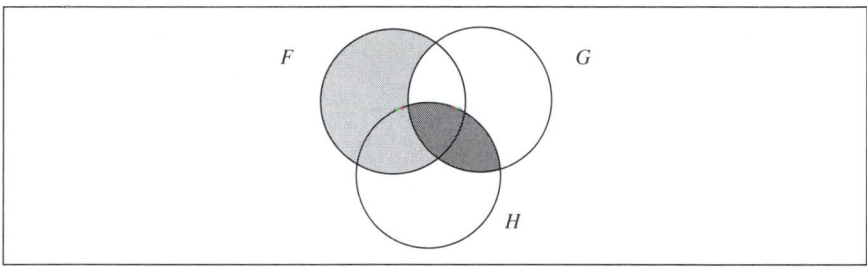

Does this diagram guarantee the truth of the conclusion, 'No *H* are *F*'? Yes: The entire intersection of the *H* and *F* circles is shaded. If the premises are true, then nothing is both an *H* and an *F*. Thus, any interpretation making the premise sentence forms true must make the conclusion sentence form true as well. The syllogism is valid.

Recall our second example:

> (35) b. Some *H* are *F*.
>   No *G* are *F*.
>   ∴ Some *G* are not *H*.

This is a form of the argument

> (37) Some political consultants work for candidates with whom they
>   disagree.
>   No ideologues work for candidates with whom they disagree.
>   ∴ Some ideologues are not political consultants.

We begin, once again, by constructing a diagram of three circles. After representing the first premise, we have:

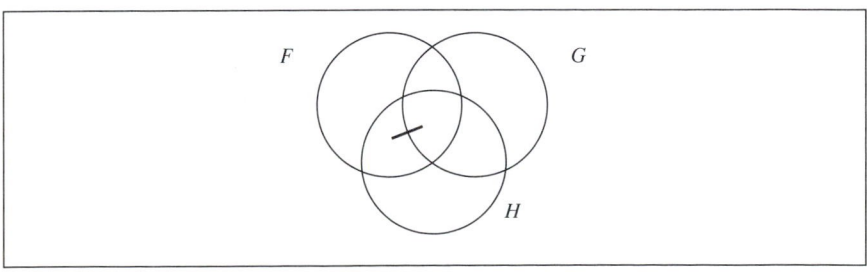

After diagramming the second, we obtain:

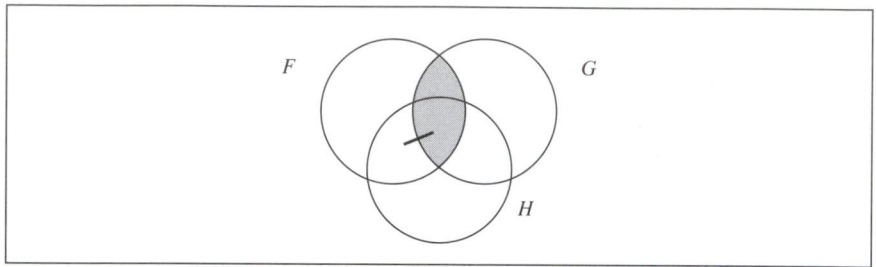

Does this guarantee the truth of the conclusion, 'Some *G* are not *H*'? Clearly, the answer is no: The diagram does not indicate that there is a *G* that is not an *H*. The diagram thus gives an interpretation of the syllogism on which the premise sentence forms are true but the conclusion is false.

We can evaluate our third example,

> (35) c. All *F* are *G*.
>   Some *F* are not *H*.
>   ∴ Some *G* are not *H*.

which is a form of the argument

> (38) Each desk in the room has some graffiti written on it.
>   Some desks in this room are not very old.
>   ∴ Some things marked with graffiti are not very old.

Diagramming the first premise results in this:

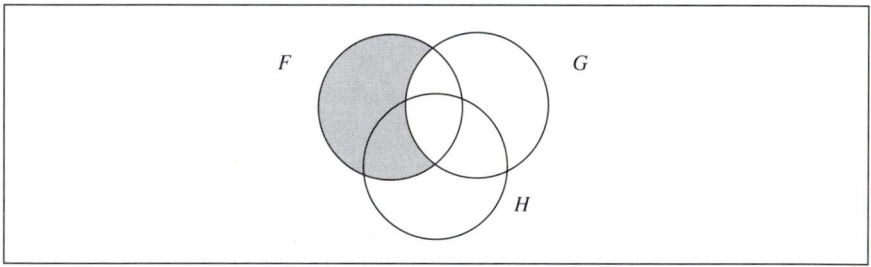

Diagramming the second produces this:

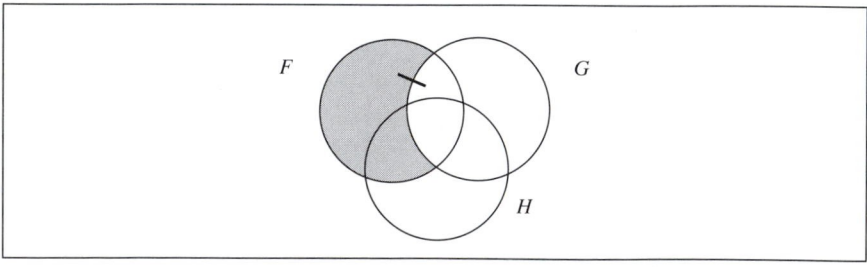

The result does guarantee the conclusion's truth; therefore, the syllogism is valid. The diagram indicates that something is both an *F* and a *G* but not an *H*, implying that some *G* are not *H*.

Finally, evaluating our fourth example, we find it invalid:

(35) d. Some *F* are not *H*.
No *H* are *G*.
∴ Some *G* are *F*.

This is a form of the following argument:

(39) Some of your friends are not very nice people.
Nobody who is very nice would insult a total stranger.
∴ Some people who would insult a total stranger are your friends.

Representing the meaning of the first premise yields this diagram:

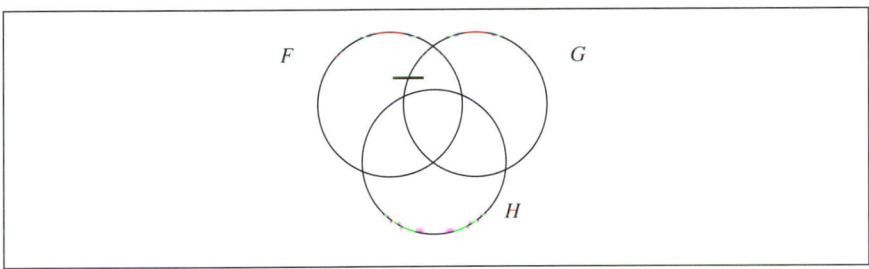

Representing the meaning of the second results in this:

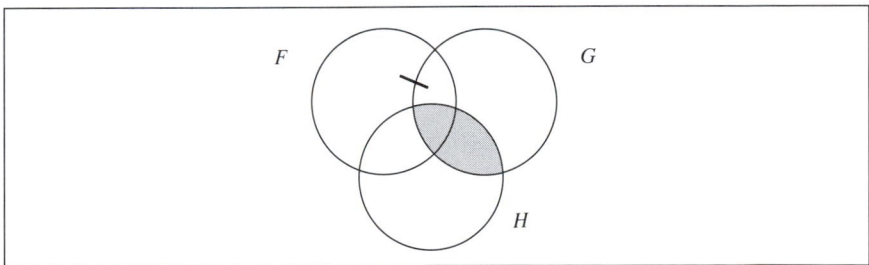

The result does not guarantee that some *F* are *G*. The diagram indicates that something is an *F* without being an *H*; however, it may or may not be a *G*. We have no guarantee that something occupies the intersection of the *F* and *G* circles. The syllogism is therefore invalid.

To summarize the Venn diagram method:

1. Construct a diagram consisting of three intersecting circles.

2. Label each circle with a predicate.

3. Diagram the first premise.

4. Diagram the second premise.

5. Check to see whether the diagram guarantees the truth of the conclusion. If it does, the syllogism is valid. If not, the syllogism is not valid.

Problems

Evaluate the following syllogisms.

▶ **1.** All *G* are *H*.
All *F* are *G*.
∴ All *F* are *H*.

▶ **2.** All *G* are *H*.
No *F* are *G*.
∴ No *F* are *H*.

▶ **3.** All *G* are *H*.
Some *F* are *G*.
∴ Some *F* are *H*.

▶ **4.** No *G* are *H*.
All *F* are *G*.
∴ No *F* are *H*.

▶ **5.** No *G* are *H*.
No *F* are *G*.
∴ All *F* are *H*.

▶ **6.** No *G* are *H*.
No *F* are *G*.
∴ Some *F* are not *H*.

7. No *G* are *H*.
Some *F* are *G*.
∴ Some *F* are not *H*.

8. No *G* are *H*.
Some *F* are not *G*.
∴ Some *F* are *H*.

9. Some *G* are *H*.
All *F* are *G*.
∴ Some *F* are *H*.

10. Some *G* are *H*.
Some *F* are *G*.
∴ Some *F* are *H*.

11. Some *G* are not *H*.
All *F* are *G*.
∴ Some *F* are not *H*.

▶ **12.** Some *G* are not *H*.
No *F* are *G*.
∴ Some *F* are not *H*.

13. Some *G* are not *H*.
Some *F* are not *G*.
∴ Some *F* are not *H*.

14. All *H* are *G*.
All *F* are *G*.
∴ All *F* are *H*.

15. All *H* are *G*.
No *F* are *G*.
∴ No *F* are *H*.

16. All *H* are *G*.
Some *F* are *G*.
∴ Some *F* are *H*.

17. All *H* are *G*.
Some *F* are not *G*.
∴ Some *F* are not *H*.

▶ **18.** No *H* are *G*.
All *F* are *G*.
∴ No *F* are *H*.

19. No *H* are *G*.
No *F* are *G*.
∴ All *F* are *H*.

20. No *H* are *G*.
No *F* are *G*.
∴ Some *F* are not *H*.

21. No *H* are *G*.
    Some *F* are *G*.
    ∴ Some *F* are not *H*.

22. No *H* are *G*.
    Some *F* are not *G*.
    ∴ Some *F* are *H*.

23. Some *H* are *G*.
    All *F* are *G*.
    ∴ Some *F* are *H*.

▸ 24. Some *H* are *G*.
    Some *F* are *G*.
    ∴ Some *F* are *H*.

25. Some *H* are not *G*.
    All *F* are *G*.
    ∴ Some *F* are not *H*.

26. Some *H* are not *G*.
    No *F* are *G*.
    ∴ Some *F* are not *H*.

27. Some *H* are not *G*.
    Some *F* are not *G*.
    ∴ Some *F* are not *H*.

28. All *G* are *H*.
    All *G* are *F*.
    ∴ All *F* are *H*.

29. All *G* are *H*.
    No *G* are *F*.
    ∴ No *F* are *H*.

▸ 30. All *G* are *H*.
    Some *G* are *F*.
    ∴ Some *F* are *H*.

31. No *G* are *H*.
    All *G* are *F*.
    ∴ No *F* are *H*.

32. No *G* are *H*.
    No *G* are *F*.
    ∴ All *F* are *H*.

33. No *G* are *H*.
    No *G* are *F*.
    ∴ Some *F* are not *H*.

34. No *G* are *H*.
    Some *G* are *F*.
    ∴ Some *F* are not *H*.

35. No *G* are *H*.
    Some *G* are not *F*.
    ∴ Some *F* are *H*.

▸ 36. Some *G* are *H*.
    All *G* are *F*.
    ∴ Some *F* are *H*.

37. Some *G* are *H*.
    Some *G* are *F*.
    ∴ Some *F* are *H*.

38. Some *G* are not *H*.
    All *G* are *F*.
    ∴ Some *F* are not *H*.

39. Some *G* are not *H*.
    No *G* are *F*.
    ∴ Some *F* are not *H*.

40. Some *G* are not *H*.
    Some *G* are not *F*.
    ∴ Some *F* are not *H*.

41. All *H* are *G*.
    All *G* are *F*.
    ∴ All *F* are *H*.

▸ 42. All *H* are *G*.
    No *G* are *F*.
    ∴ No *F* are *H*.

43. All *H* are *G*.
    Some *G* are *F*.
    ∴ Some *F* are *H*.

44. No *H* are *G*.
    All *G* are *F*.
    ∴ No *F* are *H*.

45. No *H* are *G*.
    No *G* are *F*.
    ∴ All *F* are *H*.

46. No *H* are *G*.
    No *G* are *F*.
    ∴ Some *F* are not *H*.

47. No *H* are *G*.
Some *G* are *F*.
∴ Some *F* are not *H*.

▶ **48.** No *H* are *G*.
Some *G* are not *F*.
∴ Some *F* are *H*.

49. Some *H* are *G*.
All *G* are *F*.
∴ Some *F* are *H*.

50. Some *H* are *G*.
Some *G* are *F*.
∴ Some *F* are *H*.

51. Some *H* are not *G*.
All *G* are *F*.
∴ Some *F* are not *H*.

52. Some *H* are not *G*.
No *G* are *F*.
∴ Some *F* are not *H*.

53. Some *H* are not *G*.
Some *G* are not *F*.
∴ Some *F* are not *H*.

These are arguments of syllogistic form from the Port Royal *Logic,* many of which make ethical and religious points. Translate them into Aristotelian language and evaluate them for validity.

▶ **54.** All happy persons are content. No miser is content. Therefore, no miser is happy.

55. No liar is believable. Every upright man is believable. Therefore, no upright man is a liar.

56. All bodies are divisible. All that is divisible is imperfect. Therefore, all bodies are imperfect.

57. Everything which leads toward salvation is advantageous. There are some afflictions that lead toward salvation. Therefore, there are some afflictions that are advantageous.

58. The infinite divisibility of matter is incomprehensible. The infinite divisibility of matter is most certain. Therefore, there are some most certain things that are incomprehensible.

59. No man can abandon himself. Every man is an enemy to himself. Therefore, there are some enemies whom we cannot abandon.

▶ **60.** There are some wicked men with great wealth. All wicked men are miserable. Therefore, there are some miserable men with great wealth.

61. Every servant of God is a king. There are some servants of God who are poor. Therefore, some poor people are kings.

62. There are some angers which are not blameworthy. All anger is passion. Therefore, there are some passions that are not blameworthy.

63. No folly is eloquent. Some folly is expressed syllogistically. Therefore, some syllogisms are not eloquent.

64. All the miracles of nature are ordinary. All that is ordinary fails to catch our attention. Therefore, there are things that fail to capture our attention but that are miracles of nature.

65. All the evils of this life are transitory evils. No transitory evil is to be feared. Therefore, no evil that is to be feared is an evil of this life.

▶ **66.** Some fools speak the truth. Whoever speaks the truth deserves to be imitated. Therefore, there are those who deserve to be imitated even though they are fools.

67. No virtue is a natural quality. All natural qualities have God as their author. Therefore, there are some qualities that have God as their author but are not virtues.

68. No unfortunate person is happy. Some happy persons are poor. Therefore, there are poor people who are not unfortunate.

69. Nothing that is followed by a just regret is ever to be wished for. There are some pleasures which are followed by a just regret. Therefore, there are some pleasures which are not to be wished for.

70. Whoever lets those he should support die of hunger is a murderer. All the rich who do not give alms in the time of public need let those they should support die of hunger. Therefore, all the rich who do not give alms in the time of public need are murderers.

9.5 RULES FOR VALIDITY

Before Euler and Venn developed their diagram techniques, there were two ways of evaluating syllogisms. The first, stemming from Aristotle's method, involved reducing syllogisms to those of a few special forms. According to this method, a syllogism is valid if it can be transformed by applying a specified set of rules into a paradigmatically valid form. (For more on this method, see the problems at the end of this section.) The second way of evaluating syllogisms involved applying rules for validity. A syllogism is valid, according to this method, if it violates none of the rules. This section develops the second method and presents a modern set of rules for validity.

A syllogism contains exactly three general terms.

> **DEFINITION** The conclusion's grammatical predicate is the *major term* of the syllogism. The conclusion's grammatical subject is the *minor term*. The term appearing in both premises is the *middle term*.

Each premise contains the middle term and one other. The *major premise* contains the major term; the *minor premise* contains the minor term. A syllogism is in *standard form* if and only if it's stated in this form:

Major premise
Minor premise
∴ Conclusion

Consider, for example, the syllogistic argument

(40) All cities with rent control have high occupancy rates.
Some cities with high occupancy rates have many homeless people.
∴ Some cities with rent control have many homeless people.

and the corresponding syllogism

(41) All F are H.
Some H are G.
∴ Some F are G.

The major term is G ('have many homeless people'); the minor term is F ('cities with rent control'). H ('cities having high occupancy rates') appears in both premises and is therefore the middle term. The first premise contains the minor term and is thus the minor premise. This syllogism, consequently, is not in standard form. To put it in standard form, we may switch the order of the premises:

(42) Some H are G. I
All F are H. A
∴ Some F are G. I

A syllogism's *mood* is a list of three letters signifying the form of the major premise, minor premise, and conclusion. The mood of (42) is IAI. The *figure* of a syllogism depends on the placement of its middle term. In *first figure* syllogisms, the middle term is the subject of the major premise and the predicate of the minor premise. In *second figure* syllogisms, the middle term is the predicate of both premises. In the *third figure,* the middle term is the subject of both premises. In *fourth figure* syllogisms, finally, the middle term is the predicate of the major premise and subject of the minor premise. This chart summarizes the figures according to the position of the middle term, M, in standard form (where J is the major, and N the minor, term):

	First Figure		Second Figure		Third Figure		Fourth Figure	
Major premise	M	J	J	M	M	J	J	M
Minor premise	N	M	N	M	M	N	M	N
Conclusion	N	J	N	J	N	J	N	J

The key notion behind the rules for validity is *distribution*. Medieval logicians developed the doctrine of distribution as a theory about the semantics of general terms. In particular, they held that the distribution of a term indicates whether it refers to all or only part of a set. A sentence *distributes* a term occurring in it if and only if it refers significantly to the entire extension of the term.[3] Thus, a term is distributed in a sentence if the sentence refers significantly to its entire extension. It is undistributed there if the sentence refers significantly to only part of its extension. In 'All people are mortal', for example, 'people' is distributed; the sentence refers significantly to all people, for everyone is relevant to the truth value of the sentence. In 'Some people are crazy', however, 'people' is undistributed; the sentence refers significantly only to some people, for the people who aren't crazy are irrelevant to the sentence's truth value.

In fact, the doctrine of distribution, in these terms, is nonsense. A determiner relates general terms. In most cases, we can think of it as relating extensions of terms, or sets. The sentence 'All people are mortal', for example, asserts that a certain relation holds between the set of people and the set of mortals. Similarly, 'Some people are crazy' asserts that a different relation holds between the set of people and the set of crazy things. In both cases, the sentence says something about the "entire" set of people; in that sense, the set as a whole is relevant to the sentence's truth or falsity. The idea that 'all people' refers to all people and 'some people' refers to some people rests on a mistaken conception of what determiners such as 'all' and 'some' do.

So, why consider distribution at all? First, it supplies simple rules for judging the validity of syllogisms. These rules are mechanical and effective. Second, there is a historical reason: Rules based on the doctrine of distribution offered the most popular way of evaluating syllogisms for about 600 years, from the thirteenth through the nineteenth centuries. Third, the method works because facts about distribution correspond to important features of determiners.[4]

According to the medieval doctrine, a sentence's quantity determines the distribution of its subject term. Universal sentences have distributed subjects; particular sentences have undistributed subjects. A sentence's quality determines the distribution of its grammatical predicate. Negative sentences have distributed predicate terms, whereas affirmative sentences have undistributed predicate terms. To summarize in tabular form:

Universal Affirmative:	All	$F^{Distributed}$	are	$G^{Undistributed}$
Particular Affirmative:	Some	$F^{Undistributed}$	are	$G^{Undistributed}$
Universal Negative:	No	$F^{Distributed}$	are	$G^{Distributed}$
Particular Negative:	Some	$F^{Undistributed}$	are not	$G^{Distributed}$

Rules

There are three rules for validity that any valid syllogism must satisfy:

1. The occurrences of the middle term must disagree in distribution.

2. (a) The occurrences of the major term must agree in distribution.
   (b) The occurrences of the minor term must also agree.

3. (a) If the conclusion is affirmative, both premises must be affirmative.

(b) If the conclusion is negative, exactly one premise must be negative.

We may rewrite these rules as a procedure for evaluating syllogisms.

1. Do the occurrences of the middle term agree in distribution?

> If they do: Stop. The syllogism is not valid.
> If they don't: Continue.

2. (a) Do the occurrences of the major term agree in distribution?

> If they do: Continue.
> If they don't: Stop. The syllogism is not valid.

(b) Do the occurrences of the minor term agree in distribution?

> If they do: Continue.
> If they don't: Stop. The syllogism is not valid.

3. (a) If the conclusion is affirmative: Are both premises affirmative?

> If they are: Stop. The syllogism is valid.
> If they aren't: Stop. The syllogism is not valid.

(b) If the conclusion is negative: Is exactly one premise negative?

> If exactly one is: Stop. The syllogism is valid.
> If none is, or both are: Stop. The syllogism is not valid.

To see how to apply this procedure, let's consider again the examples of syllogisms from the beginning of section 9.4.

Here is the first, with the superscripts D and U included to indicate the distribution of each occurrence of a term:

(35) a. All F^D are G^U.
No G^D are H^D.
∴ No H^D are F^D.

The middle term, G, is distributed only once; therefore, rule 1 is satisfied. The major term, F, is distributed in both occurrences, as is the minor term, H. So, the syllogism satisfies rule 2. Finally, the conclusion is negative, and exactly one premise is negative. The syllogism, therefore, is valid: It satisfies all three rules.

Consider the next example, a syllogism that is not valid.

(35) b. Some H^U are F^U.
No G^D are F^D.
∴ Some G^U are not H^D.

Do the occurrences of the middle term, F, agree in distribution? No; therefore, rule 1 is satisfied. Do the occurrences of the major term, H, agree in distribution? No: H is distributed in the conclusion but not in the major premise. The syllogism is therefore invalid. It violates rule 2(a). More specifically, it commits what traditional logicians call *an illicit process* (in this case, *of the major*), for the syllogism distributes a term in the conclusion that is undistributed in the premises.

The syllogism, incidentally, violates rule 2(b) as well. The occurrences of the minor term, G, also disagree in distribution.

The next example is valid:

(35) c. All F^D are G^U.
  Some F^U are not H^D.
  $\therefore$ Some G^U are not H^D.

The occurrences of the middle term, F, disagree in distribution; therefore, rule 1 is satisfied. Both occurrences of the major, H, are distributed, and neither occurrence of the minor term, G, is distributed; so, rule 2 is satisfied. Finally, there is a negative conclusion with exactly one negative premise. The syllogism, consequently, satisfies all three rules.

The final example fails to be valid:

(35) d. Some F^U are not H^D.
  No H^D are G^D.
  $\therefore$ Some G^U are F^U.

The middle term, H, is distributed in both its occurrences, so this syllogism violates the first rule. This violation alone makes it invalid. But the syllogism violates both other rules, as well. The major term's occurrences are both undistributed, but the occurrences of the minor term, G, disagree in distribution. So, rule 2(b) is violated. Furthermore, the conclusion is affirmative, but both premises are negative. The syllogism thus violates rule 3, too.

To repeat: A valid syllogism satisfies all three rules. Violating even one rule makes a syllogism invalid.

Problems

Use the rules of this section to evaluate these syllogisms for validity.

▶ **1.** All G are H.
  All F are G.
  $\therefore$ All F are H.

▶ **2.** All G are H.
  All F are G.
  $\therefore$ Some F are H.

▶ **3.** All G are H.
  No F are G.
  $\therefore$ Some F are not H.

▶ **4.** All G are H.
  Some F are G.
  $\therefore$ Some F are H.

▸ **5.** All G are H.
Some F are not G.
∴ Some F are not H.

7. No G are H.
All F are G.
∴ Some F are not H.

9. No G are H.
Some F are G.
∴ Some F are not H.

11. Some G are H.
No F are G.
∴ Some F are not H.

13. Some G are not H.
No F are G.
∴ Some F are H.

15. Some G are not H.
Some F are not G.
∴ Some F are H.

17. All H are G.
No F are G.
∴ No F are H.

19. All H are G.
Some F are not G.
∴ Some F are not H.

21. No H are G.
All F are G.
∴ Some F are not H.

23. No H are G.
Some F are G.
∴ Some F are not H.

25. Some H are G.
No F are G.
∴ Some F are not H.

27. Some H are not G.
No F are G.
∴ Some F are H.

29. Some H are not G.
Some F are not G.
∴ Some F are H.

▸ **6.** No G are H.
All F are G.
∴ No F are H.

8. No G are H.
No F are G.
∴ No F are H.

10. No G are H.
Some F are not G.
∴ Some F are not H.

▸ **12.** Some G are H.
Some F are not G.
∴ Some F are not H.

14. Some G are not H.
Some F are G.
∴ Some F are not H.

16. All H are G.
All F are G.
∴ Some F are H.

▸ **18.** All H are G.
No F are G.
∴ Some F are not H.

20. No H are G.
All F are G.
∴ No F are H.

22. No H are G.
No F are G.
∴ No F are H.

▸ **24.** No H are G.
Some F are not G.
∴ Some F are not H.

26. Some H are G.
Some F are not G.
∴ Some F are not H.

28. Some H are not G.
Some F are G.
∴ Some F are not H.

▸ **30.** All G are H.
All G are F.
∴ Some F are H.

31. All G are H.
No G are F.
∴ Some F are not H.

32. All G are H.
Some G are F.
∴ Some F are H.

33. All G are H.
Some G are not F.
∴ Some F are not H.

34. No G are H.
All G are F.
∴ Some F are not H.

35. No G are H.
No G are F.
∴ No F are H.

▶ **36.** No G are H.
Some G are F.
∴ Some F are not H.

37. No G are H.
Some G are not F.
∴ Some F are not H.

38. Some G are H.
All G are F.
∴ Some F are H.

39. Some G are H.
No G are F.
∴ Some F are not H.

40. Some G are H.
Some G are not F.
∴ Some F are not H.

41. Some G are not H.
All G are F.
∴ Some F are not H.

▶ **42.** Some G are not H.
No G are F.
∴ Some F are H.

43. Some G are not H.
Some G are F.
∴ Some F are not H.

44. Some G are not H.
Some G are not F.
∴ Some F are H.

45. All H are G.
All G are F.
∴ Some F are H.

46. All H are G.
No G are F.
∴ No F are H.

47. All H are G.
No G are F.
∴ Some F are not H.

▶ **48.** All H are G.
Some G are not F.
∴ Some F are not H.

49. No H are G.
All G are F.
∴ Some F are not H.

50. No H are G.
No G are F.
∴ No F are H.

51. No H are G.
Some G are F.
∴ Some F are not H.

52. No H are G.
Some G are not F.
∴ Some F are not H.

53. Some H are G.
All G are F.
∴ Some F are H.

▶ **54.** Some H are G.
No G are F.
∴ Some F are not H.

55. Some H are G.
Some G are not F.
∴ Some F are not H.

Use the rules presented in this section to evaluate the following syllogistic arguments, taken from Lewis Carroll's *Symbolic Logic,* for validity.

56. That story of yours, about your once meeting the sea-serpent, always sets me off yawning; I never yawn, unless when I'm listening to something totally devoid of interest. So, that story of yours, about your once meeting the sea-serpent, is totally devoid of interest.

57. All diligent students are successful; all ignorant students are unsuccessful. So, no diligent students are ignorant.

58. Of the prisoners who were put on trial, all against whom the verdict "guilty" was returned were sentenced to imprisonment. Some who were sentenced to imprisonment were also sentenced to hard labor. So, some against whom the verdict "guilty" was returned were sentenced to hard labor.

59. All soldiers are strong; all soldiers are brave. Therefore, some strong men are brave.

▶ 60. I admire these pictures. When I admire anything I wish to examine it thoroughly. Therefore, I wish to examine some of these pictures thoroughly.

61. None but the brave deserve the fair; some braggarts are cowards. So, some braggarts do not deserve the fair.

62. All soldiers can march; some babies are not soldiers. So, some babies cannot march.

63. All selfish men are unpopular. All obliging men are popular. So, all obliging men are unselfish.

64. Some epicures are ungenerous; all my uncles are generous. Therefore, my uncles are not epicures.

65. Gold is heavy. Nothing but gold will silence him. So, nothing light will silence him.

▶ 66. Some cravats are not artistic; I admire anything artistic. So, there are some cravats that I do not admire.

67. His songs never last an hour; a song that lasts an hour is tedious. So, his songs are never tedious.

68. Some candles give very little light. Candles are meant to give light. Therefore, some things that are meant to give light give very little.

69. All who are anxious to learn work hard. Some of these boys work hard. So, some of these boys are anxious to learn.

70. All lions are fierce. Some lions do not drink coffee. Therefore, some creatures that drink coffee are not very fierce.

71. No misers are generous. Some old men are ungenerous. So, some old men are misers.

▶ 72. Ill-managed business is unprofitable. Railways are never ill-managed. Therefore, all railways are profitable.

73. No professors are ignorant. All ignorant people are vain. So, no professors are vain.

74. All wasps are unfriendly; no puppies are unfriendly. So, puppies are not wasps.

75. No idlers win fame. Some painters are not idle. Thus, some painters win fame.

76. No monkeys are soldiers; all monkeys are mischievous. So, some mischievous creatures are not soldiers.

77. All these bonbons are chocolate creams; all these bonbons are delicious. So, all chocolate creams are delicious.

▶ 78. Bores are dreaded. No bore is ever begged to prolong his visit. So, no one who is dreaded is ever begged to prolong his visit.

79. No frogs are poetical; some ducks are unpoetical. So, some ducks are not frogs.

80. Every eagle can fly. Some pigs cannot fly. So, some pigs are not eagles.

Using the rules presented in this section and the Aristotelian rules that follow, evaluate these syllogistic arguments taken from nineteenth-century logic textbooks. When the two sets of rules disagree, explain why.

Aristotelian Rules for Validity[5]

1. The middle term must be distributed at least once.
2. No term may be distributed in the conclusion if not distributed in the premises.
3. a. If the conclusion is affirmative, both premises must be affirmative.
   b. If the conclusion is negative, exactly one premise must be negative.

81. Some truths affecting human conduct are speculations. All truths affecting human conduct are valuable. Thus, some speculations are valuable.

82. No truth applicable to practice should be neglected. Every truth applicable to practice may seem unpractical. Therefore, some seemingly impractical truths should not be neglected.

83. All wits are dreaded; all wits are admired. So, some who are admired are dreaded.

▶ **84.** All true philosophers account virtue a good in itself. The advocates of pleasure do not account virtue a good in itself. Therefore, they are not true philosophers.

85. Some slaves are not discontented. All slaves are wronged. Therefore, some who are wronged are not discontented.

86. Every true patriot is a friend to religion. Some great statesmen are not friends to religion. Thus, some great statesmen are not true patriots.

87. No one is free who is enslaved by his appetites. A sensualist is enslaved by his appetites. Therefore, a sensualist is not free.

88. No one is rich who has not enough; no miser has enough. Therefore, no miser is rich.

89. He that is of God heareth my words; ye therefore hear them not, because ye are not of God.

▶ **90.** A desire to gain by another's loss is a violation of the Tenth Commandment. All gaming, therefore, because it implies a desire to profit at the expense of another, involves a breach of the Tenth Commandment.

91. No man can possess power to perform impossibilities. A miracle is an impossibility. Therefore, no man can possess the power to perform miracles.

92. All the most bitter persecutions have been religious persecutions. Among the most bitter persecutions were those which occurred in France during the Revolution. Therefore, they were religious persecutions.

93. No evil should be allowed that good may come of it. All punishment is an evil. Therefore, no punishment should be allowed that good may come of it.

94. He who is properly called an actor does not endeavor to make his hearers believe that the sentiments he expresses and the feelings he exhibits are really his own. A barrister does this. Therefore, he is not properly to be called an actor.

95. That man is independent of the caprices of fortune who places his chief happiness in moral and intellectual excellence. A true philosopher is independent of the caprices of fortune. Therefore, a true philosopher is one who places his chief happiness in moral and intellectual excellence.

▶ **96.** Whatever is dictated by nature is allowable. Devotion to the pursuit of pleasure in youth, and to that of gain in old age, are dictated by nature. Therefore, they are allowable.

97. A man who deliberately devotes himself to a life of sensuality is deserving of strong reprobation; but those do not devote themselves to a life of sensuality who are hurried into excess by the impulse of the passions. Such, therefore, as are hurried into excess by the impulse of the passions are not deserving of strong reprobation.

98. Anyone who is candid will refrain from condemning a book without reading it. Some reviewers do not refrain from this. Therefore, some reviewers are not candid.

99. No soldiers should be brought into the field who are not well qualified to perform their part. None but veterans are well qualified to perform their part. So, none but veterans should be brought into the field.

100. No trifling business will enrich those engaged in it. A mining speculation is no trifling business. Therefore, a mining speculation will enrich those engaged in it.

These are, or contain, syllogistic arguments. Most are *enthymemes:* They have a missing premise or conclusion. Find the enthymeme. Using the rules presented in this section, determine what the missing premise or conclusion must be if the argument is to be valid.

101. Play is a sign of imperfect adaptation. It is proper to childhood. (George Santayana)

▶ **102.** Every body is in potentiality. It is therefore impossible that God should be a body. (Thomas Aquinas)

103. For we can explain nothing but what we can reduce to laws whose object is given in some possible experience. But freedom is a mere idea, the objective reality of which can in no way be shown according to natural laws or in any possible experience. (Immanuel Kant)

104. And since those who argue prove nothing, a sensible man does not argue. (Lao-Tzu)

105. How the miser is better than a slave or more free
Stooping at the crossroads to grasp the fastened coin
I do not see; Who covets, fears;
And who lives in fear for me is never free. (Horace)

Use the rules for validity to determine whether any conclusion follows from these premises. (The last three are adapted from Lewis Carroll.)

106. Cookies are sweet. Children like anything that's sweet.

107. Anyone with high cheek bones looks noble. Nobody gets a job in Hollywood who doesn't have high cheek bones.

▶ **108.** Nobody who isn't a legislator writes laws. Some judges write laws.

109. Nobody succeeds on their first try. Some of these essays are not first tries.

110. Dull people have neat kitchens. All my friends are interesting.

111. Nobody with scruples reneges on a promise. People with no scruples are deplorable.

112. Every philosopher thinks hard; some who think hard nevertheless don't think well.

113. Pigs cannot fly; pigs are greedy.

▶ **114.** Nothing unintelligible ever puzzles me. Everything about logic puzzles me.

115. No country that has been explored is infested by dragons. Unexplored countries are fascinating.

Use the rules for validity and the definitions of 'syllogism', 'figure', and 'mood' to explain why these facts hold.*

116. Every valid syllogism has at least one universal premise.

117. Every valid syllogism with a particular conclusion has one particular premise.

118. The conclusion of every valid second figure syllogism is negative.

119. The conclusion of every valid third figure syllogism is particular.

▶ **120.** No valid fourth figure syllogism has a universal affirmative conclusion.

121. The only valid syllogism whose mood is AAA is in first figure.

122. The only valid syllogism whose mood is AOO is in second figure.

123. The only valid syllogism whose mood is OAO is in third figure.

124. The only valid syllogism with an affirmative conclusion in the fourth figure has mood IAI.

125. The only valid syllogism with a universal affirmative conclusion is in first figure, with mood AAA.

▶ **126.** Every syllogism with mood EIO is valid.

127. Every valid syllogism whose major premise is particular negative is in the third figure.

128. Every valid syllogism with a particular affirmative conclusion has exactly one particular affirmative premise.

129. Every valid syllogism whose minor premise is particular negative is in second figure.

130. Every valid syllogism in first figure has an affirmative minor premise.

131. Every valid syllogism in third figure has an affirmative minor premise.

▶ **132.** No valid first figure syllogisms have a particular negative premise.

133. No valid fourth figure syllogisms have a particular negative premise.

134. No two valid syllogisms with contradictory minor premises have the same major premise.

135. No two valid syllogisms with contradictory major premises have the same minor premise.

Aristotle took two forms of the syllogism as fundamental:

All G are H.	All G are H.
All F are G.	Some F are G.
$\therefore$ All F are H.	$\therefore$ Some F are H.

He showed that all other valid forms could be reduced to these by the operations of conversion, obversion, contraposition, and substitution of terms from these forms. So, we can show syllogisms valid by reducing them to one of these forms. Using this method, show that the following are valid.

136. No G are H; All F are G; $\therefore$ No F are H.

137. No G are H; Some F are G; $\therefore$ Some F are not H.

138. All H are G; No F are G; $\therefore$ No F are H.

139. All H are G; Some F are not G; $\therefore$ Some F are not H.

140. No H are G; All F are G; $\therefore$ No F are H.

141. No H are G; Some F are G; $\therefore$ Some F are not H.

142. All G are H; Some G are F; $\therefore$ Some F are H.

143. No G are H; Some G are F; $\therefore$ Some F are not H.

144. Some G are H; All G are F; $\therefore$ Some F are H.

145. Some G are not H; All G are F; $\therefore$ Some F are not H.

146. All H are G; No G are F; $\therefore$ No F are H.

147. No H are G; Some G are F; $\therefore$ Some F are not H.

148. Some H are G; All G are F; $\therefore$ Some F are H.

9.6 EXPANDING THE ARISTOTELIAN LANGUAGE

So far we have been considering syllogisms containing only four possible sentence forms. In discussing immediate inference, however, we went beyond those forms to consider complements of predicates. It's possible to expand the Venn diagram treatment of syllogisms to incorporate complements and negations of sentence forms as well.

The expanded language AL* includes the language AL but allows us to use two forms of negation: $\neg$, which negates sentence forms, and *non,* which negates predicates or general terms. Allowing negation, $\neg$, to act as a sentential connective lets us handle sentences such as 'It's not true that some of my friends are criminals' and 'Not all the questioners were pleased with the witness's answers'. Second, AL* allows us to form complements of predicates. The syntax of AL* is:

Vocabulary

Predicates: uppercase letters, with or without numerical subscripts
Determiners: All, No, Some
Particles: $\neg$, non

Formation Rules

1. If X is a predicate, then non$X$ is a predicate.
2. If X and Y are predicates, then 'All X are Y', 'No X are Y', and 'Some X are Y' are formulas.
3. If $\mathscr{A}$ is a formula, then $\neg\mathscr{A}$ is a formula.
4. There are no other formulas.

In AL*, we can form formulas that are not formulas of AL, such as

$\neg$All non$F$ are G.
Some non$F$ are nonnon$G$.
$\neg\,\neg$No F are non$G$.

Significantly, without mentioning 'Some F are not G' in the formation rules we can construct particular negative sentences by negating the grammatical predicate:

Some *F* are non*G*.[6]

From now on, we will write particular negative sentence forms in this style.

The semantics of this language is easy to specify. The negation of a sentence form is true if and only if the sentence form itself is false. The complement of a predicate applies to those things of which the original predicate is false. The universe of discourse plays a significant role in understanding AL*, as the diagrams that follow show.

Venn Diagrams in AL*

The Venn diagram technique extends readily to AL*. We can continue drawing the sort of diagrams we drew for our original Aristotelian language, with two additional provisions. First, the circle for each predicate represents that term's extension; the area in the universe of discourse outside the circle represents the extension of the term's negation. The *F* circle represents the set of things of which *F* is true; the area outside the *F* circle represents the set of things of which *F* is false (which is, in turn, the extension of non*F*).

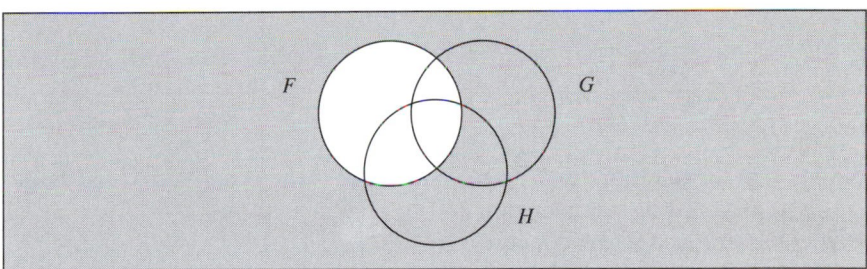

This has several consequences. First, the *F* circle represents the set of things of which *F* is true; it thus represents the set of things of which non*F* is false. So, it also represents the set of things of which nonnon*F* is true. The *F* circle, in other words, represents not only the extension of *F* but also the extensions of nonnon*F*, nonnonnonnon*F*, and so on. The area outside the *F* circle similarly represents the extensions of non*F*, nonnonnon*F*, and so on. Consequently, we can adopt a principle of *double negation:* The formula resulting from deleting two adjacent *non*s is equivalent to the original.

Second, various sentence forms lead us to draw diagrams that look somewhat different from those we've seen in our more restricted language. We can devise, for example, four different particular sentence forms (that is, those with 'some'): 'Some *F* are *G*', 'Some *F* are non*G*', 'Some non*F* are *G*', and 'Some non*F* are non*G*'. The first two are familiar, but the others are new.

Nevertheless, it's easy to see how to diagram them:

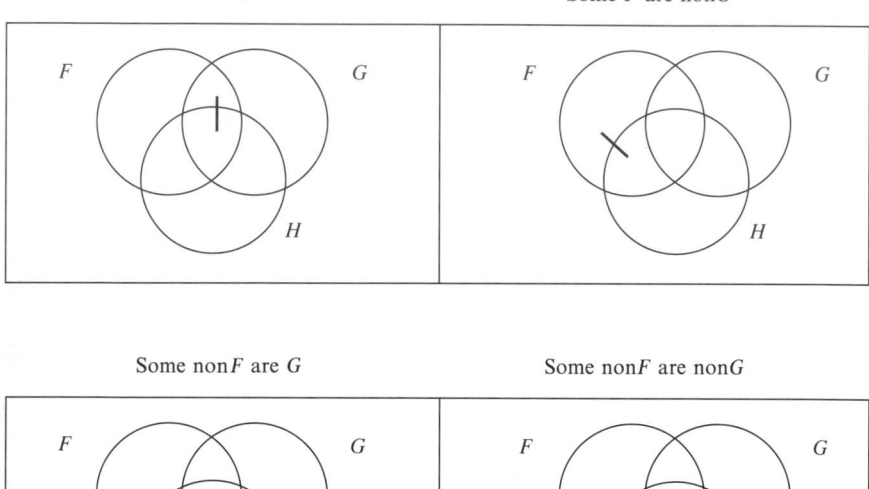

Notice that the diagram for 'Some non*F* are *G*' is the same as that for 'Some *G* are non*F*'. Adding complements to our language allows us to say that all particular sentence forms convert.

There are similarly four sentence forms with 'all' and four with 'no'. Only one in each group is familiar from our original language, though three in each group are seen to be equivalent to things that language can express. These diagrams represent the meanings of sentence forms with 'all':

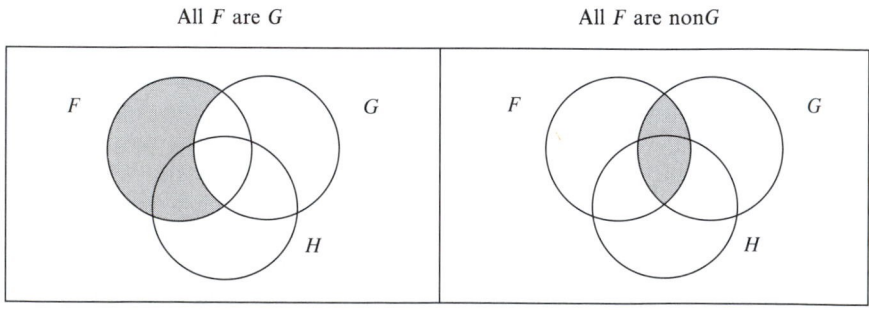

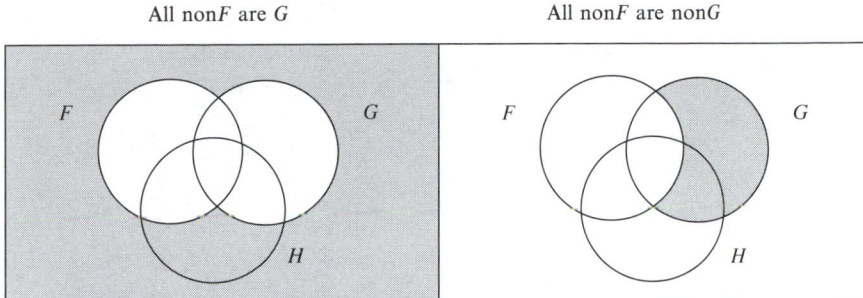

The first is familiar; the second shows that 'All *F* are non*G*' is equivalent to 'No *F* are *G*'. These sentence forms are obverses. The third, representing 'All non*F* are *G*', has no equivalent in AL. The fourth, representing 'All non*F* are non*G*', is the same as the diagram for 'All *G* are *F*'. This shows that universal affirmatives are equivalent to their contrapositives.

These diagrams represent the meanings of sentence forms with 'no'.

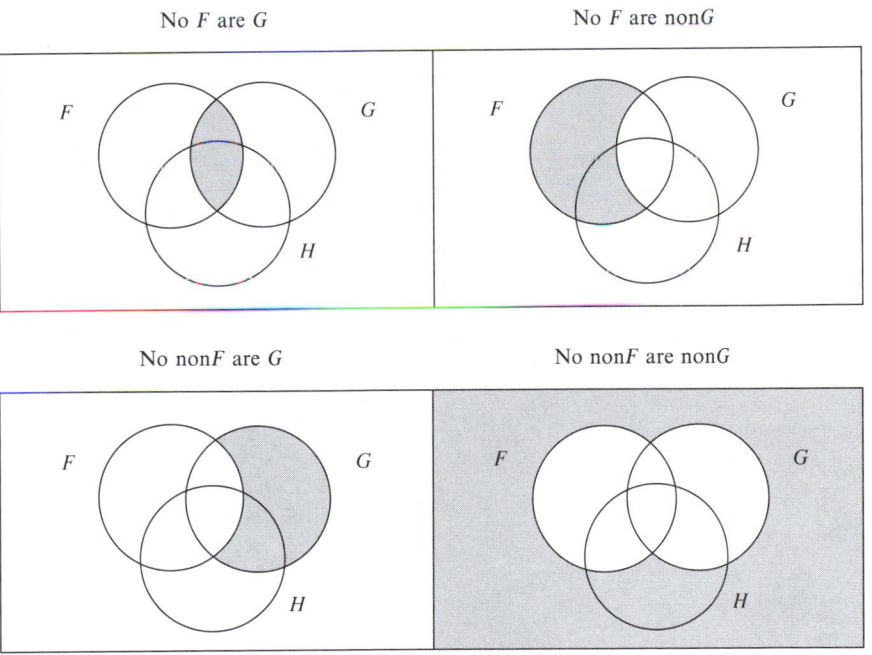

The first is familiar; the second shows that 'No *F* are non*G*' and 'All *F* are *G*' are equivalent. These sentence forms are obverses. The third shows that 'No non*F* are *G*' and 'All *G* are *F*' are equivalent; 'No non*F* are *G*' is the obverse of 'All non*F* are non*G*', which is the contrapositive of 'All *G* are *F*'. Finally, the fourth diagram represents 'No non*F* are non*G*', which has no equivalent in AL. It is, however, equivalent to its obverse 'All non*F* are *G*'.

The other provision concerns negations of entire sentence forms. How are we to diagram the negation of a sentence form? Each diagram for a sentence form indicates either that something is in a certain region or that nothing is in that region. Shading indicates that nothing is in an area, whereas the presence of a plus sign or bar indicates that something is in the area. The negation of a sentence is true exactly when the sentence itself is false. All this suggests a natural strategy for diagramming negations.

> If a sentence form asserts that a certain area is empty, then its negation asserts that the area is occupied. If the sentence form asserts that an area is occupied, then its negation asserts that the area is empty.

In accordance with this strategy, it's easy to transform negations of sentence forms into other sentence forms. Consider a particular sentence form, 'Some F are G'. It asserts that there is something that is both F and G. Its negation, then, asserts that nothing is both F and G. But this is precisely the content of 'No F are G'. '¬Some F are G' and 'No F are G' are equivalent. These rules allow us to transform the negation of 'some' or 'no' sentence forms into others:

Contradictories

¬Some X are Y	¬No X are Y
No X are Y	Some X are Y

The double line indicates that the rule inverts (that is, applies in both directions).

'All' sentence forms, when diagrammed, assert that certain areas are empty. Their negations, therefore, assert that these areas are occupied. 'All F are G' is represented by the diagram on the left. Using a bar in the diagram on the right to indicate that the area shaded in the left diagram is occupied, we obtain the diagram characteristic of 'Some F are non$G$':

All F are G ¬All F are G

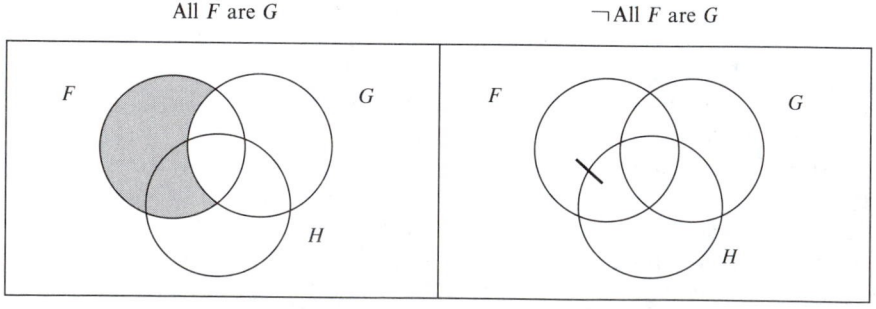

This shows that '¬All F are G' and 'Some F are non$G$' are equivalent. By generalizing, we obtain the following rule:

Contradictories

¬All X are Y

Some X are non$Y$

These relationships show that 'all' and 'no' may be defined in terms of 'some'. 'All X are Y' is equivalent to '¬Some X are non$Y$', and 'No X are Y' is equivalent to '¬Some X are Y'.

A *syllogism* within AL* is an argument form containing three AL* formulas and three predicates (with, perhaps, their complements, complements of their complements, and so on), where each predicate appears in two formulas. To summarize the Venn diagram method for these syllogisms:

1. Construct a diagram consisting of three intersecting circles inside a box (representing the universe of discourse).

2. Label each circle with a predicate.

3. Convert negations of sentence forms into equivalent, "positive" sentence forms.

4. Delete two adjacent negation signs (¬¬) or two adjacent *nons* (*nonnon*).

5. Diagram the premises.

6. Check to see whether the diagram guarantees the truth of the conclusion. If it does, the syllogism is valid. If not, the syllogism is not valid.

This adds only two steps to the usual Venn diagram method: We must "cancel" double negations and complements and convert negated sentence forms into their positive equivalents. Transforming negated sentence forms in this way applies indirectly the strategy we've outlined for dealing with negations. (Step 3 isn't necessary, of course, if we apply that strategy directly.)

Let's illustrate the method by evaluating a syllogistic argument. The argument shows, incidentally, that the rules for the syllogism no longer hold when we broaden the definition of 'syllogism'. We couldn't evaluate this argument at all using the methods we developed earlier for syllogisms in AL.

(43) No incompetent students are incapable of failing.
No lazy students are competent.
∴ All lazy students are capable of failing.

This has the form

(44) No non*F* are non*G*.
    No *H* are *F*.
    ∴ All *H* are *G*.

We begin our evaluation by drawing three intersecting circles within a box, labeling each:

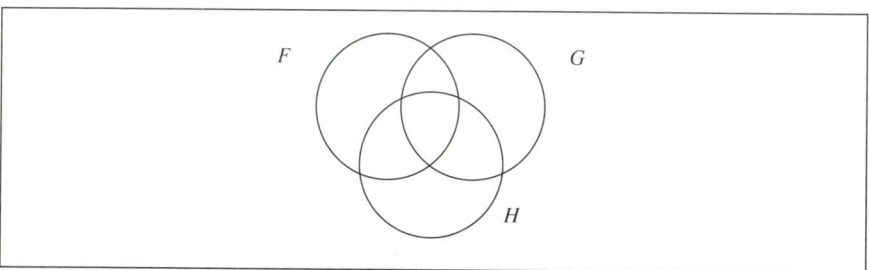

Next, we consider any negated formulas and double negations or complements. In this case, there are none. So, we proceed to diagram the first premise:

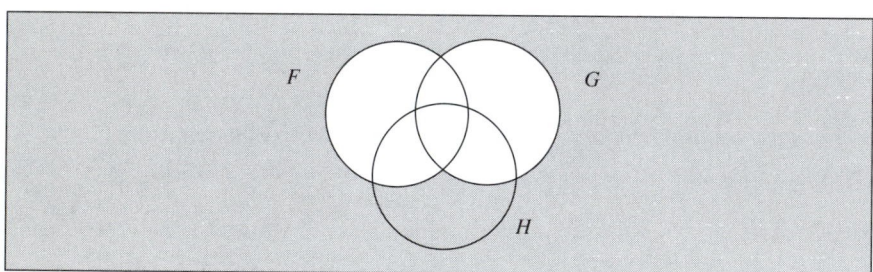

We then add a diagram of the second premise:

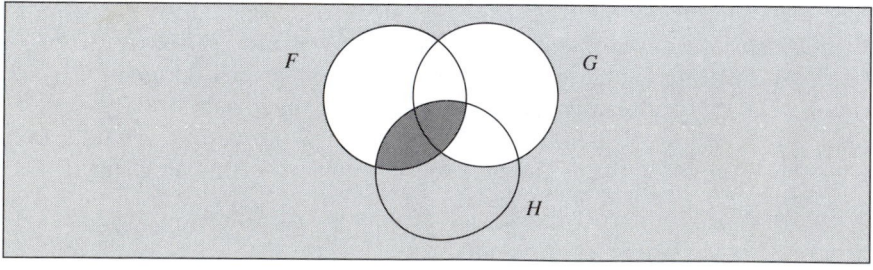

Clearly, the diagram that results guarantees the truth of the conclusion; the argument form is valid. This allows us to conclude that the argument itself is valid—despite its drawing an "affirmative" conclusion from two "negative" premises.

To take another example, consider this syllogism:

(45) All non*F* are non*G*.
   ¬ All *F* are non*H*.
   ∴ Some *G* are *H*.

We again begin by drawing three intersecting circles within a box, labeling each circle with a predicate. We then transform the second, negated premise into an equivalent:

(46) All non*F* are non*G*.
   Some *F* are nonnon*H*.
   ∴ Some *G* are *H*.

Eliminating double negations, we obtain

(47) All non*F* are non*G*.
   Some *F* are *H*.
   ∴ Some *G* are *H*.

We now diagram the first premise:

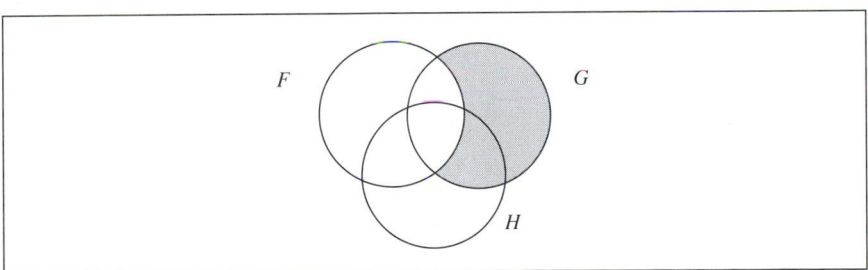

Then, we add a representation of the second premise:

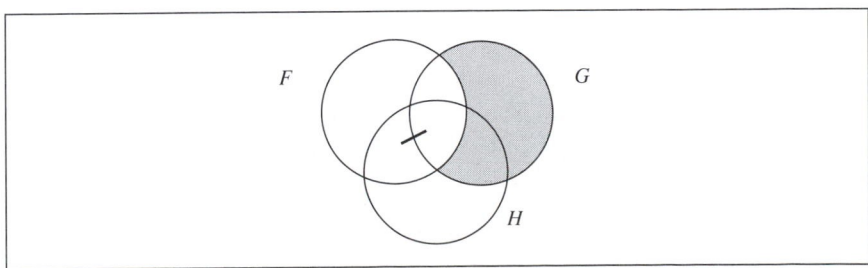

Does the result guarantee the truth of the conclusion? No: The thing that is *F* and *H* may or may not be *G*.

Problems

Evaluate these syllogisms in AL* by using Venn diagrams.

▶ **1.** No *G* are non*H*.
No *F* are non*G*.
∴ All *F* are *H*.

▶ **2.** All *G* are *H*.
All *F* are non*G*.
∴ No *F* are *H*.

▶ **3.** No *G* are non*H*.
¬All *F* are non*G*.
∴ ¬No *F* are *H*.

▶ **4.** ¬Some *G* are *H*.
All *F* are *G*.
∴ All *F* are non*H*.

▶ **5.** No *G* are *H*.
¬All *F* are non*G*.
∴ ¬All *F* are *H*.

▶ **6.** Some *G* are *H*.
¬Some *F* are non*G*.
∴ ¬No *F* are *H*.

7. All non*G* are non*H*.
¬Some *F* are non*G*.
∴ No non*H* are *F*.

8. All *H* are *G*.
All *F* are non*G*.
∴ All *F* are non*H*.

9. All *H* are *G*.
¬All non*F* are non*G*.
∴ Some non*F* are *H*.

10. All *H* are *G*.
Some *F* are non*G*.
∴ ¬All *F* are *H*.

11. All *H* are non*G*.
All *F* are *G*.
∴ ¬Some *F* are *H*.

▶ **12.** No *H* are non*G*.
¬All *F* are *G*.
∴ Some *F* are non*H*.

13. ¬All *H* are non*G*.
All *F* are *G*.
∴ ¬No *F* are *H*.

14. ¬All *H* are *G*.
¬Some *F* are non*G*.
∴ Some *F* are non*H*.

15. All *G* are *H*.
No *G* are non*F*.
∴ ¬Some *F* are non*H*.

16. No *G* are non*H*.
No *G* are *F*.
∴ No *F* are *H*.

17. All *G* are *H*.
¬No *G* are non*F*.
∴ Some non*F* are *H*.

▶ **18.** All *G* are non*H*.
¬Some *G* are non*F*.
∴ No *F* are *H*.

19. No *G* are *H*.
¬All *G* are non*F*.
∴ ¬All *F* are *H*.

20. ¬All non*G* are non*H*.
All non*G* are *F*.
∴ Some *F* are *H*.

21. ¬All *G* are *H*.
No *G* are non*F*.
∴ Some *F* are non*H*.

22. Some non*G* are non*H*.
All non*G* are non*F*.
∴ Some *F* are non*H*.

23. No *H* are *G*.
    No non*G* are non*F*.
    ∴ No *F* are non*H*.

▶ 24. No *H* are non*G*.
    No *G* are *F*.
    ∴ All *F* are non*H*.

25. ¬Some *H* are *G*.
    Some non*G* are *F*.
    ∴ Some *F* are *H*.

26. All *H* are *G*.
    All non*G* are non*F*.
    ∴ No non*F* are *H*.

27. All *H* are *G*.
    Some non*G* are *F*.
    ∴ Some *F* are non*H*.

28. Some *H* are *G*.
    All non*G* are *F*.
    ∴ Some *F* are non*H*.

Evaluate these syllogistic arguments taken from Lewis Carroll by symbolizing them in AL* and using Venn diagrams.

29. No son of mine is dishonest. People always treat an honest man with respect. Therefore, no son of mine ever fails to be treated with respect.

▶ 30. No one who means to go by the train and cannot get a conveyance, and who has not enough time to walk to the station, can do without running. This party of tourists means to go by the train and cannot get a conveyance, but they have plenty of time to walk to the station. Thus, this party of tourists need not run.

31. No misers are unselfish. None but misers save egg shells. So, no unselfish people save egg shells.

32. Some healthy people are fat. No unhealthy people are strong. So, some fat people are not strong.

33. All uneducated people are shallow. Students are all educated. So, no students are shallow.

34. All young lambs jump. No young animals are healthy unless they jump. So, all young lambs are healthy.

35. A prudent man shuns hyenas. No banker is imprudent. Thus, no banker fails to shun hyenas.

▶ 36. No muffins are wholesome. All buns are unwholesome. So, buns are not muffins.

37. Some unauthorized reports are false. All authorized reports are trustworthy. Thus, some false reports are not trustworthy.

38. Improbable stories are not easily believed. None of his stories are probable. So, none of his stories are easily believed.

39. No thieves are honest. Some dishonest people are found out. Therefore, some thieves are found out.

40. No muffins are wholesome; all puffy food is unwholesome. So all muffins are puffy.

41. All wise men walk on their feet; all unwise men walk on their hands. Therefore, no man walks on both.

▶ **42.** No wheelbarrows are comfortable. No uncomfortable vehicles are popular. So, no wheelbarrows are popular.

43. John never orders anything I ought to do; Peter never orders anything I ought not to do. So, John and Peter never give the same order.

44. None of my boys are conceited; none of my girls are greedy. Thus, no conceited child of mine is greedy.

45. None of my boys are clever; none but a clever boy could solve this problem. So, none of my boys could solve this problem.

46. None of my boys are learned; some of my boys are not choristers. So, some unlearned boys are not choristers.

Evaluate these arguments by using Venn diagrams.

47. Some illegal acts go unpunished. All blatantly wrong acts are punished. Therefore, some illegal acts are not blatantly wrong.

▶ **48.** All who do not remember the past are condemned to repeat it. No one condemned to repeat the past looks forward to the future with eagerness. So, everyone who eagerly looks forward to the future remembers the past.

49. John respects no one who insults him. Everyone who dislikes John insults him. Thus, John respects everyone who likes him.

50. I like any bread that isn't too sweet. I dislike some breads that don't contain rye flour. So, some breads that don't contain rye flour are too sweet.

51. Some untreated illnesses don't become serious. Home remedies are fine for any illness that isn't serious. Thus, home remedies are fine for some untreated illnesses.

52. Lori is unhappy with some people who didn't write thank-you notes. Lori will send presents next year to everyone with whom she's happy. Therefore, some people who didn't write thank-you notes won't get presents from Lori next year.

53. There are people without jobs who are not well nourished. Nobody who is not absent from the welfare rolls fails to be well nourished. Therefore, some people with no jobs are absent from the welfare rolls.

▶ **54.** Anyone who is not an idiot can see that Jake is lying. Some people in this room can't tell that Jake is lying. Hence, some people in this room are idiots.

55. Most people would consider anyone who shows no fear in the face of danger to be courageous. Anybody who would be considered courageous by most people deserves recognition. Therefore, only those who show fear in the face of danger deserve no recognition.

56. Genevieve befriends anyone who has been treated unfairly. But she doesn't befriend some really obnoxious people. So, some really obnoxious people receive fair treatment.

57. Not all who fail to graduate drop out. All who do not drop out eventually get their degree. Thus, not all who graduate eventually get their degree.

58. The president is willing to appoint anyone who didn't work for opposing candidates. It is not true that only people who worked for opposing candidates will accept the job. So, it's not true that nobody the president is willing to appoint will take the job.

Sorites are chains of syllogisms. Usually, only premises and the conclusion of the entire chain are stated explicitly; the unstated conclusion of one syllogism becomes an unstated premise of another. These sorites are adapted from Lewis Carroll's *Symbolic Logic*. Separate each chain into its component syllogisms and test them for validity.

59. I greatly value everything that John gives me. Nothing but this bone will satisfy my dog. I take particular care of everything I greatly value; this bone was a present from John. The things of which I take particular care are things I do not give to my dog. Therefore, my dog is not satisfied with anything I give him.

▶ 60. No experienced person is incompetent. Everyone on our staff is always blundering; no competent person is always blundering. Therefore, everyone on our staff is inexperienced.

61. No terriers wander among the signs of the zodiac. Nothing that does not wander among the signs of the zodiac is a comet. Nothing but a terrier has a curly tail. Therefore, comets do not have curly tails.

62. All members of the House of Commons have perfect self-command; no member of Parliament who wears a coronet should ride in a donkey race. All members of the House of Lords wear coronets. All members of Parliament who are not members of the House of Commons are members of the House of Lords. Therefore, no members of Parliament should ride in a donkey race, unless they have perfect self-command.

63. Showy talkers think too much of themselves. No really well-informed people are bad company. People who think too much of themselves are not good company. Therefore, showy talkers are not really well informed.

64. Things sold in the street are of no great value. Nothing but rubbish can be had for a song. Eggs of the great auk are very valuable. It is only what is sold in the street that is really rubbish. Therefore, eggs of the great auk can't be had for a song.

65. None of the unnoticed things met at sea are mermaids. Things entered in the log, as met with at sea, are sure to be worth remembering. I have never met with anything worth remembering when on a voyage. Things met with at sea that are noticed are sure to be recorded in the log. Therefore, I have never met a mermaid.

▸ 66. There is no box of mine here that I dare open. My writing desk is made of rosewood. All my boxes are painted, except what are here. There is no box of mine I dare not open, unless it is full of live scorpions. All my rosewood boxes are unpainted. Therefore, my desk is full of live scorpions.

67. Every idea of mine that cannot be expressed in a syllogism is really ridiculous; none of my ideas about bath-buns are worth writing down. No idea of mine that fails to come true can be expressed as a syllogism. I never have any really ridiculous idea that I do not at once refer to my solicitor. My dreams are all about bath-buns. I never refer any idea of mine to my solicitor unless it is worth writing down. Therefore, all my dreams come true.

68. The only animals in this house are cats. Every animal is suitable for a pet that loves to gaze at the moon. When I detest an animal, I avoid it. No animals are carnivorous, unless they prowl at night. No cat fails to kill mice. No animals ever take to me, except what are in this house. Kangaroos are not suitable for pets. None but carnivores kill mice. I detest animals that do not take to me. Animals that prowl at night always love to gaze at the moon. Therefore, I always avoid a kangaroo.

Notes

[1] Arnauld introduced this term, with its modern meaning, in the Port Royal *Logic* in 1662.

[2] Euler's version, dating from 1768, treats 'some' as meaning 'some and not all'. Venn presented his method in his *Symbolic Logic* (London: Macmillan, 1881).

[3] Peter of Spain (?–1277), who became Pope John XXI, apparently introduced the notion of distribution in connection with phrases such as *All F* in his *Summulae Logicales,* the standard logic textbook throughout the later Middle Ages and Renaissance. This general definition of distribution, however, appears only later (e.g., in the writings of Pseudo-Scot.)

[4] Replacing a distributed term with a term whose extension includes that of the original preserves the truth of the sentence or sentence form. Replacing an undistributed term with a term whose extension is a subset of that of the original similarly preserves truth.

[5] These rules were first formulated by the Jesuits of Coimbra in 1607. Arnauld adopted them in the Port Royal *Logic* in 1662.

[6] Some philosophers, including Aristotle, have objected to identifying 'Some *F* are not *G*' and 'Some *F* are non*G*' on the grounds that the latter is stronger. In English, this is sometimes true; 'Some clerks are unfriendly' implies, but isn't equivalent to, 'Some clerks aren't friendly', because clerks can be neither friendly nor unfriendly. 'Friendly' and 'unfriendly', that is, act as contraries rather than complements in English. In our artificial language, however, we assume that *non* always produces the complement of the predicate to which it attaches. And that makes 'Some *F* are not *G*' and 'Some *F* are non*G*' equivalent.

10

QUANTIFIERS

Sentential logic, by taking sentences as basic units of analysis, can handle arguments with any number of premises and any degree of complexity. Nevertheless, sentential logic is limited by narrow horizons. Consider even a simple syllogistic argument:

(1) All Greeks are human.
All humans are mortal.
∴ All Greeks are mortal.

This argument is valid, but sentential logic cannot demonstrate why. It construes (1) as

(2) p
q
∴ r

which is clearly invalid. The validity of arguments such as (1) depends on the structure *within,* not between, sentences. No theory that fails to analyze what sentential logic calls "atomic" sentences can account for such reasoning.

Around 1879, two logicians working independently—Gottlob Frege (1848–1925), a German, and Charles Sanders Peirce (1839–1914), an American—developed a way to extend sentential logic to handle arguments such as (1). They introduced symbols representing *determiners,* such as 'all', 'some', 'no', 'every', 'any', and so on. Frege and Peirce used two symbols: the *universal quantifier,* which we will write ∀ (Peirce's work uses Π), and the *existential quantifier,* ∃ (in Peirce, Σ). The universal quantifier corresponds roughly to the English 'all', 'every', and 'each'; the existential quantifier, to the English 'some', 'a', and 'an'.

10.1 Constants and Quantifiers

Sentential logic is limited precisely because it takes sentences as its basic, unanalyzed units of explanation. To expand this logic to include a broader range of arguments, we must look inside atomic sentences to see how they are put together. Uncovering this internal structure, invisible to sentential logic, allows us to develop procedures for evaluating more complex and interesting arguments than either sentential logic or the theory of the syllogism can handle.

In general, "atomic" sentences consist of a main or subject noun phrase and a main verb phrase. We can gain some insight into the internal structure of sentences by examining the character of verb phrases. Consider a few examples:

(3) a. is a man
    b. knows some people who live in Oklahoma City
    c. sleeps very soundly
    d. kicked the ball into the end zone
    e. thought that Yosemite would be more fun to visit
    f. gave Fred a copy of the letter

All verb phrases are *general terms* in the sense that they are true or false of individual objects. We can pick any object we like; it will either be a man or not be a man. It will either sleep very soundly or not sleep very soundly. It will be true either that it gave Fred a copy of the letter or that it didn't. Alone, verb phrases and other general terms are not true or false. But they yield a truth value when combined with the name of an object. Objects of which the verb phrase or general term are true *satisfy* it; the verb phrase or general term *applies to* them. Verb phrases and other general terms classify objects into two categories: those of which they are true, and those of which they are false. The set of objects of which a general term is true is called its *extension*.

Verb phrases combine with noun phrases to form sentences. Because verb phrases are true or false of particular objects, noun phrases must specify an object, or a group of objects, and specify how the verb phrase applies to them. In the sentence 'Several people gave Fred a copy of the letter', for example, the noun phrase 'Several people' specifies the set of people, and says that the verb phrase applies to several objects in that set. Noun phrases take several forms. In this chapter, we'll concentrate on two of them.

First, noun phrases may pick out a single object by naming it. A sentence with a proper name as subject is true if the verb phrase applies to the object named and false otherwise. Each of these sentences results from combining a proper name with a verb phrase from (3):

(4) a. Socrates is a man.
    b. Maria knows some people who live in Oklahoma City.

    c. Mr. Hendley sleeps very soundly.
    d. Bahr kicked the ball into the end zone.
    e. Penelope thought that Yosemite would be more fun to visit.
    f. Nate gave Fred a copy of the letter.

Our formal language will thus need at least two kinds of symbol to represent sentences such as (4)a. First, we'll use lowercase letters from the beginning of the alphabet, with or without numerical subscripts, to represent proper names and singular pronouns; we'll call these symbolic names *individual constants* or, more simply, *constants*. (We'll use constants to symbolize only those names that denote uniquely, that is, refer to exactly one thing.) Constants play several roles, corresponding to the roles of the English expressions they symbolize. They represent proper names; they also represent pronouns, which may derive their reference from a previous proper name, a feature of the context, or a previous description (such as 'an airplane' or 'the fish that saved Pittsburgh').

Second, we'll use uppercase letters, with or without numerical subscripts, as *predicate constants,* or, more simply, *predicates*. Each predicate is assigned a number as a superscript; predicates are called *n-ary* if they are assigned the number *n*. So, 'F^1', 'G^2', 'H^6_3', and 'I^{39}_{17}' will count as predicates. Every predicate yields a truth value when combined with a certain number of objects. The assigned number indicates of how many objects at once the predicate is true or false. Usually, in writing predicates, we'll omit the superscripts: We can tell what number a predicate is assigned by looking at the number of constants or other terms that follow it.

A general term is true or false of individual objects. We'll therefore symbolize simple general terms such as 'sleeps' with *unary* predicates, that is, predicates to which 1 is assigned. These predicates are true or false of single objects and produce formulas when combined with a single individual constant. Other predicates yield formulas only when combined with two names; they are true or false of two objects taken together. Such predicates are assigned the number 2 and are called *binary*. They are useful for symbolizing, among other things, transitive verbs. 'Respect', for example, applies not to objects taken individually, but to objects taken in pairs. It requires a direct object. We can ask whether Robin respects Julia, but not simply whether Robin respects.

Letting *a* symbolize 'Socrates', and *M* symbolize 'man' (or, equivalently, 'is a man'), we can symbolize 'Socrates is a man' by

(5) *Ma*

which is a symbolic version of (4)a. *Ma* is a formula of quantificational logic. One way of building formulas, then, is to combine individual constants with predicates.

A second sort of noun phrase consists of a determiner, such as 'every' or 'some', together with a common noun such as 'goose' or 'truck'. The common noun may be modified by adjectives, adjectival phrases, prepositional phrases, or relative clauses. Whatever its grammatical structure, however, the modified noun constitutes a general term.

Noun phrases of this more complex sort, when combined with the verb phrases in (3), yield the following sentences:

(6) a. One reporter who covered the match is a man.
b. A few friends know some people who live in Oklahoma City.
c. Every endomorph sleeps very soundly.
d. Several prospects kicked the ball into the end zone.
e. A taxi driver thought that Yosemite would be more fun to visit.
f. Nobody gave Fred a copy of the letter.

'Nobody', in (6)f, is a special case; the word contains both a determiner and a general term, and is equivalent to 'no person'.

To learn more about the sentences in (6), let's examine some related sentences whose subject noun phrases consist only of determiners and the rather colorless general terms 'thing' and 'object'. To begin, consider the sentence

(7) Something is peculiar.

To symbolize this sentence, we can't use an individual constant for 'something'. We don't want to say that 'peculiar' applies to any object in particular. The sentence says just that 'peculiar' applies to some object. Quantification theory allows us to represent this by using *variables*. We will say, in effect, "'x is peculiar' is true, for some object x." Variables *range over* a *domain,* a set of objects that they can take as values.

To express the idea that 'x is peculiar' is true for some x, we write the symbolic equivalent of

(8) (for some x)(x is peculiar)

which is

(9) $\exists x P x$

We may read (9) as saying the following:

(10) a. For some x, x is peculiar.
b. Some x is such that x is peculiar.
c. There is an x such that x is peculiar.
d. An x is such that x is peculiar.

In better English, these become:

(11) a. Something is peculiar.
b. There is something peculiar.
c. An object is peculiar.

The words 'thing' and 'object', in English, serve some of the purposes that variables such as x serve in quantification theory. Variables link quantifiers to the predicates they accompany.

The strategy of quantificational logic, then, requires two new sorts of symbol. First, we must introduce *individual variables,* or, more simply, *variables.* Individual variables are so called because they range over individual, particular objects. Variables will be lowercase letters from the end of the alphabet, with or without numerical subscripts. As with sentence letters, individual constants and predicate letters, subscripts allow us to have as many variables as we need. (The superscripts on predicates serve a very different purpose.) Variables in quantificational logic act, for the most part, much as variables for numbers such as n or x act in arithmetic or algebra. They denote no objects in particular; instead, they range over a set of objects. Second, the language of quantification theory must include quantifiers.

To take another simple example, suppose we want to say, recalling the title of a popular song, that everything is beautiful. To say that Pittsburgh is beautiful, or that Ingrid Bergman is beautiful, we can introduce the predicate B and the individual constants p and b and write Bp and Bb. To say that everything is beautiful, however, we need to say that 'x is beautiful' is true for every object x. The universal quantifier does just this. We can prefix the quantifier to Bx, writing the symbolic equivalent of

(12) (for every x)(x is beautiful)

or

(13) $\forall x Bx$

(13) says

(14) a. For every x, x is beautiful.
b. For all x, x is beautiful.
c. For each x, x is beautiful.
d. For any x, x is beautiful.
e. Every x is such that x is beautiful.
f. All x are such that x is beautiful.
g. Each x is such that x is beautiful.
h. Any x is such that x is beautiful.

or, in more acceptable English,

(15) a. Everything is beautiful.
b. All things are beautiful.
c. Each object is beautiful.
d. Any object is beautiful.

'All', 'every', 'each', and (usually) 'any' generally receive the same symbolization. In English, these words differ subtly but significantly in meaning. Note, for example, that though 'All things are beautiful' seems to mean just what 'Everything is beautiful' does, 'Anything is beautiful' sounds strange.

Quantification theory cannot capture all the differences among these determiners, but it can capture some, as the next chapter will show. Note also that all the sentences in (15) sound vague: Every *what* is beautiful? What is the range of the variable? Usually, context indicates what the variable ranges over.

Variables have no meanings independent of their roles in particular formulas. In (9) and (13), P and B represent 'peculiar' and 'beautiful', respectively. They cannot be interchanged without changing the translation manual relating English sentences to their symbolic representations. But variables can be interchanged, with very few restrictions, without altering meaning. 'Something is peculiar' could just as well be symbolized by

(16) $\exists y P y$

as by (9), and 'Everything is beautiful' could just as well be represented by

(17) $\forall z B z$

as by (13). We can do so because the variables x, y, and z themselves denote no particular objects but range over a domain.

10.2 CATEGORICAL SENTENCE FORMS

Sentences such as 'Something is peculiar' or 'Everything is beautiful' have limited utility. Most of the time, we want to say something about, for example, some people or every frog, not about just something or everything. We must be able to handle sentences with subject noun phrases that contain more complicated general terms. If we can do this, it will be easy to represent any sentence having one of four classic *categorical forms* in quantification theory.

Universal affirmative sentences have the structure

(18) All F are G

We might want to represent, for instance,

(19) All frogs swim.

We already know that Sa can represent, for example, 'Albert swims', and that $\forall x S x$ can symbolize 'Everything swims'. To symbolize 'All frogs swim', quantification theory focuses on the determiner 'all'. 'All' combines with a general term, in this case 'frogs', to form a noun phrase; that noun phrase in turn combines with another general term, the verb phrase 'swims'. We can see 'all', then, as relating two general terms. The general terms, in this case, are simple; thus, we can symbolize them as singulary predicates F and S. We can symbolize 'all' with the universal quantifier. To link the quantifier and the predicates together, we can use a variable, say, x. We need to search, then, for the proper logical relationship among $\forall x$, Fx, and Sx; we need to say that every x such that x is a frog swims.

In essence, the theory points out that 'All frogs swim' asserts that if an object is a frog, it swims. So, the relationship we are looking for is the conditional; we want to say something like

(20) For all x, if x is a frog, then x swims.

which we can represent, using quantifiers and sentential connectives, as

(21) $\forall x(Fx \rightarrow Sx)$.

This reasoning applies to all universal affirmative sentences. Thus, we can represent anything having the form 'All F are G' as

(22) $\forall x(Fx \rightarrow Gx)$.

Second, *particular affirmative* sentences have the structure

(23) Some F are G.

To take an example, let's try to represent

(24) Some people are bothersome.

We can represent 'Edna is bothersome' as Be, and 'Some things are bothersome' as $\exists x Bx$. (24) seems to require that we express a relationship between the general terms 'people' and 'bothersome' (or 'are bothersome') in a way corresponding to the meaning of the determiner 'some'. We want to say that some object is a person and is bothersome. Thus, conjunction expresses the right relationship: To say that some people are bothersome is to say that, for some object x, x is a person, and x is bothersome. We can write (24) as

(25) $\exists x(Px \,\&\, Bx)$

In general, particular affirmative sentences translate into quantification theory as

(26) $\exists x(Fx \,\&\, Gx)$.

Conjunction, together with the existential quantifier, succeeds in representing sentences having the form of (23).

Finally, *universal negative* sentences have the form

(27) No F are G.

They have two equivalent and equally natural symbolizations in the language of quantificational logic. Suppose we want to symbolize 'No cats are ten feet tall'. Do we need a new quantifier to symbolize the determiner 'no'? No. We can symbolize the relation between general terms that 'no' expresses by using either the existential or the universal quantifier, together with negation. Because 'No cats are ten feet tall' is a direct denial of the sentence 'Some cats are ten feet tall', we can represent it as the negation of a particular affirmative sentence form. Letting F and G represent 'cat' and 'ten feet tall', respectively, this strategy yields

(28) $\neg \exists x(Fx \mathbin{\&} Gx)$

which we can read as

(29) a. It is not the case that, for some x, x is a cat and x is ten feet tall.
   b. There is no x such that x is a cat and x is ten feet tall.

or, more naturally,

(30) a. It is not true that some cat is ten feet tall.
   b. There is no cat who is ten feet tall.
   c. There is nothing that is both a cat and ten feet tall.
   d. No cat is ten feet tall.

But 'No cat is ten feet tall' also bears some similarity to universal affirmative sentence forms, being equivalent to 'If an object is a cat, it is not ten feet tall'. It says about every cat, in other words, that it is not ten feet tall. So, adopting the same dictionary as before, we can write

(31) $\forall x(Fx \to \neg Gx)$,

which says

(32) a. For all x, if x is a cat, then x is not ten feet tall.
   b. Every x is such that, if x is a cat, then x is not ten feet tall.

or, in better English,

(33) No cat is ten feet tall.

(28) and (31) both represent universal negative sentences; they are equivalent.

Any categorical sentence form, therefore, has a representation in quantification theory. The logic of this chapter can encompass the entire realm of syllogistic reasoning. In fact, as the next few sections demonstrate, it has the power to capture an extremely wide range of English arguments.

Problems

Symbolize the following in quantificational logic.

▶ **1.** All men are born good. (Confucius)

▶ **2.** Children are always cruel. (Samuel Johnson)

▸ **3.** No man was ever wise by chance. (Seneca)

▸ **4.** He who complains, sins. (Saint Francis de Sales)

▸ **5.** There is no detail that is too small. (George Allen)

▸ **6.** All finite things reveal infinitude. (Theodore Roethke)

7. Everything is new. (Joseph Joubert)

8. All intellectual improvement arises from leisure. (Samuel Johnson)

9. Nothing is more useful than silence. (Menander)

10. No one is exempt from talking nonsense. (Michel de Montaigne)

11. It is always the adventurers who accomplish great things. (Montesquieu)

▸ **12.** No guest ever left too soon for me. (Mrs. Stuyvesant Fish)

13. No victor believes in chance. (Friedrich Nietzsche)

14. What the heart knows today the head will understand tomorrow. (James Stephens)

15. The absent are always in the wrong. (Philippe Destouches)

16. Who has the fame to be an early riser may sleep till noon. (James Howell)

17. All that time is lost which might be better employed. (Jean-Jacques Rousseau)

▸ **18.** All intelligent thoughts have already been thought. (Goethe)

19. Nothing endures but personal qualities. (Walt Whitman)

20. Only an optimist can win in playing the game of business. (J. P. Morgan)

21. There is no excellence without difficulty. (Ovid)

22. All prejudices may be traced to the intestines. (Friedrich Nietzsche)

23. There are men who are happy without knowing it. (Vauvenargues)

▸ **24.** . . . nobody has money who ought to have it. (Benjamin Disraeli)

25. There is nothing good or evil save in the will. (Epictetus)

26. Whatever men aspire to, they deem best. (Petronius)

27. The trees that are slow to grow bear the best fruit. (Molière)

28. It is only shallow people who do not judge by appearances. (Oscar Wilde)

29. No facts are to me sacred; none are profane. . . . (Ralph Waldo Emerson)

▸ **30.** He who acts, spoils; he who grasps, lets slip. (Lao-Tzu)

10.3 POLYADIC PREDICATES

General terms are true or false of objects. 'Man', 'woman', 'animal', and 'mortal', in addition to intransitive verbs such as 'swim' and 'live', all apply or fail to apply to objects considered one by one. Because general terms are true or false of single objects, we can symbolize them using *monadic* or *unary* predicates.

Some English expressions are true or false of objects taken in pairs, or even triples, quadruples, and so on. Predicates symbolizing them are *polyadic*. Consider, for example, the English verb 'like'. It makes no sense to ask whether 'like' applies to an object considered alone. Does Socrates like? Does Plato like? These questions seem incoherent. But we can ask whether Socrates likes Alcibiades (the answer: no) or whether Plato likes Socrates (the answer: yes). So, 'like' applies, or fails to apply, to objects taken in pairs. The verb needs both a subject and a direct object. The same holds of most transitive verbs. Predicates that are true or false of pairs of things are not only polyadic but, more specifically, *dyadic* (or *binary*).

To represent general terms symbolically, quantification theory uses predicates. Thus Ma might symbolize 'Alonzo is a man', and Cj might represent 'Joan lives in California'. The same strategy works for polyadic predicates. For example, let us symbolize

(34) Hanno admires Bob Dobbs.

Because it asserts that 'admires' applies to the pair of objects consisting of Hanno and Bob Dobbs, this sentence has the structure

(35) Admires (Hanno, Bob Dobbs).

We can thus symbolize it as

(36) Mhb.

Similarly, we can represent

(37) Joanie loves Chachi.

as

(38) Ljc.

Given a dyadic predicate, say, L, symbolizing 'likes', we can construct a formula of quantification theory in several ways. First, we can combine the predicate with constants, obtaining formulas such as Lab and Lcc. The first constant following the predicate marks the *subject* position; the second marks the *object* position. If we write 'x likes y' as Lxy, then x is the liker, and y is the liked. Notice that the same constant may appear more than once; this allows us to symbolize sentences such as 'Alan likes himself'.

Second, we may prefix a quantifier to the predicate and combine it with variables. We might do this in only one place, filling the other with a constant.

For example, to symbolize

(39) Sam likes everything.

we can write

(40) $\forall x Lsx$.

And, to translate

(41) Everything likes Sam.

we can write

(42) $\forall x Lxs$.

Notice that the only difference between these formulas is the order of the variables and constants. This reflects the distinction in English between subject and object. Since Lxy symbolizes 'x likes y', the first position is always occupied by the subject of 'like'; the second, by its object. So, in $\forall x Lsx$, s is in the subject position. In $\forall x Lxs$, s is in the object position.

We may construct a formula from a predicate by prefixing a quantifier for each place. There may be two variables in the formula; each may link the predicate to either a universal or an existential quantifier. Thus, using combinations of quantifiers and variables with L might yield any of the following formulas:

(43) a. $\exists x \exists y Lxy$
  b. $\exists y \exists x Lxy$
  c. $\exists x \forall y Lxy$
  d. $\exists y \forall x Lxy$
  e. $\forall x \exists y Lxy$
  f. $\forall y \exists x Lxy$
  g. $\forall x \forall y Lxy$
  h. $\forall y \forall x Lxy$
  i. $\exists x Lxx$
  j. $\forall x Lxx$

To see what these formulas mean, let's examine them one by one.

$\exists x \exists y Lxy$ asserts that for some x and some y, x likes y: that something likes something. If we take our domain, or universe of discourse—the set of objects we're talking about, over which the variables and quantifiers range— to consist only of people, the formula says that somebody likes somebody. $\exists y \exists x Lxy$ asserts that for some y and some x, x likes y: that somebody is liked by somebody. We can capture the effect of reversing the variables by using the passive voice, which reverses subject and object in English. Of course, 'Somebody likes somebody' and 'Somebody is liked by somebody' are equivalent, as are $\exists x \exists y Lxy$ and $\exists y \exists x Lxy$. Reversing the order of adjacent existential quantifiers produces an equivalent formula.

$\forall x \forall y Lxy$ asserts that, for all x and for all y, x likes y: that everybody likes everybody. $\forall y \forall x Lxy$ reverses the order of the quantifiers, saying that, for all y and all x, x likes y. Again, we can use the passive voice to reverse subject and object in English; $\forall y \forall x Lxy$ represents the English 'Everybody is liked by everybody'. 'Everybody likes everybody' and 'Everybody is liked by everybody' are also equivalent. Reversing adjacent universal quantifiers yields an equivalent formula.

Combinations of existential and universal quantifiers, however, do not allow such switches. $\exists x \forall y Lxy$ asserts that there is an x such that, for all y, x likes y. This corresponds roughly to the English 'Somebody likes everybody'. (We say it corresponds only roughly because the English sentence is ambiguous. $\exists x \forall y Lxy$ corresponds to 'Somebody in particular likes everybody' or 'There's a certain person who likes everybody'.) $\exists y \forall x Lxy$ says that there is a y such that, for all x, x likes y; that amounts to the English 'Somebody (in particular) is liked by everybody'. $\forall x \exists y Lxy$ says that, for all x, there is a y such that x likes y. It thus represents 'Everybody likes somebody (or other)'. $\forall y \exists x Lxy$ says that, for all y, there is an x such that x likes y. This corresponds to 'Everybody is liked by somebody (or other)'. Finally, $\exists x Lxx$ says that some x is such that x likes x, corresponding to the English 'Somebody likes himself' (or 'herself'), whereas $\forall x Lxx$ says that every x is such that x likes x, corresponding to 'Everybody likes himself' (or 'herself').

We can display these correspondences in a table (again assuming that we are speaking only of people):

(44)	Formula	English Sentence
a.	$\exists x \exists y Lxy$	Somebody likes somebody.
b.	$\exists y \exists x Lxy$	Somebody is liked by somebody.
c.	$\exists x \forall y Lxy$	(A certain) somebody likes everybody.
d.	$\exists y \forall x Lxy$	(A certain) somebody is liked by everybody.
e.	$\forall x \exists y Lxy$	Everybody likes somebody (or other).
f.	$\forall y \exists x Lxy$	Everybody is liked by somebody (or other).
g.	$\forall x \forall y Lxy$	Everybody likes everybody.
h.	$\forall y \forall x Lxy$	Everybody is liked by everybody.
i.	$\exists x Lxx$	Somebody likes himself or herself.
j.	$\forall x Lxx$	Everybody likes himself or herself.

No formula in this table that contains both universal and existential quantifiers is equivalent to any other. '(A certain) somebody likes everybody' and 'everybody is liked by somebody (or other)' differ in meaning. '(A certain) somebody likes everybody' means that some one person (for instance, Edgar) likes everybody. 'Everybody is liked by somebody (or other)', in contrast, means that everybody is the object of somebody-or-other's liking. In other words, the latter sentence is true even if Alvin likes you, Bertha likes me, and so on. The former requires that some one person like you, me, and everyone.

Much the same is true of 'Everybody likes somebody (or other)' and '(A certain) somebody is liked by everybody'. The former means that, for each person, there's somebody or other he or she likes; you may like Paul, I may like Laura, and so on. The latter, however, means that one person is the object of everyone's liking; you and I and everyone else like some one individual, say, Alonzo.

Quantification theory reflects these differences in meaning by assigning quantifiers different positions. When an existential quantifier appears to the left of a universal, the formula states that some one object stands in a particular relation to every object. When an existential appears to the right of a universal, the formula states that, for each object, there is some object or other standing in some relation to it.

English often distinguishes these senses by placing determiners in a particular order. The order frequently matches the order of the quantifiers. There are exceptions—'each' and 'any', as we'll see in the next chapter, almost always correspond to quantifiers at the extreme left of a formula. There are also ambiguities, as sentences such as 'Everybody likes somebody' show. Rules for ordering determiners in English are highly complex and controversial. Consequently, we often have to rely on our own intuitions about meaning to determine, in a given context, the correct order of the quantifiers.

Problems

Symbolize these sentences in quantification theory.

- **1.** All roads lead to Rome.

- **2.** All roads lead somewhere.

- **3.** No road leads everywhere.

- **4.** Nobody knows all the trouble I've seen.

- **5.** Nobody knows any of the trouble I've seen.

- **6.** Somebody knows some of the trouble I've seen.

  7. Hank admires Rose.

  8. Hank admires somebody.

  9. Somebody admires Hank.

  10. Hank admires some famous people.

  11. No famous people admire Hank.

- **12.** Life was a freshness of rain, free to all, subject to none. (Lao-Tzu)

  13. Everybody tells us everything. . . . (General Vernon Walters, quoting a Soviet intelligence officer)

14. Good merchandise finds a ready buyer. (Plautus)

15. He that hath a trade hath an estate. . . . (Benjamin Franklin)

16. Every crowd has a silver lining. (P. T. Barnum)

17. There's a sucker born every minute. (P. T. Barnum)

▸ 18. Nothing in this world can one imagine beforehand. . . . (Rainer Maria Rilke)

19. Every degree of luxury hath some connection with evil. (John Woolman)

20. Nothing is good for everyone. . . . (André Gide)

21. Every scarecrow has a secret ambition to terrorize. (Stanislaus Lec)

22. It is not every man that can afford to wear a shabby coat. (C. Colton)

23. Nobody can teach anybody to write. (Mark Medoff)

▸ 24. A dull axe never loves grindstones. (Henry Ward Beecher)

25. He that has no patience has nothing at all. (Italian proverb)

26. To do nothing is in every man's power. (Samuel Johnson)

27. A person is never happy except at the price of some ignorance. (Anatole France)

28. Everyone has a code of ethics for everyone. (Robert Half)

29. You give a guy a title and he hires someone to do his job. (Harry A. Merlo)

▸ 30. Without some dissimulation no business can be carried on at all. (G. K. Chesterton)

31. There is no moral precept that does not have something inconvenient about it. (Denis Diderot)

32. . . . every fresh experience points out some form of error which we shall afterward carefully avoid. (John Keats)

33. Rose admires somebody who admires Hank.

34. Rose admires somebody Hank admires.

35. Rose admires everybody Hank admires.

▸ 36. Rose admires everybody who admires Hank.

37. Hank admires nobody Rose admires.

38. Hank admires nobody who admires Rose.

39. Hank admires nobody who admires him.

40. Anyone who admires Hank admires everyone.

10.4 The Language QL

It's important to define the language of quantification theory more precisely. We can represent English sentences as quantificational formulas only if we know what a formula of quantification theory is.

Syntax

As we saw with the sentential language, SL, any logical language consists of a syntax and a semantics. The syntax comprises a vocabulary of symbols and a grammar, a set of formation rules for combining the symbols to form formulas. The vocabulary of our quantification language, QL, includes the following:

Vocabulary

Sentence letter constants: p, q, r, s^*
n-ary predicate constants: $A^n, B^n, \ldots, Z^{n^*}$
Individual constants: $a, b, c, \ldots, o^*$
Individual variables: t, u, v, w, x, y, z^*
Sentential connectives: $\neg, \rightarrow, \&, \vee, \leftrightarrow$
Quantifiers: $\forall, \exists$
Grouping indicators: (,)
* with or without numerical subscripts

This is the vocabulary of SL, supplemented with predicates, constants, variables, and quantifiers.

The rules for combining these symbols to construct formulas are more complex than in sentential logic. To understand them, we need to understand substitution, symbolized with '/'. Suppose that we are given an expression $\mathscr{A}$. We can construct a new expression, which we can call, abstractly, $\mathscr{A}[c/d]$ ($\mathscr{A}$, with c substituted for d), by replacing every occurrence of the constant d with an occurrence of the constant c. Similarly, we can form $\mathscr{A}[x/y]$ by replacing every occurrence of the variable y with an occurrence of the variable x. We can also substitute constants for variables, and variables for constants. To take an example, suppose $\mathscr{A}$ is Fab. Then $\mathscr{A}[c/a]$ is Fcb. Or, suppose $\mathscr{A}$ is $\forall x Fxa$; then $\mathscr{A}[y/a]$ is $\forall x Fxy$. The substitution operation is defined for all expressions, whether or not they are formulas. But applying it to a formula may yield a string of symbols that is no longer a formula. In particular, substituting a variable for a constant in a formula produces an expression that is not a formula; rather, it is what we'll call, in Chapter 13, a *protoformula*. $\forall x Fxa$, for example, is a formula according to the following rules, but $\forall x Fxy$ isn't.

Formation Rules

1. Any sentence letter constant is a formula. (Specifically, an *atomic* formula.)
2. An *n*-ary predicate followed by *n* constants is a formula. (Again, an *atomic* formula.)
3. If $\mathcal{A}$ is a formula, $\neg\mathcal{A}$ is a formula.
4. If $\mathcal{A}$ and $\mathcal{B}$ are formulas, then $(\mathcal{A} \rightarrow \mathcal{B})$, $(\mathcal{A} \,\&\, \mathcal{B})$, $(\mathcal{A} \vee \mathcal{B})$, and $(\mathcal{A} \leftrightarrow \mathcal{B})$ are formulas.
5. If $\mathcal{A}$ is a formula with a constant c, and v is a variable that does not appear in $\mathcal{A}$, then $\exists v\mathcal{A}[v/c]$ and $\forall v\mathcal{A}[v/c]$ are formulas.
6. Every formula can be constructed by a finite number of applications of these rules.

The formation rules characterize the formulas of the language of quantification theory, QL. Notice that every formula of sentential logic is also a formula of QL. In addition, QL allows us to link quantified formulas with sentential connectives and to combine sentence letters with the quantificational apparatus. When we form $\forall v\mathcal{A}[v/c]$ or $\exists v\mathcal{A}[v/c]$ in accordance with these rules, we'll say that the *scope* of $\forall v$ or $\exists v$ is all of $\forall v\mathcal{A}[v/c]$ or $\exists v\mathcal{A}[v/c]$. Thus, the quantifiers in the following formulas have these scopes:

Formula	Scope of $\forall$	Scope of $\exists$
$\exists x(Fx \,\&\, Gx)$		$\exists x(Fx \,\&\, Gx)$
$\forall x(Fx \rightarrow Gx)$	$\forall x(Fx \rightarrow Gx)$	
$\forall x\exists yFxy$	$\forall x\exists yFxy$	$\exists yFxy$
$\exists y\forall xFxy$	$\forall xFxy$	$\exists y\forall xFxy$
$\exists xFx \vee Ga$		$\exists xFx$
$\exists x(Fx \vee Ga)$		$\exists x(Fx \vee Ga)$
$\forall xHx \rightarrow Fc$	$\forall xHx$	
$\forall x(Hx \rightarrow Fc)$	$\forall x(Hx \rightarrow Fc)$	
$\forall x(Fx \rightarrow \exists yGyx)$	$\forall x(Fx \rightarrow \exists yGyx)$	$\exists yGyx$
$\exists x(\forall yFy \,\&\, Gx)$	$\forall yFy$	$\exists x(\forall yFy \,\&\, Gx)$

In formulas of QL, variables never appear outside the scope of a corresponding quantifier.

As in the case of sentential logic, we'll adopt a few simplifying conventions to make formulas more readable. First, as we've been doing already, we'll drop the superscript that indicates whether a given predicate is singulary, binary, and so on. Thus, we'll write Fa rather than F^1a, $\forall x\exists yFxy$ rather than $\forall x\exists yF^2xy$, and so on. Second, as in SL, we'll count the result of deleting a formula's outside pair of parentheses as an abbreviation of the actual formula. Thus, the first formula in each of these pairs abbreviates the second:

> (45) a. $\exists x(Fx \to Gx) \to \forall x \exists y Hxy$
> $(\exists x(Fx \to Gx) \to \forall x \exists y Hxy)$
> b. $\forall z \forall w \exists t(Fzt \,\&\, Gwz) \leftrightarrow p$
> $(\forall z \forall w \exists t(Fzt \,\&\, Gwz) \leftrightarrow p)$

Third, because we'll drop predicate superscripts, we'll avoid using the same predicate letter as both a monadic and a polyadic predicate within the same formula. Although

> (46) $\exists x \forall y(Fxy \to Fa)$

is correctly formed, using F to represent two English expressions at once tends to be confusing; the formula is more properly written out as $\exists x \forall y(F^2xy \to F^1a)$, which makes it clear that there are two different predicates.

Several points about formulas of QL deserve mention. Note that only variables may appear with quantifiers. $\exists aFa$ is not a formula; neither is $\forall p(p \to q)$ or $\exists FFa$. Intuitively, individual constants and variables take objects as values. In QL we can quantify over objects, speaking about all objects of a certain kind, or some objects of that kind, and so on. We cannot do the same with sentences or predicates. Because it allows quantification over individuals alone, QL is a system of *first-order* quantification, sometimes called *first-order logic.* Other logical theories, called *higher-order logics,* do allow quantification over sentences and predicates, but at the price of substantial complication. The higher-order logics would allow us to symbolize sentences such as 'Julio believes everything that Lucky tells him' and 'Raoul has all the qualities of a psychopath'.

Semantics

The semantics of QL is complicated. Recall that in sentential logic an interpretation is simply an assignment of truth values to atomic formulas, that is, to sentence letters. Quantificational logic includes sentential logic; therefore, interpretations within QL will incorporate such truth value assignments. But quantificational interpretations are more complex.

> **DEFINITION** An *interpretation M* of a set *S* of formulas of QL consists of a nonempty set *D* (*M*'s *domain,* or *universe of discourse*) and a function φ assigning (a) truth values to sentence letters in S, (b) elements of D to constants in S, and (c) sets of *n*-tuples of elements of *D* to *n*-ary predicates in S.

An interpretation (sometimes called a *structure* or *model*) thus has two components. The first is a set that specifies what objects the formulas in question are talking about. The quantifiers *range over* this set, in the sense that we construe 'for all x' and 'for some y' as meaning 'for all x in D' and 'for some y in D' or, in other words, 'for all elements of D' and 'for some element of D'.

The second component of an interpretation M is an *interpretation function*. This function, in effect, is a rule that assigns meaning to the constants, predicates, and sentence letters in the formulas we're interpreting. It assigns truth values to sentence letters, telling us whether the sentences they represent are true or false. It assigns elements of the domain to constants, telling us which objects they stand for. Finally, it assigns sets of n-tuples of objects to n-ary predicates. Consider a unary (or monadic) predicate, R, which informally means 'red'. The interpretation function assigns R a set of 1-tuples. Intuitively, it tells us which objects satisfy R; it tells us, in other words, which objects are red. The function assigns to a binary or dyadic predicate such as L, meaning 'loves', a set of ordered pairs. The function tells us, then, who loves whom. If $\varphi(L) = \{\langle \text{Bob, Carol}\rangle, \langle \text{Carol, Ted}\rangle, \langle \text{Ted, Alice}\rangle, \langle \text{Alice, Bob}\rangle\}$, then Bob loves Carol, Carol loves Ted, Ted loves Alice, and Alice loves Bob. (The angle brackets '$\langle$' and '$\rangle$' signify n-tuples, that is, sequences of n objects.)

This table summarizes how the interpretation function works.

Symbol	φ	Interpretation
sentence letter	$\Rightarrow$	truth value
constant	$\Rightarrow$	object in the domain
n-ary predicate	$\Rightarrow$	set of n-tuples of objects in domain

The definition of an interpretation only performs part of the task that we need to accomplish. We want to be able to produce interpretations that make various formulas true and others false. To do this, we need to know how to evaluate the truth value of a formula on an interpretation.

It's easy to judge the truth value of a sentence letter on an interpretation; we merely see what value the interpretation function assigns to it. An interpretation M consisting of D (its domain) and φ (its interpretation function) makes a sentence letter p true just in case φ assigns truth to p:

p is true on M if and only if $\varphi(p) = \text{T}$.

Other atomic formulas, consisting of an n-ary predicate followed by n constants, are also easy to evaluate. The sentence 'Bob loves Carol' is true if and only if Bob loves Carol. The sentence is true, in other words, just in case the interpretation we assign to the predicate 'loves' includes the pair $\langle \text{Bob, Carol}\rangle$. In general, then, an atomic formula of the form $\mathscr{R}a_1 \ldots a_n$ will be true on an interpretation M just in case the set the interpretation function assigns to $\mathscr{R}$ includes the n-tuple consisting of the objects that $a_1, \ldots, a_n$ stand for:

$\mathscr{R}a_1 \ldots a_n$ is true on M if and only if $\langle \varphi(a_1), \ldots, \varphi(a_n) \rangle$ belongs to $\varphi(\mathscr{R})$.

Assessing the truth values of formulas with sentential connectives as main connectives is also easy, provided that we know the truth values of the components. We can proceed exactly as in sentential logic. Given an interpretation M, we know that

$\neg \mathscr{A}$ is true on M if and only if $\mathscr{A}$ is false on M.
$(\mathscr{A} \mathbin{\&} \mathscr{B})$ is true on M if and only if $\mathscr{A}$ and $\mathscr{B}$ are both true on M.
$(\mathscr{A} \vee \mathscr{B})$ is true on M if and only if either $\mathscr{A}$ or $\mathscr{B}$ is true on M.
$(\mathscr{A} \rightarrow \mathscr{B})$ is true on M if and only if $\mathscr{A}$ is false on M or $\mathscr{B}$ is true on M.
$(\mathscr{A} \leftrightarrow \mathscr{B})$ is true on M if and only if $\mathscr{A}$ and $\mathscr{B}$ have the same truth value on M.

The real task is defining the truth value of quantified formulas. Consider an example of an existentially quantified formula, $\exists x F x$. This formula will be true if the predicate F is true of some object in the domain. We can think of ourselves as considering an instance of the formula, such as Fa, and asking whether a could name something that would make Fa true. Similarly, consider an example of a universally quantified formula, $\forall x (Fx \rightarrow Gx)$. We can think of an instance of this formula, such as $Fa \rightarrow Ga$; this instance should be true no matter what object in the domain a stands for, if the original formula is true. So, to judge the truth value of a quantified formula on an interpretation M, we can look at the truth values of an instance of that formula on interpretations which are just like M, except that they may assign different objects from the domain to the constant substituted for the quantified variable. We say that M' is a c-variant of M if and only if (iff) M and M' (a) have the same domain and (b) have interpretation functions agreeing on the interpretation of every item in the language except c. Then, for any constant c not in $\mathscr{A}$, we can say

$\exists v \mathscr{A}$ is true on M iff $\mathscr{A}[c/v]$ is true on a c-variant of M.
$\forall v \mathscr{A}$ is true on M iff $\mathscr{A}[c/v]$ is true on every c-variant of M.

Another way of thinking about the truth values of quantified formulas is this: A universally quantified formula $\forall v \mathscr{A}$ is true just in case $\mathscr{A}$ would be true no matter what object in the universe of discourse v would stand for. An existentially quantified formula $\exists v \mathscr{A}$ would similarly be true if there's an object in the domain such that, if v stood for it, $\mathscr{A}$ would be true.

The next chapter discusses symbolization: the process of using QL to represent English sentences and arguments. We've seen, in this chapter, how to symbolize sentences of certain simple forms. We'll soon extend our method to a procedure for symbolizing a large class of English sentences.

Problems

Evaluate each of the following as (a) a formula or conventional abbreviation of a formula of QL, or (b) neither of the above.

▶ **1.** F^1x ▶ **2.** F^1a ▶ **3.** $Fx \rightarrow Fy$

▶ **4.** $Fa \rightarrow Fc$ ▶ **5.** $(Fx \rightarrow Fy)$ ▶ **6.** $(F^1a \rightarrow F^1b)$

7. $\exists xFx \rightarrow Fx$ **8.** $\exists x(Fx \rightarrow Fx)$ **9.** $\exists xF^1x \rightarrow F^1a$

10. $\exists x(F^1x \rightarrow F^1a)$ **11.** $(\exists xFx \rightarrow Fa)$ ▶ **12.** $\forall x\forall yFxy \rightarrow Fyx$

13. $\forall x\forall yF^2xy \rightarrow F^2ab$ **14.** $\forall x\forall yFxy \vee Fa$

15. $\forall x\forall y(Fxy \rightarrow Fyx)$ **16.** $\forall x\forall yFxy \rightarrow \forall x\forall yFyx$

17. $(\forall x\forall yF^2xy \rightarrow \forall x\forall yF^2yx)$ ▶ **18.** $\forall x\forall yFxy \rightarrow Fy$

19. $\forall xFx \rightarrow \exists xFx$ **20.** $\forall x(Fx \rightarrow \exists xFx)$

21. $(\forall xF^1x \rightarrow \exists xF^1x)$ **22.** $\exists x\forall yGy$

23. $\forall x\forall y\forall b(Fxy \vee Fyb)$ ▶ **24.** $\forall x\exists F(Fx \rightarrow Fa)$

25. G^1y **26.** G^2b

27. $\forall xG^1x$ **28.** $\forall xGxy$

29. $\forall yG^1y \rightarrow G^1z$ ▶ **30.** $\forall y(G^1y \rightarrow G^1z)$

31. $\forall yGy \rightarrow Gy$ **32.** $\forall y(G^1y \leftrightarrow G^1y)$

33. $\forall xF^2xy \rightarrow \forall yG^2yx$ **34.** $\forall x(Fxy \rightarrow \forall yGyx)$

35. $\forall x\forall y(Fxy \rightarrow Gyx)$ ▶ **36.** $\forall y(\forall xFxy \rightarrow Gyx)$

37. $\forall x\forall y(\exists zFyz \leftrightarrow (Gy \mathbin{\&} Hzx))$

38. $\forall x(\forall y\exists zF^2yz \leftrightarrow (G^1y \mathbin{\&} H^2zx))$

39. $\forall x\forall y\exists z(Fyz \leftrightarrow (Gy \mathbin{\&} Hzy))$

40. $(\forall x\forall y\exists z(Fyz \mathbin{\&} Gx) \leftrightarrow Hzy)$

Taking each expression below as $\mathscr{A}$, write (a) $\mathscr{A}[c/d]$, (b) $\mathscr{A}[d/c]$, (c) $\mathscr{A}[x/c]$, (d) $\mathscr{A}[y/d]$, and (e) $\mathscr{A}[y/x]$, and say whether the result in each case is a formula. (Count abbreviations of formulas as formulas.)

41. Hcd ▶ **42.** Hcc

43. Hcx **44.** Hxy

45. $\forall x Fx \leftrightarrow Gc$

46. $\forall x Fxc \leftrightarrow \exists x Fdx$

47. $\forall x(Fxc \leftrightarrow \exists y Fdy)$

▶ **48.** $Fxc \leftrightarrow \exists y Fdy$

49. $\exists x Fxc \ \& \ \forall x Fxd$

50. $Fxc \ \& \ \forall x Fxd$

Let $D = \{a\}$, $\varphi(a) = a$, and $\varphi(F) = \{\langle a \rangle\}$. What is the truth value of these formulas on this interpretation?

51. Fa

52. $\neg Fa$

53. $Fa \ \& \ Fa$

▶ **54.** $Fa \vee \neg Fa$

55. $Fa \rightarrow \neg Fa$

56. $\neg Fa \rightarrow Fa$

57. $\exists x Fx$

58. $\forall x Fx$

59. $\forall x(Fx \rightarrow \exists y Fy)$

▶ **60.** $\forall x(\neg Fx \rightarrow \neg \exists y Fy)$

Let $D = \{a\}$, $\varphi(a) = a$, $\varphi(F) = \varnothing$, and $\varphi(G) = \{\langle a \rangle\}$. What is the truth value of these formulas on this interpretation?

61. Fa

62. Ga

63. $Fa \rightarrow Ga$

64. $Ga \rightarrow Fa$

65. $\exists x Fx$

▶ **66.** $\forall x Fx$

67. $\exists x Gx$

68. $\forall x Gx$

69. $\forall x(Fx \rightarrow Gx)$

70. $\forall x((Fx \vee Gx) \rightarrow Gx)$

Let $D = \{a, b\}$, $\varphi(a) = a$, $\varphi(b) = b$, and $\varphi(R) = \{\langle a, a \rangle, \langle b, a \rangle\}$. What is the truth value of these formulas on this interpretation?

71. Rab

▶ **72.** Rba

73. Rbb

74. $\exists x Rax$

75. $\exists x Rbx$

76. $\exists x Rxa$

77. $\exists x Rxb$

▶ **78.** $\forall x Rxx$

79. $\forall x \forall y(Rxy \rightarrow Ryx)$

80. $\forall x \exists y Rxy$

Let $D = \{a, b\}$, $\varphi(a) = a$, $\varphi(b) = b$, $\varphi(F) = \{\langle b \rangle\}$, and $\varphi(R) = \{\langle b, b \rangle, \langle b, a \rangle\}$. What is the truth value of these formulas on this interpretation?

81. $\exists x(Fx \ \& \ Rxx)$

82. $\exists x(Fx \ \& \ Rxa)$

83. $\forall x(Fx \rightarrow Rxx)$

▶ **84.** $\forall x(Fx \rightarrow Rax)$

85. $\forall x \forall y(Rxy \rightarrow Ryx)$

86. $\forall x \forall y(Rxy \rightarrow Rxx)$

87. $\forall x \forall y(Rxy \rightarrow Ryy)$

88. $\forall x \forall y \forall z((Rxy \ \& \ Ryz) \rightarrow Rxz)$

89. $\forall x \forall y \forall z((Rxy \ \& \ Ryz) \rightarrow \neg Rxz)$

▶ **90.** $\forall x \forall y((Fx \ \& \ Fy) \rightarrow (Rxy \ \& \ Ryx))$

Let $D = \{a, b, c\}$, $\varphi(a) = a$, $\varphi(b) = b$, and $\varphi(R) = \{\langle a, a \rangle, \langle a, b \rangle, \langle b, c \rangle,$ $\langle a, c \rangle, \langle c, b \rangle, \langle b, a \rangle\}$. What is the truth value of these formulas on this interpretation?

91. $\exists x Rxx$

92. $\forall x \forall y Rxy$

93. $\forall x \exists y Rxy$

94. $\forall x \forall y (Rxy \rightarrow Ryx)$

95. $\forall x (Rxx \rightarrow \exists y Ryx)$

▶ **96.** $\forall x (\exists y Rxy \rightarrow Rxa)$

97. $\forall x (Rxa \rightarrow Rbx)$

98. $\forall z \forall y \forall z ((Rxy \ \& \ Ryz) \rightarrow Rxz)$

99. $\forall x \forall y (Rxy \rightarrow \exists z (Rxz \ \& \ Ryz))$

100. $\forall x \forall y ((Rxy \ \& \ Ryx) \rightarrow \exists z (Rxz \ \& \ Rzz))$

Let $D =$ the set of Federal League teams in 1915, with P interpreted as 'had at least as high a winning percentage as', F as 'finished first', B as 'finished at least one game behind', G as 'won at least as many games as', and L as 'lost at least as many games as'.

The 1915 Federal League Standings

Team	Wins	Losses	Pct.	Games Behind
Chicago	86	66	.566	—
St. Louis	87	67	.565	—
Pittsburgh	86	67	.562	.5
Kansas City	81	72	.529	5.5
Newark	80	72	.526	6
Buffalo	74	78	.487	12
Brooklyn	70	82	.461	16
Baltimore	47	107	.305	40

What truth values do these formulas have on this interpretation?

101. $\forall x (Fx \rightarrow \forall y Pxy)$

▶ **102.** $\forall x (Fx \rightarrow \forall y Gxy)$

103. $\forall x (Fx \rightarrow \forall y Lyx)$

104. $\forall x (\forall y Pxy \rightarrow Fx)$

105. $\forall x (\forall y Gxy \rightarrow Fx)$

106. $\forall x (\forall y Lyx \rightarrow Fx)$

107. $\forall x \forall y (Gxy \rightarrow Lyx)$

▶ **108.** $\exists x \exists y (Bxy \ \& \ Lxy)$

109. $\exists x \exists y (Pxy \ \& \ Gyx)$

110. $\forall x \forall y (Pxy \rightarrow Lyx)$

111. $\forall x (\exists y Byx \rightarrow \neg \forall z Lxz)$

112. $\forall x \forall y (Pxy \rightarrow Gxy)$

113. $\forall x \forall y \forall z ((Pxy \ \& \ Lyx) \rightarrow Gxy)$

▶ **114.** $\forall x \forall y (Bxy \rightarrow Lxy)$

115. $\forall x \forall y (Bxy \rightarrow Gyx)$

116. $\forall x \forall y (Bxy \rightarrow Pyx)$

117. $\forall x \forall y (Lxy \rightarrow Bxy)$

118. $\forall x \forall y (Gyx \rightarrow Bxy)$

119. $\forall x \forall y (Pyx \rightarrow Bxy)$

▶ **120.** $\forall x \exists y (Gyx \ \& \ Pyx)$

11

SYMBOLIZATION

W ith the addition of polyadic predicates, quantification theory has the power to express and evaluate a very large group of sentences and arguments. This chapter presents a guide to representing English sentences in the theory. It requires some familiarity with English grammar.

To translate even a simple sentence, we must distinguish its grammatical subject from its grammatical predicate. Because the word *predicate* takes on a different meaning in logic, we'll call grammatical subjects *subject* (or *main*) *noun phrases,* and grammatical predicates *main verb phrases.* It's easy to translate simple sentences such as 'All men are mortal', 'Some computers are not reliable', and 'Nobody admires everybody' into QL. But noun and verb phrases may become far more complex.

11.1 NOUN PHRASES

Some noun phrases are easy to handle in QL. Proper names, such as 'Jane' and 'Tarzan', and singular pronouns such as 'he', 'she', or 'it', translate as individual constants; common nouns, such as 'woman' and 'chimpanzee', translate as monadic predicates. Thus, we can symbolize

(1) Jane loves Tarzan.

as

(2) *Lja,*

and

(3) Tarzan loves all chimpanzees.

as

(4) $\forall x(Cx \rightarrow Lax)$.

But here the simplicity ends.

311

Determiners

The determiners 'all', 'each', 'any', and 'every' generally translate as universal quantifiers, while 'some' and 'a(n)' generally translate as existentials. Thus, we can symbolize

(5) All chimpanzees love Jane.

as

(6) $\forall x(Cx \rightarrow Lxj)$,

and

(7) Some chimpanzees love Tarzan.

as

(8) $\exists x(Cx \ \& \ Lxa)$.

But even these rules have exceptions. First, 'a' and 'an' have a *generic* use, in which they refer to typical members of a kind. Thus

(9) A whale is a mammal.

does not mean that some whales are mammals, but that all are. In such cases, 'a' and 'an' correspond roughly to universal quantifiers.

Second, 'a', 'an', 'any', and 'some' all interact with conditionals when they are part of the antecedent. We can translate

(10) If you steal something, you'll get into trouble.

as a conditional with the quantified antecedent (where 'a' represents 'you'):

(11) You steal something.

which we can symbolize as

(12) $\exists xSax$

and the consequent

(13) You'll get into trouble.

which we can render as

(14) Ta.

As a whole, then, we can symbolize (10) as

(15) $\exists xSax \rightarrow Ta$.

But, when the consequent contains a word that refers back to something in the antecedent, this strategy doesn't work. We could try to translate

(16) If you steal something, you'll pay for it.

as

(17) $\exists x Sax \rightarrow Pax$.

But this is not a formula; Pax can't come from our formation rules because the x in Pax isn't in the scope of $\exists x$. Changing the parentheses to give the quantifier scope over the entire formula doesn't help.

(18) $\exists x(Sax \rightarrow Pax)$

is a formula, but it says the wrong thing. By the definition of the conditional, the formula is equivalent to

(19) $\exists x(\neg Sax \lor Pax)$.

But this formula says that there is an object that either you don't steal or you pay for. And this is true so long as there is an object you don't steal. The same does not hold of (16), whose truth value is not determined by whether or not there are things you don't steal.

To represent (16), we must use a universal quantifier with the entire formula as its scope:

(20) $\forall x(Sax \rightarrow Pax)$

This formula says that everything you steal, you pay for, which is equivalent to (16). So, in certain cases in which they appear in the antecedent of a conditional, with reference back to the antecedent in the consequent, the determiners 'a', 'an', and 'some' correspond to universal quantifiers in QL.

Notice that (16) is equivalent to

(21) If you steal anything, you'll pay for it.

'Any' translates as a universal quantifier, but with the widest possible scope. 'Each' usually takes wide scope among quantifiers; 'any', however, demands wide scope over connectives as well. 'Every' and 'all' make no such demand. This explains why (16) and (21) aren't equivalent to

(22) If you steal everything, you'll pay for it.

and

(23) If you steal each thing, you'll pay for it.

It also explains why 'any' often seems similar to 'some' or 'a'.

(24) John didn't see any deer.

is equivalent to

(25) John didn't see a deer.

not to

(26) John didn't see every deer.

The reason is that 'any' represents a universal quantifier to the left of the negation sign:

(27) $\forall x \neg (Sjx \ \& \ Dx)$

'Everything', 'anything', 'something', and the like all act like the corresponding determiners; 'thing' functions, more or less, as a variable. 'Everybody', 'anybody', 'somebody', 'everyone', 'anyone', and 'someone' all act like 'every person', 'any person', and so on. They generally force the use of a quantifier together with the monadic predicate P (for 'person') linked appropriately to the rest of the formula.

'No', and the related 'nobody', 'nothing', and so on all translate into QL in the ways suggested by representations of categorical sentence forms. They correspond to negations of existential quantifiers or to universal quantifiers applying to negations.

'Only', though it is not really a determiner, functions much like 'all', except that it reverses the order of the relevant expressions. 'Only F are G' amounts to 'All G are F'.

English contains many other determiners that QL can't translate. 'Many', 'several', 'a few', 'few', 'most', 'infinitely many', and 'much', for example, elude the powers of QL. Sentences containing them do not translate into quantification theory because QL contains only two quantifiers.

An important part of interpreting formulas of QL is assigning them a *universe of discourse* or *domain*. This is a set of objects. Intuitively, the universe of discourse is a set, determined by the common ground of the conversation, containing the objects the formulas are talking about. The quantifiers and variables *range over* the domain, in the following sense. We interpret the universal quantifier as asserting that something is true for all elements of the domain. We similarly interpret the existential quantifier as asserting that something is true for some element of the domain.

We can often simplify symbolization by assigning an appropriate universe of discourse. If, within the context of an argument, we are speaking of nothing but people, then we can limit the domain to the set of people. If we do, then a universal quantifier will have the effect of 'for all x in the set of people', that is, 'for all people x'. The universal quantifier, in such a case, represents the English expressions 'anybody' and 'everybody' without using a predicate meaning 'person'.

Adjectives

Adjectives, words such as 'good', 'red', 'friendly', and 'logical', modify nouns. With a few exceptions, they translate into QL as monadic predicates, linked to the predicates representing the nouns they modify by conjunctions. Thus

(28) All friendly cats purr.

becomes

(29) $\forall x((Fx \mathbin{\&} Cx) \to Px)$,

and

(30) Some artists are unhappy people.

becomes

(31) $\exists x(Ax \mathbin{\&} (Ux \mathbin{\&} Px))$.

These sentences are basically categorical sentence forms.

Adjectival phrases, consisting of an adjective modified by an adverb, for example, function in the same way. They must be treated as a single unit. Thus

(32) John is a very wealthy logician.

translates into QL as

(33) $Wj \mathbin{\&} Lj$,

where W represents 'very wealthy'.

Most adjectives and adjectival phrases thus translate as conjunctions. The set of colorless gases is the set of things that are both colorless and gases. It is the intersection of the set of colorless things and the set of gases. For this reason, we'll call adjectives that work in the standard way *intersective*.

Certain adjectives, however, aren't intersective; they don't translate into QL directly. They have meanings that relate in some way to the nouns they modify; thus, they and their nouns must translate as a single unit. Luckily, identifying these adjectives, which we'll call *nonintersective,* is easy. Wealthy logicians are both wealthy and logicians; red Chevrolets are both red and Chevrolets. But alleged criminals are not alleged and criminals. Good pianists are not simply pianists and good. Former congressmen are not former and congressmen; large mice are not large and mice. 'Good pianist' means something like 'good as a pianist'; 'large mouse', something like 'large for a mouse'. This is why the following arguments fail:

(34) a. Every pianist is a lover.
      $\therefore$ Every good pianist is a good lover.
   b. All mice are animals.
      $\therefore$ All large mice are large animals.

To avoid trouble, then, we must translate nonintersective adjectives modifying nouns as single monadic predicates. Note, however, that there is an important difference among nonintersective adjectives. The set of large mice is a subset of the set of mice; the set of good pianists is similarly a subset of the set of pianists. But other nonintersective adjectives, such as 'fake' and 'former', have a different relationship to the nouns they modify.

The set of fake diamonds is not a subset of the set of diamonds at all. Likewise, the set of former congressmen is not a subset of the set of congressmen. Such adjectives must translate, together with the nouns they modify, as a single unit. Adjectives such as 'large' and 'good', in contrast, may translate as conjunctions, but with an important difference from intersective adjectives. We can render 'large mouse' as Lx & Mx, where M represents 'mouse', but only if we construe L as translating, not 'large', but 'large for a mouse'.

Relative Clauses

Relative clauses are English expressions formed from sentences. They begin, generally, with 'that' or a word starting with 'wh-', such as 'who', 'which', 'when', or 'where', though these words are often omitted. Relative clauses frequently act like adjectives, modifying nouns or noun phrases. Thus 'that Arlene used to attend', 'who once denounced Richard Nixon', and '(when) I've placed my hopes in something' behave as relative clauses in the following sentences:

> (35) a. A school that Arlene used to attend has been closed.
> b. Senator McCarthy, who once denounced Richard Nixon, is now retired.
> c. Every time (when) I've placed my hopes in something, I've been disappointed.

Like intersective adjectives, relative clauses are conjoined to the nouns they modify. 'That Arlene used to attend', for example, derives from the open sentence 'Arlene used to attend x'. Similarly, 'who once denounced Richard Nixon' derives from 'x once denounced Richard Nixon', and '(when) I've placed my hopes in something', from 'I've placed my hopes in something at (time) x'. Using the obvious representations, we can symbolize these as Aax, Dxn, and $\exists y Hiyx$. Conjoining them in the appropriate manner to representations of their nouns, we obtain:

> (36) a. $\exists x((Sx$ & $Aax)$ & $Cx)$
> (There is an x such that x is a school, Arlene used to attend x, and x is closed.)
> b. Dmn & Rm
> (Senator McCarthy once denounced Richard Nixon, and McCarthy is now retired.)
> c. $\forall x((Tx$ & $\exists y Hiyx) \rightarrow Dix)$
> (For every x, if x is a time and, for some y, I've placed my hopes in y at x, then I've been disappointed at x.)

Relative clauses, in general, translate quite easily. Only one wrinkle ruins their simplicity. Some relative clauses restrict the group of things to which the noun phrase they modify applies. If I tell you that everyone I know prefers Mexican to Chinese food, then I am speaking, not of everyone, but just of everyone I know. (35)a and (35)c contain such *restrictive* relative clauses. Other clauses, however, make almost parenthetical comments about their nouns or noun phrases. (35)b contains such a *nonrestrictive* relative clause.

Most relative clauses in actual discourse are restrictive. To tell whether a given clause is restrictive, we can ask whether the clause is helping to specify what the sentence is talking about or providing additional information concerning an already determinate topic. English does offer two linguistic hints. First, 'that' often signals that a clause is restrictive; 'which', with some exceptions (for example, the phrases 'in which' and 'with which'), often signals a nonrestrictive. Relative clauses often begin with other 'wh-'words, however, or with no special word at all. In these cases, there are no signals. Furthermore, the use of 'that' and 'which' is not very firmly established; these words are unreliable guides. Second, and more reliably, commas often do, and always can, set off nonrestrictive clauses from the rest of the sentence. Restrictives, on the other hand, reject commas in this role. Hence, virtually all relative clauses set off by commas are nonrestrictive. For those not set off by commas, we can apply a simple test: Try inserting commas. If the result sounds acceptable, the clause is probably nonrestrictive. Otherwise, it's restrictive.

Restrictives and nonrestrictives, in symbolic representations, both connect to the remainder of the formula by conjunction. Most of the time, therefore, it makes no difference to the translation whether a given clause is restrictive. When universal quantifiers are involved, however, and the clause modifies the subject noun phrase, it does matter. Consider these sentences:

(37) a. All the Democratic candidates for president, who are already campaigning, support labor unions.
b. All the Democratic candidates for president who are already campaigning support labor unions.

The only difference is the pair of commas setting off the relative clause in (37)a. There the clause is clearly nonrestrictive. It asserts that all the Democratic candidates for president support labor unions and remarks, on the side, as it were, that all those candidates are already campaigning. (37)b, in contrast, does not claim that all the Democratic candidates support labor unions; it asserts only that all those who are already campaigning do so. (37)b is thus a weaker contention than (37)a.

To translate these sentences, we first translate the relative clause. 'Who are already campaigning' derives from 'x is(are) already campaigning', which we can write as Cx. Adopting the obvious representations (and letting Lx correspond to 'x supports labor unions'), then, we can symbolize the sentences in (37) as

(38) a. $\forall x(Dx \rightarrow Lx)$ & $\forall x(Dx \rightarrow Cx)$ (or, equivalently,
$\forall x(Dx \rightarrow (Lx \ \& \ Cx))$
b. $\forall x((Dx \ \& \ Cx) \rightarrow Lx)$.

The restrictive clause is conjoined to the rest of the subject; the nonrestrictive clause, to the rest of the entire sentence.

Prepositional Phrases

Prepositions are rather ordinary English words such as 'in', 'to', 'of', 'about', 'up', 'over', 'from', and so on. They combine with noun phrases to form prepositional phrases, which act as either adjectives or adverbs: 'in an alley', 'from Texas', and 'on the road'. We'll discuss those acting as adverbs, which translate together with the verbs or adjectives they modify as single units, in a few pages. First, we'll talk about prepositional phrases modifying nouns, which have separate translations.

In prepositional phrases that function more or less as adjectives, prepositions relate two noun phrases. They thus translate into QL as dyadic predicates. The representatives of prepositional phrases themselves connect to the symbolizations of the noun phrases they modify by conjunction. Consider these examples:

(39) a. Everyone from Pittsburgh loves the Steelers.
     b. If I don't meet you, I'll be in a jail.

(39)a contains the prepositional phrase 'from Pittsburgh'. 'From' translates into a dyadic predicate and 'the Steelers' functions as the proper name of a team). (39)a thus becomes

(40) $\forall x((Px \,\&\, Fxp) \rightarrow Lxs)$.

(39)b contains the prepositional phrase 'in a jail', which itself contains a determiner. The conjunction of prepositional phrase to noun phrase, then, occurs within the scope of a quantifier:

(41) $\neg Hab \rightarrow \exists x(Jx \,\&\, Iax)$

(41), in which a and b symbolize 'I' and 'you', respectively, symbolizes (39)b. Prepositional phrases modifying nouns thus translate readily into quantification theory.

Problems

Are the following adjectives intersective? If not, give examples to show why.

▸ **1.** blue   ▸ **2.** round   ▸ **3.** fast

▸ **4.** accelerating   ▸ **5.** gregarious   ▸ **6.** interesting

  7. wide   **8.** bad   **9.** intelligent

  10. little   **11.** famous   ▸ **12.** spherical

  13. remarkable   **14.** experienced   **15.** true

Symbolize these sentences in QL.

16. Dead men tell no tales.

17. Every tale is told by someone or other.

▶ **18.** Nobody tells every tale.

19. Every interesting tale is told by an interesting person.

20. No tales tell themselves.

21. Tales with no morals are uninteresting.

22. Complicated tales are boring unless a clever person tells them.

23. Every tale with a happy ending pleases someone.

▶ **24.** Some tales with unhappy endings please no one.

25. Someone wrote down each tale about Arthur.

26. Nobody likes a tale that has no interesting characters.

27. Some people have turned some tales into movies.

28. Every tale about Arthur pleases someone who remembers him.

29. Some people tell only tales that nobody likes.

▶ **30.** Nobody likes every tale that anyone tells.

These sentences contain relative clauses. Classify each clause as restrictive or nonrestrictive, and symbolize each sentence.

31. Every noble who has a manor has peasants.

32. All manors that are owned by nobles are large.

33. Any noble who owns any property in England pays some taxes to King John.

34. All manors, which are owned by nobles, are large.

35. Some peasants who work on manors are ill treated.

▶ **36.** King John, who collects taxes from all nobles, has a strong army.

37. King John, who has a strong army, is stronger than any other noble in England.

38. There are peasants who are fighting against King John.

39. Only nobles who are loyal to King John pay him all the taxes they owe.

40. Only nobles, who themselves collect taxes, can have armies.

41. Every noble is suspicious of every noble who has an army.

▶ **42.** Every noble is suspicious of every peasant who works for him.

43. Every noble who pays taxes to King John receives some protection from him.

44. No nobles collect all their taxes, some of which they in turn pay to King John, from a single peasant who works for them.

45. Each peasant who works on a manor pays all his or her taxes to a single noble, who in turn protects him or her.

Symbolize the following sentences in QL. If any translate with difficulty, explain why.

46. Light grows the burden which is well borne. (Ovid)

47. ... nothing great in the world has ever been accomplished without passion. (G. W. F. Hegel)

▶ **48.** Any man who has a job has a chance. (Elbert Hubbard)

49. Human beings do not do all the evil of which they are capable. (Henri de Montherlant)

50. If the only tool you have is a hammer, you tend to see every problem as a nail. (Abraham Maslow)

51. We believe easily what we fear or what we desire. (La Fontaine)

52. Blessed are those who give without remembering and take without forgetting. (Elizabeth Bibesco)

53. They also live who swerve and vanish in the river. (Archibald MacLeish)

▶ **54.** A man who cannot tolerate small ills can never accomplish great things. (Chinese proverb)

55. The man who lives for himself is a failure. (Norman Vincent Peale)

56. Nothing in business is so valuable as time. (John H. Patterson)

57. Nobody who's ever been to Gulag is a pacifist. (William F. Buckley, Jr.)

58. Every society honors its live conformists and its dead troublemakers. (Mignon McLaughlin)

59. Only the shallow know themselves. (Oscar Wilde)

▶ **60.** Only madmen and fools are pleased with themselves.... (Benjamin Whichcote)

61. Greater is he who acts from love than he who acts from fear. (Simeon Ben Eleazar)

62. We receive only what we give. (Samuel Taylor Coleridge)

63. Nothing is more boring than a man with a career. (Aleksandr Solzhenitsyn)

64. The father in praising the son extols himself. (Chinese proverb)

65. All faults may be forgiven of him who has perfect candor. (Walt Whitman)

▶ 66. You can buy anything you pay too much for. (Reza Bulbenkian)

67. There is no banquet but some dislike something in it. (Thomas Fuller)

68. He who does not know the mechanical side of a craft cannot judge it. (Goethe)

69. To whom nothing is given, of him nothing can be required. (Henry Fielding)

70. Meditation is a gift confined to unknown philosophers and cows. (Finley Peter Dunne)

71. No man is prejudiced in favor of a thing knowing it to be wrong. (Thomas Paine)

▶ 72. He that gives to be seen would never relieve a man in the dark. (Thomas Fuller)

73. One completely overcomes only what one assimilates. (André Gide)

74. They sicken of the calm, who know the storm. (Dorothy Parker)

75. Ambition is pitiless. Any merit that it cannot use it finds despicable. (Joseph Joubert)

76. ... and now nothing will be restrained from them, which they have imagined to do. (Genesis 11:6)

77. Hope is a delusion; no hand can grasp a wave or a shadow. (Victor Hugo)

▶ 78. My only books were women's looks, and folly's all they've taught me. (Thomas Moore)

79. All man's friend, no man's friend. (John Wodroephe)

80. Nobody ever did anything very foolish except from some strong principle. (William Lamb)

81. People who have no weaknesses are terrible; there is no way of taking advantage of them. (Anatole France)

82. Every great and commanding moment in the annals of the world is the triumph of some enthusiasm. (Ralph Waldo Emerson)

83. A white lie is always pardonable. But he who tells the truth without compulsion merits no leniency. (Karl Kraus)

▶ 84. The man who fears nothing is as powerful as he who is feared by everybody. (Friedrich von Schiller)

85. The sanest man sets up no deed, lays down no law, takes everything that happens as it comes. (Lao-Tzu)

11.2 VERB PHRASES

So far we've discussed how noun phrases and their modifiers translate into quantification theory. Because sentences consist of a subject noun phrase and a verb phrase, however, we also need to explain how to symbolize verb phrases and their modifiers in QL.

In any verb phrase, of course, there's a verb. Verbs fall into several categories, depending on their ability to take certain kinds of objects. Some verbs are *intransitive*; they cannot take objects at all. 'Fall', 'walk', 'expire', 'come', 'go', 'smile', and 'die' are all intransitive. *Transitive* verbs take noun phrases as direct objects. Examples are 'throw', 'win', and 'examine'. Some of these, such as 'give' and 'send', also take noun phrases as indirect objects. Other verbs take sentences, or grammatical constructions closely related to sentences, as objects. 'Believe', 'know', and 'persuade' are such *clausally complemented* verbs. The logic of verbs taking sentential complements remains the subject of much debate. Here, therefore, we'll consider only transitive and intransitive verbs.

Note that many verbs fall into more than one category. 'Believe' can take a sentence ('I believe that God exists') or a noun phrase ('I believed him'). 'Eat', for example, can have a noun phrase object (in, for example, 'We eat spaghetti every Wednesday night'), but doesn't need one ('Let's eat out'). Most transitive verbs can stand without an object; consider 'June won' and 'Orel threw'. The object, in these cases, is either supplied by the context or is simply the indefinite 'something'.

Intransitive verbs translate into QL as monadic predicates. 'John walks', for instance, becomes Wj; 'Everyone who doesn't own a car walks' becomes

(42) $\forall x((Px \ \& \ \neg \exists y(Cy \ \& \ Oxy)) \rightarrow Wx)$.

Transitive verbs translate into QL as polyadic predicates. Usually, they become dyadic predicates; Lmf represents 'Mary loves Fred', and so on. Occasionally, however, a verb relates more than two noun phrases. We can symbolize 'Mike gave John *War and Peace*', for example, as $Gmjp$. In general, predicates of more than two places prove very useful in symbolizing sentences with indirect objects or adverbial modifiers of certain kinds. In this context, however, the general issue of adverbs arises.

Adverbial Modifiers

Adverbs, such as 'quickly', 'well', 'anytime', and 'somewhere', modify verbs. They specify how, when, or where a certain condition holds or a certain activity occurs. Unfortunately, most adverbs have no direct symbolizations in quantificational logic. QL must represent them, together with the verbs they modify, as it does nonintersective adjectives; expressions such as 'walks slowly' or 'plays well' become predicates such as W or P. These adverbs are like 'large' and 'good' in that anyone who is walking slowly is walking. To express this, we can write Wx & Sx, where W symbolizes 'walks' and S symbolizes 'walks slowly'. But beware of adverbs such as 'allegedly': that John allegedly stole the money does not mean that he stole the money.

Some adverbs, however, translate into QL differently. We'll call 'always', 'anytime', 'whenever', 'wherever', 'anywhere', 'sometime', and so on *adverbs of quantification*. Consider the sentence

(43) I like Alfred sometimes.

'I like Alfred', normally, would become *Lia*. So how do we represent '*Lia*, sometimes'? 'Some' is a determiner. So, the sentence is saying, in effect, that, for some times x (Tx), 'I like Alfred' is true at x. Instead of *Lia*, then, we need *Liax*, meaning 'I like Alfred at x'. (43) thus becomes

(44) $\exists x(Tx$ & $Liax)$.

Similarly, consider

(45) Everywhere I look there are timeshare resorts.

This amounts to 'For every x, if x is a place and I look at x, then there are timeshare resorts at x', or, in symbolic notation,

(46) $\forall x((Px$ & $Lix) \rightarrow \exists y(Ry$ & $Ayx))$.

Some adverbs of quantification, however, have no correlates in QL. 'Frequently', which amounts roughly to 'at many times', and 'rarely' or 'seldom', which amount roughly to 'at few times', would translate into QL only if QL had a way of symbolizing 'many' and 'few'. Because quantification theory represents only a few determiners, it can represent only a few adverbs of quantification.

Prepositional phrases, as we've seen, can modify nouns. They can also modify verbs. 'John ran down the street', 'We're singing in the rain', and 'I'll have a hot dog on a paper plate' all contain prepositional phrases functioning adverbially. Just as adverbs, in most cases, do not translate into QL except as parts of verb phrases that become predicates, so prepositions linking noun phrases to verbs or verb phrases translate together with the modified verb or verb phrase. They don't become dyadic predicates in their own right, as they do when modifying noun phrases. Nevertheless, because prepositional phrases contain noun phrases, their symbolic representations are more interesting than those of adverbs.

Think about a sentence such as

(47) Laura lives on East 72nd Street.

This becomes, when symbolized, *Lle*, where e represents 'East 72nd Street'. 'Lives on' translates as a single dyadic predicate. We can't apply the strategy appropriate to adjectival prepositional phrases; the above sentence is not equivalent to

> (48) Laura lives and is on East 72nd Street.

To take a more complex example,

> (49) Richard has worked in every division of Reynolds Metals Company.

The sentence contains an adverbial prepositional phrase that itself contains a determiner. 'Work' here is intransitive. It would usually translate into a monadic predicate. But 'in' is a preposition that, in effect, can combine with the verb; 'work in', as a unit, is transitive. Instead of using the simple open sentence 'x works', therefore, we can use 'x works in y', a dyadic predicate, to obtain

> (50) $\forall x(Dxc \rightarrow Wrx)$.

Connectives

Quantification theory includes sentential logic. Sentential connectives can link quantified sentences together; they can even inhabit noun and verb phrases. Noun and verb phrases can be joined together by 'and', 'or', and 'if not'. In Chapter 5, we recommended a policy of splitting such phrases. Connectives linking noun or verb phrases usually can be transformed into connectives linking sentences. Thus

> (51) Abraham Lincoln and Calvin Coolidge were Republican presidents.

amounts to

> (52) Abraham Lincoln was a Republican president, and Calvin Coolidge was a Republican president.

Similarly,

> (53) Fred likes hot dogs and hamburgers.

amounts to

> (54) Fred likes hot dogs, and Fred likes hamburgers.

In quantification theory this advice becomes more important in many cases.

> (55) All lions and tigers are cats.

is equivalent to

> (56) All lions are cats, and all tigers are cats.

But the conjoined noun phrase can tempt us into a translation

> (57) $\forall x((Lx \ \& \ Tx) \rightarrow Cx)$,

which says that everything that is both a lion and a tiger is a cat. Nothing, however, is both a lion and a tiger. Separating sentences results in the formula

(58) $\forall x(Lx \rightarrow Cx)$ & $\forall x(Tx \rightarrow Cx)$,

which captures the meaning of the original. When existential quantifiers are involved, or when the connectives are in the verb phrase, splitting makes little difference. But, in subject noun phrases, it is vital.

As in the case of sentential logic, however, we must take care to split only those sentences for which the process preserves meaning.

(59) Harry loves chips and salsa.

may not be equivalent to

(60) Harry loves chips, and Harry loves salsa.

He may love the combination without being very excited about the individual components, or vice versa.

(61) Mary and Susan own the entire company.

probably does not mean that Mary owns the entire company and that Susan does too, but that they own the entire company between them. The best we can do in QL is to treat 'chips and salsa', and 'Mary and Susan', as a unit denoted by a constant. So, we could symbolize 'Harry loves chips and salsa' as Lhc, where c represents 'chips and salsa'.

Another problem pertains to connectives such as 'if', 'only if', and so on. They can't join together two noun phrases or two verb phrases, but they can appear within sentences in ways that do not reduce to simple sentential connection. Consider:

(62) A formula is contingent only if it's not valid.

We might think of this as a sentence with 'a formula' as subject noun phrase and 'is contingent only if it's not valid' as main verb phrase. The determiner 'a' is clearly functioning generically, so it translates as a universal quantifier. The common noun 'formula' appears as a monadic predicate. (62) thus looks like a complex version of a universal affirmative sentence form. Its symbolization begins with $\forall x(Fx \rightarrow$. The main verb phrase contains two connectives, 'only if' and 'not'; the adjectives 'contingent' and 'valid' appear as monadic predicates. 'It' acts much like a variable. Hence, a symbolization of (62) is

(63) $\forall x(Fx \rightarrow (Cx \rightarrow \neg Vx))$.

Alternatively, we might think of (62) as containing a connective, 'only if', joining together two sentences, 'A formula is contingent' and 'It's not valid'. On this approach, (62) resembles (16). It amounts to 'If a formula is contingent, it's not valid'. This we might be tempted to translate as

(64) $\exists x(Fx \And Cx) \rightarrow \neg Vx$,

but, in (64), the final occurrence of x isn't in the scope of the existential quantifier. Thus, (64) isn't even a formula. The solution requires using a universal quantifier with the entire formula as its scope:

(65) $\forall x((Fx \ \& \ Cx) \rightarrow \neg Vx)$

This, too, is an acceptable symbolization of (62). Fortunately, (65) is equivalent to (63). So, the two ways of construing the sentence's structure yield equivalent results.

Naturally, connectives can also join together entire sentences that have no troublesome links between them:

(66) a. If we don't hang together, we'll surely all hang separately.
      b. Some political parties die out after a short time, but others last for centuries.
      c. Unless everyone leaves, I'll refuse to come out.

All of these work as we might expect from sentential logic.

Finally, quantification theory contains not only connectives but sentence letters. It might seem that any sentence can translate into QL by using just predicates, constants, variables, and quantifiers. But a few, very simple sentences—'It's raining' and 'It's three o'clock', for example—resist this analysis. 'It', in these sentences, doesn't stand for an object; thus, it would be very odd to translate 'It's raining' as, say, Ri. To see why, we can ask, "What is raining?" The question doesn't make very good sense.

Problems

Classify these verbs as transitive, intransitive, or neither.

▶ **1.** quack ▶ **2.** walk ▶ **3.** irrigate ▶ **4.** renege

▶ **5.** turn ▶ **6.** yawn **7.** urge **8.** organize

9. persuade **10.** argue **11.** snow ▶ **12.** do

13. forget **14.** gnaw **15.** harness **16.** justify

17. lie ▶ **18.** zoom **19.** cooperate **20.** vanquish

21. burrow **22.** nullify **23.** mope ▶ **24.** consider

25. promise

These sentences contain both quantifiers and connectives. Symbolize them in QL, exposing as much structure as possible.

26. Loafing needs no explanation and is its own excuse. (Christopher Morley)

27. All men have aimed at, found, and lost. . . . (William Butler Yeats)

28. Nothing will ever be attempted if all possible objections must be first overcome. (Jules W. Lederer)

29. If you build a castle in the air, you won't need a mortgage. (Philip Lazarus)

▶ 30. I care about truth not for truth's sake, but for my own. (Samuel Butler)

31. If you run yourself, no one will run you. (David Seabury)

32. To be beloved is all I need, and whom I love, I love indeed. (Samuel Taylor Coleridge)

33. Some people with great virtues are disagreeable while others with great vices are delightful. (La Rochefoucauld)

34. If an electrical engineer has a pulse, he'll get a job. (Vicki Lynn)

35. Christmas brings out the best in all of us, but it's tiring and expensive. (William Feather)

▶ 36. Any mental activity is easy if it need not take reality into account. (Marcel Proust)

37. . . . it is not poetry, if it make no appeal to our passions or our imagination. (Samuel Taylor Coleridge)

38. When a man is wrong and won't admit it, he always gets angry. (Thomas Haliburton)

39. Every gift which is given, even though it be small, is in reality great, if it is given with affection. (Pindar)

40. Civility costs nothing, and buys everything. (Mary Wortley Montagu)

41. Nothing which is true or beautiful or good makes complete sense in any immediate context of history. . . . (Reinhold Niebuhr)

▶ 42. So then neither is he that planteth any thing, neither he that watereth; but God that giveth the increase. (I Corinthians 3:7)

43. Life does not agree with philosophy: there is no happiness that is not idleness, and only what is useless is pleasurable. (Anton Chekhov)

44. No rule for success will work if you won't. (Elmer G. Leterman)

45. The man who does not do his own thinking is a slave, and a traitor to himself and his fellowmen. (Robert Ingersoll)

46. If you have money, you will always have friends. (Monique Van Vooren)

47. Either I will find a way or I will make one. (Philip Sidney)

▶ 48. I distrust all systematizers, and avoid them. (Friedrich Nietzsche)

49. Some people will believe anything if you whisper it to them. (Louis Nizer)

50. He that is never suspected is either very much esteemed or very much despised. (Lord Halifax)

51. Always we like those who admire us, but we do not always like those whom we admire. (La Rochefoucauld)

52. Not all of those to whom we do good love us, neither do all those to whom we do evil hate us. (Joseph Roux)

53. No one can be good for long if goodness is not in demand. (Bertolt Brecht)

▶ 54. All human beings have gray little souls—and they all want to rouge them up. (Maxim Gorky)

55. You are entitled to any number of fool opinions; but there is a certain elemental wisdom every one must possess, or suffer. (Ed Howe)

56. The wretched reflect either too much or too little. (Publilius Syrus)

57. All victories breed hate, and that over your superior is foolish or fatal. (Baltasar Gracián)

58. I never speak falsehood, but I do not tell the truth to everyone. (Paolo Sarpi)

59. The fellow that agrees with everything you say is either a fool or he is getting ready to skin you. (Kin Hubbard)

▶ 60. The poor are the only consistent altruists; they sell all that they have and give to the rich. (Holbrook Jackson)

61. Sometimes a fool has talent, but never judgment. (La Rochefoucauld)

62. Every luxury must be paid for, and everything is a luxury. . . . (Cesare Pavese)

63. I've got all the money I'll ever need if I die before 4 o'clock. (Henny Youngman)

64. One either meets or one works. One cannot do both at the same time. (Peter Drucker)

65. All change is not growth, as all movement is not forward. (Ellen Glasgow)

▶ 66. Every social injustice is not only cruel, but it is economic waste. (William Feather)

67. No man is more than another unless he does more than another. (Cervantes)

68. Shallow men believe in luck, wise and strong men in cause and effect. (Ralph Waldo Emerson)

Translate the following sentences into QL, exposing as much structure as possible. If any translate only with difficulty, explain why.

69. The man who has done less than his best has done nothing. (Charles M. Schwab)

70. Only in a quiet mind is adequate perception of the world. (Hans Margolius)

71. Some degree of abuse is inseparable from the proper use of everything. (James Madison)

▶ 72. The mind, like the body, is subject to be hurt by everything it taketh for a remedy. (George Savile)

73. No one is rich enough to do without a neighbor. (Danish proverb)

74. The only true gift is a part of yourself. (Ralph Waldo Emerson)

75. Wealth serves a wise man, but commands a fool. (Thomas Fuller)

76. The less men think, the more they talk. (Montesquieu)

77. Men who are governed by reason desire nothing for themselves that they do not also desire for the rest of mankind. (Spinoza)

▶ 78. Whatever course you decide upon, there is always someone to tell you you are wrong. (Ralph Waldo Emerson)

79. Only individuals with an aberrant temperament can in the long run retain their self-esteem in the face of the disesteem of their fellows. (Thorstein Veblen)

80. No [college football] team that's ever appeared in your Top Twenty over the past 100 years is guiltless of cheating in one way or another. (Dan Jenkins)

81. That which has been believed by everyone, always and everywhere, has every chance of being false. (Paul Valéry)

82. Nothing has an uglier look to us than reason, when it is not on our side. (Lord Halifax)

83. . . . no man, deep down in the privacy of his heart, has any considerable respect for himself. (Mark Twain)

▶ 84. Logical consequences are the scarecrows of fools and the beacons of wise men. (Thomas Huxley)

85. Every beginning of an idea corresponds to an imperceptible lesion of the mind. (M. Cioran)

86. My sad conviction is that people can only agree about what they're not really interested in. (Bertrand Russell)

87. Nothing that is proved is obvious; for what is obvious shows itself and cannot be proved. (Joseph Joubert)

88. What we obtain too cheap we esteem too lightly. . . . (Thomas Paine)

89. He who wants to do good knocks at the gate; he who loves finds the gate open. (Rabindranath Tagore)

▸ 90. What the superior man seeks is in himself. (Confucius)

91. We live in an age when unnecessary things are our only necessities. (Oscar Wilde)

92. Men are not against you; they are merely for themselves. (Gene Fowler)

93. It is only the cynicism that is born of success that is penetrating and valid. (George Jean Nathan)

94. Only the man who finds everything wrong and expects it to get worse is thought to have a clear brain. (John Kenneth Galbraith)

95. Only what proceeds from emotion or cynicism is real. All the rest is "talent." (M. Cioran)

▸ 96. To be a prophet it is sufficient to be a pessimist. (Elsa Triolet)

97. All men that are ruined, are ruined on the side of their natural propensities. (Edmund Burke)

98. A wise man is cured of ambition by ambition itself. (Jean de la Bruyère)

99. It is only the fools who keep straining at high C all their lives. (Charles Dudley Warner)

100. Each concession we make is accompanied by an inner diminution of which we are not immediately conscious. (M. Cioran)

101. The only way to make a man trustworthy is to trust him. (Henry Stimson)

▸ 102. In an honest man there is always something of a child. (Martial)

103. There are well-dressed foolish ideas just as there are well-dressed fools. (Nicolas Chamfort)

104. When all is summed up, a man never speaks of himself without loss; his accusations of himself are always believed; his praises never. (Michel de Montaigne)

105. Great is the hand that holds dominion over man by a scribbled name. (Dylan Thomas)

106. There has never been any thirty-hour week for men who had anything to do. (Charles F. Kettering)

107. Work is a grand cure of all the maladies that ever beset mankind. (Thomas Carlyle)

▶ **108.** Every man without passions has within him no principle of action, no motive to act. (Claude-Adrien Helvétius)

11.3 DEFINITIONS

In Chapter 4, we examined traditional and modern rules for definitions. The traditional rules require that definitions state the essence of the kind of thing being defined; that they be noncircular; that they be expressed in clear, rather than figurative, obscure, or ambiguous language; and that they be affirmative whenever possible. The traditional rules of definition are useful for constructing and evaluating definitions. But they're not very precise. Moreover, they concentrate on what a definition should not be, saying relatively little about what it should be. Finally, a definition may satisfy all four traditional rules while being seriously inadequate. Suppose we try to define being a boss as follows.

(67) x is y's boss if and only if y must follow x's orders.

This satisfies the traditional criteria. It states the essence of being a boss; it isn't negative, circular, or expressed in obscure, figurative, or ambiguous language. Nevertheless, it leads to an absurd result. Say that Larry must follow the orders of two people, Mary and Chuck. (67) implies that Mary is Larry's boss, but also that Chuck is Larry's boss. But it follows that Chuck is Mary, a ridiculous conclusion.

The Polish logician Stanislaw Lesniewski (1886–1939) devised two modern rules for definition. Definitions satisfying these rules are formally acceptable. That is, such definitions have the proper form of a definition. Purported definitions violating one or both of them are flawed and should not be counted as definitions at all. Lesniewski's rules are as follows:

1. *Eliminability.* A defined term must be eliminable, without ambiguity, from any sentence in which it occurs.
2. *Noncreativity.* A definition must imply nothing that does not contain the term it defines.

The first rule asserts that a definition acts like an abbreviation. The defined term, in effect, abbreviates the expression defining it. But we use abbreviations for the sake of convenience; they aren't absolutely necessary. We should therefore be able to replace the abbreviation with what it abbreviates. The eliminability rule means that, for each sentence containing the newly defined term, there must be an equivalent sentence without it. Consider a simple definition. Edith Summerskill defines 'nagging' as 'the repetition of unpalatable truths'. This definition allows us to substitute 'the repetition of unpalatable truths' for 'nagging' in any sentence, to obtain an equivalent sentence. For example,

> (68) I finally surrendered to the boss's nagging and turned in my report.

becomes

> (69) I finally surrendered to the boss's repetition of unpalatable truths and turned in my report.

Rule 1 has an interesting relation to one of the traditional rules for definition. No definition satisfying the eliminability rule is circular. In a circular definition, the defined term would appear in the defining expression, and, therefore, replacing the latter for the former would not eliminate it.

The second rule asserts that adding a definition to a language should give us no new information, except, of course, how to use a new term. Definitions aren't axioms, principles, or facts. They provide information only about the use of a linguistic expression. Whenever that expression is absent, consequently, the definition should tell us nothing. This is the rule violated by our earlier definition of 'x is y's boss'. That definition implied 'Chuck is Mary'. This sentence doesn't contain the defined term. So, it shouldn't follow from this or any other legitimate definition of 'x is y's boss'. Whereas we might think of the eliminability rule as generalizing the traditional rule concerning noncircularity, the noncreativity rule has no counterpart in the traditional theory.

How can we make sure that the modern rules for definition are satisfied? Because noncreativity is difficult to establish, the best method is indirect. It's possible to develop some patterns of definition that satisfy the criteria of eliminability and noncreativity. Any definition meeting the appropriate pattern automatically fulfills the modern requirements. Because QL has only two kinds of nonlogical constants—predicate and individual constants—we need only two patterns for it.

Before specifying these patterns, we need to suppose that we're introducing definitions in a particular order. To avoid circles, we need to suppose that we can begin with undefined terms (often called *primitives*) and define other expressions in terms of the primitive and previously defined expressions. The patterns below all assume that the definition being characterized is part of a series of definitions.

First, consider predicates. QL represents common nouns, adjectives, and verbs, as well as phrases formed from them, as predicates. How can we frame a legitimate definition of a predicate? Suppose we're interested in defining an n-ary predicate F. We want the defining expression to be equivalent to F, no matter what objects both apply to; thus, the definition must take the form of a universally quantified biconditional.

> To define an n-ary predicate F: devise a formula of the form
> $$\forall x_1 \dots \forall x_n(Fx_1 \dots x_n \leftrightarrow \mathcal{A}),$$
> where $\mathcal{A}$ contains only primitive and previously defined expressions as nonlogical symbols.

Suppose we want to define the English verb 'kick'. The pattern tells us that the definition should have the form

> (70) $\forall x \forall y(x \text{ kicks } y \leftrightarrow \mathcal{A})$,

since 'kick' is a transitive verb. We might, for example, try this definition:

> (71) $\forall x \forall y(x \text{ kicks } y \leftrightarrow x \text{ strikes } y \text{ with } x\text{'s foot})$.

This fits the pattern, assuming that we already understand 'strikes', 'with', and 'foot of'. So, this definition satisfies the requirements of eliminability and noncreativity.

Similarly, let's try to define the English adjective 'bald'. The pattern tells us that the definition should have the form

> (72) $\forall x(x \text{ is bald } \leftrightarrow \mathcal{A})$,

where $\mathcal{A}$ contains only already understood expressions. If we understand 'have', 'hair', 'on', and 'head', then we can frame the definition

> (73) $\forall x(x \text{ is bald } \leftrightarrow x \text{ has no hair on } x\text{'s head})$.

This, too, succeeds in fitting the pattern and satisfying the two modern criteria for definitions.

To understand how this pattern functions, it's important to see what it rules out as illegitimate. Consider, for example, this attempted definition of 'bald':

> (74) $\forall x(x \text{ is bald } \leftrightarrow x \text{ has less hair than } y)$.

This doesn't fit the pattern, for the definition isn't a formula: The variable y isn't quantified. In English, it amounts to saying that being bald is the same as having less hair than y. That obviously fails as a definition, unless we know who y is. In formal terms, (74) violates the eliminability criterion. Replacing the defined term 'bald' with the defining expression would convert formulas into nonformulas. We can fix the flawed definition in several ways. We might say who y is; we might, in other words, pick a person with very little hair— Mikhail Gorbachev, perhaps—and declare that being bald is having less hair than that person.

(75) $\forall x(x$ is bald $\leftrightarrow x$ has less hair than Gorbachev did in 1989).

Alternatively, we could make the predicate binary rather than unary, and adopt the definition

(76) $\forall x(x$ is balder than $y \leftrightarrow x$ has less hair than $y)$.

This, however, no longer defines 'bald' but something else.

Another attempted definition ruled out as illegitimate is this definition of 'kick':

(77) $\forall x(x$ kicks $x \leftrightarrow x$ strikes x with x's foot).

'Kick' is transitive, but this formula uses only one quantifier and one variable. It defines, not 'kick', but 'kick oneself'. As a definition of 'kick', (77) also violates the eliminability criterion: It doesn't show how to eliminate 'kick' in a sentence such as 'John kicked the football'.

Finally, consider an attempted definition like (78).

(78) $\forall x(x$ is bald $\leftrightarrow x$ is bald).

This is blatantly circular. It fails to fit the pattern, because the definiens must contain only primitive and previously defined expressions. That is, an expression must be defined in terms that are already understood. If we already understood 'bald', however, the attempt at definition would be pointless. (78) violates the eliminability criterion, for replacing 'bald' with 'bald' doesn't eliminate 'bald' at all.

A second pattern specifies the form of definitions of constants.

> To define an individual constant c: devise a formula of the form
> $\quad \forall x(x$ is $c \leftrightarrow \mathscr{A})$,
> where $\mathscr{A}$ contains only primitive and previously defined expressions as nonlogical symbols, and where it is possible to prove that one and only one thing satisfies $\mathscr{A}$.

This pattern says that defining a constant c is just like defining the unary predicate 'is identical with c', except that we must be able to show that one and only one thing satisfies the definiens. Why is that required? The form of the definiendum, x is c, guarantees that it holds of one and only one thing, assuming appropriate principles for 'is'. But $\mathscr{A}$ may have a wide variety of forms; no similar guarantee is built into its logical structure. Therefore, we have to impose that demand separately.

To see why this is important, consider these attempted definitions:

(79) $\forall x(x$ is $c \leftrightarrow x$ lives in New York City).

(80) $\forall x(x$ is $d \leftrightarrow x$ is the largest unicorn in Texas).

The first fails because many people live in New York City. Given that George Steinbrenner and Amy Irving both live in New York City, (79) would let us infer that George Steinbrenner is Amy Irving. The second fails because there are no unicorns, large or otherwise, in Texas. (80) lets us infer, contrary to fact, that there is such a thing as the largest unicorn in Texas. Both (79) and (80) imply formulas not containing the constants c and d and therefore violate the condition of noncreativity.

The following definition fits the pattern:

(81) $\forall x(x = 0 \leftrightarrow \forall y x \times y = x)$

There is one and only one number in arithmetic that, multiplied by any number, yields itself. A slight alteration produces a definition of one:

(82) $\forall x(x = 1 \leftrightarrow \forall y x \times y = y)$

Notice that (81) is not the only formally and mathematically correct definition of zero. The following, for example, also work:

(83) $\forall x(x = 0 \leftrightarrow \forall y x + y = y)$
(84) $\forall x(x = 0 \leftrightarrow \forall y y^x = 1)$
(85) $\forall x(x = 0 \leftrightarrow \forall y y - y = x)$

Although definitions of constants are especially common in mathematics, they appear in other contexts as well. These definitions fit the pattern for definitions of constants and thus meet the modern criteria.

(86) $\forall x(x$ is Pluto $\leftrightarrow x$ is the ninth planet from the sun).
(87) $\forall x(x$ is Eve $\leftrightarrow x$ was the first woman to inhabit the earth).
(88) $\forall x(x$ is Daniel Bonevac $\leftrightarrow x$ wrote this book).

These definitions are formally acceptable, if we can show that there was a unique first woman and a unique author of this book.

We've noted that the traditional rules for definitions don't characterize the notion of a successful definition fully. A definition may meet all four traditional criteria and still be completely unacceptable. Similarly, a definition may meet both modern rules and be completely unacceptable. The modern rules pertain solely to the form of the definition; they say little about its content. These definitions meet the conditions of eliminability and noncreativity, although they violate the traditional rule requiring that definitions state essential attributes of a kind.

(89) $\forall x(x$ is bald $\leftrightarrow x$ watches *Alf*).
(90) $\forall x \forall y(x$ kicks $y \leftrightarrow x$ has less hair than y).
(91) $\forall x(x$ is Zeus $\leftrightarrow x$ is the oldest member of the Partridge family).
(92) $\forall x(x$ is clever $\leftrightarrow x$ understands this chapter).

These definitions are too broad, too narrow, and silly. But they allow for the elimination of their defined terms, without implying things independent of their usage. In a stipulative definition, like most appearing in mathematics, nothing else matters. When we want a definition to reflect the actual use of an expression, however, we must turn to both the modern and the traditional rules for guidance.

Problems

Using the modern criteria for definitions, evaluate the formal adequacy of these definitions.

▶ **1.** Thrift is care and scruple in the spending of one's means. It is not a virtue, and it requires neither skill nor talent. (Immanuel Kant)

▶ **2.** Education is what survives when what has been learned has been forgotten. (B. F. Skinner)

▶ **3.** Education is a state-controlled manufactory of echoes. (Norman Douglas)

▶ **4.** Education: that which discloses to the wise and disguises from the foolish their lack of understanding. (Ambrose Bierce)

▶ **5.** Education is the process of casting false pearls before real swine. (Irwin Edman)

▶ **6.** Education is the process of driving a set of prejudices down your throat. (Martin Fischer)

7. A tout is a guy who goes around a race track giving out tips on the races, if he can find anybody who will listen to his tips, especially suckers, and a tout is nearly always broke. If he is not broke, he is by no means a tout, but a handicapper, and is respected by one and all. (Damon Runyan)

8. He's the player to be named later in the Buddy Bell trade. (Pete Rose, asked if he believed Elvis were still alive)

9. The American Medical Association announced . . . a redefinition of "unnecessary surgery" as that performed on patients who can't pay, and most important, stricter licensing requirements to reduce the number of new physicians to zero. (*National Lampoon,* 1983)

10. Democracy demands that all of its citizens begin the race even. Egalitarianism insists that they all finish even. (Roger Price)

11. Courage is a special kind of knowledge: the knowledge of how to fear what ought to be feared and how not to fear what ought not to be feared. (David Ben-Gurion)

▶ **12.** The obvious is that which is never seen until someone expresses it simply. (Kahlil Gibran)

13. Interest is the birth of money from money. Breeding of money is most unnatural. (Aristotle)

14. Diplomacy: the art of saying "nice doggie" until you can find a rock. (Wynn Catlin—also attributed to Will Rogers)

15. Politicians are people who resolve through linguistic processes conflicts that would otherwise have to be solved by force. (S. I. Hayakawa)

16. The greatest fool is he who thinks he is not one and all others are. (Baltasar Gracián)

17. Confidence is that feeling by which the mind embarks on great and honorable courses with a sure hope and trust in itself. (Cicero)

▶ 18. The art of investment banking consists of taking a button and making a suit out of it. (Andre Meyer)

19. An executive is a man who decides. (John H. Patterson)

20. Positive means being mistaken at the top of one's voice. (Ambrose Bierce)

21. Maturity of mind is the capacity to endure uncertainty. (John Finley)

22. A lie is an excuse guarded. (Jonathan Swift)

23. Originality is the art of concealing your source. (Franklin P. Jones)

▶ 24. Wisdom denotes the pursuing of the best ends by the best means. (Frances Hutcheson)

25. An intellectual is someone whose mind watches itself. (Albert Camus)

26. Common sense is genius dressed in its working clothes. (Ralph Waldo Emerson)

27. Politics is the art of looking for trouble, finding it everywhere, diagnosing it incorrectly, and applying the wrong remedies. (Groucho Marx)

28. Anger is momentary madness. (Horace)

29. Character is that which reveals moral purpose, exposing the class of things a man chooses or avoids. (Aristotle)

▶ 30. What is virtue? To hold yourself to your fullest development as a person and as a responsible member of the human community. (Arthur Dobrin)

31. Love is liking someone better than you like yourself. (Frank Tyger)

32. Political power is the power to oppress others. (Lin Piao)

33. Kindness. The most unkindest thing of all. (Edna O'Brien)

34. Brain: the apparatus with which we think we think. (Ambrose Bierce)

35. Prejudice: n. A vagrant opinion without visible means of support. (Ambrose Bierce)

▶ 36. Abstainer: n. A weak person who yields to the temptation of denying himself pleasure. (Ambrose Bierce)

37. Charity is the sterilized milk of human kindness. (Oliver Herford)

38. Philanthropist: A rich (and usually bald) old gentleman who has trained himself to grin while his conscience is picking his pocket. (Ambrose Bierce)

39. Courage is almost a contradiction in terms. It means a strong desire to live taking the form of a readiness to die. (G. K. Chesterton)

40. Democracy is a process by which the people are free to choose the man who will get the blame. (Laurence J. Peter)

41. A man is called selfish, not for pursuing his own good, but for neglecting his neighbor's. (Richard Whately)

▸ **42.** Patience is the art of hoping. (Vauvenargues)

43. Cynic: n. A blackguard whose faulty vision sees things as they are, not as they ought to be. (Ambrose Bierce)

44. Cynicism is an unpleasant way of telling the truth. (Lillian Hellman)

45. A pessimist is a man who has been compelled to live with an optimist. (Elbert Hubbard)

46. Optimism is the content of small men in high places. (F. Scott Fitzgerald)

47. The optimist proclaims that we live in the best of all possible worlds; and the pessimist fears this is true. (James Branch Cabell)

▸ **48.** Achievement, *n*. The death of endeavor and the birth of disgust. (Ambrose Bierce)

49. A liberal is a man too broadminded to take his own side in a quarrel. (Robert Frost)

50. Conservatism is the policy of make no change and consult your grandmother when in doubt. (Woodrow Wilson)

51. A neoconservative is a liberal who's been mugged by reality. A neoliberal is a liberal who's been mugged by reality but has refused to press charges. (Irving Kristol)

52. Once an editor explained to me that a journalist was just an out-of-work reporter. (Linda Ellerbee)

53. Altruism is the art of using others with the air of loving them. (René Dubreuil)

▸ **54.** Action is but coarsened thought—thought become concrete, obscure, and unconscious. (Frédéric Amiel)

55. Acquaintance, *n*. A person whom we know well enough to borrow from, but not well enough to lend to. (Ambrose Bierce)

56. Gossip is when you hear something you like about someone you don't. (Earl Wilson)

57. Hope: a pathological belief in the occurrence of the impossible. (H. L. Mencken)

58. Charm is a way of getting the answer yes without having asked any clear question. (Albert Camus)

59. A fanatic is a man that does what he thinks th' Lord wud do if He knew th' facts iv th' case. (Finley Peter Dunne)

▸ **60.** Life is just one damned thing after another. (Frank O'Malley)

12

QUANTIFIED
TABLEAUX

The method of semantic tableaux extends easily to incorporate quantifiers. As in sentential logic, semantic tableaux provide a very powerful and efficient means of determining whether argument forms are valid. Nevertheless, tableaux fall short of being decision procedures for validity and related semantic concepts in quantification theory. Within the bounds of sentential logic, tableaux constitute decision procedures for determining validity. They remain such a technique in certain limited fragments of quantificational logic. In the full language QL, however, this decision procedure breaks down. The method of semantic tableaux is still mechanical, but some tableaux don't terminate after a finite time. Applying tableau rules sometimes results in infinitely long tableaux.

This fact might tempt us to search for another method that would constitute a decision procedure for quantificational logic. In 1936, however, the American logician Alonzo Church proved that quantification theory is *undecidable*—that is, that there is no decision procedure for quantificational validity.[1] Any method for demonstrating validity, or satisfiability, or contradictoriness, and so on within this logic must at some point yield infinite procedures or require the use of nonmechanical insights. Quantification theory is thus so powerful that no effective procedure can capture it. Nevertheless, semantic tableaux can demonstrate the validity or invalidity of a very wide range of quantificational argument forms.

12.1 QUANTIFIER TABLEAU RULES

Semantic tableaux for quantificational logic use all the sentential tableau rules, together with four new rules for the quantifiers. Each quantifier has two associated rules: one for its occurrences on the left side of tableau branches, the other for its occurrences on the right.

The quantifier rules all rely on the notion of an instance. Say that $\mathcal{A}[c/v]$ is the result of substituting c for every occurrence of v throughout the formula $\mathcal{A}$. If $\forall v \mathcal{A}$ and $\exists v \mathcal{A}$ are formulas, then $\mathcal{A}[c/v]$ is called an *instance* of them. Conversely, $\forall v \mathcal{A}$ and $\exists v \mathcal{A}$ are *generics* of $\mathcal{A}[c/v]$.

The left side of a tableau represents truth, while the right represents falsity. "Left" rules thus tell us what we can infer from the supposition that a quantified formula is true; "right" rules tell us what we can infer from the assumption that such a formula is false.

Existential Left (∃L)

$$\begin{array}{c|c} \checkmark & \exists v \mathcal{A} \\ & \mathcal{A}[c/v] \end{array}$$

Here c must be a constant new to the tableau.

This rule asserts that we may replace an existential formula on the left by one of its instances, provided that constant which we substitute for the variable is new to the tableau. To see why the rule has this form, assume that an existential sentence—say,

(1) Someone in this room is a spy.

is true.[2] The truth of this assumption, by itself, tells us nothing about who is the spy. Nevertheless, it's important to introduce some way of referring to the spy, so that we can record additional information about the same person. In English, we might just use 'the spy' in this role, as we've in fact been doing in the last two sentences. Or, we might use a pronoun. In our system of tableaux, we achieve the same effect by introducing a name for the spy—as we might also in English by saying, "call the spy *Karla*"—in the guise of a constant that hasn't appeared anywhere on the tableau before. We must use a new constant precisely because we can't say who the spy is. It's hardly fair to say to Fred, "Someone in this room is a spy. Let's call him *Fred*." Similarly, it would be outrageous for a mathematician to say, "So, there's a point on the interval at which the derivative is zero. Let's call this point '9.3.'" If we don't know which objects make the existential sentence true, we need a new constant to avoid making illicit identifications.

To take an example, suppose that we want to learn whether the formula $\exists x(Fx \ \& \ \neg Fx)$—'something is both F and not F'—is satisfiable or contradictory. As in sentential logic, we place the formula on the left of a tableau, assuming that it is true, and see whether a contradiction results.

$$\begin{array}{c}
\checkmark \quad \exists x(Fx \ \& \ \neg Fx) \\
\checkmark \quad Fa \ \& \ \neg Fa \\
Fa \\
\checkmark \quad \neg Fa
\end{array} \Big| \begin{array}{c} \\ \\ \\ \\ Fa \end{array}$$

Cl

The tableau closes, so the formula is contradictory; nothing can be both F and not F at the same time.

Existential Right (∃R)

$$\Big| \begin{array}{c} \exists v \mathscr{A} \ * \\ \mathscr{A}[c/v] \end{array}$$

Here c may be any constant.

This rule asserts that we may dispatch an existential formula on the right by writing, also on the right, any instance of that formula. The constant we use in ∃R need not be new, though it may be; any constant whatever will do. Furthermore, we may apply this rule more than once. The *temporary dispatch mark* '*' indicates that although we have already applied ∃R to this formula, we may come back and apply it again. To see why we may repeat this rule, suppose that we know it's false that someone in this room is a spy. Then we can infer that it's false that Al is a spy, that Beth is a spy, that Carl is a spy, that Dorothy is a spy, and so on for each person in the room.

To take an example, suppose we want to find out whether the formula $\exists x(Fx \lor \neg Fx)$—'something is either F or not F'—is valid. We place it on the right side of a tableau, assuming that it can be false.

$$\begin{array}{c|c} & \exists x(Fx \lor \neg Fx) \ * \\ & Fa \lor \neg Fa \ \checkmark \\ & Fa \\ & \neg Fa \ \checkmark \\ Fa & \end{array}$$

Cl

Since the tableau closes, the formula is valid. The instance here contains a new constant. It must, not because the rule demands it, but because no constants had yet appeared on the branch. In general, we'll introduce new constants on a tableau branch under only two circumstances: (a) when a rule (existential left or universal right) requires it; and (b) when the branch contains no constants.

Universal Left (∀L)

$$* \forall v \mathscr{A} \mid$$
$$\mathscr{A}[c/v] \mid$$

Here c may be any constant.

This rule asserts that a universal formula on the left allows us to write any instance of it on the left. Again, the constant we use doesn't have to be new. In fact, any instance of the formula will do. Furthermore, we can repeat this rule, too. If everyone here knows logic, then it follows that I know logic, you know logic, Fred knows logic, Samantha knows logic, and so on for each person here.

Suppose that we want to discover whether $\forall x F x$ implies $\exists x F x$. We place these formulas on the left and right sides of a tableau, respectively, and find out whether there is any interpretation making $\forall x F x$ true but $\exists x F x$ false.

$$* \forall x F x \mid$$
$$\mid \exists x F x *$$
$$\mid F a$$
$$F a \mid$$
$$Cl$$

As this tableau shows, there's no such interpretation; therefore, $\forall x F x$ does imply $\exists x F x$. Notice that neither quantifier rule used here requires the use of new constants. We can use a single constant for both instances, no matter in what order we applied the rules.

Universal Right (∀R)

$$\mid \forall v \mathscr{A} \; \checkmark$$
$$\mid \mathscr{A}[c/v]$$

Here c must be a constant new to the tableau.

This rule asserts that we can replace a universal formula on the right by an instance of it on the right, using a constant that hasn't appeared before on the tableau. Suppose it's false that everyone in the department has a PhD. It follows that at least one person in the department doesn't have a PhD. We can't infer anything about who these persons are, but we want to reason about them; so, we need some way of referring to them. To correspond roughly to the English 'the person or persons in the department without a PhD', we introduce a new constant. If the constant were not new, we would be illicitly assuming something about the identity of those without PhDs.

For example, suppose that we want to know whether $\forall x(Fx \to Fx)$—'all Fs are Fs'—is valid.

$$
\begin{array}{c|l}
 & \forall x(Fx \to Fx) \quad \checkmark \\
 & Fa \to Fa \quad \checkmark \\
Fa & \\
 & Fa \\
\hline
\text{Cl} &
\end{array}
$$

This tableau tells us that it is. Our search for an interpretation making the formula false results in contradiction.

12.2 STRATEGIES

In sentential logic, any way of applying tableau rules produces the same result. Nevertheless, some ways of reaching that result are more efficient than others. We thus adopted two strategies for simplifying tableaux. The first was to *close branches as soon as possible*. Once some formula has appeared on both sides of a branch, applying further rules to the branch can make no difference; the branch—or branches, if further applications split the original—will still have a formula that appears on both sides and so will close. The second was to *avoid splitting tableaux as long as possible*. Once a branch splits, applying rules to the formulas above the split forces us to write the result on each resulting branch.

These strategies remain useful in quantificational logic. Furthermore, two other strategies help to simplify tableaux. Here is the third strategy:

> Introduce the constants we need as quickly as possible by applying $\exists$L and $\forall$R before applying $\exists$R and $\forall$L. That is, apply the quantifier rules introducing new constants as soon as possible.

Observing this principle minimizes the number of constants in a tableau.

Let's consider an example. Suppose that we want to evaluate the argument

(2) Some rulers are dictators.
All dictators have absolute power.
∴ Some rulers have absolute power.

We can symbolize this as

(3) $\exists x(Fx \,\&\, Gx)$
  $\forall x(Gx \rightarrow Hx)$
  $\therefore\ \exists x(Fx \,\&\, Hx)$

Following the third strategy results in the first tableau, while introducing the new constant after applying the other quantifier rules results in the longer, second tableau.

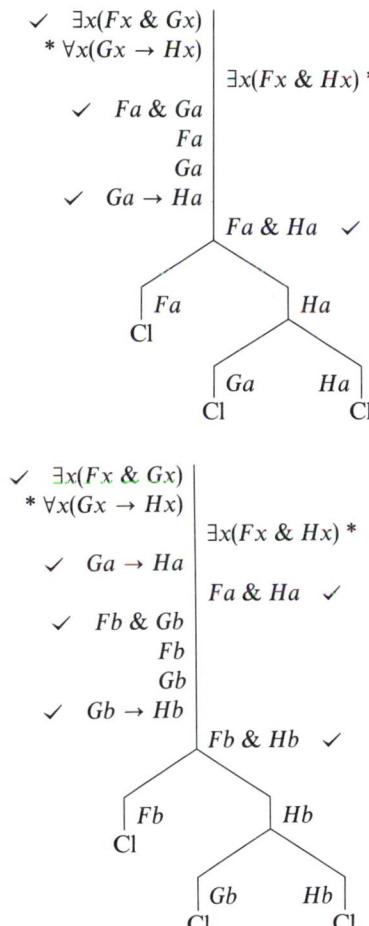

Our fourth strategy is the following:

Use constants already on the tableau whenever possible.

Two quantifier rules, ∃R and ∀L, don't require a new constant. They accept any constant, whether or not it's already on the tableau. Consequently, when applying these rules, we use any available constants. We introduce new ones only if a rule requires it or no constants are available on the tableau.

To see why, again consider an example:

(4) Some conservative Southerners are Democrats.
∴. Some Democrats are conservative.

This argument has the following form:

(5) $\exists x((Fx \,\&\, Gx) \,\&\, Hx)$
∴. $\exists x(Hx \,\&\, Fx)$

Following the fourth strategy produces the first tableau, while ignoring it results in the second tableau.

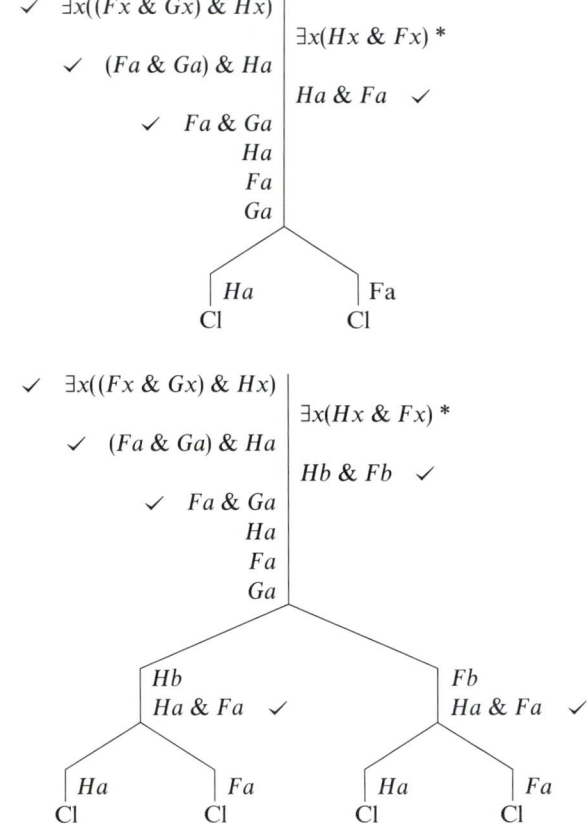

The second tableau closes only because we returned to instantiate the existential formula on the right a second time using the original constant.

This example points out an important fact: Some tableaux will close only if we use the correct constants in applying quantifier rules. The last tableau we saw, for instance, would not have closed if we had given up too early. Consequently, it's important to follow one more policy:

> Continue instantiating as far as possible using the constants on the branch.

∃R and ∀L don't require new constants and can be repeated. Indeed, they must be repeated, using the constants available on the tableau, until (a) the tableau closes or (b) the available constants are exhausted or (c) it seems clear that the tableau isn't going to close. The last case is possible precisely because tableaux do not constitute a decision procedure for quantificational logic. If applying the rules for tableau construction results in an infinite tableau in a particular case, then the tableau will never close, but the opportunities for further instantiation will never be exhausted. Sometimes it will become obvious that a repeating pattern has developed, but not always.

Some tableaux close only through the return to a previously instantiated formula. In the last chapter, we saw that there is a great difference between the quantifier strings $\forall x \exists y$ and $\exists y \forall x$. The former says that each thing stands in some relation to something or other, allowing the possibility that a stands in the relation to b, c to d, and so on. The latter, in contrast, says that there is a single object to which everything stands in some relation. It should be clear that if this is true, then the former is true as well. That is, if everything relates to some one thing, then everything relates to something or other. Thus, if God created everything, then everything was created (by something or other). So, switching the order of quantifiers in a string by moving universals to the left preserves truth. Normally, however, the reverse is not true; switching existentials to the left results in a stronger assertion that doesn't follow from the original. In a moment, we'll consider a fallacious argument of this form that some people think Saint Thomas Aquinas advocated: the inference from 'Everything has a cause' to 'Something is the cause of everything'.

For now, however, we will consider an unusual case. Sometimes moving an existential quantifier to the left does preserve truth. Consider the argument form

(6) $\forall x \exists y (Fx \ \& \ Gy)$
   $\therefore \ \exists y \forall x (Fx \ \& \ Gy)$

Switching the quantifiers results in a valid argument form here only because the variables x and y have no relation in the formula. No atomic portion of it contains both variables. In fact, both premise and conclusion are equivalent to the much clearer formula

(7) $\forall x Fx \ \& \ \exists y Gy.$

We could begin a tableau to evaluate the above argument form in the following way, observing our strategy rules:

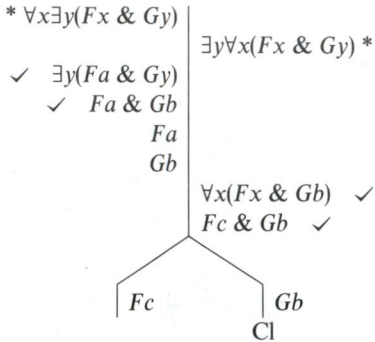

At this point, the fainthearted might stop and declare the argument form invalid. But there is still a universal formula on the left that has been dispatched only temporarily; we have taken an instance using the constant a, but not using b or c. Similarly, we've instantiated the existential formula on the right using b, without trying a or c. It seemed wise for us to use b here because doing so gave us a portion of the formula, Gb, that matched a formula on the other side of the branch. Thinking about possible matches may lead us to look for something that might match the newly introduced Fc. The best hope for doing so seems to reside in instantiating the universal formula on the left, again using c. This instantiation allows us to close the tableau:

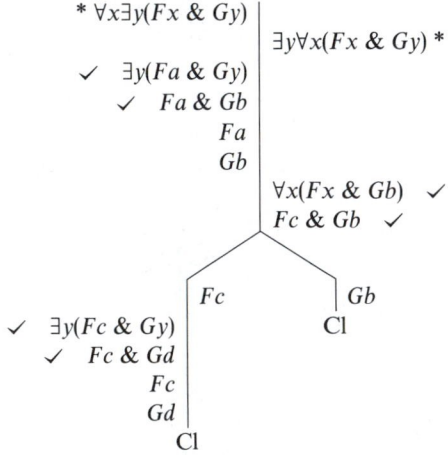

To see an example of the second possibility, let's consider a case where we exhaust the opportunities for instantiation without closing the tableau. A good example concerns properties of relations. A relation R is *reflexive* if every object stands in R to itself. R is *symmetric* if, whenever it holds between objects in one direction, it holds between them in the other direction. R is *transitive* if, whenever it holds between x and y and between y and z, it also holds between x and z. This table summarizes these definitions and provides a few examples, using relations between numbers.

R is	If and only if	Examples
reflexive	$\forall x Rxx$	$=, \leq, \geq$
symmetric	$\forall x \forall y (Rxy \rightarrow Ryx)$	$=$
transitive	$\forall x \forall y \forall z ((Rxy \ \& \ Ryz) \rightarrow Rxz)$	$=, <, \leq, >, \geq$

Suppose we want to find out whether all symmetric and transitive relations are reflexive. We can assume that R is symmetric and transitive and construct a tableau to determine whether that fact implies that R is reflexive. Following our strategy principles, we can produce the tableau

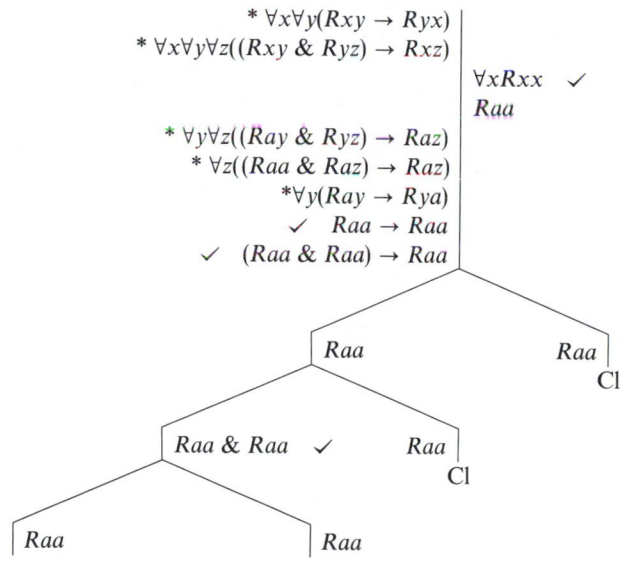

Notice that we've exhausted the available instances. Our strategy principles tell us that it's pointless to instantiate with constants not already available on the branch if we don't have to. So, introducing a constant b would be of no help here. Once we finish instantiating with a throughout, we are finished. The argument form is invalid.

This tableau points out that instantiating a string of universal quantifiers on the left, or a string of existential quantifiers on the right, is dull. We can substitute any constant for any variable. Our rules instruct us to take instances, dropping one quantifier at a time. It's far more convenient, however, to drop several quantifiers and make several substitutions at once. Therefore, we'll apply the rules $\forall$L and $\exists$R in tandem, to move from formulas to instances of their instances, or instances of instances of their instances, and so on. So, supposing that we have the formula $\forall x \forall y (Rxy \to Ryx)$ on the left, we can move immediately to the formulas $Raa \to Raa$, $Rab \to Rba$, $Rba \to Rab$, $Rbb \to Rbb$, and so on.

Similarly, it can be convenient to treat several consecutive existential quantifiers on the left, or universal quantifiers on the right, at the same time. Each application of these rules, however, requires a new constant. We can take the quantifiers together as a short cut only if we use a new constant for each quantifier. Thus, assuming that a is the only constant appearing earlier on the tableau, we can move from the formula $\exists x \exists y \exists z (Fxy \;\&\; Fxz)$ to $Fbc \;\&\; Fbd$.

Finally, some tableaux never close, but neither do they allow us to deplete their stores of available constants. These infinite, nonterminating tableaux are the source of the undecidability of quantificational logic. They also present a serious practical problem. There is no way of telling when a particular tableau construction will be nonterminating. In many simple cases, nonetheless, it's easy to tell that the tableau will never close; it traps us in a loop that continually forces us to introduce new constants.

Consider the argument mentioned earlier, which Aquinas allegedly advanced:

(8) Everything has a cause.
∴ Something is the cause of everything.

We can symbolize the argument as

(9) $\forall x \exists y Cyx$
∴ $\exists y \forall x Cyx$

Constructing a tableau for this argument quickly leads into a loop in which we introduce new constants, take new instances, introduce new constants, and so on in a never-ending cycle.

$*\ \forall x \exists y Cyx$	$\exists y \forall x Cyx\ *$
✓ $\exists y Cya$	
Cba	
	$\forall x Cbx$ ✓
	Cbc
✓ $\exists y Cyc$	
Cdc	
	$\forall x Cdx$ ✓
	Cde
⋮	

This tableau will never close; the argument form is not valid.

Problems

Evaluate these arguments for validity by using tableaux.

▶   **1.** All tableau problems are easy. Everything that isn't easy gives me a headache. Therefore, some things that give me a headache aren't tableau problems.

▶   **2.** Something about the way she moves excites me. Some songs are about the way she moves. Thus, some songs excite me.

▶   **3.** All flying horses are quick and clever; all flying horses live forever. And sad but true, all horses die. It follows that no horses fly.

▶   **4.** Some illegal acts go unpunished. All blatantly wrong acts are punished. Therefore, some illegal acts are not blatantly wrong.

▶   **5.** All who do not remember the past are condemned to repeat it. No one condemned to repeat the past looks forward to the future with eagerness. So, everyone who eagerly looks forward to the future remembers the past.

▶   **6.** I like any bread that isn't too sweet. I dislike some breads that don't contain rye flour. So, some breads that don't contain rye flour are too sweet.

7. Some untreated illnesses don't become serious. Home remedies are fine for any illness that isn't serious. Thus, home remedies are fine for some untreated illnesses.

8. Lori is unhappy with some people who didn't write thank-you notes. Lori will send presents next year to everyone with whom she's happy. Therefore, some people who didn't write thank-you notes won't get presents from Lori next year.

9. There are people without jobs who are not well nourished. Nobody who is not absent from the welfare rolls fails to be well nourished. Therefore, some people with no jobs are absent from the welfare rolls.

10. Anyone who is not an idiot can see that Jake is lying. Some people in this room can't tell that Jake is lying. Hence, some people in this room are idiots.

11. Genevieve befriends anyone who has been treated unfairly. But she doesn't befriend some really obnoxious people. So, some really obnoxious people receive fair treatment.

▶   **12.** Not all who fail to graduate drop out. All who do not drop out eventually get their degree. Thus, not all who graduate eventually get their degree.

13. The president is willing to appoint anyone who didn't work for opposing candidates. It is not true that only people who worked for opposing candidates will accept the job. So, it's not true that nobody the president is willing to appoint will take the job.

Evaluate these arguments taken from Lewis Carroll by symbolizing them in QL and using semantic tableaux.

14. No one who means to go by the train and cannot get a conveyance, and who has not enough time to walk to the station, can do without running. This party of tourists means to go by the train and cannot get a conveyance, but they have plenty of time to walk to the station. Thus, this party of tourists need not run.

15. Some healthy people are fat. No unhealthy people are strong. So, some fat people are not strong.

16. All uneducated people are shallow. Students are all educated. So, no students are shallow.

17. No muffins are wholesome. All buns are unwholesome. So, buns are not muffins.

▶ 18. Some unauthorized reports are false. All authorized reports are trustworthy. Thus, some false reports are not trustworthy.

19. No thieves are honest. Some dishonest people are found out. Therefore, some thieves are found out.

20. No muffins are wholesome; all puffy food is unwholesome. So, all muffins are puffy.

21. All wise men walk on their feet; all unwise men walk on their hands. Therefore, no man walks on both.

22. None of my boys are learned; some of my boys are not choristers. So, some unlearned boys are not choristers.

These arguments involve polyadic predicates. Evaluate them by using semantic tableaux.

23. Abu Nidal hates everyone. Qadhafy hates everyone who hates Abu Nidal. So, Abu Nidal and Qadhafy hate each other.

▶ 24. All Frenchmen are afraid of Socialists, and Socialists fear all Communists. Thus, every French Socialist is a Communist.

25. A psychiatrist can help all those who cannot help themselves. So, a psychiatrist can help someone who can help himself.

26. All Don Juans love all women. All who have a conscience treat all whom they love well. If some Don Juans have consciences, therefore, all women are treated well.

27. I like everyone who likes everyone I like. So, I don't dislike everyone.

28. Something is truly ugly just in case, if it is beautiful, then anything is. Some things, therefore, are truly ugly.

Evaluate these sentences as valid, contingent, or contradictory.

29. Something is either physical or nonphysical.

▸ 30. Something is both physical and nonphysical.

31. Everything that's physical is nonphysical.

32. Everything nonphysical is physical.

33. Everything is neither physical nor nonphysical.

34. If everything is physical, then something is physical.

35. If nothing is physical, then something is nonphysical.

▸ 36. If everything is physical, then nothing is nonphysical.

37. If nothing is physical, then nothing is nonphysical.

38. Either everything is physical, or everything is nonphysical.

39. There is a barber who shaves all those who don't shave themselves.

40. There is a barber who shaves only those who don't shave themselves.

41. There is a barber who shaves all and only those who don't shave themselves.

▸ 42. Nobody's seen all the trouble I've seen.

43. Nobody's seen any of the trouble I've seen.

44. There is something such that, if it's an object of art, anything is.

45. Existence, by nothing bred, breeds everything. (Lao-Tzu)

46. God created everything, but nothing created God.

47. Given any gun, there is a faster gun.

▸ 48. A gun is faster than every gun only if it's faster than itself.

49. There's a gun that's faster than every gun only if some gun is faster than itself.

50. If, for any gun, there is a faster gun, then no gun is faster than itself.

51. There are people who love each other only if they both love some one person.

52. Somebody respects everyone unless he or she respects somebody who has self-respect.

53. Somebody respects everyone unless he or she respects only somebody who has self-respect.

The philosopher Gottfried Leibniz defined a good person as one who loves everyone (as much as reason allows). If we accept this definition,

$$\forall x(Gx \leftrightarrow \forall yLxy)$$

then which of these statements follow?

▶ **54.** All good people love somebody or other.

55. All good people love themselves.

56. Someone is loved by all good people.

57. Somebody loves all good people.

58. Everyone good is loved by somebody or other.

59. All good people love all good people.

▶ **60.** Everybody is loved by somebody or other.

61. If there are any good people, then everybody is loved by somebody.

62. Nobody who is not good loves anybody.

63. Everyone who is good loves everyone who is not good.

Use tableaux to evaluate the following argument forms of validity.

64. $\exists x(Gx \ \& \ \neg Fx)$; $\forall x(Gx \rightarrow Hx)$; $\therefore \ \exists x(Hx \ \& \ \neg Fx)$

65. $\exists x(Gx \ \& \ Fx)$; $\forall x(Fx \rightarrow \neg Hx)$; $\therefore \ \exists x \neg Hx$

66. $\forall x(Gx \rightarrow \neg Fx)$; $\forall x(Fx \rightarrow \neg Hx)$; $\therefore \ \forall x(Gx \rightarrow Hx)$

▶ **67.** $\forall x(Gx \rightarrow \exists y(Fy \ \& \ Hy))$; $\therefore \ \forall x \neg Fx \rightarrow \neg \exists z Gz$

68. $\forall x(Gx \rightarrow (Hx \ \& \ Jx))$; $\forall x((Fx \vee \neg Jx) \rightarrow Gx)$; $\therefore \ \forall x(Fx \rightarrow Hx)$

69. $\forall x((Gx \vee Kx) \rightarrow Hx)$; $\neg \exists x(Fx \ \& \ Gx)$; $\therefore \ \forall x \neg (Fx \ \& \ Hx)$

70. $\forall x(Gx \rightarrow Hx)$; $\exists x(Fx \ \& \ Gx \ \& \ Mx)$; $\therefore \ \exists x(Fx \ \& \ Hx \ \& \ Mx)$

71. $\forall x(\neg Gx \vee \neg Hx)$; $\forall x((Jx \rightarrow Fx) \rightarrow Hx)$; $\therefore \ \neg \exists x(Fx \ \& \ Hx)$

72. $\neg \exists x(Gx \ \& \ \neg Hx)$; $\forall x(Fx \rightarrow \neg Gx)$; $\therefore \ \forall x((Fx \ \& \ \neg Gx) \rightarrow \neg Hx)$

▶ **73.** $\forall x \neg (Gx \ \& \ Hx)$; $\exists x(Fx \ \& \ Gx)$; $\therefore \ \exists x(Fx \ \& \ \neg Hx)$

74. $\exists x(Gx \ \& \ Hx \ \& \ Jx)$; $\forall x((Fx \vee Jx) \rightarrow Gx)$; $\therefore \ \exists x(Fx \ \& \ Hx)$

75. $\exists x(Gx \ \& \ \neg Hx)$; $\neg \exists x(Fx \ \& \ \neg Gx)$; $\therefore \ \neg \forall x(Fx \rightarrow Hx)$

76. $\forall x((Hx \vee Kx) \rightarrow Gx) \ \& \ \forall x(\neg Fx \vee \neg Gx)$; $\therefore \ \forall x \neg (Fx \ \& \ (Kx \vee Hx))$

77. $\forall x((Hx \vee Jx) \rightarrow (Gx \ \& \ Kx))$; $\exists x(Fx \ \& \ Gx \ \& \ (Jx \rightarrow Kx))$; $\therefore \ \exists x(Fx \ \& \ Hx)$

78. $\forall x(Hx \rightarrow (Hx \& Gx)); \exists x(\neg Gx \& Fx); \therefore \exists x(Fx \& \neg Hx)$

▶ **79.** $\forall x(Hx \rightarrow \neg Gx); \neg \exists x(Fx \& \neg Gx); \therefore \forall x\neg(Fx \& Hx)$

80. $\forall x(\neg Hx \vee \neg Gx); \exists x(Fx \& Gx \& Mx); \therefore \exists x(Fx \& Mx \& \neg Hx)$

81. $\exists xFx \leftrightarrow \exists xGx; \therefore \exists x(Fx \leftrightarrow Gx)$

82. $\exists xFx \vee \exists xGx; \therefore \exists x(Fx \vee Gx)$

83. $\forall x(Fx \leftrightarrow Gx); \therefore \forall xFx \leftrightarrow \forall xGx$

84. $\exists x(Fx \vee Gx); \therefore \exists xFx \vee \exists xGx$

▶ **85.** $\exists xFx \rightarrow \forall y(Gy \rightarrow Hy); \exists xJx \rightarrow \exists xGx; \therefore \exists x(Fx \& Jx) \rightarrow \exists zHz$

86. $\exists xFx \vee \exists xGx; \forall x(Fx \rightarrow Gx); \therefore \exists xGx$

87. $\neg \exists x(Fx \& Gx); \therefore \forall x(Fx \rightarrow \neg Gx)$

88. $\forall x(Fx \rightarrow \neg Gx); \therefore \neg \exists x(Fx \& Gx)$

89. $\forall x((Fx \vee Hx) \rightarrow (Gx \& Kx)); \neg \forall x(Kx \& Gx); \therefore \exists x\neg Hx$

90. $\forall x(Fx \rightarrow (Gx \vee Hx)); \forall x((Jx \& Fx) \rightarrow \neg Gx); \forall x(\neg Fx \rightarrow \neg Jx);$
$\therefore \forall x(Jx \rightarrow Hx)$

▶ **91.** $\forall x((Fx \& Gx) \rightarrow Hx); Ga \& \forall xFx; \therefore Fa \& Ha$

92. $\forall x(Fx \leftrightarrow Gx); \therefore \forall xFx \leftrightarrow \forall xGx$

93. $\forall x(Fx \leftrightarrow Gx); \therefore \exists xFx \leftrightarrow \exists xGx$

94. $\exists x(Fx \leftrightarrow Gx); \therefore \forall xFx \leftrightarrow \exists xGx$

95. $\exists x(Fx \& \forall y(Gy \rightarrow Hy)); \forall x(Fx \rightarrow (\neg Lx \rightarrow \neg \exists z(Kz \& Hz)));$
$\therefore \exists x(Kx \& Gx) \rightarrow \exists xLx$

96. $\forall x(Fx \leftrightarrow \forall yGy); \therefore \forall xFx \vee \forall x\neg Fx$

▶ **97.** $\forall y(Fa \rightarrow (\exists xGx \rightarrow Gy)); \forall x(Gx \rightarrow Hx); \forall x(\neg Jx \rightarrow \neg Hx);$
$\therefore \exists x\neg Jx \rightarrow (\neg Fa \vee \forall x\neg Gx)$

98. $\forall x(Dx \rightarrow Fx); \therefore \forall z(Dz \rightarrow (\forall y(Gy \rightarrow Fy) \rightarrow Gz))$

99. $\exists xFx \leftrightarrow \forall y((Fy \vee Gy) \rightarrow Hy); \exists xHx; \neg \forall z\neg Fz; \therefore \exists x(Fx \& Hx)$

100. $\forall xFx; \therefore \neg \exists xGx \leftrightarrow \neg(\exists x(Fx \& Gx) \& \forall y(Gy \leftrightarrow Fy))$

101. $\exists x(Px \& \neg Mx) \rightarrow \forall y(Py \rightarrow Ly); \exists x(Px \& Nx); \forall x(Px \rightarrow \neg Lx);$
$\therefore \exists x(Nx \& Mx)$

Although, in general, we can't switch existential and universal quantifiers to reach an equivalent formula, we can do this in special circumstances. Use semantic tableaux to show that each of these switches is legitimate.

102. $\forall x\exists y(Fx \& Gy); \therefore \exists y\forall x(Fx \& Gy)$

▶ **103.** $\forall x\exists y(Fx \vee Gy); \therefore \exists y\forall x(Fx \vee Gy)$

104. $\forall x \exists y (Fx \rightarrow Gy)$; $\therefore$ $\exists y \forall x (Fx \rightarrow Gy)$

105. $\forall x \exists y (Gy \rightarrow Fx)$; $\therefore$ $\exists y \forall x (Gy \rightarrow Fx)$

These argument forms contain polyadic predicates. Evaluate them, using semantic tableaux.

106. $\forall x (\exists y Fyx \rightarrow \forall z Fxz)$; $\therefore$ $\forall y \forall x (Fyx \rightarrow Fxy)$

107. $\exists x (Gx \,\&\, \forall y Gxy)$; $\forall x \forall y (Gxy \rightarrow Gyx)$; $\therefore$ $\exists x (Gx \,\&\, \forall y Gyx)$

108. $\exists x \forall y (Gxy \rightarrow Fyx)$; $\therefore$ $\exists x \exists y (Gxy \,\&\, Gyx)$

▶ **109.** $\forall x (Gx \rightarrow \forall y (Fy \rightarrow Hxy))$; $\exists x (Fx \,\&\, \forall z \neg Hxz)$; $\therefore$ $\neg \forall x Gx$

110. $\forall x \forall y (Fxy \rightarrow Gxy)$; $\therefore$ $\forall x (Gxx \rightarrow \exists y (Gxy \,\&\, Fyx))$

111. $\forall x \forall y (Gxy \rightarrow (Gyx \rightarrow \exists z Hxyz))$; $\forall x Gax$; $\therefore$ $\exists x \exists y Hyyx$

112. $\forall x (Fx \rightarrow \forall y (Gy \rightarrow Hxy))$; $\forall x (Dx \rightarrow \forall y (Hxy \rightarrow Cy))$; $\therefore$ $\exists x (Fx \,\&\, Dx) \rightarrow \forall y (Gy \rightarrow Cy)$

113. $\forall x (Kx \rightarrow (\exists y Lxy \rightarrow \exists z Lzx))$; $\forall x (\exists z Lzx \rightarrow Lxx)$; $\neg \exists x Lxx$; $\therefore$ $\forall x (Kx \rightarrow \forall y \neg Lxy)$

114. $\forall x (\neg Fxx \lor Hx)$; $\neg \exists x Hx \lor \neg \exists y Gy$; $\therefore$ $\forall x (Gx \rightarrow \neg \exists z Fzz)$

▶ **115.** $\neg \exists x (Hxa \,\&\, \neg Gxb)$; $\forall x \neg (Fxc \,\&\, Fbx)$; $\forall x (Gdx \rightarrow Fxe)$; $\therefore$ $\neg (Hea \,\&\, Fec)$

116. $\forall x (\exists y (Ay \,\&\, Bxy) \rightarrow Cx)$; $\exists y (Dy \,\&\, \exists x ((Fx \,\&\, Gx) \,\&\, Byx))$; $\forall x (Gx \rightarrow Ax)$; $\therefore$ $\exists x (Cx \,\&\, Dx)$

117. $\forall x \forall y \forall z ((Fxy \,\&\, Fyz) \rightarrow Fxz)$; $\neg \exists x Fxx$; $\therefore$ $\forall x \forall y (Fxy \rightarrow \neg Fyx)$

118. $\exists x (Fx \,\&\, \forall y (Ty \rightarrow Gy))$; $\forall x (Fx \rightarrow (\exists y (Ay \,\&\, Gy) \rightarrow Bxx))$; $\exists z (Az \,\&\, Tz)$; $\therefore$ $\exists x Bxx$

119. $\forall x \neg Fxc \rightarrow \exists x Gxb$; $\therefore$ $\exists x (\neg Fxc \rightarrow Gxb)$

120. $\forall x (Fx \rightarrow \neg \exists y (Gy \,\&\, Hxy))$; $\forall x (Fx \rightarrow \exists y (Fy \,\&\, Hxy))$; $\therefore$ $\forall x \forall y (Hxy \rightarrow Hyx) \rightarrow \forall x \neg (Fx \,\&\, Gx)$

▶ **121.** $\forall x \neg Fxx$; $\therefore$ $\neg \exists x \forall y (Fyx \leftrightarrow \exists z \forall w ((Fwz \rightarrow Fwy) \,\&\, \neg Fzy))$

122. $\forall x (Fx \rightarrow \forall y (Gy \rightarrow Hxy))$; $\exists x (Fx \,\&\, \exists y \neg Hxy)$; $\therefore$ $\exists x \neg Gx$

123. $\exists x (Fx \,\&\, \forall y (Gy \rightarrow Hxy))$; $\therefore$ $\exists x (Fx \,\&\, (Ga \rightarrow Hxa))$

124. $\forall x (\exists y Fxy \rightarrow \exists y \neg Gy)$; $\exists x \exists y Fxy$; $\forall x (Gx \leftrightarrow \neg Hx)$; $\therefore$ $\exists x Hx$

125. $\forall x (Mx \rightarrow Hx)$; $\exists x \exists y ((Fx \,\&\, Mx) \,\&\, (Gy \,\&\, Jyx))$; $\exists x Hx \rightarrow \forall y \forall z (\neg Hy \rightarrow \neg Jyz)$; $\therefore$ $\exists x (Gx \,\&\, Hx)$

126. $\forall x (\exists y Fxy \rightarrow \forall y Fyx)$; $\exists x \exists y Fxy$; $\therefore$ $\forall x \forall y Fxy$

▶ **127.** $\exists x \forall y (\exists z Fyz \rightarrow Fyx)$; $\forall x \exists y Fxy$; $\therefore \exists x \forall y Fyx$

128. $\exists x \forall y \neg Fxy;\ \therefore\ \exists x \forall y \forall z(Fxz \rightarrow Fzy)$

129. $\forall x \forall y(Fxy \rightarrow Fyx);\ \therefore\ \forall x \forall y(Fxy \leftrightarrow Fyx)$

130. $\forall x \forall y((Ax\ \&\ By) \rightarrow Cxy);\ \exists y(Fy\ \&\ \forall z(Hz \rightarrow Cyz));$
$\forall x \forall y \forall z((Cxy\ \&\ Cyz) \rightarrow Cxz);\ \forall x(Fx \rightarrow Bx);\ \therefore\ \forall z \forall y((Az\ \&\ Hy) \rightarrow Czy)$

131. $\exists x(Gxb\ \&\ \forall z(Fz \rightarrow Gzx));\ \forall x \forall y(Hxy \leftrightarrow ((Fx\ \&\ Fy)\ \&\ Gxy));$
$\therefore\ \exists xHxx \rightarrow \exists y \forall z \forall w((Hwz \lor Hzw) \rightarrow (Gzy\ \&\ Gyb))$

132. Use semantic tableaux to do the problems at the end of Sections 13.1, 13.2, 13.3, and 13.4.

Notes

[1] "A Note on the Entscheidungsproblem," *Journal of Symbolic Logic* 1 (1936): 40–41. (Correction on 101–2.)

[2] 'Someone in this room is a spy' asserts that there is at least one spy in the room. What follows in the text assumes, for the sake of simplicity, that there is only a single spy. If there is more than one, then what is said about 'the spy' applies to any of the spies; we cannot distinguish among them with the information at hand.

13

QUANTIFIED DEDUCTION

Natural deduction extends easily to predicate logic. All rules of sentential deduction apply in quantification theory. To deal with quantifiers, the system adds several new rules. The deduction system that emerges shares the virtues of its sentential cousin. The system is sound, for every provable formula is valid, and every conclusion provable from a set of premises follows from them. The system is also complete, for every valid formula of quantification theory can be proved in the system, and every valid argument can be shown valid within it. Furthermore, the system mirrors closely the processes of reasoning that people use in a wide variety of contexts.

13.1 DEDUCTION RULES FOR QUANTIFIERS

The deduction rules needed for quantificational logic are very straightforward. Say that $\mathscr{A}[c/v]$ is the result of substituting c for every occurrence of v throughout the formula $\mathscr{A}$. If $\forall v \mathscr{A}$ and $\exists v \mathscr{A}$ are formulas, then $\mathscr{A}[c/v]$ is called an *instance* of them. Conversely, $\forall v \mathscr{A}$ and $\exists v \mathscr{A}$ are *generics* of $\mathscr{A}[c/v]$. If $\mathscr{A}[c/v]$ is an instance of $\forall v \mathscr{A}$ and $\exists v \mathscr{A}$, and those formulas do not contain c, then $\mathscr{A}[c/v]$ is a *conservative instance* of $\forall v \mathscr{A}$ and $\exists v \mathscr{A}$.

Each connective has two rules. One rule introduces the connective into proofs, whereas the other allows us to exploit its presence. The existential quantifier similarly comes with two rules: an introduction rule and an exploitation rule. The introduction rule, in essence, allows us to move to an existentially quantified formula from any instance of that formula.[1] Called *existen-*

tial generalization, the rule takes the form:

Existential Generalization (EG)

n. $\quad \mathscr{A}\left[c/v\right]$

n + p. $\quad \exists v \mathscr{A} \qquad$ EG, n

Here c may be any constant.

Existential generalization allows us to infer an existentially quantified formula from any instance of it. It sanctions the step from an instance to its corresponding existential generic. Suppose that our universe of discourse consists entirely of people. If Jones, for example, is a spy, then we may conclude that someone is a spy. If Susan suspects Harry, then Susan suspects someone; of course, it's also true that somebody suspects Harry and that somebody suspects somebody. Finally, if Frank doesn't trust himself to work around large sums of money, then Frank doesn't trust somebody to work around large sums of money. Additionally, somebody doesn't trust Frank to work around large sums, and someone doesn't trust himself to do so. Each of the following is an acceptable application of existential generalization.

Premise	Conclusion
Fa	$\exists x Fx$
Gab	$\exists x Gax$
Gab	$\exists x Gxb$
Hcc	$\exists x Hcx$
Hcc	$\exists x Hxc$
Hcc	$\exists x Hxx$
$\exists x Fxa$	$\exists y \exists x Fxy$
$\forall x Fx \rightarrow Gb$	$\exists z(\forall x Fx \rightarrow Gz)$

In each case, the premise is an instance of the conclusion.

The rule of *existential specification* allows us to move from an existentially quantified formula to an instance of it.[2] This rule is almost exactly the reverse, then, of the existential generalization rule. But it imposes a restriction: The instance must involve a constant new to the proof. The rule asserts that we may (a) drop an existential quantifier serving as a main connective in a formula and (b) substitute for the quantified variable a constant that hasn't appeared earlier in the proof or in the conclusion. The constant must have appeared nowhere in the deduction. And it must not appear in the deduction's conclusion.

Existential Specification (ES)

$$n. \qquad \exists v \mathscr{A}$$
$$n + p. \quad \mathscr{A}[c/v] \qquad \text{ES, } n$$

Here c must be a constant new to the proof and must not appear in the proof's conclusion.

This rule reflects a very important feature of indefinite descriptions like 'a house' or 'a room with a view': They not only assert existence but, like proper names, introduce a constant that can figure in subsequent discourse. The existential quantifier itself plays only the first role. The rule of existential specification, however, allows us to simulate the second. It allows us to refer back to the object whose existence is asserted in the existentially quantified formula.

Consider, for example, this simple discourse:

(1) Wanda lives in *a house* on Speedway. *Her house* is convenient to campus. More important, *it*'s close to Rosie's Cantina.

We would ordinarily symbolize the first sentence as

(2) $\exists x(Hx \,\&\, Oxs \,\&\, Lax)$.

But this step raises a problem about how to symbolize the second and third sentences. If we use a constant to translate 'her house' and 'it', as seems natural, we have no way of making it clear that we're talking about the object, Wanda's house, that the first sentence introduces. If we use existential quantifiers for 'her house' and 'it' in separate translations of the last two sentences, we also fail to express the idea that we're talking about one object; we would have instead formulas like these:

(3) a. $\exists x(Hx \,\&\, Oxs \,\&\, Lax)$
     (There's a house on Speedway Wanda lives in.)
   b. $\exists x(Hx \,\&\, Wax \,\&\, Cxc)$
     (There's a house Wanda owns that's convenient to campus.)
   c. $\exists x Sxr$
     (Something is close to Rosie's Cantina.)

Nothing here indicates that we're talking about one and the same object. We can symbolize the entire discourse in a single formula as

(4) $\exists x(Hx \,\&\, Oxs \,\&\, Lax \,\&\, Wax \,\&\, Cxc \,\&\, Sxr)$.

But doing so forces us to symbolize the discourse as a whole unit; we can't proceed sentence by sentence. In a proof, however, we must proceed line by line as we deduce more and more information. The existential specification rule allows us to refer back to the object introduced by an existentially quantified formula while still proceeding line by line in the usual manner of a proof.

The restriction on the rule—that we use a constant appearing neither in the proof above nor in the conclusion—prevents us from using it to derive invalid conclusions. To see why the constant must be new, consider this argument:

(5) Officer O'Malley shot someone.
∴ Officer O'Malley shot himself.

Plainly, the argument is invalid. But, if we were to ignore the requirement that we use a new constant in applying ES, we could show the corresponding argument form to be valid:

1. ∃xSmx   A
2. Smm   ES, 1   (Wrong!)

To understand why we must not use a constant appearing in the conclusion, consider this argument:

(6) Some people are crazy.
∴ You're crazy.

This, too, is a terrible argument. But, if we were to ignore the requirement that no conclusion of a proof contain a constant introduced by ES, we could show the argument to have a valid form (where *a* symbolizes 'you'):

1. ∃xCx   A
2. Ca   ES, 1   (Wrong!)

This proof is flawed. But there would be nothing wrong with step 2 if the proof didn't end at that line and didn't conclude with a formula containing a.[3]

The third rule for quantifiers is *universal specification*. If we know that something is true about every object, then we can conclude that it is true for each particular object we consider. If God loves everyone, then God loves you, me, and the Earl of Roxburgh. If Jane likes everyone she meets, then she likes you, if she's met you; she likes me, if she's met me; and so on. The rule of universal specification asserts that from a universally quantified formula, we may infer any of its instances.

Universal Specification (US)

n. $\forall v \mathscr{A}$
n + p. $\mathscr{A}[c/v]$ US, n

Here c may be any constant.

This rule does not require a new constant. In fact, it is silly to use a new constant in applying US unless no constants at all appear in the proof up to this line. If constants *a* and *b* appear earlier, then, from ∀*xFx*, we can infer *Fa*, or *Fb*, or both. From a formula ∀*xGxx*, we can infer *Gaa* or *Gbb*. And, from ∀*x*∀*yHxy*, we can obtain ∀*yHay* or ∀*yHby* and, in another step, any of *Haa*, *Hab*, *Hba*, and *Hbb*. We could also, of course, infer similar formulas with other constants. Unless we are forced to introduce those constants in other ways, however, using them to exploit a universal formula serves no purpose.

To see how these rules work, let's demonstrate the validity of a simple argument:

(7) Something is rotten in the state of Denmark.
    Whatever is in Denmark is in Europe.
    ∴ Something's rotten in Europe.

1.	∃*x*(*Rx* & *Ixd*)	A
2.	∀*y*(*Iyd* → *Iye*)	A
3.	*Ra* & *Iad*	ES, 1
4.	*Iad* → *Iae*	US, 2
5.	*Iad*	S, 3
6.	*Iae*	MP, 4, 5
7.	*Ra*	S, 3
8.	*Ra* & *Iae*	C, 7, 6
9.	∃*z*(*Rz* & *Ize*)	EG, 8

Problems

Use deduction to show that these arguments are valid. Symbolize universal negative sentences with universal quantifiers.

▶ **1.** God created everything. So, God created Texas.

▶ **2.** God created everything. So, God created something.

▶ **3.** God created everything. So, God created Himself.

▶ **4.** God created everything. So, something created God.

▶ **5.** Nothing logical frustrates me. This book frustrates me; so, this book is illogical.

▶ **6.** Any player who bats over .300 could be a hot item in the free agent market. There is a player on the Pirates who bats over .300. So, some Pirate could be a hot free agent.

7. There are new houses that are very large but that are not very well built. Every very large house is impressive to visitors. Therefore, some houses that impress visitors are not very well built.

8. All insects in this house are large and hostile. Some insects in this house are impervious to pesticides. Thus, some large, hostile insects are impervious to pesticides.

9. Some students can't succeed at the university. All students who are bright and mature can succeed. It follows that some students are either not bright or immature.

10. Everyone is afraid of Dracula; Dracula fears only those capable of destroying him. So, Dracula can destroy himself.

11. Nothing written by committee is easy to write or easy to read. Some documents written by committee are nevertheless extremely insightful. So, some extremely insightful documents are not easy to read.

▶ 12. Some of the cleverest people I know are clearly insane. Any of the cleverest people I know could prove that this argument is valid. Hence, some people who could prove this argument valid are clearly insane.

13. All managers who put their own welfare above that of their company endanger the interests of stockholders. Some CEOs put their own welfare above that of their company. Thus, some managers who endanger stockholder interests are CEOs.

14. Some business professors spend their time on highly esoteric, theoretical questions. Nobody who spends his or her time on such matters does research that has much to do with the real world. Consequently, some business professors do research that has little to do with the real world.

15. Some utility companies are predicting brownouts in their service regions during this summer. No utilities that can easily and affordably purchase power from other utilities are predicting brownouts for this summer. Hence, some utility companies cannot easily and affordably purchase power from other utilities.

16. Some analysts insist that we are in the middle of a historic bull market, but others say that the market will soon collapse. Nobody who is expecting the market to collapse is recommending anything but utility stocks. None who believe that M1 controls the direction of the economy contend that we are in the midst of a historic bull market. Thus, some analysts are recommending only utility stocks, but some don't believe that M1 controls the economy's direction.

17. Wild Bill can outdraw everyone who can outdraw someone he can. Wild Bill can outdraw some gunfighters. Therefore Wild Bill can outdraw himself.

▶ **18.** One prosecutor can convict another only if the former can convict every-one the latter can. There are prosecutors who can convict each other. So, there are prosecutors who can convict themselves.

These are some of the syllogisms that Aristotle considered valid, together with their medieval names. Show that each is valid in QL. (Some require extra assumptions; they are listed in parentheses. Translate universal negative sentence forms with a universal quantifier.)

19. Darii: Every M is L; Some S is M; ∴ Some S is L.

20. Ferio: No M is L; Some S is M; ∴ Some S is not L.

21. Festino: No L is M; Some S is M; ∴ Some S is not L.

22. Baroco: Every L is M; Some S is not M; ∴ Some S is not L.

23. Darapti: Every M is L; Every M is S; (There are Ms;) ∴ Some S is L.

▶ **24.** Felapton: No M is L; Every M is S; (There are Ms;) ∴ Some S is not L.

25. Disamis: Some M is L; Every M is S; ∴ Some S is L.

26. Datisi: Every M is L; Some M is S; ∴ Some S is L.

27. Bocardo: Some M is not L; Every M is S; ∴ Some S is not L.

28. Ferison: No M is L; Some M is S; ∴ Some S is not L.

Medieval logicians added other syllogistic patterns to those Aristotle explic-itly held valid. Show that these "subaltern moods" are valid, at least with the added assumptions in parentheses.

29. Barbari: Every M is L; Every S is M; (There are Ss;) ∴ Some S is L.

▶ **30.** Celaront: No M is L; Every S is M; (There are Ss;) ∴ Some S is not L.

31. Cesaro: No L is M; Every S is M; (There are Ss;) ∴ Some S is not L.

32. Camestros: Every L is M; No S is M; (There are Ss;) ∴ Some S is not L.

Theophrastus, who succeeded Aristotle as head of the Lyceum, also added additional syllogistic principles. Show that these too are valid, with the added assumptions in parentheses.

33. Baralipton: Every M is L; Every S is M; (There are Ss;) ∴ Some L is S.

34. Dabitis: Every M is L; Some S is M; ∴ Some L is S.

35. Fapesmo: Every M is L; No S is M; (There are Ms;) ∴ Some L is not S.

▶ **36.** Frisesomorum: Some M is L; No S is M; ∴ Some L is not S.

Use deduction to establish the validity of these argument forms.

37. $\forall x Fx$; $\therefore$ $\exists x Fx$

38. $\exists x Fx$; $\forall x Gx$; $\therefore$ $\exists x(Fx \,\&\, Gx)$

39. $\exists x Fx$; $\forall x(Fx \to \neg Gx)$; $\therefore$ $\exists x \neg Gx$

40. $\forall x(Gx \to Hx)$; $\exists x(Fx \,\&\, Gx)$; $\therefore$ $\exists x(Fx \,\&\, Hx)$

41. $\forall x \neg(Gx \,\&\, Hx)$; $\exists x(Fx \,\&\, Gx)$; $\therefore$ $\exists x(Fx \,\&\, \neg Hx)$

▶ **42.** $\forall x(Hx \to Gx)$; $\exists x(\neg Gx \,\&\, Fx)$; $\therefore$ $\exists x(Fx \,\&\, \neg Hx)$

43. $\forall x(\neg Gx \to \neg Hx)$; $\exists x(Fx \,\&\, \neg Gx)$; $\therefore$ $\exists x(Fx \,\&\, \neg Hx)$

44. $\forall x(Gx \to Hx)$; $\exists x(Gx \,\&\, Fx)$; $\therefore$ $\exists x(Fx \,\&\, Hx)$

45. $\forall x(Gx \to \neg Hx)$; $\exists x(Gx \,\&\, \neg Fx)$; $\therefore$ $\exists x(\neg Fx \,\&\, \neg Hx)$

46. $\exists x(Gx \,\&\, Hx)$; $\forall x(Gx \to Fx)$; $\therefore$ $\exists x(Fx \,\&\, Hx)$

47. $\exists x(Gx \,\&\, \neg Hx)$; $\forall x(Gx \to Fx)$; $\therefore$ $\exists x(Fx \,\&\, \neg Hx)$

▶ **48.** $\forall x(Hx \to \neg Gx)$; $\exists x(Gx \,\&\, Fx)$; $\therefore$ $\exists x(Fx \,\&\, \neg Hx)$

49. $\exists x(Hx \,\&\, Gx)$; $\forall x(Gx \to Fx)$; $\therefore$ $\exists x(Fx \,\&\, Hx)$

50. $\exists x(\neg Fx \,\&\, \neg Gx)$; $\forall x(\neg Gx \to \neg Hx)$; $\therefore$ $\exists x(\neg Hx \,\&\, \neg Fx)$

51. $\forall x(Fx \leftrightarrow Gx)$; $\forall x(Fx \leftrightarrow Hx)$; $\exists x(\neg Hx \lor Gx)$; $\therefore$ $\exists x(\neg Fx \lor (Gx \,\&\, Hx))$

52. $\forall x(Fx \leftrightarrow Gx)$; $\forall x(Fx \leftrightarrow Hx)$; $\exists x(\neg Hx \lor Gx)$; $\therefore$ $\exists x(\neg Hx \lor (Gx \,\&\, Fx))$

53. $\forall x(Fx \to (Gx \to \neg Hx))$; $\exists y(Hy \,\&\, Fy)$; $\therefore$ $\exists x \neg Gx$

▶ **54.** $\forall x(Fx \lor \neg Gx)$; $\forall x(Fx \to Hx)$; $\forall x(\neg Gx \to Jx)$; $\exists x \neg Jx$; $\therefore$ $\exists x Hx$

55. $\forall x(Fx \leftrightarrow Gx)$; $\forall x(Gx \to Hx)$; $\exists x(Fx \lor Gx)$; $\therefore$ $\exists x(Fx \,\&\, Hx)$

56. $\exists y Fyy$; $\exists x \forall z Gxz$; $\therefore$ $\exists x \exists y(Gyx \,\&\, Fxx)$

57. $\exists x \exists y Fxy$; $\forall x \forall y(Fxy \leftrightarrow (Gx \,\&\, \neg Gy))$; $\therefore$ $\exists x Gx \,\&\, \exists x \neg Gx$

58. $\exists x Gx \,\&\, \exists x \neg Gx$; $\forall x \forall y(Fxy \leftrightarrow (Gx \,\&\, \neg Gy))$; $\therefore$ $\exists x \exists y Fxy$

59. $\exists x(Gx \,\&\, \forall z \neg Hxz)$; $\forall x Fx$; $\therefore$ $\exists x(Fx \,\&\, \exists y \neg(Gy \to Hxy))$

▶ **60.** $\forall x(Fx \to Gx)$; $\therefore$ $\exists x(\neg Fx \lor Gx)$

61. $\forall x \forall y(Fxy \leftrightarrow (Gx \,\&\, \neg Gy))$; $\exists x \exists y(Fxy \,\&\, Fyx)$; $\therefore$ $\exists x(Gx \,\&\, \neg Gx)$

62. $\exists x \exists y(Fx \,\&\, Gyx)$; $\forall x \forall y((Fx \,\&\, Hy) \to \neg Jxy)$; $\therefore$ $\exists x \exists y(Gxy \,\&\, \neg(Hx \,\&\, Jyx))$

63. $\forall x \forall y \forall z((Fxy \,\&\, Fxz) \to Fyz)$; $\exists x \exists y(Fxy \,\&\, \neg Fyx)$; $\therefore$ $\exists x \neg Fxx$

64. $\forall z \forall x(\neg Hz \leftrightarrow (Fx \,\&\, Gz))$; $\forall x \exists y(Gy \,\&\, Fx)$; $\therefore$ $\exists x \neg Hx$

13.2 UNIVERSAL GENERALIZATION

Introducing a universal formula requires a new rule.

Universal Generalization (UG)

$$n. \quad \mathscr{A}[c/v]$$
$$n + p. \quad \forall v \mathscr{A} \qquad \text{UG, n}$$

Here 1. c must not occur in $\forall v \mathscr{A}$;
2. c must not occur in the assumptions or conclusion of the proof;
3. c must not have been introduced by ES;
4. No term remaining in $\forall v \mathscr{A}$ may depend on c.

The last of these restrictions is needed only for proofs involving formulas with quantifiers that overlap in scope. For simpler formulas, it may be ignored. For that reason, let's set the last restriction aside for the moment and examine the rest of the rule.

Basic Conditions

To prove a universal conclusion, this rule asserts, we prove a conservative instance of it. In general, it's best to try to derive an instance that results from substituting a constant new to the proof for the quantified variable. Since no information will appear anywhere earlier in the proof regarding the new constant, it stands for no object in particular. It represents, as it were, an arbitrarily chosen object. Because the proof puts no constraints on it, absolutely any object could play this role. Consequently, though we prove something about c, we've shown how to prove it about anything. And this justifies our drawing a universal conclusion.

The restrictions prevent this form of proof from allowing us to prove very silly arguments valid. Consider the first restriction, that c not appear in $\forall v \mathscr{A}$. The restriction requires that we derive a universal from a *conservative* instance of it. To see why this is necessary, suppose we tried to argue

(8) Everyone respects himself or herself.
∴ Everyone respects Qadhafy.

Clearly, the argument fails. We might attempt this proof:

1. $\forall x Rxx$ A
2. Rgg US, 1
3. $\forall x Rxg$ UG, 2 (Wrong!)

We must derive a universal generic from one of its conservative instances. Since g occurs in $\forall x Rxg$, line 3 violates the first restriction on UG.

The second restriction prohibits c from appearing in the assumptions or conclusion of the proof. If we allowed c to appear in the assumptions, we could prove valid poor arguments such as:

(9) Eliot Ness sent Al Capone to jail.
∴ Eliot Ness sent everybody to jail.

Ignoring the second restriction, we could attempt the proof:

1. Snc A
2. $\forall x Snx$ UG, 1 (Wrong!)

We can't go from the information that Ness sent Capone to jail to the conclusion that he sent everyone there. The constant c, on which line 2 tries to generalize, appears in an assumption. So, UG can't apply.

A similar argument shows the point of the third restriction, that c not have been introduced by ES. Consider this invalid argument:

(10) There is a pope.
∴ Everybody is pope.

We might try to prove it valid as follows:

1. $\exists x Px$ A
2. Pa ES, 1
3. $\forall x Px$ UG, 2 (Wrong)

We used existential specification to introduce a; therefore, we can't later universally generalize on it.

To take an example of a successful universal generalization, consider this inference:

(11) Everything created by God is good.
Everything is a creation of God.
∴ Everything is good.

To establish its validity, we construct a universal proof:

1. $\forall x(Cgx \rightarrow Gx)$ A
2. $\forall x Cgx$ A
3. Cga US, 2
4. $Cga \rightarrow Ga$ US, 1
5. Ga MP, 4, 3
6. $\forall x Gx$ UG, 5

To show that everything is G, we show that some arbitrarily chosen object a is G. UG succeeds because a occurs in neither assumptions (lines 1 and 2) nor in the universal conclusion (line 6), and was not introduced by ES.

Problems

Aristotle considered the first four of these syllogisms valid; Theophrastus added the last. Show that each is valid in quantification theory. (Symbolize universal negative sentence forms with universal quantifiers.)

▸ **1.** Barbara: Every M is L; Every S is M; ∴ Every S is L.

▸ **2.** Celarent: No M is L; Every S is M; ∴ No S is L.

▸ **3.** Cesare: No L is M; Every S is M; ∴ No S is L.

▸ **4.** Camestres: Every L is M; No S is M; ∴ No S is L.

▸ **5.** Celantes: No M is L; Every S is M; ∴ No L is S.

These arguments are adapted from Lewis Carroll's *Symbolic Logic*. Symbolizing universal negative sentences with universal quantifiers, use deduction to show that each is valid.

▸ **6.** All diligent students are successful; all ignorant students are unsuccessful. So, no diligent students are ignorant.

7. All selfish men are unpopular. All obliging men are popular. So, all obliging men are unselfish.

8. Gold is heavy. Nothing but gold will silence him. So, nothing light will silence him.

9. His songs always last an hour; a song that lasts an hour is tedious. So, his songs are always tedious.

10. Ill-managed business is unprofitable. Universities are invariably ill managed. Therefore, all universities are unprofitable.

11. No professors are ignorant. All vain people are ignorant. So, no professors are vain.

▸ **12.** All wasps are unfriendly; no puppies are unfriendly. So, puppies are not wasps.

13. Bores are dreaded. No one who is dreaded is ever begged to prolong his visit. So, no bore is ever begged to prolong his visit.

14. No son of mine is dishonest. People always treat an honest man with respect. Therefore, no son of mine ever fails to be treated with respect.

15. No misers are unselfish. None but misers save egg shells. So, people who save egg shells are selfish.

16. All young lambs jump. No young animals are unhealthy if they jump. So, all young lambs are healthy.

17. A prudent man shuns hyenas. No banker is imprudent. Thus, no banker fails to shun hyenas.

▶ **18.** Improbable stories are not easily believed. None of his stories are probable. So, none of his stories are easily believed.

19. No thieves are honest. All dishonest people are found out. Therefore, all thieves are found out.

20. All wise men walk on their feet; all unwise men walk on their hands. Therefore, every man walks on either his hands or his feet.

21. No wheelbarrows are comfortable. No uncomfortable vehicles are popular. So, no wheelbarrows are popular.

22. John never orders anything I ought to do; Peter never orders anything I ought not to do. So, John and Peter never give the same order.

23. None of my boys are conceited; none of my girls are greedy. All my children are either boys or girls. Thus, no conceited child of mine is greedy.

▶ **24.** None of my boys are clever; none but a clever boy could solve this problem. So, none of my boys could solve this problem.

25. No experienced person is incompetent. Everyone on our staff is always blundering; no competent person is always blundering. Therefore, everyone on our staff is inexperienced.

26. No terriers wander among the signs of the zodiac. Nothing that does not wander among the signs of the zodiac is a comet. Nothing but a terrier has a curly tail. Therefore, comets do not have curly tails.

27. All members of the House of Commons have perfect self-command; no member of Parliament who wears a coronet should ride in a donkey race. All members of the House of Lords wear coronets. All members of Parliament who are not members of the House of Commons are members of the House of Lords. Therefore, no members of Parliament should ride in a donkey race, unless they have perfect self-command.

28. Showy talkers think too much of themselves. No really well-informed people are bad company. People who think too much of themselves are not good company. Therefore, showy talkers are not really well informed.

29. Things sold in the street are of no great value. Nothing but rubbish can be had for a song. Eggs of the great auk are very valuable. It is only what is sold in the street that is really rubbish. Therefore, eggs of the great auk can't be had for a song.

▶ **30.** None of the unnoticed things met at sea are mermaids. Things entered in the log, as met with at sea, are sure to be worth remembering. I have never met with anything worth remembering when on a voyage. Things met with at sea that are noticed are sure to be recorded in the log. Therefore, I have never met a mermaid.

31. There is no box of mine here that I dare open. My writing desk is made of rosewood. All my boxes are painted, except those here. There is no box of mine I dare not open, unless it is full of live scorpions. All my rosewood boxes are unpainted. Therefore, my desk is full of live scorpions.

32. Every idea of mine that cannot be expressed in a syllogism is really ridiculous; none of my ideas about bath-buns are worth writing down. No idea of mine that fails to come true can be expressed as a syllogism. I never have any really ridiculous idea that I do not at once refer to my solicitor. My dreams are all about bath-buns. I never refer any idea of mine to my solicitor unless it is worth writing down. Therefore, all my dreams come true.

33. The only animals in this house are cats. Every animal that loves to gaze at the moon is suitable for a pet. When I detest an animal, I avoid it. No animals are carnivorous, unless they prowl at night. No cat fails to kill mice. No animals ever take to me, except those in this house. Kangaroos are not suitable pets. None but carnivores kill mice. I detest animals that do not take to me. Animals that prowl at night always love to gaze at the moon. Therefore, I always avoid a kangaroo.

Use deduction to show that these arguments are valid. (Symbolize universal negative sentences with universal quantifiers.)

34. Only clever students can solve this problem, and all clever students have taken logic. So, only students who have taken logic can solve this problem.

35. All who do not remember the past are condemned to repeat it. No one condemned to repeat the past looks forward to the future with eagerness. So, everyone who eagerly looks forward to the future remembers the past.

▶ **36.** John respects no one who insults him. Everyone who dislikes John insults him. Thus, John respects only those who like him.

37. Anyone who is not an idiot can see that Jake is lying. Nobody in this room can tell that Jake is lying. Hence, all the people in this room are idiots.

38. Most people would consider anyone who shows no fear in the face of danger to be courageous. Anybody who would be considered courageous by most people deserves recognition. Therefore, only those who show fear in the face of danger deserve no recognition.

39. Genevieve befriends anyone who has been treated unfairly. But she doesn't befriend any really obnoxious people. So, all really obnoxious people receive fair treatment.

40. All who are either insecure or frightened face new situations with dread. Only those who have had bad experiences in the past and have not overcome them dread new situations. Everyone who has been threatened is frightened, and everyone who lacks confidence is insecure. Thus, only those confident people who have not been threatened either have had no bad experiences or have overcome them.

Show, using deduction, that these argument forms are valid.

41. $\forall x(Fx \mathrel{\&} Gx)$; $\therefore$ $\forall xFx \mathrel{\&} \forall xGx$

▶ **42.** $\forall xFx \mathrel{\&} \forall xGx$; $\therefore$ $\forall x(Fx \mathrel{\&} Gx)$

43. $\forall x(Fx \leftrightarrow Gx)$; $\forall xFx$; $\therefore$ $\forall xGx$

44. $\forall x(Fx \leftrightarrow (Gx \mathrel{\&} Hx))$; $\therefore$ $\forall x(Fx \rightarrow Gx) \mathrel{\&} \forall x(Fx \rightarrow Hx)$

45. $\forall x((Fx \lor Gx) \rightarrow Hx)$; $\therefore$ $\forall x(Fx \rightarrow Hx) \mathrel{\&} \forall x(Gx \rightarrow Hx)$

46. $\forall x(Fx \rightarrow Hx)$; $\forall x(Gx \rightarrow Hx)$; $\therefore$ $\forall x((Fx \lor Gx) \rightarrow Hx)$

47. $\forall x(Fx \leftrightarrow (\neg Gx \mathrel{\&} \neg Fx))$; $\therefore$ $\forall xGx$

▶ **48.** $\forall x(Fx \leftrightarrow (\neg Gx \lor \neg Fx))$; $\therefore$ $\forall x \neg Gx$

49. $\forall x(Fx \leftrightarrow (\neg Gx \rightarrow \neg Fx))$; $\therefore$ $\forall xGx$

50. $\forall x(Fx \leftrightarrow (\neg Gx \leftrightarrow \neg Fx))$; $\therefore$ $\forall xGx$

51. $\forall x(Fx \rightarrow Hx)$; $\forall x(\neg Gx \rightarrow \neg(Hx \lor Jx))$; $\therefore$ $\forall x(\neg Fx \lor Gx)$

52. $\forall x((Fx \mathrel{\&} Gx) \rightarrow Hx)$; $\forall xGx \mathrel{\&} \forall xFx$; $\therefore$ $\forall x(Fx \mathrel{\&} Hx)$

53. $\forall x((Fx \lor Gx) \rightarrow (Hx \mathrel{\&} Jx))$; $\forall x(Rx \rightarrow Fx)$; $\forall x(\neg Gx \rightarrow Rx)$; $\therefore$ $\forall x(Hx \mathrel{\&} Jx)$

▶ **54.** $\forall x(Fx \rightarrow (Gx \lor Hx))$; $\forall x((Jx \mathrel{\&} Fx) \rightarrow \neg Gx)$; $\forall x(\neg Fx \rightarrow \neg Jx)$; $\therefore$ $\forall x(Jx \rightarrow Hx)$

55. $\forall x((Fx \rightarrow \neg Gx) \rightarrow (\neg Hx \mathrel{\&} \neg Jx))$; $\forall x(Kx \rightarrow Hx)$; $\therefore$ $\forall x(Kx \rightarrow (Fx \mathrel{\&} Gx))$

Use deduction to show that these argument forms involving polyadic predicates are valid.

56. $\forall x \forall y(Fxy \rightarrow Fyx)$; $\therefore$ $\forall x \forall y(Fxy \leftrightarrow Fyx)$

57. $\forall x \forall y \forall z((Fxy \mathrel{\&} Fyz) \rightarrow \neg Fxz)$; $\therefore$ $\forall x \neg Fxx$

58. $\forall x \forall y(Fxy \lor Fyx)$; $\forall x \forall y(Fxy \rightarrow Fyx)$; $\therefore$ $\forall x \forall y Fxy$

59. $\forall x \forall y \forall z((Fxy \mathrel{\&} Fyz) \rightarrow Fxz)$; $\forall x \neg Fxx$; $\therefore$ $\forall x \forall y(Fxy \rightarrow \neg Fyx)$

▶ **60.** $\forall x \forall y \forall z((Fxy \mathrel{\&} Fxz) \rightarrow Fyz)$; $\therefore$ $\forall x \forall y \forall z((Fxy \mathrel{\&} Fxz) \rightarrow Fzy)$

61. $\forall x \forall y \forall z((Fxy \mathrel{\&} Fxz) \rightarrow Fyz)$; $\forall x \neg Fxx$; $\therefore$ $\forall x \forall y \neg Fxy$

62. $\forall x \forall y \forall z((Fxy \ \& \ Fyz) \rightarrow Fxz)$; $\forall x \forall y(Fxy \rightarrow Fyx)$; $\exists x \exists y Fxy$; $\therefore \ \exists x Fxx$

63. $\forall x \forall y \forall z((Fxy \ \& \ Fyz) \rightarrow Fxz)$; $\forall x \neg Fxx$; $\therefore \ \forall x \forall y(Fxy \rightarrow \neg Fyx)$

64. $\forall x \forall y \forall z((Fxy \ \& \ Fxz) \rightarrow Fyz)$; $\forall x \forall y(Fxy \rightarrow Fyx)$; $\forall x Fxx$;
    $\therefore \ \forall x \forall y \forall z((Fxy \ \& \ Fyz) \rightarrow Fxz)$

65. $\forall x \forall y \forall z((Fxy \ \& \ Fyz) \rightarrow Fxz)$; $\forall x \forall y(Fxy \rightarrow Fyx)$; $\forall x Fxx$;
    $\therefore \ \forall x \forall y \forall z((Fxy \ \& \ Fxz) \rightarrow Fyz)$

13.3 Formulas with Overlapping Quantifiers

The final restriction on UG is needed only to cope with formulas having quantifiers that overlap in scope. It provides a way to distinguish in a proof 'something or other' from 'some one thing' or 'something in particular'. It requires that no constant in $\forall v \mathcal{A}$ depend on c. To understand this idea, we need to define *dependence* among constants.

> **Definition** A constant c *immediately depends on* a constant d in a proof if and only if c is introduced into the proof by applying ES to a formula containing d.

> **Definition** A constant c *depends on* a constant d if and only if there is a chain of constants $c_1, \dots, c_n$ such that c immediately depends on c_1, c_1 immediately depends on $c_2, \dots$, and c_n immediately depends on d. (The chain may be empty; immediate dependence is a kind of dependence.)

Suppose that we apply ES at some stage of a proof:

    n. $\exists v \mathcal{A}$
    m. $\mathcal{A}[c/v]$ ES, n

Then c depends on all other constants in $\exists v \mathcal{A}$. Moreover, c depends on all constants on which those constants depend. To take a concrete example:

    1. $\exists x(\exists y(Fx \ \& \ Fy) \ \& \ Fa)$ A
    2. $\exists y(Fb \ \& \ Fy) \ \& \ Fa$ ES, 1 (*b* depends on *a*)
    3. $\exists y(Fb \ \& \ Fy)$ S, 2
    4. $Fb \ \& \ Fc$ ES, 3 (*b* depends on *a*;
                                  c depends on *b* and *a*)

On line 2, we apply ES to a formula containing the constant *a*, thereby introducing *b*. So, *b* immediately depends on *a*. On line 4, we again apply ES. This time, the constant *b* is already present; applying the rule introduces *c*. So, *c* immediately depends on *b*. Since *b* immediately depends on *a*, *c* also depends on *a*.

The fourth restriction on UG sounds complicated; it may seem to make applying UG more trouble than it's worth. But we can keep track of dependence among constants very easily in a *dependency diagram*. These diagrams aren't official parts of proofs, but they make it easier to check whether the restrictions on UG are being obeyed. To construct a dependency diagram, wait until the first application of ES. Suppose the proof, so far, looks like this:

1. $\exists x(Fx \rightarrow (Ga \;\&\; Hb))$ A
2. $\exists x(Gx \;\&\; Fa)$ A
3. $Fc \rightarrow (Ga \;\&\; Hb)$ ES, 1

First, list horizontally the constants in the formula to which the rule has been applied (if there are any). Here, we've applied the rule to the formula on line 1, which contains a and b. So, we write a and b horizontally:

$a \qquad b$

Then, we write the new constant introduced below them and circle it, drawing lines to connect it to the others in the formula. Here, we've introduced c:

$a \qquad b$

$\widehat{c}$

Continuing the proof, we might apply ES again:

1. $\exists x(Fx \rightarrow (Ga \;\&\; Hb))$ A
2. $\exists x(Gx \;\&\; Fa)$ A
3. $Fc \rightarrow (Ga \;\&\; Hb)$ ES, 1
4. $Gd \;\&\; Fa$ ES, 2

First, we add to the diagram any constants appearing in the formula to which we've applied the rule—in this case, $\exists x(Gx \;\&\; Fa)$, on line 2—that aren't already there. In this case, a is already on the diagram. Then, we write the new constant we've introduced—here, d—below the other nodes, circling it and linking it to the others in the resulting formula (here, a). So, we obtain:

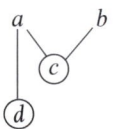

This diagram indicates that c depends on both a and b and that d depends on a.

What is the intuitive significance of dependence? In Chapter 10, we saw that there is a difference between

(12) Everyone likes someone (or other).

and

(13) Some one person is liked by everyone.

In (12), the identity of the 'someone'—the person liked—depends on who's doing the liking. Our diagrams reflect this fact. We would symbolize (12) as

(14) $\forall x \exists y Lxy$,

which, applying the obvious rules, might lead to these steps in a deduction:

(15)　n.　$\forall x \exists y Lxy$

　　　　m.　$\exists y Lay$　　　US, n　　　a

　　　　k.　Lab　　　　　ES, m　　Ⓑ

(Again, the dependency diagram is on the right.) Notice that b depends on a; who is being liked depends on who is liking. The situation is very different with (13), which we could symbolize as

(16) $\exists x \forall y Lyx$

This might lead to these deduction steps:

(17)　n.　$\exists x \forall y Lyx$

　　　　m.　$\forall y Lyb$　　　ES, n　　Ⓑ

　　　　k.　Lab　　　　US, m

Here, a and b are independent. Who is liked does not depend on who is liking. The notion of dependence thus reflects concepts that in English we capture by ordering noun phrases, choosing determiners, and using phrases such as 'or other', 'a certain', 'in particular', 'one', and so on.

To summarize: Dependency diagrams change only when we apply ES. When we do apply existential specification, moving from $\exists v \mathcal{A}$ to $\mathcal{A}[c/v]$, we follow these rules:

> 1. Write, horizontally, the constants in $\exists v \mathcal{A}$ not already in the diagram.
> 2. Add the new constant c below the constants in $\exists v \mathcal{A}$, circling it and drawing lines linking it to them.

We can use these diagrams to check the fulfillment of the third and fourth restrictions on UG. The third bans the use of the same constant in ES and UG. Dependency diagrams show which constants have been introduced by ES: They appear circled. So, applying UG to a constant circled in the diagram is prohibited. The fourth restriction requires that in moving from $\mathcal{A}[c/v]$ to $\forall v \mathcal{A}$, no constant in $\forall v \mathcal{A}$ depend on c. The restriction is satisfied provided that no constant in $\mathcal{A}[c/v]$ is linked upward to c.

To see why the fourth restriction is needed and to see how to use dependency diagrams to check on its satisfaction, consider this invalid argument.

(In the last chapter, we saw that it generates an infinite tableau.)

(18) Everything has a cause.

∴ Something is the cause of everything.

We could try to prove it valid by constructing this deduction. The corresponding dependency diagram, constructed in one step (because there is one application of ES in the proof), appears on the right:

1. $\forall x \exists y C y x$ A
2. $\exists y C y a$ US, 1
3. $C b a$ ES, 2
4. $\forall x C b x$ UG, 3 (Wrong!)
5. $\exists y \forall x C y x$ EG, 4

Step 4 fails because b is linked upward to a in the diagram. That is, b depends on a. So, we can't universally generalize on a.

This example illustrates why dependence is important. Imagine an extended English argument mirroring the flawed proof:

(19)
1. Everything has a cause.   A
2. Take your passing this course (a); it has a cause.   US, 1
3. Passing the exam (b), let us say, causes you to pass the course (a).   ES, 2
4. Passing the exam (b) causes everything.   UG, 3 (Wrong!)
5. Something causes everything.   EG, 4

The proof introduces b (passing the exam) as the cause of a (passing the course). The identity of b depends on the identity of a; different events have different causes.

Problems

In Chapter 10, we asserted that the order of existential quantifiers within a string of such quantifiers makes no difference; the same holds true for universal quantifiers. Illustrate this assertion by showing valid both these argument forms:

▶ **1.** $\exists x \exists y F x y$; ∴ $\exists y \exists x F x y$ ▶ **2.** $\forall x \forall y F x y$; ∴ $\forall y \forall x F x y$

Although, in general, we can't switch existential and universal quantifiers in order to reach an equivalent formula, we can do so in special circumstances. Show that each of these switches is legitimate.

▶ **3.** $\exists x \forall y F x y$; ∴ $\forall y \exists x F x y$

▶ **4.** $\forall x \exists y (F x \ \& \ G y)$; ∴ $\exists y \forall x (F x \ \& \ G y)$*

These argument forms are invalid. (a) Show that, without restriction 4 on UG, they would be provable. (b) Show where your "proofs" violate restriction 4.

5. $\forall x \exists y (Fx \rightarrow Gxy)$; $\therefore$ $\exists y \forall x (Fx \rightarrow Gxy)$

6. $\forall x \forall y \exists z (Fxz \& Fzy)$; $\forall x \forall y (Fxy \rightarrow Gyx)$; $\therefore$ $\exists x \forall y \forall z (Gxy \& Gzx)$

7. $\forall x \exists y \forall z (\exists w Fwy \& (Gxy \rightarrow Gzy))$; $\therefore$ $\exists w \forall x \exists y \forall z (Fwy \& (Gxy \rightarrow Gzy))$

Use deduction to show that these argument forms are valid.

8. $\forall x (Fx \rightarrow \forall y (Gy \rightarrow Hxy))$; $\exists x (Fx \& \exists y \neg Hxy)$; $\therefore$ $\exists x \neg Gx$

9. $\exists x (Fx \& \forall y (Gy \rightarrow Hxy))$; $\therefore$ $\exists x (Fx \& (Ga \rightarrow Hxa))$

10. $\forall x (\exists y Fxy \rightarrow \exists y \neg Gy)$; $\exists x \exists y Fxy$; $\forall x (Gx \leftrightarrow \neg Hx)$; $\therefore$ $\exists x Hx$

11. $\forall x (Mx \rightarrow Hx)$; $\exists x \exists y ((Fx \& Mx) \& (Gy \& Jyx))$;
$\exists x Hx \rightarrow \forall y \forall z (\neg Hy \rightarrow \neg Jyz)$; $\therefore$ $\exists x (Gx \& Hx)$

▶ **12.** $\forall x (\exists y Fxy \rightarrow \forall y Fyx)$; $\exists x \exists y Fxy$; $\therefore$ $\forall x \forall y Fxy$

13. $\exists x \forall y (\exists z Fyz \rightarrow Fyx)$; $\forall x \exists y Fxy$; $\therefore$ $\exists x \forall y Fyx$

14. $\exists x \forall y \neg Fxy$; $\therefore$ $\exists x \forall y \forall z (Fxz \rightarrow Fzy)$

15. $\forall x (Sx \rightarrow \exists y (Sy \& \forall z (Bzy \leftrightarrow (Bzx \& Bzz))))$; $\forall x \neg Bxx$; $\exists x Sx$;
$\therefore$ $\exists x (Sx \& \forall y \neg Byx)$

16. $\forall x (\exists y (Ay \& Bxy) \rightarrow Cx)$; $\exists y (Dy \& \exists x (Fx \& Gx \& Byx))$; $\forall x (Fx \rightarrow Ax)$;
$\exists x (Cx \& Dx) \rightarrow (\exists y (Dy \& \exists z Byz) \rightarrow \forall x Fx)$; $\therefore$ $\forall x Ax$

17. $\forall x \forall y ((Ax \& By) \rightarrow Cxy)$; $\exists y (Fy \& \forall z (Hz \rightarrow Cyz))$;
$\forall x \forall y \forall z ((Cxy \& Cyz) \rightarrow Cxz)$; $\forall x (Fx \rightarrow Bx)$; $\therefore$ $\forall z \forall y ((Az \& Hy) \rightarrow Czy)$

13.4 QUANTIFIERS AND CONNECTIVES

It's useful to have a way of relating quantifiers and connectives. Our rules allow us to attack formulas with quantifiers as main connectives in one step. But, if a negation precedes a quantifier, or if the quantified formula is part of a disjunction, the proof strategy becomes much more complicated. Luckily, negations, disjunctions, and other relationships among quantified formulas are equivalent to formulas with quantifiers as main connectives. Rules expressing these equivalences are called *rules of passage*.

Stating these rules requires an additional bit of terminology. We say that quantifiers $\exists v$ and $\forall v$ are *on* the variable v.

> **DEFINITION** A protoformula of QL is a string of symbols that results from deleting one or more quantifiers from a formula of QL. If a deleted quantifier was on a variable v, then v is *free* in the protoformula.

Thus, the formulas on the left below are formulas; those on the right are protoformulas. (The free variables are listed to the right.)

Formula of QL	Protoformula of QL	Free Variables
$\exists x F x$	$F x$	x
$\forall y F a y$	$F a y$	y
$\exists x \forall y G x y$	$\forall y G x y$	x
$\exists x \forall y G x y$	$\exists x G x y$	y
$\exists x \forall y G x y$	$G x y$	x, y
$\exists x F x \rightarrow \forall z H z$	$\exists x F x \rightarrow H z$	z
$\exists x F x \rightarrow \forall z H z$	$F x \rightarrow H z$	x, z

The rules of this section (except VR) apply to protoformulas as well as formulas.

Quantifier Negation

Two *quantifier negation* rules relate quantified formulas to their negations. In the process, these rules relate the universal and existential quantifiers. In fact, they show how to define each quantifier in terms of the other. They underlie the equivalence of the following pairs of sentences:

(20) a. Not everyone will show up.
  b. Somebody will fail to show up.

(21) a. Jerry couldn't see a thing.
  b. Everything was such that Jerry couldn't see it.

Quantifier Negation (QN)

n.	$\neg \exists v \mathscr{A}$	QN, m
m.	$\forall v \neg \mathscr{A}$	QN, n
n.	$\neg \forall v \mathscr{A}$	QN, m
m.	$\exists v \neg \mathscr{A}$	QN, n

Both versions of quantifier negation invert. That is, the premise and conclusion are equivalent; therefore, the rules work in both directions. We can infer $\exists x \neg F x$ from $\neg \forall x F x$, and vice versa. Similarly, just by adding a negation sign, we can see that $\exists x F x$ is equivalent to $\neg \forall x \neg F x$, and that $\forall x F x$ is equivalent to $\neg \exists x \neg F x$. So, we can define the quantifiers in terms of each other.

Because QN takes the form of an equivalence, and because it involves protoformulas as well as formulas, the replacement principle allows us to apply it to portions of formulas as well as to entire formulas. Each of the following is thus a legitimate application of QN.

$$\neg \exists x Fxx \qquad\qquad \forall x \neg Fxx$$
$$\neg \forall x \forall y Gxy \qquad\qquad \exists x \neg \forall y Gxy$$
$$\forall x \forall y \neg \forall z(Fxz \,\&\, Fyz) \qquad \forall x \forall y \exists z \neg (Fxz \,\&\, Fyz)$$
$$\exists x \neg \exists y Gyx \qquad\qquad \exists x \forall y \neg Gyx$$

We can apply QN several times in a single step: We can abbreviate

$\neg \forall x \forall y \forall z((Rxy \,\&\, Ryz) \to Rxz)$	
$\exists x \neg \forall y \forall z((Rxy \,\&\, Ryz) \to Rxz)$	QN
$\exists x \exists y \neg \forall z((Rxy \,\&\, Ryz) \to Rxz)$	QN
$\exists x \exists y \exists z \neg ((Rxy \,\&\, Ryz) \to Rxz)$	QN

to

$\neg \forall x \forall y \forall z((Rxy \,\&\, Ryz) \to Rxz)$	
$\exists x \exists y \exists z \neg ((Rxy \,\&\, Ryz) \to Rxz)$	QN^3

We can use quantifier negation to demonstrate the validity of

(22) Everyone who came to the party was arrested.
Not all my friends were arrested.
∴ Not all my friends came to the party.

After symbolizing, we can construct this proof:

1. $\forall x(Cx \to Ax)$	A		
2. $\neg \forall x(Fx \to Ax)$	A		
3. $\exists x \neg (Fx \to Ax)$	QN, 2		
4. $\neg (Fa \to Aa)$	ES, 3		ⓐ
5. $Fa \,\&\, \neg Aa$	NC, 4		
6. Fa	S, 5		
7. $\neg Aa$	S, 5		
8. $Ca \to Aa$	US, 1		
9. $\neg Ca$	MT, 8, 7		
10. $Fa \,\&\, \neg Ca$	C, 6, 9		
11. $\neg (Fa \to Ca)$	NC, 10		
12. $\exists x \neg (Fx \to Cx)$	EG, 11		
13. $\neg \forall x(Fx \to Cx)$	QN, 12		

Other Rules of Passage

Another rule of passage relates quantifiers to disjunctions. It underlies the equivalence of sentences such as:

(23) a. There's a witness who lied unless Hank did.
b. Unless Hank lied, there's a witness who did.

(24) a. Each of us will come unless it rains.
b. Unless it rains, we'll all come.

Rule of Passage—Disjunction (RP∨)

Existential:

n.	$\underline{\exists v \mathcal{A} \vee \mathcal{B}}$ (or $\mathcal{B} \vee \exists v \mathcal{A}$)	RP∨, m
m.	$\exists v(\mathcal{A} \vee \mathcal{B})$ (or $\exists v(\mathcal{B} \vee \mathcal{A})$)	RP∨, n

Here v is in $\mathcal{A}$ but not $\mathcal{B}$.

Universal:

n.	$\underline{\forall v \mathcal{A} \vee \mathcal{B}}$ (or $\mathcal{B} \vee \forall v \mathcal{A}$)	RP∨, m
m.	$\forall v(\mathcal{A} \vee \mathcal{B})$ (or $\forall v(\mathcal{B} \vee \mathcal{A})$)	RP∨, n

Here v is in $\mathcal{A}$ but not $\mathcal{B}$.

We can use this rule to show that this argument is valid:

(25) Either something is missing, or something is out of place.
Anything missing should be reported.
Anything out of place should be found.
∴ Something should be reported or found.

Symbolizing the argument as $\exists x M x \vee \exists y P y$; $\forall x(M x \to R x)$; $\forall x(P x \to F x)$; ∴ $\exists x(R x \vee F x)$, we can construct this proof:

1.	$\exists x M x \vee \exists y P y$	A
2.	$\forall x(M x \to R x)$	A
3.	$\forall x(P x \to F x)$	A
4.	$\exists x(M x \vee \exists y P y)$	RP∨, 1
5.	$M a \vee \exists y P y$	ES, 4
6.	$\exists y(M a \vee P y)$	RP∨, 5
7.	$M a \vee P b$	ES, 6
8.	$M a \to R a$	US, 2
9.	$P b \to F b$	US, 3
10.	$R a \vee F b$	CD, 7, 8, 9
11.	$R a \to (R a \vee F a)$	W
12.	$\neg R a \vee (R a \vee F a)$	MC, 11
13.	$\exists x(\neg R a \vee (R x \vee F x))$	EG, 12
14.	$\neg R a \vee \exists x(R x \vee F x)$	RP∨, 13
15.	$R a \to \exists x(R x \vee F x)$	MC, 14
16.	$F b \to (R b \vee F b)$	W
17.	$\neg F b \vee (R b \vee F b)$	MC, 16
18.	$\exists x(\neg F b \vee (R x \vee F x))$	EG, 17
19.	$\neg F b \vee \exists x(R x \vee F x)$	RP∨, 18
20.	$F b \to \exists x(R x \vee F x)$	MC, 19
21.	$\exists x(R x \vee F x)$	CD, 10, 15, 20

This proof suggests other rules of passage that we can derive from the rules already presented. Conditionals, by MC, are equivalent to certain disjunctions. So, we can derive rules of passage involving conditionals from the rule for disjunctions. Because $\mathscr{A} \to \mathscr{B}$ is equivalent to $\neg\mathscr{A} \vee \mathscr{B}$, however, we must take care to distinguish the antecedent from the consequent of a conditional. They require different rules. The first rules concern quantifiers in the consequent of a conditional. They underlie the equivalence of these pairs of sentences:

(26) a. If McCartney doesn't perform, everyone will be upset.
   b. Each person will be upset if McCartney doesn't perform.

(27) a. If the FBI suspects Glenda, someone will tail her.
   b. There's someone who will tail Glenda if the FBI suspects her.

Rule of Passage—Conditional (Consequents) (RP→)

Existential:

n. $\underline{\mathscr{A} \to \exists v\mathscr{B}}$ RP→, m
m. $\exists v(\mathscr{A} \to \mathscr{B})$ RP→, n

Universal:

n. $\underline{\mathscr{A} \to \forall v\mathscr{B}}$ RP→, m
m. $\forall v(\mathscr{A} \to \mathscr{B})$ RP→, n

Here v is in $\mathscr{B}$ but not $\mathscr{A}$.

We can use these rules to demonstrate that this argument is valid:

(28) Ann knows of some programs that will shut down if the budget isn't increased.
   ∴ If the budget isn't increased, some programs will shut down.

We can symbolize this as $\exists x(Kax \ \& \ Px \ \& \ (\neg Ib \to Sx))$;
∴ $\neg Ib \to \exists x(Px \ \& \ Sx)$ and construct the following proof:

1. $\exists x(Kax \ \& \ Px \ \& \ (\neg Ib \to Sx))$ A
2. $Kac \ \& \ Pc \ \& \ (\neg Ib \to Sc)$ ES, 1
3. $\neg Ib \to Sc$ S, 2
4. Pc S, 2
5. $Ib \vee Pc$ Ad, 4
6. $\neg Ib \to Pc$ MC, 5
7. $\neg Ib \to (Pc \ \& \ Sc)$ CC, 6, 3
8. $\exists x(\neg Ib \to (Px \ \& \ Sx))$ EG, 7
9. $\neg Ib \to \exists x(Px \ \& \ Sx)$ RP→, 8

The rules for antecedents of conditionals look surprising, because they switch quantifiers. They underlie the equivalence of pairs of sentences like these:

(29) a. If you laugh at everything, you'll embarrass us.
   b. Something is such that you'll embarrass us if you laugh at it.

(30) a. If you steal something, you'll be prosecuted.
   b. Everything is such that you'll be prosecuted if you steal it.

Rule of Passage—Conditional (Antecedents) (RP→)

Existential:

н.	$\exists v \mathscr{A} \to \mathscr{B}$	RP→, m
m.	$\forall v(\mathscr{A} \to \mathscr{B})$	RP→, n

Universal:

n.	$\forall v \mathscr{A} \to \mathscr{B}$	RP→, m
m.	$\exists v(\mathscr{A} \to \mathscr{B})$	RP→, n

Here v is in $\mathscr{A}$ but not $\mathscr{B}$.

These rules allow a straightforward proof of the validity of the following argument:

(31) If Stan raises anything that makes Denise upset, he'll be sorry.
   Any objection will make Francis look bad.
   Anything that makes Francis look bad upsets Denise.
   ∴ If Stan raises an objection, he'll be sorry.

We might symbolize this as $\forall x((Rsx \ \& \ Uxd) \to Ss)$; $\forall x(Ox \to Mxf)$; $\forall x(Mxf \to Uxd)$; ∴ $\exists x(Ox \ \& \ Rsx) \to Ss$, proceeding with the proof:

1.	$\forall x((Rsx \ \& \ Uxd) \to Ss)$	A
2.	$\forall x(Ox \to Mxf)$	A
3.	$\forall x(Mxf \to Uxd)$	A
4.	$(Rsa \ \& \ Uad) \to Ss$	US, 1
5.	$Oa \to Maf$	US, 2
6.	$Maf \to Uad$	US, 3
7.	$Oa \to Uad$	HS, 5, 6
8.	$(Oa \ \& \ Rsa) \to Oa$	W
9.	$(Oa \ \& \ Rsa) \to Uad$	HS, 8, 7
10.	$(Oa \ \& \ Rsa) \to Rsa$	W
11.	$(Oa \ \& \ Rsa) \to (Rsa \ \& \ Uad)$	CC, 10, 9
12.	$(Oa \ \& \ Rsa) \to Ss$	HS, 11, 4

13. $\forall x((Ox \ \& \ Rsx) \rightarrow Ss)$ UG, 12
14. $\exists x(Ox \ \& \ Rsx) \rightarrow Ss$ RP$\rightarrow$, 13

The final rules of passage relate quantifiers and conjunctions.

Rules of Passage—Conjunction (RP&)

Existential:

n. $\underline{\exists v \mathcal{A}} \ \& \ \mathcal{B}$ (or $\mathcal{B} \ \& \ \exists v \mathcal{A}$)   RP&, m
m. $\exists v(\mathcal{A} \ \& \ \mathcal{B})$ (or $\exists v(\mathcal{B} \ \& \ \mathcal{A})$)   RP&, n

Universal:

n. $\underline{\forall v \mathcal{A}} \ \& \ \mathcal{B}$ (or $\mathcal{B} \ \& \ \forall v \mathcal{A}$)   RP&, m
m. $\forall v(\mathcal{A} \ \& \ \mathcal{B})$ (or $\forall v(\mathcal{B} \ \& \ \mathcal{A})$)   RP&, n

Here v is in $\mathcal{A}$ but not $\mathcal{B}$.

Rewriting Variables

Variables have no independent meanings. The formulas $\forall x F x$ and $\forall z F z$ function in logically similar ways; so do $\exists y G y$ and $\exists w G w$. Indeed, it's easy to show that these pairs are equivalent. Here are the proofs in one direction:

1.	$\forall x F x$	A		1.	$\exists y G y$	A	
2.	$F a$	US, 1		2.	$G a$	ES, 1	$\textcircled{a}$
3.	$\forall z F z$	UG, 2		3.	$\exists w G w$	EG, 2	

The proofs of the other directions follow exactly the same pattern.

Thus, we can substitute one variable for another throughout a formula. The only restriction we must observe is that we shouldn't introduce into a formula a variable that is already there; otherwise we could go from the legitimate formula $\forall x \forall y F x y$ to the very different nonformula $\forall x \forall x F x x$.

Variable Rewrite (VR)

n. $\underline{\mathcal{A}}$ VR, m
m. $\mathcal{A}[v/u]$ VR, n

Here u is in $\mathcal{A}$ but v is not.

This rule applies to subformulas as well as entire formulas. It's useful chiefly in combination with rules of passage. Suppose that, at some stage in a proof, we have the formula $\exists x Fx \lor \exists x Gx$. Because disjunctions can be hard to exploit, especially when the disjuncts contain quantifiers, it would help to transform this formula into one with a quantifier as main connective. But we can't apply RP∨; x is in both disjuncts. Trying to apply the rule would lead us to $\exists x(Fx \lor \exists x Gx)$, which isn't a formula. Our formation rules never allow quantifiers on the same variable to overlap in scope. But we can apply the rule of passage if we first switch variables in one disjunct. $\exists x Gx$ and $\exists y Gy$, for example, are equivalent. So, we can first obtain $\exists x Fx \lor \exists y Gy$ by variable rewrite, and then apply RP∨ to reach $\exists x(Fx \lor \exists y Gy)$.

This rule, for example, allows us to show the validity of

(32) All mentally deranged people are dangerous.
    ∴ If there are mentally deranged people, some people are
      dangerous.

Taking the universe of discourse to be the set of people, we can symbolize this argument as $\forall x(Mx \to Dx)$; ∴ $\exists x Mx \to \exists x Dx$. The proof uses VR and rules of passage.

   1. $\forall x(Mx \to Dx)$ A
   2. $Ma \to Da$ US, 1
   3. $\exists y(Ma \to Dy)$ EG, 2
   4. $Ma \to \exists y Dy$ RP→, 3
   5. $\forall x(Mx \to \exists y Dy)$ UG, 4
   6. $\exists x Mx \to \exists y Dy$ RP→, 5
   7. $\exists x Mx \to \exists x Dx$ VR, 6

Variable rewrite also allows us to show that this argument is valid:

(33) Either some bats are vampires, or no stories about Dracula
    are true.
    All vampires drink blood.
    Some people believe some Dracula stories.
    ∴ Unless some bats drink blood, some people believe stories
      that aren't true.

The proof is difficult, and uses VR and rules of passage repeatedly.

   1. $\exists x(Bx \,\&\, Vx) \lor \neg\exists x(Sx \,\&\, Axd$
     $\&\, Tx)$ A
   2. $\forall x(Vx \to Dx)$ A

3. $\exists x(Px \ \& \ \exists y(Sy \ \& \ Ayd \ \& \ Bxy))$ ⟶ A

4. $Pa \ \& \ \exists y(Sy \ \& \ Ayd \ \& \ Bay)$ ⟶ ES, 3

5. Pa ⟶ S, 4

6. $\exists y(Sy \ \& \ Ayd \ \& \ Bay)$ ⟶ S, 4

7. $Sb \ \& \ Abd \ \& \ Bab$ ⟶ ES, 6

8. $\exists z(Bz \ \& \ Vz) \lor \neg \exists x(Sx \ \& \ Axd \ \& \ Tx)$ ⟶ VR, 1

9. $\exists z((Bz \ \& \ Vz) \lor \neg \exists x(Sx \ \& \ Axd \ \& \ Tx))$ ⟶ RP$\lor$, 8

10. $(Bc \ \& \ Vc) \lor \neg \exists x(Sx \ \& \ Axd \ \& \ Tx)$ ⟶ ES, 9

11. $(Bc \ \& \ Vc) \lor \forall x \neg (Sx \ \& \ Axd \ \& \ Tx)$ ⟶ QN, 10

12. $\forall x((Bc \ \& \ Vc) \lor \neg (Sx \ \& \ Axd \ \& \ Tx))$ ⟶ RP$\lor$, 11

13. $(Bc \ \& \ Vc) \lor \neg (Sb \ \& \ Abd \ \& \ Tb)$ ⟶ US, 12

14. $Vc \rightarrow Dc$ ⟶ US, 2

15. $(Bc \ \& \ Vc) \rightarrow Bc$ ⟶ W

16. $(Bc \ \& \ Vc) \rightarrow Vc$ ⟶ W

17. $(Bc \ \& \ Vc) \rightarrow Dc$ ⟶ HS, 16, 14

18. $(Bc \ \& \ Vc) \rightarrow (Bc \ \& \ Dc)$ ⟶ CC, 15, 17

19. $Sb \ \& \ Abd$ ⟶ S, 7

20. $\neg Tb \lor (Sb \ \& \ Abd)$ ⟶ Ad, 19

21. $Tb \rightarrow (Sb \ \& \ Abd)$ ⟶ MI, 20

22. $Tb \rightarrow Tb$ ⟶ SI

23. $Tb \rightarrow (Sb \ \& \ Abd \ \& \ Tb)$ ⟶ CC, 21, 22

24. $\neg (Sb \ \& \ Abd \ \& \ Tb) \rightarrow \neg Tb$ ⟶ Tr, 23

25. $(Bc \ \& \ Dc) \lor \neg Tb$ ⟶ CD, 13, 18, 24

26. Sb ⟶ S, 19

27. Bab ⟶ S, 7

28. $Pa \ \& \ Sb$ ⟶ C, 5, 26

29. $Pa \ \& \ Sb \ \& \ Bab$ ⟶ C, 28, 27

30. $Tb \lor (Pa \ \& \ Sb \ \& \ Bab)$ ⟶ Ad, 29

31. $\neg Tb \rightarrow (Pa \ \& \ Sb \ \& \ Bab)$ ⟶ MI, 30

32. $\neg Tb \rightarrow \neg Tb$ ⟶ SI

33. $\neg Tb \rightarrow (Pa \ \& \ Sb \ \& \ Bab \ \& \ \neg Tb)$ ⟶ CC, 31, 32

34. $(Bc \ \& \ Dc) \rightarrow (Bc \ \& \ Dc)$ ⟶ SI

35. $(Bc \ \& \ Dc) \lor (Pa \ \& \ Sb \ \& \ Bab \ \& \ \neg Tb)$ ⟶ CD, 25, 34, 33

36. $(Bc \ \& \ Dc) \lor (Pa \ \& \ Sb \ \& \ \neg Tb \ \& \ Bab)$ ⟶ Cm, 35

37. $\exists x((Bx \ \& \ Dx) \lor (Pa \ \& \ Sb \ \& \ \neg Tb \ \& \ Bab))$ ⟶ EG, 36

38. $\exists x(Bx \ \& \ Dx) \lor (Pa \ \& \ Sb \ \& \ \neg Tb \ \& \ Bab)$ ⟶ RP$\lor$, 37

39. $\exists y(\exists x(Bx \ \& \ Dx) \lor (Pa \ \& \ Sy$
    $\& \ \neg Ty \ \& \ Bay))$ EG, 38
40. $\exists x(Bx \ \& \ Dx) \lor \exists y(Pa \ \& \ Sy$
    $\& \ \neg Ty \ \& \ Bay)$ RP$\lor$, 39
41. $\exists x(Bx \ \& \ Dx) \lor (Pa \ \& \ \exists y(Sy \ \&$
    $\neg Ty \ \& \ Bay))$ RP&, 40
42. $\exists z(\exists x(Bx \ \& \ Dx) \lor (Pz \ \& \ \exists y(Sy$
    $\& \ \neg Ty \ \& \ Bzy)))$ EG, 41
43. $\exists x(Bx \ \& \ Dx) \lor \exists z(Pz \ \& \ \exists y(Sy$
    $\& \ \neg Ty \ \& \ Bzy))$ RP$\lor$, 42
44. $\exists x(Bx \ \& \ Dx) \lor \exists x(Px \ \& \ \exists y(Sy$
    $\& \ \neg Ty \ \& \ Bxy))$ VR, 43

Here is a summary of our rules for quantifiers:

Rules Applying Only to Entire Formulas

Existential Generalization (EG)

n. $\mathcal{A}[c/v]$
n + p. $\exists v \mathcal{A}$ EG, n

Here c may be any constant.

Existential Specification (ES)

n. $\exists v \mathcal{A}$
n + p. $\mathcal{A}[c/v]$ ES, n

Here c must be a constant new to the proof and must not appear in the proof's conclusion.

Universal Specification (US)

n. $\forall v \mathcal{A}$
n + p. $\mathcal{A}[c/v]$ US, n

Here c may be any constant.

Universal Generalization (UG)

$$n. \quad \mathscr{A}[c/v]$$
$$n + p. \; \forall v \mathscr{A} \qquad \text{UG, n}$$

Here 1. c must not occur in $\forall v \mathscr{A}$;
2. c must not occur in the assumptions or conclusion of the proof;
3. c must not have been introduced by ES;
4. No term remaining in $\forall v \mathscr{A}$ may depend on c.

INVERTIBLE RULES

Quantifier Negation (QN)

$$n. \quad \neg \exists v \mathscr{A} \qquad \text{QN, m}$$
$$m. \; \forall v \neg \mathscr{A} \qquad \text{QN, n}$$

$$n. \quad \neg \forall v \mathscr{A} \qquad \text{QN, m}$$
$$m. \; \exists v \neg \mathscr{A} \qquad \text{QN, n}$$

Rule of Passage—Disjunction (RP∨)

Existential:

$$n. \quad \exists v \mathscr{A} \vee \mathscr{B} \; (\text{or } \mathscr{B} \vee \exists v \mathscr{A}) \qquad \text{RP}\vee, \text{m}$$
$$m. \; \exists v (\mathscr{A} \vee \mathscr{B}) \, (\text{or } \exists v (\mathscr{B} \vee \mathscr{A})) \qquad \text{RP}\vee, \text{n}$$

Here v is in $\mathscr{A}$ but not $\mathscr{B}$.

Universal:

$$n. \quad \forall v \mathscr{A} \vee \mathscr{B} \; (\text{or } \mathscr{B} \vee \forall v \mathscr{A}) \qquad \text{RP}\vee, \text{m}$$
$$m. \; \forall v (\mathscr{A} \vee \mathscr{B}) \, (\text{or } \forall v (\mathscr{B} \vee \mathscr{A})) \qquad \text{RP}\vee, \text{n}$$

Here v is in $\mathscr{A}$ but not $\mathscr{B}$.

Rule of Passage—Conditional (Consequents) (RP→)

Existential:

n. $\underline{\mathscr{A} \rightarrow \exists v \mathscr{B}}$ RP→, m

m. $\exists v(\mathscr{A} \rightarrow \mathscr{B})$ RP→, n

Universal:

n. $\underline{\mathscr{A} \rightarrow \forall v \mathscr{B}}$ RP→, m

m. $\forall v(\mathscr{A} \rightarrow \mathscr{B})$ RP→, n

Here v is in $\mathscr{B}$ but not $\mathscr{A}$.

Rule of Passage—Conditional (Antecedents) (RP→)

Existential:

n. $\underline{\exists v \mathscr{A} \rightarrow \mathscr{B}}$ RP→, m

m. $\forall v(\mathscr{A} \rightarrow \mathscr{B})$ RP→, n

Universal:

n. $\underline{\forall v \mathscr{A} \rightarrow \mathscr{B}}$ RP→, m

m. $\exists v(\mathscr{A} \rightarrow \mathscr{B})$ RP→, n

Here v is in $\mathscr{A}$ but not $\mathscr{B}$.

Rules of Passage—Conjunction (RP&)

Existential:

n. $\underline{\exists v \mathscr{A} \mathbin{\&} \mathscr{B}}$ (or $\mathscr{B} \mathbin{\&} \exists v \mathscr{A}$)   RP&, m

m. $\exists v(\mathscr{A} \mathbin{\&} \mathscr{B})$ (or $\exists v(\mathscr{B} \mathbin{\&} \mathscr{A})$ RP&, n

Universal:

n. $\underline{\forall v \mathscr{A} \mathbin{\&} \mathscr{B}}$ (or $\mathscr{B} \mathbin{\&} \forall v \mathscr{A}$)   RP&, m

m. $\forall v(\mathscr{A} \mathbin{\&} \mathscr{B})$ (or $\forall v(\mathscr{B} \mathbin{\&} \mathscr{A})$ RP&, n

Here v is in $\mathscr{A}$ but not $\mathscr{B}$.

> ### Variable Rewrite (VR)
>
> n. $\mathscr{A}$ VR, m
>
> m. $\mathscr{A}[v/u]$ VR, n
>
> Here u is in $\mathscr{A}$ but v is not.

Problems

Using deduction, show that these arguments are valid.

▶ **1.** Every team that finishes in last place declares its next year a rebuilding year. So, no teams from Chicago will declare next year a rebuilding year only if no Chicago team finishes in last place.

▶ **2.** No Ivy League colleges have tuitions of under $8000 per year. Every state-affiliated college has a tuition under $8000 per year. A college is private if and only if it is not state affiliated. It follows that every Ivy League college is private.

▶ **3.** No mammals but bats can fly. Every commonly kept house pet is a mammal, but none are bats. So nothing that can fly is a commonly kept house pet.

▶ **4.** Nothing stupid is difficult. Everything you can do is stupid; anything that isn't difficult, I can do better than you. So anything you can do, I can do better.

▶ **5.** There are no good books that do not require their readers to think. Every book that has inspired acts of terror has been inflammatory. No inflammatory books require their readers to think. Therefore, all books that have inspired acts of terror are no good.

▶ **6.** Anyone with some brains can do logic. Nobody who has no brains is fit to program computers. No one who reads this book can do logic. So, no one who reads this book is fit to program computers.

7. A person is humble if and only if he or she doesn't admire himself or herself. It follows that nobody who admires all humble people is humble.

8. An Olympic athlete could outrun everyone on our team. Since none on our team can outrun themselves, there is no one on our team who is an Olympic athlete.

9. If nobody comes forward and confesses, then someone will be punished. So, someone will be punished if he or she doesn't confess.

10. An archetypal pig is something such that, if anything at all is a pig, *it* is. Therefore, there is an archetypal pig.

Although, in general, we can't switch existential and universal quantifiers in order to reach an equivalent formula, we can do so in special circumstances. Using rules of passage, show that each of these switches is legitimate.

11. $\exists x \forall y F x y; \therefore \forall y \exists x F x y$

► **12.** $\forall x \exists y (F x \& G y); \therefore \exists y \forall x (F x \& G y)$

13. $\forall x \exists y (F x \lor G y); \therefore \exists y \forall x (F x \lor G y)$

14. $\forall x \exists y (F x \rightarrow G y); \therefore \exists y \forall x (F x \rightarrow G y)$

15. $\forall x \exists y (G y \rightarrow F x); \therefore \exists y \forall x (G y \rightarrow F x)$

Use deduction to establish the validity of these argument forms.

16. $\exists x F x \rightarrow \exists x G x; \therefore \exists x (F x \rightarrow G x)$

17. $\exists x F x \lor \exists x G x; \therefore \exists x (F x \lor G x)$

► **18.** $\forall x (F x \rightarrow G x); \therefore \forall x F x \rightarrow \forall x G x$

19. $\exists x (F x \lor G x); \therefore \exists x F x \lor \exists x G x$

20. $\exists x F x \rightarrow \forall y (G y \rightarrow H y); \exists x J x \rightarrow \exists x G x; \therefore \exists x (F x \& J x) \rightarrow \exists z H z$

21. $\exists x F x \lor \exists x G x; \forall x (F x \rightarrow G x); \therefore \exists x G x$

22. $\forall x (\exists y F y x \rightarrow \forall z F x z); \therefore \forall y \forall x (F y x \rightarrow F x y)$

23. $\neg \exists x (F x \& G x); \therefore \forall x (F x \rightarrow \neg G x)$

► **24.** $\forall x (F x \rightarrow \neg G x); \therefore \neg \exists x (F x \& G x)$

25. $\forall x \exists y ((F x y \lor W x y) \& G y); \forall x (G x \rightarrow \forall y (F y x \rightarrow L y x));$
$\therefore \forall x \forall y (W x y \rightarrow L x y) \rightarrow \forall x \exists y (G y \& (L x y \lor L y x))$

Establish the validity of these argument forms by means of deduction.

26. $\forall x (F x \rightarrow \forall y (G y \rightarrow H x y)); \forall x (D x \rightarrow \forall y (H x y \rightarrow C y));$
$\therefore \exists x (F x \& D x) \rightarrow \forall y (G y \rightarrow C y)$

27. $\forall x ((F x \lor H x) \rightarrow (G x \& K x)); \neg \forall x (K x \& G x); \therefore \exists x \neg H x$

28. $\forall x \forall y (G x y \leftrightarrow (F y \rightarrow H x)); \forall z G a z; \therefore \exists x F x \rightarrow \exists x H x$

29. $\forall x (F x \leftrightarrow G x); \therefore \forall x F x \leftrightarrow \forall x G x$

► **30.** $\forall x (F x \leftrightarrow G x); \therefore \exists x F x \leftrightarrow \exists x G x$

31. $\exists x (F x \rightarrow G x); \therefore \forall x F x \rightarrow \exists x G x$

32. $\exists x (F x \& \forall y (G y \rightarrow H y)); \forall x (F x \rightarrow (\neg L x \rightarrow \neg \exists z (K z \& H z)));$
$\therefore \exists x (K x \& G x) \rightarrow \exists x L x$

33. $\forall x (K x \rightarrow (\exists y L x y \rightarrow \exists z L z x)); \forall x (\exists z L z x \rightarrow L x x); \neg \exists x L x x;$
$\therefore \forall x (K x \rightarrow \forall y \neg L x y)$

34. $\neg\forall x(Hx \lor Kx); \forall x((Fx \lor \neg Kx) \to Gxx); \therefore \exists x Gxx$

35. $\forall x(Fxx \to Hx); \exists x Hx \to \neg\exists y Gy; \therefore \forall x(Gx \to \neg\exists z Fzz)$

▸ 36. $\neg\exists x(Hxa \And \neg Gxb); \forall x \neg(Fxc \And Fbx); \forall x(Gex \to Fxe);$
    $\therefore \neg(Hea \And Fec)$

37. $\forall x(\exists y(Ay \And Bxy) \to Cx); \exists y(Dy \And \exists x((Fx \And Gx) \And Byx)); \forall x(Gx \to Ax);$
    $\therefore \exists x(Cx \And Dx)$

38. $\forall x\forall y\forall z((Fxy \And Fyz) \to Fxz); \neg\exists x Fxx; \therefore \forall x\forall y(Fxy \to \neg Fyx)$

39. $\forall x(Fx \leftrightarrow \forall y Gy); \therefore \forall x Fx \lor \forall x \neg Fx$

40. $Fa \to (\exists x Gx \to Gb); \forall x(Gx \to Hx); \forall x(\neg Jx \to \neg Hx);$
    $\therefore \neg Jb \to (\neg Fa \lor \forall x \neg Gx)$

41. $\forall x(Dx \to Fx); \therefore Da \to (\forall y(Fy \to Gy) \to Ga)$

▸ 42. $\exists x Fx \to \forall y((Fy \lor Gy) \to Hy); \exists x Hx; \neg\forall z \neg Fz; \therefore \exists x(Fx \And Hx)$

43. $\exists x(Fx \And \forall y(Ty \to Gy)); \forall x(Fx \to (\exists y(Ay \And Gy) \to Bxx));$
    $\exists z(Az \And Tz); \therefore \exists x Bxx$

44. $\forall x \neg Fxc \to \exists x Gxb; \therefore \exists x(\neg Fxc \to Gxb)$

45. $\forall x Fx; \therefore \neg\exists x Gx \leftrightarrow \neg(\exists x(Fx \And Gx) \And \forall y(Gy \to Fy))$

46. $\exists x(Px \And \neg Mx) \to \forall y(Py \to Ly); \exists x(Px \And Nx); \forall x(Px \to \neg Lx);$
    $\therefore \exists x(Nx \And Mx)$

47. $\forall x(Fx \to \neg\exists y(Gy \And Hxy)); \forall x(Fx \to \exists y(Fy \And Hxy));$
    $\therefore \forall x\forall y(Hxy \to Hyx) \to \forall x \neg(Fx \And Gx)$

▸ 48. $\forall x \neg Fxx; \therefore \neg\exists x\forall y(Fyx \leftrightarrow \exists z\forall w((Fwz \to Fwy) \And \neg Fzy))$

These arguments are "from straight to slanting," in the terminology of Joachim Junge, who discussed such arguments in his 1638 textbook. They played an important role in leading logicians beyond Aristotelian logic to a comprehensive theory of relations. Show that each is valid.

49. Knowledge is a conceiving; $\therefore$ The object of knowledge is an object of conception. (Aristotle, *Topics*)

50. A circle is a figure; $\therefore$ Whoever draws a circle draws a figure. (Junge)

51. All horses are animals; $\therefore$ All heads of horses are heads of animals. (DeMorgan)

Use deduction to show that these arguments are valid.

52. Mary was Jesus' parent. Mary's parents were born with the taint of original sin. But Jesus wasn't tainted by original sin. Therefore, not everyone who has a parent born with the taint of original sin is also tainted by original sin.

53. All who are moral respect all in their community if they respect themselves. Everyone here is in the same community. Every moral person has self-respect. So, all here who are moral respect each other.

54. Ralph can outsmart anybody who can outsmart everybody he can. Therefore, Ralph can outsmart himself.

55. Anybody who thinks distrusts every sophist. Sophists distrust everyone. Since there are sophists, every thinking person distrusts someone who, in turn, distrusts him or her.

56. All Frenchmen are afraid of Socialists, and Socialists fear only Communists. Thus, every French Socialist is a Communist.

57. A person is famous if and only if everyone has heard of him or her. So, all famous people have heard of each other.

58. All people like everyone who likes them. A person has Will Rogers's philosophy if and only if he or she likes everyone. Somebody or other can take advantage of anyone who shares Will Rogers's view. Some people can't be taken advantage of by anybody. It follows that some people are disliked.

59. No one who lacks self-respect respects anyone who respects him or her. No insecure people respect anyone respected by someone they respect. Thus, no insecure people respect each other.

60. Yoda knows everyone. Someone can defeat Luke if and only if he or she can do anything. All inability results from lack of self-knowledge. Therefore, Yoda can defeat Luke.

61. The government chooses to do x rather than y just in case it doesn't choose to do y over x. A person has veto power just in case the government can choose to do x over y only if that person doesn't prefer y to x. A person is a dictator just in case the government chooses to do x rather than y if he prefers x to y. Consequently, everyone with veto power is a dictator.

Notes

[1] This rule was first formulated by the English philosopher William of Ockham in the fourteenth century.

[2] The American philosopher W. V. Quine first formulated existential exploitation in this way in 1950, in his *Methods of Logic* (Cambridge: Harvard University Press, 1950, 1982).

[3] The system of rules in this chapter is sound in the sense that the rules never lead us astray; they never allow us to prove a formula that isn't valid or permit us to establish the validity of an invalid argument form. Nevertheless, the existential specification rule is unsound; it justifies the inference from $\exists v \mathscr{A}$ to $\mathscr{A}[c/v]$, provided that c is new to the proof. To preserve the system's soundness, we need to add restrictions to our proof system.

Most of our rules are *truth-preserving:* The truth of the rules' premises guarantees the truth of their conclusions. Existential specification, however, is not truth-preserving. We should hardly be able to argue, 'Some philosophers have been bachelors. Therefore, Socrates was a bachelor'. This form of inference is fallacious. The same is true of universal generalization; the inference from 'Gorbachev is Russian' to 'Everybody's Russian' fails. But, although ES and UG are not truth-preserving, they never lead us to an illegitimate conclusion. Rule ES is *conservative* in that any formula without the constant introduced or generalized on that follows from the conclusion of the rule also follows from the rule's premise.

To put this another way: Our system of rules as a whole is sound, but proofs are not sound line by line. We can never prove a conclusion that doesn't follow from the premises, but we may deduce intermediate formulas in the proof that don't follow from them. The restrictions make sure that these deviations don't affect the outcome of the proof.

Some logicians believe that proofs must be sound line by line; therefore, they formulate ES and UG differently. There is, however, a way of interpreting our system as sound line by line that does not require us to reformulate our rules. This method requires that we reinterpret constants—in particular, constants used in ES and UG. So far, we've thought of constants, relative to a context, as standing for objects. We could choose to think of them as marking places for objects but without necessarily standing for anything in particular. Or, we could think of them as standing for a different kind of object. Developing these strategies goes beyond the scope of this book. But both lead to serious and interesting analyses of logic. For the first, see Hans Kamp, "A Theory of Truth and Semantic Representation," in J. Groenendijk, T. Janssen, and M. Stockhof, *Formal Methods in the Study of Language* (Amsterdam: Mathematisch Centrum Tracts, 1981), and Irene Heim, *The Syntax and Semantics of Definite and Indefinite Noun Phrases* (PhD dissertation: University of Massachusetts at Amherst, 1983). For the second, see Kit Fine, *Reasoning with Arbitrary Objects* (Oxford: Basil Blackwell, 1985).

IV

INDUCTIVE REASONING

14

GENERALIZATIONS

art II and Part III of this book discuss deductive validity. An argument is valid if and only if the truth of its premises guarantees the truth of its conclusion. Any valid argument meets at least one condition of success—the condition of reliability. But many successful, commonly advanced arguments are not deductively valid. Indeed, most of our general knowledge about the world rests on induction, reasoning "from the known to the unknown," in the words of John Stuart Mill (1806–1873). Such reasoning is reliable but not meant to be valid deductively. Deduction dominates mathematics, logic itself, and a few other highly abstract disciplines. In all other areas, induction is far more prevalent. For this reason, Mill called induction "the main question of the science of logic."[1]

Consider a very simple argument:

(1) Every cat I've ever known liked to eat fish.
∴ All cats like to eat fish.

The premise of this argument could be true even if the conclusion were false. There may be cats I've never met who hate fish. Nevertheless, the premise does offer some evidence for the conclusion. There is a logical relation between the two, although that relation is not implication. If I've known a wide variety of cats, moreover, the argument is fairly reliable.

An argument that is reliable without being deductively valid is *inductively reliable*. The premises of such an argument support the conclusion but don't establish it conclusively. This chapter discusses the notion of inductive reliability and probes two of the most common types of inductive arguments. The next three chapters discuss progressively more complex topics in the logic of induction.

14.1 INDUCTIVE RELIABILITY

So far we've said that inductively reliable arguments are successful without being valid deductively. Reliable arguments thus fall into two classes:

Reliable Arguments
Inductively Reliable   Deductively Reliable (Valid)

To understand the general concept of reliability, we must understand inductive reliability. What relation must hold between the premises and conclusion of such an argument?

The mark of validity is that the premises imply the conclusion; the premises can't all be true while the conclusion is false. The truth of the premises guarantees the truth of the conclusion. In an inductively reliable argument, there is no guarantee. But, in any reliable argument, the truth of the premises does provide evidence for the truth of the conclusion. The truth of the premises makes the truth of the conclusion probable. That is, if the premises are true, the conclusion is likely to be true also.

> **DEFINITION**   An argument is *reliable* if and only if the truth of the premises makes the truth of the conclusion probable.

> **DEFINITION**   An argument is *inductively reliable* if and only if it is reliable but not valid.

Any valid argument is reliable; if the truth of the premises guarantees the truth of the conclusion, then the truth of the premises certainly makes the truth of the conclusion probable. Inductively reliable arguments are reliable but not valid. The truth of the premises of such an argument makes the truth of the conclusion probable but does not guarantee it. So, although it's possible for an inductively reliable argument to have true premises and a false conclusion, such an outcome is unlikely. It's probable that whenever all the premises are true, the conclusion is true as well.

Here's an argument that is inductively reliable:

(2) All the crows that have ever been observed have been black.
∴ All crows are black.

People have observed a great many crows, of many different shapes and sizes, in many different places, and at many different times. If all have been black, it seems probable that all crows are black. Drawing this conclusion from the collected observations of crowwatchers through the ages seems quite reasonable. Nevertheless, the truth of the conclusion isn't guaranteed; a fuchsia crow may lurk somewhere unobserved. The argument is reliable but not valid.

Here is another, more complex example:

(3) 51 percent of voters surveyed leaving the polls voted Democratic.
∴ 51 percent of all voters voted Democratic.

If the poll was taken correctly, then the premise of this argument supports its conclusion. The survey results indicate that it's probable that 51 percent of all voters voted Democratic. The results don't, however, guarantee this conclusion. In 1988, two major news networks declared, on the basis of exit surveys, that Michael Dukakis had won Illinois. The survey methods were sophisticated; the surveys were conducted properly. But, when all the votes were counted, it was found that George Bush had won the state.

There are two major differences between inductively reliable and deductively valid arguments. First, can adding a premise make a reliable argument unreliable? If the reliability is deductive, no. The truth of the premises guarantees the truth of the conclusion. So, no matter what information is added to the premises, the conclusion still follows. For example, this argument is valid:

(4) Barry and Bernice love opera.
∴ Bernice loves opera.

The argument remains valid, no matter what premises we add.

(5) Barry and Bernice love opera.
Sam prefers rock and roll, but Susan agrees with Barry and Bernice.
Bernice has seen the Met's production of *Aida*.
Barry has seen operas only on television.
∴ Bernice loves opera.

In fact, the argument remains valid even if we add information that directly contradicts our premise.

(6) Barry and Bernice love opera.
Bernice hates opera.
Barry hates opera.
∴ Bernice loves opera.

Any argument with inconsistent premises, after all, is valid.

But adding premises to an inductively reliable argument may make it unreliable. The premises of such an argument support the conclusion but don't establish it conclusively. So, additional information may indicate that the support offered by the original premises is weak. For example,

(7) Barry and Bernice love opera.
People tend to become friends with people who share their
interests.
∴ Many of Bernice's friends love opera.

Bernice's love for opera may suggest that many of her friends love opera, too. So, the premise offers some support for the conclusion. Adding premises, however, may destroy whatever reliability the argument has.

(8) Barry and Bernice love opera.
People tend to become friends with people who share their
interests.
Bernice's other friends are Sam, Susan, Max, Mindy, and Pat.
Sam, Max, Mindy, and Pat think opera is stupid.
∴ Many of Bernice's friends love opera.

So, adding premises may make an inductively reliable argument unreliable, although adding premises never makes a valid argument invalid.

The second major difference between inductively and deductively reliable arguments is this: Deductive reliability—validity—is an all-or-nothing affair, while inductive reliability is a matter of degree. An argument is valid if the truth of its premises guarantees the truth of its conclusion and is invalid otherwise. All valid arguments are equally valid. Some may be more convincing than others, but all are valid. It makes no sense to make comparative judgments of validity—to say, for example, that one valid argument is more valid than another. Nor does it make sense to speak of an argument as "somewhat valid," "moderately valid," "highly valid," or "very valid."

Inductive reliability, in contrast, comes in degrees. The truth of the premises of an inductively reliable argument makes the conclusion probable, and probability is a matter of degree. The premises may offer more or less support for the conclusion. So, some inductively reliable arguments may be more reliable than others. We can speak sensibly of arguments being "somewhat reliable," "moderately reliable," "highly reliable," "very reliable," and the like.

Suppose that we're investigating a murder. We find a witness who says that she heard three gunshots. We may conclude, provisionally, that there were three gunshots.

(9) Ms. Anderson says she heard three gunshots.
∴ There were three gunshots.

How reliable is this argument? That depends on how reliable the witness, Ms. Anderson, is. If we find additional witnesses who also report three shots, we can construct a stronger, more reliable argument.

> (10) Ms. Anderson, Mr. Baldwin, Mr. Crittenden, and Ms. Donnally
>   all say they heard three gunshots.
>   ∴ There were three gunshots.

Of course, as we've already observed, further information may lead to a weaker, less reliable argument.

> (11) Four witness say they heard three gunshots.
>   Six witnesses say they heard four gunshots.
>   One witness reports hearing five gunshots.
>   ∴ There were three gunshots.

This argument seems very weak, perhaps so weak as to be unreliable. The witness reports strongly support the assertion that there were at least three gunshots, but offer weak support for the conclusion that there were exactly three.

Problems

Say whether each argument in Chapter 1, section 1.2, is deductively valid, inductively reliable, or neither.

14.2 ENUMERATION

The simplest kind of inductively reliable argument is argument by enumeration. Arguments by enumeration try to justify a general conclusion by listing instances of that conclusion. Suppose we want to argue that all cats like fish. We might take as premises sentences such as

> (12) Jessica is a cat, and Jessica likes fish.
>   Gwen is a cat, and Gwen likes fish.
>   Sarah Jane is a cat, and Sarah Jane likes fish.

No matter how many such sentences we accumulate, the conclusion 'all cats like fish' will not follow deductively. Nevertheless, these sentences do support that conclusion. The more premises of this form we acquire, the stronger that support becomes. The argument having the sentences in (12) as premises is not very reliable; it mentions only three of the millions of cats covered by the conclusion. If we add premises such as

> (13) Tina is a cat, and Tina likes fish.
>   Leela is a cat, and Leela likes fish.
>   Penelope is a cat, and Penelope likes fish.

the argument becomes slightly more reliable. The conclusion follows with a greater degree of probability.

This example suggests a general pattern. The form of arguments by enumeration is from instances to generalization. The instances used to support a conclusion of the form 'All Fs are Gs'—'All cats are fish-likers', for example—have the form 'x is both F and G'—for instance, 'x is a cat and likes fish'. They are often called supporting or confirming instances of the conclusion. Arguments by enumeration thus have the basic structure:

Argument by Enumeration

Supporting instances: a_1 is both F and G.
a_2 is both F and G.
$\vdots$
a_n is both F and G.
Generalization: $\therefore$ All Fs are Gs.

If the conclusion has the form 'No F are G', the supporting instances follow the pattern 'x is F and not G'. To show that no cats eat fruit, for example, we can enumerate premises of the form 'x is a cat and does not eat fruit'.

Arguments by enumeration can adopt two forms closely related to, but not identical with, this basic structure. The first provides an alternative form for the premises. Instead of listing the supporting instances one by one, we could group instances together, presenting, in effect, subgeneralizations.

(14) All tabbies that have been observed like fish.
All calicos that have been observed like fish.
$\therefore$ All cats like fish.

Or, we could combine all the observed supporting instances together into a single group.

(15) All cats that have been observed like fish.
$\therefore$ All cats like fish.

This makes clear a central feature of arguments by enumeration: They argue from observed instances to generalizations. The observed instances may be listed, or presented in groups, or bunched together into a single group in the premises. The key move is from facts about observed instances in the premises to a generalization, to observed and unobserved cases in the conclusion.

There is another alternative form in which arguments by enumeration may appear. The conclusion may concern another, unobserved instance.

(16) Jessica, Gwen, Sarah Jane, Tina, Leela, and Penelope are all cats who like fish.
Isis is a cat.
$\therefore$ Isis likes fish.

This argument is very similar to arguments from analogy, which the final section of this chapter discusses in detail. In most circumstances, however, we would interpret this as a combination of two arguments: the first, an argument by enumeration, and the second, a deductive argument using the conclusion of the first as a premise. That is, we'd interpret (16) as a combination of (17) and (18).

(17) Jessica, Gwen, Sarah Jane, Tina, Leela, and Penelope are all cats who like fish.
∴ All cats like fish.

(18) All cats like fish.
Isis is a cat.
∴ Isis likes fish.

14.3 EVALUATING ENUMERATIONS

Arguments by enumeration generalize on the basis of observed instances. They are never deductively valid. Even if we were to enumerate all instances of a certain kind, our list of premises would not by itself imply the generalized conclusion. As Bertrand Russell (1872–1970) noted, we'd also need the premise that we've in fact listed all the instances of the relevant kind. Suppose that Ann has two brothers, Jake and Harry. The argument

(19) Jake and Harry are both dentists.
∴ All Ann's brothers are dentists.

is not valid. We would need to supplement (19) with an additional premise to obtain a valid argument.

(20) Jake and Harry are both dentists.
Jake and Harry are Ann's only brothers.
∴ All Ann's brothers are dentists.

Even though they are not valid, some arguments by enumeration are very reliable. Dogs of all known breeds, for example, have noses. It seems reasonable to conclude that dogs of all breeds, known and unknown, observed and unobserved, have noses. There could be a breed of dog, never before encountered, that features a very unusual head with nothing that we would call a nose. But this possibility seems very unlikely. That all known breeds of dogs have a certain feature provides strong evidence that all breeds of dogs have that feature.

Other arguments by enumeration, however, are unreliable. A child who has seen only one dog, which happens to be gentle, might infer that all dogs are gentle. The evidence presented by observation of one dog offers weak support for any generalization about all dogs.

This raises the question: What distinguishes reliable from unreliable arguments by enumeration? Several factors help to determine the reliability of these arguments. These factors relate to characteristics of the *sample,* the class of objects appealed to in the premises.

1. *Sample Size.* How many objects of the appropriate kind have been observed? What percentage of the total population is in the sample? In general, the more objects that have been observed, the more reliable the argument from the premises to the conclusion. Inferring things about all federal agencies on the basis of observations about just one agency, for example, is not very reliable. Generalizing from observations of two agencies is somewhat better; generalizing from observations of six agencies is much more reliable. Percentages, as well as absolute numbers, make a difference. Six agencies may constitute a reasonable percentage of all federal agencies to survey, but six people would constitute a much smaller percentage of the total number of people. A conclusion based on an enumeration involving six agencies, all other things being equal, would be far more reliable than a conclusion based on an enumeration involving six people.

Generalizations obtained from inadequate enumeration are called *hasty.* Concluding that all government employees are underpaid because a few observed ones are, or that welfare cheating is widespread because of one or two highly publicized cases, is to make a hasty generalization.

2. *Sample Variation.* How varied are the observed instances? How homogeneous is the sample? In general, the more varied the sample, the more reliable the argument. If we make a generalization about all government agencies on the basis of our experiences with six agencies, all of which were involved in military affairs, our argument is less reliable than one generalizing from experiences with six very different agencies. Similarly, our generalizations about people are more reliable if we've observed a wide variety of people. Suppose we want to learn what Soviet citizens think about the United States. If we ask only Communist party members, we will get one set of answers. If we ask only dissidents and emigres, we will get another. If we ask only schoolchildren, or only farmworkers, or only city dwellers, we will get still different results. To generalize accurately, we need to ask people in different parts of the Soviet Union, of different ages, ethnic backgrounds, political persuasions, and professions. Ideally, we want our sample to be *representative*—to mirror the total population in its relevant characteristics. (Unrepresentative samples are *biased.*) The more varied our sample, the greater its chances of being representative.

As the philosopher Ludwig Wittgenstein (1889–1951) pointed out, looking at just one kind of example is a common source of philosophical error. The same holds true in all fields. Unless a sample is varied enough, it's likely to be biased. The bias may arise from limitations of the method used to gather the sample. It may result from habitual ways of thinking that are hard to break. And, bias may arise from a tendency, conscious or unconscious, to ignore contrary evidence.

Problems

For each of the following generalizations, say whether each additional premise listed makes the inference more or less reliable, and explain. (Consider each added premise separately.)

▶ **1.** All my cats like turkey. So, all cats like turkey.
   (a) I have two cats.
   (b) I have six cats.
   (c) All my cats are calicos.
   (d) One of my cats is a calico; several are tabbies; one is a Persian, and one is a Siamese.
   (e) All my cats are former strays.

▶ **2.** Werner has taken several philosophy courses with professors who smoke pipes. He concludes that all philosophy professors smoke pipes.
   (a) Werner takes several more philosophy courses, and all those professors also smoke pipes.
   (b) All Werner's philosophy courses have been taken at the same university.
   (c) All Werner's philosophy professors studied under Gentzen at Göttingen.
   (d) Almost all professors on Werner's campus smoke pipes.
   (e) Werner takes another philosophy course and never sees the professor smoke.

3. Abigail meets some people from the Maritime provinces; all are named 'Leblanc'. She concludes that everyone in the Maritimes is named 'Leblanc'.
   (a) Everyone Abigail met belongs to the same family.
   (b) Everyone Abigail met is a teacher at a college or university.
   (c) Abigail met the Leblancs at different times and in different places.
   (d) The Leblancs Abigail met all know each other.
   (e) Abigail met the Leblancs many years ago.

4. Orlando knows several people who spent some of their childhood in France. All are very fond of wine. He concludes that everyone who lived for a while in France as a child likes wine.
   (a) One person Orlando knows is an accountant; one is a museum curator; one is a lawyer.
   (b) Everyone else Orlando knows likes wine, too.
   (c) Orlando meets people who spent part of their childhood in Spain; they are also very fond of wine.
   (d) Most of Orlando's other acquaintances prefer beer to wine.
   (e) Orlando visits France and finds that most people drink wine with meals.

5. Millie knows several friends who own Vauxhalls and like them; she concludes that she'll like her new Vauxhall.
   (a) Millie's friends all live in York.
   (b) Some of Millie's friends take good care of their cars; others are negligent about maintenance.
   (c) Some of Millie's neighbors also drive Vauxhalls; most like them.
   (d) One of Millie's friends bought her car in Glasgow; the others bought theirs in York or Leeds.
   (e) Most of Millie's friends drive only around town; one drives to Edinburgh and back each week.

14.4 STATISTICAL GENERALIZATIONS

Rare before the twentieth century, and unheard of before the development of modern science, statistical arguments are now commonplace. In a typical newspaper, statistics fill the financial pages, the sports pages, and some of the advertising. The national news pages may discuss inflation rates and results of the latest poll; the local pages may discuss a survey of city residents' attitudes on a particular issue. Each of these headlines, for example, would accompany an article (or advertisement) prominently featuring statistical reasoning:

> LOW P/E STOCKS OUTPERFORM MARKET, STUDY FINDS
> GOODEN AND HERSHISER BATTLE FOR ERA LEAD
> NEW IMPROVED SCRUB GETS CLOTHES 20% BRIGHTER
> INFLATION SLOWS IN AUGUST; TRADE GAP NARROWS
> RACE TOO CLOSE TO CALL, POLL SHOWS
> "BUILD IT SOMEWHERE ELSE":
> CITY RESIDENTS WANT NEW AIRPORT, BUT NOT NEAR THEM

Because statistical reasoning is so common, no study of logic would be complete without some examination of it.

Evaluating statistical arguments, however, is difficult. Statistics is a significant and complex field of mathematics. Moreover, many frequently used English words pertaining to statistics, such as 'average', have somewhat different and more specific uses in statistics than in everyday discourse. Finally, statistical arguments often omit important information. When the *Wall Street Journal* reports poll results, it publishes nearby a brief summary of how the poll was conducted. Few news sources report such information, however, and few readers know how to interpret it. Yet, how the poll was conducted may have a large bearing on how we should interpret its results.

Polls and surveys rely on a form of argument known as *statistical* or *inductive generalization*. They seek to learn what percentage of people prefer the Republican candidate for president, or have incomes over $100,000 per year, or feel unsatisfied with their current toothpaste. To find out, they ask, not everyone, but a relatively small collection of people, called a *sample*. They use information about the sample to draw a conclusion about the total population under study.

Roughly speaking, a statistical generalization has the following form:

Statistical Generalization

$n\%$ of observed Fs are G.
$\therefore$ $n\%$ of Fs are G.

For example, a poll may find that 52 percent of those surveyed who said they planned to vote preferred the Republican presidential candidate. From this premise, we might conclude that 52 percent of all likely voters prefer that candidate. Or, a quality control study may find that 3.2 percent of the bumpers tested from a certain factory are defective. We might conclude from this study that 3.2 percent of the bumpers made at that factory are defective.

Arguments by enumeration are really simple statistical generalizations. If the percentage in both premise and conclusion is 100 percent, then the form of the statistical generalization is

All observed Fs are G.
$\therefore$ All Fs are G.

which is one form of argument by enumeration.

Evaluating statistical generalizations requires examining several factors. Some are those factors relevant to evaluating arguments by enumeration. But others are introduced by the statistical nature of the argument.

Sample Size

When we infer something about a large group from information gathered about a small group, we assume that the small group sampled is *representative* of the large group: that the relevant characteristics of the sample are typical of the large group as a whole. An unrepresentative sample is *biased*. The reliability of a statistical generalization thus depends crucially on how accurately the sample represents the population being studied.

All other things being equal, larger samples are more likely to be representative than smaller samples. The more cases observed, the more reliable the generalization based on them. How large a sample must we consider to establish the reliability of a generalization based on that sample? There is no simple, definite answer to this question. Too small a sample leads to unreliability; too large a sample wastes resources. To determine an appropriate sample size, we need to specify two factors: the *confidence interval,* or *margin of error,* or *accuracy* we want, and the *degree of confidence* or *reliability* we want. Only relative to these can we determine an appropriate sample size.

An example may clarify the distinction between accuracy and confidence. Suppose we are trying to describe the performance of an archer—Xerxes, let's call him—trying to hit a target. We can describe how Xerxes does by indicating how many arrows fall within various circles around the center of the target:

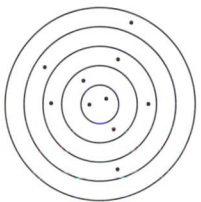

Suppose that the bull's-eye, the innermost circle, has a radius of two inches; the next circle, four inches; the next, six inches; and so on. If the ten arrows are representative, then Xerxes is accurate to within two inches 20 percent of the time; to within four inches, 40 percent of the time; to within six inches, 70 percent of the time; to within eight inches, 90 percent of the time; and, to within ten inches, all the time. The radius of each circle corresponds to a margin of error, or level of accuracy; the percentage of times an arrow falls within that circle corresponds to a level of confidence or reliability. The bull's-eye thus corresponds to a margin of error of two inches. Xerxes hits the center 20 percent of the time. So, we may have 20 percent confidence that Xerxes will hit within two inches of the center. We may have 40 percent confidence that he'll hit within four inches of the center; 70 percent confidence that he'll hit within six inches of the center; and so on.

Here is another analogy: The difference between accuracy and reliability is like the difference between a point spread and odds in betting on a game. The odds indicate the level of confidence the parties have about the performances of the teams; the point spread indicates something about the accuracy of their estimate of the score. Clearly, the odds and the point spread are interrelated: The same bettors would assign different odds to a bet, depending on the point spread. Similarly, the accuracy and reliability of a sample interrelate. The confidence interval is so called because it is the range into which *n* percent of the actual values for the population will fall, where *n* percent is the confidence level.

Let's represent these concepts visually:

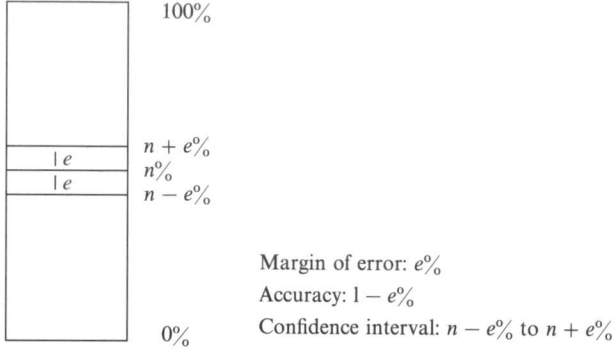

Let us illustrate how these concepts apply to statistical generalizations. Suppose we want to find out how many of 50,000 students at the university consider themselves Democrats. How many do we need to survey to obtain an adequate sample? Before answering, we must specify a desired margin of error. Suppose we say that we want the answer to be correct to within a 5 percent margin of error. That is, if our poll finds that 40 percent of the students sampled consider themselves Democrats, we will draw the conclusion that between 35 and 45 percent of the student body at large consider themselves Democrats. The range of 35 to 45 percent in this case is the confidence interval established for the survey. The margin of error (and, indirectly, the confidence interval) is often reported in poll results in phrases such as 'within 3 points', 'plus or minus 5 percent', and so on. The poll is said to be accurate to within the margin of error.

Second, we must specify a desired degree of reliability or confidence. Just how reliable, in other words, do we want our generalization to be? We can't guarantee that the sample's characteristics will be within 5 percent of those of the entire student body without asking everyone. So, we need to know what degree of reliability is acceptable. We might specify a confidence level of 90 percent: Nine times out of ten, the percentage of, perhaps, Democrats in the entire population will fall within the confidence interval we've specified. We could represent these decisions as follows. The form of the generalization will be

(21) $n\%$ of the sample are F.
∴ $n\%$, $\pm e\%$, of the population are F.
Confidence: $m\%$

where e is the margin of error; $n - e$ to $n + e$ is the confidence interval; and m is the confidence limit, the measure of the reliability of the inference. In our example, choosing 5 percent for a margin of error (or, equivalently, 95 percent accuracy) and 90 percent reliability, the generalization will have the form

(22) $n\%$ of the sample consider themselves Democrats.
∴ $n\%$, $\pm 5\%$, of the students consider themselves Democrats.
Confidence: 90%

This means that the percentage of students considering themselves Democrats will lie between $n - 5\%$ and $n + 5\%$, except for a one in ten chance. To obtain this level of confidence and margin of error, we would have to survey about 270 students. (This is true, incidentally, provided that the university has more than about 6,000 students. The sample of 270 will allow us to generalize to populations of 6000, 25,000, 50,000, or 500,000, with almost exactly the same confidence and margin of error. In statistical generalizations, the percentage of the population sampled is usually irrelevant to their reliability. This fact is surprising; explaining why it's true goes beyond the scope of this book. But this property enables opinion polls to be economically and practically feasible.)

Supposing, again, that we find 40 percent of the sample calling themselves Democrats, our resulting generalization will have the form

(23) 40% of the sample consider themselves Democrats.
∴ 40%, $\pm 5\%$, of the students consider themselves Democrats.
Confidence: 90%

The smaller the margin of error we're willing to tolerate and the more reliability we demand, the larger the sample must be. If we require 95 percent reliability, for example, we'll have to interview about 400 students. Shrinking the margin of error below 5 percent, or increasing the reliability above 95 percent, requires a sharper increase in the size of the sample. This table indicates how large a sample is needed in a large population (that is, for the purposes of the table, one over about 330,000) to obtain various margins of error and levels of confidence.

		Confidence			
		99%	95%	90%	80%
	1%	16,650	9,600	6,725	4,100
Margin	2%	4,163	2,400	1,681	1,025
of	3%	1,850	1,067	747	456
Error	4%	1,041	600	420	256
	5%	666	384	269	164
	10%	154	96	68	41

Our assumption here is that about half the population will exhibit the trait we're interested in and that the population being studied is relatively homogeneous—that is, that it doesn't divide naturally into subpopulations with very different characteristics. We need to take the variation of the population into account to determine both how big and how varied the sample ought to be.

Sample Variation

Groups are rarely completely homogeneous; their members typically display some degree of variation. The more varied the sample we take, the more likely it is to represent accurately the variation in the group as a whole. Increasing the variation in a sample, therefore, is one way to increase the reliability of a statistical generalization.

Suppose, for example, that we want to compare several supermarkets to see which has the lowest prices. Supermarkets sell many different products; their wares vary greatly. If we compare the supermarkets by examining their prices on a single item—rutabagas, perhaps—any argument concerning their pricing across the board will be unreliable. Considering prices of lettuce, carrots, oranges, and jalapeno peppers will increase the reliability somewhat, but not much, because all these items are fresh produce; their prices may not reflect the prices of other kinds of goods. An adequate sample would have to include items of different kinds, reflecting more of the variation in products. A sample consisting of rutabagas, pork chops, canned beets, corn flakes, shampoo, bread, cheese, and milk, for example, would allow a much more reliable generalization than one consisting solely of eight fruits, or eight breakfast cereals, or eight brands of dog food.

How do we ensure that our sample is varied enough for a reliable generalization? The most common technique is to use a random sample: one drawn randomly from the population.

> **DEFINITION** A sample of a population is *random* if and only if every member of the population has an equal chance of being included in it.

Random sampling doesn't guarantee a representative or even widely varied sample, but it does make one likely.

Random sampling works well with populations that are fairly homogeneous or about which we have little further information. When considering populations that divide into quite distinct subgroups with different characteristics, we can do better with *stratified random sampling:* applying random sampling techniques separately to each subgroup. Stratified sampling also provides more detailed information; it permits generalizations about the various subgroups, or *strata,* as well as about the population as a whole. In surveying our university students for political affiliations, for example, we might want to poll students in business, liberal arts, and education colleges separately. In addition, we might want to distinguish graduate from undergraduate students. This would lead to a survey with six separate random samplings.

Obtaining a random sample within a strata or in the population at large is extremely difficult. An ideal method is to number all the population's members and then choose the sample using a random number sequence. But this method poses two problems. First, many populations are difficult to number. Imagine facing Winnie-the-Pooh's task of counting the bees in even a single hive! Even already-numbered populations, like the student body at a college or university, may present problems because Social Security numbers, student numbers, and the like aren't public information. A statistician can't simply send in a fee and get a list of everyone in the United States by Social Security number; questions of privacy rule out the use of these already-available numbering systems. Second, there's no way to force people to respond to survey questions. Even if everyone selected for the sample can be found—and this isn't a trivial matter—many will typically decline to answer. People may be pressed for time, or be concerned about privacy, or hate surveys. This presents a serious problem to the statistician, for it may introduce bias.

Suppose that only 80 percent of those questioned in a randomly chosen sample respond. Is the responding sample still representative? Perhaps, if the unresponsive people were distributed randomly. In many cases, however, reasons why people respond, or fail to respond, are relevant to the survey's topic. People at the top and bottom of the socioeconomic ladder are notoriously hard to find and also notoriously unresponsive; consequently, few opinion polls reflect their views. Because social and economic standing are relevant to opinions on many topics, omission of these groups introduces bias into many surveys. In general, the greater the response rate, the less significant a source of bias unresponsive members of the sample constitute. So, to evaluate a survey based on even a carefully drawn random sample, we look at the response rate. If it's low—and some surveys have response rates well below 50 percent—we should interpret the results with caution.

Because numbering a population can be difficult, most samples are selected in a less than ideal way. Sometimes, pollsters choose a system that numbers many, but not all people: a voter registration list, for example, a driver's license list, or the telephone book. These, too, can introduce bias. Many people don't register to vote; many people don't have licenses to drive; and many people have either no telephone or an unlisted number. If any of these factors relates statistically to what is being studied, omitting such people creates bias.

Sometimes, pollsters choose samples in even less reliable ways. Someone may stand on a street corner or in a shopping mall and ask questions of passersby. Clearly, this is not a random sample—not everyone has an equal chance of passing by a given point on a given street during a given time. A magazine's survey of its readers may reveal something about the people who read it, but it's very unlikely to reveal much about the population at large.

Perhaps the worst are surveys with self-selected samples. A television program, for example, may flash a number and ask people to call to register their views. The sample that results is self-selected: People choose whether to be a part of it or not. Such samples are almost always biased, because a person's decision to respond or not depends on his or her feelings about the issue in question. For this reason, the selection almost always relates to the issue at hand and distorts the result. Consequently, surveys with self-selected samples are usually so flawed as to be virtually meaningless. Yet newspapers or magazines still occasionally conduct surveys by soliciting readers to mail back an insert expressing some opinion. Members of Congress still count the letters they receive on opposing sides of issues, and consumer's groups still base ratings of automobiles on surveys mailed to subscribers. Several widely publicized studies of female sexuality published in the 1970s and 1980s used self-selected samples. One magazine asked readers to fill out a questionnaire, and another researcher distributed questionnaires through women's groups (mostly, chapters of the National Organization for Women). Although such studies may turn up interesting information, their samples are almost sure to be unrepresentative, and any statistical generalizations drawn from those samples are suspect.

Problems

For each of the following survey topics, evaluate the sampling methods proposed. Do they contain sources of bias?

▶ **1.** How many students are happy with the education they're receiving at State?
  (a) Pass out questionnaires in large introductory courses.
  (b) Pass out questionnaires at registration.
  (c) Ask students in lines at registration.
  (d) Interview students chosen at random from each floor of each dormitory.
  (e) Put a questionnaire in the student newspaper, to be mailed in.

▶ **2.** Which of three factories produces the smallest percentage of flawed widgets?
  (a) Test every hundredth widget produced at each factory between 9:00 A.M. and 5:00 P.M. for a week.
  (b) Test randomly selected widgets produced at each factory between 9:00 A.M. and 5:00 P.M. for a week.
  (c) Test randomly selected widgets produced at each factory during any shift for a week.
  (d) Test randomly selected widgets produced at each factory during any shift for a month.
  (e) Test randomly selected widgets produced at each factory, separately for each shift, for a month.

  3. How many students at Tech support raising the university's admissions standards?
  (a) Ask representatives in the student government.
  (b) Ask students at the Union at lunchtime.
  (c) Ask students in randomly selected classes.

(d) Ask students in the library.
(e) Put up posters asking students to write their comments.

4. What percentage of El Paso residents will vote Republican in the next election?
   (a) Survey people in each El Paso shopping center.
   (b) Call randomly selected telephone numbers with El Paso exchanges.
   (c) Survey randomly selected people from voter registration lists.
   (d) Run a TV ad asking people to call one number if they plan to vote Democratic and another if they plan to vote Republican.
   (e) Divide the city into census tracts, group them by income and education levels, and survey people at randomly selected addresses in each group.

The following are especially difficult topics to examine using surveys. Can you suggest any methods for each? Do the methods contain sources of bias?

5. How many residents of San Diego are illegal aliens?

▸ 6. How many husbands cheat on their wives?

7. How many people have seen or are seeing a psychiatrist?

8. How many people did the last census fail to count?

9. How many people are homeless?

10. How many people cheat on their taxes?

A common statistical fallacy results from making precise numerical assertions concerning things that can't, or can't easily, be quantified. Another results from making comparative judgments, such a 'n% better', without specifying one term of the comparison. (n% better than what?) In each of the following, what is the precise numerical measure measuring? What are the terms of any comparisons made? Are there any reasons to be suspicious of the claim?

11. New SoothTooth gets your teeth 50% brighter!

▸ 12. Now, 20% more bleach!

13. Two out of three doctors surveyed prefer Curital.

14. The group eating a strict, low-fat diet experienced an average 30% drop in blood sugar.

15. Children in affluent schools learning 30% more, study finds.

16. New, improved Whitewash gets your laundry 42% whiter!

17. Married men 15% happier than bachelors, psychologist says.

▸ 18. Married men live 15% longer.

19. 10% more fiber than other leading brands.

20. Pitching is 75% of baseball.

Here are two opinions concerning a presidential election as a survey of public opinion. Using the concepts of this chapter, analyze and evaluate each argument.

21. Only about half the eligible electorate went to the polls November 8 [1988]. . . . the half-nation that votes is not what statisticians would call a random sampling. . . . [It] is heavily skewed toward the rich and well-educated, the white and the conservative. . . . Factoring out the gender gap and the minorities gap from the turnout figures, the electoral equation brutally belies the myth that "the American people" gave Bush his victory. (*The Nation*)

22. Yet the *New York Times* and CBS News tested the impact of voter turnout by polling a single sample of voters both before and after the election to record the preferences of those who failed to vote. On the basis of this survey, the *Times* reported that if everyone had voted, Bush would have won by an even larger margin—about 11 percentage points. (Joshua Muravchik)

23. Consider teaching evaluations in which students, near the end of a semester, fill out a questionnaire about their opinion of a course and its instructor. (The instructor typically doesn't see the surveys until well after grades are submitted.) Can you name any sources of bias in this procedure?

24. Suppose that you are writing an article for your school or town newspaper and want to include a survey of students' (or residents') attitudes about a particular question. How can you draw an adequate sample? (a) Describe a method for choosing your sample and then (b) critique it, analyzing it for possible sources of bias. (c) If feasible, exchange your answer to (a) with other students and critique their methods.

14.5 ANALOGIES

Many inductive arguments are arguments by analogy. The word 'analogy' derives, by way of Middle English, Old French, and Latin, from the Greek word for proportion. As this suggests, an analogical argument is an argument by proportion or ratio. Mathematical problems concerning ratios often have the form

$$A:B = C:D$$

where, given values for three quantities, we can compute the fourth. We can read this formula as follows: 'As A is to B, so C is to D'. A proportion or ratio involves relating things according to certain similarities. This is the essence of analogy. An analogy is a similarity, in certain respects, between distinct things. And an argument by analogy is an argument inferring a similarity from other similarities.

Most often, analogies fulfill nonargumentative roles. They help to describe, to illustrate, and to explain. In literature, similes and metaphors are kinds of analogy. Consider, for example, these speeches from Shakespeare:

(24) No, no, no, no! Come, let's away to prison;
We two alone will sing like birds i' th' cage.
When thou dost ask me blessing, I'll kneel down
And ask of thee forgiveness. So we'll live,
And pray, and sing, and tell old tales, and laugh
At gilded butterflies, and hear poor rogues
Talk of court news; and we'll talk with them too,
Who loses and who wins; who's in, who's out;
And take upon 's the mystery of things
As if we were God's spies; and we'll wear out,
In a wall'd prison, packs and sects of great ones
That ebb and flow by th' moon. (*King Lear* V, iii, 8–19)

(25) ... Out, out, brief candle!
Life's but a walking shadow, a poor player
That struts and frets his hour upon the stage
And then is heard no more. It is a tale
Told by an idiot, full of sound and fury,
Signifying nothing. (*Macbeth* V, v, 23–28)

The first of these speeches compares the speaker and listener, in prison, to birds in a cage, singing regardless of what's happening outside the confines of their allotted space. The speech goes on to compare the speaker and listener to spies of God, capable of seeing and knowing anything without actually being a part of it. The second speech contains several metaphors for life: as a candle, about to be blown out; as a shadow, an ephemeral, elusive, dependent bit of reality; as an actor, on a stage only temporarily; as a tale told by an idiot, without meaning or design. Much of the power of great literature depends on the use of simile and metaphor to shed new light on familiar scenes and situations.

Analogy is also extremely useful in science. Modern science has made its most powerful advances by developing theories of entities beyond the realm of our senses: atoms, molecules, subatomic particles, waves, and fields. Mathematical equations define their character. But using analogies to relate them to more familiar things helps to make them more intelligible. Contemporary cosmology, for example, holds that the universe is expanding outward in all directions, without any center to the expansion. This concept is difficult to picture. But suppose we consider a balloon being inflated, visualizing the stars and galaxies as dots on the balloon's surface. No dot is in the center; yet, from the perspective of each dot, all other dots are moving away from it. The analogy helps to explain how an uncentered expansion is possible.[2] Perhaps the most dramatic example of analogy in science has been the conception of the atom as a minute planetary system, with the nucleus as sun and electrons as planets. Charles Darwin used a variety of metaphors for the process of natural selection. He described nature as a "tangled bank," the development of species as a "piece of seaweed endlessly branching," natural selection as "war," and variation as "wedging." Darwin also relied on an extended analogy between Malthus's economic portrait of scarcity and competition in the natural world. Indeed, some scientists hold that analogy is the key to scientific discovery: ". . . Hypotheses," geologist G. K. Gilbert wrote, "are always suggested through analogy."[3]

How are analogies used in argument? An analogical argument infers a similarity from other similarities. Consider, for example, this argument from Henry Kissinger's *White House Years:*

(26) The superpowers often behave like two heavily armed blind men feeling their way around a room, each believing himself in mortal peril from the other, whom he assumes to have perfect vision. Each side should know that frequently uncertainty, compromise, and incoherence are the essence of policymaking. Yet each tends to ascribe to the other side a consistency, foresight and coherence that its own experience belies. Of course, over time even two armed blind men in a room can do enormous damage to each other, not to speak of the room.

This argument begins by comparing the superpowers to two heavily armed blind men. After listing several similarities, the argument points out that the two men present extreme danger to each other and to their surroundings. The unstated conclusion is that the superpowers also pose a serious threat to each other and to their surroundings—the world as a whole.

As this example suggests, arguments by analogy have the forms:

Argument by Analogy

$a_1, \ldots, a_n$ and b are all $F_1, F_2, \ldots$ and F_k.
$a_1 \ldots a_n$ are G.
$\therefore b$ is G.

All H and all J are $F_1, F_2, \ldots$ and F_k.
All H are G.
$\therefore$ All J are G.

We may write Kissinger's argument in this form, as follows:

(27) Both the superpowers and two heavily armed blind men feeling their way around a room
   a. believe themselves to be in mortal peril from the other;
   b. assume the other to have perfect vision;
   c. should know that frequently uncertainty, compromise, and incoherence are the essence of policymaking;
   d. ascribe to the other side a consistency, foresight, and coherence that their own experiences belie.
   Over time, even two armed blind men in a room can do enormous damage to each other, not to speak of the room.
   ∴ Over time, the superpowers can do enormous damage to each other, not to mention their surroundings (the world).

Arguments by analogy proceed by listing similarities between two objects or circumstances and concluding that because one has some characteristic, so does the other.

Analogical arguments, in effect, are arguments by modeling. Using models, we can draw conclusions from one situation by analyzing another, similar situation. The situation we analyze directly serves as a model for the situation about which we wish to draw a conclusion. Modeling a situation offers many advantages. The model is usually clearer, better understood, and more familiar than the circumstance being modeled. Consequently, analyzing the model—seeing how its parts relate and interact, seeing how it evolves, reacts, and causes changes in other circumstances—is easier than reasoning directly about the less familiar and less comprehensible situation we want to understand. Kissinger, for example, reasons about the superpowers indirectly, by drawing inferences from a more easily visualized situation—two heavily armed, suspicious blind men in a room. We can analyze the model of the blind men to draw conclusions about the superpowers.

Evaluating Analogical Arguments

Arguments by analogy are inductive. The truth of the premises doesn't guarantee the truth of the conclusion, but it does lend it some degree of probability. In other words, the existence of some similarities may make probable, but doesn't guarantee, the existence of further similarities. The reliability of an analogical argument depends on several factors. They include the number and relevance of the similarities; the number and relevance of dissimilarities; the variety and number of analogous objects or circumstances; and the strength of premises and conclusion.

1. *The number and relevance of similarities.* The more relevant similarities the premises offer, the more reliable the analogical inference. Arguments mentioning only a single similarity of dubious causal relevance to the desired

conclusion are extremely weak:

> (28) Darryl is a man, and so is Jerryl.
> Darryl is an engineer.
> ∴ Jerryl is an engineer.

This argument offers very little support for its conclusion. Adding similarities that have no causal connection to the conclusion doesn't really help:

> (29) Darryl and Jerryl are both men who are over forty and like beets.
> Darryl is an engineer.
> ∴ Jerryl is an engineer.

This argument is still terrible. Adding relevant similarities, however, strengthens the argument:

> (30) Darryl and Jerryl are both men who wear short-sleeved shirts, polyester pants, and plastic pocket guards to work.
> Darryl is an engineer.
> ∴ Jerryl is an engineer.

This argument is hardly overwhelming, but it's much better than (29) and (28); how people dress for work is connected to their occupation. If we add further similarities, the argument becomes more reliable:

> (31) Darryl and Jerryl are both men who wear short-sleeved shirts, polyester pants, and plastic pocket guards to work.
> Both Darryl and Jerryl work for the local power company and have offices on the second floor of the same building.
> Both Darryl and Jerryl took calculus from Professor Munk at A&M.
> Darryl is an engineer.
> ∴ Jerryl is an engineer.

2. *The number and relevance of dissimilarities.* Any two objects or circumstances differ in indefinitely many ways. The mere existence of differences doesn't undermine the reliability of an analogical argument. When the differences are causally relevant to the issue at hand, however, they do undermine the argument's reliability. In general, the more relevant dissimilarities there are, the weaker the argument.

Consider our case about Darryl and Jerryl above. By the time we reach (31), we have a fairly strong argument for the conclusion that Jerryl is an engineer. Adding information about irrelevant dissimilarities to the premises takes nothing away from the argument's strength:

> (32) Darryl and Jerryl are both men who wear short-sleeved shirts, polyester pants, and plastic pocket guards to work.
> Both Darryl and Jerryl work for the local power company and have offices on the second floor of the same building.

> Both Darryl and Jerryl took calculus from Professor Munk at A&M.
>
> Darryl's favorite color is green, his favorite food is meat loaf, and his favorite drink is milk; Jerryl's favorites are blue, turkey, and beer, respectively.
>
> Darryl is an engineer.
>
> ∴ Jerryl is an engineer.

Adding relevant dissimilarities, however, weakens the argument:

> (33) Darryl and Jerryl are both men who wear short-sleeved shirts, polyester pants, and plastic pocket guards to work.
>
> Both Darryl and Jerryl work for the local power company and have offices on the second floor of the same building.
>
> Both Darryl and Jerryl took calculus from Professor Munk at A&M.
>
> Darryl has an M.S. in electrical engineering and works entensively with computers; Jerryl has a B.S. in accounting and works with spreadsheets, an adding machine, tax forms, and a green eyeshade.
>
> Darryl is an engineer.
>
> ∴ Jerryl is an engineer.

This argument is no longer very reliable. Indeed, we'd be tempted to draw the conclusion that Jerryl is an accountant.

3. *The variety and number of analogous objects or circumstances.* That Darryl and Jerryl dress similarly for work lends some support to the conclusion that they have the same occupation. We would strengthen this support by noting other engineers who dress in the same way. Darryl's habits of dress may be due to his personal preferences, his alma mater, or some limited local practice; his habits may be unusual for people in his profession. The more engineers we observe with similar habits, the more reliable the argument. Also, the more varied a group we observe dressing the same way, the stronger the argument. If we point to Darryl and his friends, the argument is more reliable than if we point to Darryl alone. But the argument becomes still more reliable if we point to engineers in different places, companies, and social settings who dress similarly.

4. *The strength of premises and conclusion.* The stronger a conclusion we try to derive—the more informative and detailed we wish it to be—the weaker the argument becomes. If, given the similarities between Darryl and Jerryl mentioned in (30), we conclude that Jerryl is an engineer, the argument seems reasonable. If, mentioning that Darryl is an engineer working in transmission and distribution, we conclude that Jerryl also works in transmission and distribution, the argument becomes much weaker. A more detailed conclusion requires more extensive similarities, while it opens the door more widely for relevant dissimilarities.

Problems

Analyze the following literary analogies. (a) Explain what is related to what, and (b) explain in what respects. Also, (c) mention some dissimilarities.

▸ **1.** As my hand hath found the kingdoms of the idols, and whose graven images did excel them of Jerusalem and of Samaria; Shall I not, as I have done unto Samaria and her idols, so do to Jerusalem and her idols? (Isaiah 10:10–11)

▸ **2.** Beware of false prophets, which come to you in sheep's clothing, but inwardly they are ravening wolves. (Matthew 7:15)

▸ **3.** Would that you knew what the Disaster is! On that day men shall become like scattered moths and the mountains like tufts of carded wool. (Koran 101:1)

▸ **4.** Unholy Mars bends all to his mad will:
The world is like a chariot run wild
That rounds the course unchecked and, gaining speed,
Sweeps the helpless driver on to his doom. (Virgil)

▸ **5.** We are such stuff
As dreams are made on, and our little life
Is rounded with a sleep. (William Shakespeare)

▸ **6.** All the world's a stage,
And all the men and women merely players;
They have their exits and their entrances;
And one man in his time plays many parts. . . . (William Shakespeare)

7. Like to the Pontic sea,
Whose icy current and compulsive course
Ne'er feels retiring ebb, but keeps due on
To the Propontic and the Hellespont;
Even so my bloody thoughts, with violent pace,
Shall ne'er look back, ne'er ebb to humble love,
Till that a capable and wide revenge
Swallow them up. (William Shakespeare)

8. This city now doth, like a garment, wear
The beauty of the morning. . . . (William Wordsworth)

9. It is beauteous evening, calm and free,
The holy time is quiet as a Nun
Breathless with adoration. . . . (William Wordsworth)

10. Then felt I like some watcher of the skies
When a new planet swims into his ken;
Or like stout Cortez when with eagle eyes

He stared at the Pacific—and all his men
Looked at each other with a wild surmise—
Silent, upon a peak in Darien. (John Keats)

11. He mourns that day so soon has glided by:
E'en like the passage of an angel's tear
That falls through the clear ether silently. (John Keats)

▸ 12. And this gray spirit yearning in desire
To follow knowledge like a sinking star,
Beyond the utmost bound of human thought. (Alfred, Lord Tennyson)

13. Many a night I saw the Pleiads, rising through the mellow shade,
Glitter like a swarm of fire-flies tangled in a silver braid. (Alfred, Lord
Tennyson)

14. I love thee freely, as men strive for Right;
I love thee purely, as they turn from Praise. (Elizabeth Barrett Browning)

15. Ah, love, let us be true
To one another! for the world, which seems
To lie before us like a land of dreams,
So various, so beautiful, so new,
Hath really neither joy, nor love, nor light,
Nor certitude, nor peace, nor help for pain;
And we are here as on a darkling plain
Swept with confused alarms of struggle and flight,
Where ignorant armies clash by night. (Matthew Arnold)

16. My heart is like a singing bird
Whose nest is in a watered shoot;
My heart is like an apple-tree
Whose boughs are bent with thickset fruit;
My heart is like a rainbow shell
That paddles in a halcyon sea;
My heart is gladder than all these
Because my love is come to me. (Christina Rossetti)

17. Language is like a cracked kettle on which we beat out tunes for bears
to dance to, while all the time we long to move the stars to pity. (Gustave
Flaubert)

Analyze the following analogies: (a) Explain what is related to what. (b) Describe in what respects they are related. (c) Indicate some dissimilarities between the items. If the analogy is part of an analogical argument, (d) evaluate the argument's strength.

▸ 18. Seeing Yankee fans for the first time is like waking up in a Brazilian jail.
(Art Hill)

19. College is like an imprimatur. It's like having an American Express card. (Clare Boothe Luce)

20. It struck me that this task force [Democratic Task Force on high interest rates, Senate Banking Committee] was a little like mosquitoes investigating the cause of malaria. (James Balog)

21. Television is to news what bumper stickers are to philosophy. (Richard Nixon)

22. Asking a working writer what he thinks about critics is like asking a lamppost what it feels about dogs. (John Osborne)

23. Going to church doesn't make you a Christian any more than going to the garage makes you a car. (Laurence J. Peter)

▶ 24. 'Tis with our judgments as our watches: none go just alike, yet each believes his own. (Alexander Pope)

25. My country, right or wrong, is a thing no patriot would think of saying, except in a desperate case. It is like saying, "my mother, drunk or sober." (G. K. Chesterton)

26. The universe of ideas is just as little independent of the nature of our experiences as clothes are of the form of the human body. (Albert Einstein)

27. Light and other forms of radiation are analogous to water ripples or waves, in that they distribute energy from a central source. (James Jeans)

28. The difficulty [the Reagan administration faces to hold down future spending] is that the budget is like a supertanker. It acquires tremendous momentum that cannot be arrested quickly and that comes from several sources. (Edward Cowan)

29. *Q.* Some of the major carriers in the New York area want restrictions placed on private and corporate aviation. What about that?
    A. Let me draw a parallel. If, on the New Jersey Turnpike, it became crowded, would you like it if all automobiles were kept off the New Jersey Turnpike and only buses could run? (Rear Admiral Donald Engen)

▶ 30. High interest rates and slow growth reduce inflation in the way that chemotherapy works on cancer. It kills the good along with the bad cells and makes the patient dreadfully sick. Physicians, to their credit, are trying to find therapies that will kill cancer cells without killing the patient. But America's economic policymakers have not made the same intellectual leap. (Paul A. London)

31. With big headlines telling us that unemployment, at 9.4%, is at the highest level in 40 years, the political balance shifts in favor of advocates of an instant fix. Their typical prescription: federal "jobs" programs and gun-

ning the money supply. That's like ordering a sunlamp for a heat stroke victim. (*Wall Street Journal*)

32. ... "You can't put the clock back." The simple and obvious answer is "You can." A clock, being a piece of human construction, can be restored by the human finger to any figure or hour. In the same way society, being a piece of human construction, can be reconstructed upon any plan that has ever existed. (G. K. Chesterton)

33. For seven months now, ever since my arrest and trial, I have been living like a queen here in prison: doors are flung open before me wherever I go—into cells, interrogation rooms, the courtroom. . . . Other hands close these doors behind me, too. . . . Mostly I am driven from place to place. An impressive number of people are employed in "serving" me: just to get a pencil sharpened I summon a junior officer of the guard. (Irina Ratushinskaya)

34. My aim is to show that the celestial machine is to be likened not to a divine organism but rather to a clockwork. (Johannes Kepler)

35. The people who bind themselves to systems are those who are unable to encompass the whole truth and try to catch it by the tail; a system is like the tail of truth, but truth is like a lizard; it leaves its tail in your fingers and runs away knowing full well that it will grow a new one in a twinkling. (Ivan Turgenev)

▶ 36. The earth is an element placed in the middle of the world, as the yoke in the middle of an egg; around it is the water, like the white surrounding the yoke; outside that is the air, like the membrane of the egg; and around all is the fire, which closes it in as the shell does. (The Venerable Bede)

37. The easiest way to think of the electrons is as small "planets" circling round a central nucleus which is made up of neutrons and protons. . . . We can imagine electrons as planets whirling around the central sun in a solar system. . . . (A. M. Low)

38. As the mistletoe is disseminated by birds, its existence depends on them; and it may metaphorically be said to struggle with other fruit-bearing plants, in tempting the birds to devour and thus disseminate its seeds. (Charles Darwin)

39. Just as in astronomy the difficulty of admitting the motion of the earth lay in the immediate sensation of the earth's stationariness and of the planet's motion, so in history the difficulty of recognizing the subjection of the personality to the laws of space and time and causation lies in the difficulty of surmounting the direct sensation of the independence of one's personality. (Leo Tolstoy)

40. Supposing the light of any given colour to consist of undulations of a given breadth, or of a given frequency, it follows that these undulations

must be liable to those effects which we have already examined in the case of the waves of water, and the pulses of sound. (Thomas Young)

41. The first stages ... consisted of a rapid expansion determined by the mass of the initial atom. ... The atom-world was broken into fragments, each fragment into still smaller pieces. ... The evolution of the world can be compared to a display of fireworks that has just ended. (Georges Lemaitre)

▸ 42. In mechanism, when two wheels are intended to revolve in the same direction, a wheel is placed between them so as to be in gear with both, and this wheel is called an "idle wheel." The hypothesis about the vortices which I have to suggest is that a layer of particles, acting as idle wheels, is interposed between each vortex. (James Maxwell)

43. Malcolm Forbes, Jr. ... attacked the Federal Reserve for clamping down too tightly on interest rates—slowing down and almost killing the economic recovery. "It would be as if a doctor had a patient who made a quick comeback from the operation, and the doctor thought the patient was getting too healthy and induced a relapse. Well, in medicine you'd get sued for malpractice. In economics they make you the head of the Federal Reserve." (WKRN-TV, Nashville)

44. The relation which the several parts or members, of the natural body have to each other and to the whole body, is here compared to the relation which each particular person in society has to the whole society: and the latter is intended to be illustrated by the former. And if there be a likeness between these two relations, the consequence is obvious: that the latter shows us we were intended to do good to others, as the former shows us that the several members of the natural body were intended to be instruments of good to each other and to the whole body. (Joseph Butler)

45. Electric displacement, according to our theory, is a kind of elastic yielding to the action of the force, similar to that which takes place in structures and machines owing to the want of perfect rigidity of the connexions. ... Energy may be stored in the field ... by the action of electromotive force in producing electric displacement. ... [I]t resides in the space surrounding the electrified and magnetic bodies ... as the motion and strain of one and the same medium. (James Maxwell)

46. For instance, there can hardly be a doubt that the animals which fight with their teeth, have acquired the habit of drawing back their ears closely to their heads, when feeling savage, from their progenitors having voluntarily acted in this manner in order to protect their ears from being torn by antagonists. ... We may infer as highly probable that we ourselves have acquired the habit of contracting the muscles round the eyes, whilst crying gently, that is, without the utterance of any loud sound,

from our progenitors, especially during infancy, having experienced during the act of screaming, an uncomfortable sensation in the eyeballs. (Charles Darwin)

47. And why are we not willing to acknowledge that the appearance of a daily revolution belongs to the heavens, its actuality to the earth? The relation is similar to that of which Virgil's Aeneas says: "We sail out of the harbor and the countries and cities recede." For when a ship is sailing along quietly, everything which is outside of it will appear to those on board to have a motion corresponding to the movement of the ship, and the voyagers are of the erroneous opinion that they with all that they have with them are at rest. This can without doubt apply to the motion of the earth, and it may appear as if the whole universe were revolving. . . . (Nicolaus Copernicus)

▶ 48. Then I began to suspect whether the rays, after their trajection through the prism, did not move in curved lines, and according to their more or less curvity tend to divers parts of the wall. And it increased my suspicion, when I remembered that I had often seen a tennis ball struck with an oblique racket describe such a curved line . . . v. For the same reason, if the rays of light should possibly be globular bodies, and by their oblique passage out of one medium into another, acquire a circulating motion, they ought to feel the greater resistance from the ambient ether on that side where the motions conspire, and hence be continually bowed to the other. (Isaac Newton)

For each of the following analogical arguments, consider whether adding each listed premise would make the argument more or less reliable.

49. Twice before you've asked Joyce for a favor, and she's always agreed to help. You conclude that she'll probably agree to help again.
   (a) Before, you've asked her for rides; this time, you're asking for a loan.
   (b) Before, Joyce was single; now she's married.
   (c) Before, you were single; now you're married.
   (d) Joyce is now extremely busy; she's just had a baby.
   (e) Bart has also asked Joyce for favors, and she's granted them.

50. Norbert has taken one philosophy course and hated it. He refuses to sign up for another, reasoning that he'd hate it, too.
   (a) This course and that were taught by the same professor.
   (b) This course is on logic; that was on ancient skepticism.
   (c) Norbert has hated every humanities course he's taken.
   (d) This course and that both meet on Tuesdays and Thursdays.
   (e) Norbert has just spent a year off from school working on an oil rig.

51. Fanny has made As on both exams during the semester and infers that she'll probably get an A on the final.
   (a) The three exams cover different, nonoverlapping material.

(b) The same instructor made up all three exams.

(c) Fanny studied hard for the first two exams but isn't bothering to study for the final.

(d) Fanny's grades on the two exams were the highest in the class.

(e) Fanny's professor has gotten sick, and someone else is making up the final.

Notes

[1] John Stuart Mill, *A System of Logic* (University of Toronto Press, 1963; originally published 1843), p. 283.

[2] Alan P. Lightman discusses this example in "Magic on the Mind: Physicists' Use of Metaphor," *American Scholar* 58 (1989): 97–101.

[3] G. K. Gilbert, "The Origin of Hypotheses, Illustrated by the Discussion of a Topographic Problem," *Science* 3 (1896): 1–13.

CHAPTER

15

CAUSES

I f "all Inference, consequently all Proof, and all discovery of truths not self-evident, consists of inductions, and the interpretation of inductions," as John Stuart Mill believed, then virtually all knowledge depends on reasoning about causes, for the notion of causation is "the root of the whole theory of Induction."[1] Indeed, outside mathematics and logic itself, most knowledge involves causal relations. Engineers, for example, need to know what causes a bridge to withstand forces, what causes a power plant to produce electricity, and what causes a machine to perform a task. Doctors need to know what causes illness and what causes recovery. Something as simple as making a sandwich requires knowing that pulling on the refrigerator door will cause it to open, that twisting a bottle cap will cause it to come off, and so on.

Understanding causal reasoning, therefore, is fundamental to logic. This chapter discusses the idea of causation and presents methods, first developed by Mill, for establishing or disproving a causal relation. These methods offer some general principles for evaluating causal arguments.

15.1 KINDS OF CAUSES

To cause, in essence, is to bring about or produce. In English, we can speak of actions, events, objects, and perhaps even facts and states of affairs as causes.

(1) a. The Fed's announcement caused the dollar to drop.
   b. The dollar's slide caused investors to sell.
   c. Jill caused the accident.
   d. The fact that she ignored him caused Karl to fly into a jealous rage.
   e. Lou's persistent slovenliness caused his wife to leave him.

As these examples suggest, however, what is caused is almost always an action or event. Sometimes we speak of something causing a state—as in 'A genetic abnormality caused Frank to be obese'—but these seem to depend on causation of events ('A genetic abnormality caused Frank to become obese'). Nevertheless, throughout this chapter we'll think of actions as events of a special kind and treat effects as events or collections thereof.

Similarly, we seem to speak of objects, facts, and states as causes only when some event or collection of events acts as a cause. Jill caused the accident, for example, only if something Jill did caused it. Lou's persistent slovenliness caused his wife to leave him, similarly, only if a series of Lou's actions caused her departure. Throughout this chapter, then, we'll think of causation as relating events or collections of events.

Philosophers have disagreed about what causation is. Usually, they have analyzed it in terms of necessary and sufficient conditions.

> **DEFINITION** A condition is *necessary* for an event if and only if the event can't occur when the condition doesn't hold.

> **DEFINITION** A condition is *sufficient* for an event if and only if the event must occur when the condition holds.

Consider a classic case: the lighting of a match. The match can't light unless oxygen is present. The presence of oxygen, in other words, is a necessary condition of the lighting. If the match is dry and struck with enough force in the presence of oxygen, then the match must light. So, that joint condition is a sufficient condition of the lighting.

There may be more than one necessary condition of an event. The match's lighting requires, for example, not only the presence of oxygen but also the dryness of the match. There may be more than one sufficient condition as well. The match will light if we toss it, dry and in the presence of oxygen, into a blazing fire. By definition, all the necessary conditions must be included in each sufficient condition. If one weren't included in some sufficient condition, the event could take place without it, in which case it wouldn't be necessary after all.

Consider another example: A Texas university admits all Texas high school graduates who apply and who scored at least 1200 on the SAT or finished in the top quarter of their high school class. Applying and graduating from a Texas high school in the top quarter of the class is a sufficient condition for admission. So is applying, graduating from a Texas high school, and scoring at least 1200 on the SAT. Neither, however, is necessary. The university admits some who scored below 1200, some who finished below the top quarter in their high school classes, and some who didn't graduate from Texas high schools. Applying, however, is a necessary condition.

Some philosophers have defined causes as sufficient conditions. While this has appeal, it doesn't quite match our intuitive concept of causation. This exchange sounds odd:

(2) *A*: What caused the match to light?
B: Striking it, its dryness, and the presence of oxygen.

Sufficient conditions usually include more than an event, or even a set of events. They include at least some features of the background against which an event or set of events occurs. But we don't ordinarily count features of the background as causes or even parts of causes. Asked what caused the match to light, we'd ordinarily mention only the striking.

We might try to improve on this proposed definition by requiring that causes be events that are part of sufficient conditions. This would rule out the dryness of the match and the presence of oxygen and leave us with the striking alone. But, in other cases, we'd be left with many events, not all of which are causes. If we ask, "What caused it to snow today?" any account of sufficient conditions probably must mention many events: a collision between cold and warm air masses, the rising of the warm air, the condensation of moisture, the movement of the front through our area, and so on. But answering the question doesn't require mentioning them all.

Some philosophers have argued that causes are necessary conditions. But not all necessary conditions count as causes. No combustion can take place without oxygen; the presence of oxygen is a necessary condition of combustion. Oxygen's presence, however, isn't generally counted as the (or even a) cause of combustion. It doesn't help to require that causes be events. The university admits only those whose applications have been delivered by the post office, but we don't consider the delivery a cause of a student's being admitted.

Philosophers have advanced many other more complicated proposals for defining causation. Some have suggested that *A* causes *B* if and only if *A* is either necessary or sufficient for *B*. This definition suffers from several difficulties we've noted. It also implies that if *A* causes *B*, then *B* causes *A*, an erroneous suggestion. Other philosophers have suggested that 'cause' is ambiguous: It may mean either 'is a necessary condition for' or 'is a sufficient condition for'. Such an ambiguity would be surprising. It's often very important to know whether something is a necessary or a sufficient condition. For example, to cook a roast for supper, it's important to know that turning on the oven is necessary, but not sufficient; it's necessary to do more than that. So, it would be very odd to use the same word for both necessary and sufficient conditions. Whenever someone asserted a causal relation, we'd have to ask which kind of cause was meant. But people feel no need to resolve any persistent ambiguity about causation.

In fact, we can give a unified definition of causation that explains why the above attempts at definition fail. Causation is a context-relative notion.

To use Mill's example, if we ask why a stone thrown into a pond sinks to the bottom, a huge and indefinite amount of information is relevant to the question. A complete explanation would have to include the gravitational attraction between the earth and the stone, the chemical composition of the stone, a comparison of the specific gravities of the stone and the water, together with explanations for all of these. Yet, if asked what caused the stone to fall to the bottom of the pond, we'd ordinarily respond with a simple answer: "Johnny threw it in," "It's heavy," or something similar, depending on context. We assume a certain amount of information as background, and supply only whatever else the listener needs to understand why the event happened.

This returns us to the notion that figured so heavily in Chapters 2 and 3 of the common ground of a conversation. The participants in a conversation share a certain amount of information. They have in common certain items of knowledge, beliefs, and assumptions. The collection of those shared items is the conversation's common ground. When we allege a causal relation, we rely on the common ground to provide background information and specify only the aspect of the relationship that changes prior circumstances and offers our listeners new information. So, we don't discuss all the necessary or sufficient conditions of an event in indicating its cause. Instead, we specify what must be added to the common ground, or to a certain context, to yield a sufficient condition for the event.

> **DEFINITION**   An event A *causes* an event B *relative to* a context
> C if and only if A, together with C, is a sufficient condition for B.

Thus, we say that striking the match causes it to light. Striking, by itself, is neither a sufficient nor a necessary condition of the lighting. But, relative to typical circumstances—in which the match is dry and oxygen is present—the striking causes the match to light. Striking, in addition to the conditions that are part of the context or common ground, is sufficient for the event of the match's lighting.

Sometimes events occur in causal chains: A causes B, B causes C, C causes D, and so on. Striking the match, say, causes it to light; lighting the match causes the gas grill to start; starting the gas grill causes the temperature inside it to rise; the rising temperature causes the steak to cook. These chains play an extremely important role in explanations, as we'll see in the next chapter. We can often think of each member of a chain as an effect of the events preceding it. That is, we can often think of D as an effect of A, of B, and of C. C is the *proximate* or *immediate* cause of D; A and B are *remote* causes. Whether we think of earlier members of a chain as causes of later events depends on how the context shifts as we move from considering one causal relation to considering the next. We'd generally count starting the gas grill as a cause of the steak's cooking, for example, but we might not count striking the match as a cause.

Problems

Below are some typical sentences about causal relations. For each case, answer these questions: (a) Is the cause a necessary condition for the effect, independent of the context? (b) Is the cause a sufficient condition, independent of the context? (c) What context must we assume for the cause to be sufficient? (d) Is the cause proximate or remote?

▶ **1.** The infection caused the illness.

▶ **2.** Taking the drug caused the patient's recovery.

▶ **3.** Imbibing poison was the cause of death.

▶ **4.** A computer crash caused the delay in our sending you the information.

▶ **5.** John's tardiness caused the meeting to start an hour late.

▶ **6.** Gary's question caused the discussion to stray far from the topic.

7. Injecting dye into the vat caused the fabric to change color.

8. Turning the key caused the car to start.

9. Scattering salt on the ice caused it to melt.

10. Putting ice in the drink caused it to cool.

11. The heating of the oven caused the bread to rise.

▶ **12.** The activity of the yeast caused the bread to rise.

13. Turning the knob caused the door to open.

14. Something Fran said caused Deborah to become very angry.

15. A letter from the IRS caused Alex to leave the country.

16. Zeke's punch caused Charley's nose to bleed.

17. Hearing Val's story caused Bonnie to feel sorry for her.

▶ **18.** The flood caused widespread destruction.

19. Applying the fertilizer caused the plants to grow much more quickly.

20. Heating the mixture caused a violent reaction.

21. Flipping the switch caused the light to come on.

22. Nora's testimony caused the jury to change its mind.

23. Hank's departure caused the team's fall into the second division.

▶ **24.** Waving the red cloth caused the bull to charge.

25. The increase in atmospheric pressure caused the rise in the barometer reading.

These are causal chains. (a) Say whether, in each link, the cause is a necessary or sufficient condition independent of the context. (b) Say whether, in your opinion, each event prior to the proximate cause of the last event in the chain should count as a cause of that event, and explain your judgment.

26. (a) The leak in the fuel line caused the engine failure.
    (b) The engine failure caused the plane to crash.
    (c) The plane crash caused the deaths of more than one hundred people.

27. (a) Pulling the trigger caused the rifle to fire.
    (b) Firing the rifle caused its barrel to heat.
    (c) The heating of the barrel caused the rifle to emit an infrared glow.

28. (a) The scandal caused the party's defeat in the elections.
    (b) The party's electoral defeat caused a change in leadership.
    (c) The change in leadership caused a sweeping revision of government policy.
    (d) The sweeping revision of government policy caused widespread turmoil.

29. (a) The shooting of the archduke caused his government to issue an ultimatum.
    (b) The issuance of the ultimatum caused the Russians to mobilize.
    (c) The Russian mobilization caused the rejection of the ultimatum.
    (d) The ultimatum's rejection caused Austria-Hungary to declare war.
    (e) Austria-Hungary's declaration of war caused Serbia to declare war.
    (f) Serbia's declaration of war caused Russia's declaration of war.
    (g) Russia's declaration of war caused Germany to declare war.

▶ **30.** (a) The assassin's anger caused him to pull the trigger.
    (b) Pulling the trigger caused the gun to fire.
    (c) The gun's firing caused a loud noise.
    (d) The loud noise caused the crowd to react.
    (e) The reaction of the crowd caused the assassin to flee.
    (f) The assassin's fleeing caused some members of the crowd to follow him.
    (g) The crowd members following him caused the police to seize the assassin.
    (h) Being seized by the police caused the assassin to swallow his cyanide capsule.
    (i) Swallowing the cyanide capsule caused the assassin's death.

We ordinarily think that a variety of different events could produce the same effect: that, for example, either dieting or getting more exercise can cause a person to lose weight. This has been called the doctrine of the plurality of causes. Some philosophers have denied this doctrine, claiming that no event could be the effect of more than one possible event.

31. Does the doctrine of the plurality of causes conflict with (a) the view that causes are sufficient conditions; (b) the view that causes are necessary conditions; (c) the view that causes are sufficient conditions relative to a context?

Can you think of more than one cause that could produce each of these effects?

32. Karen wins one million dollars.

33. Linda gets married.

34. Pablo becomes an uncle.

35. Oliver is arrested.

▸ **36.** Irene dies of blood poisoning.

37. The cafeteria explodes.

38. Yolanda falls from a twenty-seven story building.

39. The potatoes in the pantry spoil.

40. The eight-ball moves in a straight line and falls into the corner pocket.

41. Three desert travelers, *A*, *B*, and *C*, stopped for the night before setting out on separate journeys. Both *A* and *B* hated *C*. *A* poisoned *C*'s only water supply, his canteen; *B*, not knowing what *A* did, drilled a small hole in *C*'s canteen so that the water would leak out. Several days later, *C* died of thirst. Which action—*A*'s or *B*'s—caused *C*'s death? Explain your answer.[2]

15.2 AGREEMENT AND DIFFERENCE

The British philosopher Francis Bacon (1561–1626) recognized that there was more to induction than generalization. He saw the importance of causal reasoning and developed some methods for devising and evaluating causal claims. John Stuart Mill developed these methods further, formulating them so clearly that they are now called "Mill's methods." The methods pertain particularly to causal generalizations: assertions that events of one kind cause events of another kind. The first two of Mill's canons for inductive procedure are the methods of *agreement* and *difference*.

Agreement

The central idea behind Mill's first method is that any factor that can be absent while the effect still results can't be the cause of that effect. If all factors that might be present or absent are eliminated and only one factor remains, that factor must be the cause. Similarly, anything that can be absent while the same cause is operating can't be an effect of that cause. If all features of the circumstances that follow a cause and might be either present or absent are eliminated, and only one remains, that circumstance must be the effect. As Mill himself expresses his first canon:

> If two or more circumstances of the phenomenon under investigation have only one circumstance in common, the circumstance in which alone all the instances agree, is the cause (or effect) of the given phenomenon (*A System of Logic,* 390).

Schematically, suppose that we are seeking the cause of a kind of event *E*. In different circumstances, we find *E* following events of various other kinds, as detailed in this table:

Case	Antecedent Events			Followed by
1	*A*	*B*		*E*
2		*B*	*D*	*E*
3	*A*	*B* *C*		*E*
4		*B* *C*	*D*	*E*
5	*A*	*B*	*D*	*E*

Mill's method of agreement says that *B* is a likely candidate for being the cause of *E*. Events of type *E* may or may not follow events of types *A*, *C*, or *D*; thus, according to Mill's principle, those are unlikely to be causally connected to *E*.

In short, then, the method of agreement is as follows. To find the cause of a kind of event, see what the antecedent circumstances have in common. To find the effect of a given event, see what the subsequent circumstances have in common.

An excellent example of applying the method of agreement occurred in a puzzling medical case in 1944, detailed by Berton Roueche in *Eleven Blue Men.*[3] Throughout the day on Monday, September 25, 1944, Beekman-Downtown Hospital in New York City received eleven ragged old men with similar and unusual symptoms. Each patient had collapsed. At first the extremities, and gradually the remainder of the body, of each patient became sky blue. The physician who examined the first patient at 8:30 A.M. attributed his blue color to cyanosis resulting from insufficient levels of oxygen in the blood and diagnosed carbon monoxide poisoning. The tenth patient arrived at noon; the eleventh and last was found in a flophouse that evening. The Health Department had begun to investigate by afternoon. One patient died; the other ten, given heart stimulants, oxygen, and bed rest, began to recover.

Questioning the patients yielded the following information. All the patients collapsed in the Bowery area. Five patients were stricken in the Globe

Hotel, two in the Star Hotel, one in the Lion Hotel, and three on the street. Already Mill's method of agreement applied. It indicated that the cause was unlikely to involve any of the flophouses specifically but probably did involve the Bowery area. If indeed the cause were gas poisoning, the method would signal that the source must have been around the Bowery.

More interestingly, all the patients had eaten breakfast at a single Bowery area eating place, the Eclipse Cafeteria. Agreement on this feature of the antecedent circumstances strongly suggested, by Mill's method of agreement, that the cafeteria was the source of the poisoning. All the men, moreover, had gotten sick within half an hour after eating; all but one had eaten oatmeal, rolls, and coffee, and the remaining one had eaten oatmeal. Again Mill's method applied: The cause probably involved the oatmeal.

Furthermore, the men had not been in the cafeteria at the same time. They had eaten at various times in a busy three-hour period, during which many other customers ate breakfast without incident. This led the doctors to abandon the hypothesis of gas poisoning. If carbon monoxide had filled the cafeteria, the gas would probably have been present for only a short time and, moreover, would have affected everyone there. Again, the reasoning relied on the method of agreement. Suppose the Eclipse Cafeteria had contained toxic amounts of carbon monoxide. Then, to find the effects, we should look at all the relevant cases—all the people who were there while the gas was—and see what they have in common later. But most of the morning customers were fine; only eleven were ill.

The Health Department, therefore, conjectured that the oatmeal had been poisoned. Tests on blood samples from the affected men confirmed the conjecture, and chemical analysis of the oatmeal ingredients indicated that what should ordinarily have been sodium chloride—salt—was in fact sodium nitrite, a compound sometimes substituted for sodium nitrate in curing meats during World War II. The investigators thus concluded that the eleven old men were victims of sodium nitrite poisoning, an extremely rare type of poisoning. Before 1944, only ten cases had ever been reported in the medical literature.

This account of the causal reasoning in the case of the eleven blue men is simplified, though quite accurate to the actual reasoning of the Health Department officials. A careful reader may have noticed, however, that the afflicted men had other things in common. All were old, and all were heavy drinkers. These initially overlooked features became important at a later stage of the investigation. They also illustrate an important philosophical point. The method of agreement, like Mill's other methods, relies on an assumption that all and only relevant features of the circumstances are being taken into account. Two cases, after all, never have just one feature or circumstance in common. Any two people, for example, have a great many things in common, simply because they are human beings. Mill's description of the method makes sense, therefore, only if we understand it to concern relevant features or circumstances. But this interpretation means that success of the method depends on correctly judging what factors are relevant to explaining the phenomenon in question. If we exclude as irrelevant items that play a causal role, the method may lead us to partially or totally incorrect conclusions.

Mill's methods also rely on another assumption concerning the phenomena to be discussed. We must assume that we've analyzed the circumstances correctly. That is, the success of the method of agreement, as well as Mill's other methods to follow, depends on a proper division of the circumstances into distinct causal factors. If we incorrectly identify the factors that might play a causal role from the beginning, the methods are unlikely to yield any helpful results. For example, applying the method of agreement to chemical reactions is helpful only if we've properly distinguished and perhaps even identified the various compounds involved. If we haven't—if, perhaps, some of our samples marked 'X' are sodium nitrate, while others are sodium nitrite—then the method may find no interesting causal relations at all. To work, the method requires that we sort objects and circumstances into appropriate kinds before searching for agreement and drawing causal conclusions.

Difference

Mill's second canon, the method of difference, seeks to discover causes and effects not by examining similar cases and identifying what they have in common but by examining cases that differ and identifying those differences. If one case demonstrates a certain effect and if another, similar case doesn't, the method says to look for other differences which can account for the presence of the effect in only one case. Similarly, if a cause is operating in one case but not in another very similar case, we can find the effect by comparing the two and seeing what other differences follow. As Mill himself describes the canon,

> If an instance in which the phenomenon under investigation occurs, and an instance in which it does not occur, have every circumstance in common save one, that one occurring only in the former; the circumstance in which alone the two instances differ, is the effect, or the cause, or an indispensable part of the cause, of the phenomenon (*A System of Logic,* 391).

Once again, we should understand that Mill is referring to circumstances that might be relevant to the phenomenon. So, let us suppose that we can find two very similar cases: one in which the effect we're investigating occurs, and another, very similar case in which it doesn't. We look to see what other differences are present. The method of difference states that if we can find just one other difference, it is the cause, or "an indispensable part of the cause," of the effect. If we are seeking the cause of the effect E, then we seek two cases very similar except that only one demonstrates the effect. Suppose we find:

Case	Antecedent Circumstances	Effect
1	A B C	E
2	A B	F

The method of difference indicates that C is the cause, or part of the cause, of E. We cannot infer that C is the entire cause; C may be only "part of the cause." C might not produce the effect E except in the presence of B, or under other special conditions. The same reasoning holds for finding effects. Suppose we find two similar cases and apply the cause we want to investigate only to one. We can observe differences in effects to determine the effect of that additional cause.

Case	Antecedent Circumstances	Effects
1	A B C D	E F
2	A B C	E

The results described in the table indicate that D causes, or is part of the cause, of F.

The method of difference also played an important role in the case of the eleven blue men, but at a later stage of the investigation. Health Department officials traced the illness afflicting the eleven elderly residents of Manhattan to oatmeal served at the Eclipse Cafeteria. However, a new puzzle emerged. The Eclipse prepared enough oatmeal to serve around 125 breakfast customers, and on September 25, 1944, all of it was consumed. Therefore, the cause of the illness could not be attributed to the oatmeal alone. Out of roughly 125 people who had eaten it, only 11 got sick. Why?

The method of difference says that, to find the cause, we must consider differences between the 11 sick men and the approximately 114 other individuals who had eaten oatmeal yet showed no ill effects. Health Department officials, making up a batch of oatmeal following the recipe of the Eclipse cook and chemically analyzing it, were able to explain why most customers did not get sick: The oatmeal contained only about 80% of the minimum toxic dose of sodium nitrite. The eleven sick men must have somehow received a greater dose. How? One doctor conjectured that if the salt container in the kitchen contained sodium nitrite, salt shakers on the tables might also. Testing them showed that all contained table salt but one, which contained a mixture of salt and sodium nitrite. So, the investigation uncovered two hypotheses about very significant differences between the sick men and the healthy customers. The sick men all sat at one table, and they all salted their oatmeal. (Unfortunately, this hypothesis could not be checked: By the time investigators had formulated it, the surviving patients had been released.)

The method of difference indicates that adding more sodium nitrite to the already poisoned oatmeal at that one table was the cause of the illness.

This assumption raised yet another question. Some people salt oatmeal. To obtain a toxic dose, however, the men had to add at least a teaspoon of salt to their oatmeal. Why would they add so much? Here, the method of agreement helped. The men had a number of things in common. They were found in the Bowery area; they had eaten oatmeal at the Eclipse, apparently at a single table; they were old; and they were heavy drinkers. Alcoholics tend to have lower sodium chloride levels in the blood than other people; they need to consume more salt to provide what their bodies require. Thus, the men probably used an excessive amount of salt because they were alcoholics.

Joint Method of Agreement and Difference

The methods of agreement and difference may be used together. As in the case of the eleven blue men, first one, then another, may be used to isolate the cause of some phenomenon. But they may also be used jointly. Doing so produces an improvement of the method of agreement, which, in Mill's words, has as its canon:

> If two or more instances in which the phenomenon occurs have only one circumstance in common, while two or more instances in which it does not occur have nothing in common save the absence of that circumstance; the circumstance in which alone the two sets of instances differ, is the effect, or the cause, or an indispensable part of the cause, of the phenomenon (*A System of Logic,* 396).

Schematically, we can see the pattern of the joint method of agreement and difference:

Case	Antecedent Circumstances	Effects
1	A B	E F
2	A C	E G
3	B C	F G
4	D	H

Here, the antecedent circumstances of cases 1 and 2 have only A in common; the antecedent circumstances of cases 3 and 4 have nothing in common but the absence of A. Cases 1 and 2 exhibit the effect E, but cases 3 and 4 don't. The joint method of agreement and difference states that A is probably the cause, or an indispensable part of the cause, of E.

This method corresponds to the familiar experimental technique of using a control group. In the table, cases 1 and 2 are used to test the effects of A; cases 3 and 4 are controls used to discover what happens without A. Using a control group of this kind greatly increases the reliability of a causal inference, for it indicates whether the effect—here, E—would have occurred even without A.

Problems

Find and assess applications of the methods of agreement, difference, and agreement and difference in these passages.

▸ **1.** Texas is a key to Republican presidential victories. No Democrat has ever won the White House without carrying Texas.

▸ **2.** In the past few years, dozens of countries have cut marginal tax rates. Almost everywhere, the cuts have been followed by increased economic growth and, in the presence of monetary policy keeping the currency stable, vastly reduced inflation.

▸ **3.** Andy was a top graduate of a department ranked second in the country and got tenure. Beth was a top graduate of a school ranked fifteenth; she got tenure. Claire was an above-average graduate of a school ranked third, and she got tenure. Derek was an above-average graduate from a school ranked twelfth, and Eric was an above-average graduate from a school ranked tenth; they were denied tenure.

▸ **4.** The commission studied ratings of departments of various universities, finding that every great university ranked among the top ten in English and history, and all but one ranked in the top ten in philosophy. Universities just below them in stature might have great departments of anthropology, or linguistics, or zoology, but invariably fell short of the mark in English, history, or philosophy.

5. The starting roster of the Cincinnati Reds, 1960:

Player	Pos	HR	RBI	Avg.	SB
Ed Bailey	c	13	67	.261	1*
Frank Robinson	1b	31	83	.297	13
Billy Martin	2b	3	16	.246	0*
Eddie Kasko	3b	6	51	.292	2
Roy McMillan	ss	10	42	.236	9*
Wally Post	lf	19	50	.282	4
Vada Pinson	cf	20	61	.287	32
Gus Bell	rf	12	62	.262	0*

Player	Pos	W	L	ERA	
Bob Purkey	p	17	11	3.59	
Jim O'Toole	p	12	12	3.81	
Jay Hook	p	11	18	4.50*	
Cal McLish	p	4	14	4.17*	

Players whose lines are marked with an asterisk were traded before the 1961 season. A sixth-place team thereby rose to win the National League pennant. Using Mill's methods, explain why the players who were kept were kept and why those who were traded were traded.

6. Several students from a single college have applied to one particular graduate program. Here are the students' records and the graduate school's decisions:

Student	GPA	GRE-V	GRE-M	Decision
A	3.9	750	620	admit, with fellowship
B	3.8	680	760	admit, with assistantship
C	3.6	730	780	waiting list, possible assistantship
D	3.5	650	670	waiting list, no aid
E	3.3	660	610	reject

Use Mill's methods to explain the results.

7. A glance was all he needed. It was enough to convince him that he was indeed up against a series of related cases of tetanus. It was also enough to give him an excellent idea of how they must have originated. Like Williams, Bab Miller, Ida Metcalf, Juanita Jackson, Josephine Dozier, and Ruby Bowers had all been firmly addicted to heroin.[4] (Berton Roueche)

8. "I don't know what she cut it with, but you know how those addicts operate. They'll use anything that's handy. My guess is she mixed in a pinch of dust."

"I suppose that's as good a guess as any," Dr. Greenberg said. "Except for one thing. It doesn't explain why Lulu is still alive."

"I was coming to that," Dr. Clarke said. "As a matter of fact, it does. It's about the only explanation that seems to stand up. The last few times Lulu and her friends met, Lulu didn't get a regular shot. She didn't have any money for drugs. All she got, she says, was what she could cadge from the others. And they weren't overly generous. They only gave her just enough to keep her going."[5] (Berton Roueche)

9. In 1947, there was an outbreak of smallpox in New York City. Health department officials studied the cases of two smallpox patients at Willard Parker Hospital, Acosta and Patricia. Acosta was married, from the East Bronx, and worked as a porter at another hospital. He had entered Willard Parker on March 27. Patricia had been admitted to Willard Parker on March 21. Both patients had been in the hospital previously. Acosta had been in Willard Parker from February 27 to March 11, suf-

fering from mumps; Patricia, suffering from croup, had been there from February 28 to March 13. Soon, a two and a half year old boy, John, contracted smallpox; he had been in the hospital, suffering from whooping cough, since March 6. The Health department officials concluded that Acosta, Patricia, and John had contracted smallpox at Willard Parker, from somebody who had been there between March 6 and March 13.[6]

10. In 1945, there was an outbreak of psittacosis, parrot fever, on Long Island. Initially, everyone who contracted the disease worked on a duck farm. Additional cases began to appear, however, among people who had no link to duck farms. One patient worked on the Long Island Railroad; one ran a farm in Riverhead. Both kept chickens, and a neighbor of the first owned pigeons. Ten other patients raised chickens, and a few patients enjoyed feeding wild pigeons.[7]

11. In 1980, Dr. Richard B. Shekelle of Rush-Presbyterian-St. Luke's Medical Center in Chicago analyzed deaths among 1,900 middle-aged American men whose diets were first examined more than 20 years earlier. The analysis showed that those who consumed large amounts of cholesterol had a much greater chance of dying prematurely of a heart attack. And a national study completed in 1983 among 3,806 men by the National Heart, Lung, and Blood Institute showed that reducing cholesterol in the blood can indeed be life-saving. When the men, all of whom faced a high risk of developing heart disease, were treated with a cholesterol-reducing drug and dietary advice, each 1-percent fall in cholesterol produced a 2-percent drop in their rate of coronary heart disease. (Jane Brody)

12. John T. Molloy describes an experiment concerning the importance of ties:

> ... I panhandled money around the Port Authority Bus Terminal and Grand Central Station in New York. My approach was to stop people, say I was terribly embarrassed, but had left my wallet home, and needed 75 cents to get home. I did this for two hours at rush hour. During the first hour, I wore a suit, but no tie; for the second hour, I added my tie. In the first hour, I made $7.23, but in the second, with my tie on, I made $26.00, and one man even gave me extra money for a newspaper.

(a) What can we conclude, given Mill's methods? (b) Imagine repeating this experiment with other articles of clothing or aspects of grooming: with and without glasses, watch, jacket, shirt, belt, shoes, socks, pants; hair combed and uncombed, shaved and unshaved, and so on. What results would you predict? What would the results allow us to conclude about these items?

15.3 Residues and Concomitant Variation

Residues

Mill's fourth method is the method of *residues*. Aptly named, it rests on the idea that if we "subtract out" all effects of known causes, the remainder or residue must be the effect of some other cause or causes. In other words, if we can explain some aspects of the phenomenon, we can consider the other as yet unexplained aspects as effects of causes still to be determined. As Mill expresses this canon of inductive reasoning:

> Subduct from any phenomenon such part as is known by previous inductions to be the effect of certain antecedents, and the residue of the phenomenon is the effect of the remaining antecedents (*A System of Logic,* p. 398).

"Of all the methods of investigating laws of nature," Mill declared, "this is the most fertile in unexpected results" (p. 398).

The method of residues is so familiar that it counts as common sense. Suppose that Meg wants to weigh a fairly light object—a baby, perhaps—but has a bathroom scale accurate only for fairly heavy objects. Meg can step on the scale without the baby to determine her own weight and then step on it again with the baby to determine their combined weight. Subtracting her weight from the combined weight yields the baby's weight. Here, Meg's weight is the portion of the phenomenon known to be the effect of a certain cause—the gravitational attraction between the earth and her own body—while the difference between the combined weight and her weight is the residue to be explained by the additional factor of the baby's weight.

Schematically, we can see the pattern behind the method of residues:

Case	Antecedent Circumstances	Effects
1	*A* *B* *C*	*E* *F*

If *A* and *B* are known to cause *E*, then we can infer that *C* must be responsible for *F*.

This method is unlike the others in at least two respects. First, it applies to even a single case. Second, it requires reference to prior knowledge of causal relationships. The other methods allow us to infer causal relations from examining several cases; the method of residues allows us to draw causal inferences from examining one or more cases in conjunction with already understood causal laws.

Concomitant Variation

Mill's fifth and final method is that of *concomitant variation*. The previous methods have involved cases that vary in their antecedent circumstances and their effects. The method of difference and the joint method of agreement and difference require that we be able to isolate cases not exhibiting the cause or effect we want to investigate. The method of agreement similarly requires that we be able to eliminate as possible causes all those antecedent circumstances without which the effect we wish to study can occur. These methods are therefore *eliminative*. Sometimes, however, eliminating circumstances is impossible. Suppose we want to study the earth's gravity. We can't, at least in the macroscopic realm, find any object immune from gravity. But we can observe variations in gravitational attraction reflected in differences in weight. When antecedent circumstances and/or effects involve quantities that vary, we can apply the method of concomitant variations. This method indicates how to relate variations in the antecedent circumstances to variations in effects.

Mill expresses the canon of this method as follows:

> Whatever phenomenon varies in any manner whenever another phenomenon varies in some particular manner, is either a cause or an effect of that phenomenon, or is connected with it through some fact of causation (*A System of Logic*, p. 401).

In more modern terms, we might call this the method of correlations. When variations in the antecedent circumstances correlate with variations in effects, we can infer some causal connection between these variations.

Schematically, we can see the pattern behind applications of the method of concomitant variation. Here, 'A+' represents an increased quantity of A, while 'A−' represents a decreased quantity.

Case	Antecedent Circumstances			Effects
1	A	B	C	E
2	$A+$	B	C	$E+$
3	$A-$	B	C	$E-$

This allows us to infer that A and E are causally linked.

Let us consider a simple example: The harder a driver presses on a car's gas pedal, the faster the car moves. Movements of the accelerator correlate with increases in the car's velocity. We can infer from this that there is a causal connection between pressing on the gas pedal and increasing the speed of the car. The former, in particular, causes the latter. Another simple example concerns summer temperatures and the use of electricity. The hotter the day, the more electricity people use. We can infer by the method of concomitant variation that there is a causal link between temperatures and electricity use. In this case, the link is slightly more complicated. The hotter the day, the higher the temperature, and the more electricity air conditioners require to maintain comfortable indoor temperatures.

As this example shows, the method of concomitant variation allows us to infer the existence of causal connections, but not their specific form. We can't assume that one varying factor must be the cause while the other must be the effect. Suppose that we find a correlation in various economies between rates of inflation and interest rates. This allows us to infer that inflation and interest rates are causally connected. We can't, however, infer that increases in inflation cause increases in interest rates. Nor can we infer that increases in interest rates cause increases in inflation. Both kinds of variation might result from some third factor or some collection of factors that causes increases in both. So, from the kind of information in our table above, we can infer that A and E are causally linked but not that A causes E or that E causes A. Both A and E may be effects of some common cause.

The kind of variation occurring in the above table is *direct:* Increases in one quantity occur in conjunction with increases in another. But the variation may also be *inverse:* Increases in one quantity may occur in conjunction with decreases in another. That is, we might find the pattern:

Case	Antecedent Circumstances			Effects
1	A	B	C	E
2	$A+$	B	C	$E-$
3	$A-$	B	C	$E+$

Quantities that vary inversely aren't uncommon. The volume of a quantity of gas, for example, varies inversely with the pressure applied to it. The more pressure, the smaller the gas's volume; the less pressure, the larger the volume. We can infer a causal connection between the pressure applied and the volume of the gas. Here is another simple example: The harder a driver presses on the brake pedal, the more the car slows down. The movement of the brake pedal correlates with the car's deceleration. Again, we can infer a causal link. Finally, demand for electricity varies inversely with its price. The more electricity costs, the less people tend to use. The method of concomitant variation allows us to conclude that some causal relation lies behind the correlation.

Problems

Discuss the applications of Mill's methods in these bits of reasoning.

▶ **1.** Since going from 65-mph and 70-mph state speed limits to a national 55-mph rule, traffic fatality rates have dropped from 3.5 per 100 million vehicle miles in 1975 to 2.9 in 1982, with or without safety devices, the National Safety Council says. (*Forbes*)

▶ **2.** Well, true enough—as far as it goes. But the statement leaves us with a serious question: Did that editor not know what else the Council says, that fatality rates dropped from 18.2 in 1925 to 3.6 in 1974, with no national speed laws at all? (Kevin Smith)

▶ **3.** Ancient Rome declined because it had a Senate; now what's going to happen to us with both a Senate and a House? (Will Rogers)

▶ **4.** From 1981 to 1983, the federal deficit skyrocketed—from 2.6% of national income in 1981 to 6% in 1982 and 6.9% in 1983. At the same time, nominal interest rates fell sharply—the three-month T-bill rate, for example, averaged 14% in 1981, 10.7% in 1982 and 8.6% in 1983. Real interest rates—the excess of nominal interest rates over the rate of inflation—remained roughly constant, averaging 4.7% in 1981 and 1982 and 4.4% in 1983, if inflation is measured by the GNP deflator. Nonetheless, neither this dramatic counterexample nor the more extensive empirical studies by respected economists that have found no historical relation between deficits and interest rates has shaken the confidence of Wall Street and Washington that deficits raise interest rates. Unexamined repetition works wonders. (Milton Friedman)

▶ **5.** Every time we have reduced taxes, we have increased the total revenue paid in taxes by the people to the government, because there is an incentive for people to earn more, and to go out and experiment and so forth. And so, no, the deficit has not been caused by the cut in taxes. The deficit would increase if we yielded to those who want us to increase taxes. (Ronald Reagan)

▶ **6.** Mama believed that garlic was the cure-all for any disease. Every morning she'd line us all up and she'd rub garlic on a little hankie and tie it around our necks. We'd say, "Mama, don't do that." She'd say, "Shut up." (She was a very loving woman.) She'd send us off to school with this garlic around our necks and we stunk to high heaven. But I want to tell you a secret; I was never sick a day. My theory about it is that no one ever got close enough to me to pass the germs. (Leo Buscaglia)

7. Liberals often assert that punishment does not deter crime, but James Q. Wilson and Richard J. Herrnstein, in *Crime and Human Nature,* cite evidence to the contrary from several countries. What does fail, it seems clear, is *not* punishing—putting offenders on probation, for example. Failing to punish sends pernicious messages—encouraging offenders, perplexing nonoffenders, subverting parents and impairing the prospects of civilized life. (William Bowen)

8. Advertisement appearing in magazines on San Diego newsstands:

Last year, Handguns killed
48 people in Japan
8 in Great Britain
34 in Switzerland
52 in Canada
58 in Israel
21 in Sweden
42 in West Germany
10,728 in the United States (James McClure)

9. There is no connection between New Hampshire's reputation as an outstanding ski state and the fact that we make 75 per cent of all wooden crutches. (State Planning and Development Commission)

10. *Q*: What if I'm still not convinced helmets work?
    A: Try this experiment. Put on a helmet and have a friend whack you on the head with a baseball bat. Now try the same experiment without the helmet. If you're still not convinced, you're probably too hard-headed to need a helmet. (Jerry Smith)

11. For instance, there can hardly be a doubt that the animals which fight with their teeth, have acquired the habit of drawing back their ears closely to their heads, when feeling savage, from their progenitors having voluntarily acted in this manner in order to protect their ears from being torn by antagonists; for those animals which do not fight with their teeth do not thus express a savage state of mind. (Charles Darwin)

▶ 12. ... researchers studying the relationship between married couples' work commitments and their love lives found that people with M.B.A. degrees have "significantly better" sex lives than other advanced-degree professionals. Even more surprising is the group found at the bottom of the sexual-satisfaction scale: Doctors of Philosophy, or Ph.D.s. Is this yet another sign of the times—that lucre is a greater turn-on than learning? (*Forbes*)

13. Both were delivered at the same instant; so that both were constrained to allow the same constellations, even to the minutest points, the one for his son, the other for his new-born slave. ... and yet Firminus, born in a high estate in his parents' house, ran his course through the gilded paths of life, was increased in riches, raised to honours; whereas that slave continued to serve his masters, without any relaxation of his yoke. ... (Saint Augustine)

14. [Jacob and Esau were] two twins born so near together that the second held the first by the heel; yet in their lives, manners, and actions, was such a disparity, that that very difference made them enemies to one another. (Saint Augustine)

15. Beethoven played a more decisive role in the evolution of music than any other single figure, not excepting Bach. It is only necessary to compare his earliest works with his last ones to recognize what progress the art of music made in his time—and largely owing to him. (David Ewen)

16. The generally accepted theory that both the Greeks and the Jews owe their systems of writing to the Phoenicians is strongly supported by the similarity in the names of the symbols: compare the Greek *alpha, beta, gamma,* with the Hebrew *aleph, beth, ghimel.* (Tobias Dantzig)

17. This tide increases with the declination of the moon till the 7th or 8th day; then for the 7 or 8 days following it decreases at the same rate as

it had increased before, and ceases when the moon changes its declination, crossing over the equator to the south. (Isaac Newton)

▶ **18.** Take away oxygen from the blood. The mind loses its reasoning ability. (Waldemar Kaempffert)

19. The ultimate fate of an ounce of uranium may be expressed by the equation:

$$1 \text{ ounce uranium} = \begin{cases} 0.8653 \text{ ounce lead,} \\ 0.1345 \text{ ounce helium,} \\ 0.0002 \text{ ounce radiation.} \end{cases}$$

The lead and helium together contain just as many electrons and just as many protons as did the original ounce of uranium, but their combined weight is short of the original uranium by about one part in 4000. Where 4000 ounces of matter originally existed, only 3999 now remain; the missing ounce has gone off in the form of radiation. (James Jeans)

20. During the campaign, the "racism" issue coalesced around Bush's attacks on the Massachusetts prison-furlough program and in particular around the case of Willie Horton, a murderer who escaped while on furlough and committed a brutal assault and rape upon a Maryland couple. . . . [T]he implication that voters hate blacks *per se* more than they fear criminals, or that weekend passes for murderers and other forms of coddling felons would stir little protest if the convicts were white, is absurd. The state of Maryland is currently being convulsed by a scandal: a rehabilitation-oriented penal institution is in danger of being closed down by legislators irate over the discovery that weekend furloughs were granted to a triple murderer, and work release to a rapist suspected of having used the occasion to commit another rape. Both convicts were white, and, to boot, the murderer was upper-class while the victim of his most heinous killing was black. But the people of Maryland—surprise?—are outraged nevertheless. (Joshua Muravchik)

21. Throughout the history of the game, almost every significant increase in offense has been accompanied by an increase in attendance, and almost every decrease in offense has been accompanied by a decrease in attendance. With the sole exception of the 1930s, every hitter's era in baseball history has been a period of growth, and every pitcher's era has been a period of stagnation. When runs per game dropped from 4.5 in 1911 to 3.7 in 1914, attendance dwindled from 6.6 million to 4.5 million. . . . When runs per game jumped from 3.8 in 1919 to 4.4 in 1920, attendance exploded. . . . When the ball was deadened in 1931, runs per game dropped from 5.5 to 4.8 and attendance dropped from 10.1 million to 8.5. By 1933, runs were down to 4.4 per game, and attendance was down to 6.1 million. . . . In the late 1940s, runs per game were back up in the 4.7 range, and attendance shot up to over 20 million; in 1952, runs were down to a little below 4.2, and attendance was down under 15 million. (Bill James)

How might the following causal claims be defended, using Mill's methods?

22. The United States has become great not because of things but because of ideas. (James Michener)

23. Kindness in words creates confidence, kindness in thinking creates profoundness, kindness in giving creates love. (Lao-Tzu)

▸ 24. Things are interesting because we care about them, and important because we need them. (George Santayana)

25. As a humanist, I am bound to reply that almost all important questions are important precisely because they are not susceptible to quantitative answers. (Arthur Schlesinger, Jr.)

26. Beggars get handouts before philosophers because people have some idea what it's like to be blind and lame. (Diogenes of Sinope)

27. Neighbors praise unselfishness because they profit by it. (Friedrich Nietzsche)

28. The ultimate result of shielding men from the effects of folly is to fill the world with fools. (Herbert Spencer)

29. You are free and that is why you are lost. (Franz Kafka)

▸ 30. If there's one major cause for the spread of mass illiteracy, it's the fact that everybody can read and write. (Peter de Vries)

31. It sounds too simple to say that lack of self-insight causes our griefs, but that is the plain fact. (Vernon Howard)

32. In the old *Amos 'n Andy Show* on radio Amos once asked the Kingfish why he had such good judgment.
    "Well," said the Kingfish, "good judgment comes from experience."
    "Then where does experience come from?" asked Amos.
    "Experience comes from bad judgment," was the Kingfish's answer. (David Mahoney)

33. In the following well-known passage, William James reverses the usual conception of the causal order of emotions and physiological reactions:

> Common-sense says, we lose our fortune, are sorry and weep; we meet a bear, are frightened and run; we are insulted by a rival, are angry and strike. The hypothesis here to be defended says that the order of this sequence is incorrect, that one mental state is not immediately induced by the other, that the more rational statement is that we feel sorry because we cry, angry because we strike, afraid because we tremble, not that we cry, strike or tremble because we are sorry, angry, or fearful as the case may be.[8]

How, using Mill's methods, might we test James's hypothesis?

15.4 Causal Fallacies

Mill's methods provide paradigms of good causal reasoning. They aren't deductively valid; they don't guarantee their conclusions. But they are reliable. Indeed, they are models of inductive inference. They play an important role in devising experiments and drawing conclusions from them in fields as diverse as astronomy, medicine, physics, economics, linguistics, and psychology.

Two argument patterns concerning causal reasoning occur frequently enough to be mentioned here, although they aren't reliable at all. The first has a Latin name, *post hoc, ergo propter hoc*—"after this, therefore because of this." As the name suggests, this type of argument involves drawing a causal conclusion simply from the temporal ordering of events. So, the form of the argument is the following:

> E preceded F.
> $\therefore$ E caused F.

or, in terms of causal generalizations,

> Events of kind E precede events of kind F.
> $\therefore$ Events of kind E cause events of kind F.

Clearly, this is a poor and unreliable form of argument. The Hundred Years' War occurred before the discovery of uranium, but it would be preposterous to conclude that the Hundred Years' War caused uranium to be discovered. Similarly, the moon landing occurred before the Pittsburgh Pirates won the 1971 World Series, but the moon landing didn't cause the Pirates to win. Nevertheless, arguments of this form are tempting. Political candidates rely on them constantly, proclaiming proudly that the economy did well during their tenure, concluding that they were responsible for its excellent performance, or decrying the unfortunate events occurring during their opponent's tenure, concluding that their opponent was the cause of all that misfortune. Political commentators also tend to be glib about extending temporal relations to causal relations. Large U.S. government budget deficits were a consistent feature of the world economy of the 1980s. At various times, commentators seemed to reach a consensus that the deficits caused a recession, an economic expansion, increases in interest rates, decreases in interest rates, increases in inflation rates, decreases in inflation rates, rises in the value of the dollar, declines in the value of the dollar, and almost every other economic occurrence of the decade. Sometimes these hypotheses gained some support from economic theory. Often, however, they were little more than *post hoc, ergo propter hoc* arguments. The budget deficit was large, then the price of gold fell; therefore, commentators concluded, the budget deficit caused the drop.

A second seductive but unreliable form of causal inference concerns Mill's method of concomitant variation. We've seen that the method allows inferring the existence of some causal connection but yields no information about its exact form or nature. If one quantity varies with another, changes in the former may cause changes in the latter, or changes in the latter may cause changes in the former, or changes in both quantities may result from some other causal mechanism. Finally, of course, the correlation may be just a coincidence. But it can be tempting to draw a straightforward causal conclusion from a correlation, bypassing Mill's caution. That constitutes a fallacy of induction, an unreliable form of argument.

Sports figures and fans seem especially prone to such arguments. The Dallas Cowboys, for example, declined to wear their blue home uniforms for years because they believed them to be unlucky; they seemed to lose more often while wearing those uniforms. Probably, however, there was no causal relationship; any correlation between wearing blue jerseys and losing was just chance. Similarly, the career of Lyman Bostock, a Detroit outfielder during the 1970s, tracked very closely the career of Austin McHenry, a St. Louis outfielder who played during the first decades of the twentieth century. Their achievements correlate very closely but almost certainly by coincidence.

These arguments are more tempting, and more deceptive, when the correlation probably isn't coincidental. As most barometer faces indicate explicitly, low barometric pressure correlates closely with rain. It can be tempting to conclude that low atmospheric pressure causes rain, or that rain causes low pressure. In fact, however, both tend to be effects of a common cause, namely, the movements of an air mass. During the 1970s, medical researchers established a correlation between heart disease and what they called "Type A" behavior—aggressiveness, hard work, ambition, and so on. Some people were tempted to conclude that Type A behavior causes heart disease. That inference may be true, but it may also be true that some common genetic or environmentally produced characteristic produces both Type A behavior and a tendency toward heart disease.

The moral, then, is that correlations, even when not coincidental, signal the existence of a causal link but reveal nothing about its nature.

Problems

Evaluate these causal arguments. Do they contain causal fallacies? Explain.

▶ 1. The harsh terms of the Versailles conference were followed by ruinous inflation in Germany in the early 1920s, which in turn preceded the rise of National Socialism. So, the harsh Versailles settlement caused the Nazi rise to power.

▶ 2. Experience shows that, when hemlines rise, stock prices also rise. Conversely, times of falling hemlines are also times of falling stock prices. Long skirts were fashionable during the Depression, whereas miniskirts were the rage during the booming 1960s. Thus, trends in women's fashion are effects of economic trends.

▶ **3.** Michael had problems with cholesterol until he began eating large amounts of oat bran. Then, his cholesterol level returned to normal. So, eating oat bran lowered his cholesterol level.

4. All fifty people in the study had high cholesterol levels before the study, during which they ate a diet high in oat bran. At the end of the study, the participants' cholesterol levels were 15 percent lower than at the beginning. So, eating oat bran lowers cholesterol levels.

5. People who have been audited have a high chance of being audited again. So, the IRS audits many people simply because it has audited them in the past.

Notes

[1] John Stuart Mill, *A System of Logic* (University of Toronto Press, 1963; originally published 1843), pp. 283, 326.

[2] This puzzle is from Raymond Smullyan, *What Is the Name of This Book?* (Englewood Cliffs, N. J.: Prentice-Hall, 1978), p. 9.

[3] Berton Roueche, *Eleven Blue Men* (Boston: Little, Brown and Company, 1947, 1953).

[4] Roueche, "A Pinch of Dust," *Eleven Blue Men.*

[5] Roueche, "A Pinch of Dust," *Eleven Blue Men.*

[6] Adapted from Roueche, "A Man from Mexico," *Eleven Blue Men.*

[7] Adapted from Roueche, "Birds of a Feather," *Eleven Blue Men.*

[8] William James, *Psychology* (Cleveland and New York: World Publishing, 1948), p. 376.

16

EXPLANATIONS

The goal of science is to achieve reliable knowledge and understanding. Almost all science involves careful observation—of the natural world, of people and their behavior, of social organizations, or of events in a laboratory. Scientists generalize on the basis of these observations, constructing laws and theories to explain what they observe. Because science seeks reliable knowledge, logic plays an important role in this process. Scientists seek to gain knowledge by reliable means.

Science goes far beyond generalizations of experience. We want to know, not only what happens, and under what circumstances, but why. Answering the "Why?" questions is crucial to understanding, rather than merely cataloguing, the world. Consequently, explanation is one of science's most important concepts. Often, explanation is causal; it proceeds by finding causes for the phenomena to be explained. This chapter will therefore relate very closely to the last. But not all explanations are causal. Indeed, scientists disagree about whether, in the final analysis, physical laws will make any reference to causation at all.

16.1 EXPLANATIONS AND HYPOTHETICAL REASONING

On November 22, 1963, President John F. Kennedy rode in a motorcade through downtown Dallas. Shots rang out; the presidential limousine raced to Parkland Memorial Hospital. Half an hour later, the president was dead. Why?, asked a shocked and mourning nation.

This question divides into many others. Why did Kennedy die? The immediate answer was discovered by attending physicians almost immediately. Kennedy suffered a massive gunshot wound to the head. Why and how was he wounded? Here, the answer is far less clear. The Warren Commission held that a single assassin hit the president with two bullets, one in the neck or upper back and one in the head. Critics have argued that as many as three assassins were involved. Whether the fatal shot was fired from the Texas School Book Depository building or the grassy knoll remains controversial. Why did the assassin or assassins kill the president? Here, too, controversy reigns. If Lee Harvey Oswald was the lone gunman, as the Warren Report argued, his motives are still obscure. If other conspirators were involved, it remains unknown who they were, much less why they shot Kennedy.

Consider the first question: Why did Kennedy die? The doctors explained his death by saying that he suffered a massive gunshot wound to the head. This explanation is causal, for the gunshot caused the wound that caused his death. It is also a *covering law* explanation. It explains a particular occurrence by relating it to a general law. We might explain why leaves, once detached from trees, fall to the ground by pointing out that all objects dropped near the earth fall toward it. Similarly, we might explain why a particular crow is black by pointing out that all crows are black. Covering law explanations of particular events or states of the world thus have the form of simple deductive arguments.

(1) Covering law
Particular circumstances
∴ Particular event or state

In the case of the crow, for example, the explanation has the form

(2) All crows are black.
This is a crow.
∴ This is black.

In the case of President Kennedy, it has the form

(3) People who suffer massive gunshot wounds to the head die.
Kennedy suffered a massive gunshot wound to the head.
∴ Kennedy died.

Covering law explanations can account for general as well as particular truths. We might explain why all crows on campus are black by saying that all crows are black. Similarly, we might explain why batted baseballs travel in parabolic arcs by pointing out that all projectiles travel in parabolic arcs. The form of these explanations is syllogistic, for example, the case of the campus crows:

(4) All crows are black.
All crows on campus are crows.
∴ All crows on campus are black.

This example suggests that covering law explanations of general truths have this form:

(5) Covering law
Universal affirmative relating general truth to covering law
∴ General truth

Often, this sort of explanation is said to *subsume* a generalization under the covering law.

Scientific explanations often involve more than one law. The explanation of Kennedy's death in (3) summarizes a much more complete medical explanation that would cite damage to parts of the brain, the importance of their functioning, and so on. The laws appealed to here might be very complex, hardly intelligible to anyone without medical training. But, in general terms, we can think of a law as asserting that if certain conditions hold, then certain other conditions hold, or a certain kind of event will occur. Explanations can thus explain a complex of conditions or events in terms of several laws and conditions.

(6) Laws
    Conditions
    ∴ Conditions or Events

These examples might suggest that explanation is a topic for the theory of deduction, not induction. But such a suggestion is misleading. In a deductive argument, we start with premises and deduce some conclusion. In a covering law explanation, we start with the fact to be explained. This will be, in effect, the conclusion of the explanation. We then work to develop a hypothesis that allows us to explain what we want to explain. And any such hypothesis is developed and justified inductively. In other words, given a covering law and a general truth or particular fact to be explained, devising and assessing an explanation of the latter by the former is like devising and assessing a deductive argument. But we need induction to derive the covering law.

Covering laws and explanations involving them arise by a process called *hypothetical reasoning.* Scientists accept or reject sentences as laws depending on whether there is evidence to support them. Before the evidence is assessed, proposed laws are *hypotheses:* sentences tentatively proposed as laws or explanations. Hypotheses are not themselves facts; they are proposed to explain facts and are subject to investigation. Hypothetical reasoning is the process of proposing hypotheses, testing them, and accepting, rejecting, or modifying them in light of evidence. Reasoning toward a goal of explaining certain phenomena consists of four stages, which are often repeated:

Hypothetical Reasoning

1. Formulate a hypothesis to explain the phenomena in question.
2. Determine what the hypothesis implies or predicts about the phenomena.
3. Test these implications or predictions.
4. Accept, reject, or modify the hypothesis.

We can express this in a diagram:

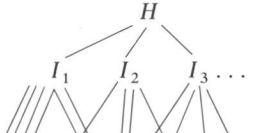

Hypothesis
Inference
Implications (Predictions)

Evidence

Consider again the Kennedy assassination. The Dallas police and later the Warren Commission hypothesized that Lee Harvey Oswald, acting alone, killed the president. To test this hypothesis, they explored its implications and tested them against the available evidence. For example, films of the assassination show that the shots were all fired within six seconds. A single gunman could have fired only three shots during that time. So, the hypothesis entails that there were at most three shots. Is this conclusion compatible with the evidence? Unfortunately, the evidence is quite unclear. A Dallas police radio was left on inadvertently during the shooting, but acoustic tests have not established whether three or four shots were fired. A single gunman would have taken about two seconds to reload and fire a rifle. The hypothesis also entails, therefore, that about three seconds elapsed between shots. Does this square with the evidence? Again, the answer is unclear. The Zapruder film of the assassination seems to show Kennedy react to being hit about a second before Governor John Connally reacted, too long for a single bullet to have hit both, but too short for a second bullet to have been fired by the same gunman. Critics of the commission have argued on this basis for revising the single-gunman hypothesis. Defenders of the commission have maintained that Connally's reaction was delayed.

The first stage—formulating a hypothesis—requires imagination. There's no rule for devising hypotheses; thinking of them demands intelligence, insight, ingenuity, creativity, and hard work. Some philosophers have thought that we need only to collect the facts, generalize on them to obtain a hypothesis, and test the hypothesis. But where do we begin collecting facts? There are infinitely many facts we could collect; we need to know where to begin. We might say, "Collect the relevant facts"—but relevant to what? Moreover, even if we begin with a well-defined problem to be solved, we won't know what's relevant to it without having some proposal for solving it. Suppose we want to find the cause of a newly discovered disease. What facts are relevant? Until we have a hypothesis about whether it is contagious, how it may be transmitted, and so on, we can't begin to know how to distinguish relevant from irrelevant facts. Hypotheses, therefore, are crucial to scientific activity. They are not dictated by the data, but are proposals for organizing and explaining the data.

The second stage—determine what the hypothesis implies or predicts—is largely deductive, although it may also involve inductive reasoning. Once we've formulated a hypothesis, we need to determine how to test it. So, we must see which of its implications we can test. These implications may concern the future, in which case they are *predictions*. But they may also concern the present or the past.

Often, the hypothesis alone does not imply anything we can test. To derive something we can test, we need to introduce other assumptions, items of knowledge, hypotheses, principles, and facts. These are called *auxiliary assumptions*. They may be well established, or they may be mere conjecture. But we assume them to be true for the purposes of testing the hypothesis. For example, in inferring from the single-gunman hypothesis that at most three shots were fired, we used the auxiliary assumptions that all the shots were fired within six seconds and that about three seconds were needed between shots.

The third stage, testing the hypothesis, is fundamental to the scientific method. It distinguishes science from intuition and superstition. Having derived some testable implications of our hypothesis, we proceed to test them. This may require great cleverness and technical skill. Testing the single-gunman hypothesis, for example, has required sophisticated work in acoustics, photographic analysis, ballistics, and forensics, which has nevertheless failed to yield a clear answer. Testing hypotheses in modern particle physics tends to require very complex, sophisticated, and expensive equipment.

If we discover through testing that the implications are true, our test *confirms* the hypothesis (together with any auxiliary assumptions we used). If we discover that at least one implication is false, our test *disconfirms* or *infirms* our hypothesis (assuming that all auxiliary assumptions hold).

Confirmation and disconfirmation are quite different from a logical point of view. Tests that confirm a hypothesis constitute evidence in its favor; they support it inductively. Tests that disconfirm a hypothesis, however, show conclusively that it, or some auxiliary assumption accompanying it, is false. Confirming tests, that is, have inductive force. Disconfirming tests have deductive force. Disconfirming tests, therefore, require revision or outright rejection of the hypothesis or some auxiliary assumption.

To see why, recall the definition of implication. One sentence implies another if the truth of the first guarantees the truth of the second. So, the truth of a hypothesis, together with auxiliary assumptions, guarantees the truth of implications or predictions drawn from the hypothesis. But the truth of some of those implications or predictions doesn't guarantee the truth of the hypothesis, although the truth of the implications does support it inductively. The falsehood of some implications or predictions, in contrast, guarantees the falsehood of the hypothesis or an auxiliary assumption. So, a disconfirming test guarantees that the hypothesis or an auxiliary assumption is false.

Put more simply: suppose A implies B. Then the truth of A guarantees the truth of B. If B is false, then A must be false. But, if B is true, we can deduce nothing at all about A. The truth of B may constitute evidence for A, but it doesn't conclusively establish the truth of A.

Consider once again the single-gunman hypothesis. If we were able to show that there were only three shots, then we would have evidence in favor of the hypothesis. We would not, however, have proved it to be true. Several gunmen might have fired a total of three shots between them. If we were to show that there were more than three shots, however, we'd have established that the hypothesis, or some auxiliary assumption we used to derive implications from it, is false.

Let's analyze an actual case of scientific reasoning to see how hypothetical reasoning works. Recall from Chapter 15 the case of the eleven blue men. The story involves repeated applications of the hypothetical method. It begins early on the morning of September 25, 1944, with a policeman's discovery of an old man on the street who had vomited and collapsed. The policeman, accustomed to Bowery residents who drank too much, conjectured that the old man was suffering from a bout with alcohol. Here arose the first hypothesis about the cause of illness. The hypothesis posited implications concerning the old man's condition. A closer examination, however, did not bear out those implications: The old man's fingers and nose were blue. This information disconfirmed the policeman's hypothesis.

The doctor who treated the old man upon his arrival at Beekman-Downtown Hospital tentatively diagnosed carbon monoxide poisoning. That diagnosis explained the sky blue color of the man's extremities, as well as his collapse. But the diagnosis also posited implications that weren't borne out. The old man didn't exhibit the dopiness and headache that typically accompany gas poisoning, but he did experience abdominal cramps and vomiting. As these aspects of the patient's condition became clear, the doctor was forced to abandon the hypothesis of carbon monoxide poisoning.

Once Health Department officials learned that all ten surviving patients suffering from the same symptoms had eaten breakfast at the Eclipse Cafeteria, they conjectured that food poisoning caused the old men's afflictions. This hypothesis explained the cramps and vomiting. However, five to twenty-four hours typically elapse before the symptoms of food poisoning appear; the old men collapsed within thirty minutes after eating. Therefore, that hypothesis also had to be rejected.

Tracing the problem to the oatmeal eaten by all the men and, in particular, to the accidental substitution of sodium nitrite for sodium chloride in the cereal, the Health Department officials hypothesized that the men suffered from sodium nitrite poisoning induced by eating chemically contaminated oatmeal. This conjecture correctly accounted for all their symptoms but also led to some false consequences. The men could have been poisoned only if they had ingested a toxic amount of sodium nitrite. But the oatmeal, mixed according to the cook's recipe, contained less than a toxic amount. Moreover, if the oatmeal had been toxic, all 125 people who had eaten it should have become ill. Yet only eleven were sick.

These facts required revising the hypothesis. The officials hypothesized that the men suffered from sodium nitrite poisoning, the source of which was the Eclipse Cafeteria oatmeal and "salt," actually sodium nitrite, from a table shaker. This hypothesis no longer implied that the other patrons should have become sick. It continued to explain the men's symptoms. Furthermore, it predicted that at least one table at the Eclipse would have a shaker containing a significant amount of sodium nitrite. Testing the shakers confirmed that prediction. Thus, the hypothesis was confirmed.

The process of investigation in the case of the eleven blue men is fairly typical of scientific inquiry. Actually, this case is simpler than many. In essence, it's a case of puzzle solving: The case of the eleven blue men occurs against a background of well-developed medical knowledge. Sometimes, there is no theoretical framework in the background. Then, the problem is not just to apply a framework to a particular case but to devise a framework and then apply it.

Problems

Analyze the structure of each of the following explanations, identifying the covering law or laws used as well as the structure of any hypothetical reasoning.

▶ **1.** They said today we should stock up on canned goods. So I went out and bought a case of beer. (John Gretchen III, Galveston carpenter, preparing for a hurricane)

▶ **2.** People in capitalist countries do not earn enough money to buy products and therefore they remain on the shelves. The income of the Soviet peoples has been rising steadily so that now they can buy everything they desire. It is the buying power of the Soviet people that keeps the store shelves empty. (Soviet schoolteacher)

▶ **3.** If a man is wise, he gets rich an' if he gets rich, he gets foolish, or his wife does. That's what keeps the money movin' around. (Finley Peter Dunne)

▶ **4.** People were forced to be with their loved ones. (Police officer Dave Gaouette, explaining an increase in domestic disturbances during two days of heavy snow)

▶ **5.** The "housing crisis" agitating Mayor Koch and Governor Cuomo is actually a product of local attempts to suspend economic law. Everybody who isn't a tenant admits how destructive the city's World War II rent controls have been, but tenants have the most votes. An extralegal free market in abandoned factory-loft conversions compensated somewhat, but City Hall's first instinct was to prohibit most conversions. Anyone fool enough to want to build new apartments has to pay double the standard price for concrete because of a Mafia stranglehold on the commodity. Vast areas of New York City are a wasteland of abandoned housing and rubble. (*Wall Street Journal*)

▸ **6.** The moon's orbit is elliptical, and departs by an angle of about five degrees from the earth's orbit around the sun. This explains why eclipses of the sun do not occur every month. (Daniel J. Boorstin)

7. Furthermore the sphericity of the earth is proved by the evidence of our senses, for otherwise lunar eclipses would not take such forms; for whereas in the monthly phases of the moon the segments are of all sorts—straight, gibbous and crescent—in eclipses the dividing line is always rounded. Consequently, if the eclipse is due to the interposition of the earth, the rounded line results from its spherical shape. (Aristotle)

8. Now it is scarcely possible to conceive how the aggregates of dissimilar particles should be so uniformly the same. If some of the particles of water were heavier than others; if a parcel of the liquid on any occasion were constituted principally of these heavier particles, it must be supposed to affect the specific gravity of the mass, a circumstance not known. Similar observations may be made on other substances. Therefore, we may conclude that the ultimate particles of all homogeneous bodies are perfectly alike in weight, figure, etc. In other words, every particle of water is like every other particle of water; every particle of hydrogen is like every other particle of hydrogen; etc. (John Dalton)

9. Their [the Mayas'] world, once so certain, stable, dependable, and definite is gone. And why? Here of course is a first-rate mystery for modern skill and knowledge to unravel. The people were not exterminated, nor their cities taken over by an enemy. Plagues may cause temporary migrations, but not the permanent abandonment of established and prosperous centers. The present population to the north has its share of debilitating infections, but its ancestors were not too weak or wasted to establish the Second Empire after they left the First. Did the climate in the abandoned cities become so much more humid that the invasion of dense tropical vegetation could not be arrested, while fungous pests, insects, and diseases took increasing toll? This is hard to prove. Were the inhabitants starved out because they had no steel tools or draft animals to break the heavy sod which formed over their resting fields? Many experts think so. (Paul B. Sears)

10. Are not the rays of light very small bodies emitted from shining substances? For such bodies will pass through uniform mediums in right lines without bending into the shadow, which is the nature of the rays of light. They will also be capable of several properties and be able to conserve their properties unchanged in passing through several mediums, which is another condition of the rays of light. (Isaac Newton)

11. ... the country now called Hellas had in ancient times no settled population; on the contrary, migrations were of frequent occurrence, the several tribes readily abandoning their homes under the pressure of superior numbers. Without commerce, without freedom of communication either by land or sea, cultivating no more of their territory than the exigencies of life required, destitute of capital, never planting their land (for they could not tell when an invader might not come and take it all away, and when he did come they had no walls to stop him), thinking that the necessities of daily sustenance could be supplied at one place as well as another, they cared little for shifting their habitation, and consequently neither built large cities nor attained to any other form of greatness. (Thucydides)

▶ **12.** This morning the windowsills were wet. Overnight, the outside temperature fell, cooling the window glass. The air inside contained water vapor, which condenses on any surface that's cold enough. So, the water vapor condensed when it came in contact with the cooler glass, and the resulting drops of water fell to the sill.

13. Wood floats on water because its density is lower than that of water. Archimedes discovered that a liquid supports a body immersed in it with a force equal to the weight of the liquid the body displaces. So, any body floats if its weight is less than the weight of an equal volume of water.

14. Children of blue-eyed parents invariably have blue eyes. Why? Eye color is determined by a pair of genes, and having blue eyes is a recessive trait. So, if the parents have blue eyes, both genes of each must be for blue eyes. The child gets one eye color gene from each parent. The child, therefore, must end up with two blue-eye genes, making his or her eyes blue.

15. Why did Hitler wait until June 22, 1941, to attack Russia, when his generals pleaded for an early spring invasion? There were at least two factors. He had had to send Rommel to Africa to bail out Mussolini in February and wanted to wait until that campaign was over. And, Hitler underestimated Soviet strength; he thought that Russia would fall within weeks, calling the Red Army "no more than a joke." So, he hardly felt constrained to maintain a rigid timetable.

16.2 Scientific Theories

Earlier, we saw that tests confirming a hypothesis support it but don't conclusively establish it. Tests disconfirming a hypothesis, in contrast, show that the hypothesis or an auxiliary assumption must be false. This raises the question: Can evidence ever conclusively prove or disprove a scientific hypothesis?

Clearly, evidence can't prove a hypothesis. No matter how many implications of a hypothesis we observe to hold, no matter how great the inductive evidence in favor of the hypothesis, its truth isn't guaranteed. John Hunter (1728–1793), an English biologist, hypothesized that the same biological agent was responsible for both syphilis and gonorrhea. He tested the hypothesis on himself, infecting himself with gonorrhea. He thought he could cure both diseases; he was tragically wrong. But he did come down with syphilis, confirming his hypothesis. Despite this development, his hypothesis was false: Different agents cause the two diseases. Classical physics, developed by Isaac Newton (1642–1727), was confirmed by observation after observation, experiment after experiment, for more than a century; we now believe it to be, strictly speaking, false, although it approximates the truth very closely. Several dramatic tests during this century have confirmed Albert Einstein's (1879–1955) theory of relativity, but it could still turn out to be false.

Some tests are nevertheless very compelling. Very good confirming experiments can tempt us to think that the hypothesis is the only explanation for the data. But this assumption is never literally true. Scientific laws are always asserted on the basis of incomplete evidence. At any point, only a finite number of tests of a law could have been performed. But any law has infinitely many consequences. So, the body of empirical evidence at any stage of investigation is incomplete; many different hypotheses would explain the same data. For example, suppose that we have conducted experiments relating the mass of an object to its acceleration in free fall. Suppose that we've recorded our observations in a graph:

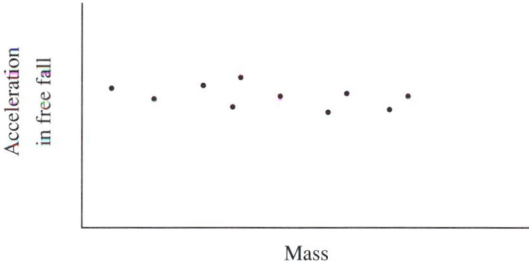

No matter how many points we record, an infinite number of curves can pass through those points. Here, for example, are several.

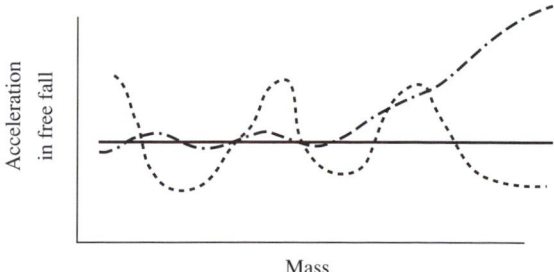

Even a million points do not determine what relation holds between mass and free fall acceleration.

This example has historical significance. Aristotle had held that free-fall acceleration depended on the mass of the falling object. Galileo (1564–1642) formulated a law holding that acceleration in free fall toward the earth is independent of mass and, in fact, constant. (Galileo's law corresponds to the straight line in the graph above.) Newton's law of gravitation explained this hypothesis. According to Newtonian physics, gravitational attraction depends on the mass of the falling object and the distance between the object and the center of the earth. So, the earth will attract a heavier object with greater force than it will attract a lighter object. But, according to Newton's second law, force—in this case, gravitational attraction—is equal to mass times acceleration. The effects of mass thus cancel each other; the greater gravitational force accelerates the greater mass at the same rate as lighter objects.

The Newtonian theory does differ from Galileo's in an important way. Newton's law of gravitation predicts that gravitational force is stronger near the earth's surface than it is farther away. For medium-sized objects relatively near the earth's surface, these effects are tiny: The predictions of Newton's law differ only minutely from those of Galileo's law. In the absence of extremely sophisticated and sensitive equipment, tests using such objects would seem to confirm both laws. Two stones dropped from different heights will accelerate at what appears to be the same rate. But the laws differ in their predictions when one of the objects involved is very far from the earth.

Experimental findings, then, can't prove laws conclusively. Laws say something about the future and about unexamined circumstances in the past; in this sense, the laws go beyond the evidence. No scientific laws, therefore, can be proved from observations alone. But this overall limitation doesn't mean that one law is as good as another or that there can be no scientific knowledge. It simply means that there are degrees of confirmation. The evidence may support—indeed, overwhelmingly support—a particular theory or hypothesis.

Negative results, as we've seen, are more powerful than positive results in that they prove that something is wrong somewhere. The argument form

(6) $(h \mathbin{\&} a) \to p$
p
$\therefore h \mathbin{\&} a$

isn't valid, but

(7) $(h \mathbin{\&} a) \to p$
$\neg p$
$\therefore \neg(h \mathbin{\&} a)$

is valid.

Nevertheless, negative results almost never conclusively refute a hypothesis. This is true for two reasons. First, between a hypothesis and falsified predictions are auxiliary assumptions. The negative results show that the hypothesis and auxiliary assumptions are not all true. But the results don't locate the source of the falsehood. So, disconfirming tests don't prove that the hypothesis is false. They prove only that it or an auxiliary assumption is false. Recall the reaction of the defenders of the Warren Commission to the Zapruder film, claiming that Governor Connally showed a delayed reaction to being hit by a bullet. Faced with recalcitrant evidence, they reject, not the hypothesis of the lone gunman, but the auxiliary assumption that people react to bullets as soon as those bullets strike.

Second, the negative results might themselves be due to error. The observations may be mistaken, or the deduction of the predictions from the hypothesis and assumptions may contain a mistake. So, in the face of a disconfirming test, we can always deny the accuracy of the test or deny that the hypothesis really implied what the test shows to be false. A well-known acoustic study of the Kennedy assassination, for example, found evidence of four shots, leading a congressional committee to conclude that there was a conspiracy. But others claimed that the acoustic findings were mistaken, the fourth "shot" being due to crosstalk between channels rather than an actual gunshot.

These are not idle possibilities. Both factors have played an important role in the history of science. Consider first the problem posed by auxiliary assumptions. Tycho Brahe (1546–1601), contemplating the controversy between theories of the solar system devised by Ptolemy (second century A.D.) and Copernicus (1473–1543), devised an interesting test to determine which theory was accurate. If the earth revolved around the sun, as Copernicus claimed, then fixed stars should not remain in the same position in the sky, as judged by a sextant or other navigational device; the stars should appear at different angles, depending on the position of the earth in its orbit. This phenomenon is called the parallax of the stars. Tycho recorded the positions of the stars and found, over the course of six months, that they did not change. He therefore rejected the Copernican hypothesis and tried to combine the Copernican and Ptolemaic approaches.

But the parallax of the stars doesn't follow from Copernicus's theory alone. Auxiliary assumptions are needed. Tycho had no telescope; the parallax, as he well knew, would be observable only if the stars were fairly close to the earth. He thought they must be close to earth because they appear as small disks rather than mere points of light. In fact, the stars are very distant. If we were to model the solar system with an orange representing the sun and a pea, about 20 feet from the orange, representing the earth, the nearest star would be about 500 miles away. Stars appear as disks, not points, only because the atmosphere diffuses their light. Tycho's negative result, then, showed that the Copernican theory, together with some auxiliary assumptions, couldn't be entirely correct. But the problem lay in the auxiliary assumptions, not in the Copernican theory. (The parallax was first observed, with a telescope, in 1838.)

The possibility of observational or calculational error is also real. Reports of observation may be in error because of an observer's fatigue, distraction, inebriation, incompetence, wishful thinking, or falsification of data. High school students routinely obtain results in chemistry and physics laboratory experiments that contradict current scientific theory. No one takes this to refute modern chemistry or physics; the errors are chalked up to incompetence. Even great scientists, however, have made serious mistakes in observation. Gregor Mendel (1822–1884), who founded modern genetics, counted flowers having various traits to confirm his genetic hypotheses. His counts conform so precisely to his theory's predictions that his observations are unlikely to have been accurate. Some modern astronomers have claimed that Ptolemy's data contain substantial errors. In these cases, the source of the error is not clear.

A researcher may also make a mathematical or logical mistake about what a hypothesis predicts or implies. Newton's theory failed to explain some aspects of the perturbations in the moon's orbit. But this failure was due to a mathematical error in Newton's work; if the mistake is corrected, the theory's predictions are accurate. (Newton himself found this error but didn't bother to publicize it.)

For all of these reasons, then, negative results do not unequivocally refute a hypothesis. The problem may lie in auxiliary assumptions, observations, or deductions. Disconfirming tests definitively indicate the presence of falsehood but not its location.

Problems

What is some confirming evidence for the following widely accepted hypotheses?

▸ **1.** The earth is round.

▸ **2.** The earth has a gravitational field.

3. Electricity is a form of energy.

4. The moon revolves around the earth.

5. The earth rotates on its axis.

Discuss the appeals to confirming or disconfirming evidence in the following. What hypothesis do these appeals address? What do they imply about that hypothesis? What auxiliary assumptions might be involved?

▸ **6.** Ptolemy's astronomy predicted the motions of the stars and planets in the sky fairly successfully but had at least one unfortunate consequence. Ptolemy's theory required that the orbit of the moon bring it, at certain times, twice as close to the earth as at other times. It follows that the moon should sometimes appear twice as big as at other times. But, of course, it doesn't.

7. Ptolemy's theory also held that everything in the heavens revolved around the earth. Galileo, however, discovered the moons of Jupiter, which revolve around Jupiter, not the earth.

8. Newtonian physics held that there were infinitely many "fixed" stars that seemed not to change position, relative to each other, in the sky. But, since they exert gravitational attraction for each other, why don't they move closer and eventually collapse?

9. If there were infinitely many "fixed" stars, roughly evenly distributed throughout the universe, every line of sight would end at a star. So, the heavens as a whole would be as bright, from our perspective, as the sun. Obviously, that's not the case.

10. Einstein proposed three tests for the general theory of relativity. First, the theory predicts that light should bend, or be deflected, in the vicinity of massive objects like the sun to a greater extent than Newtonian physics allows. On May 29, 1919, a day which one historian has called the beginning of the modern world, a British expedition in Principe confirmed this experimentally by photographing a solar eclipse. Second, general relativity also implies that Mercury's orbit should turn, its perihelion advancing very slightly with each trip around the sun. Observations have indicated that this prediction is correct. Third, the theory predicts a reddening of light from strong gravitational fields. Observations of "white dwarfs," small, very dense stars, have borne out the theory's prediction.

11. The wave theory of light had been attacked on various grounds. One was that the theory had bizarre consequences. Waves, for example, intersect to form characteristic patterns of interference; if light were passed through two small slits in a screen, and light consisted of waves, the result would be a pattern of alternating bands of light and shadow:

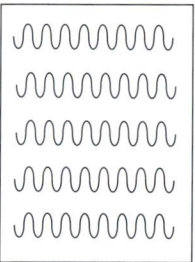

This idea was thought to be absurd. But Thomas Young did the experiment and found that the pattern was exactly what the wave theory predicted.

▶ **12.** He hath brought many captives home to Rome,
Whose ransoms did the general coffers fill;
Did this in Caesar seem ambitious?
When that the poor have cried, Caesar hath wept;
Ambition should be made of sterner stuff:
Yet Brutus says he was ambitious,
And Brutus is an honourable man.
You all did see that on the Lupercal
I thrice presented him a kingly crown,
Which he did thrice refuse. Was this ambition? (Shakespeare)

13. The great opportunity for the Jesuits came when an eclipse was expected on the morning of June 21, 1629. The Imperial astronomers predicted that the eclipse would occur at 10:30 and would last for two hours. The Jesuits forecast that the eclipse would not come until 11:30 and would last for only two minutes. On the crucial day, as 10:30 came and went the sun shone in full brilliance. The Imperial astronomers were wrong, but were the Jesuits right? Then, just at 11:30, the eclipse began and lasted for a brief two minutes, as the Jesuits had predicted. (Daniel J. Boorstin)

14. Sir: For the past six months, miniskirts have been coming back into style and look what has happened to the market. Just how high do skirts have to go for the market to act in the traditional fashion? (Alan R. Greenwald)

15. The value of the instrument [the sextant] has been proved in a splendid way by the fact that the distances found by its aid in Kassel agree within a minute, indeed within one half minute with those found by us in Denmark with our sextants. (Tycho Brahe)

16.3 EVALUATING EXPLANATIONS

Explanations have the form of arguments. Although they play a different role in communication, we can evaluate them using many of the same criteria we used to evaluate arguments. Recall that we required arguments to satisfy five conditions:

1. *Evidence.* The premises should offer evidence for the conclusion.

2. *Relevance.* The argument should be relevant to the issue at hand.

3. *Grounding.* The argument should assume only what occupies the common ground between speaker and audience.

4. *Truth.* The premises should be true.

5. *Reliability.* The forms of inference used in the argument should be reliable.

Applied to explanations, the last two of these are straightforward. We want our laws, descriptions of circumstances, and assumptions to be true; we want our explanations to use reliable forms of inference. The grounding condition is also easy to apply to explanations. An explanation should use only those auxiliary assumptions that occupy the common ground between speaker and audience. In the case of science, this condition requires that an explanation not use auxiliary assumptions that aren't accepted by the scientist and the scientific community in general. That's not to say that new assumptions can never arise but that any assumption not already in the common ground must be identified and argued for independently.

Evidence

The evidence condition for explanations is very important but has a form somewhat different from that applying to arguments. In Chapter 2, we took the evidence condition to imply that the premises of an argument be more evident than the conclusion. In an explanation, that will generally not be true. The fact to be explained may be quite evident, while the hypothesis introduced to explain it may be anything but. Consider, for example, the falling of an apple. The fact is quite plain, but the laws explaining it—a universal law of gravitation, in Newton's theory, or the curvature of space, in Einstein's— are quite abstract.

In fact, we want this characteristic to be true of all explanations. Arguments start with premises and try to justify conclusions; explanations start with things to be explained—conclusions—and try to find general principles—premises—that explain them. "In the order of knowledge," therefore, explanations are the reverse of arguments. The fact to be explained should provide evidence for the covering law or laws used in the explanation. To do so, the conclusion must be more evident than the covering law. So, we want the conclusion to be more evident than at least one premise. Otherwise, the explanation would be little more than a list of facts.

This criterion rules out a kind of explanation often called the "dormitive virtue" explanation. It is so called because of a well-known example in a Molière (1622–1673) play:

> I, a learned scholar, am asked the cause and reason why opium puts me to sleep. To which I reply: Because it possesses a dormitive virtue whose nature it is to make the senses drowsy.

This, plainly, is no explanation. The doctor Molière ridicules tries to explain the power of opium to induce sleep in terms of its power to induce sleep. Expressing this explanation as an argument, we obtain

(8) Opium has dormitive virtue.
∴ Opium has the power to induce sleep.

This argument begs the question; the premise possesses the same degree of evidence as the conclusion. Here is another example of a dormitive virtue explanation:

(9) Cities tend to have high rates of violent crime because large population centers experience high levels of violence.

The explanation does little more than repeat the fact to be explained.

Relevance

The condition of relevance, applied to explanations, requires that the explanation be relevant to the issue at hand. This criterion demands more than that the fact to be explained follow from laws, auxiliary assumptions, sentences describing the circumstances, and so on. As with arguments, the condition of relevance demands that the explanation be directed at the proper question. What the proper question is depends on context: on the nature of the conversation in which the explanation occurs. Just as with arguments, the common ground of a conversation contains information about the problem that the argument or explanation addresses. To be relevant, an explanation must address that problem.

A violation of the condition of relevance may make this requirement clearer. A famous bank robber, Willie Sutton, was asked why he robbed banks. "That's where the money is," he replied. Sutton, of course, was joking. His response is funny because it's a peculiar explanation. We want to know why he *robbed* banks, not why he robbed *banks*. So, the explanation addresses the wrong issue. It may nevertheless be a perfectly good explanation in another context. If we imagine that a thief asked Sutton the question, his reply makes good sense. So, an explanation must be relevant; what is relevant depends on the context and, in particular, on the interests of the participants in the conversation.[1]

Here is another example: A professor is found stark naked in the girls' dormitory at midnight. To explain his presence, we say, "He was there, stark naked, one billionth of a second before midnight, and he couldn't put his clothes on or leave without going faster than the speed of light. But no professor travels faster than light." The covering law here—'no professor travels faster than light'—is true, as is the fact that he couldn't move much in a billionth of a second without going faster than light. And, it is less evident than the fact to be explained. Together with the information that he was there at a billionth of a second before midnight, the premises entail that he was there, stark naked, at midnight. So, the conditions of truth, reliability, and evidence are satisfied. The explanation is unhelpful because we don't want an explanation of why he was still in the girls' dormitory at midnight but of why he was there at all. We aren't interested in physical but in psychological or moral explanations. The explanation violates the relevance condition because it addresses the wrong problem.

We may summarize the five conditions, applied to explanations, as follows:

1. *Evidence.* The conclusion should offer evidence for the covering law. Thus, the conclusion should be more evident than at least one premise.

2. *Relevance.* The explanation should be relevant to the issue at hand.

3. *Grounding.* The explanation should use only those auxiliary assumptions that occupy the common ground between speaker and audience.

4. *Truth.* The premises should be true.

5. *Reliability.* The forms of inference used in the explanation should be reliable.

Inductive Criteria

There are other, peculiarly inductive criteria for evaluating explanations. Unlike the first five criteria, these are matters of degree. An explanation does not simply satisfy, or fail to satisfy, these conditions but satisfies them to a greater or lesser degree. The most important are confirmation, power, and simplicity.

6. *Confirmation.* An explanation should be confirmed from both above and below.

7. *Power.* An explanation should lead to conclusions or predictions about more than the case at hand.

8. *Simplicity.* An explanation should be uniform and economical.

Confirmation, power, and simplicity, because they are matters of degree, are not absolute requirements for inductive explanations. Perhaps we should call them desiderata rather than conditions or criteria. The more highly confirmed, powerful, and simple an explanation is, the better it is.

Confirmation

Explanations typically employ covering laws and various other principles. The more evidence supports these laws and principles, the stronger the explanation. The quantity of evidence is important, but so is its quality and variety. Reliably observing more objects and more kinds of objects in various circumstances and obtaining positive results adds to a principle's confirmation.

The confirmation criterion asserts that an explanation should be confirmed from above and from below. An explanation is confirmed to the degree its laws, assumptions, and other principles are confirmed. They may be confirmed as hypotheses are confirmed by confirming tests: Their implications may be confirmed through observation. This concept is known as confirmation from below. Principles may also be confirmed from above, that is, by being deduced from other principles with inductive support. A typical law, then, may be confirmed by tests of its implications as well as by being deduced from more general laws.

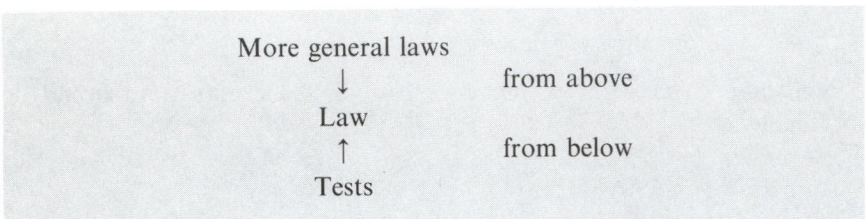

Consider, for example, the earth's rotation. Initially considered an absurd supposition by Ptolemaic astronomers, the rotation of the earth is now highly confirmed. Much confirmation comes from below: the rising and setting of the sun, stars, and planets; the Coriolis effect; the rotation of free-swinging pendulums; and the trajectories of objects falling from high places. But confirmation from above—from Newtonian physics and the laws developed by Johannes Kepler (1571–1630)—is also very important.

The importance of confirmation from below is obvious. But confirmation from above also matters. Without it, principles tend to look weak and ad hoc. Consider, for example, a proposed generalization that all U.S. presidents have brown eyes. We can check this generalization by checking the eye color of each past president, but regardless of the number of brown-eyed presidents we find, we're unlikely to count the generalization as a law. There is no reason why presidents should have brown eyes. The lack of support from above makes us distrust the principle. The moral, then, is that all but the most abstract and general principles themselves require explanations. Explained principles are, all other things being equal, more trustworthy and better confirmed than unexplained ones.

Power

The more powerful an explanation is, the better it is. That is, all other things being equal, we prefer explanations that have implications for more than the case at hand. The more situations to which the explanation could apply—the more general it is, in other words—the better.

Explaining the earth's motion by appeal to Newton's theory, for example, is preferable to explaining the same thing by appeal to Kepler's laws. Newton's theory is more general; indeed, it implies a very close approximation of Kepler's laws. It also explains much more: Galileo's law of falling bodies, the orbit of the moon, the paths of comets, the shape of the earth, the wobble of its axis, and the action of its tides. For this reason, a Newtonian explanation is more profound than one grounded in Kepler's laws. The goal of explanation is understanding. And a more powerful explanation provides a deeper understanding. Explaining the earth's motion by appeal to Newton's theory explains not only why the earth moves as it does but also why other planets obey Kepler's laws and why many other phenomena occur as they do.

To put this concept another way, Newton's theory is richer and more fruitful than Kepler's. Kepler's laws explain the orbits of the planets: in particular, why those orbits are roughly elliptical. But they have no implications about other phenomena. Newton's theory bears more fruit. It explains much more and has many more observational consequences.

Another factor makes power preferable. Theories that explain other theories, as Newton's explains Kepler's and Galileo's, often show that those theories are true only approximately and in a limited realm. As we've seen, Newton's law of gravitation implies that the gravitational attraction between two objects depends on the masses of the objects and the distance between them. So, it implies that the attraction between the earth and an object depends on the mass of the object and its distance from the earth. Galileo's law ignored these dependencies. Within the realm of medium-sized objects near the earth's surface, they make little difference. Outside that realm, the differences can be significant. But, even within the realm, they are there. Newton's theory not only explains everything Galileo's law does but also shows that the law is a simplification. The same is true of Kepler's laws. Newton's theory shows that they hold only approximately. Each planet is affected by the gravitational pull of the others, as well as by that of the sun. These other forces distort each planet's orbit slightly. More powerful explanations, then, are often more accurate as well as more profound.

Simplicity

The criterion of simplicity asserts that explanations should be uniform and economical. Given two hypotheses explaining the same class of phenomena, and otherwise equally acceptable, we should prefer the simpler.

The classic formulation of the demand for economy is *Ockham's razor*, so named for William of Ockham: "Entities should not be multiplied beyond necessity." That is, omit unnecessary entities. Explanations should posit the existence of entities, kinds, and processes only when necessary. Newton formulated a similar principle: "We are to admit no more causes of natural things than such as are both true and sufficient to explain their appearances." The demand for economy, therefore, is a demand that an explanation appeal only to what it must.

Newton also formulated a principle of uniformity: "To the same natural effects we must, as far as possible, assign the same causes." We should prefer explanations that explain the phenomena more uniformly, that attribute more uniformity to nature. This principle is much older than Newton. Ancient Greek philosophers argued about which hypotheses accounted for natural events most uniformly; indeed, uniformity, rather than data from observation, was the chief strength of Copernicus's sun-centered theory of the solar system against Ptolemy's earth-centered one.

Why prefer a simpler theory to one more complex? Economy is a way of minimizing the risk of error. Introducing unnecessary elements into a theory or explanation adds to the possibility of falsehood with no balancing gain in explanatory power. So, economy is a form of safety. Uniformity relates to our preference for deeper, more powerful explanations. Explanations attributing a higher degree of uniformity explain a range of phenomena with fewer independent hypotheses. Whenever a single explanation can be found for what formerly had been two independent hypotheses, we gain power and insight. Indeed, this sort of increase in uniformity has marked most of the great scientific advances of the past few centuries. Newton's theory, for example, reduces the laws of motion to three. Consequently, the quest for uniformity is one of science's most important driving principles. Scientists often proceed by considering distinct principles or classes of phenomena and trying to find a single account for all. The search for field theories and theories of quantum gravity in twentieth-century physics has been motivated, in large part, by a desire for uniformity.

Nevertheless, making the criterion of simplicity precise, or even very clear, is extremely difficult. What, for example, is the simplest function linking two variables? What's the simplest two-dimensional curve? How can we count the hypotheses a theory or explanation invokes? (Any sentence is equivalent to a conjunction of two other sentences, and any two sentences are equivalent to a single sentence—for example, their conjunction.) So, simplicity is an important goal of scientific inquiry, but measuring it seems to be impossible.

Problems

What, if anything, is wrong with the following explanations?

▸ **1.** *Child:* Why can't I go to the fair?
Parent: Because I said so.

▸ **2.** *A:* Why do I have to fill out all these forms?
B: That's the procedure.

▸ **3.** *A:* Why do brides wear white?
B: It's always been done that way.

4. *A:* Why can't I have the loan?
B: You don't have enough income.
A: If I had enough income, I wouldn't need the loan.

5. *A:* Why does everyone get the same, across-the-board raise, no matter how well or poorly they've done?

   B: That's company policy.

6. Objects fall toward the earth because they have a natural place on its surface, and every object seeks its natural place.

7. Men have beards, and women do not, because men's heads are warmer; the increased heat provides better growing conditions for hair.

8. Why did the chicken cross the road? To get to the other side.

9. Evaluate, by the criteria of this section, the explanations following sections 16.1 and 16.2.

Notes

[1] This and the following example are from Hilary Putnam, *Meaning and the Moral Sciences* (Boston: Routledge and Kegan Paul, 1978), p. 42. He credits the use of the Willie Sutton example in this context to Alan Garfinkel.

I

DEDUCTION
STYLE
TWO

A

SENTENTIAL LOGIC

Truth tables and semantic tableaux can evaluate arguments clearly and efficiently. But they say almost nothing about how to *construct* arguments. In this appendix we'll develop a system designed to simulate people's construction of arguments. The deduction system is natural in the sense that it is supposed to reflect the way people construct arguments in legal, scientific, philosophical, and mathematical contexts. It differs from the system in Chapter 8 by containing complex rules that allow drawing conclusions, not just from formulas established on previous lines, but from other proofs.

A.1 PROOFS

A *natural deduction system* is a set of rules: specifically, *rules of inference* that allow the deduction of formulas from other formulas. Central to the concept of a natural deduction system is the idea of *proof*. Proofs are extended arguments. There are two kinds of proofs. *Hypothetical* proofs begin with *assumptions* (or *hypotheses*). The assumptions act as premises; the conclusion of the proof follows from them. Such proofs show that the conclusion is true, not unconditionally, but if the assumptions are true. Other proofs are categorical: They use no assumptions. They show that their conclusions are true outright. We'll use hypothetical proofs to show that argument forms are valid and categorical proofs to show that formulas are tautologies.

   A *proof* in a natural deduction system is a series of *lines*. On each line appears a formula. Each formula in a proof (a) is an assumption or (b) derives from formulas on previously established lines by a rule of inference. In the system of this appendix, the last line of a proof is its conclusion; the proof *proves* that formula *from* the assumptions. Formulas proved from no assumptions at all are *theorems* of the system.

Rules of Inference

Rules of inference are either *simple* or *complex*. Simple rules allow us to derive formulas of certain kinds in a proof if other formulas of certain kinds occupy lines already established there. For example, our system has a rule letting us write $\mathscr{A}$ or $\mathscr{B}$, whichever we choose, if we've already established $\mathscr{A}$ & $\mathscr{B}$ on a previous line.

Complex rules allow us to derive a formula of a certain kind in a proof if we've completed some other proof. Our system has a rule, for instance, allowing us to write $\neg \mathscr{A}$ if we've proved a contradiction from the assumption $\mathscr{A}$. Another complex rule allows us to assert a conditional formula $\mathscr{A} \rightarrow \mathscr{B}$ if we can, in a subordinate proof, assume $\mathscr{A}$ and derive $\mathscr{B}$.

Because some rules are complex, proofs sometimes appear within other proofs. A proof appearing within another is *subordinate* to it. The larger, *superordinate* proof uses the subordinate proof's information by means of a complex rule. The larger proof may use the fact that the subordinate was able to prove a conclusion from a given assumption to derive something that doesn't itself depend on that assumption. (Assertions established by subordinate proofs are *lemmas*.)

Our deduction system has a pair of rules for most connectives. One rule indicates how to derive a formula with a certain connective as main connective. In short, it specifies how to *introduce* formulas of that form into proofs. The other rule indicates how to use information encoded in a formula having that connective as main connective. That is, it specifies how to *exploit* formulas of that kind in proofs. The basic rules of the system, therefore, will fall into two groups: *introduction* rules and *exploitation* rules. Strategies for constructing proofs derive from this distinction. Strategy depends, primarily, on what we're trying to prove, and, secondarily, on what we already have. Our system is organized to make proof strategies apparent. To prove a formula with a given main connective, we try using the introduction rule for that connective. To use a formula with a given main connective, we try using that connective's exploitation rule.

Proof Format

Here's an example of a simple, hypothetical proof:

1. p A
2. $p \rightarrow q$ A
3. q MP, 1, 2

All proofs are series of lines structured in certain ways. As in this example, proofs have three columns. The middle column consists of a sequence of formulas. The left column numbers these formulas; the right column provides justifications for them. Thus, if a formula derives from previously established formulas by a rule of inference, the right column will show what rule of inference and what earlier lines were used. If the formula is an assumption, the right column will so indicate.

> ### Proof Lines
>
> Number   Formula   Justification

The proof above is a successful, completed proof of q from p and $p \to q$. The 'A's in the right column of lines 1 and 2 indicate that p and $p \to q$ are assumptions, thus signaling that the proof is hypothetical. The 'MP, 1, 2' on line 3 indicates that q is derived from the formulas on lines 1 and 2 by the rule MP (*modus ponens*).

Any hypothetical proof begins with assumptions and proceeds to its conclusion. A successful, completed proof of $\mathscr{B}$ from the premises $\mathscr{A}_1, \ldots, \mathscr{A}_n$ thus always looks like this:

> ### Proof
>
> 1. $\mathscr{A}_1$
> $\vdots$
> n + m. $\mathscr{A}_n$
> $\vdots$
> n + p. $\mathscr{B}$

Obtaining $\mathscr{B}$ completes the proof only if a condition is satisfied. Certain rules in our system will cause lines in proofs to be bracketed. The bracketed segments will introduce assumptions that go beyond the hypotheses of the proof itself. Lines within such brackets therefore may not follow from the hypotheses alone; they may require the extra assumptions of the bracketed portion. So,

> $\mathscr{B}$, on line n + p, must not be enclosed in a set of brackets.

We want to show that $\mathscr{B}$ follows from what has gone before. If $\mathscr{B}$, on line n + p, were enclosed in a bracket, we could not be sure that $\mathscr{B}$ followed from what we were given. We would know only that $\mathscr{B}$ followed from what we were given together with some additional assumptions.

The same would hold if there were any unbracketed assumptions between our initial hypotheses and the conclusion. The conclusion would depend not only on the hypotheses but also on the further, unbracketed assumptions. A proof with additional unbracketed assumptions remains a proof, but it proves the conclusion, not from the hypotheses alone, but from them together with the additional assumptions.

Central to the idea of hypothetical proof, then, is the *assumption rule*, which allows a proof to begin with a list of premises or assumptions. At any point in a proof, we may write premises. Any conclusion we derive, of course, may depend on these premises.

Assumption
n. $\mathscr{A}$ A

To prove q hypothetically from $p \rightarrow q$ and $p \vee q$, we write the premises, hoping to obtain the conclusion:

1. $p \rightarrow q$ A
2. $p \vee q$ A
    $\vdots$
n. q

In every hypothetical proof, we list the assumptions (that is, premises) of the proof at the beginning.

A.2 Conjunction and Negation Rules

Conjunction

The rule of *simplification* indicates how we can use the information encoded in a conjunction. What follows from the truth of a conjunction? The truth of both conjuncts. If $\mathscr{A}$ & $\mathscr{B}$ is true, both $\mathscr{A}$ and $\mathscr{B}$ must be true. Simplification underlies arguments such as

(1) a. Lupe and Kimo saw.
     $\therefore$ Lupe saw.
   b. I ate rice and beans.
     $\therefore$ I ate beans.

The rule allowing us to exploit conjunctions thus takes two forms:

Simplification (S)

$$
\begin{array}{ll}
\text{n.} & \underline{\mathscr{A} \ \& \ \mathscr{B}} \\
\text{n + m.} \ \mathscr{A} & \text{S, n}
\end{array}
$$

$$
\begin{array}{ll}
\text{n.} & \underline{\mathscr{A} \ \& \ \mathscr{B}} \\
\text{n + m.} \ \mathscr{B} & \text{S, n}
\end{array}
$$

Hereafter, we'll abbreviate rules having two forms by using parentheses. We can write S as

---

$$
\begin{array}{ll}
\text{n.} & \underline{\mathscr{A} \ \& \ \mathscr{B}} \\
\text{n + m.} \ \mathscr{A} \ (\text{or } \mathscr{B}) & \text{S, n}
\end{array}
$$

This rule asserts that from a conjunction, we can derive each conjunct. We may write the conjuncts on any later line. When we apply this rule, we write a conjunct together with the explanation that the line comes by application of S—simplification—to the formula on line n. (The line just above the formula that results from applying this rule separates the formula deduced from its necessary antecedents; it won't appear in actual proofs.) To apply S to a formula, conjunction must be its main connective. We can move from $p \ \& \ (q \rightarrow r)$ to $q \rightarrow r$, but we cannot go from $(p \ \& \ q) \rightarrow r$ to $p \rightarrow r$. Indeed, such a move would be invalid.

To demonstrate this rule, let's show that this argument is valid:

(2) Jorge and Holly liked the movie, but George didn't.
∴. Holly liked the movie.

Let's assume $((p \ \& \ q) \ \& \ \neg r)$ and prove q. We begin with an assumption.

1. $(p \ \& \ q) \ \& \ \neg r$ A

Now, we can exploit the conjunction to derive a smaller conjunction, $(p \ \& \ q)$. We can't derive q directly: The connective to which we apply the rule must be the main connective of the formula.

1. $(p \ \& \ q) \ \& \ \neg r$ A
2. $(p \ \& \ q)$ S, 1

The right column tells us that the formula on line 2 comes from line 1 by applying S. We can easily apply that same rule again to obtain q, thereby finishing the proof.

1. $(p \& q) \& \neg r$ A
2. $(p \& q)$ S, 1
3. q S, 2

The rule of *conjunction* indicates how to prove conjunctions. It's a very simple rule; to prove a conjunction, it asserts, we prove each conjunct. This rule reflects the reasoning in the following:

(3) Feodor thinks the time is right.
    Deidre thinks the time is right.
    ∴ Feodor and Deidre think the time is right.

If $\mathscr{A}$ is true, and $\mathscr{B}$ is true also, then $\mathscr{A} \& \mathscr{B}$ is true. So, from the two formulas $\mathscr{A}$ and $\mathscr{B}$ we can derive $\mathscr{A} \& \mathscr{B}$:

Conjunction (C)

n. $\mathscr{A}$
m. $\mathscr{B}$
p. $\mathscr{A} \& \mathscr{B}$ C, n, m

The right column indicates that $\mathscr{A} \& \mathscr{B}$ comes from conjoining the formulas on lines n and m. The order in which $\mathscr{A}$ and $\mathscr{B}$ occur in the proof does not matter. We could just as easily have concluded $\mathscr{B} \& \mathscr{A}$.

To see how we might use C in a proof, let's show that $(p \& q)$ allows us to derive $(q \& p)$. Again, we begin by using the assumption rule.

1. $p \& q$ A

To show $q \& p$, we need to separate the two conjuncts. We can derive them separately, using S, and put them back together in the other order, using C.

1. $p \& q$ A
2. p S, 1
3. q S, 1
4. $q \& p$ C, 3, 2

Negation

One negation rule acts as both an introduction and an exploitation rule. It always introduces or exploits two negation symbols at once. We'll therefore refer to it as DN, the *double negation* rule. We can add or delete two consecutive negation signs without affecting truth values.

Double Negation (DN)

n.	$\mathscr{A}$	
n + p.	$\neg\,\neg\,\mathscr{A}$	DN, n
n.	$\neg\,\neg\,\mathscr{A}$	
n + p.	$\mathscr{A}$	DN, n

We can express this rule more compactly by writing a double line between $\mathscr{A}$ and $\neg\,\neg\,\mathscr{A}$ to indicate that the rule *inverts*—that we can go from what is above the lines to what is below them, or from what is below the lines to what is above them. The rule works in both directions.

---

n.	$\mathscr{A}$	DN, m
m.	$\neg\,\neg\,\mathscr{A}$	DN, n

To illustrate this rule, let's show that we can derive $\neg\,\neg\,p\ \&\ \neg q$ from $\neg\,\neg(p\ \&\ \neg\,\neg\,\neg q)$.

1. $\neg\,\neg(p\ \&\ \neg\,\neg\,\neg q)$ A
2. $p\ \&\ \neg\,\neg\,\neg q$ DN, 1
3. p S, 2
4. $\neg\,\neg\,p$ DN, 3
5. $\neg\,\neg\,\neg q$ S, 2
6. $\neg q$ DN, 5
7. $\neg\,\neg\,p\ \&\ \neg q$ C, 4, 6

Replacement

In general, we can apply rules only to formulas with the appropriate main connectives. For instance, we can apply S only to conjunctions—formulas with & as their main connectives. Invertible rules, however, have a special and important feature: They apply to parts of formulas—more precisely, subformulas—as well as to entire formulas. Invertible rules are justified by the equivalence of the formulas they link. If, in any formula, we replace a subformula with an equivalent subformula, we obtain a formula equivalent to the original. If p and $\neg\,\neg p$ are equivalent, for instance, then so are $p \to q$ and $\neg\,\neg p \to q$. In addition to our derivable rules, therefore, we'll adopt a principle of *replacement*, allowing us to apply invertible rules to subformulas as well as to entire formulas. So we can use DN to move not only from $\neg \neg p$ to p, but also from $\neg \neg p \to q$ to $p \to q$.

We can therefore streamline the previous proof to

1.	$\neg \neg (p \,\&\, \neg \neg \neg q)$	A
2.	$p \,\&\, \neg \neg \neg q$	DN, 1
3.	$p \,\&\, \neg q$	DN, 2
4.	$\neg \neg p \,\&\, \neg q$	DN, 3

Indirect Proof

Another, more powerful negation rule is the method of *indirect proof*. Essentially another negation introduction rule, indirect proof is complex. It asserts that we can derive $\neg \mathscr{A}$ if we can deduce a contradiction from the assumption $\mathscr{A}$. An indirect proof always introduces an assumption. We'll label these *assumptions for indirect proof (AIPs)*. From them and from formulas already available, we deduce contradictions. If an assumption leads to a contradiction, the assumption must be false. Consequently, indirect proofs establish the negations of their assumptions.

An indirect proof begins with an assumption, namely, the formula we're trying to establish, but with its main negation omitted. An indirect proof thus begins as follows:

  n. $\mathscr{A}$ AIP

To establish $\neg \mathscr{A}$, we must prove a contradiction. The contradiction need not relate directly to the assumption; we do not have to prove $\mathscr{A} \,\&\, \neg \mathscr{A}$, or anything else containing $\mathscr{A}$. In fact, we don't even have to use $\mathscr{A}$ in deriving a contradiction. We want, for any formula $\mathscr{B}$, to prove $\mathscr{B} \,\&\, \neg \mathscr{B}$. A completed indirect proof looks like this:

Indirect Proof

n.	$\mathscr{A}$	AIP
$\vdots$	$\vdots$	
n + p.	$\mathscr{B} \,\&\, \neg \mathscr{B}$	$\vdots$
n + r.	$\neg \mathscr{A}$	IP, n–n + p

Once we complete the proof, we bracket the area from the assumption for indirect proof to the contradiction. $\mathscr{B} \,\&\, \neg \mathscr{B}$ must not already be enclosed in brackets on line n + p, and we may enclose no unbracketed assumptions when we draw a bracket to complete the proof.

This rule allows us to prove, for instance, that a contradiction implies anything. To see this, take a contradiction, say, $p \mathbin{\&} \neg p$, and any formula q. From $p \mathbin{\&} \neg p$, we can derive q. We begin with an assumption.

    1. $p \mathbin{\&} \neg p$ A

We can't derive q directly in this system, since it bears no relation to our assumption. We must instead use indirect proof. (In general, it's wise to resort to indirect proof when nothing else suggests itself as a good proof technique.) As we've so far characterized indirect proof, we can use it to prove only negated formulas. But our double negation rule indicates that q and $\neg \neg q$ are equivalent. So, we can prove $\neg \neg q$ and use DN to obtain q.

    1. $p \mathbin{\&} \neg p$ *A*
    2. $\neg q$ AIP
    3. p S, 1
    4. $\neg p$ S, 1
    5. $p \mathbin{\&} \neg p$ C, 3, 4
    6. $\neg \neg q$ IP, 2–5
    7. q DN, 6

Restrictions

Let's call any line we can use in a proof at a given point *free* at that point. In sentential logic, every line is free, except lines imprisoned within a bracket. Access to bracketed lines is prohibited, for they depend on a particular assumption. Both indirect and, as we'll soon see, conditional proofs introduce assumptions; the lines that depend on them hold only given those assumptions. They might not hold in general.

In the preceding proof, for example, we introduced a contradiction—$p \mathbin{\&} \neg p$—as an assumption. We proceeded to show that if this were true, then anything would be true. We didn't want to say that the contradiction was true; we merely pretended that it was. The contradiction served only as a dialectical premise, in Aristotle's terminology: We assumed it, not because we thought it was true, but because we wanted to see what followed from it. If this proof were part of a larger proof, it would be a terrible mistake to claim that, in general, we could prove $p \mathbin{\&} \neg p$ because it was introduced earlier as an assumption within a subordinate proof.

A line is free, then, only if it is not imprisoned within a bracket. This "proof," consequently, makes a serious error:

    1. $[\,p \mathbin{\&} \neg p$ AIP
    2. $\neg(p \mathbin{\&} \neg p)$ IP, 1–1
    3. p S, 1 (Wrong)

To summarize: Formulas within a completed prison are sentenced to life. They are inaccessible.

Problems

Do problems 1–9 in Chapter 8, section 8.2.

A.3 Conditional and Biconditional Rules

The Conditional

Some axiom systems have only one rule of inference: the rule of conditional exploitation. Called *modus ponens,* it sanctions the inference from p and $p \rightarrow q$ to q. It stands behind arguments such as

(4) If it rains, the game will be postponed.
It will rain.
∴ The game will be postponed.

(5) If Socrates is human, then Socrates is mortal.
Socrates is human.
∴ Socrates is mortal.

Modus Ponens (MP)	
n. $\mathcal{A} \rightarrow \mathcal{B}$	
m. $\mathcal{A}$	
p. $\mathcal{B}$	MP, n, m

This rule, for example, lets us show the validity of this argument:

(6) Maxine will be happy if Newton visits Lubbock.
Newton will visit Lubbock and Tucumcari.
∴ Newton will visit Tucumcari, and Maxine will be happy.

Symbolizing the argument, we derive $p \& q$ from the premises $r \rightarrow q$ and $r \& p$.

1. $r \rightarrow q$	A
2. $r \& p$	A
3. r	S, 2
4. p	S, 2
5. q	MP, 1, 3
6. $p \& q$	C, 4, 5

Conditional Proof

Conditional introduction is a complex rule, often called *conditional proof.* Like an indirect proof, a conditional proof may use some premises or earlier lines of a proof, but it doesn't have to. It always establishes a formula with a conditional as its main connective. It makes an *assumption for conditional proof (ACP)*, which is the antecedent of the conditional we're trying to establish. A conditional proof, then, begins as follows:

n. $\mathscr{A}$ ACP
          ⋮
n + m. $\mathscr{A} \rightarrow \mathscr{B}$ CP

A successful conditional proof derives a conditional's consequent from its antecedent. To show that 'If $\mathscr{A}$, then $\mathscr{B}$', we assume $\mathscr{A}$ and try to show that $\mathscr{B}$ follows.

Conditional Proof (CP)

n. $\begin{bmatrix} \mathscr{A} \\ \vdots \end{bmatrix}$ ACP

n + p. $\mathscr{B}$
n + q. $\mathscr{A} \rightarrow \mathscr{B}$ CP, n–n + p

Obtaining the subordinate conclusion $\mathscr{B}$ allows us to count the conditional formula as established, thus completing the conditional proof. Drawing a bracket around the proof indicates that it is complete; the bracket allows us to see which lines justify the conditional. Just as in indirect proofs, we may not draw the bracket if $\mathscr{B}$, on line n + p, appears inside another bracket or if we would thereby enclose another unbracketed assumption.

To take an example, we can derive $r \rightarrow q$ from $p \,\&\, q$, showing this argument to be valid:

(7) There's ham and roast beef.
    ∴ There's roast beef, if you want some.

1. $p \,\&\, q$ A
2. $\begin{bmatrix} r \end{bmatrix}$ ACP
3. q S, 1
4. $r \rightarrow q$ CP, 2–3

Conditional proof also allows us to prove $(p \rightarrow \neg q) \rightarrow (q \rightarrow \neg p)$.

1. $p \rightarrow \neg q$ ACP
2. q ACP
3. p AIP
4. $\neg q$ MP, 1, 3
5. $q \,\&\, \neg q$ C, 2, 4
6. $\neg p$ IP, 3–5
7. $q \rightarrow \neg p$ CP, 2–6
8. $(p \rightarrow \neg q) \rightarrow (q \rightarrow \neg p)$ CP, 1–7

Here, an indirect proof is subordinate to a conditional proof that is, in turn, subordinate to another conditional proof.

The Biconditional

When may we introduce a biconditional into a proof? What does it take to establish the truth of a biconditional? A biconditional is so called because it amounts to two conditionals. Mathematicians, for example, often prove biconditionals in two steps. They prove the "left-to-right" and "right-to-left" directions separately. In other words, they prove two conditionals. Our rule for biconditional introduction similarly requires two conditionals:

Biconditional (B)

$$
\begin{array}{ll}
\text{n.} & \mathscr{A} \to \mathscr{B} \\
\text{m.} & \underline{\mathscr{B} \to \mathscr{A}} \\
\text{p.} & \mathscr{A} \leftrightarrow \mathscr{B} \qquad \text{B, n, m}
\end{array}
$$

To show how this rule works, let's show

(8) Ben will help if you'd like him to; in fact, he'll help, and you
      would like him to.
  ∴ Ben will help if and only if you'd like him to.

to be valid by deriving $p \leftrightarrow q$ from $(p \to q)$ & $(q$ & $p)$.

$$
\begin{array}{lll}
1. & (p \to q) \,\&\, (q \,\&\, p) & \text{A} \\
2. & p \to q & \text{S, 1} \\
3. & q \,\&\, p & \text{S, 1} \\
4. & \lceil q & \text{ACP} \\
5. & \lfloor p & \text{S, 3} \\
6. & q \to p & \text{CP, 4–5} \\
7. & p \leftrightarrow q & \text{B, 2, 6}
\end{array}
$$

To exploit biconditionals, recall that a biconditional asserts that two statements have the same truth value. If we've established a biconditional and one of its components, we can deduce the other.

Modus Both-ends (MB)

$$
\begin{array}{ll}
\text{n.} & \mathscr{A} \leftrightarrow \mathscr{B} \\
\text{m.} & \mathscr{A} \ (\text{or } \mathscr{B}) \\
\text{p.} & \mathscr{B} \ (\text{or } \mathscr{A}) \qquad \text{MB, n, m}
\end{array}
$$

This rule differs from *modus ponens* by allowing us to deduce $\mathscr{A}$ from $\mathscr{B}$ or vice versa. If we have one component, we can derive the other; it makes no difference which appears on which side of the biconditional. *Modus ponens*, in contrast, works only in one direction. It allows us to derive the consequent from the antecedent of the conditional. However, we can't go from the consequent to the antecedent.

To illustrate, let's show that $p \leftrightarrow q$ implies $(p \rightarrow q)$ & $(\neg p \rightarrow \neg q)$.

1.	$p \leftrightarrow q$	A
2.	p	ACP
3.	q	MB, 1, 2
4.	$p \rightarrow q$	CP, 2–3
5.	$\neg p$	ACP
6.	q	AIP
7.	p	MB, 1, 6
8.	p & $\neg p$	C, 7, 5
9.	$\neg q$	IP, 6–8
10.	$\neg p \rightarrow \neg q$	CP, 5–9
11.	$(p \rightarrow q)$ & $(\neg p \rightarrow \neg q)$	C, 4, 10

Problems

Do the problems in Chapter 8, section 8.3.

A.4 Disjunction Rules

Like most connectives, disjunction has an introduction and an exploitation rule. The introduction rule, called *addition,* reflects the reasoning manifested in arguments such as

(9) Vinnie won the "best speaker" trophy.
∴ Vinnie or Carlo won the "best speaker" trophy.

It says that we may introduce a disjunction into a proof if we've already obtained either disjunct.

Addition (Ad)
n. $\mathscr{A}$ (or $\mathscr{B}$)
n + p. $\mathscr{A} \vee \mathscr{B}$ Ad, n

To see how this rule works in practice, let's prove 'the law of the excluded middle', $p \vee \neg p$. We can't prove either disjunct separately—neither p nor $\neg p$ is valid—therefore, we must use indirect proof. We need to prove $\neg \neg (p \vee \neg p)$. Introducing the assumption for indirect proof, however, helps us little; how we can get anything out of $\neg (p \vee \neg p)$? From a contradiction, anything follows. So, let's begin by trying to show $\neg p$.

1. $\neg(p \lor \neg p)$ AIP
2. p AIP
3. $p \lor \neg p$ Ad, 2
4. $(p \lor \neg p) \mathbin{\&} \neg(p \lor \neg p)$ C, 3, 1
5. $\neg p$ IP, 2–4
6. $p \lor \neg p$ Ad, 5
7. $(p \lor \neg p) \mathbin{\&} \neg(p \lor \neg p)$ C, 6, 1
8. $\neg \neg (p \lor \neg p)$ IP, 1–7
9. $p \lor \neg p$ DN, 8

How can we exploit the information encoded in a disjunction? How can we use a disjunction to derive a conclusion? The answer lies in our rule of disjunction exploitation, called *disjunctive syllogism*. It underlies arguments such as

(10) a. Zach or Levi will go to town.
       Zach won't go to town.
       ∴ Levi will.
    b. The film was made in either Kenya or Tanzania.
       It wasn't made in Tanzania.
       ∴ The film was made in Kenya.

If at least one of $\mathscr{A}$ or $\mathscr{B}$ is true, and $\mathscr{A}$ is false, $\mathscr{B}$ must be true. Similarly, if $\mathscr{A}$ or $\mathscr{B}$ is true, $\mathscr{A}$ must be true if $\mathscr{B}$ is false.

Disjunctive Syllogism (DS)

n. $\mathscr{A} \lor \mathscr{B}$
m. $\neg \mathscr{A}$ (or $\neg \mathscr{B}$)
p. $\mathscr{B}$ (or $\mathscr{A}$)   MB, n, m

To illustrate this rule, let's show that this argument form is valid: $p \lor q$; $p \lor \neg q$; ∴ p.

1. $p \lor q$ A
2. $p \lor \neg q$ A
3. $\neg p$ AIP
4. q DS, 1, 3
5. $\neg q$ DS, 2, 3
6. $q \mathbin{\&} \neg q$ C, 4, 5
7. $\neg \neg p$ IP, 3–6
8. p DN, 7

Problems

Do the problems in Chapter 8, sections 8.4 and 8.5.

A.5 DERIVED RULES

The basic idea of a system of symbolic logic is that by evaluating a symbolic argument form, we can evaluate an argument in English or any other language. We symbolize the argument, obtaining an argument form. We use some formal technique to evaluate it. Then, we try to infer the validity or invalidity of the original argument.

The key to this strategy is the evaluation of argument forms. To work, the formal methods we use must allow us to recognize valid forms. Specifically, they must count valid every argument form that is valid. And they must count invalid every argument form that is invalid.

Our proof methods and rules meet these criteria. They allow us to prove the validity of any valid argument form in sentential logic. Our system is *complete*—every valid argument form can be proved valid in the system. Completeness guarantees that we have enough rules. Our system is also *sound*—we can derive a conclusion from some premises only if the argument form is valid. Our rules never lead us astray. To speak in terms of formulas rather than argument forms, all tautologies—and only tautologies—are provable. Our system's completeness guarantees that every tautology is a theorem; its soundness guarantees that every theorem is a tautology. Establishing the soundness and completeness of this appendix's natural deduction system requires a sophisticated proof beyond the scope of this book.

To encompass sentential logic, therefore, we need no further rules or proof techniques. Nevertheless, this section develops some added rules. Everything we can prove with them is still valid. Indeed, they are all *derived* rules; they abbreviate series of proof lines that we could write in terms of our basic rules. They are short cuts that force us to accept nothing new about the logical connectives.

Indirect Proof Expanded

First, we can amend a basic rule. An indirect proof shows something to be false by showing that assuming its truth leads to a contradiction. The conclusion of an indirect proof is always a negation. But the method extends to any formula. To show that a formula $\mathscr{A}$ is true, we can assume that $\mathscr{A}$ is false—by assuming $\neg \mathscr{A}$—and show that a contradiction follows. The extended method of indirect proof works as follows:

Indirect Proof (extended)		
n.	$\neg \mathscr{A}$	AIP
⋮	⋮	⋮
n + p.	$\mathscr{B} \& \neg \mathscr{B}$	
n + q.	$\mathscr{A}$	IP, n–n + p

This extension eliminates at least one application of negation exploitation. For example, we can use two applications of it to show 'Peirce's law', $((p \rightarrow q) \rightarrow p) \rightarrow p$.

1.	$(p \rightarrow q) \rightarrow p$	ACP
2.	$\neg p$	AIP
3.	p	ACP
4.	$\neg q$	AIP
5.	$p \,\&\, \neg p$	C, 3, 2
6.	q	IP, 4–5
7.	$p \rightarrow q$	CP, 3–6
8.	p	MP, 1, 7
9.	$p \,\&\, \neg p$	C, 8, 2
10.	p	IP, 2–9
11.	$((p \rightarrow q) \rightarrow p) \rightarrow p$	CP, 1–10

Negations of Complex Formulas

Several derived rules pertain to negated formulas. Negations can be difficult to exploit in our basic system; we can eliminate negations only in pairs. To help simplify formulas beginning with a negation, these derivable rules all give equivalents for negated formulas. They work in either direction; the first two are called *DeMorgan's laws*.

The first reflects the equivalence of sentences such as

(11) a. Jane and Horace won't both have a good time.
    b. Either Jane or Horace won't have a good time.

DeMorgan's Law #1 (DM)

n.	$\neg(\mathscr{A} \,\&\, \mathscr{B})$	DM, m
m.	$\neg\mathscr{A} \lor \neg\mathscr{B}$	DM, n

If not both $\mathscr{A}$ and $\mathscr{B}$ are true, then either $\mathscr{A}$ is false or $\mathscr{B}$ is; and vice versa. This rule lets us show the validity of

(12) Ginny and Diego aren't both coming to the talk.
    If Ginny isn't coming, neither is Diego.
    $\therefore$ Diego isn't coming.

which we can symbolize as $\neg(p \,\&\, q)$; $\neg p \rightarrow \neg q$; $\therefore \neg q$. DeMorgan's law enables us to prove the argument's validity much more easily than do our basic rules alone.

$$
\begin{array}{lll}
1. & \neg(p \,\&\, q) & \text{A} \\
2. & \neg p \to \neg q & \text{A} \\
3. & \quad q & \text{AIP} \\
4. & \quad \neg p \vee \neg q & \text{DM, 1} \\
5. & \quad \neg\neg q & \text{DN, 3} \\
6. & \quad \neg p & \text{DS, 4, 5} \\
7. & \quad \neg q & \text{MP, 2, 6} \\
8. & \quad q \,\&\, \neg q & \text{C, 3, 7} \\
9. & \neg q & \text{IP, 3–9}
\end{array}
$$

The second of DeMorgan's laws underlies the equivalence of sentences such as

(13) a. Neither Fred nor Sam believes you.
     b. Fred doesn't believe you, and neither does Sam.

DeMorgan's Law #2 (DM)

$$
\begin{array}{lll}
\text{n.} & \underline{\neg(\mathscr{A} \vee \mathscr{B})} & \text{DM, m} \\
\text{m.} & \neg\mathscr{A} \,\&\, \neg\mathscr{B} & \text{DM, n}
\end{array}
$$

If neither $\mathscr{A}$ nor $\mathscr{B}$ is true, then $\mathscr{A}$ and $\mathscr{B}$ are both false. This rule allows a shortened proof of the validity of

(14) Neither Aswan nor Cairo will have many tourists this time of year.
    ∴ Either Aswan won't have many tourists this time of year, or I'll be disappointed.

which we can symbolize as $\neg(p \vee q)$; ∴ $\neg p \vee \neg r$.

$$
\begin{array}{lll}
1. & \neg(p \vee q) & \text{A} \\
2. & \neg p \,\&\, \neg q & \text{DM, 1} \\
3. & \neg p & \text{S, 2} \\
4. & \neg p \vee \neg r & \text{Ad, 3}
\end{array}
$$

The next rule, *negated conditional,* rests on the truth-table definition of the conditional.

$\mathscr{A}$	$\mathscr{B}$	$\mathscr{A} \to \mathscr{B}$
T	T	T
T	F	F
F	T	T
F	F	T

$\mathscr{A} \to \mathscr{B}$ is false only on the row on which $\mathscr{A}$ is true and $\mathscr{B}$ is false.

Negated Conditional (NC)

n. $\dfrac{\neg(\mathcal{A} \to \mathcal{B})}{}$ NC, m

m. $\mathcal{A} \,\&\, \neg\mathcal{B}$ NC, n

If $\mathcal{A} \to \mathcal{B}$ is false, then $\mathcal{A}$ must be true and $\mathcal{B}$ must be false. This rule allows a shortened proof of

(15) If Orlando is crowded, we'll go to Tampa.
      It's not true that we'll be late if Orlando is crowded.
      $\therefore$ It's not true that we'll be late if we go to Tampa.

Symbolizing, we arrive at $p \to r;\ \neg(p \to q);\ \therefore\ \neg(r \to q)$.

1. $p \to r$ A
2. $\neg(p \to q)$ A
3. $p \,\&\, \neg q$ NC, 2
4. p S, 3
5. r MP, 1, 4
6. $\neg q$ S, 3
7. $r \,\&\, \neg q$ C, 5, 6
8. $\neg(r \to q)$ NC, 7

This proof uses NC to go from a negation to a conjunction on line 3 and then uses the rule in the opposite direction to derive a negation on line 8 from a conjunction.

    Yet another rule allows for the introduction and exploitation of negated biconditionals.

Negated Biconditional (NB)

n. $\dfrac{\neg(\mathcal{A} \leftrightarrow \mathcal{B})}{}$ NB, m

m. $\neg\mathcal{A} \leftrightarrow \mathcal{B}$ (or $\mathcal{A} \leftrightarrow \neg\mathcal{B}$)   NB, n

If '$\mathcal{A}$ if and only if $\mathcal{B}$' is false, then $\mathcal{A}$ and $\mathcal{B}$ must have opposite truth values. $\mathcal{A}$ is false if and only if $\mathcal{B}$ is true. Equivalently, $\mathcal{A}$ is true if and only if $\mathcal{B}$ is false. This rule allows a shortened proof of the validity of

(16) It's not the case that India will withdraw if and only if Uganda doesn't.
    India and Uganda won't both withdraw.
    $\therefore$ It's not true that India will withdraw if Uganda doesn't.

which, symbolized, becomes $\neg(p \leftrightarrow \neg q);\ \neg(p \,\&\, q);\ \therefore\ \neg(\neg q \to p)$.

1. $\neg(p \leftrightarrow \neg q)$		A
2. $\neg(p \mathbin{\&} q)$		A
3.	$\neg q \to p$	AIP
4.	$p \leftrightarrow \neg\neg q$	NB, 1
5.	$\neg q$	AIP
6.	p	MP, 3, 5
7.	$\neg\neg q$	MB, 4, 6
8.	$\neg q \mathbin{\&} \neg\neg q$	C, 5, 7
9.	$\neg\neg q$	IP, 5–8
10.	q	DN, 8
11.	p	MB, 4, 8
12.	$p \mathbin{\&} q$	C, 10, 9
13.	$(p \mathbin{\&} q) \mathbin{\&} \neg(p \mathbin{\&} q)$	C, 12, 2
14. $\neg(\neg q \to p)$		IP, 3–13

Closely related to these rules are several others that define a connective in terms of other connectives. The first allows us to transform disjunctions into conditionals, and vice versa. It reflects the equivalence of sentences such as

(17) a. If Yvonne doesn't stop insulting me, I'll kill her.
   b. Unless Yvonne stops insulting me, I'll kill her.

Material Conditional (MC)

n.	$\underline{\mathscr{A} \to \mathscr{B}}$	MC, m
m.	$\neg\mathscr{A} \lor \mathscr{B}$	MC, n

'If $\mathscr{A}$ then $\mathscr{B}$' is equivalent to '$\mathscr{B}$ unless not $\mathscr{A}$'. This rule allows an easier demonstration of the validity of

(18) If Tony accepts, Rhonda will become manager.
   Tony will accept if you don't talk him out of it.
   $\therefore$ Unless you talk Tony out of it, Rhonda will become manager.

by permitting a shortened proof of $r \to q; \neg p \to r; \therefore p \lor q$.

1. $r \to q$		A
2. $\neg p \to r$		A
3.	$\neg p$	ACP
4.	r	MP, 2, 3
5.	q	MP, 1, 4
6. $\neg p \to q$		CP, 3–5
7. $p \lor q$		MC, 6

The next rule allows us to characterize the biconditional in terms of the conditional:

Biconditional-Conditional (BC)

> n. $\mathcal{A} \leftrightarrow \mathcal{B}$
> m. $\mathcal{A} \rightarrow \mathcal{B}$ (or $\mathcal{B} \rightarrow \mathcal{A}$)   BC, n

---

This rule asserts that we can deduce from a conditional either of the conditionals included in it. 'If and only if', as we might expect, implies both 'if' and 'only if'.

Order and Grouping

Next, four rules assert that the order and grouping of subformulas in continued conjunctions and continued disjunctions make no difference. The first rule indicates that the order of conjuncts doesn't matter: '$\mathcal{A}$ & $\mathcal{B}$' is equivalent to '$\mathcal{B}$ & $\mathcal{A}$'. It states that conjunction is *commutative*. This rule underlies the equivalence of such sentences as

(19) a. Edwin and Werner drink too much.
     b. Werner and Edwin drink too much.

Commutativity of Conjunction (Cm)

> n. $\mathcal{A}$ & $\mathcal{B}$ Cm, m
> m. $\mathcal{B}$ & $\mathcal{A}$ Cm, n

The second rule asserts that the grouping of conjuncts makes no difference; conjunction is *associative*. It underlies the equivalence of sentences such as

(20) a. Aristotle and Aquinas were great philosophers, and so was Kant.
     b. Aristotle was a great philosopher, and so were Aquinas and Kant.

Associativity of Conjunction (As)

> n. $(\mathcal{A}$ & $\mathcal{B})$ & $\mathcal{C}$ As, m
> m. $\mathcal{A}$ & $(\mathcal{B}$ & $\mathcal{C})$ As, n

The third and fourth rules assert the same principle for disjunctions, underlying the equivalence of these pairs of sentences:

(21) a. He called Marlene or Darlene.
    b. He called Darlene or Marlene.

(22) a. Either Nellie or Benjy finished the work, or Verne did.
    b. Either Nellie finished the work, or Benjy or Verne did.

Commutativity of Disjunction (Cm)

n. $\mathcal{A} \,\&\, \mathcal{B}$ Cm, m

m. $\mathcal{B} \,\&\, \mathcal{A}$ Cm, n

Associativity of Disjunction (As)

n. $(\mathcal{A} \lor \mathcal{B}) \lor \mathcal{C}$ As, m

m. $\mathcal{A} \lor (\mathcal{B} \lor \mathcal{C})$ As, n

We'd already assumed in Chapter 5 that these principles hold when we allowed $p \lor q \lor r$, for example, as an abbreviation for either $(p \lor q) \lor r$ or $p \lor (q \lor r)$.

Abbreviations

Finally, four rules abbreviate commonly used proof steps. The first two allow negations to function readily, without detours, in exploiting conditionals and biconditionals. The third provides an alternative technique for exploiting disjunctions. The fourth expresses the principle that anything follows from a contradiction.

The first abbreviation rule, *modus tollens,* underlies the reasoning in arguments such as this:

(23) Charlie will accept the settlement only if you do.
    You won't accept the settlement.
    ∴ Charlie won't accept the settlement.

Modus Tollens (MT)

n. $\mathcal{A} \rightarrow \mathcal{B}$

m. $\neg \mathcal{B}$

p. $\neg \mathcal{A}$ MT, n, m

If $\mathcal{A}$ is true only if $\mathcal{B}$ is, and $\mathcal{B}$ is false, then $\mathcal{A}$ must also be false. This rule allows an easier demonstration of the validity of

(24) If Louis denies the allegation, so will Doug.
     Neither Kim nor Doug will deny the allegation.
     $\therefore$ Neither Kim nor Louis will deny it.

by permitting a shortened proof of $p \rightarrow q$; $\neg(r \vee q)$; $\therefore \neg(r \vee p)$. (Notice the use of both directions of DM.)

1.	$p \rightarrow q$	A
2.	$\neg(r \vee q)$	A
3.	$\neg r \;\&\; \neg q$	DM, 2
4.	$\neg r$	S, 3
5.	$\neg q$	S, 3
6.	$\neg p$	MT, 1, 5
7.	$\neg r \;\&\; \neg p$	C, 4, 6
8.	$\neg(r \vee p)$	DM, 7

The second abbreviation rule is similar to *modus tollens,* but it involves the biconditional. It relates to *modus tollens,* in fact, as 'modus both-ends' relates to *modus ponens.* The rules involving the conditional work in only one direction; those for the biconditional work in both directions. Because of the similarity of the rules, we'll consider this rule an expanded form of 'modus both-ends'. It underlies arguments such as

(25) a. Laramie will send someone if and only if Casper does.
       Laramie won't send anyone.
       $\therefore$ Neither will Casper.
    b. Jim will come if and only if Hattie is invited.
       Hattie isn't invited.
       $\therefore$ Jim won't come.

Modus Both-ends, Expanded (MB)

n.	$\mathcal{A} \leftrightarrow \mathcal{B}$	
m.	$\neg\mathcal{A}$ (or $\neg\mathcal{B}$)	
p.	$\neg\mathcal{B}$ (or $\neg\mathcal{A}$)	MB, n, m

If '$\mathcal{A}$ if and only if $\mathcal{B}$' is true, and $\mathcal{A}$ is false, $\mathcal{B}$ must also be false. The biconditional asserts that $\mathcal{A}$ and $\mathcal{B}$ agree in truth value. This rule allows a shortened proof of

(26) Gilda really said that if and only if she was livid.
       Gilda was irritated, but she didn't really say that.
       $\therefore$ Gilda wasn't livid.

which we can symbolize as $p \leftrightarrow q; r \;\&\; \neg p; \therefore \neg q$.

1. $p \leftrightarrow q$ A
2. $r \;\&\; \neg p$ A
3. $\neg p$ S, 2
4. $\neg q$ MB, 1, 3

The third abbreviation rule offers an alternate way of exploiting disjunctions. It reflects the reasoning in

(27) Phillip or Desmond is carrying a gun.
    If Phillip's carrying a gun, we're in trouble.
    If Desmond's carrying a gun, we're in trouble.
    $\therefore$ We're in trouble.

Constructive Dilemma (CD)

n. $\mathscr{A} \vee \mathscr{B}$
m. $\mathscr{A} \to \mathscr{C}$
p. $\mathscr{B} \to \mathscr{C}$
q. $\mathscr{C}$ CD, n, m, p

To see how CD works, let's derive q from $p \vee q$ and $p \to q$.

1. $p \vee q$ A
2. $p \to q$ A
3. $[q$ ACP
4. $q \to q$ CP, 3–3
5. q CD, 1, 2, 4

We can prove $q \to q$ in just one step because the antecedent and consequent are the same.

Finally, a derived rule allows us to deduce anything from a contradiction.

Contradiction (!)

n. $\mathscr{A}$
m. $\neg \mathscr{A}$
p. $\mathscr{B}$!, n, m

If $\mathscr{A}$ is both true and false, then anything follows. This is our most surprising derivable rule. We've already seen how it follows from basic rules. More illuminating, perhaps, is the original medieval deduction of the contradiction rule.

1. p A
2. $\neg p$ A
3. $\quad\neg q$ AIP
4. $\quad p \vee q$ Ad, 1
5. $\quad q$ DS, 4, 2
6. $\quad q \,\&\, \neg q$ C, 5, 3
7. q IP, 3–6

The contradiction rule allows us to count a proof complete whenever we obtain a contradiction within it. If we reach a contradiction in an indirect proof, of course, that proof is complete. If we reach a contradiction in a conditional proof, the contradiction rule guarantees that we can write the conditional's consequent on the next line. Similarly, reaching a contradiction in a direct proof indicates that we can write the desired conclusion on the next line.

Strategy

Overall proof strategies derive, primarily, from what we're trying to prove, and, secondarily, from what we already have. Our system is organized to make proof strategies apparent. To prove a formula with a given main connective, we try using the introduction rule for that connective. To use a formula with a given main connective, we try using that connective's exploitation rule. The following table contains some of the most important strategies. If it can be achieved, a direct proof is usually easiest. But, if it's not obvious how to prove the conclusion directly, then use the strategies listed.

Proof Strategies

To get	Try to
$\neg \mathscr{A}$	Use indirect proof.
$\mathscr{A} \,\&\, \mathscr{B}$	Prove $\mathscr{A}$ and $\mathscr{B}$ separately.
$\mathscr{A} \vee \mathscr{B}$	(a) Use indirect proof, or (b) prove $\mathscr{A}$ or $\mathscr{B}$ separately.
$\mathscr{A} \to \mathscr{B}$	Use conditional proof.
$\mathscr{A} \leftrightarrow \mathscr{B}$	Prove the two conditionals $\mathscr{A} \to \mathscr{B}$ and $\mathscr{B} \to \mathscr{A}$.

To exploit	Try to
$\neg \mathscr{A}$	(a) Use it with other lines that have $\mathscr{A}$ as a part, or (b) use a derived rule.
$\mathscr{A} \,\&\, \mathscr{B}$	Use S to get $\mathscr{A}$ and $\mathscr{B}$ individually.
$\mathscr{A} \vee \mathscr{B}$	(a) Get the negation of one disjunct and use DS to get the other, or (b) use CD by taking each case separately.
$\mathscr{A} \to \mathscr{B}$	(a) Get $\mathscr{A}$ and then reach $\mathscr{B}$ by MP, or (b) get $\neg \mathscr{B}$ and then reach $\neg \mathscr{A}$ by MT.
$\mathscr{A} \leftrightarrow \mathscr{B}$	(a) Get either component and then reach the other by MB, or (b) get the negation of either component and then the negation of the other by our expanded MB.

These strategies indicate how to construct proofs of various kinds. They are helpful in a wide variety of situations. Sometimes, however, the obvious tactics don't work. Our system offers two "safety valves"—strategies that work well under pressure. First, when in doubt, use indirect proof. Anything that can be proved can be proved indirectly. Second, if it's not clear within an indirect proof how to derive a contradiction, choose any sentence letter that is not already established and whose negation is not yet established, and try to prove that sentence letter or its negation. The assumption for indirect proof, together with other information in the proof, will lead to a contradiction; therefore, anything follows. No matter what letter you select, therefore, you should be able to prove it.

Problems

Do the problems in Chapter 8, section 8.6.

SUMMARY OF RULES
RULES APPLYING ONLY TO ENTIRE FORMULAS
BASIC RULES

Assumption (A)

$$n. \quad \mathscr{A} \qquad A$$

Simplification (S)

$$
\begin{array}{ll}
n. & \underline{\mathscr{A} \ \& \ \mathscr{B}} \\
n + m. & \mathscr{A} \ (\text{or} \ \mathscr{B}) \qquad S, n
\end{array}
$$

Conjunction (C)

$$
\begin{array}{ll}
n. & \mathscr{A} \\
m. & \underline{\mathscr{B}} \\
p. & \mathscr{A} \ \& \ \mathscr{B} \qquad C, n, m
\end{array}
$$

Indirect Proof (IP)

$$
\begin{array}{lll}
n. & \lceil \mathscr{A} & \text{AIP} \\
\vdots & & \vdots \\
n + p. & \lfloor \mathscr{B} \ \& \ \neg \mathscr{B} & \\
n + r. & \neg \mathscr{A} & \text{IP}, n\text{--}n + p
\end{array}
$$

Modus Ponens (MP)

n. $\mathscr{A} \rightarrow \mathscr{B}$
m. $\underline{\mathscr{A}}$
p. $\mathscr{B}$ MP, n, m

Conditional Proof (CP)

n.   ⌈$\mathscr{A}$ ACP
      │ ⋮   ⋮
n + p. ⌊$\mathscr{B}$
n + q. $\mathscr{A} \rightarrow \mathscr{B}$ CP, n–n + p

Biconditional (B)

n. $\mathscr{A} \rightarrow \mathscr{B}$
m. $\mathscr{B} \rightarrow \mathscr{A}$
p. $\mathscr{A} \leftrightarrow \mathscr{B}$ B, n, m

Modus Both-ends (MB)

n. $\mathscr{A} \leftrightarrow \mathscr{B}$
m. $\underline{\mathscr{A}}$ (or $\mathscr{B}$)
p. $\mathscr{B}$ (or $\mathscr{A}$)   MB, n, m

Addition (Ad)

n. $\underline{\mathscr{A}}$ (or $\mathscr{B}$)
n + p. $\mathscr{A} \vee \mathscr{B}$ Ad, n

Disjunctive Syllogism (DS)

n. $\mathscr{A} \vee \mathscr{B}$
m. $\underline{\neg \mathscr{A}}$ (or $\neg \mathscr{B}$)
p. $\mathscr{B}$ (or $\mathscr{A}$)   DS, n, m

DERIVED RULES

Indirect Proof (extended)

n. $\lceil \neg \mathscr{A}$ AIP
⋮ | ⋮   ⋮
n + p. $\lfloor \mathscr{B} \,\&\, \neg \mathscr{B}$
n + q. $\mathscr{A}$ IP, n–n + p

Modus Tollens (MT)

n. $\mathscr{A} \rightarrow \mathscr{B}$
m. $\neg \mathscr{B}$
p. $\neg \mathscr{A}$ MT, n, m

Modus Both-ends, Expanded (MB)

n. $\mathscr{A} \leftrightarrow \mathscr{B}$
m. $\neg \mathscr{A}$ (or $\neg \mathscr{B}$)
p. $\neg \mathscr{B}$ (or $\neg \mathscr{A}$)   MB, n, m

Biconditional-Conditional (BC)

n. $\mathscr{A} \leftrightarrow \mathscr{B}$
m. $\mathscr{A} \rightarrow \mathscr{B}$ (or $\mathscr{B} \rightarrow \mathscr{A}$)   BC, n

Constructive Dilemma (CD)

n. $\mathscr{A} \vee \mathscr{B}$
m. $\mathscr{A} \rightarrow \mathscr{C}$
p. $\mathscr{B} \rightarrow \mathscr{C}$
q. $\mathscr{C}$ CD, n, m, p

Contradiction (!)

n. $\mathcal{A}$
m. $\neg\mathcal{A}$
p. $\mathcal{B}$!, n, m

RULES APPLYING TO PARTS OF FORMULAS
AS WELL AS ENTIRE FORMULAS
BASIC RULES

Double Negation (DN)

n. $\mathcal{A}$ DN, m
m. $\neg\neg\mathcal{A}$ DN, n

DERIVED RULES

DeMorgan's Law #1 (DM)

n. $\neg(\mathcal{A} \& \mathcal{B})$ DM, m
m. $\neg\mathcal{A} \vee \neg\mathcal{B}$ DM, n

DeMorgan's Law #2 (DM)

n. $\neg(\mathcal{A} \vee \mathcal{B})$ DM, m
m. $\neg\mathcal{A} \& \neg\mathcal{B}$ DM, n

Negated Conditional (NC)

n. $\neg(\mathcal{A} \rightarrow \mathcal{B})$ NC, m
m. $\neg\mathcal{A} \& \neg\mathcal{B}$ NC, n

Negated Biconditional (NB)

n. $\underline{\neg(\mathcal{A} \leftrightarrow \mathcal{B})}$ NB, m

m. $\neg \mathcal{A} \leftrightarrow \mathcal{B}$ (or $\mathcal{A} \leftrightarrow \neg \mathcal{B}$)   NB, n

Material Conditional (MC)

n. $\underline{\mathcal{A} \rightarrow \mathcal{B}}$ MC, m

m. $\neg \mathcal{A} \lor \mathcal{B}$ MC, n

Commutativity of Conjunction (Cm)

n. $\underline{\mathcal{A}\ \&\ \mathcal{B}}$ Cm, m

m. $\mathcal{B}\ \&\ \mathcal{A}$ Cm, n

Associativity of Conjunction (As)

n. $\underline{(\mathcal{A}\ \&\ \mathcal{B})\ \&\ \mathcal{C}}$ As, m

m. $\mathcal{A}\ \&\ (\mathcal{B}\ \&\ \mathcal{C})$ As, n

Commutativity of Disjunction (Cm)

n. $\underline{\mathcal{A} \lor \mathcal{B}}$ Cm, m

m. $\mathcal{B} \lor \mathcal{A}$ Cm, n

Associativity of Disjunction (As)

n. $\underline{(\mathcal{A} \lor \mathcal{B}) \lor \mathcal{C}}$ As, m

m. $\mathcal{A} \lor (\mathcal{B} \lor \mathcal{C})$ As, n

I

DEDUCTION
STYLE
TWO

B

ADDING QUANTIFIERS

Natural deduction extends easily to predicate logic. All rules of sentential deduction apply in quantification theory. To deal with quantifiers, the system adds four new rules. The deduction system that emerges shares the virtues of its sentential cousin. The system is sound, for every provable formula is valid, and every conclusion provable from a set of premises follows from them. The system is also complete, for every valid formula of quantification theory can be proved in the system, and every valid argument can be shown valid within it. Furthermore, the system mirrors closely the processes of reasoning that people use in a wide variety of contexts.

B.1 DEDUCTION RULES FOR QUANTIFIERS

The deduction rules needed for quantificational logic are very straightforward. Suppose that $\mathscr{A}[c/v]$ is the result of substituting c for every occurrence of v throughout the formula $\mathscr{A}$. If $\forall v \mathscr{A}$ and $\exists v \mathscr{A}$ are formulas, then $\mathscr{A}[c/v]$ is called an *instance* of them. Conversely, $\forall v \mathscr{A}$ and $\exists v \mathscr{A}$ are *generics* of $\mathscr{A}[c/v]$. If $\mathscr{A}[c/v]$ is an instance of $\forall v \mathscr{A}$ and $\exists v \mathscr{A}$, and those formulas do not contain c, then $\mathscr{A}[c/v]$ is a *conservative instance* of $\forall v \mathscr{A}$ and $\exists v \mathscr{A}$.

Each connective has two rules. One rule introduces the connective into proofs, whereas the other allows us to exploit its presence. The existential quantifier similarly comes with two rules: an introduction rule and an exploitation rule. The introduction rule, in essence, allows us to move to an existentially quantified formula from any instance of that formula.[1] Called *existential generalization,* it takes this form:

Existential Generalization (EG)

$$
\begin{array}{ll}
\text{n.} & \mathscr{A}[c/v] \\
\text{n + p.} & \exists v \mathscr{A} \qquad \text{EG, n}
\end{array}
$$

Here c may be any constant.

Existential generalization allows us to infer an existentially quantified formula from any instance of it. It sanctions the step from an instance to its corresponding existential generic. Suppose that our universe of discourse consists of people. If Jones, for example, is a spy, then we may conclude that someone is a spy. If Susan suspects Harry, then Susan suspects someone; of course, it's also true that somebody suspects Harry and that somebody suspects somebody. Finally, if Frank doesn't trust himself to work around large sums of money, then Frank doesn't trust somebody to work around large sums of money. Additionally, somebody doesn't trust Frank to work around large sums, and someone doesn't trust himself to do so. Each of the following is an acceptable application of existential generalization:

Fa	$\exists x Fx$
Gab	$\exists x Gax$
Gab	$\exists x Gxb$
Hcc	$\exists x Hcx$
Hcc	$\exists x Hxc$
Hcc	$\exists x Hxx$
$\exists x Fxa$	$\exists y \exists x Fxy$
$\forall x Fx \rightarrow Gb$	$\exists z(\forall x Fx \rightarrow Gz)$

In each case, the premise is an instance of the conclusion.

The rule of *existential specification* allows us to move from an existentially quantified formula to an instance of it.[2] This rule is almost exactly the reverse, then, of the existential generalization rule. But it imposes a restriction: The instance must involve a constant new to the proof. The rule asserts that we may (a) drop an existential quantifier serving as a main connective in a formula and (b) substitute for the quantified variable a constant that hasn't appeared earlier in the proof. The constant must have appeared nowhere in the deduction. (Actually, no harm would result from allowing us to use, for ES, constants that appear earlier only on already bracketed lines. But, to minimize confusion, we'll always use completely new constants.)

Existential Specification (ES)

n. $\exists v \mathscr{A}$

n + p. $\mathscr{A}[c/v]$ ES, n

Here c must be a constant new to the proof.

Suppose that we have the information that someone in our department is selling trade secrets to a competitor. We don't know who this person is—or, perhaps, who these people are—but we want to reason from what we know to find out. We know that at least one person has been selling secrets; our reasoning and our communication will proceed much more readily if we give this person some name—'John Doe', perhaps, or just 'the mole'—so that we can refer to him or her in various contexts. We can't simply say, "Someone has been selling our trade secrets. Someone must have joined the department around the middle of 1981, because that's when secrets began to leak. Someone is a bad person." Nothing here indicates that the "someones" are the same. To tie these assertions to the same individual, we must have a way of referring to that person. Introducing a name accomplishes this goal. It's critical that the name we choose be new. If Ingrid is the head of the department, and we decide to call the seller of trade secrets 'Ingrid', we'll be led to conclusions that don't follow.

The existential specification rule reflects a very important feature of indefinite descriptions like 'a house' or 'a room with a view': They not only assert existence but also, like proper names, introduce a constant that can figure in subsequent discourse. The existential quantifier itself plays only the first role. The rule of existential specification, however, allows us to simulate the second. It allows us to refer back to the object whose existence is asserted in the existentially quantified formula.

Consider, for example, this simple discourse:

(1) Wanda lives in *a house* on Speedway. *Her house* is convenient to campus. More important, *it*'s close to Rosie's Tamale House.

We would ordinarily symbolize the first sentence as

(2) $\exists x(Hx \,\&\, Oxs \,\&\, Lax)$.

But this step raises a problem about how to symbolize the second and third sentences. If we use a constant to translate 'her house' and 'it', as seems natural, we have no way of making it clear that we're talking about the object, Wanda's house, that the first sentence introduces. If we use existential quantifiers for 'her house' and 'it' in separate translations of the last two sentences, we also fail to express the idea that we're talking about one object; we would have instead formulas like these:

(3) a. $\exists x(Hx \ \& \ Oxs \ \& \ Lax)$
      (There's a house on Speedway Wanda lives in.)
   b. $\exists x(Hx \ \& \ Wax \ \& \ Cxc)$
      (There's a house Wanda owns that's convenient to campus.)
   c. $\exists xSxr$
      (Something is close to Rosie's Tamale House.)

Nothing here indicates that we're talking about one and the same object.
   We can symbolize the entire discourse in a single formula as

(4) $\exists x(Hx \ \& \ Oxs \ \& \ Lax \ \& \ Wax \ \& \ Cxc \ \& \ Sxr)$.

But doing so forces us to symbolize the discourse as a whole unit; we can't proceed sentence by sentence. In a proof, however, we must proceed line by line as we deduce more and more information. The existential specification rule allows us to refer back to the object introduced by an existentially quantified formula while still proceeding line by line in the usual manner of a proof.
   To preserve the overall soundness of the system, we need to add a restriction.

> A proof must never end with a formula containing a constant introduced by ES.

This restriction, together with the restriction on ES requiring a new constant, prevents us from using it to derive invalid conclusions. To see why the constant must be new, consider this argument:

(5) Officer O'Malley shot someone.
   ∴ Officer O'Malley shot himself.

Plainly, the argument is invalid. But, if we were to ignore the requirement that we use a new constant in applying ES, we could show the corresponding argument form to be valid:

1. $\exists xSmx$ A
2. Smm ES, 1   (Wrong!)

To understand why we must not use a constant appearing in the conclusion, consider this argument:

(6) Some people are crazy.
   ∴ You're crazy.

This, too, is a terrible argument. But, if we were to ignore the requirement that no conclusion of a proof contain a constant introduced by ES, we could prove the argument (where a symbolizes 'you').

1. $\exists xCx$ A
2. Ca ES, 1   (Wrong!)

This proof is flawed. But there would be nothing wrong with step 2 if the proof didn't end at that line and didn't conclude with a formula containing a.[3]

The third rule for quantifiers is *universal specification*. If we know that something is true about every object, then we can conclude that it is true for each particular object we consider. If God loves everyone, then God loves me, you, and the Earl of Roxburgh. If Jane likes everyone she meets, then she likes you, if she's met you; she likes me, if she's met me; and so on. The rule of universal specification asserts that from a universally quantified formula, we may infer any of its instances.

Universal Specification (US)

n. $\forall v \mathcal{A}$
n + p. $\mathcal{A}[c/v]$ US, n

Here c may be any constant.

This rule does not require a new constant. In fact, it's silly to use a new constant in applying US unless no constants at all appear in the proof up to this line. If constants a and b appear earlier, then, from $\forall xFx$, we can infer Fa, or Fb, or both. If we also have a formula $\forall xGxx$, we can infer Gaa or Gbb. And, from $\forall x\forall yHxy$, we can obtain $\forall yHay$ or $\forall yHby$ and, in another step, any of Haa, Hab, Hba, and Hbb. We could also, of course, infer similar formulas with other constants. Unless we are forced to introduce those constants in other ways, however, using them to exploit a universal formula serves no purpose.

To see how these rules work, let's demonstrate the validity of a simple argument.

(7) Something is rotten in the state of Denmark.
     Whatever's in Denmark is in Europe.
     $\therefore$ Something's rotten in Europe.

1. $\exists x(Rx \mathbin{\&} Ixd)$ A
2. $\forall y(Iyd \rightarrow Iye)$ A
3. $Ra \mathbin{\&} Iad$ ES, 1
4. $Iad \rightarrow Iae$ US, 2
5. Iad S, 3
6. Iae MP, 4, 5
7. Ra S, 3
8. $Ra \mathbin{\&} Iae$ C, 7, 6
9. $\exists z(Rz \mathbin{\&} Ize)$ EG, 5

Problems

Do the problems in Chapter 13, section 13.1.

B.2 Universal Generalization

Introducing a universal formula requires a new rule.

Universal Generalization (UG)

$$n. \quad \mathscr{A}[c/v]$$
$$n + p. \quad \forall v \mathscr{A} \qquad \text{UG, n}$$

Here 1. c must not occur in $\forall v \mathscr{A}$.
2. c must not occur in any free assumptions or in the conclusion of the proof.
3. c must not have been introduced by ES.
4. No term remaining in $\forall v \mathscr{A}$ may depend on c.

The last of these restrictions is needed only for proofs involving formulas with quantifiers that overlap in scope. For simpler formulas, it may be ignored. For that reason, let's set the last restriction aside for the moment and examine the rest of the rule.

Basic Conditions

To prove a universal conclusion, this rule asserts, we prove a conservative instance of it. In general, it's best to try to derive an instance that results from substituting a constant new to the proof for the quantified variable. Because no information regarding the new constant will appear anywhere earlier in the proof, the constant stands for no object in particular. It represents an arbitrarily chosen object. Because the proof puts no constraints on it, absolutely any object could play this role. Consequently, though we prove something about c, we've shown how to prove that assertion about anything. And this justifies our drawing a universal conclusion.

The restrictions prevent this form of proof from allowing us to prove very silly arguments valid. Consider the first restriction, that c not appear in $\forall v \mathscr{A}$. The restriction requires that we derive a universal from a *conservative* instance of it. To see why this is necessary, suppose we tried to argue

(8) Everyone respects himself or herself.
∴ Everyone respects Qadhafy.

Clearly, the argument fails. We might attempt this proof:

1. $\forall x Rxx$ A
2. Rgg US, 1
3. $\forall x Rxg$ UG, 2   (Wrong!)

We must derive a universal generic from one of its conservative instances. Since g occurs in $\forall x Rxg$, line 3 violates the first restriction on UG.

The second restriction prohibits c from appearing in the free assumptions or conclusion of the proof. If we allowed c to appear in the assumptions (including those for indirect or conditional proof), we could prove the validity of poor arguments, such as

(9) Eliot Ness sent Al Capone to jail.
     $\therefore$ Eliot Ness sent everybody to jail.

Ignoring the second restriction, we could attempt this proof:

1. Snc A
2. $\forall x Snx$ UG, 1   (Wrong!)

We can't go from the information that Ness sent Capone to jail to the conclusion that he sent everyone there. The constant c, which line 2 tries to generalize, appears in an assumption. So, UG can't apply.

A similar argument shows the point of the third restriction, that c must not have been introduced by ES. Consider this invalid argument:

(10) There is a pope.
     $\therefore$ Everybody is pope.

We might try to prove it valid as follows:

1. $\exists x Px$ A
2. Pa ES, 1
3. $\forall x Px$ UG, 2   (Wrong!)

We used existential specification to introduce a; therefore, we can't later universally generalize it.

As an example of a successful universal generalization, consider this inference:

(11) Everything created by God is good.
     Everything is a creation of God.
     $\therefore$ Everything is good.

To establish its validity, we construct a universal proof.

1. $\forall x(Cgx \rightarrow Gx)$ A
2. $\forall x Cgx$ A
3. Cga US, 2
4. $Cga \rightarrow Ga$ US, 1
5. Ga MP, 4, 3
6. $\forall x Gx$ UG, 5

To show that everything is *G*, we show that some arbitrarily chosen object *a* is *G*. UG succeeds because *a* occurs in neither assumptions (lines 1 and 2) nor in the universal conclusion (line 6), and was not introduced by ES.

Problems

Do the problems in Chapter 13, section 13.2.

B.3 Formulas with Overlapping Quantifiers

The final restriction on UG is needed only to cope with formulas having quantifiers that overlap in scope. It provides a way to distinguish in a proof 'something or other' from 'some one thing' or 'something in particular'. It requires that no constant in $\forall v \mathscr{A}$ depend on *c*. To understand this idea, we need to define *dependence* among constants.

> **Definition** A constant *c* *immediately depends on* a constant *d* in a proof if and only if *c* is introduced into the proof by applying ES to a formula containing *d*.

> **Definition** A constant *c* *depends on* a contant *d* if and only if there is a chain of constants $c_1, \ldots, c_n$ such that *c* immediately depends on c_1, c_1 immediately depends on $c_2, \ldots,$ and c_n immediately depends on *d*. (The chain may be empty; immediate dependence is a kind of dependence.)

Suppose that we apply ES at some stage of a proof:

> n. $\exists v \mathscr{A}$
> m. $\mathscr{A}[c/v]$ ES, n

Then *c* depends on all other constants in $\exists v \mathscr{A}$. Moreover, *c* depends on all constants on which those constants depend. Here is a concrete example:

> 1. $\exists x(\exists y(Fx \ \& \ Fy) \ \& \ Fa)$ A
> 2. $\exists y(Fb \ \& \ Fy) \ \& \ Fa$ ES, 1 (*b* depends on *a*)
> 3. $\exists y(Fb \ \& \ Fy)$ S, 2
> 4. $Fb \ \& \ Fc$ ES, 3 (*b* depends on *a*; *c* depends on *b* and *a*)

On line 2, we apply ES to a formula containing the constant *a*, thereby introducing *b*. So, *b* immediately depends on *a*. On line 4, we again apply ES. This time, the constant *b* is already present; applying the rule introduces *c*. So, *c* immediately depends on *b*. Since *b* immediately depends on *a*, *c* also depends on *a*.

The fourth restriction on UG sounds complicated; it may seem to make applying UG more trouble than it's worth. But we can keep track of dependence among constants very easily in a *dependency diagram*.[4] These diagrams aren't official parts of proofs, but they make it easier to check whether the restrictions on UG are being obeyed. To construct a dependency diagram, we wait until the first application of ES. Suppose the proof, so far, looks like this:

1. $\exists x(Fx \rightarrow (Ga \mathbin{\&} Hb))$ A
2. $\exists x(Gx \mathbin{\&} Fa)$ A
3. $Fc \rightarrow (Ga \mathbin{\&} Hb)$ ES, 1

First, we make a horizontal list of the constants in the formula to which the rule has been applied (if there are any). Here, we've applied the rule to the formula on line 1, which contains a and b. So, we write a and b horizontally.

$a \qquad b$

Then, we write the new constant introduced below them and circle it, drawing lines to connect it to the others in the formula. Here, we've introduced c.

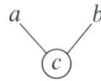

Continuing the proof, we might apply ES again.

1. $\exists x(Fx \rightarrow (Ga \mathbin{\&} Hb))$ A
2. $\exists x(Gx \mathbin{\&} Fa)$ A
3. $Fc \rightarrow (Ga \mathbin{\&} Hb)$ ES, 1
4. $Gd \mathbin{\&} Fa$ ES, 2

First, we add to the diagram any constants appearing in the formula to which we've applied the rule—in this case, $\exists x(Gx \mathbin{\&} Fa)$, on line 2—that aren't already there. In this case, a is already on the diagram. Then, we write the new constant we've introduced—here, d—below the other nodes, circling it and linking it to the others in the resulting formula (here, a). So, we obtain

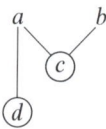

This diagram indicates that c depends on both a and b and that d depends on a.

What is the intuitive significance of dependence? In Chapter 10, we saw that there is a difference between

(12) Everyone likes someone (or other).

and

(13) Some one person is liked by everyone.

In (12), the identity of the 'someone'—the person liked—depends on who's doing the liking. Our diagrams reflect this fact. We would symbolize (12) as

(14) $\forall x\exists y Lxy$,

which, applying the obvious rules, might lead to these steps in a deduction:

(15) n. $\forall x\exists y Lxy$

   m. $\exists y Lay$ US, n a

   k. Lab ES, m $\textcircled{b}$

(The dependency diagram is on the right.) Notice that b depends on a; who is being liked depends on who is liking. The situation is very different with (13), which we could symbolize as

(16) $\exists x\forall y Lyx$.

This might lead to these deduction steps:

(17) n. $\exists x\forall y Lyx$

   m. $\forall y Lyb$ ES, n $\textcircled{b}$

   k. Lab US, m

Here, a and b are independent. Who is liked does not depend on who is liking. The notion of dependence thus reflects concepts that in English we capture by ordering noun phrases, choosing determiners, and using phrases such as 'or other', 'a certain', 'in particular', 'one', and so on.

   To summarize: Dependency diagrams change only when we apply ES. When we do apply existential specification, moving from $\exists v\mathscr{A}$ to $\mathscr{A}[c/v]$, we follow these rules:

1. Write, horizontally, the constants in $\exists v\mathscr{A}$ not already in the diagram.
2. Add the new constant c below the constants in $\exists v\mathscr{A}$, circling it and drawing lines linking it to them.

We can use these diagrams to check the fulfillment of the third and fourth restrictions on UG. The third bans the use of the same constant in ES and UG. Dependency diagrams show which constants have been introduced by ES: They appear circled. So, we cannot apply UG to a constant circled in the diagram. The fourth restriction requires that as we move from $\mathscr{A}[c/v]$ to $\forall v\mathscr{A}$, no constant in $\forall v\mathscr{A}$ depend on c. The restriction is satisfied provided that no constant in $\mathscr{A}[c/v]$ is linked upward to c.

   To see why the fourth restriction is needed and how to use dependency diagrams to check on its satisfaction, consider this invalid argument. (In Chapter 12, we saw that it generates an infinite tableau.)

(18) Everything has a cause.
∴ Something is the cause of everything.

We could try to prove it valid by constructing this deduction. The corresponding dependency diagram, constructed in one step (because there is one application of ES in the proof), appears on the right:

1. $\forall x \exists y C y x$ A
2. $\exists y C y a$ US, 1
3. $C b a$ ES, 2
4. $\forall x C b x$ UG, 3   (Wrong!)
5. $\exists y \forall x C y x$ EG, 4

Step 4 fails because b is linked upward to a in the diagram. That is, b depends on a. So, we can't universally generalize on a.

This example illustrates why dependence is important. Imagine an extended English argument mirroring the flawed proof.

(19) 1. Everything has a cause.   A
    2. Take your passing this course (a); it has a cause.   US, 1
    3. Passing the exam (b), let us say, causes you to pass the course (a).   ES, 2
    4. Passing the exam (b) causes everything.   UG, 3   (Wrong!)
    5. Something causes everything.   EG, 4

The proof introduces b (passing the exam) as the cause of a (passing the course). The identity of b depends on the identity of a; different events have different causes.

To see why dependence, and not just immediate dependence, matters, we consider this more complicated but still erroneous proof for a related argument form:

1. $\forall x \exists y (F x y \ \& \ \exists z F y z)$ A
2. $\exists y (F a y \ \& \ \exists z F y z)$ US, 1

3. $F a b \ \& \ \exists z F b z$ ES, 2
4. $F a b$ S, 3
5. $\exists z F b z$ S, 3
6. $F b c$ ES, 5
7. $F a b \ \& \ F b c$ C, 4, 6
8. $\exists y (F a y \ \& \ F y c)$ EG, 7
9. $\forall x \exists y (F x y \ \& \ F y c)$ UG, 8   (Wrong!)
10. $\exists z \forall x \exists y (F x y \ \& \ F y z)$ EG, 9

On line 9, the application of UG is incorrect because c depends on a.

Problems

Do the problems in Chapter 13, section 13.3.

B.4 Derived Rules for Quantifiers

The system resulting from adding these four rules to our natural deduction system for sentential logic has all the power it needs. It can demonstrate the validity of any valid argument form in quantification theory. Nevertheless, adding some further rules can increase its efficiency and naturalness. This section presents some derived rules which, while theoretically superfluous, make the proof system more pleasant to work with.

Combining Steps

First, we can apply quantifier rules several times in a single step. Suppose, for example, that we want to take instances of $\forall x \forall y F xy$. The universal specification rule requires us to move first to the instance $\forall y Fay$, let us say, and then to its instance Faa. But any constant can substitute for both x and y here because both are universally quantified. So, it's easy to perform the operation in one step. We can move directly from $\forall x \forall y F xy$ to an instance of an instance of it, Faa. Similarly, we could move to Fab, Fba, Fbb, Fac, and so on. We can record that we've exploited a series of n universal quantifiers at once by writing, not US, but US^n. The application would look like this:

m. $\forall x \forall y F xy$
m + n. Faa US^2, m

We can do the same for existential quantifiers if we replace each quantified variable with a new constant. So, we may move from $\exists x \exists y \exists z (Fxy \ \& \ Fxz)$ to $Fab \ \& \ Fac$, citing the rule as ES^3.

Similarly, we can compress a sequence of universal generalizations into a single step. We can prove a formula with an initial string of n universal quantifiers by proving an instance of an instance ... of an instance of the formula, using n different new constants to replace the n quantified variables. For example, we can prove $\forall x \forall y (Fxy \rightarrow \neg Fyx)$ by proving $Fab \rightarrow \neg Fba$, where neither a nor b has appeared earlier in the proof and then inferring $\forall x \forall y (Fxy \rightarrow \neg Fyx)$ by UG^2.

Although these combinations of rules or proofs are very convenient, it's not a good idea to combine exploitations of universal and existential quantifiers. While US^2 and ES^4 are fairly easy to follow, US^2ES^3US is unintelligible.

Rewriting Variables

Variables have no independent meanings. The formulas $\forall x Fx$ and $\forall z Fz$ function in logically similar ways; so do $\exists y Gy$ and $\exists w Gw$. Indeed, it's easy to show that these pairs are equivalent. Here are the proofs in one direction:

1. $\forall x F x$	A	1. $\exists y G y$	A
2. $F a$	US, 1	2. $G a$	ES, 1
3. $\forall z F z$	UG, 2	3. $\exists w G w$	EG, 2

The proofs of the other directions follow exactly the same pattern.

Thus, we can substitute one variable for another throughout a formula. The only restriction we must observe is that we should not introduce into a formula a variable that is already there; otherwise we could go from the legitimate formula $\forall x \forall y F x y$ to the very different nonformula $\forall x \forall x F x x$. The derived rule, then, is this:

Variable Rewrite (VR)

n. $\mathcal{A}$
m. $\mathcal{A}[v/u]$ VR, n

Here v is foreign to $\mathcal{A}$.

Exploiting Negations

It's extremely useful to have a direct way of dealing with negations of quantified formulas. Our rules allow us to attack formulas with quantifiers as main connectives in one step. But, if a negation precedes a quantifier, the proof strategy becomes much more complicated. Luckily, negations of quantified formulas are equivalent to formulas with quantifiers as main connectives. Two *quantifier negation* rules relate quantified formulas to their negations. In the process, these rules relate the universal and existential quantifiers. In fact, they show how to define each quantifier in terms of the other. They underlie the equivalence of the following pairs of sentences:

(20)   a. Not everyone will show up.
      b. Somebody will fail to show up.

(21)   a. Jerry couldn't see a thing.
      b. Everything was such that Jerry couldn't see it.

Quantifier Negation (QN)

n. $\neg \exists v \mathcal{A}$ QN, m
m. $\forall v \neg \mathcal{A}$ QN, n

n. $\neg \forall v \mathcal{A}$ QN, m
m. $\exists v \neg \mathcal{A}$ QN, n

Both versions of quantifier negation invert. That is, the premise and conclusion are equivalent; therefore, the rules work in both directions. We can infer $\exists x \neg Fx$ from $\neg \forall x Fx$, and vice versa. Similarly, just by adding a negation sign, we can see that $\exists x Fx$ is equivalent to $\neg \forall x \neg Fx$, and that $\forall x Fx$ is equivalent to $\neg \exists x \neg Fx$. So, we can define the quantifiers in terms of each other.

Because QN takes the form of an equivalence, the replacement principle allows us to apply it to portions of formulas as well as to entire formulas. Each of the following is thus a legitimate application of QN.

$\neg \exists x Fxx$	$\forall x \neg Fxx$
$\neg \forall x \forall y Gxy$	$\exists x \neg \forall y Gxy$
$\forall x \forall y \neg \forall z(Fxz \ \& \ Fyz)$	$\forall x \forall y \exists z \neg(Fxz \ \& \ Fyz)$
$\exists x \neg \exists y Gyx$	$\exists x \forall y \neg Gyx$

We can apply this rule several times in a single step. We can abbreviate

$\neg \forall x \forall y \forall z((Rxy \ \& \ Ryz) \rightarrow Rxz)$	
$\exists x \neg \forall y \forall z((Rxy \ \& \ Ryz) \rightarrow Rxz)$	QN
$\exists x \exists y \neg \forall z((Rxy \ \& \ Ryz) \rightarrow Rxz)$	QN
$\exists x \exists y \exists z \neg((Rxy \ \& \ Ryz) \rightarrow Rxz)$	QN

as

$\neg \forall x \forall y \forall z((Rxy \ \& \ Ryz) \rightarrow Rxz)$	
$\exists x \exists y \exists z \neg((Rxy \ \& \ Ryz) \rightarrow Rxz)$	QN³

Finally, we can use quantifier negation to demonstrate, more easily than from our basic rules alone, the validity of

(22) Everyone who came to the party was arrested.
Not all my friends were arrested.
∴ Some of my friends didn't come to the party.

After symbolizing, we can construct this proof:

1.	$\forall x(Cx \rightarrow Ax)$	A
2.	$\neg \forall x(Fx \rightarrow Ax)$	A
3.	$\exists x \neg(Fx \rightarrow Ax)$	QN, 2
4.	$\neg(Fa \rightarrow Aa)$	ES, 3
5.	$Fa \ \& \neg Aa$	NC, 4
6.	Fa	S, 5
7.	$\neg Aa$	S, 5
8.	$Ca \rightarrow Aa$	US, 1
9.	$\neg Ca$	MT, 8, 7
10.	$Fa \ \& \neg Ca$	C, 6, 9
11.	$\exists x(Fx \ \& \neg Cx)$	EG, 10

Problems

Do the problems in Chapter 13, Section 13.4.

SUMMARY OF RULES
RULES APPLYING ONLY TO ENTIRE FORMULAS
BASIC RULES

Existential Generalization (EG)

$$n. \qquad \mathcal{A}[c/v]$$
$$n + p. \ \exists v \mathcal{A} \qquad\qquad \text{EG, } n$$

Here c may be any constant.

Existential Specification (ES)

$$n. \qquad \exists v \mathcal{A}$$
$$n + p. \ \mathcal{A}[c/v] \qquad \text{ES, } n$$

Here c must be a constant new to the proof.

Universal Specification (US)

$$n. \qquad \forall v \mathcal{A}$$
$$n + p. \ \mathcal{A}[c/v] \qquad \text{US, } n$$

Here c may be any constant.

Universal Generalization (UG)

$$n. \qquad \mathcal{A}[c/v]$$
$$n + p. \ \forall v \mathcal{A} \qquad\qquad \text{UG, } n$$

Here 1. c must not occur in $\forall v \mathcal{A}$;
    2. c must not occur in any free assumptions or the conclusion of the proof;
    3. c must not have been introduced by ES;
    4. No term remaining in $\forall v \mathcal{A}$ may depend on c.

DERIVED RULE

Variable Rewrite (VR)

n. $\mathscr{A}$
m. $\mathscr{A}[v/u]$ VR, n

Here v is foreign to $\mathscr{A}$.

RULES APPLYING TO PARTS OF FORMULAS
AS WELL AS ENTIRE FORMULAS

Quantifier Negation (QN)

n. $\underline{\neg \exists v \mathscr{A}}$ QN, m
m. $\forall v \neg \mathscr{A}$ QN, n

n. $\underline{\neg \forall v \mathscr{A}}$ QN, m
m. $\exists v \neg \mathscr{A}$ QN, n

Notes

[1] This rule was first formulated by the English philosopher William of Ockham in the fourteenth century.

[2] The American philosopher W. V. Quine first formulated existential exploitation in this way in 1950, in his *Methods of Logic* (Cambridge: Harvard University Press, 1950, 1982).

[3] The system of rules in this chapter is sound in the sense that the rules never lead us astray; they never allow us to prove a formula that isn't valid or permit us to establish the validity of an invalid argument form. Nevertheless, the existential specification rule is not sound, considered in itself; it justifies the invalid inference from $\exists v \mathscr{A}$ to $\mathscr{A}[c/v]$, provided that c is new to the proof. Our proof system, therefore, is not sound line by line. To preserve the overall soundness of the system, we need to add restrictions.

Most of our rules are *truth-preserving:* The truth of the premises of the rules guarantees the truth of their conclusions. Existential specification, however, is not truth-preserving. We should hardly be able to argue, 'Some philosophers have been bachelors. Therefore, Socrates was a bachelor'. This form of inference is fallacious. The same is true of universal generalization; the inference from 'Gorbachev is Russian' to 'Everybody is Russian' fails. But, although ES and UG are not truth-preserving, they never lead us to an illegitimate conclusion. Rule ES is *conservative* in that any formula that follows from the conclusion of the rule also follows from the rule's premise, provided the formula does not contain the introduced constant.

Thus, our system of rules as a whole is sound, but proofs are not sound line by line. We can never prove a conclusion that doesn't follow from the premises, but we may deduce intermediate formulas in the proof that don't follow from them. The restrictions make sure that these deviations don't affect the outcome of the proof.

Some logicians believe that proofs must be sound line by line; therefore, they formulate ES and UG differently. There is, however, a way of interpreting our system as sound line by line that does not require us to reformulate our rules. This method requires that we reinterpret constants—in particular, constants used in ES and UG. So far, we've thought of constants, relative to a context, as standing for objects. We could choose to think of them as marking places for objects but without necessarily standing for anything in particular. Or, we could think of them as standing for a different kind of object. Developing these strategies goes beyond the scope of this book. But both lead to serious and interesting analyses of logic. For the first, see Hans Kamp, "A Theory of Truth and Semantic Representation," in J. Groenendijk, T. Janssen, and M. Stockhof, *Formal Methods in the Study of Language* (Amsterdam: Mathematisch Centrum Tracts, 1981), and Irene Heim, *The Syntax and Semantics of Definite and Indefinite Noun Phrases* (PhD dissertation: University of Massachusetts at Amherst, 1983). For the second, see Kit Fine, *Reasoning with Arbitrary Objects* (Oxford: Basil Blackwell, 1985).

[4] Kit Fine introduced dependency diagrams in *Reasoning with Arbitrary Objects*.

II

DEDUCTION
STYLE
THREE

A

SENTENTIAL LOGIC

Truth tables and semantic tableaux can evaluate arguments clearly and efficiently. But they say almost nothing about how to *construct* arguments. In this appendix we'll develop a system designed to simulate people's construction of arguments. The deduction system is natural in the sense that it is meant to reflect the way people construct arguments in legal, scientific, philosophical, and mathematical contexts.

The deduction system of this appendix differs from that of Chapters 8 and 13 in two fundamental ways. First, this system allows complex as well as simple rules; we'll treat the complex rules as methods of proof. Second, we'll declare at the outset what we're trying to prove, as a part of the proof. These two differences allow for greatly simplified versions of several deduction rules.

A.1 PROOFS

A *natural deduction system* is a set of rules: specifically, *rules of inference* that allow us to derive formulas from other formulas. Central to the concept of a natural deduction system is the idea of *proof*. Proofs are extended arguments. There are two kinds of proofs. *Hypothetical* proofs begin with *assumptions* (or *hypotheses*). The assumptions act as premises; the proof's conclusion follows from them. Such proofs show that the conclusion is true, not unconditionally, but if the assumptions are true. These proofs are the most direct way of showing the validity of an argument form. Other proofs are *categorical:* They use no assumptions. They show that their conclusions are true outright. Categorical proofs are the most direct way to show that a certain formula is a tautology.

A *proof* in a natural deduction system is a series of *lines*. On each line appears a formula. Each formula in a proof (a) is an assumption, (b) occurs on a *Show* line, or (c) derives from formulas on previously established lines by a rule of inference. In the system of this appendix, the formula on the topmost *Show* line of a proof is its conclusion; the proof *proves* that formula *from* the assumptions. Formulas proved from no assumptions at all are *theorems* of the system.

Hypothetical Proof	Categorical Proof
Assumptions	*Show* Conclusion (Theorem)
Show Conclusion	⋮
⋮	

Rules of Inference

Rules of inference are either *simple* or *complex*. Simple rules allow us to derive formulas of certain kinds in a proof if other formulas of certain kinds occupy lines already established there. For example, our system has a rule letting us write $\mathcal{A}$ or $\mathcal{B}$, whichever we choose, if we've already established $\mathcal{A}$ & $\mathcal{B}$.

Complex rules allow us to derive a formula of a certain kind in a proof if we've completed some other proof. Our system has a rule, for instance, allowing us to write $\neg\mathcal{A}$ if we've proved a contradiction from the assumption $\mathcal{A}$. Another complex rule allows us to assert a conditional formula $\mathcal{A} \rightarrow \mathcal{B}$ if we can, in a subordinate proof, assume $\mathcal{A}$ and derive $\mathcal{B}$. Throughout this appendix, we'll treat complex rules as methods of proof.

Because some rules are complex, proofs sometimes appear within other proofs. A proof appearing within another is *subordinate* to it. The larger, *superordinate* proof uses the subordinate proof's information by means of a complex rule. The larger proof may take over the conclusion of its smaller partner. The larger proof may also use the fact that the subordinate was able to prove a conclusion from a given assumption to derive something that doesn't itself depend on that assumption. Assertions established by subordinate proofs are *lemmas.*

Our deduction system has a pair of rules for most connectives. One rule indicates how to derive a formula with a certain connective as main connective. In short, it specifies how to *introduce* formulas of that form into proofs. The other rule indicates how to use information encoded in a formula having that connective as main connective. That is, it specifies how to *exploit* formulas of that kind in proofs. The basic rules of the system, therefore, will fall into two groups: *introduction* rules and *exploitation* rules.

Methods of Proof

Before discussing these rules in detail, we need to know more about the kinds of proofs our system allows. Proofs can appear inside other proofs. In this chapter, subordinate proofs fulfill three functions; accordingly, there will be three methods of proof. Two are really complex connective-introduction rules. The remaining method is that of *direct proof*.

Here's a simple example of a hypothetical, direct proof:

1. p A
2. $p \to q$ A
3. ~~Show~~ q
4. $[q$ $\to$E, 1, 2

All proofs are series of lines structured in certain ways. As in this example, proofs have three columns. The middle column consists of a sequence of formulas, some of which may be preceded by the word *Show*. The left column numbers these formulas; the right column provides justifications for them. Thus, if a formula derives from previously established formulas by a rule of inference, the right column will show what rule of inference and what earlier lines were used. If the formula is an assumption, the right column will so indicate. Only when the formula derives from an entire subordinate proof will the right column be empty. The bracket appearing in our example signals that the proof is complete; for this reason, the 'Show' in line 3 is canceled. The formula on that line is no longer a goal, but an achievement.

Proof Lines

Number   Formula   Justification

A direct proof begins with assumptions—or, if it appears within another proof, formulas deduced from earlier lines—and proceeds to its conclusion. We'll begin a direct proof, once we record any assumptions or earlier lines, by stating what we want to show:

n. Show $\mathcal{A}$

Lines we hope to establish by doing proofs always have this form. The left column contains a line number; the right column is empty. The formula we hope to prove is prefaced by the word 'Show' to indicate that we haven't yet proved the formula.

If we can prove $\mathcal{A}$ from the information available, then we can cross out the 'Show' on line n. The proof allowing us to do so justifies canceling the 'Show', and follows line n immediately. To show graphically which lines constitute the proof, we draw a bracket encompassing those lines to the left of the formulas in the proof. A successful, completed direct proof thus looks like this:

Direct Proof

$$
\begin{array}{ll}
\text{n.} & \text{Show } \mathscr{A} \\
\ \ \vdots & \\
\text{n + m.} & \left[\ \vdots \atop \mathscr{A}\right. \quad \vdots
\end{array}
$$

The example above is a successful, completed proof of q from the assumptions p and $p \to q$. The 'A' in the justification column indicates that p and $p \to q$ are assumptions; the '$\to$E, 1, 2' in line 4 indicates that q follows from the formulas on lines 1 and 2 by the rule $\to$E (Conditional Exploitation). The bracket and canceled 'Show' signal that the proof is complete. The bracket also allows us to see which lines justify the conclusion.

To complete a direct proof of $\mathscr{A}$, we must obtain $\mathscr{A}$ on a subsequent line of the proof. But obtaining $\mathscr{A}$ completes the proof only if two conditions are satisfied:

1. $\mathscr{A}$, on line n + m, must not already be enclosed in another set of brackets.
2. No uncanceled 'Show' statements may occupy the area to be bracketed.

We want to show that $\mathscr{A}$ follows from what has gone before. If $\mathscr{A}$, on line n + m, were already enclosed in a bracket, or if we were to enclose any uncanceled 'Show' statements by drawing a new bracket to complete the proof, we could not be sure that $\mathscr{A}$ followed from what we were given. We would know only that $\mathscr{A}$ followed from what we were given together with some additional assumptions, for other proof methods introduce assumptions into the proof.

Neither of the following, then, count as legitimate instances of direct proof:

$$
\begin{array}{ll}
\qquad\qquad \text{(a)} & \qquad\qquad \text{(b)} \\
\text{n.} \quad \text{Show } p & \text{n.} \quad \text{Show } r \\
\text{m.} \quad \left[\text{Show } q\right. & \text{m.} \quad \left[\text{Show } q\right. \\
\qquad\ \ \vdots & \qquad\ \ \vdots \\
\text{k.} \quad \left[\, p \right. \qquad \text{(Wrong)} & \text{k.} \quad \left[\, r \right. \qquad \text{(Wrong)}
\end{array}
$$

In (a), the occurrence of p on line k purportedly completes a direct proof of p. But, on that line, another set of brackets already encloses p. This attempted proof therefore violates the first condition. Because the proof of q may have begun with an added assumption, we have no guarantee that p follows solely from the formulas above line n. In (b), an uncanceled 'Show' statement appears within the bracket. This procedure, too, may have allowed added assumptions into the proof; (b) violates the second condition.

Central to the idea of a hypothetical proof is the *assumption rule,* which allows a proof to begin with a list of premises or assumptions. That is, before the very first 'Show' line, we may write premises. Any conclusion we derive, of course, may depend on them.

Assumption

n. $\mathscr{A}$ A

Here line n must precede the first 'Show' line in the proof.

To prove q hypothetically from $p \rightarrow q$ and $p \vee q$, we write the premises followed by a 'Show' line containing the conclusion.

1. $p \rightarrow q$ A
2. $p \vee q$ A
3. Show q

In every hypothetical proof, we list the proof's assumptions above the first 'Show' line.

A.2 CONJUNCTION AND NEGATION RULES

Conjunction

The rule of conjunction exploitation indicates how we can use the information encoded in a conjunction. What follows from the truth of a conjunction? The truth of both conjuncts. If $\mathscr{A}$ & $\mathscr{B}$ is true, both $\mathscr{A}$ and $\mathscr{B}$ must be true. The rule of conjunction exploitation reflects the reasoning in these arguments:

(1) a. Molly and Nate ran in the Capitol 10,000.
      ∴ Molly ran in the Capitol 10,000.
   b. Bas didn't like the painting, but Verna did.
      ∴ Verna liked the painting.

Thus, the rule of conjunction exploitation takes two forms:

Conjunction Exploitation (&E)

n.	$\mathcal{A}$ & $\mathcal{B}$	
n + m.	$\mathcal{A}$	&E, n
n.	$\mathcal{A}$ & $\mathcal{B}$	
n + m.	$\mathcal{B}$	&E, n

Hereafter, we'll abbreviate rules having two forms by using parentheses. We can write &E as

n.	$\mathcal{A}$ & $\mathcal{B}$	
n + m.	$\mathcal{A}$ (or $\mathcal{B}$)	&E, n

This rule asserts that from a conjunction, we can derive each conjunct. We may write the conjuncts on any later line. When we apply this rule, we write a conjunct together with the explanation that the line comes by application of &E—conjunction exploitation—to the formula on line n. (The line just above the formula that results from applying this rule separates the formula deduced from its necessary antecedents; it won't appear in actual proofs.) To apply &E to a formula, conjunction must be its main connective. We can move from p & $(q \rightarrow r)$ to $q \rightarrow r$, but we cannot go from $(p$ & $q) \rightarrow r$ to $p \rightarrow r$. The latter, in fact, would be plainly invalid.

To demonstrate this rule, let's show this argument to be valid:

(2) Cedric and Lynn ate heartily, but Kurt hardly touched a thing.
∴ Lynn ate heartily.

Let's assume $((p$ & $q)$ & $\neg r)$ and prove q. We begin with an assumption and a 'Show' statement.

1. $(p$ & $q)$ & $\neg r$ A
2. Show q

Now, we can exploit the conjunction to derive a smaller conjunction, $(p$ & $q)$. We can't derive q directly: The connective to which we apply the rule must be the main connective of the formula.

1. $(p$ & $q)$ & $\neg r$ A
2. Show q
3. $(p$ & $q)$ &E, 1

The right column tells us that the formula on line 3 comes from line 1 by applying &E. We can easily apply that same rule again to obtain q, thereby finishing the proof. We can therefore bracket the proof and cancel the 'Show' on line 2.

1. $(p \& q) \& \neg r$ A
2. ~~Show~~ q
3. ⌈ $(p \& q)$ &E, 1
4. ⌊ q &E, 3

Conjunction Introduction

The rule of conjunction introduction indicates how to prove conjunctions. It's a very simple rule; to prove a conjunction, it asserts, we prove each conjunct. The rule reflects the reasoning in the following:

(3) Jerry knows when we arrive in Houston.
    Gabrielle knows when we arrive in Houston.
    ∴ Both Jerry and Gabrielle know when we arrive in Houston.

If $\mathscr{A}$ is true, and $\mathscr{B}$ is true also, then $\mathscr{A} \& \mathscr{B}$ is true. So, from the two formulas $\mathscr{A}$ and $\mathscr{B}$ we can derive $\mathscr{A} \& \mathscr{B}$:

Conjunction Introduction (&I)

n. $\mathscr{A}$
m. $\mathscr{B}$
p. $\mathscr{A} \& \mathscr{B}$ &I, n, m

The right column indicates that $\mathscr{A} \& \mathscr{B}$ comes from applying conjunction introduction to the formulas on lines n and m. The order in which $\mathscr{A}$ and $\mathscr{B}$ occur in the proof doesn't matter. We could just as easily have concluded $\mathscr{B} \& \mathscr{A}$.

To see how we might use &I in a proof, let's show that these sentences are equivalent:

(4) a. France and Denmark have joined the United States in condemning the action.
    b. Denmark and France have joined the United States in condemning the action.

(p & q) allows us to derive (q & p), and vice versa. Because these two deductions have the same form, we'll do only the first. Again, we begin by using the assumption rule and writing a 'Show' line.

1. p & q A
2. Show q & p

To show q & p, we need to separate the two conjuncts. We can derive them separately, using &E, and put them back together in the other order, using &I.

1. p & q A
2. Show q & p
3. $\lceil p$ &E, 1
4. $\quad q$ &E, 1
5. $\lfloor q$ & p &I, 4, 3

Negation

One negation rule acts as both an introduction and an exploitation rule. It always introduces or exploits two negation symbols at once. We'll therefore refer to it as $\neg\,\neg$, the *double negation* rule. It says that $\neg\,\neg\mathcal{A}$ is equivalent to $\mathcal{A}$. We can add or delete two consecutive negation signs without affecting truth values.

Negation Introduction/Exploitation ($\neg\,\neg$)

n. $\mathcal{A}$
n + p. $\neg\,\neg\mathcal{A}$ $\neg\,\neg$, n

n. $\neg\,\neg\mathcal{A}$
n + p. $\mathcal{A}$ $\neg\,\neg$, n

We can express this rule more compactly by writing a double line between $\mathcal{A}$ and $\neg\,\neg\mathcal{A}$ to indicate that the rule *inverts*—that we can go from what is above the lines to what is below them, or from what is below the lines to what is above them. The rule works in both directions.

n. $\mathcal{A}$ $\neg\,\neg$, m
m. $\neg\,\neg\mathcal{A}$ $\neg\,\neg$, n

To illustrate this rule, let's show that we can derive $\neg\neg p \,\&\, \neg q$ from $\neg\neg(p \,\&\, \neg\neg\neg q)$.

$$
\begin{array}{lll}
1. & \neg\neg(p \,\&\, \neg\neg\neg q) & \text{A} \\
2. & \text{Show } \neg\neg p \,\&\, \neg q & \\
3. & \lceil\, p \,\&\, \neg\neg\neg q & \neg\neg,\ 1 \\
4. & |\ p & \&\text{E},\ 3 \\
5. & |\ \neg\neg p & \neg\neg,\ 4 \\
6. & |\ \neg\neg\neg q & \&\text{E},\ 3 \\
7. & |\ \neg q & \neg\neg,\ 6 \\
8. & \lfloor\, \neg\neg p \,\&\, \neg q & \&\text{I},\ 5,\ 7
\end{array}
$$

Invertible rules have a special and important feature: They apply to parts of formulas as well as to entire formulas. In general, we can apply rules only to formulas with the appropriate main connectives. For instance, we can apply &E only to conjunctions—formulas with & as their main connectives. Invertible rules, however, are justified by the equivalence of the formulas they link. If, in any formula, we replace a subformula with an equivalent subformula, we obtain a formula equivalent to the original. If p and $\neg\neg p$ are equivalent, for instance, then so are $p \to q$, $\neg\neg(p \to q)$, $p \to \neg\neg q$, and $\neg\neg p \to q$. In addition to our derivable rules, therefore, we'll adopt a principle of *replacement*, allowing us to apply invertible rules to subformulas as well as to entire formulas. So, we can use $\neg\neg$ to move not only from $\neg\neg p$ to p, but also from $\neg\neg p \to q$ to $p \to q$.

We can therefore streamline the previous proof to

$$
\begin{array}{lll}
1. & \neg\neg(p \,\&\, \neg\neg\neg q) & \text{A} \\
2. & \text{Show } \neg\neg p \,\&\, \neg q & \\
3. & \lceil\, p \,\&\, \neg\neg\neg q & \neg\neg,\ 1 \\
4. & |\ p \,\&\, \neg q & \neg\neg,\ 3 \\
5. & \lfloor\, \neg\neg p \,\&\, \neg q & \neg\neg,\ 4
\end{array}
$$

Indirect Proof

Another, more powerful negation rule is the method of *indirect proof*. Essentially another negation introduction rule, indirect proof is complex. It asserts that we can derive $\neg \mathscr{A}$ if we can deduce a contradiction from the assumption $\mathscr{A}$. Indirect proofs always introduce *assumptions for indirect proof* (AIPs), from which they deduce contradictions. If an assumption leads to a contradiction, the assumption must be false. Consequently, indirect proofs establish the negations of their assumptions.

Here's an example of a categorical indirect proof, establishing a theorem often called 'the law of noncontradiction'—$\neg(p \,\&\, \neg p)$.

$$
\begin{array}{lll}
1. & \text{Show } \neg(p \,\&\, \neg p) & \\
2. & \lceil\, p \,\&\, \neg p & \text{AIP} \\
3. & |\ p & \&\text{E},\ 2 \\
4. & \lfloor\, \neg p & \&\text{E},\ 2
\end{array}
$$

An indirect proof begins with a statement of what we want to prove: a formula, in this case $\neg(p \& \neg p)$, prefaced by the word 'Show'. This formula must have a negation as main connective. The proof then makes an assumption, namely, the formula we're trying to establish, but with its main negation omitted—here, $p \& \neg p$. Thus, an indirect proof always begins this way:

> n.   Show $\neg \mathscr{A}$
> n + 1. $\mathscr{A}$ AIP

To complete the proof, we must prove a contradiction. The contradiction need not relate directly to the assumption; we do not have to use the assumption $\mathscr{A}$ to prove $\mathscr{A} \& \neg \mathscr{A}$, or anything else containing $\mathscr{A}$. In fact, we don't even have to use $\mathscr{A}$ in deriving a contradiction. Furthermore, we don't have to establish a single, contradictory formula; two formulas, one of which is the negation of the other, suffice. We want, then, to prove both a formula $\mathscr{B}$ and its negation $\neg \mathscr{B}$. Above, we accomplished this by proving p and $\neg p$, both by conjunction exploitation. A completed indirect proof always looks like this:

Indirect Proof

> n.   Show $\neg \mathscr{A}$
> n + 1. $\quad \mathscr{A}$ AIP
> $\vdots$
> n + p. $\quad \mathscr{B}$
> n + q. $\quad \neg \mathscr{B}$

Either $\mathscr{B}$ or $\neg \mathscr{B}$ may be established first. Once we complete the proof, we cancel the word 'Show'. Again, neither $\mathscr{B}$ nor $\neg \mathscr{B}$ may already be enclosed in brackets on lines n + p and n + q, and we may enclose no uncanceled 'Show' statements when we draw a bracket to complete the proof.

Restrictions

If we could use 'Show' lines whenever we wanted, we could easily prove anything. Consider, for instance, this "proof" of an arbitrary sentence letter p.

> 1. Show p
> 2. $\quad \neg \neg p$ $\neg \neg, 1$ (Wrong)
> 3. $\quad p$ $\neg \neg, 2$

We need to restrict the circumstances in which we can use such lines.

Any line we can use in a proof at a given point is *free* at that point. In sentential logic, every line is free, except (a) lines beginning with an uncanceled 'Show'; and (b) lines imprisoned within a bracket. Lines beginning with an uncanceled 'Show' contain formulas that we haven't yet proved. So, we have no access to the information on those lines. Thus, the proof of p above seems silly; we used what we wanted to prove, namely, p, in order to prove p. After a 'Show' has been canceled, however, we've proved the formula; so, we can proceed to use it.

The second restriction prohibits access to bracketed lines. Lines enclosed in a completed bracket or "prison" may depend on a particular assumption. Both indirect and conditional proofs introduce assumptions; the assumptions and the lines that depend on them hold only given those assumptions. They may not hold in general. In Aristotle's terminology, they serve only as dialectical premises; we assume them because we want to see what follows from them, not because we have reason to believe that they're true.

A line is free, then, only if it is neither prefaced with an uncanceled 'Show' nor imprisoned within a bracket (that is, a completed proof). These "proofs," consequently, make grave errors:

1. Show $\neg p$
2. Show $\neg(p \,\&\, \neg p)$
3. $p \,\&\, \neg p$ AIP
4. p &E, 3
5. $\neg p$ &E, 3
6. $\neg p$ &E, 3   (Wrong)

1. Show $p \,\&\, \neg p$
2. p &E, 1   (Wrong)
3. $\neg p$ &E, 1   (Wrong)
4. $p \,\&\, \neg p$ &I, 2, 3

To summarize: Formulas preceded by an uncanceled 'Show' have not yet reached "legal age," and those within a completed prison are "sentenced to life." Neither sort of formula is accessible.

Reiteration

The *reiteration* rule allows repeating a formula that appeared earlier in the proof, provided that the line containing that formula is still free.

Reiteration
n. $\mathcal{A}$
n + p. $\mathcal{A}$ R, n

This rule states that whatever we've shown to be true is still true. To see how it works, consider a simple argument form

$\neg p$
$\therefore \neg (p \mathbin{\&} \neg q)$

corresponding to a simple argument:

> (5) Sonya doesn't like chocolate.
> $\therefore$ It's not true that Sonya likes chocolate and Alice doesn't.

We begin by using the rule of assumption to introduce the premise and then trying to show the conclusion.

> 1. $\neg p$ A
> 2. Show $\neg (p \mathbin{\&} \neg q)$

We choose a proof method by looking at the main connective of the formula being proved. In trying to prove a negation, we use indirect proof.

> 1. $\neg p$ A
> 2. Show $\neg (p \mathbin{\&} \neg q)$
> 3. $p \mathbin{\&} \neg q$ AIP

Applying &E to derive p, we then get a contradiction by reiterating the premise.

> 1. $\neg p$ A
> 2. Show $\neg (p \mathbin{\&} \neg q)$
> 3. $\lceil\, p \mathbin{\&} \neg q$ AIP
> 4. $\mid\, p$ &E, 3
> 5. $\lfloor\, \neg p$ R, 1

Reiteration is useful chiefly for completing indirect and other subordinate proofs.

Problems

Do problems 1–9 from Chapter 8, section 8.2.

A.3 Conditional and Biconditional Rules

The Conditional

Some axiom systems have only one rule of inference: the rule of conditional exploitation. Often called *modus ponens,* it sanctions the inference from p

and $p \rightarrow q$ to q. It stands behind arguments such as

(6) If Socrates is human, then Socrates is mortal.
Socrates is human.
∴ Socrates is mortal.

Conditional Exploitation

n. $\mathscr{A} \rightarrow \mathscr{B}$
m. $\mathscr{A}$
p. $\mathscr{B}$ →E, n, m

This rule, for example, lets us show the validity of the argument

(7) If Paulette calls, I'll scream.
Paulette and Cal will call.
∴ Cal will call, and I'll scream.

by letting us derive $p \,\&\, q$ from the premises $r \rightarrow q$ and $r \,\&\, p$.

1. $r \rightarrow q$ A
2. $r \,\&\, p$ A
3. Show $p \,\&\, q$
4. ⌈ r &E, 2
5. | p &E, 2
6. | q →E, 1, 4
7. ⌊ $p \,\&\, q$ &I, 5, 6

Conditional Proof

Conditional introduction is a complex rule that constitutes the method of *conditional proof*. Like an indirect proof, a conditional proof may use some premises or earlier lines of a proof, but it doesn't have to. It always establishes a formula with a conditional as its main connective. Beginning with a statement of what we want to prove, it makes an *assumption for conditional proof (ACP)*, which is the antecedent of the conditional we're trying to establish. A conditional proof, then, begins as follows:

n.   Show $\mathscr{A} \rightarrow \mathscr{B}$
n + 1. $\mathscr{A}$ ACP

A successful conditional proof derives a conditional's consequent from its antecedent. To show that 'If $\mathscr{A}$, then $\mathscr{B}$', we assume $\mathscr{A}$ and try to show that $\mathscr{B}$ follows.

> ### Conditional Proof
>
> $$
> \begin{array}{lll}
> \text{n.} & \text{Show } \mathcal{A} \to \mathcal{B} & \\
> \text{n + 1.} & \lceil\ \mathcal{A} & \text{ACP} \\
> \quad\vdots & \mid\ \vdots & \vdots \\
> \text{n + p.} & \lfloor\ \mathcal{B} &
> \end{array}
> $$

Obtaining the subordinate conclusion $\mathcal{B}$ allows us to cancel the 'Show' above it and count the conditional formula as established, thereby completing the conditional proof. Drawing a bracket around the proof indicates that it is complete; the bracket allows us to see which lines justify the conditional. Just as in direct and indirect proofs, we may not draw the bracket if $\mathcal{B}$, on line n + p, appears inside another bracket or if we would be enclosing any uncanceled 'Show' statements.

For example, we can derive $r \to q$ from $p \ \& \ q$, showing that this argument is valid:

(8) We have pickles and chutney.
   $\therefore$ We have chutney, if you want some.

1. $p \ \& \ q$ A
2. Show $r \to q$
3. $\lceil\ r$ ACP
4. $\lfloor\ q$ &E, 1

Conditional proof also allows us to prove $(p \to \neg q) \to (q \to \neg p)$.

1. Show $(p \to \neg q) \to (q \to \neg p)$
2. $\lceil\ p \to \neg q$ ACP
3. $\mid$ Show $q \to \neg p$
4. $\mid\ \lceil\ q$ ACP
5. $\mid\ \mid$ Show $\neg p$
6. $\mid\ \mid\ \lceil\ p$ AIP
7. $\mid\ \mid\ \mid\ \neg q$ $\to$E, 2, 6
8. $\lfloor\lfloor\lfloor\ q$ R, 4

Here, an indirect proof is subordinate to a conditional proof that is, in turn, subordinate to another conditional proof.

The Biconditional

When may we introduce a biconditional into a proof? What does it take to establish the truth of a biconditional? A biconditional is so called because it amounts to two conditionals. Mathematicians, for example, often prove biconditionals in two steps. They prove the "left-to-right" and "right-to-left" directions separately. In other words, they prove two conditionals. Our rule for biconditional introduction similarly requires two conditionals:

Biconditional Introduction ($\leftrightarrow$I)

$$
\begin{array}{ll}
\text{n.} & \mathcal{A} \rightarrow \mathcal{B} \\
\text{m.} & \underline{\mathcal{B} \rightarrow \mathcal{A}} \\
\text{p.} & \mathcal{A} \leftrightarrow \mathcal{B} \qquad \leftrightarrow\text{I, n, m}
\end{array}
$$

To show how this rule works, let's derive $p \leftrightarrow q$ from $(p \;\&\; q) \;\&\; (q \rightarrow p)$.

$$
\begin{array}{lll}
1. & (p \;\&\; q) \;\&\; (q \rightarrow p) & \text{A} \\
2. & \text{Show } p \leftrightarrow q & \\
3. & \quad p \;\&\; q & \&\text{E, 1} \\
4. & \quad q \rightarrow p & \&\text{E, 1} \\
5. & \quad \text{Show } p \rightarrow q & \\
6. & \qquad p & \text{ACP} \\
7. & \qquad q & \&\text{E, 3} \\
8. & \quad p \leftrightarrow q & \leftrightarrow\text{I, 7, 4}
\end{array}
$$

To exploit biconditionals, recall that a biconditional asserts that two statements have the same truth value. If we've established a biconditional and one of its components, we can deduce the other.

Biconditional Exploitation ($\leftrightarrow$E)

$$
\begin{array}{ll}
\text{n.} & \mathcal{A} \leftrightarrow \mathcal{B} \\
\text{m.} & \mathcal{A} \text{ (or } \mathcal{B}) \\
\text{p.} & \mathcal{B} \text{ (or } \mathcal{A}) \qquad \leftrightarrow\text{E, n, m}
\end{array}
$$

This rule differs from conditional exploitation by allowing us to deduce $\mathcal{A}$ from $\mathcal{B}$ or vice versa. If we have one component, we can derive the other; it makes no difference which appears on which side of the biconditional. The rule of conditional exploitation, in contrast, works only in one direction. It allows us to derive the consequent from the antecedent of the conditional. But we can't go from the consequent to the antecedent.

To illustrate, let's show the validity of the argument

(9) Ozzie will play if and only if Harriet does.
Ozzie won't play.
∴ Harriet won't play.

by showing that $p \leftrightarrow q$ and $\neg p$ imply $\neg q$.

1. $p \leftrightarrow q$ A
2. $\neg p$ A
3. Show $\neg q$
4. q AIP
5. p $\leftrightarrow$E, 1, 4
6. $\neg p$ R, 2

Problems

Do the problems in Chapter 8, section 8.3.

A.4 Disjunction Rules

Like most connectives, disjunction has an introduction and an exploitation rule. The introduction rule asserts that we may introduce a disjunction into a proof if we've already obtained either disjunct. It reflects the reasoning manifested in these arguments:

(10) a. Joe will be there.
∴ Either Jaime or Joe will be there.
    b. The earth is round.
∴ The earth is round, or I'm a monkey's uncle.

Disjunction Introduction (∨I)

n. $\mathscr{A}$ (or $\mathscr{B}$)
n + p. $\mathscr{A} \vee \mathscr{B}$ ∨I, n

To see how this rule works in practice, let's prove 'the law of the excluded middle', $p \vee \neg p$. We can't prove either disjunct separately—neither p nor $\neg p$ is valid—therefore, we must use indirect proof. So, we need to prove $\neg\neg(p \vee \neg p)$. Introducing the assumption for indirect proof, however, helps us little; how can we get anything out of $\neg(p \lor \neg p)$? From a contradiction, anything follows. So, let's begin by trying to show $\neg p$.

1. Show $p \lor \neg p$
2. Show $\neg \neg (p \lor \neg p)$
3. $\neg(p \lor \neg p)$ AIP
4. Show $\neg p$
5. p AIP
6. $p \lor \neg p$ $\lor$I, 5
7. $\neg(p \lor \neg p)$ R, 3
8. $p \lor \neg p$ $\lor$I, 4
9. $p \lor \neg p$ $\neg \neg$, 2

Disjunction Exploitation

How can we exploit the information encoded in a disjunction? We can again take inspiration from mathematicians, who exploit disjunctions by doing "proofs by cases." The rule of disjunction exploitation reflects the reasoning in

(11) The venture will either fail or succeed.
    If the venture fails, we'll be better off (because of the tax losses).
    If the venture succeeds, we'll be better off (because we'll
      make money).
    $\therefore$ We'll be better off.

Disjunction Exploitation ($\lor$E)

n. $\mathscr{A} \lor \mathscr{B}$
m. $\mathscr{A} \to \mathscr{C}$
p. $\mathscr{B} \to \mathscr{C}$
q. $\mathscr{C}$ $\lor$E, n, m, p

A disjunction usually forces us to prove our conclusion in each case the disjunction presents.

To see how $\lor$E works, let's derive q from $p \lor q$ and $p \to q$.

1. $p \lor q$ A
2. $p \to q$ A
3. Show q
4. Show $q \to q$
5. q ACP
6. q $\lor$E, 1, 2, 4

We can prove $q \to q$ in just one step because the antecedent and consequent are the same.

Problems

Do the problems in Chapter 8, sections 8.4 and 8.5.

A.5 DERIVED RULES

Our proof methods and rules allow us to prove the validity of any valid argument form in sentential logic. Our system is deductively *complete*—every valid argument form can be proved valid in the system. This result guarantees that we have enough rules. Our system is also *sound*—we can derive a conclusion from some premises only if the argument form is valid. Our rules never lead us astray. To speak in terms of formulas rather than argument forms, all tautologies—and only tautologies—are provable. Our system's completeness guarantees that every tautology is a theorem; its soundness guarantees that every theorem is a tautology. The goal of a deduction system is to provide a way to prove that valid arguments are valid. Ideally, then, a deduction system should allow proofs of all and only valid argument forms. The soundness and completeness of our system show that it fulfills this ideal. (Establishing these features of this appendix's natural deduction system requires a sophisticated proof beyond the scope of this book.)

To encompass sentential logic, therefore, we need no further rules or proof techniques. Nevertheless, this section develops some additional rules. Everything we can prove with them is still valid. Indeed, they are all *derived* rules; they abbreviate series of proof lines that we could write in terms of our basic rules. They are short cuts that force us to accept nothing new about the logical connectives.

Indirect Proof Expanded

First, we can amend a basic proof method. An indirect proof shows something to be false by showing that assuming its truth leads to a contradiction. The conclusion of an indirect proof is always a negation. But the method extends to any formula. To show that a formula $\mathcal{A}$ is true, we can assume that $\mathcal{A}$ is false—by assuming $\neg\mathcal{A}$—and show that a contradiction follows. The extended method of indirect proof works as follows:

Indirect Proof (extended)		
n.	~~Show~~ $\mathcal{A}$	
n + 1.	$\neg\mathcal{A}$	AIP
⋮	⋮	⋮
p.	$\mathcal{B}$	
q.	$\neg\mathcal{B}$	

This extension eliminates at least one application of negation exploitation. For example, we can use two applications of it to show 'Peirce's law', $((p \to q) \to p) \to p$.

1. Show $((p \to q) \to p) \to p$
2. $(p \to q) \to p$ ACP
3. Show p
4. $\neg p$ AIP
5. Show $p \to q$
6. p ACP
7. Show q
8. $\neg q$ AIP
9. p R, 6
10. $\neg p$ R, 4
11. p $\to$E, 2, 5

Negations of Complex Formulas

Several derivable rules pertain to negated formulas. Negations can be difficult to exploit in our basic system; we can eliminate negations only in pairs. To help simplify formulas beginning with a negation, these derivable rules all give equivalents for negated formulas. They are invertible; they work in either direction. The first two are often called *DeMorgan's laws*.

Negation-Conjunction ($\neg$ &)

n. $\underline{\neg(\mathscr{A} \,\&\, \mathscr{B})}$ $\neg$&, m

m. $\neg \mathscr{A} \vee \neg \mathscr{B}$ $\neg$&, n

If not both $\mathscr{A}$ and $\mathscr{B}$ are true, then either $\mathscr{A}$ is false or $\mathscr{B}$ is; and vice versa. This rule, reflecting the equivalence of sentences such as

(12) a. My aunt and my uncle won't both come to the reception.
     b. Either my aunt or my uncle won't come to the reception.

lets us show the validity of

(13) Roberto and Van won't both be hired.
     If Roberto isn't hired, Van won't be.
     $\therefore$ Van won't be hired.

or, symbolizing, $\neg(p \,\&\, q)$; $\neg p \to \neg q$; $\therefore$ $\neg q$. DeMorgan's law enables us to prove the argument's validity much more easily than do our basic rules alone.

1. $\neg(p \mathbin{\&} q)$ A
2. $\neg p \rightarrow \neg q$ A
3. Show $\neg q$
4. $\neg p \vee \neg q$ $\neg\&$, 1
5. Show $\neg q \rightarrow \neg q$
6. $\neg q$ ACP
7. $\neg q$ $\vee$E, 4, 2, 5

The second of DeMorgan's laws underlies the equivalence of sentences like these:

(14) a. Neither Alabama nor Georgia will play in the Sugar Bowl.
  b. Alabama won't play in the Sugar Bowl, and neither will Georgia.

Negation-Disjunction ($\neg\vee$)

n. $\neg(\mathcal{A} \vee \mathcal{B})$ $\neg\vee$, m

m. $\neg\mathcal{A} \mathbin{\&} \neg\mathcal{B}$ $\neg\vee$, n

If neither $\mathcal{A}$ nor $\mathcal{B}$ is true, then $\mathcal{A}$ and $\mathcal{B}$ are both false. This rule allows a shortened proof of the validity of

(15) Neither Patricia nor Quincy agreed to loan us the money.
 $\therefore$ Patricia didn't agree to loan us the money, unless I didn't understand what she said.

which we can symbolize as $\neg(p \vee q)$; $\therefore \neg p \vee \neg r$.

1. $\neg(p \vee q)$ A
2. Show $\neg p \vee \neg r$
3. $\neg p \mathbin{\&} \neg q$ $\neg\vee$, 1
4. $\neg p$ $\&$E, 3
5. $\neg p \vee \neg r$ $\vee$I, 4

Another derived rule allows the exploitation and introduction of negated conditionals. It rests on the truth table definition of the conditional:

$\mathcal{A}$	$\mathcal{B}$	$\mathcal{A} \rightarrow \mathcal{B}$
T	T	T
T	F	F
F	T	T
F	F	T

$\mathscr{A} \rightarrow \mathscr{B}$ comes out false only on the row on which $\mathscr{A}$ is true and $\mathscr{B}$ is false.

Negation-Conditional ($\neg \rightarrow$)

$$
\begin{array}{lll}
\text{n.} & \underline{\neg(\mathscr{A} \rightarrow \mathscr{B})} & \neg \rightarrow, \text{m} \\
\text{m.} & \mathscr{A} \,\&\, \neg \mathscr{B} & \neg \rightarrow, \text{n}
\end{array}
$$

If $\mathscr{A} \rightarrow \mathscr{B}$ is false, then $\mathscr{A}$ must be true and $\mathscr{B}$ must be false. This rule allows a shortened proof of $p \rightarrow r; \neg(p \rightarrow q); \therefore \neg(r \rightarrow q)$, a form of the argument

> (16) If the company earns a profit, it will owe additional taxes.
> It's not true that, if the company earns a profit, it will raise dividends.
> ∴ It's not true that, if the company owes additional taxes, it will raise dividends.

$$
\begin{array}{lll}
1. & p \rightarrow r & \text{A} \\
2. & \neg(p \rightarrow q) & \text{A} \\
3. & \text{Show } \neg(r \rightarrow q) & \\
4. & \quad p \,\&\, \neg q & \neg \rightarrow, 2 \\
5. & \quad p & \&\text{E}, 4 \\
6. & \quad r & \rightarrow\text{E}, 1, 5 \\
7. & \quad \neg q & \&\text{E}, 4 \\
8. & \quad r \,\&\, \neg q & \&\text{I}, 6, 7 \\
9. & \quad \neg(r \rightarrow q) & \neg \rightarrow, 8
\end{array}
$$

This proof uses $\neg \rightarrow$ to go from a negation to a conjunction on line 4, and then uses the rule in the opposite direction to derive a negation on line 9 from a conjunction.

A similar rule let's us exploit and introduce negated biconditionals.

Negation-Biconditional ($\neg \leftrightarrow$)

$$
\begin{array}{lll}
\text{n.} & \underline{\neg(\mathscr{A} \leftrightarrow \mathscr{B})} & \neg \leftrightarrow, \text{m} \\
\text{m.} & \neg\mathscr{A} \leftrightarrow \mathscr{B} \text{ (or } \mathscr{A} \leftrightarrow \neg\mathscr{B}) & \neg \leftrightarrow, \text{n}
\end{array}
$$

If '$\mathscr{A}$ if and only if $\mathscr{B}$' is false, then $\mathscr{A}$ and $\mathscr{B}$ must have opposite truth values. $\mathscr{A}$ is false if and only if $\mathscr{B}$ is true. Equivalently, $\mathscr{A}$ is true if and only if $\mathscr{B}$

is false. This rule allows a shortened proof of

(17) It's not the case that Zambia will declare war if and only if Xanthu is not released.
It won't happen that Zambia declares war and Xanthu is released.
∴ It's not true that, if Xanthu isn't released, Zambia will declare war.

which we can symbolize as $\neg(p \leftrightarrow \neg q)$; $\neg(p \& q)$; $\therefore \neg(\neg q \rightarrow p)$.

1.	$\neg(p \leftrightarrow \neg q)$	A
2.	$\neg(p \& q)$	A
3.	Show $\neg(\neg q \rightarrow p)$	
4.	$\neg q \rightarrow p$	AIP
5.	$p \leftrightarrow \neg \neg q$	$\neg \leftrightarrow$, 1
6.	Show $\neg \neg q$	
7.	$\neg q$	AIP
8.	p	→E, 4, 7
9.	$\neg \neg q$	↔E, 5, 8
10.	q	$\neg \neg$, 6
11.	p	↔E, 5, 6
12.	$p \& q$	&I, 11, 10
13.	$\neg(p \& q)$	R, 2

Closely related to these rules are several others that define a connective in terms of other connectives. The first allows us to transform disjunctions into conditionals, and vice versa. It underlies the equivalence of sentences such as

(18) a. The patient will live only if we operate.
b. The patient will die unless we operate.

Conditional-Disjunction (→∨)

n.	$\mathscr{A} \rightarrow \mathscr{B}$	→∨, m
m.	$\neg \mathscr{A} \vee \mathscr{B}$	→∨, n

'If $\mathscr{A}$ then $\mathscr{B}$' is equivalent to '$\mathscr{B}$ unless not $\mathscr{A}$'. This rule allows a shortened proof of the validity of

(19) If Rollie denies it, he's lying.
If Emma doesn't offer to help, Rollie will deny it.
∴ Unless Emma offers to help, Rollie will lie.

or, symbolizing, $r \rightarrow q$; $\neg p \rightarrow r$; $\therefore$ $p \lor q$.

1. $r \rightarrow q$	A	
2. $\neg p \rightarrow r$	A	
3. Show $p \lor q$		
4. Show $\neg p \rightarrow q$		
5. $\neg p$	ACP	
6. r	$\rightarrow$E, 2, 5	
7. q	$\rightarrow$E, 1, 6	
8. $p \lor q$	$\rightarrow\lor$, 4	

The next rule allows us to characterize the biconditional in terms of the conditional. The rule allows us to go from 'if and only if' to 'if' and to 'only if'.

Biconditional-Conditional ($\leftrightarrow\rightarrow$)

n. $\mathcal{A} \leftrightarrow \mathcal{B}$
m. $\mathcal{A} \rightarrow \mathcal{B}$ (or $\mathcal{B} \rightarrow \mathcal{A}$) $\leftrightarrow\rightarrow$, n

This rule asserts that we can deduce from a biconditional either of the conditionals included in it.

Order and Grouping

Next, four rules assert that the order and grouping of subformulas in continued conjunctions and continued disjunctions makes no difference. The first indicates that the order of conjuncts doesn't matter: '$\mathcal{A}$ & $\mathcal{B}$' is equivalent to '$\mathcal{B}$ & $\mathcal{A}$', reflecting the equivalence of sentences such as

(20) a. Yuri and Uwe are here.
      b. Uwe and Yuri are here.

The first of these rules states that conjunction is *commutative*.

Commutativity of Conjunction (&C)

n. $\mathcal{A}$ & $\mathcal{B}$ &C, m
m. $\mathcal{B}$ & $\mathcal{A}$ &C, n

The second rule asserts that the grouping of conjuncts makes no difference; conjunction is *associative*. The rule underlies the equivalence of

(21) a. I've been to Ipswich and Orkney, as well as Oban.
      b. I've been to Ipswich, as well as Orkney and Oban.

Associativity of Conjunction (&A)

n.	$(\mathcal{A} \,\&\, \mathcal{B}) \,\&\, \mathcal{C}$	&A, m
m.	$\mathcal{A} \,\&\, (\mathcal{B} \,\&\, \mathcal{C})$	&A, n

---

The third and fourth rules assert the same principle for disjunctions. One reflects the equivalence of

(22) a. Either Porky or Donald is on.
 b. Either Donald or Porky is on.

Commutativity of Disjunction (∨C)

n.	$\mathcal{A} \lor \mathcal{B}$	∨C, m
m.	$\mathcal{B} \lor \mathcal{A}$	∨C, n

The other rule reflects the equivalence of

(23) a. I'll bring either hamburgers or hot dogs, or a dessert.
 b. I'll bring hamburgers, or either hot dogs or a dessert.

Associativity of Disjunction (∨A)

n.	$(\mathcal{A} \lor \mathcal{B}) \lor \mathcal{C}$	∨A, m
m.	$\mathcal{A} \lor (\mathcal{B} \lor \mathcal{C})$	∨A, n

We'd already assumed in Chapter 5 that these principles hold, when we allowed $p \lor q \lor r$, for example, to abbreviate either $(p \lor q) \lor r$ or $p \lor (q \lor r)$.

Abbreviations

Finally, four rules abbreviate commonly used proof steps. Three allow negations to function readily, without detours, in exploiting conditionals, biconditionals, and disjunctions. The fourth expresses the principle that anything follows from a contradiction.

The first rule underlies such arguments as

(24) If you passed the exam, you passed the course.
 You didn't pass the course.
 ∴ You didn't pass the exam.

Conditional Exploitation * (→E*)

> n. $\mathscr{A} \rightarrow \mathscr{B}$
> m. $\underline{\neg \mathscr{B}}$
> p. $\neg \mathscr{A}$ →E*, n, m

If $\mathscr{A}$ is true only if $\mathscr{B}$ is, and $\mathscr{B}$ is false, then $\mathscr{A}$ must also be false. This rule, traditionally called *modus tollens,* allows a shortened proof of

(25) Serge is happy only if Danielle is happy.
     Neither Forrest nor Danielle is happy.
     ∴ Neither Forrest nor Serge is happy.

which we can symbolize as $p \rightarrow q$; $\neg(r \vee q)$; ∴ $\neg(r \vee p)$. (Notice the use of both directions of $\neg \vee$.)

1. $p \rightarrow q$	A	
2. $\neg(r \vee q)$	A	
3. Show $\neg(r \vee p)$		
4. $\lceil \neg r \,\&\, \neg q$	$\neg \vee$, 2	
5. $\mid \neg r$	&E, 4	
6. $\mid \neg q$	&E, 4	
7. $\mid \neg p$	→E*, 1, 6	
8. $\mid \neg r \,\&\, \neg p$	&I, 5, 7	
9. $\lfloor \neg(r \vee p)$	$\neg \vee$, 8	

The next rule allows negations to interact with biconditionals. It reflects the reasoning in the following:

(26) That argument is good if and only if it's valid.
     That argument is no good.
     ∴ That argument isn't valid.

Biconditional Exploitation * (↔E*)

> n. $\mathscr{A} \leftrightarrow \mathscr{B}$
> m. $\underline{\neg \mathscr{A}}$ (or $\neg \mathscr{B}$)
> p. $\neg \mathscr{B}$ (or $\neg \mathscr{A}$)   ↔E*, n, m

If '$\mathscr{A}$ if and only if $\mathscr{B}$' is true, and $\mathscr{A}$ is false, $\mathscr{B}$ must also be false. The biconditional asserts that $\mathscr{A}$ and $\mathscr{B}$ agree in truth value. This rule allows a shortened proof of

> (27) Gene will object if and only if he thinks he's being ignored.
> We'll be careful, and Gene won't object.
> ∴ Gene won't think he's being ignored.

or, symbolizing, $p \leftrightarrow q$; r & $\neg p$; ∴ $\neg q$.

1. $p \leftrightarrow q$ A
2. r & $\neg p$ A
3. Show $\neg q$
4. $\neg p$ &E, 2
5. $\neg q$ $\leftrightarrow$E*, 1, 4

Another derived rule allows negations to interact with disjunctions, reflecting the reasoning in

> (28) Either Emporia State or Wichita is playing on Friday.
> Emporia State isn't playing on Friday.
> ∴ Wichita is playing on Friday.

Disjunction Exploitation * (∨E*)

n. $\mathscr{A} \vee \mathscr{B}$
m. $\neg \mathscr{A}$ (or $\neg \mathscr{B}$)
p. $\mathscr{B}$ (or $\mathscr{A}$)   ∨E*, n, m

If $\mathscr{A}$ or $\mathscr{B}$ is true, and $\mathscr{A}$ is false, $\mathscr{B}$ must be true. Similarly, $\mathscr{A}$ must be true if $\mathscr{B}$ is false. This rule, often called *disjunctive syllogism,* allows a shortened proof of $p \vee q$; $p \vee \neg q$; ∴ p.

1. $p \vee q$ A
2. $p \vee \neg q$ A
3. Show p
4. $\neg p$ AIP
5. q ∨E*, 1, 4
6. $\neg q$ ∨E*, 2, 4

The last derived rule allows us to deduce anything from a contradiction.

Contradiction (!)

n. $\mathscr{A}$
m. $\neg \mathscr{A}$
p. $\mathscr{B}$!, n, m

If $\mathcal{A}$ is both true and false, then anything follows. This is our most surprising derived rule; therefore, it's worth seeing how it follows from basic rules.

1.	p	A
2.	$\neg p$	A
3.	Show q	
4.	Show $\neg \neg q$	
5.	$\neg q$	AIP
6.	p	R, 1
7.	$\neg p$	R, 2
8.	q	$\neg \neg$, 4

Reiterating p and $\neg p$, when they have nothing to do with $\neg q$, may seem suspicious to some. More illuminating, perhaps, is the original medieval derivation of the contradiction rule. It uses a derived rule and the expanded indirect proof method.

1.	p	A
2.	$\neg p$	A
3.	Show q	
4.	$\neg q$	AIP
5.	$p \vee q$	$\vee$I, 1
6.	q	$\vee$E*, 5, 2

The contradiction rule allows us to count a proof complete whenever we obtain a contradiction within it. If we reach a contradiction in an indirect proof, of course, that proof is complete. If we reach a contradiction in a conditional proof, the contradiction rule guarantees that we can write the conditional's consequent on the next line. Similarly, reaching a contradiction in a direct proof indicates that we can write the desired conclusion on the next line.

Strategy

Overall proof strategies derive, primarily, from what we're trying to prove, and, secondarily, from what we already have. Our system is organized to make proof strategies apparent. To prove a formula with a given main connective, we try using the introduction rule for that connective. To use a formula with a given main connective, we try using that connective's exploitation rule. The following table contains some of the most important strategies. If it can be achieved, a direct proof is usually easiest. But, if it's not obvious how to prove the conclusion directly, then use the strategies listed.

Proof Strategies

To get	Try to
$\neg \mathcal{A}$	Use indirect proof.
$\mathcal{A} \& \mathcal{B}$	Prove $\mathcal{A}$ and $\mathcal{B}$ separately.
$\mathcal{A} \vee \mathcal{B}$	(a) Use indirect proof, or (b) prove $\mathcal{A}$ or $\mathcal{B}$ separately.
$\mathcal{A} \to \mathcal{B}$	Use conditional proof.
$\mathcal{A} \leftrightarrow \mathcal{B}$	Prove the two conditionals $\mathcal{A} \to \mathcal{B}$ and $\mathcal{B} \to \mathcal{A}$.

To exploit	Try to
$\neg \mathcal{A}$	(a) Use it with other lines that have $\mathcal{A}$ as a part, or (b) use a derivable rule.
$\mathcal{A} \& \mathcal{B}$	Use &E to get $\mathcal{A}$ and $\mathcal{B}$ individually.
$\mathcal{A} \vee \mathcal{B}$	(a) Get the negation of one disjunct and use $\vee$E* to get the other, or (b) use $\vee$E by taking each case separately.
$\mathcal{A} \to \mathcal{B}$	(a) Get $\mathcal{A}$ and then reach $\mathcal{B}$ by $\to$E, or (b) get $\neg \mathcal{B}$ and then reach $\neg \mathcal{A}$ by $\to$E*.
$\mathcal{A} \leftrightarrow \mathcal{B}$	(a) Get either component and then reach the other by $\leftrightarrow$E, or (b) get the negation of either component and then the negation of the other by $\leftrightarrow$E*, or (c) get one or both conditionals by $\leftrightarrow \to$.

These strategies indicate how to construct proofs of various kinds. They are helpful in a wide variety of situations. Sometimes, however, the obvious tactics don't work. Our system offers two "safety valves"—strategies that work well under pressure. First, when in doubt, use indirect proof. Anything that can be proved can be proved indirectly. Second, if it's not clear within an indirect proof how to derive a contradiction, choose any sentence letter that is not already established and whose negation is not yet established, and try to prove that sentence letter or its negation. The assumption for indirect proof, together with other information in the proof, will lead to a contradiction; therefore, anything will follow. No matter what letter you select, therefore, you should be able to prove it.

Problems

Do the problems in Chapter 8, section 8.6.

SUMMARY OF RULES
PROOF METHODS

Direct Proof

n.	Show $\mathcal{A}$	
⋮	⋮	⋮
n + m.	$\mathcal{A}$	

Indirect Proof

n.   Show ¬ 𝒜
n + 1. ⌈ 𝒜   AIP
⋮ | ⋮   ⋮
n + p. | ℬ
n + q. ⌊ ¬ ℬ

Indirect Proof (extended)

n.   Show 𝒜
n + 1. ⌈ ¬ 𝒜   AIP
⋮ | ⋮   ⋮
p. | ℬ
q.   ⌊ ¬ ℬ

Conditional Proof

n.   Show 𝒜 → ℬ
n + 1. ⌈ 𝒜   ACP
⋮ | ⋮   ⋮
n + p. ⌊ ℬ

BASIC RULES, APPLYING ONLY TO ENTIRE FORMULAS

Assumption (A)

n. 𝒜   A

Here line n must precede the first 'Show' line in the proof.

Conjunction Exploitation (&E)

n.   𝒜 & ℬ
n + m. 𝒜 (or ℬ)   &E, n

Conjunction Introduction (&I)

n. $\mathcal{A}$
m. $\underline{\mathcal{B}}$
p. $\mathcal{A}$ & $\mathcal{B}$ &I, n, m

Reiteration (R)

n. $\underline{\mathcal{A}}$
n + p. $\mathcal{A}$ R, n

Conditional Exploitation (→E)

n. $\mathcal{A} \rightarrow \mathcal{B}$
m. $\underline{\mathcal{A}}$
p. $\mathcal{B}$ →E, n, m

Biconditional Introduction (↔I)

n. $\mathcal{A} \rightarrow \mathcal{B}$
m. $\underline{\mathcal{B} \rightarrow \mathcal{A}}$
p. $\mathcal{A} \leftrightarrow \mathcal{B}$ ↔I, n, m

Biconditional Exploitation (↔E)

n. $\mathcal{A} \leftrightarrow \mathcal{B}$
m. $\underline{\mathcal{A}}$ (or $\mathcal{B}$)
p. $\mathcal{B}$ (or $\mathcal{A}$)   ↔E, n, m

Disjunction Introduction (∨I)

n. $\underline{\mathcal{A}}$ (or $\mathcal{B}$)
n + p. $\mathcal{A} \vee \mathcal{B}$ ∨I, n

Disjunction Exploitation (∨E)

n. $\mathcal{A} \vee \mathcal{B}$
m. $\mathcal{A} \rightarrow \mathcal{C}$
p. $\underline{\mathcal{B} \rightarrow \mathcal{C}}$
q. $\mathcal{C}$ ∨E, n, m, p

BASIC RULES, APPLYING TO PARTS OF FORMULAS AS WELL AS ENTIRE FORMULAS

Negation Introduction/Exploitation (¬ ¬)

n. $\underline{\underline{\mathcal{A}}}$ ¬ ¬, m
m. $\neg \neg \mathcal{A}$ ¬ ¬, n

DERIVED RULES, APPLYING ONLY TO ENTIRE FORMULAS

Biconditional-Conditional (↔→)

n. $\underline{\mathcal{A} \leftrightarrow \mathcal{B}}$
m. $\mathcal{A} \rightarrow \mathcal{B}$ (or $\mathcal{B} \rightarrow \mathcal{A}$)   ↔→, n

Conditional Exploitation * (→E*)

n. $\mathcal{A} \rightarrow \mathcal{B}$
m. $\underline{\neg \mathcal{B}}$
p. $\neg \mathcal{A}$ →E*, n, m

Biconditional Exploitation * (↔E*)

n. $\mathcal{A} \leftrightarrow \mathcal{B}$
m. $\neg \mathcal{A}$ (or $\neg \mathcal{B}$)
p. $\neg \mathcal{B}$ (or $\neg \mathcal{A}$)   ↔E*, n, m

Disjunction Exploitation * (∨E*)

n. $\mathcal{A} \vee \mathcal{B}$
m. $\neg \mathcal{A}$ (or $\neg \mathcal{B}$)
p. $\mathcal{B}$ (or $\mathcal{A}$)   ∨E*, n, m

Contradiction (!)

n. $\mathcal{A}$
m. $\neg \mathcal{A}$
p. $\mathcal{B}$!, n, m

DERIVED RULES, APPLYING TO PARTS OF FORMULAS AS WELL AS TO ENTIRE FORMULAS

Negation-Conjunction (¬&)

n. $\neg(\mathcal{A} \ \& \ \mathcal{B})$ ¬&, m
m. $\neg \mathcal{A} \vee \neg \mathcal{B}$ ¬&, n

Negation-Disjunction (¬∨)

n. $\neg(\mathcal{A} \vee \mathcal{B})$ ¬∨, m
m. $\neg \mathcal{A} \ \& \ \neg \mathcal{B}$ ¬∨, n

Negation-Conditional (¬→)

n. $\neg(\mathcal{A} \rightarrow \mathcal{B})$ ¬→, m
m. $\mathcal{A} \ \& \ \neg \mathcal{B}$ ¬→, n

Negation-Biconditional (¬↔)

n. $\neg(\mathcal{A} \leftrightarrow \mathcal{B})$ ¬↔, m
m. $\neg \mathcal{A} \leftrightarrow \mathcal{B}$ (or $\mathcal{A} \leftrightarrow \neg \mathcal{B}$)   ¬↔, n

Conditional-Disjunction ($\rightarrow\lor$)

n. $\underline{\mathcal{A} \rightarrow \mathcal{B}}$ $\rightarrow\lor$, m

m. $\neg\mathcal{A} \lor \mathcal{B}$ $\rightarrow\lor$, n

Commutativity of Conjunction (&C)

n. $\underline{\mathcal{A} \ \& \ \mathcal{B}}$ &C, m

m. $\mathcal{B} \ \& \ \mathcal{A}$ &C, n

Commutativity of Disjunction ($\lor$C)

n. $\underline{\mathcal{A} \lor \mathcal{B}}$ $\lor$C, m

m. $\mathcal{B} \lor \mathcal{A}$ $\lor$C, n

Associativity of Conjunction (&A)

n. $\underline{(\mathcal{A} \ \& \ \mathcal{B}) \ \& \ \mathcal{C}}$ &A, m

m. $\mathcal{A} \ \& \ (\mathcal{B} \ \& \ \mathcal{C})$ &A, n

Associativity of Disjunction ($\lor$A)

n. $\underline{(\mathcal{A} \lor \mathcal{B}) \lor \mathcal{C}}$ $\lor$A, m

m. $\mathcal{A} \lor (\mathcal{B} \lor \mathcal{C})$ $\lor$A, n

II

DEDUCTION STYLE THREE

B

ADDING QUANTIFIERS

Natural deduction extends easily to predicate logic. All rules of sentential deduction apply in quantification theory. To deal with quantifiers, the system adds three new, simple rules and a complex rule that has the form of a new method of proof. The deduction system that emerges shares its sentential cousin's virtues. The system is sound, for every provable formula is valid, and every conclusion provable from a set of premises follows from them. The system is also complete, for every valid formula of quantification theory can be proved in the system, and every valid argument can be shown valid within it. Furthermore, the system mirrors closely the processes of reasoning that people use in a wide variety of contexts.

B.1 DEDUCTION RULES FOR QUANTIFIERS

The deduction rules needed for quantificational logic are very straightforward. Suppose that $\mathscr{A}[c/v]$ is the result of substituting c for every occurrence of v throughout the formula $\mathscr{A}$. If $\forall v \mathscr{A}$ and $\exists v \mathscr{A}$ are formulas, then $\mathscr{A}[c/v]$ is called an *instance* of them. Conversely, $\forall v \mathscr{A}$ and $\exists v \mathscr{A}$ are *generics* of $\mathscr{A}[c/v]$.

Each connective has two rules. One rule introduces the connective into proofs, whereas the other allows us to exploit its presence. The existential quantifier similarly comes with two rules: an introduction rule and an exploitation rule. The introduction rule, in essence, allows us to move to an existentially quantified formula from any instance of that formula.[1] Often called *existential generalization*, it takes the form:

Existential Introduction (∃I)

> n. $\mathscr{A}[c/v]$
> n + p. $\exists v \mathscr{A}$ ∃I, n

Here c may be any constant.

Existential introduction allows us to infer an existentially quantified formula from any instance of it. It sanctions the step from an instance to its corresponding existential generic. Suppose that our universe of discourse consists of people. If Jones, for example, is a spy, then we may conclude that someone is a spy. If Susan suspects Harry, then Susan suspects someone; of course, it's also true that somebody suspects Harry and that somebody suspects somebody. Finally, if Frank doesn't trust himself to work around large sums of money, then Frank doesn't trust somebody to work around large sums of money. Additionally, somebody doesn't trust Frank to work around large sums, and someone doesn't trust himself to do so. Each of the following is an acceptable application of existential introduction:

Fa	$\exists x Fx$
Gab	$\exists x Gax$
Gab	$\exists x Gxb$
Hcc	$\exists x Hcx$
Hcc	$\exists x Hxc$
Hcc	$\exists x Hxx$
$\exists x Fxa$	$\exists y \exists x Fxy$
$\forall x Fx \to Gb$	$\exists z(\forall x Fx \to Gz)$

In each case, the premise is an instance of the conclusion.

The rule of existential exploitation allows us to move from an existentially quantified formula to an instance of it. This rule is almost exactly the reverse, then, of the existential introduction rule. But it imposes a restriction: The instance must involve a constant new to the proof. The rule says that we may (a) drop an existential quantifier serving as a main connective in a formula, and (b) substitute for the quantified variable a constant that hasn't appeared earlier in the proof. The constant must have appeared nowhere in the deduction, not even in a 'Show' line. (Actually, no harm would result from allowing us to use, for ∃E, constants that appear earlier only on already bracketed lines. But, to minimize confusion, we'll always use completely new constants.)

Existential Exploitation (∃E)

n. $\exists v.\mathscr{A}$

n + p. $\mathscr{A}[c/v]$ ∃E, n

Here c must be a constant new to the proof.

Suppose that we have the information that someone in our department is selling trade secrets to a competitor. We don't know who this person is—or, perhaps, who these people are—but we want to reason from what we know to find out. We know that at least one person has been selling secrets; our reasoning and our communication will proceed much more readily if we give this person some name—'John Doe', perhaps, or just 'the mole'—so that we can refer to him or her in various contexts. We can't simply say, "Someone has been selling our trade secrets. Someone must have joined the department around the middle of 1981, because that's when secrets began to leak. Someone is a bad person." For nothing here indicates that the "someones" are the same. To tie these assertions to the same individual, we must have a way of referring to that person. Introducing a name accomplishes this goal. It's critical that the name we choose be new. If Sarah Freeland is the head of the department, and we decide to call the seller of trade secrets 'Sarah Freeland', then we'll be led to conclusions that don't follow from the information we have.

The existential exploitation rule reflects a very important feature of indefinite descriptions like 'a house' or 'a room with a view': They not only assert existence but, like proper names, introduce a constant that can figure in subsequent discourse. The existential quantifier itself plays only the first role. The rule of existential exploitation, however, allows us to simulate the second. It allows us to refer back to the object whose existence is asserted in the existentially quantified formula.

Consider, for example, this simple discourse:

(1) Wanda lives in *a house* on Speedway. *Her house* is convenient to campus. More important, *it*'s close to Rosie's Cantina.

We would ordinarily symbolize the first sentence as

(2) $\exists x(Hx \ \& \ Oxs \ \& \ Lax)$.

But this step raises a problem about how to symbolize the second and third sentences. If we use a constant to translate 'her house' and 'it', as seems natural, we have no way of making it clear that we're talking about the object, Wanda's house, that the first sentence introduces. If we use existential quantifiers for 'her house' and 'it' in separate translations of the last two sentences, we also fail to express the idea that we're talking about one object; we would have instead formulas like these:

(3) a. $\exists x(Hx \ \& \ Oxs \ \& \ Lax)$
       (There's a house on Speedway Wanda lives in.)
    b. $\exists x(Hx \ \& \ Wax \ \& \ Cxc)$
       (There's a house Wanda owns that's convenient to campus.)
    c. $\exists xSxr$
       (Something is close to Rosie's Cantina.)

Nothing here indicates that we're talking about one and the same object.
       We can symbolize the entire discourse in a single formula as

(4) $\exists x(Hx \ \& \ Oxs \ \& \ Lax \ \& \ Wax \ \& \ Cxc \ \& \ Sxr)$.

But doing so forces us to symbolize the discourse as a whole unit; we can't proceed sentence by sentence. In a proof, however, we must proceed line by line as we deduce more and more information. The existential exploitation rule allows us to refer back to the object introduced by an existentially quantified formula while still proceeding line by line in the usual manner of a proof.
       The restriction on the rule—that we use a constant appearing nowhere above in the proof—prevents us from using it to derive invalid conclusions. To see why the constant must be new, consider this argument:

(5) Officer O'Malley shot someone.
    ∴ Officer O'Malley shot himself.

Plainly, the argument is invalid. But, if we were to ignore the requirement that we use a new constant in applying ∃E, we could show the corresponding argument form to be valid:

1. $\exists xSmx$ A
2. Smm ES, 1   (Wrong!)

To see why we must not use a constant appearing in a 'Show' line, consider this argument:

(6) Some people are crazy.
    ∴ You're crazy.

This, too, is a terrible argument. But, if we were to ignore the requirement that ∃E not introduce a constant appearing in the conclusion, we could show the argument to have a valid form (where a symbolizes 'you'):

1. $\exists xCx$ A
2. ~~Show~~ Ca
3. [Ca ES, 1   (Wrong!)

This proof is flawed. But there would be nothing wrong with step 3 if the 'Show' line, 2, didn't contain a.[3]

The third rule for quantifiers is *universal exploitation*. If we know that something is true about every object, then we can conclude that it is true for each particular object we consider. If God loves everyone, then God loves me, you, and the Earl of Roxburgh. If Jane likes everyone she meets, then she likes you, if she's met you; she likes me, if she's met me; and so on. The rule of universal exploitation asserts that from a universally quantified formula, we may infer any of its instances.

Universal Exploitation (∀E)

n. $\forall v \mathscr{A}$

n + p. $\mathscr{A}[c/v]$ ∀E, n

Here c may be any constant.

This rule does not require a new constant. In fact, it is silly to use a new constant in applying ∀E unless no constants at all appear in the proof up to this line. If constants a and b appear earlier, then, from $\forall x F x$, we can infer Fa, or Fb, or both. If we also have a formula $\forall x G x x$, we can infer Gaa or Gbb. And, if we have $\forall x \forall y H x y$, then we can obtain $\forall y H a y$ or $\forall y H b y$ and, in another step, any of Haa, Hab, Hba, and Hbb. We could also, of course, infer similar formulas with other constants. Unless we are forced to introduce those constants in other ways, however, using them to exploit a universal formula serves no purpose.

To see how these rules work, let's demonstrate the validity of a simple argument.

(7) Something is rotten in the state of Denmark.
    Whatever is in Denmark is in Europe.
    ∴ Something's rotten in Europe.

1.	$\exists x(Rx \ \& \ Ixd)$	A
2.	$\forall y(Iyd \rightarrow Iye)$	A
3.	Show $\exists z(Rz \ \& \ Ixe)$	
4.	$Ra \ \& \ Iad$	∃E, 1
5.	$Iad \rightarrow Iae$	∀E, 2
6.	Ra	&E, 4
7.	Iad	&E, 4
8.	Iae	→E, 5, 7
9.	$Ra \ \& \ Iae$	&I, 6, 8
10.	$\exists z(Rz \ \& \ Ize)$	∃I, 9

Problems

Use this deduction system to solve the problems at the end of section 13.1.

B.2 UNIVERSAL PROOF

Introducing a universal formula requires a new method of proof. We already have three proof techniques: direct proof, indirect proof, and conditional proof. Quantificational logic adds *universal proof*.

Universal Proof

$$n. \quad \text{Show } \forall v \mathscr{A}$$
$$n + 1. \quad \left[\text{Show } \mathscr{A}[c/v] \right.$$
$$\left[\vdots \right.$$

Here c must be a constant new to the proof.

To prove a universal conclusion, in other words, we prove an instance of it. The instance must result from substituting a constant new to the proof for the quantified variable. Since no information will appear anywhere earlier in the proof regarding the new constant, it stands, in effect, for no object in particular. It represents an arbitrarily chosen object. Because the proof puts no constraints on it, absolutely any object could play this role. Consequently, though we prove something about c, we've shown how to prove that assertion about anything. And this justifies our drawing a universal conclusion.

It might seem that this form of proof allows us to prove the validity of very silly arguments. It lets us derive a universal formula from one of its instances. So, can't we show that, if Nicholas loves the Go-Gos, everybody loves the Go-Gos? Fortunately, no, because of the new-constant requirement.

1. *Lfg*	A	Nicholas loves the Go-Gos.
2. Show $\forall x Lxg$		Show everybody loves the Go-Gos.
3. Show *Lag*		Show *a* loves the Go-Gos.

We can't go from the information that Nicholas loves the Go-Gos to the conclusion that some arbitrarily selected *a* does.

As an example of a universal proof, consider this inference:

(8) Everything created by God is good.
  Everything is a creation of God.
  ∴ Everything is good.

To establish its validity, we construct a universal proof.

1. $\forall x(Cgx \rightarrow Gx)$ A
2. $\forall xCgx$ A
3. Show $\forall xGx$
4. ⌜Show Ga
5.   ⌜Cga $\forall$E, 2
6. $Cga \rightarrow Ga$ $\forall$E, 1
7.   ⌞Ga $\rightarrow$E, 5, 6

To show that everything is G, we show that some arbitrarily chosen object a is G.

Problems

Use this deduction system to solve the problems at the end of sections 13.2 and 13.3.

B.3 Derived Rules for Quantifiers

The system resulting from adding these three rules and universal proof to our natural deduction system for sentential logic has all the power it needs. It can demonstrate the validity of any valid argument form in quantification theory. Nevertheless, adding some further rules can increase its efficiency and naturalness considerably. This section presents some derived rules which, while theoretically superfluous, make the proof system more pleasant to work with.

Combining Steps

First, we can apply quantifier rules several times in a single step. Suppose, for example, that we want to take instances of $\forall x\forall yFxy$. The universal exploitation rule requires us to move first to the instance $\forall yFay$, let us say, and then to its instance Faa. But any constant can substitute for both x and y here because both are universally quantified. So, it's easy to perform the operation in one step. We can move directly from $\forall x\forall yFxy$ to an instance of an instance of it, Faa. Similarly, we could move to Fab, Fba, Fbb, Fac, and so on. We can record that we've exploited a series of n universal quantifiers at once by writing, not $\forall$E, but $\forall$E^n. The application would look like this:

m. $\forall x\forall yFxy$
m + n. Faa $\forall$E^2, m

We can do the same for existential quantifiers if we replace each quantified variable with a new constant. So, we may move from $\exists x\exists y\exists z(Fxy \,\&\, Fxz)$ to $Fab \,\&\, Fac$, citing the rule as $\exists$E^3.

Similarly, we can compress a sequence of universal proofs into a single proof. We can prove a formula with an initial string of n universal quantifiers by proving an instance of an instance ... of an instance of the formula, using n different new constants to replace the n quantified variables. For example, we can prove $\forall x \forall y (Fxy \rightarrow \neg Fyx)$ by proving $Fab \rightarrow \neg Fba$, where neither a nor b have appeared earlier in the proof.

Although these combinations of rules or proofs are very convenient, it's not a good idea to combine exploitations of universal and existential quantifiers. While $\forall E^2$ and $\exists E^4$ are fairly easy to follow, citing a rule such as $\forall E^2 \exists E^3 \forall E$ would be virtually unintelligible.

Rewriting Variables.

Variables have no independent meanings. The formulas $\forall x Fx$ and $\forall z Fz$ function in logically similar ways, as do $\exists y Gy$ and $\exists w Gw$. Indeed, it's easy to show that these pairs are equivalent. Here are the proofs in one direction:

1. $\forall x Fx$	A		1. $\exists y Gy$	A
2. ~~Show~~ $\forall z Fz$			2. ~~Show~~ $\exists w Gw$	
3. ⌈ ~~Show~~ Fa			3. ⌈ Ga	$\exists E, 1$
4. ⌊ [Fa	$\forall E, 1$		4. ⌊ $\exists w Gw$	$\exists I, 3$

The proofs of the other directions follow exactly the same pattern.

Thus, we can substitute one variable for another throughout a formula. The only restriction we must observe is that we should not introduce into a formula a variable that is already there; otherwise we could go from the legitimate formula $\forall x \forall y Fxy$ to the very different nonformula $\forall x \forall x Fxx$.[4] The derived rule, then, is this:

Variable Rewrite (VR)

n. $\mathcal{A}$
m. $\mathcal{A}[v/u]$ VR, n

Here v is foreign to $\mathcal{A}$.

Exploiting Negations

It's extremely useful to have a direct way of dealing with negations of quantified formulas. Our rules allow us to attack formulas with quantifiers as main connectives in one step. But, if a negation precedes a quantifier, the proof strategy becomes much more complicated. Luckily, negations of quantified formulas are equivalent to formulas with quantifiers as main connectives. Two *quantifier negation* rules relate quantified formulas to their negations.

In the process, these rules relate the universal and existential quantifiers. In fact, they show how to define each quantifier in terms of the other.

Quantifier Negation (QN)

n.	$\neg \exists v \mathcal{A}$	QN, m
m.	$\forall v \neg \mathcal{A}$	QN, n
n.	$\neg \forall v \mathcal{A}$	QN, m
m.	$\exists v \neg \mathcal{A}$	QN, n

Both versions of quantifier negation invert. That is, the premise and conclusion are equivalent; therefore, the rules work in both directions. We can infer $\exists x \neg Fx$ from $\neg \forall x Fx$, and vice versa. Similarly, just by adding a negation sign, we can see that $\exists x Fx$ is equivalent to $\neg \forall x \neg Fx$, and that $\forall x Fx$ is equivalent to $\neg \exists x \neg Fx$. So, we can define the quantifiers in terms of each other.

Deriving even simple applications of these rules from our basic quantifier rules shows how much work they can save. These two proofs are necessary to show, for example, that $\exists x \neg Fx$ and $\neg \forall x Fx$ are equivalent.

1.	$\exists x \neg Fx$	A
2.	Show $\neg \forall x Fx$	
3.	$\forall x Fx$	AIP
4.	$\neg Fa$	$\exists$E, 1
5.	Fa	$\forall$E, 3

1.	$\neg \forall x Fx$	A
2.	Show $\exists x \neg Fx$	
3.	$\neg \exists x \neg Fx$	AIP
4.	Show $\forall x Fx$	
5.	Show Fa	
6.	$\neg Fa$	AIP
7.	$\exists x \neg Fx$	$\exists$I, 6
8.	$\neg \exists x \neg Fx$	R, 3
9.	$\neg \forall x Fx$	R, 1

Deriving the other equivalence is similar.

Because QN takes the form of an equivalence, the replacement principle allows us to apply it to portions of formulas as well as to entire formulas. Each of the following is thus a legitimate application of QN.

$\neg \exists x Fxx$	$\forall x \neg Fxx$
$\neg \forall x \forall y Gxy$	$\exists x \neg \forall y Gxy$
$\forall x \forall y \neg \forall z (Fxz \ \& \ Fyz)$	$\forall x \forall y \exists z \neg (Fxz \ \& \ Fyz)$
$\exists x \neg \exists y Gyx$	$\exists x \forall y \neg Gyx$

This rule, too, can be applied several times in a single step: We can abbreviate

$$\neg \forall x \forall y \forall z((Rxy \ \& \ Ryz) \rightarrow Rxz)$$
$$\exists x \neg \forall y \forall z((Rxy \ \& \ Ryz) \rightarrow Rxz) \qquad \text{QN}$$
$$\exists x \exists y \neg \forall z((Rxy \ \& \ Ryz) \rightarrow Rxz) \qquad \text{QN}$$
$$\exists x \exists y \exists z \neg ((Rxy \ \& \ Ryz) \rightarrow Rxz) \qquad \text{QN}$$

as

$$\neg \forall x \forall y \forall z((Rxy \ \& \ Ryz) \rightarrow Rxz)$$
$$\exists x \exists y \exists z \neg ((Rxy \ \& \ Ryz) \rightarrow Rxz) \qquad \text{QN}^3$$

Problems

Use this style of deduction to solve the problems at the end of section 13.4.

SUMMARY OF RULES
BASIC RULES, APPLYING ONLY TO ENTIRE FORMULAS

Existential Introduction ($\exists$I)

$$
\begin{array}{ll}
\text{n.} & \dfrac{\mathcal{A}[c/v]}{} \\
\text{n + p.} & \exists v \mathcal{A} \qquad \exists \text{I, n}
\end{array}
$$

Here c may be any constant.

Existential Exploitation ($\exists$E)

$$
\begin{array}{ll}
\text{n.} & \dfrac{\exists v \mathcal{A}}{} \\
\text{n + p.} & \mathcal{A}[c/v] \qquad \exists \text{E, n}
\end{array}
$$

Here c must be a constant new to the proof.

Universal Exploitation ($\forall$E)

$$
\begin{array}{ll}
\text{n.} & \dfrac{\forall v \mathcal{A}}{} \\
\text{n + p.} & \mathcal{A}[c/v] \qquad \forall \text{E, n}
\end{array}
$$

Here c may be any constant.

Universal Proof

n.	Show $\forall v \mathcal{A}$
n + 1.	Show $\mathcal{A}[c/v]$
	$\square$

Here c must be a constant new to the proof.

DERIVED RULE, APPLYING ONLY TO ENTIRE FORMULAS

Variable Rewrite (VR)

n.	$\mathcal{A}$	
m.	$\mathcal{A}[v/u]$	VR, n

Here v is foreign to $\mathcal{A}$.

DERIVED RULE, APPLYING TO PARTS OF FORMULAS AS WELL AS TO ENTIRE FORMULAS

Quantifier Negation (QN)

n.	$\underline{\neg \exists v \mathcal{A}}$	QN, m
m.	$\forall v \neg \mathcal{A}$	QN, n
n.	$\underline{\neg \forall v \mathcal{A}}$	QN, m
m.	$\exists v \neg \mathcal{A}$	QN, n

Notes

[1] This rule was first formulated by the English philosopher William of Ockham in the fourteenth century.

[2] The American philosopher W. V. Quine first formulated existential exploitation in this way in 1950, in his *Methods of Logic* (Cambridge: Harvard University Press, 1950, 1982).

[3] The system of rules in this chapter is sound in the sense that the rules never lead us astray; they never allow us to prove a formula that isn't valid or permit us to establish the validity of an invalid argument form. Nevertheless, the existential exploitation rule is, by itself, unsound; it justifies the inference from $\exists v \mathcal{A}$ to $\mathcal{A}[c/v]$, provided that c is new to the proof. To preserve the system's soundness, we need to add restrictions to our proof system.

Most of our rules are *truth-preserving:* The truth of the rules' premises guarantees the truth of their conclusions. Existential exploitation, however, is not truth-preserving. We should hardly be able to argue, 'Some philosophers have been bachelors. Therefore, Socrates was a bachelor'. This form of inference is fallacious. The same is true of universal proof; the inference from 'Gorbachev is Russian' to 'Everybody's Russian' fails. But, although ∃E and universal proof are not truth-preserving, they never lead us to an illegitimate conclusion. Rule ∃E is *conservative* in that any formula that follows from the conclusion of the rule also follows from the rule's premise, provided the formula does not contain the introduced constant.

To put this idea another way, our system of rules as a whole is sound, but proofs are not sound line by line. We can never prove a conclusion that doesn't follow from the premises, but we may deduce intermediate formulas in the proof that don't follow from them. The restrictions make sure that these deviations don't affect the outcome of the proof. Some logicians believe that proofs must be sound line by line; therefore, they formulate ∃E and universal proof differently. There is a way, however, of interpreting our system as sound line by line that does not require us to reformulate our rules. This method requires that we reinterpret constants—in particular, constants used in applications of those two rules. So far, we've thought of constants, relative to a context, as standing for objects. We could choose to think of them as marking places for objects but without necessarily standing for anything in particular. Or, we could think of them as standing for a different kind of object. Developing these strategies goes beyond the scope of this book. But both lead to serious and interesting analyses of logic. For the first, see Hans Kamp, "A Theory of Truth and Semantic Representation," in J. Groenendijk, T. Janssen, and M. Stockhof, *Formal Methods in the Study of Language* (Amsterdam: Mathematisch Centrum Tracts, 1981), and Irene Heim, *The Syntax and Semantics of Definite and Indefinite Noun Phrases* (PhD dissertation: University of Massachusetts at Amherst, 1983). For the second, see Kit Fine, *Reasoning with Arbitrary Objects* (Oxford: Basil Blackwell, 1985).

[4] $\forall x \forall x F x x$ can't arise from our formation rules, which allow us to build formulas by adding quantifiers and substituting only when the quantified variable doesn't already appear in the formula. From Faa we can obtain $\forall x F x x$; from Fab, $\forall x F x b$; and from $\forall x F x b$, $\forall y \forall x F x y$. But we can't obtain $\forall x \forall x F x x$.

BIBLIOGRAPHY

WORKS IN THE HISTORY OF LOGIC

Aristotle. *Prior Analytics.*

Arnauld, Antoine. *Logic, or, the Art of Thinking.* Indianapolis: Bobbs-Merrill, 1964; originally published in 1662.

Carroll, Lewis. (Dodgson, C. L.) *Symbolic Logic and the Game of Logic.* New York: Dover, 1958.

Gilbert, G. K. "The Origin of Hypotheses, Illustrated by the Discussion of a Topographic Problem," *Science* 3 (1896): 1–13.

Keynes, J. N. *Studies and Exercises in Formal Logic.* London: Macmillan, 1884.

Mill, John Stuart. *A System of Logic.* Toronto: University of Toronto Press, 1963; originally published in 1843.

Venn, John. *Symbolic Logic.* London: Macmillan, 1881.

Whately, Richard. *Elements of Logic.* New York: Sheldon and Company, 1869.

WORKS ON THE HISTORY OF LOGIC

Geach, Peter T. *Reference and Generality.* Ithaca, N.Y.: Cornell University Press, 1962, 1980.

Kneale, William, and Kneale, Martha. *The Development of Logic.* Oxford: Oxford University Press, 1964, 1984.

CONTEMPORARY LOGIC TEXTBOOKS

Copi, Irving M. *Introduction to Logic.* New York: Macmillan, 1978.

Quine, W. V. O. *Methods of Logic.* Cambridge, Mass.: Harvard University Press, 1950, 1982.

Smullyan, Raymond. *What Is the Name of This Book?* Englewood Cliffs, N.J.: Prentice-Hall, 1978.

TWENTIETH-CENTURY RESEARCH RELEVANT TO LOGIC

Beth, E. W. "Semantic Entailment and Formal Derivability," in Hintikka, K. J. J. (ed.), *Philosophy of Mathematics.* Oxford: Oxford University Press, 1969.

Cherniak, Christopher. *Minimal Rationality.* Cambridge, Mass.: Bradford Books, 1986.

Fine, Kit. *Reasoning with Arbitrary Objects.* Oxford: Basil Blackwell, 1985.

Fischer, David Hackett. *Historian's Fallacies.* New York: Harper and Row, 1970.

Gentzen, Gerhard. "An Investigation into Logical Deduction," in Szabo, M. (ed.), *The Collected Papers of Gerhard Gentzen.* Amsterdam: North-Holland, 1969.

Heim, Irene. *The Syntax and Semantics of Definite and Indefinite Noun Phrases.* PhD dissertation: University of Massachusetts at Amherst, 1983.

Hintikka, K. J. J. "Form and Content in Quantification Theory," *Acta Philosophica Fennica* 8 (1955): 7–55.

James, William. *Psychology.* Cleveland and New York: World Publishing, 1948.

Kamp, Hans. "A Theory of Truth and Semantic Representation," in J. Groenendijk, T. Janssen, and M. Stokhof (ed.), *Formal Methods in the Study of Language.* Amsterdam: Mathematisch Centrum Tracts, 1981.

Karttunen, Lauri. "Presupposition and Linguistic Context," *Theoretical Linguistics* 1 (1974): 182–194.

Levin, Richard. *New Readings v. Old Plays.* Chicago: University of Chicago Press, 1979.

Lewis, David. "Scorekeeping in a Language Game," *Journal of Philosophical Logic* 8 (1979): 339–59.

Lightman, Alan P. "Magic on the Mind: Physicists' Use of Metaphor," *American Scholar* 58 (1989): 97–101.

Roueche, Berton. *Eleven Blue Men.* Boston: Little, Brown and Company, 1947, 1953.

Stalnaker, Robert. "Assertion," in Peter Cole (ed.), *Syntax and Semantics 9: Pragmatics.* New York: Academic Press, 1978.

ANSWERS TO SELECTED PROBLEMS

Chapter 1
TRUTH AND VALIDITY

1.2 Recognizing Arguments

There is rarely exactly one way to state the premises and conclusion of an argument. The answers given below are not the only correct ones.

1. Contains a simple argument:
   If a slave can survive without a master, it is awful to admit that the master cannot live without the slave.
   ∴ It is absurd to bring back a runaway slave.

2. Contains a simple argument:
   At Scrabble, children are both easy to beat and fun to cheat.
   ∴ Children make the most desirable opponents in Scrabble.

3. Contains a simple argument:
   A man with one watch knows what time it is.
   A man with two watches is never quite sure what time it is.
   ∴ It is possible to own too much.

4. Contains a simple argument:
   If you are on good terms with yourself, it is an impertinence to love your neighbor as yourself.
   If you are on bad terms with yourself, it is an injury to love your neighbor as yourself.
   ∴ You should not love your neighbor as yourself.

5. Contains a simple argument:
   It is very selfish to mind strictly our own business.
   ∴ The idea of strictly minding our own business is moldy rubbish.

6. Contains a simple argument:
   We made civilization in order to impress our girlfriends.
   ∴ If there hadn't been women, we'd still be squatting in a cave eating raw meat.

12. Does not contain an argument.

18. Contains an extended argument:
Man is a reasonable creature.
∴ Man is a thinking creature.
Man is a thinking creature.
Upon the right direction and employment of a man's thoughts depends both his usefulness to the public, and his own present and future benefits in all respects.
∴ There is nothing more worthy of a man's being than the right direction and employment of his thoughts.

24. Contains an extended argument pattern (take any volume, call it *x*):
x is a volume.
x does not contain any abstract reasoning concerning quantity or number.
x does not contain any experimental reasoning concerning matter of fact and existence.
∴ *x* contains nothing but sophistry and illusion.
x contains nothing but sophistry and illusion.
∴ *x* should be committed to the flames.

30. Contains a simple argument:
Everybody who isn't a tenant admits how destructive the city's World War II rent controls have been, but tenants have the most votes.
An extralegal free market in abandoned factory-loft conversions compensated somewhat, but City Hall's first instinct was to prohibit most conversions.
Anyone fool enough to want to build new apartments has to pay double the standard price for concrete because of a Mafia stranglehold on the commodity.
As a result of all this, vast areas of New York City are a wasteland of abandoned housing and rubble.
∴ The "housing crisis" agitating Mayor Koch and Governor Cuomo is actually a product of local attempts to suspend economic law.

36. Contains an extended argument:
In 1983 government agents in South Florida seized some six tons of cocaine and 850 tons of marijuana.
In 1985 the figures were twenty-five and 750 tons respectively.
∴ Seizures of cocaine have quadrupled while seizures of marijuana have fallen off.
Seizures of cocaine have quadrupled while seizures of marijuana have fallen off.
It is generally believed that the amounts of drugs seized reflect the amounts coming in.
∴ Almost certainly, more cocaine is being imported now than ever before.
The heightened risk of interdiction (as a result of the government's strategy in the war on drugs) has prompted smugglers to favor drugs that are compact and expensive, like cocaine, over drugs that are bulky and relatively cheap, like marijuana.
∴ The government's strategy in the war on drugs may be partly to blame for the sudden abundance of cocaine.

42. Contains an extended argument:
Whatever must be thought to exist is greater than whatever can be thought not to exist.
∴ If the greatest conceivable being can be thought not to exist, then it is not the greatest conceivable being, which is absurd.
If the greatest conceivable being can be thought not to exist, then it is not the greatest conceivable being, which is absurd.
∴ Something so great that a greater cannot be conceived exists so truly that it cannot even be thought not to exist.

48. Contains an extended argument:
To cause change is to bring into being what was before only potential, and only something that already is can do this.
∴ Nothing changes except what can but does not yet have some actuality; something that causes change has that actuality already.

Nothing changes except what can but does not yet have some actuality; something that causes change has that actuality already.

It is impossible for the same thing to be simultaneously actually F and potentially F, though it can be actually F and potentially G.

∴ It is impossible that something undergoing a change cause itself to undergo that very change.

It is impossible that something undergoing a change cause itself to undergo that very change.

∴ Anything changing must be changed by something else. If this other thing is also changing, it is being changed by another thing, and that by another.

Certainly, our senses show us that some things in the world are changing.

Anything changing must be changed by something else.

If this other thing is also changing, it is being changed by another thing, and that by another. This does not go on to infinity, or else there would be no first cause of the change and, consequently, no other changes.

∴ The intermediate causes will not produce change unless they are affected by the first change. It is necessary to arrive at some first cause of change, itself changed by nothing, and this all understand to be God.

1.4 Reliability

1. valid   **2.** valid   **3.** valid   **4.** valid   **5.** invalid; everything might be easy.

6. valid   **12.** valid   **18.** valid

1.5 Implication and Equivalence

1. (b) implies (a)   **2.** (a) implies (b)   **3.** equivalent   **4.** (b) implies (a)

5. no implications   **6.** no implications   **12.** (b) implies (a)   **18.** (b) implies (a)

24. (a) implies (b)   **30.** equivalent   **36.** We will operate immediately.

42. neither follows from nor implies   **48.** neither follows from nor implies

54. Nothing relevant.   **60.** You are not single.

1.6 Logical Properties of Sentences

1. contingent   **2.** tautologous   **3.** contingent   **4.** tautologous

5. contradictory   **6.** tautologous   **12.** tautologous   **18.** contingent

24. tautologous   **30.** contradictory   **36.** tautologous

42. (a) nothing   (b) A is not a tautology   (c) nothing   (d) A is contradictory

48. true: whatever follows from a sentence is true in any circumstance in which that sentence is true; a valid sentence (tautology) is true in all circumstances; thus, so is what follows from a valid sentence.

54. true: a contradiction is always false, so two contradictions always agree in truth value.

60. It could be true for every visitor. It implies that Donora is worse than every one of the towns of the visitors (and also that if any visitors come from different towns, these towns are equally nice).

66. Judy is a knight.   **72.** Punch and Judy are both knights.

78. Moe is a knight; either Curly or Larry is a knave.

84. "You know your brother" does not entail that you will recognize him in every circumstance, but only that you will recognize him under certain "normal" conditions.

90. Suppose I keep the promise; then I must have broken it. So, the promise cannot be kept. But if it isn't kept, then I do keep it. So, it can't be broken, either.

Chapter 2
EVIDENCE AND RELEVANCE

Note: Many of the following have more than one defensible answer.

2.1 Begging the Question

1. Quincy and Wanda exist.

2. Ellen, Rick, and Ted exist; Rick and Ted were somewhere last night.

3. Irma exists and was complaining about the price.

4. Polly exists and has a cat.

5. Alan exists and has friends.

6. Saul exists; others were angry; Saul was less likely than they to have become angry.

12. France exists and has a King.

18. Carla, Violet, and France exist; France has a King.

24. Does not beg the question. 'Abortion is tantamount to murder' does not presuppose that abortion is wrong. Murder is a legal concept that doesn't, in itself, involve moral pre-suppositions.

30. Does not beg the question. It's unclear whether this is an argument at all. If it is, then the conclusion 'Some form of mind-reading exists' isn't contained in or presupposed by the premises. It isn't supported by them either.

2.2 Complex Questions

In the following answers, presuppositions involving the existence of the people mentioned are omitted.

1. You've been poisoning people.   2. You've seen roaches in your apartment.

3. It's some time or other.   4. You were embezzling money from the bank.

5. You took the money; it was wrong to do so.   6. You cheated on the test.

12. A nation (France) has 246 kinds of cheese.

2.3 Relevance: Refutations

1. Clearly ad hominem and thus fallacious, but may be either abusive or circumstantial, depending on context. 'Nerd' may be an insult, or may describe the listener's characteristics, as one who places undue emphasis on studying.

2. Tu quoque, alleging hypocrisy.   3. Ad hominem circumstantial.

4. Ad hominem circumstantial.   5. Ad hominem abusive.

6. Not fallacious. This does not attack the actresses, or claim that they held their positions because of self-interest, or allege hypocrisy or inconsistency. It simply questions their expertise.

12. This is very close to a tu quoque. The fish, however, could hardly be said to be hypocritical or inconsistent.

18. Ad hominem. It could be interpreted as abusive (calling Fast a Stalinist) or as circumstantial (saying that he held his views because he was a Stalinist). The best interpretation, perhaps, is that this is tu quoque, alleging hypocrisy in that Fast parades as a peace activist.

2.4 Relevance: Confusing the Issue

1. No. These are relevant to the need for new legislation.

2. The demand for a definition is probably a red herring. And the argument that the relatives don't need help is attacking a straw man.

3. Standardized tests seem to be a red herring. Without further argument, it's hard to see why they are relevant.

4. The American way and the Constitution are surely red herrings here.

5. No. Ned doesn't address the issue of human rights abuses, but what he says isn't irrelevant.

6. This appears to be a straw man; there's no indication why restricting foreign investment is the best response to the facts cited.

Chapter 3
GROUNDING

Note: Many of the following have more than one defensible answer.

3.1 Appeals to Emotion

1. a. crucify, upon a cross of gold;
  b. You will not adopt a gold standard.
  c. You will not give our money a firm foundation in something with timeless and universal value, gold.

2. a. finest, succumb, dehumanizing, worship at the shrine of the Bitch-Goddess
  b. The best-known historians will not adopt the mathematical methods of social science, whatever their uses and values, which I hasten to acknowledge. Nor will historians place undue value on quantification.
  c. The historians perched at the top of their profession will not recognize and adapt to modern methods of social science, which are extremely useful and valuable. Nor will historians give proper respect to quantification.

3. a. spur action, enhance collective responsibility, egocentricity, personal fulfillment through social participation
  b. Right-wing ideologies are modes of thought designed not to make people do things, at least in groups, but to provide a moral justification for doing things for oneself. Insofar as political commitment requires qualities of self-sacrifice or a capacity to enjoy doing things with others, such personal qualities do not resonate well with right-wing political perspectives.
  c. Right-wing ideologies are modes of thought designed not to inspire "activists" or lead people to hide behind groups, but to provide a moral justification for individualism and self-reliance. Insofar as political commitment requires qualities of self-sacrifice or a capacity to enjoy hob-nobbing with like-minded folk, such personal qualities do not resonate well with right-wing political perspectives.

4. a. repudiate, deception, fraud, befogging
  b. We reject all morality taken apart from human society and classes. We say that it is inaccurate and used by landlords and capitalists to confuse workers and peasants.
  c. We fail to appreciate the importance of morality taken apart from human society and classes. It represents an ideal, fostered by the landlords and capitalists and enlightening the workers and peasants.

5. a. petty, reassure, regard, serve
  b. ... we refuse to be influenced by objections, since we are convinced this will not disturb those who work in the nation's interest.
  c. ... we refuse to be influenced by even the most serious and reasonable objections, since we are convinced this will increase the self-satisfaction of those who are blindly nationalistic.

6. a. rotating, add his bit, among other insults to human intelligence, indulged, demagogue, he'd be run out of town

b. The Reverend Jesse Jackson has been traveling around the world, broadcasting over Radio Havana to speak about the South African mess and comparing Botha to Adolf Hilter. Americans have listened to this politician too long. Official Democrats do not dare criticize him because he allegedly speaks for blacks, who vote Democratic. If that is so, at least non-Democrats can make the point that needs making, namely that if Mr. Jackson were white, people would publicly disagree with him.

c. The Reverend Jesse Jackson has been touring the world, broadcasting over Radio Havana to give an address about the South African mess and comparing Botha to Adolf Hitler. Americans have nourished this statesman too long. Official Democrats do not dare chide him because he allegedly speaks for blacks, who vote Democratic. If that is so, at least non-Democrats can make the point that needs making, namely that if Mr. Jackson were white, his views would stir controversy.

12. a. unifying, initiating resurgence, rise, distress, misery, shameful disregard, renaissance, encirclement against, hatred, plot, inhibiting, people's State, plunging, impotence, misery

b. . . . the National Socialist movement began its work of organizing the people and starting to change the Reich. The improvement in the people's circumstances bore all the signs of an internal movement. Nevertheless, a new policy of alliance on the part of Germany's neighbors began immediately. Internally and externally there resulted that agreement familiar to us all . . . with the sole aim of affecting Germany and limiting its power.

c. . . . the National Socialist movement began to control the people and started to repair the Reich. The people's increased satisfaction bore all the signs of an internal revolution. Nevertheless, a new policy of containment on the part of Germany's neighbors began immediately. Internally and externally there resulted that alliance familiar to us all . . . with the sole aim of discouraging German militarism and defending against its aggression.

3.2 Practical Fallacies

1. This is not an argument but a joke. In the right context, it could be an appeal to fear.

2. This is an appeal to common practice and, so, a bad argument.

3. This is an appeal to pity, combined with a hypothetical tu quoque. Whether the argument is good depends on how the hunger of children compares to the harm caused by working off the books.

4. An appeal to common practice—bad.

5. If this is an argument, it is an appeal to force. But it is probably a threat.

6. If, in context, this is an argument for condoning cheating, it's a bad argument, an appeal to common practice.

3.3 Superficiality

1. An allegation of a fallacy of accident, probably justified.

2. This argument seems to apply the silly rule "Nobody who can't get a cab in the rain is really powerful" and so exhibits the fallacy of accident.

3. As it stands, this isn't an argument. If, in context, it were used as an argument that Nelson was no more powerful than a flea, it would exhibit the fallacy of accident.

4. Arguably a fallacy of misapplication. The principle that consuming large numbers of trees is bad is sensible, but newspapers do have balancing virtues.

5. Arguably misapplication—the principle that manners should be rectified is not silly, but why it should be applied to "all recreations and pasttimes" seems unclear.

6. An appeal to ignorance. Whether it is fallacious depends on how many have made this charge before, whether anyone "on the Left" has had opportunity to respond, and so on.

12. The captain seems guilty of an appeal to authority.

18. Application: research a company before you invest in it.
Misapplication: don't accept gifts from friends without questioning them about their motives. (This is not a misapplication if you are a government official.)

24. Application: People will like you better if you're nice to them.
Misapplication: In warfare, surrender is more effective than counterattack.

30. a. There's no conclusive evidence that there's not;
b. There's no conclusive evidence that there is.

Chapter 4
MEANING

Note: Many problems have more than one defensible answer.

4.1 Equivocation

1. XV, XVI, and so on don't indicate size

2. 'his place'—as 'the place he held' (head of customs) or 'The place he now holds' (in a casket)

3. This explains an equivocation in the word 'imperialist'

4. 'get up' as 'become psychologically ready' or 'awaken'

5. 'anti-Communist' as kind of Communist or opponent of Communism

6. 'picture-taking' as 'photography' or 'removing paintings'

12. odd, humorous   **18.** mound, forget

24. move rapidly, take part in (a race), function, ravel lengthwise, continue

30. center of egg, harness for oxen, burden

4.2 Amphiboly

1. Equivocation: 'pest' as 'bothersome person' or 'insect'

2. Equivocation: 'comb' as 'object for grooming hair' or 'honeycomb'

3. Equivocation: 'race for' as 'race having as its goal' or 'race for the purpose of'

4. Equivocation: 'key' as 'means to' or 'lock opener'

5. Equivocation and amphiboly: 'pro' as 'in favor of' or 'professional'

6. Amphiboly: 'them' as referring to cars or potholes

12. Equivocation: 'man' as 'humanity' or 'individual man'

18. Equivocation: 'give everyone equal shares' as 'distribute equal amounts' or 'distribute so that resulting amounts are equal'

24. Amphiboly: 'blew' + 'down the Rockies' (meaning 'descended from the Rockies'), or 'blew down' + 'the Rockies' (meaning 'collapsed the Rockies')

30. Amphiboly: 'his high-school sweetheart' as relative clause giving added information about his wife or as distinct entry in list

36. Equivocation: 'bunch' as 'group of people' or 'group of bananas'; tempting amphiboly (treating 'banana' as verb). To correct; replace 'bunch' with 'group'

42. Amphiboly: 'talk rubbish' as 'talk (about) rubbish' or as idiom meaning 'say nothing useful'. To correct: supply 'about'

48. Amphiboly: 'antique' as adjective or as noun. To correct: replace with 'stripper of antiques'

54. Amphiboly: 'pair' of ears or earrings. To correct: add 'of earrings'

4.3 Accent

1. a. Someone has killed Tom.
   b. John has done something to Tom.
   c. John's killed someone else.

2. a. Someone sees roaches around here.
   b. I encounter roaches around here in some way.
   c. I see other things around here.
   d. I see roaches elsewhere.

4.4 Composition and Division

1. Division. Inferring property of members from property of society.

2. Division. Inferring property of member from property of team.

3. Composition. Inferring property of society from property of members.

4. Composition. Inferring property of Socrates from property of his parts.

5. Division. Inferring property of room from property of house.

6. Division. Inferring property of employees from property of company.

12. Division. Inferring property of member from property of family.

18. Division. Inferring property of partygoer from property of party.

24. All seven of the patients who died never recovered from the disease being studied. This is hard to understand because it sounds like a tautology.

4.5 Traditional Criteria for Definitions

3. description, analysis; changed. Now, too broad (not everything unpublished is an anecdote) and too narrow (there may be published anecdotes).

4. description, analysis; changed. Now, too broad; ejecting nongaseous substances is not belching but vomiting.

5. description, analysis; unchanged.

6. description, analysis; changed. Now, too narrow; bugs needn't stink and may be bred anywhere.

12. description, synonymy; changed. Now, too broad and too narrow.

18. description, analysis; unchanged.

24. description, synonymy; unchanged.

30. description, analysis; unchanged.

Chapter 5
SENTENCES

5.1 Sentence Connectives

1. Binary; truth-functional. 'A or B' is true unless A and B are both false, in which case 'A or B' is false.

2. Binary; not truth-functional. Suppose A and B are both true. 'A because B' might be true or false.

3. Binary; not truth-functional. Suppose A and B are true. 'A before B' might be true or false.

4. Singulary; truth-functional. A and 'not A' have opposite truth values.

5. Singulary; truth-functional. 'It is true that A' has the same truth value as A.

6. Singulary; not truth-functional. Some truths are obvious, but many are not.

12. Binary; not truth-functional. If A is false, 'A in order that B' is false. But, if A is true, 'A in order that B' might be true or false.

18. Binary; truth-functional. 'A whether or not B' has the same truth value as 'A'.

24. Binary; truth-functional. 'A nevertheless B' is true if and only if A and B are true.

5.2 A Sentential Language

1. a. $\neg$.   **2.** b. &.   **3.** a. $\vee$.   **4.** b. $\vee$.   **5.** a. $\neg$.   **6.** c.   **12.** a. $\vee$.

18. c.   **24.** a. $\neg$.

5.3 Truth Functions

1. The 'and' here does not conjoin two sentences. 'John is a brother and Sam is a brother' follows from but isn't equivalent to 'John and Sam are brothers'.

2. The definition of the conditional suggests that this should be true if nobody insults Kate. In English, however, we wouldn't tend to count it as true automatically if nobody happened to insult her.

3. The definition of the conditional suggests that this is true automatically if I have thirty days, whether or not I needed them and whether or not I finish the work.

4. The sentence implies neither that thirty undergraduates have been given, nor that thirty-five opinions have been offered. The 'and' here may best be translated as a conditional.

5. Similar to 4.   **6.** Similar to 4.

5.4 Symbolization

1. p: life is daring adventure; q: life is nothing

$$p \vee q$$

2. p: God is; q: all is well

$$p \ \& \ q$$

3. p: excellence can be bought; q: excellence must be paid for

$$\neg p \ \& \ q$$

4. p: wealth serves a wise man; q: wealth commands a fool

$$p \ \& \ q$$

5. p: money is a terrible master; q: money is an excellent servant

$$p \ \& \ q$$

6. p: activity conquers cold; q: stillness conquers heat

$$p \ \& \ q$$

12. p: wealth brings excellence; q: wealth comes from excellence

$$\neg p \ \& \ q$$

18. p: opposition enflames the enthusiast; q: opposition converts the enthusiast

$$p \ \& \ \neg q$$

24. p: progress might have been all right once; q: progress has gone on too long

$$p \ \& \ q$$

30. p: God can alter the past; q: historians can alter the past

$$\neg p \ \& \ q$$

36. *p*: I am opposed to millionaires; *q*: it would be dangerous to offer me the position

$$p \& q$$

42. *p*: the idea that all wealth is acquired through stealing is popular in prisons; *q*: the idea that all wealth is acquired through stealing is popular at Harvard.

$$p \& q$$

48. *p*: the hard fact was, circumstances rarely misled; *q*: the hard fact was, appearances were always full of truth

$$p \& q$$

54. *p*: other people are going to talk: *q*: conversation becomes impossible

$$p \to q$$

60. *p*: the lion and the calf shall lie down together (Note: this can't be broken down into a conjunction; it isn't equivalent to 'the lion shall lie down and the calf shall lie down'); *q*: the calf won't get much sleep

$$p \& \neg q$$

5.5 Validity

1. Correct. Where the conclusion is always true, the argument form must be valid.

2. Incorrect. Where all the premises cannot be true, the definition of validity is satisfied; the premises cannot be all true while the conclusion is false.

3. Correct. A contradictory formula implies every other.

4. Incorrect. For example, a contradictory formula cannot be equivalent to a valid one.

5. Correct. If $\mathscr{A}$ is satisfiable, it is true on at least one interpretation of it. And, if $\mathscr{A}$ implies $\mathscr{B}$, any interpretation making $\mathscr{A}$ true makes $\mathscr{B}$ true. So, there is an interpretation making $\mathscr{B}$ true.

6. Correct. A valid formula cannot imply a formula that is false on any interpretation.

12. Correct. They are all true, on any interpretation of them.

18. Truth.   24. Truth.   30. Falsehood.

36. (a) contingent; (b) satisfiable; (c) not valid; (d) satisfiable; (e) satisfiable; (f) nothing.

Chapter 6
TRUTH TABLES

6.1 Truth Tables for Formulas

1. p Contingent

p
T
F

2. p $p \to p$ Tautologous

p	$p \to p$
T	T T T
F	F T F

3. p $p \to \neg p$ Contingent

p	$p \to \neg p$
T	T F FT
F	F T TF

4. p $p \vee \neg p$ Tautologous

p	$p \vee \neg p$
T	TT FT
F	FT TF

5. p $p \leftrightarrow \neg p$ Contradictory

p	$p \leftrightarrow \neg p$
T	T F FT
F	F F TF

6. p $p \& \neg p$ Contradictory

p	$p \& \neg p$
T	T F FT
F	F F TF

12. p q $(q \to p) \to q$ Contingent

p q	$(q \to p) \to q$
T T	T T T T T
T F	F T T F F
F T	T F F T T
F F	F T F F F

18. $p\ q$ $p \to (q\ \&\ p)$ Contingent

T T	T **T** T T T
T F	T **F** F F T
F T	F **T** T F F
F F	F **T** F F F

24. $p\ q$ $(p \to q) \leftrightarrow (q \to p)$ Contingent

T T	T T T **T** T T T
T F	T F F **F** F T T
F T	F T T **F** T F F
F F	F T F **T** F T F

30. $p\ q$ $\neg(p \to q) \to \neg(q \to p)$ Contingent

T T	F T T T **T** F T T T
T F	T T F F **F** F F T T
F T	F F T T **T** T T F F
F F	F F T F **T** F F T F

36. $p\ q$ $p \vee ((p \leftrightarrow q)\ \&\ (p \leftrightarrow \neg q))$ Contingent

T T	T **T** T T T F T F F T
T F	T **T** T F F F T T T F
F T	F **F** F F T F F T F T
F F	F **F** F T F F F F T F

42. $p\ q\ r$ $(q\ \&\ r) \leftrightarrow ((p \leftrightarrow q) \vee (p \leftrightarrow r))$ Contingent

T T T	T T T **T** T T T T T T T
T T F	T F F **F** T T T T T F F
T F T	F F T **F** T F F T T T T
T F F	F F F **T** T F F F T F F
F T T	T T T **F** F F T F F F T
F T F	T F F **F** F F T T T F F
F F T	F F T **F** F T F T F F T
F F F	F F F **F** F T F T F T F

48. $p\ q\ r$ $(p \leftrightarrow (q \to r)) \leftrightarrow ((p \leftrightarrow q) \to (p \leftrightarrow r))$ Contingent

T T T	T T T T T **T** T T T T T T T
T T F	T F T F F **T** T T T F T F F
T F T	T T F T T **T** T F F T T T T
T F F	T T F T F **T** T F F T T F F
F T T	F F T T T **F** F F T T F F T
F T F	F T T F F **T** F F T T F T F
F F T	F F F T T **T** F T F F F F T
F F F	F F F T F **F** F T F T F T F

6.2 Other Uses of Truth Tables

1. $p \vee q$

	$p\ q$	$p \vee q$	p	$\neg q$	invalid
p	T T	T **T** T	**T**	F T	
$\therefore \neg q$	T F	T **T** F	**T**	T F	
	F T	F **T** T	**F**	F T	
	F F	F **F** F	**F**	T F	

2. $p \vee q$

	$p\ q$	$p \vee q$	$\neg q$	p	valid
$\neg q$	T T	T **T** T	F T	**T**	
$\therefore p$	T F	T **T** F	T F	**T**	
	F T	F **T** T	F T	**F**	
	F F	F **F** F	T F	**F**	

3. $p \rightarrow q$

	$p\ q$	$p \rightarrow q$	$q \rightarrow \neg p$	$\neg q$	invalid
$q \rightarrow \neg p$	T T	T T T	T F FT	FT	
$\therefore \neg q$	T F	T F F	F T FT	TF	
	F T	F T T	T T TF	FT	
	F F	F T F	F T TF	TF	

4. $p \rightarrow q$

	$p\ q$	$p \rightarrow q$	$q \rightarrow \neg p$	$\neg p$	valid
$q \rightarrow \neg p$	T T	T T T	T F FT	FT	
$\therefore \neg p$	T F	T F F	F T FT	FT	
	F T	F T T	T T TF	TF	
	F F	F T F	F T TF	TF	

5. $p \vee q$

	$p\ q$	$p \vee q$	$q \rightarrow p$	p	valid
$q \rightarrow p$	T T	T T T	T T T	T	
$\therefore p$	T F	T T F	F T T	T	
	F T	F T T	T F F	F	
	F F	F F F	F T F	F	

6. $p \rightarrow q$

	$p\ q\ r$	$p \rightarrow q$	$r \rightarrow \neg p$	$q \rightarrow p$	$q \vee r$	invalid
$r \rightarrow \neg p$	T T T	T T T	T F FT	T T T	T T T	
$q \rightarrow p$	T T F	T T T	F T FT	T T T	T T F	
$\therefore q \vee r$	T F T	T F F	T F FT	F T T	F T T	
	T F F	T F F	F T FT	F T T	F F F	
	F T T	F T T	T T TF	T F F	T T T	
	F T F	F T T	F T TF	T F F	T T F	
	F F T	F T F	T T TF	F T F	F T T	
	F F F	F T F	F T TF	F T F	F F F	

12. $p \leftrightarrow \neg q$

	$p\ q\ r$	$p \leftrightarrow \neg q$	$q\ \&\ p$	r	valid
$q\ \&\ p$	T T T	T F FT	T T T	T	
$\therefore r$	T T F	T F FT	T T T	F	
	T F T	T T TF	F F T	T	
	T F F	T T TF	F F T	F	
	F T T	F T FT	T F F	T	
	F T F	F T FT	T F F	F	
	F F T	F F TF	F F F	T	
	F F F	F F TF	F F F	F	

18. $p \rightarrow (q \vee r)$

	$p\ q\ r$	$p \rightarrow (q \vee r)$	$\neg q\ \&\ \neg r$	$\neg p$	valid
$\neg q\ \&\ \neg r$	T T T	T T T T T	FT F FT	FT	
$\therefore \neg p$	T T F	T T T T F	FT F TF	FT	
	T F T	T T F T T	TF F FT	FT	
	T F F	T F F F F	TF T TF	FT	
	F T T	F T T T T	FT F FT	TF	
	F T F	F T T T F	FT F TF	TF	
	F F T	F T F T T	TF F FT	TF	
	F F F	F T F F F	TF T TF	TF	

24.

$p\ q$	$p \vee q$	p	$\neg q$	invalid
T T	T T T	T	FT	
T F	T T F	T	TF	
F T	F T T	F	FT	
F F	F F F	F	TF	

30.

p	$p \rightarrow p$	$\neg p \rightarrow p$	p	valid
T	T T T	FT T T	T	
F	F T F	TF F F	F	

36.

p q	$\neg(q \leftrightarrow p)$	$\neg q \leftrightarrow p$	equivalent
T T	F T T T	FT F T	
T F	T F F T	TF T T	
F T	T T F F	FT T F	
F F	F F T F	TF F F	

42.

p q	$q \,\&\, p$	$(q \vee p) \,\&\, (p \to q)$	$q \,\&\, p$ implies $(q \vee p) \,\&\, (p \to q)$
T T	T T T	T T T T T T T	
T F	F F T	F T T F T F F	
F T	T F F	T T F T F T T	
F F	F F F	F F F F F T F	

48.

p q	$q \leftrightarrow p$	$(q \,\&\, p) \,\&\, (\neg q \,\&\, \neg p)$	$(q \,\&\, p) \,\&\, (\neg q \,\&\, \neg p)$ implies $q \leftrightarrow p$
T T	T T T	T T T F FT F FT	
T F	F F T	F F T F TF F FT	
F T	T F F	T F F F FT F TF	
F F	F T F	F F F F TF T TF	

54.

p q r	$r \to (\neg\,\neg p \to q)$	$(r \,\&\, \neg q) \to \neg p$	yes
T T T	T T T FT T T	T F FT T FT	
T T F	F T T FT T T	F F FT T FT	
T F T	T F T FT F F	T T TF F FT	
T F F	F T T FT F F	F F TF T FT	
F T T	T T F TF T T	T F FT T TF	
F T F	F T F TF T T	F F FT T TF	
F F T	T T F TF T F	T T TF T TF	
F F F	F T F TF T F	F F TF T TF	

60.

p q r	$\neg(r \leftrightarrow \neg p)$	$r \leftrightarrow (q \leftrightarrow p)$	$\neg(p \to (r \leftrightarrow q))$	no
T T T	T T F FT	T T T T T	F T T T T T	
T T F	F F T FT	F F T T T	T T F F F T	
T F T	T T F FT	T F F F T	T T F T F F	
T F F	F F T FT	F T F F T	F T T F T F	
F T T	F T T TF	T F T F F	F F T T T T	
F T F	T F F TF	F T T F F	F F T F F T	
F F T	F T T TF	T T F T F	F F T T F F	
F F F	T F F TF	F F F T F	F F T F T F	

66.

p q	$p \,\&\, q$	$p \vee q$
T T	T T T	T T T
T F	T F F	T T F
F T	F F T	F T T
F F	F F F	F F F

72.

p q	$\neg(p \,\&\, q)$	$((\neg p \to q) \,\&\, \neg q) \to \neg(p \to q)$	yes
T T	F T T T	FT T T F FT T F T T T	
T F	T T F F	FT T F T TF T T T T F F	
F T	T F F T	TF T T F FT T F F T T	
F F	T F F F	TF F F F TF T F F T F	

Chapter 7
SEMANTIC TABLEAUX

1. (Branch 1)   True: $p \vee q$ False: p open
   (Branch 2)   True: $p \vee q$ False: r open
The tableau is open and unfinished.

2. (Branch 1)   True: p False: p closed
   (Branch 2)   True: q False: p open
   (Branch 3)   True: q, p False: open
   (Branch 4)   True: q False: open
The tableau is open and finished.

3. (Branch 1)   True: p False: p, q closed
   (Branch 2)   True: q False: p open
   (Branch 3)   True: q, p False: q closed
   (Branch 4)   True: q False: p open
The tableau is open and finished.

4. (Branch 1)   True: r, p False: $p \,\&\, r$ open
   (Branch 2)   True: $r, \neg r$ False: $p \,\&\, r, r$ closed
The tableau is open and unfinished.

5. (Branch 1)   True: p, q False: p closed
   (Branch 2)   True: p, q False: r open
   (Branch 3)   True: p, q False: r, q closed
The tableau is open and finished.

6. (Branch 1)   True: q, p False: r, p closed
   (Branch 2)   True: q False: r, p, q closed
   (Branch 3)   True: q, r, p False: r closed
   (Branch 4)   True: q, r False: r, p, q closed
The tableau is closed and finished.

7.1 Rules for Negation, Conjunction, and Disjunction

1.
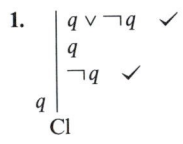

2.
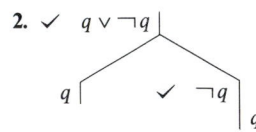

3.   **4.**
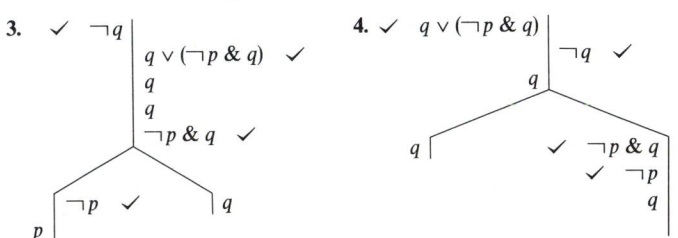

5.   ✓ *q & p*   **6.**   ✓ *s ∨ q*

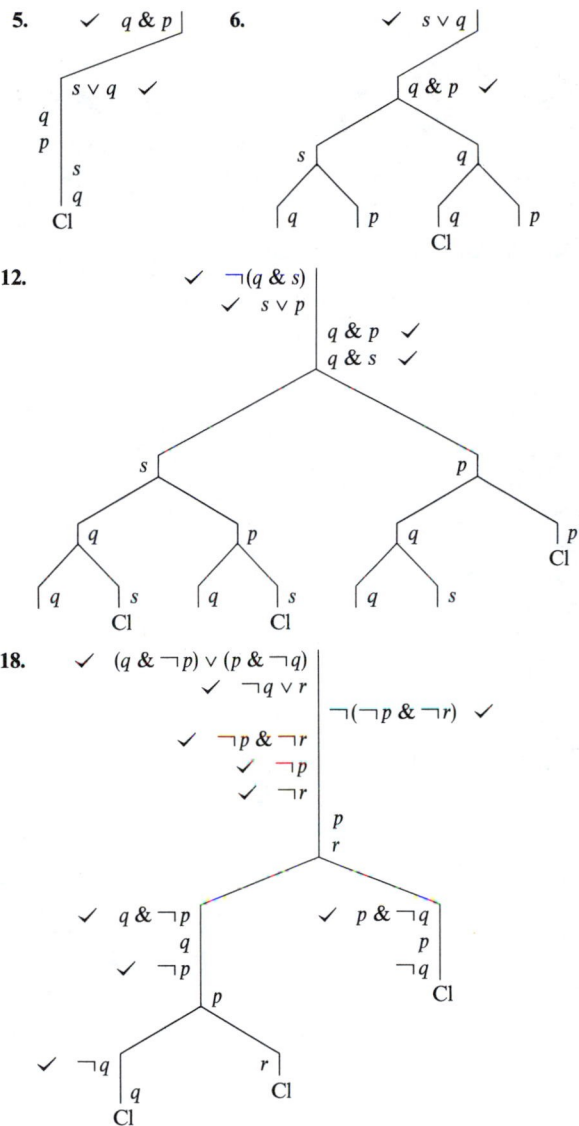

12.

18.

7.2 Rules for the Conditional and Biconditional

1. ✓ ¬(*p* → *r*)

¬*p* → ¬*r* ✓
p → *r* ✓

✓ ¬*p*

¬*r*

p

r
p
Cl

No interpretation exists.

2.

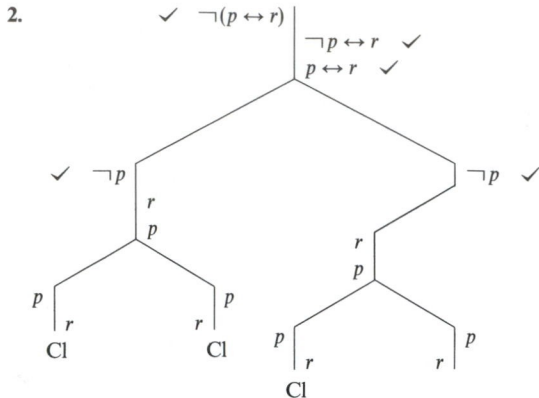

No interpretation exists.

3.

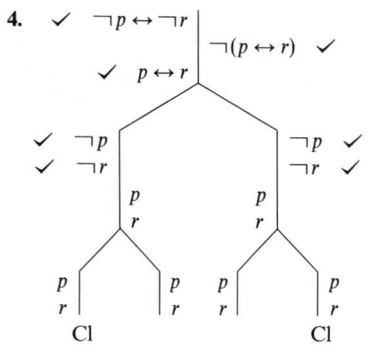

No interpretation exists.

4.

Two possible interpretations: Branches 2 (False: p, r) and 3 (True: p, r).

5.

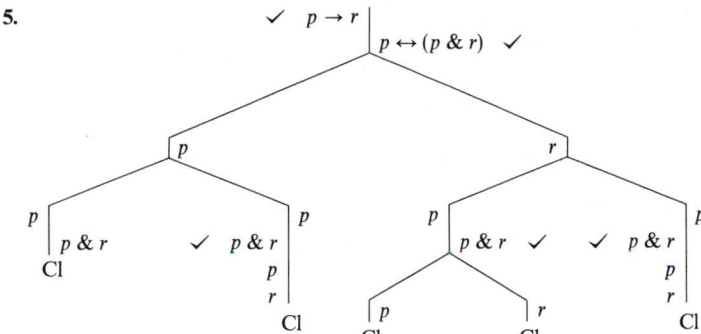

No interpretations exist.

6.

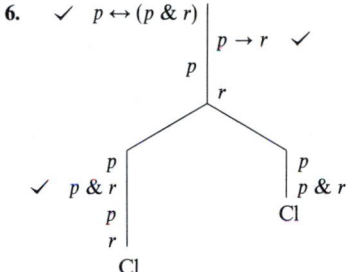

No interpretation exists.

12.

No interpretation exists.

18.

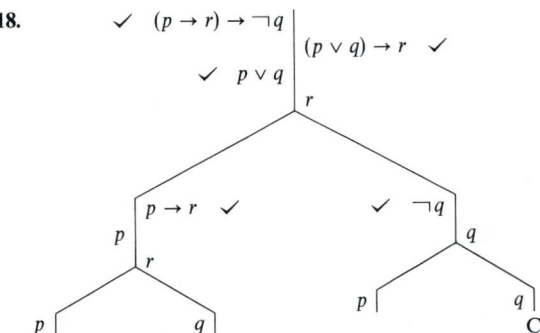

Two interpretations: Branches 1 and 2 (True: p, q; False: r) and Branches 1 and 3 (True: p; False: q, r).

24.

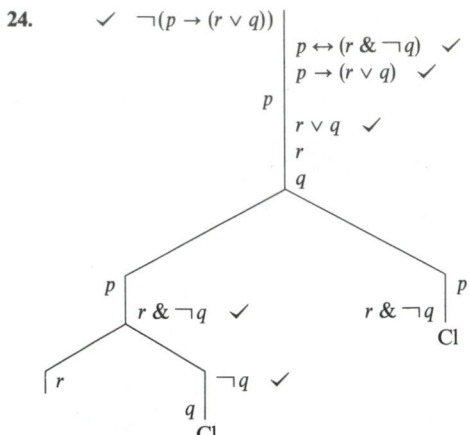

One interpretation: Branch 1 (True: p; False: r, q).

30.

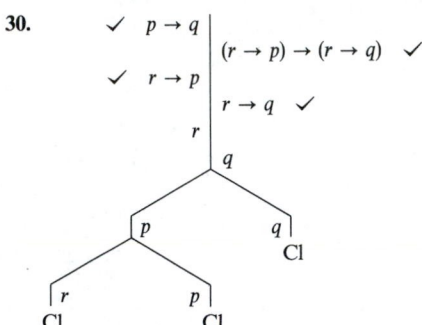

No interpretation exists.

7.3 Decision Procedures

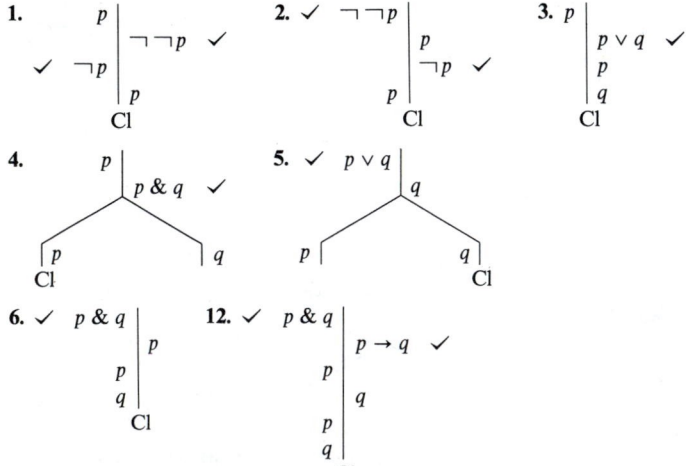

18. ✓ $p \to q$

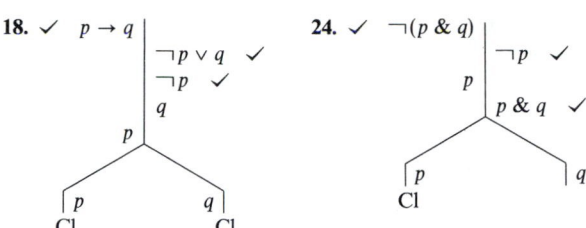

24. ✓ $\neg(p \,\&\, q)$

30. ✓ $\neg(p \to q)$

36. ✓ $p \to (q \vee r)$

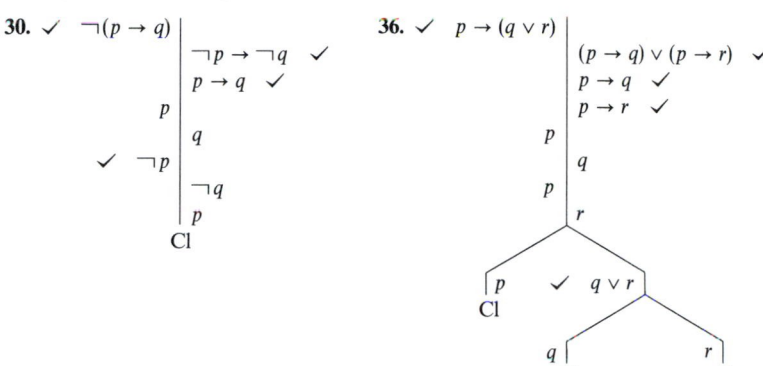

42. ✓ $p \to q$ ✓ $\neg q$

Valid.

48. ✓ $\neg p \vee q$ ✓ $\neg q$ ✓ $\neg p \to r$ ✓ $\neg r$

Valid.

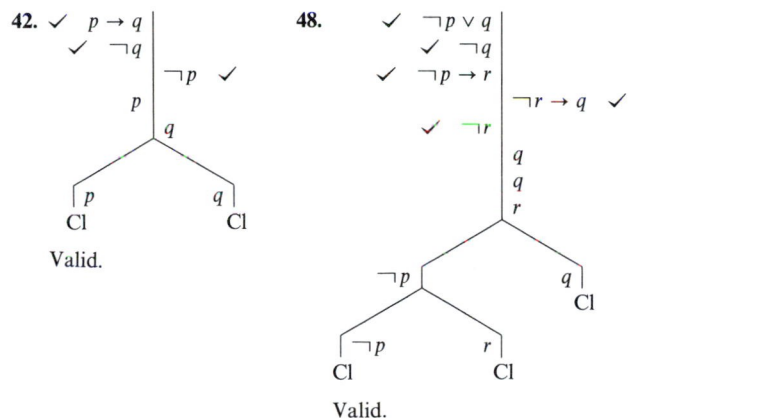

60. *p*: Nathan publishes several more papers; *q*: Nathan gets tenure

✓ $\neg(p \to q)$

Valid.

66. *p*: God is all powerful; *q*: God is able to prevent evil; *r*: God is willing to prevent evil; *s*: evil exists; *t*: God is all good; *u*: God exists

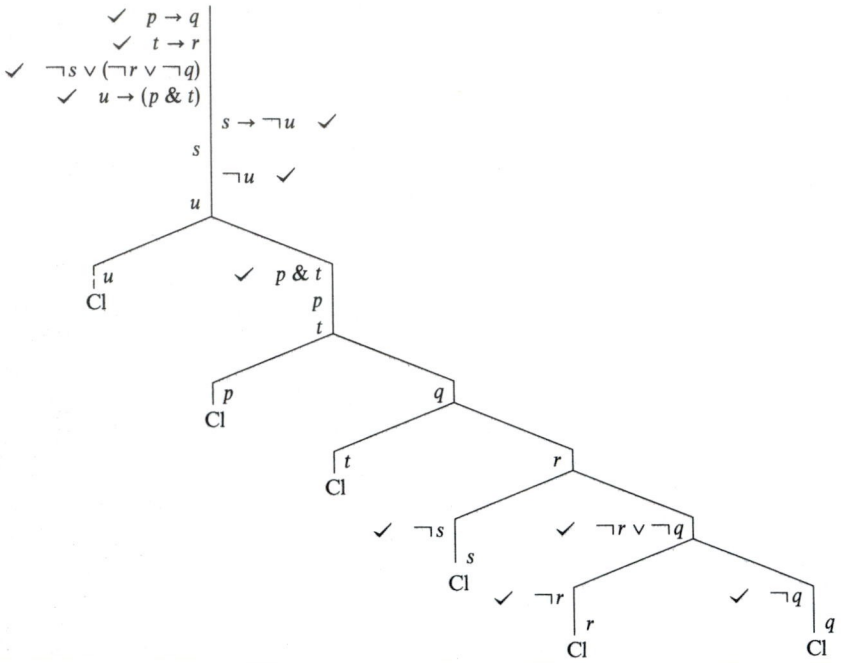

Valid.

72. *p*: you want to maximize your job opportunities after graduation; *q*: you major in business; *r*: you succeed in the top ranks of industry; *s*: you can write effectively; *t*: you major in liberal arts

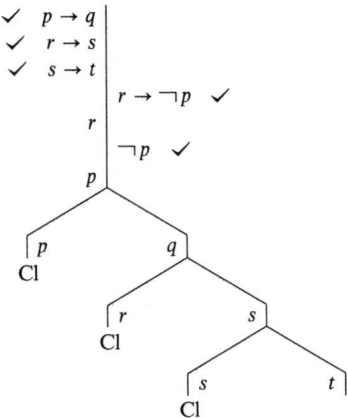

Not valid.

78. *p*: people conserve energy; *q*: people tolerate much greater despoiling of the environment; *r*: utilities will rely on something other than nuclear power; *s*: nuclear power remains prohibitively expensive; *t*: nuclear power is risky

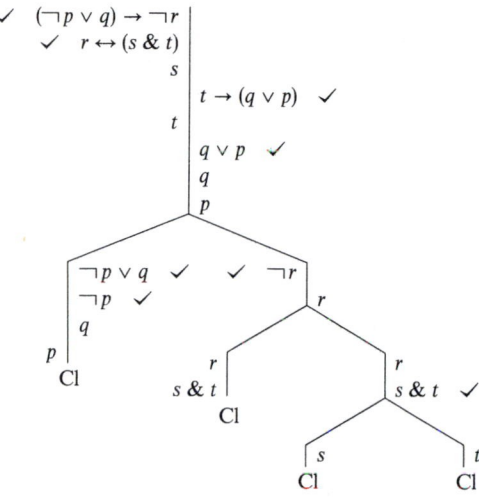

Valid.

84. *p*: advertisers continue to use cartoons to sell toys by having toys as their main characters; *q*: pressure will build for legislation; *r*: ratings will decline; *s*: parents understand what's going on; *t*: Congress will act; *u*: children will become obsessed with material goods; *v*: American culture will irrevocably decline

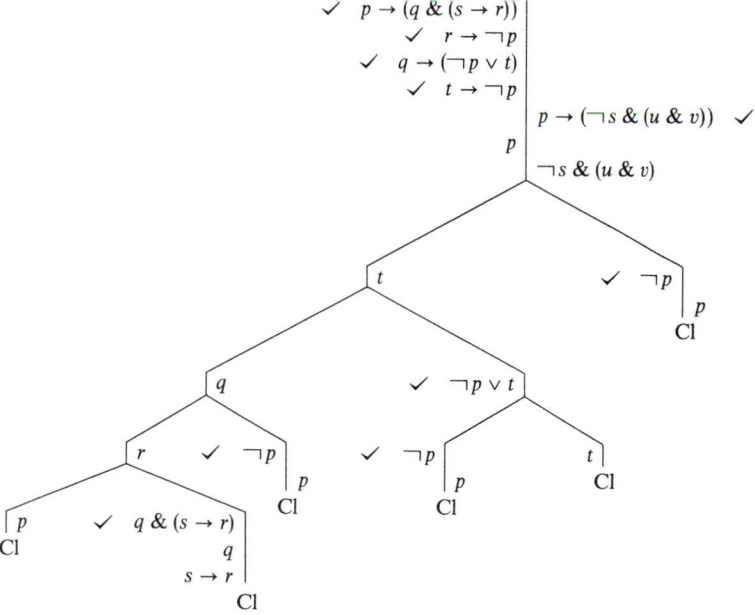

Valid.

Use the following dictionary for problems 93–111:
p: Punch is a knight $\neg p$: Punch is a knave
j: Judy is a knight $\neg j$: Judy is a knave

96.   ✓ $j \leftrightarrow (j \vee \neg j)$

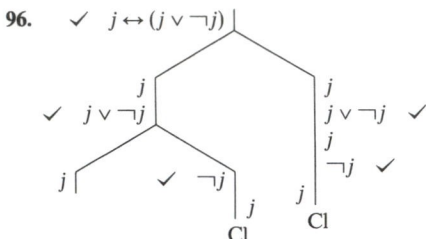

Judy is a knight.

102.   ✓ $j \leftrightarrow (p \,\&\, \neg j)$

Punch and Judy are knaves.

108.   ✓ $p \leftrightarrow (p \leftrightarrow j)$
                          ✓ $j \leftrightarrow p$

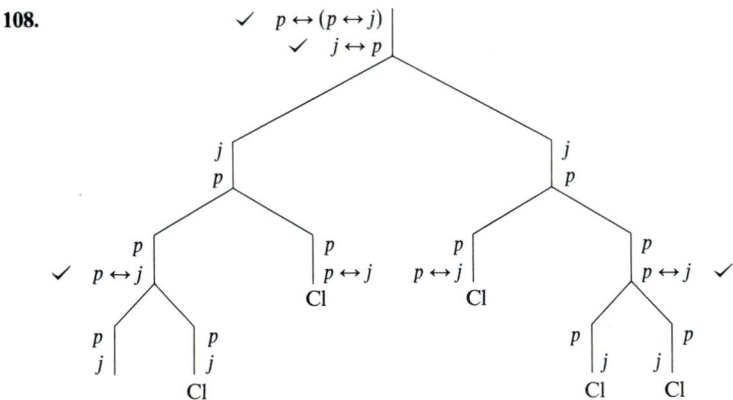

Punch and Judy are knights.

114.

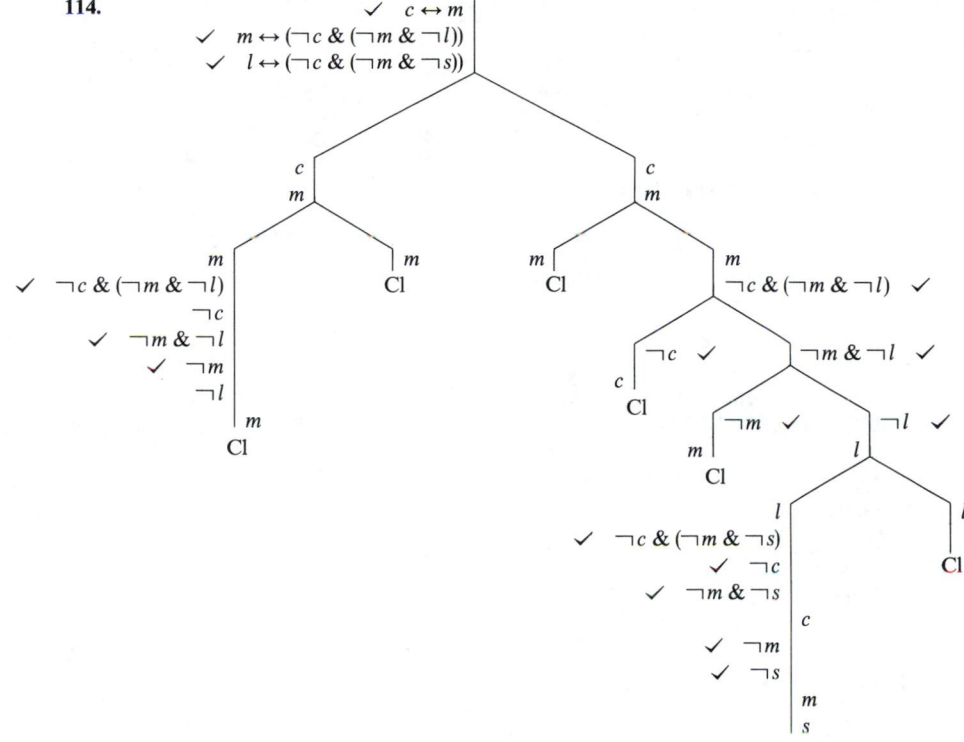

Larry is a knight; Curly, Moe, and all their cousins are knaves.

Chapter 8
DEDUCTION

8.2 Conjunction and Negation Rules

1. 1. $p \& q$ A
       2. q S, 1

2. 1. $p \& (q \& r)$ A
       2. $q \& r$ S, 1
       3. r S, 2

3. 1. $p \& \neg\neg q$ A
       2. $\neg\neg q$ S, 1
       3. q DN, 2

4. 1. $\neg\neg p \& \neg q$ A
       2. $\neg\neg p$ S, 1
       3. p DN, 2
       4. $\neg q$ S, 1
       5. $\neg\neg\neg q$ DN, 4
       6. $\neg\neg\neg q \& p$ C, 5, 3

5. 1. $p \& \neg q$ A
       2. $\neg r \& s$ A
       3. p S, 1
       4. s S, 2
       5. $s \& p$ C, 4, 3

6. 1. $(p \& q) \& r$ A
       2. $p \& q$ S, 1
       3. p S, 2
       4. q S, 2
       5. r S, 1
       6. $q \& r$ C, 4, 5
       7. $p \& (q \& r)$ C, 3, 6

12. 1. $p \to q$ A
        2. $(p \to \neg r) \& s$ A
        3. $p \to \neg r$ S, 2
        4. $p \to (q \& \neg r)$ CC, 1, 3
        5. $\neg\neg p \to (q \& \neg r)$ DN, 4

18.
1.	$\neg q \to r$	A
2.	$\neg(p \,\&\, q) \,\&\, \neg p$	A
3.	$\neg q \to (r \to s)$	A
4.	$\neg p$	S, 2
5.	$\neg q \to ((r \to s) \,\&\, r)$	CC, 3, 1
6.	$\neg p \,\&\, (\neg q \to ((r \to s) \,\&\, r))$	C, 4, 5

8.3 Conditional and Biconditional Rules

1.
1.	$p \to q$	A
2.	p	A
3.	q	MP, 1, 2

2.
1.	$p \leftrightarrow q$	A
2.	p	A
3.	$(p \to q) \,\&\, (q \to p)$	B, 1
4.	$p \to q$	S, 3
5.	q	MP, 4, 2

3.
1.	$p \leftrightarrow q$	A
2.	q	A
3.	$(p \to q) \,\&\, (q \to p)$	B, 1
4.	$q \to p$	S, 3
5.	p	MP, 4, 2

4.
1.	$(p \to p) \to p$	A
2.	$p \to p$	SI
3.	p	MP, 1, 2

5.
1.	$p \leftrightarrow \neg q$	A
2.	$\neg \neg p$	A
3.	$(p \to \neg q) \,\&\, (\neg q \to p)$	B, 1
4.	$p \to \neg q$	S, 3
5.	p	DN, 2
6.	$\neg q$	MP, 4, 5

6.
1.	$p \to q$	A
2.	$p \,\&\, r$	A
3.	p	S, 2
4.	q	MP, 1, 3
5.	r	S, 2
6.	$r \,\&\, q$	C, 5, 4

12.
1.	$\neg q \,\&\, (r \to p)$	A
2.	$\neg \neg r$	A
3.	$\neg q$	S, 1
4.	$r \to p$	S, 1
5.	r	DN, 2
6.	p	MP, 4, 5
7.	$p \,\&\, \neg q$	C, 6, 3

18.
1.	$\neg p \leftrightarrow \neg q$	A
2.	$\neg q \to \neg r$	A
3.	$\neg p \to \neg s$	A
4.	$\neg p \,\&\, t$	A
5.	$(\neg p \to \neg q) \,\&\, (\neg q \to \neg p)$	B, 1
6.	$\neg p \to \neg q$	S, 5
7.	$\neg p$	S, 4
8.	$\neg q$	MP, 6, 7
9.	$\neg r$	MP, 2, 8
10.	$\neg s$	MP, 3, 7
11.	$\neg s \,\&\, \neg r$	C, 10, 9

24.
1.	$p \to p$	SI
2.	$p \to \neg \neg p$	DN, 1
3.	$\neg \neg p \to p$	DN, 1
4.	$(p \to \neg \neg p) \,\&\, (\neg \neg p \to p)$	C, 2, 3
5.	$p \leftrightarrow \neg \neg p$	B, 4

30. p: this product will succeed; q: this product is given adequate advertising support; r: the company will show a profit for the year; s: the Vice-President believes that another product has more potential; t: this product is great

1.	$\neg p \leftrightarrow \neg q$	A
2.	$\neg p \to \neg r$	A
3.	$\neg q \to s$	A
4.	$t \,\&\, \neg p$	A
5.	$\neg p$	S, 4
6.	$(\neg p \to \neg q) \,\&\, (\neg q \to \neg p)$	B, 1
7.	$\neg p \to \neg q$	S, 6
8.	$\neg q$	MP, 7, 5
9.	s	MP, 3, 8

10. $\neg r$ MP, 2, 5
11. $s \,\&\, \neg r$ C, 9, 10

8.4 Disjunction Rules

1. 1. p A
    2. $p \lor q$ Ad, 1

2. 1. $p \,\&\, q$ A
    2. p S, 1
    3. $p \lor q$ Ad, 2

3. 1. $p \lor q$ A
    2. $\neg q$ A
    3. $q \lor p$ Cm, 1
    4. $\neg\neg q \lor p$ DN, 3
    5. $\neg q \to p$ MC, 4
    6. p MP, 5, 2

4. 1. $\neg p \lor q$ A
    2. p A
    3. $p \to q$ MC, 1
    4. q MP, 3, 2

5. 1. $q \to r$ A
    2. $p \lor q$ A
    3. $p \to s$ A
    4. $q \lor p$ Cm, 2
    5. $r \lor s$ CD, 4, 1, 3

6. 1. $p \lor q$ A
    2. $\neg r$ A
    3. $p \to r$ A
    4. $q \to q$ SI
    5. $r \lor q$ CD, 1, 3, 4
    6. $\neg\neg r \lor q$ DN, 5
    7. $\neg r \to q$ MC, 6
    8. q MP, 7, 2

12. 1. $(p \,\&\, q) \lor (r \lor s)$ A
     2. $((p \,\&\, q) \lor r) \lor s$ As, 1

18.   1. $\neg p \lor q$ A
      2. $\neg q \lor r$ A
      3. $\neg r$ A
      4. $\neg p \to \neg p$ SI
      5. $q \to r$ MC, 2
      6. $\neg p \lor r$ CD, 1, 4, 5
      7. $r \lor \neg p$ Cm, 6
      8. $\neg\neg r \lor \neg p$ DN, 7
      9. $\neg r \to \neg p$ MC, 8
    10. $\neg p$ MP, 9, 3

24.   1. $p \,\&\, (q \to r)$ A
      2. $q \lor \neg p$ A
      3. $(r \lor s) \to t$ A
      4. p S, 1
      5. $\neg p \lor q$ Cm, 2
      6. $p \to q$ MC, 5
      7. q MP, 6, 4
      8. $q \to r$ S, 1
      9. r MP, 8, 7
    10. $r \lor s$ Ad, 9
    11. t MP, 3, 10
    12. $t \lor m$ Ad, 11

30. p: someone knows where Rick was last night; q: Rick has an alibi; r: Rick is the prime suspect; s: new evidence points to someone else

    1. $\neg p$ A
    2. $q \lor r$ A
    3. $q \to p$ A
    4. $r \to r$ SI
    5. $p \lor r$ CD, 2, 3, 4
    6. $\neg\neg p \lor r$ DN, 5
    7. $\neg p \to r$ MC, 6
    8. r MP, 7, 1
    9. $r \lor s$ Ad, 8
    10. $s \lor r$ Cm, 9

8.5 Rules of Definition

1.
1. $r \to p$ A
2. $p \to q$ A
3. $\neg r \lor p$ MC, 1
4. $\neg r \to \neg r$ SI
5. $\neg r \lor q$ CD, 3, 4, 2
6. $r \to q$ MC, 5

2.
1. $r \to p$ A
2. $p \to q$ A
3. $\neg r \lor p$ MC, 1
4. $p \lor \neg r$ Cm, 3
5. $\neg r \to \neg r$ SI
6. $q \lor \neg r$ CD, 4, 2, 5
7. $\neg \neg q \lor \neg r$ DN, 6
8. $\neg q \to \neg r$ MC, 7

3.
1. $r \to p$ A
2. $\neg r \to q$ A
3. $\neg \neg r \lor q$ MC, 2
4. $r \lor q$ DN, 3
5. $q \to q$ SI
6. $p \lor q$ CD, 4, 1, 5
7. $\neg \neg p \lor q$ DN, 6
8. $\neg p \to q$ MC, 7

4.
1. $r \to p$ A
2. $\neg r \to q$ A
3. $\neg r \lor p$ MC, 1
4. $p \to p$ SI
5. $q \lor p$ CD, 3, 2, 4
6. $\neg \neg q \lor p$ DN, 5
7. $\neg q \to p$ MC, 6

6.
1. $\neg r \lor \neg p$ A
2. $\neg p \lor \neg r$ Cm, 1
3. $p \to \neg r$ MC, 2

7.
1. $r \to p$ A
2. $r \to r$ SI
3. $r \to (r \& p)$ CC, 1, 2
4. $\neg r \lor r$ MC, 2
5. $(\neg r \lor r) \lor \neg p$ Ad, 4
6. $(r \lor \neg r) \lor \neg p$ Cm, 5
7. $r \lor (\neg r \lor \neg p)$ As, 6
8. $(\neg r \lor \neg p) \lor r$ Cm, 7
9. $\neg (r \& p) \lor r$ DM, 8
10. $(r \& p) \to r$ MC, 9
11. $(r \to (r \& p)) \& ((r \& p) \to r)$ C, 3, 10
12. $r \leftrightarrow (r \& p)$ B, 11

8.
1. $r \leftrightarrow (r \& p)$ A
2. $(r \to (r \& p)) \& ((r \& p) \to r)$ B, 1
3. $r \to (r \& p)$ S, 2
4. $\neg r \lor (r \& p)$ MC, 3
5. $\neg r \to \neg r$ SI
6. $p \to p$ SI
7. $\neg p \lor p$ MC, 6
8. $(\neg p \lor p) \lor \neg r$ Ad, 7
9. $\neg r \lor (\neg p \lor p)$ Cm, 8
10. $(\neg r \lor \neg p) \lor p$ As, 9
11. $\neg (r \& p) \lor p$ DM, 10
12. $(r \& p) \to p$ MC, 11
13. $\neg r \lor p$ CD, 4, 5, 12
14. $r \to p$ MC, 13

9.
1. $r \lor p$ A
2. $\neg r \& s$ A
3. $\neg r \to p$ MC, 1
4. $\neg r$ S, 2
5. p MP, 3, 4
6. $p \lor q$ Ad, 5

10.
1. $r \to p$ A
2. $q \to r$ A
3. $\neg q \to \neg q$ SI
4. $\neg q \lor r$ MC, 2
5. $\neg q \lor p$ CD, 4, 3, 1

11.
1. $\neg r \lor \neg q$ A
2. $\neg (r \& q)$ DM, 1
3. $\neg (r \& \neg \neg q)$ DN, 2

12.
1. $\neg(r \& \neg p) \vee \neg r$ — A
2. $\neg r \vee \neg(r \& \neg p)$ — Cm, 1
3. $\neg r \vee (\neg r \vee \neg \neg p)$ — DM, 2
4. $(\neg r \vee \neg r) \vee \neg \neg p$ — As, 3
5. $r \to r$ — SI
6. $r \to (r \& r)$ — CC, 5, 5
7. $\neg r \vee (r \& r)$ — MC, 6
8. $(r \& r) \vee \neg r$ — Cm, 7
9. $\neg \neg (r \& r) \vee \neg r$ — DN, 8
10. $\neg(\neg r \vee \neg r) \vee \neg r$ — DM, 9
11. $(\neg r \vee \neg r) \to \neg r$ — MC, 10
12. $\neg \neg \neg p \to \neg \neg p$ — SI
13. $\neg r \vee \neg \neg p$ — CD, 4, 11, 12
14. $\neg r \vee p$ — DN, 13
15. $r \to p$ — MC, 14

18.
1. $(r \& \neg p) \to \neg q$ — A
2. q — A
3. $\neg(r \& \neg p) \vee \neg q$ — MC, 1
4. $\neg q \vee \neg(r \& \neg p)$ — Cm, 3
5. $q \to \neg(r \& \neg p)$ — MC, 4
6. $\neg(r \& \neg p)$ — MP, 5, 2
7. $\neg r \vee \neg \neg p$ — DM, 6
8. $\neg r \vee p$ — DN, 7
9. $r \to p$ — MC, 8
10. $r \to r$ — SI
11. $r \to (r \& p)$ — CC, 10, 9
12. $\neg r \vee (r \& p)$ — MC, 11

24.
1. $r \leftrightarrow p$ — A
2. $(r \to p) \& (p \to r)$ — B, 1
3. $r \to p$ — S, 2
4. $p \to r$ — S, 2
5. $\neg r \vee p$ — MC, 3
6. $\neg p \vee r$ — MC, 4
7. $p \vee \neg r$ — Cm, 5
8. $r \vee \neg p$ — Cm, 6
9. $\neg \neg p \vee \neg r$ — DN, 7
10. $\neg \neg r \vee \neg p$ — DN, 8
11. $\neg p \to \neg r$ — MC, 9
12. $\neg r \to \neg p$ — MC, 10
13. $(\neg p \to \neg r) \& (\neg r \to \neg p)$ — C, 11, 12
14. $\neg p \leftrightarrow \neg r$ — B, 13

30.
1. $(s \& \neg q) \to \neg r$ — A
2. $(p \to \neg s) \leftrightarrow \neg r$ — A
3. $((p \to \neg s) \to \neg r) \& (\neg r \to (p \to \neg s))$ — B, 2
4. $\neg r \to (p \to \neg s)$ — S, 3
5. $\neg \neg r \vee (p \to \neg s)$ — MC, 4
6. $r \vee (p \to \neg s)$ — DN, 5
7. $r \vee (\neg p \vee \neg s)$ — MC, 6
8. $(r \vee (\neg p \vee \neg s)) \vee \neg q$ — Ad, 7
9. $r \vee ((\neg p \vee \neg s) \vee \neg q)$ — As, 8
10. $((\neg p \vee \neg s) \vee \neg q) \vee r$ — Cm, 9
11. $((\neg s \vee \neg p) \vee \neg q) \vee r$ — Cm, 10
12. $(\neg q \vee (\neg s \vee \neg p)) \vee r$ — Cm, 11
13. $(\neg q \vee \neg(s \& p)) \vee r$ — DM, 12
14. $\neg(q \& (s \& p)) \vee r$ — DM, 13
15. $(q \& (s \& p) \to r$ — MC, 14
16. $\neg(s \& \neg q) \vee \neg r$ — MC, 1
17. $\neg r \vee \neg(s \& \neg q)$ — Cm, 16
18. $\neg r \vee (\neg s \vee \neg \neg q)$ — DM, 17
19. $\neg r \vee (\neg s \vee q)$ — DN, 18
20. $(\neg r \vee \neg s) \vee q$ — As, 19
21. $(\neg s \vee \neg r) \vee q$ — Cm, 20
22. $\neg s \vee (\neg r \vee q)$ — As, 21

23. $\neg s \lor (r \to q)$	MC, 22
24. $s \to (r \to q)$	MC, 23
25. $(p \to \neg s) \to \neg r$	S, 3
26. $\neg (p \to \neg s) \lor \neg r$	MC, 25
27. $\neg (\neg p \lor \neg s) \lor \neg r$	MC, 26
28. $\neg r \lor \neg (\neg p \lor \neg s)$	Cm, 27
29. $\neg r \lor \neg (\neg s \lor \neg p)$	Cm, 28
30. $\neg r \lor \neg \neg (s \& p)$	DM, 29
31. $\neg r \lor (s \& p)$	DN, 30
32. $\neg r \to \neg r$	SI
33. $s \to s$	SI
34. $\neg s \lor s$	MC, 33
35. $\neg p \lor (\neg s \lor s)$	Ad, 34
36. $(\neg p \lor \neg s) \lor s$	As, 35
37. $(\neg s \lor \neg p) \lor s$	Cm, 36
38. $\neg (s \& p) \lor s$	DM, 37
39. $(s \& p) \to s$	MC, 38
40. $\neg r \lor s$	CD, 31, 32, 39
41. $r \to r$	SI
42. $\neg r \lor r$	MC, 41
43. $r \lor \neg r$	Cm, 42
44. $(r \lor \neg r) \lor q$	Ad, 43
45. $r \lor (\neg r \lor q)$	As, 44
46. $\neg \neg r \lor (\neg r \lor q)$	DN, 45
47. $\neg r \to (\neg r \lor q)$	MC, 46
48. $\neg r \to (r \to q)$	MC, 47
49. $(r \to q) \lor (r \to q)$	CD, 40, 24, 48
50. $\neg (r \to q) \to \neg (r \to q)$	SI
51. $\neg \neg (r \to q) \lor (r \to q)$	DN, 49
52. $\neg (r \to q) \to (r \to q)$	MC, 51
53. $\neg (r \to q) \to ((r \to q) \& \neg (r \to q))$	CC, 52, 50
54. $\neg \neg (r \to q) \lor ((r \to q) \& \neg (r \to q))$	MC, 53
55. $((r \to q) \& \neg (r \to q)) \lor \neg \neg (r \to q)$	Cm, 54
56. $((r \to q) \& \neg (r \to q)) \lor (r \to q)$	DN, 55
57. $\neg \neg ((r \to q) \& \neg (r \to q)) \lor (r \to q)$	DN, 56
58. $\neg ((r \to q) \& \neg (r \to q)) \to (r \to q)$	MC, 57
59. $(r \to q) \to (r \to q)$	SI
60. $\neg (r \to q) \lor (r \to q)$	MC, 59
61. $\neg (r \to q) \lor \neg \neg (r \to q)$	DN, 60
62. $\neg ((r \to q) \& \neg (r \to q))$	DM, 61
63. $r \to q$	MP, 58, 62
64. $r \to (s \& p)$	MC, 31
65. $r \to (q \& (s \& p)$	CC, 63, 64
66. $(r \to (q \& (s \& p)) \& ((q \& (s \& p) \to r)$	C, 15, 65
67. $r \leftrightarrow (q \& (s \& p))$	B, 66

36.
1. $p \& \neg q$	A	
2. $\neg \neg (p \& \neg q)$	DN, 1	
3. $\neg (\neg p \lor \neg \neg q)$	DM, 2	
4. $\neg (\neg p \lor q)$	DN, 3	
5. $\neg (p \to q)$	MC, 4	

42.
1. $p \to p$	SI
2. $\neg p \lor p$	MC, 1
3. $(\neg p \lor p) \lor \neg q$	Ad, 2
4. $(p \lor \neg p) \lor \neg q$	Cm, 3
5. $p \lor (\neg p \lor \neg q)$	As, 4
6. $(\neg p \lor \neg q) \lor p$	Cm, 5
7. $\neg (p \& q) \lor p$	DM, 6
8. $(p \& q) \to p$	MC, 7

48.
1. $(p \;\&\; q) \lor r$ A
2. $\neg\neg(p \;\&\; q) \lor r$ DN, 1
3. $\neg(\neg p \lor \neg q) \lor r$ DM, 2
4. $\neg(\neg q \lor \neg p) \lor r$ Cm, 3
5. $\neg\neg(q \;\&\; p) \lor r$ DM, 4
6. $(q \;\&\; p) \lor r$ DN, 5

54. p: a man can serve god; q: a man can serve Mammon; r: a man starves

1.	$\neg(p \;\&\; q)$	A
2.	$\neg q \rightarrow r$	A
3.	$r \rightarrow \neg p$	A
4.	$\neg p \lor \neg q$	DM, 1
5.	$q \lor r$	MC, 2
6.	$\neg q \lor \neg p$	Cm, 4
7.	$q \rightarrow \neg p$	MC, 6
8.	$\neg p \lor \neg p$	CD, 5, 7, 3
9.	$p \rightarrow p$	SI
10.	$p \rightarrow (p \;\&\; p)$	CC, 9, 9
11.	$\neg p \lor (p \;\&\; p)$	MC, 10
12.	$(p \;\&\; p) \lor \neg p$	Cm, 11
13.	$\neg\neg(p \;\&\; p) \lor \neg p$	DN, 12
14.	$\neg(\neg p \lor \neg p) \lor \neg p$	DM, 13
15.	$(\neg p \lor \neg p) \rightarrow \neg p$	MC, 14
16.	$\neg p$	MP, 15, 8

8.6 Derived Rules

1. p: you are ambitious; q: you'll achieve your goals; r: life has meaning

1.	$p \rightarrow \neg q$	A
2.	$r \rightarrow p$	A
3.	$r \rightarrow \neg q$	HS, 2,1
4.	$\neg\neg q \rightarrow \neg r$	Tr, 3
5.	$q \rightarrow \neg r$	DN, 4

2. p: Adam comes to the party; q: Barbara comes to the party; r: Carlos will be happy

1.	$p \rightarrow q$	A
2.	$q \rightarrow p$	A
3.	$\neg q \lor p$	MC, 2
4.	$(\neg q \lor p) \lor r$	Ad, 3
5.	$(p \lor \neg q) \lor r$	Cm, 4
6.	$p \lor (\neg q \lor r)$	As, 5
7.	$r \rightarrow r$	SI
8.	$\neg r \lor r$	MC, 7
9.	$(\neg r \lor r) \lor \neg q$	Ad, 8
10.	$\neg r \lor (r \lor \neg q)$	As, 9
11.	$\neg r \lor (\neg q \lor r)$	Cm, 10
12.	$(p \lor (\neg q \lor r)) \;\&\; (\neg r \lor (\neg q \lor r))$	C, 6, 11
13.	$(p \;\&\; \neg r) \lor (\neg q \lor r)$	D, 12
14.	$\neg(\neg p \lor \neg\neg r) \lor (\neg q \lor r)$	DM, 13
15.	$\neg(\neg p \lor r) \lor (\neg q \lor r)$	DN, 14
16.	$(\neg p \lor r) \rightarrow (\neg q \lor r)$	MC, 15
17.	$(p \rightarrow r) \rightarrow (\neg q \lor r)$	MC, 16
18.	$(p \rightarrow r) \rightarrow (q \rightarrow r)$	MC, 17

3. *p*: interest rates will rise; *q*: Congress enacts a tax increase; *r*: the unemployment level will increase; *s*: the budget deficit will increase

1.	$p \lor q$	A
2.	$q \to p$	A
3.	$p \to r$	A
4.	$\neg r \lor s$	A
5.	$q \to r$	HS, 2, 3
6.	$r \to s$	MC, 4
7.	$q \to s$	HS, 5, 6
8.	$p \to s$	HS, 3, 6
9.	$s \lor s$	CD, 1, 8, 7
10.	s	I, 9

4. *p*: God is omnipotent; *q*: God can do everything; *r*: God can make a stone so heavy he can't lift it

1.	$p \leftrightarrow q$	A
2.	$\neg r \to \neg q$	A
3.	$r \to \neg q$	A
4.	$r \to r$	SI
5.	$\neg r \lor r$	MC, 4
6.	$\neg q \lor \neg q$	CD, 5, 2, 3
7.	$\neg q$	I, 6
8.	$\neg p$	BE, 1, 7
9.	$\neg p \lor \neg s$	Ad, 8

5. *p*: the President pursues arms limitations talks; *q*: the President gets the foreign policy mechanism working harmoniously; *r*: the European left will acquiesce to the placement of additional nuclear weapons in Europe

1.	$p \to (q \to r)$	A
2.	$\neg r$	A
3.	$\neg p \lor (q \to r)$	MC, 1
4.	$\neg p \lor (\neg q \lor r)$	MC, 3
5.	$(\neg p \lor \neg q) \lor r$	As, 4
6.	$\neg p \lor \neg q$	DS, 5, 2
7.	$\neg q \lor \neg p$	Cm, 6

6. *p*: we introduce a new product line; *q*: we give an existing line a new advertising image; *r*: we take risks; *s*: we may lose market share; *t*: we have to make large expenditures on advertising

1.	$(p \lor q) \to (r \,\&\, s)$	A
2.	$\neg p \to \neg t$	A
3.	$\neg (p \lor q) \lor (r \,\&\, s)$	MC, 1
4.	$(\neg p \,\&\, \neg q) \lor (r \,\&\, s)$	DM, 3
5.	$((\neg p \,\&\, \neg q) \lor r) \,\&\, ((\neg p \,\&\, \neg q) \lor s)$	D, 4
6.	$(\neg p \,\&\, \neg q) \lor r$	S, 5
7.	$r \lor (\neg p \,\&\, \neg q)$	Cm, 6
8.	$(r \lor \neg p) \,\&\, (r \lor \neg q)$	D, 7
9.	$r \lor \neg p$	S, 8
10.	$r \to r$	SI
11.	$r \lor \neg t$	CD, 9, 10, 2
12.	$\neg \neg r \lor \neg t$	DN, 11
13.	$\neg r \to \neg t$	MC, 12

12. *p*: the president retaliates against Libya with military force; *q*: the public will be ambivalent; *r*: Libya directs terrorist attacks toward Americans on American soil

1. $p \rightarrow q$	A
2. $r \rightarrow \neg q$	A
3. $\neg\neg q \rightarrow \neg r$	Tr, 2
4. $q \rightarrow \neg r$	DN, 3
5. $p \rightarrow \neg r$	HS, 1, 4
6. $\neg p \lor \neg r$	MC, 5
7. $\neg r \lor \neg p$	Cm, 6

18. *p*: Congress erects trade barriers; *q*: Congress grants further subsidies to American farmers; *r*: other countries will retaliate, *s*: the economy will slow down; *t*: Congress will find new sources of revenue

1. $(p \ \& \ q) \rightarrow r$	A
2. $r \rightarrow s$	A
3. $s \rightarrow (\neg q \lor t)$	A
4. $\neg p \rightarrow (\neg q \ \& \ \neg r)$	A
5. $\neg\neg p \lor (\neg q \ \& \ \neg r)$	MC, 4
6. $p \lor (\neg q \ \& \ \neg r)$	DN, 5
7. $(\neg q \ \& \ \neg r) \lor p$	Cm, 6
8. $(\neg q \lor p) \ \& \ (\neg r \lor p)$	D, 7
9. $\neg q \lor p$	S, 8
10. $q \rightarrow p$	MC, 9
11. $q \rightarrow q$	SI
12. $q \rightarrow (p \ \& \ q)$	CC, 10, 11
13. $q \rightarrow r$	HS, 12, 1
14. $q \rightarrow s$	HS, 13, 2
15. $q \rightarrow (\neg q \lor t)$	HS, 14, 3
16. $\neg q \lor (\neg q \lor t)$	MC, 15
17. $(\neg q \lor \neg q) \lor t$	As, 16
18. $\neg q \lor t$	I, 17
19. $t \lor \neg q$	Cm, 18

24.

1. p	A
2. $\neg(p \lor r)$	A
3. $\neg p \ \& \ \neg r$	DM, 2
4. $\neg p$	S, 3
5. q	!, 1, 4

30.

1. $(\neg p \rightarrow q) \lor r$	A
2. $(\neg\neg p \lor q) \lor r$	MC, 1
3. $(p \lor q) \lor r$	DN, 2
4. $p \lor (q \lor r)$	As, 3
5. $\neg p \rightarrow (q \lor r)$	MC, 4

36.

1. $p \leftrightarrow q$	A
2. $\neg\neg(p \leftrightarrow q)$	DN, 1
3. $\neg\neg((p \rightarrow q) \ \& \ (q \rightarrow p))$	B, 2
4. $\neg\neg((q \rightarrow p) \ \& \ (p \rightarrow q))$	Cm, 3
5. $\neg\neg(q \leftrightarrow p)$	B, 4
6. $\neg(\neg q \leftrightarrow p)$	NB, 5
7. $\neg q \leftrightarrow \neg p$	NB, 6

42.

1. $p \lor q$	A
2. $\neg q \lor r$	A
3. $\neg\neg p \lor q$	DN, 1
4. $\neg p \rightarrow q$	MC, 3
5. $q \rightarrow r$	MC, 2
6. $\neg p \rightarrow r$	HS, 4, 5
7. $\neg\neg p \lor r$	MC, 6
8. $p \lor r$	DN, 7

48.

1. $\neg s \rightarrow \neg k$	A
2. $(s \ \& \ t) \rightarrow (p \leftrightarrow q)$	A
3. $\neg(\neg p \lor q)$	A
4. $\neg(p \rightarrow q)$	MC, 3
5. $\neg(p \rightarrow q) \lor \neg(q \rightarrow p)$	Ad, 4
6. $\neg((p \rightarrow q) \ \& \ (q \rightarrow p))$	DM, 5

7. $\neg(p \leftrightarrow q)$ B, 6
8. $\neg(s \,\&\, t)$ MT, 2, 7
9. $\neg s \vee \neg t$ DM, 8
10. $\neg t \rightarrow \neg t$ SI
11. $\neg k \vee \neg t$ CD, 9, 1, 10
12. $\neg t \vee \neg k$ Cm, 11
13. $t \rightarrow \neg k$ MC, 12

54. 1. $(p \rightarrow q) \rightarrow (p \rightarrow q)$ SI
     2. $(p \rightarrow q) \rightarrow (\neg q \rightarrow \neg p)$ Tr, 1

60. 1. $(p \vee (q \vee r)) \rightarrow (p \vee (q \vee r))$ SI
     2. $(p \vee (q \vee r)) \rightarrow ((q \vee r) \vee p)$ Cm, 1
     3. $(p \vee (q \vee r) \rightarrow (q \vee (r \vee p))$ As, 2
     4. $(p \vee (q \vee r)) \rightarrow (q \vee (p \vee r))$ Cm, 3

8.7 Indirect Proof from 8.5

1. 1. $r \rightarrow p$ A
     2. $p \rightarrow q$ A
     3. $\neg(r \rightarrow q)$ AIP
     4. $r \rightarrow q$ HS, 1, 2
     5. $(r \rightarrow q) \,\&\, \neg(r \rightarrow q)$ C, 4, 3

2. 1. $r \rightarrow p$ A
     2. $p \rightarrow q$ A
     3. $\neg(\neg q \rightarrow \neg r)$ AIP
     4. $\neg q \,\&\, \neg \neg r$ NC, 3
     5. $\neg q$ S, 4
     6. $\neg \neg r$ S, 4
     7. $\neg p$ MT, 2, 5
     8. $\neg r$ MT, 1, 7
     9. $\neg r \,\&\, \neg \neg r$ C, 8, 6

3. 1. $r \rightarrow p$ A
     2. $\neg r \rightarrow q$ A
     3. $\neg(\neg p \rightarrow q)$ AIP
     4. $\neg p \,\&\, \neg q$ NC, 3
     5. $\neg p$ S, 4
     6. $\neg q$ S, 4
     7. $\neg r$ MT, 1, 5
     8. q MP, 2, 7
     9. $q \,\&\, \neg q$ C, 8, 6

4. 1. $r \rightarrow p$ A
     2. $\neg r \rightarrow q$ A
     3. $\neg(\neg q \rightarrow p)$ AIP
     4. $\neg q \rightarrow \neg \neg r$ Tr, 2
     5. $\neg q \rightarrow r$ DN, 4
     6. $\neg q \rightarrow p$ HS, 5, 1
     7. $(\neg q \rightarrow p) \,\&\, \neg(\neg q \rightarrow p)$ C, 6, 3

6. 1. $\neg r \vee \neg p$ A
     2. $\neg(p \rightarrow \neg r)$ AIP
     3. $p \,\&\, \neg \neg r$ NC, 2
     4. $\neg \neg r$ S, 3
     5. $\neg p$ DS, 1, 4
     6. p S, 3
     7. $p \,\&\, \neg p$ C, 6, 5

7. 1. $r \rightarrow p$ A
     2. $\neg(r \leftrightarrow (r \,\&\, p))$ AIP
     3. $r \leftrightarrow \neg(r \,\&\, p)$ NB, 2
     4. $(r \rightarrow \neg(r \,\&\, p)) \,\&\, (\neg(r \,\&\, p) \rightarrow r)$ B, 3
     5. $r \rightarrow \neg(r \,\&\, p)$ S, 4
     6. $r \rightarrow r$ SI
     7. $r \rightarrow (r \,\&\, p)$ CC, 6, 1
     8. $(r \,\&\, p) \rightarrow (r \,\&\, p)$ SI
     9. $\neg(r \,\&\, p) \vee (r \,\&\, p)$ MC, 8
     10. $\neg \neg(\neg(r \,\&\, p) \vee (r \,\&\, p))$ DN, 9
     11. $\neg(\neg \neg(r \,\&\, p) \,\&\, \neg(r \,\&\, p))$ DM, 10
     12. $\neg((r \,\&\, p) \,\&\, \neg(r \,\&\, p))$ DN, 11
     13. $r \rightarrow ((r \,\&\, p) \,\&\, \neg(r \,\&\, p))$ CC, 5, 7
     14. $\neg r$ MT, 13, 12
     15. $\neg \neg(r \,\&\, p)$ BE, 3, 14
     16. $r \,\&\, p$ DN, 15
     17. r S, 16
     18. $r \,\&\, \neg r$ C, 17, 14

8.
1.	$r \leftrightarrow (r \& p)$	A
2.	$\neg(r \to p)$	AIP
3.	$r \& \neg p$	NC, 2
4.	r	S, 3
5.	$r \& p$	BE, 1, 4
6.	p	S, 5
7.	$\neg p$	S, 3
8.	$p \& \neg p$	C, 6, 7

9.
1.	$r \vee p$	A
2.	$\neg r \& s$	A
3.	$\neg(p \vee q)$	AIP
4.	$\neg p \& \neg q$	DM, 3
5.	$\neg p$	S, 4
6.	r	DS, 1, 5
7.	$\neg r$	S, 2
8.	$r \& \neg r$	C, 6, 7

10.
1.	$r \to p$	A
2.	$q \to r$	A
3.	$\neg(\neg q \vee p)$	AIP
4.	$\neg\neg q \& \neg p$	DM, 3
5.	$\neg p$	S, 4
6.	$\neg r$	MT, 1, 5
7.	$\neg q$	MT, 2, 6
8.	$\neg\neg q$	S, 4
9.	q	DN, 8
10.	$q \& \neg q$	C, 9, 7

11.
1.	$\neg r \vee \neg q$	A
2.	$\neg\neg(r \& \neg\neg q)$	AIP
3.	$r \& \neg\neg q$	DN, 2
4.	r	S, 3
5.	$\neg q$	DS, 1, 4
6.	$\neg\neg q$	S, 3
7.	$\neg q \& \neg\neg q$	C, 5, 6

12.
1.	$\neg(r \& \neg p) \vee \neg r$	A
2.	$\neg(r \to p)$	AIP
3.	$r \& \neg p$	NC, 2
4.	$\neg\neg(r \& \neg p)$	DN, 3
5.	$\neg r$	DS, 1, 4
6.	r	S, 3
7.	$r \& \neg r$	C, 6, 5

18.
1.	$(r \& \neg p) \to \neg q$	A
2.	q	A
3.	$\neg(\neg r \vee (r \& p))$	AIP
4.	$\neg\neg r \& \neg(r \& p)$	DM, 3
5.	$\neg\neg q$	DN, 2
6.	$\neg(r \& \neg p)$	MT, 1, 5
7.	$\neg r \vee \neg\neg p$	DM, 6
8.	$\neg\neg r$	S, 4
9.	$\neg\neg p$	DS, 7, 8
10.	$\neg(r \& p)$	S, 4
11.	$\neg r \vee \neg p$	DM, 10
12.	$\neg p$	DS, 11, 8
13.	$\neg p \& \neg\neg p$	C, 12, 9

24.
1.	$r \leftrightarrow p$	A
2.	$\neg(\neg r \leftrightarrow \neg p)$	AIP
3.	$\neg\neg r \leftrightarrow \neg p$	NB, 2
4.	$r \leftrightarrow \neg p$	DN, 3
5.	$(r \to p) \& (p \to r)$	B, 1
6.	$(r \to \neg p) \& (\neg p \to r)$	B, 4
7.	$r \to p$	S, 5
8.	$r \to \neg p$	S, 6
9.	$r \to (p \& \neg p)$	CC, 7, 8
10.	$p \to p$	SI
11.	$\neg p \vee p$	MC, 10
12.	$\neg\neg(\neg p \vee p)$	DN, 11
13.	$\neg(\neg\neg p \& \neg p)$	DM, 12
14.	$\neg(p \& \neg p)$	DN, 13
15.	$\neg r$	MT, 9, 14
16.	$\neg p$	BE, 1, 15
17.	$\neg\neg p$	BE, 4, 15
18.	$\neg p \& \neg\neg p$	C, 16, 17

30.

1.	$(s \mathbin{\&} \neg q) \to \neg r$	A
2.	$(p \to \neg s) \leftrightarrow \neg r$	A
3.	$\neg(r \leftrightarrow (q \mathbin{\&} (s \mathbin{\&} p)))$	AIP
4.	$\neg r \leftrightarrow (q \mathbin{\&} (s \mathbin{\&} p))$	NB, 3
5.	$(\neg r \to (q \mathbin{\&} (s \mathbin{\&} p))) \mathbin{\&} ((q \mathbin{\&} (s \mathbin{\&} p)) \to \neg r)$	B, 4
6.	$\neg r \to (q \mathbin{\&} (s \mathbin{\&} p))$	S, 5
7.	$(q \mathbin{\&} (s \mathbin{\&} p)) \to (s \mathbin{\&} p)$	W
8.	$\neg r \to (s \mathbin{\&} p)$	HS, 6, 7
9.	$\neg r \to (p \mathbin{\&} s)$	Cm, 8
10.	$\neg r \to \neg(p \to \neg s)$	NC, 9
11.	$(p \to \neg s) \to r$	Tr, 10
12.	$((p \to \neg s) \to \neg r) \mathbin{\&} (\neg r \to (p \to \neg s))$	B, 2
13.	$\neg r \to (p \to \neg s)$	S, 12
14.	$\neg r \to r$	HS, 13, 11
15.	$\neg\neg r \vee r$	MC, 14
16.	$r \vee r$	DN, 15
17.	r	I, 16
18.	$(p \to \neg s) \to \neg r$	S, 12
19.	$\neg\neg r$	DN, 17
20.	$\neg(p \to \neg s)$	MT, 18, 19
21.	$p \mathbin{\&} \neg\neg s$	NC, 20
22.	p	S, 21
23.	$\neg\neg s$	S, 21
24.	s	DN, 23
25.	$\neg(s \mathbin{\&} \neg q)$	MT, 1, 19
26.	$\neg s \vee \neg\neg q$	DM, 25
27.	$\neg\neg s$	DN, 24
28.	$\neg\neg q$	DS, 26, 27
29.	q	DN, 28
30.	$s \mathbin{\&} p$	C, 24, 22
31.	$q \mathbin{\&} (s \mathbin{\&} p)$	C, 29, 30
32.	$(q \mathbin{\&} (s \mathbin{\&} p)) \to \neg r$	S, 5
33.	$\neg r$	MP, 32, 31
34.	$r \mathbin{\&} \neg r$	C, 17, 33

36.

1.	$p \mathbin{\&} \neg q$	A
2.	$\neg\neg(p \to q)$	AIP
3.	$p \to q$	DN, 2
4.	p	S, 1
5.	q	MP, 3, 4
6.	$\neg q$	S, 1
7.	$q \mathbin{\&} \neg q$	C, 5, 6

42.

1.	$\neg((p \mathbin{\&} q) \to p)$	AIP
2.	$(p \mathbin{\&} q) \mathbin{\&} \neg p$	NC, 1
3.	$p \mathbin{\&} q$	S, 2
4.	$\neg p$	S, 2
5.	p	S, 3
6.	$p \mathbin{\&} \neg p$	C, 5, 4

48.

1.	$(p \mathbin{\&} q) \vee r$	A
2.	$\neg((q \mathbin{\&} p) \vee r)$	AIP
3.	$\neg(q \mathbin{\&} p) \mathbin{\&} \neg r$	DM, 2
4.	$\neg r$	S, 3
5.	$p \mathbin{\&} q$	DS, 1, 4
6.	$\neg(q \mathbin{\&} p)$	S, 3
7.	$q \mathbin{\&} p$	Cm, 5
8.	$(q \mathbin{\&} p) \mathbin{\&} \neg(q \mathbin{\&} p)$	C, 7, 6

54.

1.	$\neg(p \mathbin{\&} q)$	A
2.	$\neg q \to r$	A
3.	$r \to \neg p$	A
4.	$\neg\neg p$	AIP
5.	$\neg p \vee \neg q$	DM, 1
6.	$\neg q$	DS, 5, 4
7.	$\neg r$	MT, 3, 4
8.	$\neg\neg q$	MT, 2, 6
9.	$\neg q \mathbin{\&} \neg\neg q$	C, 6, 8

8.7 Indirect Proof from 8.6

1.
1.	$p \rightarrow \neg q$	A
2.	$r \rightarrow p$	A
3.	$\neg(q \rightarrow \neg r)$	AIP
4.	$q \& \neg \neg r$	NC, 3
5.	q	S, 4
6.	$\neg \neg q$	DN, 5
7.	$\neg p$	MT, 1, 6
8.	$\neg r$	MT, 2, 7
9.	$\neg \neg r$	S, 4
10.	$\neg r \& \neg \neg r$	C, 8, 9

2.
1.	$p \rightarrow q$	A
2.	$q \rightarrow p$	A
3.	$\neg((p \rightarrow r) \rightarrow (q \rightarrow r))$	AIP
4.	$(p \rightarrow r) \& \neg(q \rightarrow r)$	NC, 3
5.	$\neg(q \rightarrow r)$	S, 4
6.	$q \& \neg r$	NC, 5
7.	q	S, 6
8.	p	MP, 2, 7
9.	$p \rightarrow r$	S, 4
10.	r	MP, 9, 8
11.	$\neg r$	S, 6
12.	$r \& \neg r$	C, 10, 11

3.
1.	$p \vee q$	A
2.	$q \rightarrow p$	A
3.	$p \rightarrow r$	A
4.	$\neg r \vee s$	A
5.	$\neg s$	AIP
6.	$\neg r$	DS, 4, 5
7.	$\neg p$	MT, 3, 6
8.	q	DS, 1, 7
9.	$\neg q$	MT, 2, 7
10.	$q \& \neg q$	C, 8, 9

4.
1.	$p \leftrightarrow q$	A
2.	$\neg r \rightarrow \neg q$	A
3.	$r \rightarrow \neg q$	A
4.	$\neg(\neg p \vee \neg s)$	AIP
5.	$\neg \neg p \& \neg \neg s$	DM, 4
6.	$p \& \neg \neg s$	DN, 5
7.	p	S, 6
8.	q	BE, 1, 7
9.	$\neg \neg q$	DN, 8
10.	$\neg \neg r$	MT, 2, 9
11.	$\neg r$	MT, 3, 9
12.	$\neg r \& \neg \neg r$	C, 11,10

5.
1.	$p \rightarrow (q \rightarrow r)$	A
2.	$\neg r$	A
3.	$\neg(\neg q \vee \neg p)$	AIP
4.	$\neg \neg q \& \neg \neg p$	DM, 3
5.	$\neg \neg q$	S, 4
6.	q	DN, 5
7.	$q \& \neg r$	C, 6, 2
8.	$\neg(q \rightarrow r)$	NC, 7
9.	$\neg p$	MT, 1, 8
10.	$\neg \neg p$	S, 4
11.	$\neg p \& \neg \neg p$	C, 9, 10

6.
1.	$(p \vee q) \rightarrow (r \& s)$	A
2.	$\neg p \rightarrow \neg t$	A
3.	$\neg(\neg r \rightarrow \neg t)$	AIP
4.	$\neg r \& \neg \neg t$	NC, 3
5.	$\neg \neg t$	S, 4
6.	$\neg \neg p$	MT, 2, 5
7.	p	DN, 6
8.	$p \vee q$	Ad, 7
9.	$r \& s$	MP, 1, 8
10.	r	S, 9
11.	$\neg r$	S, 4
12.	$r \& \neg r$	C, 10, 11

12.
1.	$p \rightarrow q$	A
2.	$r \rightarrow \neg q$	A
3.	$\neg(\neg r \vee \neg p)$	AIP
4.	$\neg \neg r \& \neg \neg p$	DM, 3
5.	$\neg \neg r$	S, 4
6.	r	DN, 5
7.	$\neg q$	MP, 2, 6
8.	$\neg \neg p$	S, 4
9.	p	DN, 8
10.	q	MP, 1, 9
11.	$q \& \neg q$	C, 10, 7

18.
1.	$(p \& q) \rightarrow r$	A
2.	$r \rightarrow s$	A
3.	$s \rightarrow (\neg q \vee t)$	A
4.	$\neg p \rightarrow (\neg q \& \neg r)$	A
5.	$\neg(t \vee \neg q)$	AIP
6.	$\neg(\neg q \vee t)$	Cm, 5
7.	$\neg s$	MT, 6, 3
8.	$\neg r$	MT, 2, 7
9.	$\neg(p \& q)$	MT, 1, 8
10.	$\neg p \vee \neg q$	DM, 9
11.	$\neg t \& \neg \neg q$	DM, 5
12.	$\neg \neg q$	S, 11
13.	$\neg p$	DS, 10, 12
14.	$\neg q \& \neg r$	MP, 4, 13
15.	$\neg q$	S, 14
16.	$\neg q \& \neg \neg q$	C, 15, 12

24.
1.	p	A
2.	$\neg(p \vee r)$	A
3.	$\neg q$	AIP
4.	$\neg p \,\&\, \neg r$	DM, 2
5.	$\neg p$	S, 4
6.	$p \,\&\, \neg p$	C, 1, 5

30.
1.	$(\neg p \to q) \vee r$	A
2.	$\neg(\neg p \to (q \vee r))$	AIP
3.	$\neg p \,\&\, \neg(q \vee r)$	NC, 2
4.	$\neg p$	S, 3
5.	$\neg(q \vee r)$	S, 3
6.	$\neg q \,\&\, \neg r$	DM, 5
7.	$\neg r$	S, 6
8.	$\neg p \to q$	DS, 1, 7
9.	q	MP, 8, 4
10.	$\neg q$	S, 6
11.	$q \,\&\, \neg q$	C, 9, 10

36.
1.	$p \leftrightarrow q$	A
2.	$\neg(\neg q \leftrightarrow \neg p)$	AIP
3.	$q \leftrightarrow \neg p$	NB, 2
4.	$(p \to q) \,\&\, (q \to p)$	B, 1
5.	$p \to q$	S, 4
6.	$(q \to \neg p) \,\&\, (\neg p \to q)$	B, 3
7.	$q \to \neg p$	S, 6
8.	$p \to \neg p$	HS, 5, 7
9.	$\neg p \vee \neg p$	MC, 8
10.	$\neg p$	I, 9
11.	q	BE, 3, 10
12.	p	BE, 1, 11
13.	$p \,\&\, \neg p$	C, 12, 10

42.
1.	$p \vee q$	A
2.	$\neg q \vee r$	A
3.	$\neg(p \vee r)$	AIP
4.	$\neg p \,\&\, \neg r$	DM, 3
5.	$\neg p$	S, 4
6.	q	DS, 1, 5
7.	$\neg r$	S, 4
8.	$\neg q$	DS, 2, 7
9.	$q \,\&\, \neg q$	C, 6, 8

48.
1.	$\neg s \to \neg k$	A
2.	$(s \,\&\, t) \to (p \leftrightarrow q)$	A
3.	$\neg(\neg p \vee q)$	A
4.	$\neg(t \to \neg k)$	AIP
5.	$\neg\neg p \,\&\, \neg q$	DM, 3
6.	$t \,\&\, \neg\neg k$	NC, 4
7.	$\neg\neg k$	S, 6
8.	$\neg\neg s$	MT, 1, 7
9.	s	DN, 8
10.	t	S, 6
11.	$s \,\&\, t$	C, 9, 10
12.	$p \leftrightarrow q$	MP, 2, 11
13.	$\neg\neg p$	S, 5
14.	p	DN, 13
15.	q	BE, 12, 14
16.	$\neg q$	S, 5
17.	$q \,\&\, \neg q$	C, 15, 16

54.
1.	$\neg((p \to q) \to (\neg q \to \neg p))$	AIP
2.	$(p \to q) \,\&\, \neg(\neg q \to \neg p)$	NC, 1
3.	$(p \to q) \,\&\, \neg(p \to q)$	Tr, 2

60.
1.	$\neg((p \vee (q \vee r)) \to (q \vee (p \vee r)))$	AIP
2.	$(p \vee (q \vee r)) \,\&\, \neg(q \vee (p \vee r))$	NC, 1
3.	$(p \vee (q \vee r)) \,\&\, \neg((p \vee r) \vee q)$	Cm, 2
4.	$(p \vee (q \vee r)) \,\&\, \neg(p \vee (r \vee q))$	As, 3
5.	$(p \vee (q \vee r)) \,\&\, \neg(p \vee (q \vee r))$	Cm, 4

Chapter 9
SYLLOGISMS

9.1 Categorical Sentences

1. No.   **2.** No.   **3.** General.   **4.** No.   **5.** General.   **6.** No.   **12.** General.

18. General.   **24.** Categorical-Universal affirmative.

30. Categorical-Universal affirmative.   **36.** Categorical-Universal affirmative.

9.2 Diagramming Categorical Sentence Forms

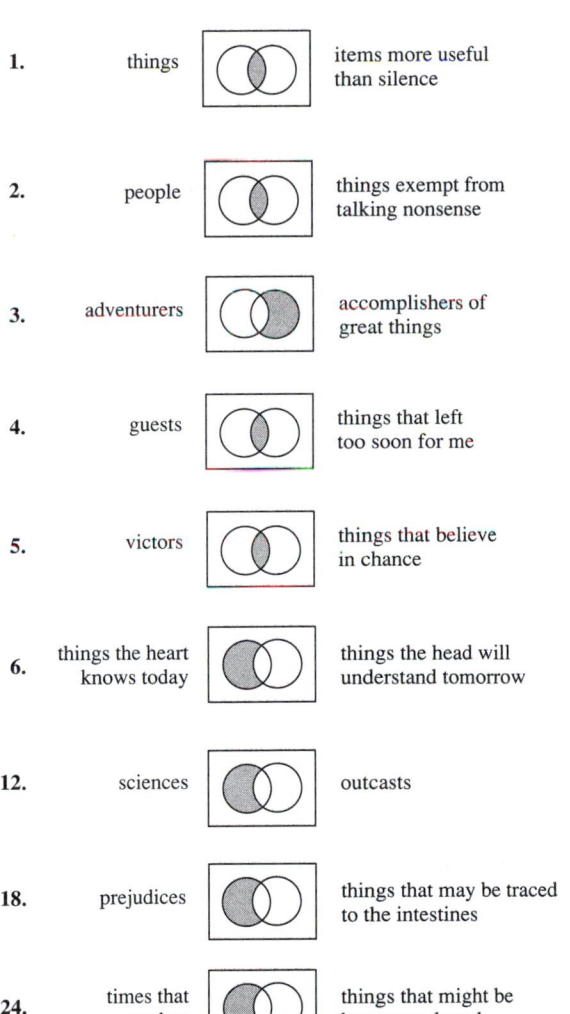

1. things — items more useful than silence

2. people — things exempt from talking nonsense

3. adventurers — accomplishers of great things

4. guests — things that left too soon for me

5. victors — things that believe in chance

6. things the heart knows today — things the head will understand tomorrow

12. sciences — outcasts

18. prejudices — things that may be traced to the intestines

24. times that are lost — things that might be better employed

30. those who have money those who ought to have money

36. facts sacred things

facts profane things

9.3 Immediate Inference

1. (a) All things worth two in the bush are birds in hand. (b) No birds in hand are not worth two in the bush. Equivalent. (c) All things not worth two in the bush are not birds in hand. Equivalent. (d) Some birds in the hand are not worth two in the bush.

2. (a) All blessed things are peacemakers. (b) No peacemakers are not blessed. Equivalent. (c) All nonblessed things are nonpeacemaking things. Equivalent. (d) Some peacemakers are not blessed.

3. (a) Some things worth reading twice are books. Equivalent. (b) Some things worth reading twice are not nonbooks. Equivalent. (c) Some things not worth reading twice are not books. (d) No books are worth reading twice.

4. (a) All things which save nine are stitches in time. (b) No stitches in time do not save nine. Equivalent. (c) All things which do not save nine are not stitches in time. Equivalent. (d) Some stitches in time do not save nine.

5. This sentence may be ambiguous. On one reading: (a) All those who never felt a wound jest at scars. (b) No one who jests at scars has ever felt a wound. Equivalent. (c) All those who have felt a wound do not jest at scars. Equivalent. (d) Some of those who jest at scars have felt a wound. On the other: (a) All those who jest at scars never felt a wound. (b) No one who has never felt a wound fails to jest at scars. Equivalent. (c) All those who do not jest at scars have felt a wound. Equivalent. (d) Some of those who have never felt a wound do not jest at scars.

6. (a) Not one of those who escaped was a Greek at Thermopylae. Equivalent. (b) All of the Greeks at Thermopylae did not escape. Equivalent. (c) Not one of those who did not escape was not a Greek at Thermopylae. (d) Some of the Greeks at Thermopylae escaped.

12. (a) Some men who know they're happy are not happy. (b) Some men who are happy are ignorant that they're happy. Equivalent. (c) Some men who don't know they're happy are not unhappy. Equivalent. (d) All men who are happy know they're happy.

18. (a) No too small things are details. Equivalent. (b) All details are big enough. Equivalent. (c) No thing that's big enough is not a detail. (d) Some details are too small.

24. (a) Nobody saw us. (b) Somebody both saw us and didn't see us. (c) Somebody didn't see us.

30. (a) Either all of us got away, or none of us did. (b) None of us got away. (c) Either all of us got away, or none of us did, or some of us were killed.

36. (a) True. (b) Unknown. (c) Unknown. (d) False. (e) Unknown.
(f) Unknown. (g) True. (h) Unknown. (i) True.

9.4 Syllogisms

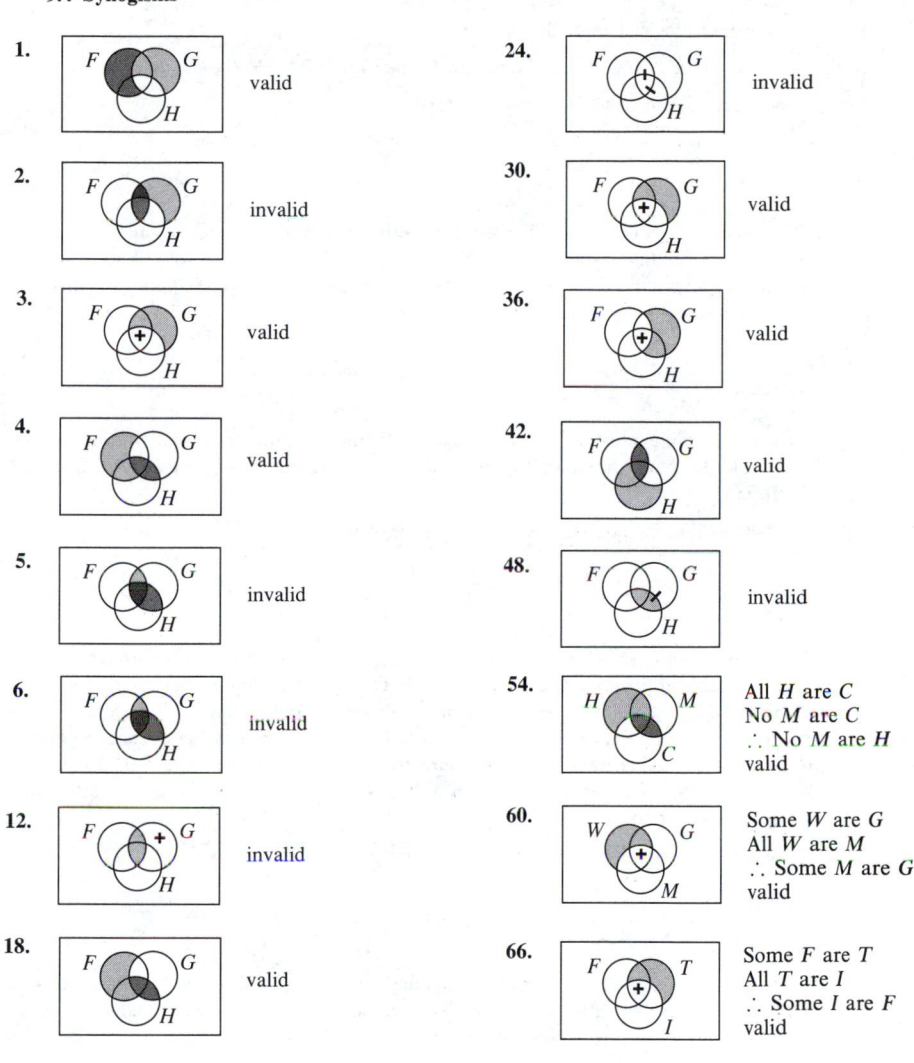

1. valid

2. invalid

3. valid

4. valid

5. invalid

6. invalid

12. invalid

18. valid

24. invalid

30. valid

36. valid

42. valid

48. invalid

54.
All *H* are *C*
No *M* are *C*
∴ No *M* are *H*
valid

60.
Some *W* are *G*
All *W* are *M*
∴ Some *M* are *G*
valid

66.
Some *F* are *T*
All *T* are *I*
∴ Some *I* are *F*
valid

9.5 Rules for Validity

1. Valid. **2.** Invalid (Rule 2b). **3.** Invalid (Rules 1, 2a, and 2b). **4.** Valid.

5. Invalid (Rules 1 and 2a). **6.** Valid. **12.** Invalid (Rule 2a).

18. Invalid (Rule 2b). **24.** Invalid (Rules 1 and 3b). **30.** Invalid (Rule 1).

36. Valid. **42.** Invalid (Rules 2a, 2b, and 3a). **48.** Invalid (Rules 1 and 2b).

54. Invalid (Rules 2a and 2b). **60.** Invalid (Rule 2a). **66.** Invalid (Rules 1 and 2a).

72. Invalid (Rule 1). **78.** Invalid (Rules 1 and 2a). **84.** Valid under both sets of rules.

90. Valid under both sets of rules. **96.** Valid under both sets of rules.

102. God is not in potentiality.   **108.** Some judges are legislators.

114. Nothing about logic is unintelligible.

In the following three answers, F is the minor, G the middle, and H the major term.

120. In the fourth figure, syllogisms have the form:

$$
\begin{array}{cc}
H & G \\
G & F \\
\therefore \quad F & H
\end{array}
$$

If the conclusion is universal affirmative, its subject term is distributed, but its predicate term is undistributed. Occurrences of the major term must agree in distribution, by the rules for validity; similarly for the minor term (Rules 2a and 2b). So, the pattern of distribution would have to be

$$
\begin{array}{cc}
H^U & G \\
G & F^D \\
\therefore \quad F^D & H^U
\end{array}
$$

But then the minor premise would be negative, while the conclusion was affirmative, violating rule 3a. No valid fourth figure syllogism, therefore, has a universal affirmative conclusion.

126. Any syllogism in mood EIO has the pattern of distribution

$$
\begin{array}{cc}
D & D \\
U & U \\
\therefore \quad U & D
\end{array}
$$

No matter which term is the middle term, it must be distributed in the major premise and undistributed and the minor, satisfying Rule 1. The major term must be distributed in the major premise, because both terms there are distributed, and is similarly distributed in the conclusion, satisfying Rule 2a. The minor term is undistributed in the conclusion and in the minor premise, because both terms there are undistributed, satisfying Rule 2b. Finally, the syllogism has a negative conclusion and exactly one negative premise. Thus, every syllogism with mood EIO is valid.

132. Terms in a first figure syllogism have the pattern:

$$
\begin{array}{cc}
G & H \\
F & G \\
\therefore \quad F & H
\end{array}
$$

Suppose such a syllogism had a particular negative premise. By Rule 3a, it would have to have a negative conclusion. H, therefore, would be distributed in the conclusion. By Rule 2a, it would have to be distributed in the major premise as well:

$$
\begin{array}{cc}
G & H^D \\
F & G \\
\therefore \quad F & H^D
\end{array}
$$

Now if G were distributed in the minor premise, the syllogism would have two negative premises, violating Rule 3b. Hence, G must be undistributed there. By Rule 1, however, the occurrences of the middle term must disagree in distribution; G must be distributed in the major premise:

$$
\begin{array}{cc}
G^D & H^D \\
F & G^U \\
\therefore \quad F & H^D
\end{array}
$$

So, if a valid first figure syllogism has a negative premise, it must have a universal negative major premise. No valid first figure syllogisms have a particular negative premise.

9.6 Expanding the Aristotelian Language

1. 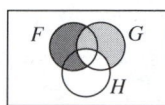 valid

2. 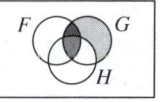 invalid

3. 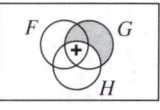 valid

4. 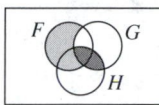 valid

5. 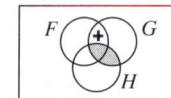 valid

6. 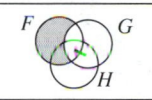 invalid

12. 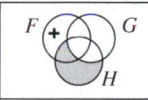 valid

18. 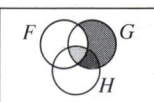 invalid

24. 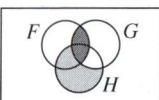 valid

30. 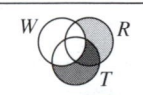 No nonW are R
All T are W
∴ All T are R
invalid

36. 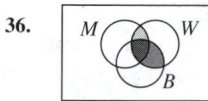 No M are W
All B are nonW
∴ All B are nonM
invalid

42. 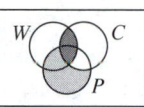 No W are C
No nonC are P
∴ No W are P
valid

48. 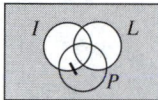 All F are R
No R are E
∴ All E are nonF
valid

54. 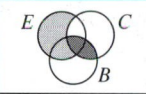 All nonI are L
Some P are nonL
∴ Some P are I
valid

60a. 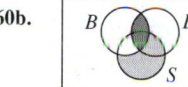 No E are nonC
No C are B
∴ No B are E
valid

60b. 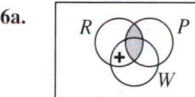 No B are E
All S are B
∴ All S are nonE
valid

66a. 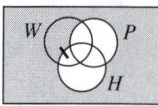 All R are nonP
Some W are R
∴ Some W are nonP
valid

66b. Some W are nonP
All nonH are P
∴ Some W are H
valid

66c. 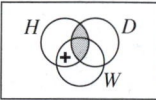 No H are D
Some W are H
∴ Some W are nonD
valid

66d. 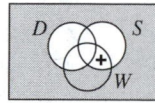 All nonD are S
Some W are nonD
∴ Some W are S
valid

Chapter 10
QUANTIFIERS

10.2 Categorical Sentence Forms

Many English sentences have alternative symbolizations of equal merit. The answers below are not the only ones possible.

1. $\forall x(Mx \rightarrow Gx)$ **2.** $\forall x(Cx \rightarrow Gx)$ **3.** $\neg\exists x(Mx \,\&\, Wx)$ **4.** $\forall x(Cx \rightarrow Sx)$

5. $\neg\exists x(Dx \,\&\, Sx)$ **6.** $\forall x(Fx \rightarrow Rx)$ **12.** $\forall x(Gx \rightarrow \neg Lx)$ **18.** $\forall x(Ix \rightarrow Ax)$

24. $\neg\exists x(Mx \,\&\, Ox)$ **30.** $\forall x(Ax \rightarrow Sx) \,\&\, \forall x(Gx \rightarrow Lx)$

10.3 Polyadic Predicates

Throughout the following, 'P' symbolizes 'is a person'.

1. $\forall x(Rx \rightarrow Lxm)$ **2.** $\forall x(Rx \rightarrow \exists yLxy)$ **3.** $\neg\exists x(Rx \,\&\, \forall yLxy)$

4. $\neg\exists x(Px \,\&\, \forall y((Ty \,\&\, Siy) \rightarrow Kxy))$ **5.** $\neg\exists x(Px \,\&\, \exists y((Ty \,\&\, Siy) \,\&\, Kxy))$

6. $\exists x(Px \,\&\, \exists y((Ty \,\&\, Siy) \,\&\, Kxy))$ **12.** $Rl \,\&\, (\forall xFlx \,\&\, \forall x\neg Slx)$

18. $\neg\exists x\exists y(Px \,\&\, Ixy)$ **24.** $\forall x((Dx \,\&\, Ax) \rightarrow \forall y(Gy \rightarrow \neg Lxy))$

30. $\neg\exists x(Bx \,\&\, \neg\exists y(Dy \,\&\, Cxy))$, where '$C$' symbolizes 'is carried on with'

36. $\forall x(Axh \rightarrow Arx)$

10.4 The Language QL

1. (b)   **2.** (a)   **3.** (b)   **4.** (a)   **5.** (b)   **6.** (a)   **12.** (b)   **18.** (b)

24. (b)   **30.** (b)   **36.** (b)

42. (a) Hcc; formula   (b) Hdd; formula   (c) Hxx; not a formula
     (d) Hcc; formula   (e) Hcc; formula

48. (a) $Fxc \leftrightarrow \exists yFcy$; not a formula   (b) $Fxd \leftrightarrow \exists yFdy$; not a formula
     (c) $Fxx \leftrightarrow \exists yFdy$; not a formula   (d) $Fxc \leftrightarrow \exists yFyy$; not a formula
     (e) $Fyc \leftrightarrow \exists yFdy$; not a formula

54. true   **60.** true   **66.** false   **72.** true   **78.** false   **84.** false   **90.** true

96. false   **102.** false   **108.** true   **114.** true   **120.** true

Chapter 11
SYMBOLIZATION

11.1 Noun Phrases

1. intersective   **2.** intersective

3. nonintersective: e.g., the same person may be a fast typist and a slow runner.

4. intersective   **5.** intersective   **6.** intersective   **12.** intersective

18. $\neg\exists x(Px \,\&\, \forall y(Ty \rightarrow Rxy))$, where '$R$' symbolizes 'tell'.

24. $\exists x((Tx \,\&\, \exists y(Uy \,\&\, Wxy)) \,\&\, \forall z(Pz \rightarrow \neg Rxz))$, where '$R$' symbolizes 'please'.

30. Ambiguous: $\neg\exists x(Px \,\&\, \forall y\forall z((Py \,\&\, Tz \,\&\, Ryz) \rightarrow Lxz))$ or
     $\forall y(Py \rightarrow \neg\exists x(Px \,\&\, \forall z((Tz \,\&\, Ryz) \rightarrow Lxz)))$

36. nonrestrictive: $\exists x((Ax \& Sx) \& Hjx) \& \forall x(Nx \rightarrow \exists y(Ty \& Cjyx))$, where '$S$' symbolizes 'strong for an army' and 'C' symbolizes 'collect . . . from'.

42. restrictive: $\forall x(Nx \rightarrow \forall y((Py \& Wyx) \rightarrow Sxy))$

48. Both of the following are options, depending on how literally one wants to take the English sentence. (The same sort of choice arises with some of the sentences below.) $\forall x((Mx \& \exists y(Jy \& Hxy)) \rightarrow \exists y(Cy \& Hxy))$ or $\forall x((Mx \& \exists y(Jy \& Hxy)) \rightarrow Fy)$, where '$F$' symbolizes 'has a chance'.

54. $\forall x((Mx \& \forall y(Sy \rightarrow \neg Txy)) \rightarrow \forall y(Gy \rightarrow \neg Axy))$, where '$S$' symbolizes 'small ill' and 'G' symbolizes 'great thing'. This symbolization doesn't do full justice to the meaning of the English sentence, since a person who cannot tolerate small ills isn't necessarily bothered by absolutely every small ill (but certainly is put off by more than one).

60. $\forall x(Pxx \rightarrow (Mx \lor Fx))$, where '$P$' symbolizes 'is pleased with'.

66. $\forall x \forall y(Pxy \rightarrow Cxy)$, where '$P$' symbolizes 'pay too much for' and 'C' symbolizes 'can buy'.

72. $\forall x(Gx \rightarrow \forall y((My \& Iyd) \rightarrow \neg Rxy))$

78. $\forall x((Bx \& Oxi) \rightarrow (Wx \& \forall z(Txiz \rightarrow Fz)))$ This symbolization doesn't do full justice to the meaning of the English sentence, since the latter suggests that it is the aggregate of the women's looks encountered which did the teaching, and not each of the looks individually.

84. $\forall x((Mx \& \forall y \neg Fxy) \rightarrow \forall y((Py \& \forall z(Pz \rightarrow Fzy)) \rightarrow Axy))$, where '$A$' corresponds to 'is as powerful as.'

11.2 Verb Phrases

1. intransitive

2. ambiguous: on one meaning, intransitive: 'John walks fast'; on another, transitive: 'John walks the dog'

3. transitive   **4.** intransitive

5. ambiguous: transitive ('Pat turned the corner', 'Moose turned the box on its side') or intransitive ('Pat turned to see where the noise had come from')

6. intransitive

12. ambiguous: transitive ('John did the dishes') or intransitive ('How do you do?')

18. intransitive

24. transitive or clausally complemented: 'Mary considered the plan'; 'Mary considered the plan to be too risky'

30. $Cih \& (\exists x((Sx \& Oxh) \& \neg Rihx) \& \exists x((Sx \& Oxi) \& Rihx))$, where '$C$' corresponds to 'care about', 'h' to 'truth', 'S' to 'sake', 'O' to 'is of', and 'R' to 'care about . . . for'; or $\neg Fihh \& Fihi$, where 'F' symbolizes 'care about . . . for the sake of'.

36. $\forall x(Mx \rightarrow (\neg Nxo \rightarrow Ex))$, where '$N$' symbolizes 'need to take . . . into account' and 'o' symbolizes 'reality'.

42. $\forall x \forall y \forall z(((Pxz \lor Wyz) \rightarrow (\neg Gxz \& \neg Gyz)) \& Ggz)$, where '$G$' symbolizes 'giveth the increase in'.

48. $\forall x(Sx \rightarrow (Dix \& Aix))$

54. $\forall x(Bx \rightarrow \exists y(((Gy \& (Sy \& Ly)) \& Hxy) \& Wxy))$, where '$B$' symbolizes 'human being', 'L' 'little for a soul', 'H' 'have', and 'W' 'want to rouge . . . up'.

60. $\forall x(Cx \rightarrow Px) \& \forall x(Px \rightarrow (\forall y(Hxy \rightarrow Sxy) \& \exists y(Ry \& Gxy)))$, where '$C$' symbolizes 'consistent altruist' and 'P' symbolizes 'poor'.

66. $\forall x(Sx \rightarrow (Cx \,\&\, Ex))$ **72.** $\forall x(Tmx \rightarrow Smx) \,\&\, \forall x(Tbx \rightarrow Sbx)$

78. $\forall x(Cx \rightarrow \forall y(Py \rightarrow (Dyx \rightarrow \exists z(Pz \,\&\, Tzyy))))$, where '$T$' symbolizes 'tell . . . that . . . is wrong'.

84. $\forall x(Lx \rightarrow (\forall y(Fy \rightarrow Sxy) \,\&\, \forall y(Wy \rightarrow Bxy)))$

90. $\forall x \forall y(((Mx \,\&\, Sx) \,\&\, Fxy) \rightarrow Iyx)$, where '$S$' symbolizes 'superior for a man' and 'F' symbolizes 'seek'.

96. $\forall x(Px \rightarrow Qx)$, where '$P$' symbolizes 'pessimist' and 'Q' symbolizes 'prophet'.

102. $\forall x((Hx \,\&\, Mx) \rightarrow \exists y \exists z((Cz \,\&\, Oyz) \,\&\, Iyx))$, where '$O$' symbolizes 'is of'; or $\forall x((Hx \,\&\, Mx) \rightarrow Sx)$, where '$S$' symbolizes 'in . . . there is something of a child'.

108. $\forall x((Mx \,\&\, \neg\exists y(Py \,\&\, Wxy)) \rightarrow \neg\exists y((Ay \vee By) \,\&\, Hxy))$, where '$P$' symbolizes 'passion', 'W' 'with', 'A' 'principle of action', and 'B' 'motive to act'.

11.3 Definitions

1. not formally adequate: ineliminable ('one's': not a formula)

2. formally adequate   **3.** not formally adequate: creative (no uniqueness)

4. formally adequate   **5.** formally adequate   **6.** formally adequate

12. formally adequate   **18.** formally adequate   **24.** formally adequate

30. not formally adequate: ineliminable ('yourself': not a formula)

36. formally adequate   **42.** formally adequate   **48.** formally adequate

54. formally adequate   **60.** not formally adequate: creative (no uniqueness)

Chapter 12
QUANTIFIED TABLEAUX

12.2 Strategies

1.

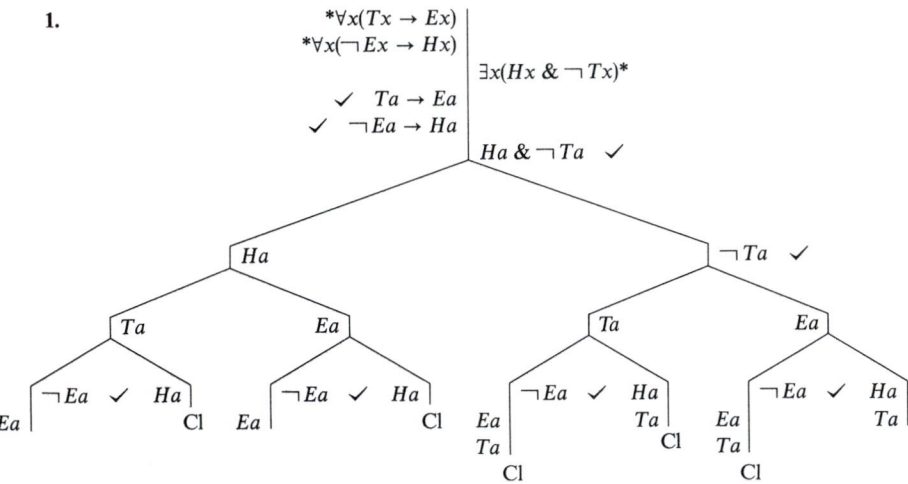

Invalid

2.   ✓ ∃x(Mx & Ex)
          ✓ ∃x(Sx & Mx)

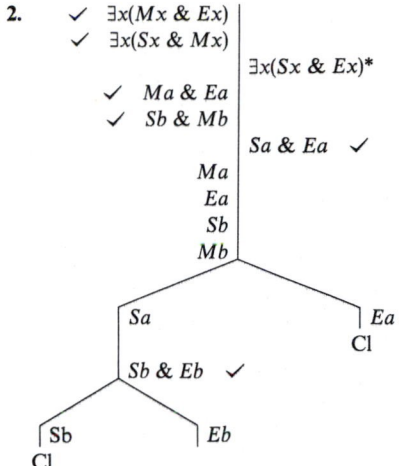

                     ∃x(Sx & Ex)*

    ✓ Ma & Ea
    ✓ Sb & Mb

               Sa & Ea ✓

          Ma
          Ea
          Sb
          Mb

      Sa   Ea
                      Cl

    Sb & Eb ✓

  Sb   Eb
  Cl

Invalid.

3. *∀x((Hx & Fx) → (Qx & Cx))
     *∀x((Hx & Fx) → ¬Dx)
        *∀x(Hx → Dx)

                ¬∃x(Hx & Fx) ✓

     ✓ ∃x(Hx & Fx)
       ✓ Ha & Fa
  ✓ (Ha & Fa) → (Qa & Ca)
    ✓ (Ha & Fa) → ¬Da
      ✓ Ha → Da
        Ha
        Fa

     Ha & Fa ✓   ✓ ¬Da
                       Da

  Ha   Fa   Ha   Da
  Cl   Cl   Cl   Cl

Valid.

4.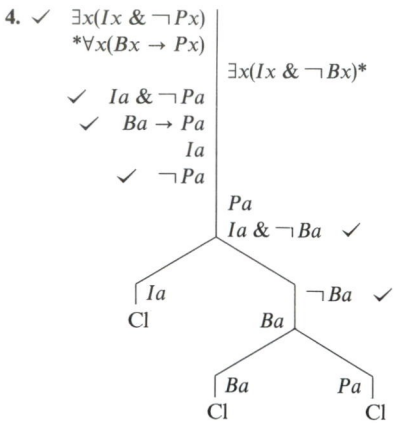

Valid.

5.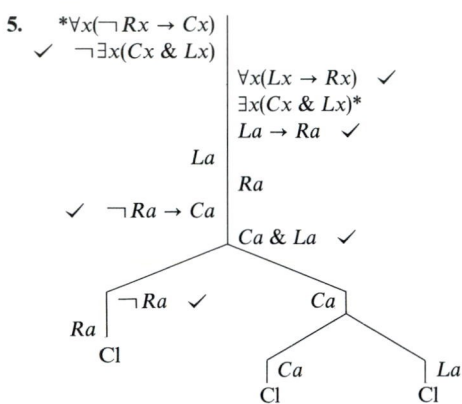

Valid.

6. ✓   *∀x((Bx & ¬Sx) → Lx)

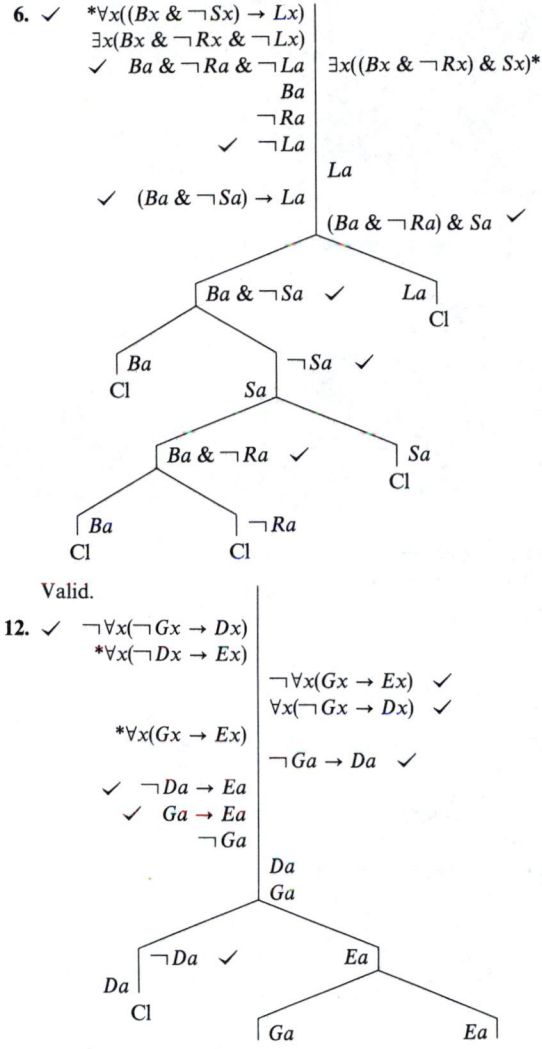

Valid.

12. ✓   ¬∀x(¬Gx → Dx)

Invalid.

18.

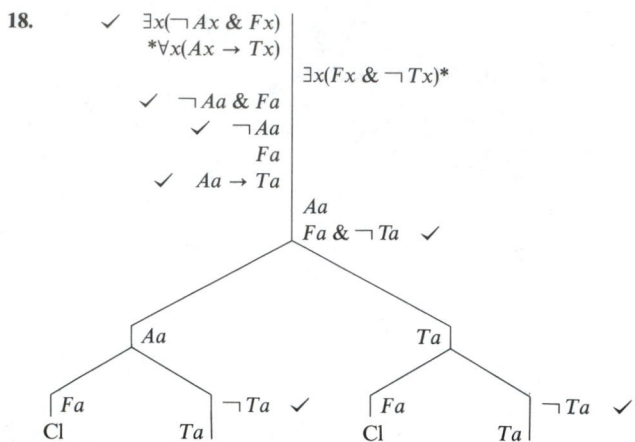

Invalid.

24. *∀x(Fx → ∀y(Sy → Axy))
  *∀x(Sx → ∀y(Cy → Axy))

  ∀x((Fx & Sx) → Cx) ✓
  (Fa & Sa) → Ca ✓

  ✓ Fa → ∀y(Sy → Aay)
  ✓ Sa → ∀y(Cy → Aay)
        ✓ Fa & Sa

                    Ca
              Fa
              Sa

        Fa   *∀y(Sy → Aay)
        Cl

              Sa   *∀y(Cy → Aay)
              Cl   ✓ Sa → Aaa
                        ✓ Ca → Aaa

                    Sa   Aaa
                    Cl

                          Ca   Aaa

Invalid.

30. ✓ ∃x(Px & ¬Px)
      ✓ Pa & ¬Pa
              Pa
        ✓ ¬Pa
                      | Pa
                      Cl

Contradictory.

36.   ∀xPx → ¬∃x¬Px ✓
              *∀xPx
                        ¬∃x¬Px ✓
        ✓ ∃x¬Px
        ✓ ¬Pa
                        Pa
                    Pa |
                        Cl

Valid.

42. ✓ ¬∃x∀y((Ty & Siy) → Sxy)

$$
\begin{array}{l}
\exists x \forall y((Ty \ \& \ Siy) \rightarrow Sxy) \ * \\
\forall y((Ty \ \& \ Siy) \rightarrow Siy) \ \checkmark \\
(Ta \ \& \ Sia) \rightarrow Sia \ \checkmark
\end{array}
$$

✓ Ta & Sia

Sia

Ta
Sia

Cl

Contradictory.

48.

$$
\begin{array}{l}
\forall x((Gx \ \& \ \forall y(Gy \rightarrow Fxy)) \rightarrow Fxx) \ \checkmark \\
(Ga \ \& \ \forall y(Gy \rightarrow Fay)) \rightarrow Faa \ \checkmark
\end{array}
$$

✓ Ga & ∀y(Gy → Fay)

Faa

Ga
*∀y(Gy → Fay)
✓ Ga → Faa

| Ga | Faa |
| Cl | Cl |

Valid.

54. *∀x(Gx ↔ ∀yLxy)

∀x(Gx → ∃yLxy) ✓
Ga → ∃yLay ✓

✓ Ga ↔ ∀yLay
Ga

∃yLay*

Ga	Ga
*∀yLay	∀yLay
Laa	Cl

Laa
Cl

Follows.

60. *∀x(Gx ↔ ∀yLxy)

∀x∃yLyx ✓
∃yLya*

Ga ↔ ∀yLay

Laa

Ga	Ga
*∀yLay	∀yLay ✓
Laa	Lab
Cl	Lba

Gb	Gb
*∀yLby	∀yLby ✓
Lba	Lbc
Cl	

Does not follow.

67. $*\forall x(Gx \rightarrow \exists y(Fy \& Hy))$

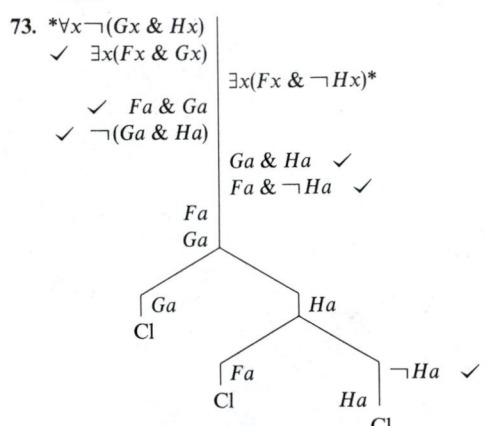

$\forall x \neg Fx \rightarrow \neg \exists z Gz$ ✓

$*\forall x \neg Fx$

$\neg \exists z Gz$ ✓

✓ $\exists z Gz$

Ga

✓ $Ga \rightarrow \exists y(Fy \& Hy)$

Ga ✓ $\exists y(Fy \& Hy)$
Cl   ✓ $Fb \& Hb$
         Fb
         Hb
      ✓ $\neg Fb$ | Fb
               Cl

Valid.

73. $*\forall x \neg (Gx \& Hx)$

✓ $\exists x(Fx \& Gx)$

$\exists x(Fx \& \neg Hx)*$

✓ $Fa \& Ga$

✓ $\neg (Ga \& Ha)$

$Ga \& Ha$ ✓
$Fa \& \neg Ha$ ✓

Fa
Ga

Ga | Ha
Cl

Fa | $\neg Ha$ ✓
Cl Ha |
          Cl

Valid.

79. $*\forall x(Hx \rightarrow \neg Gx)$

✓ $\neg \exists x(Fx \& \neg Gx)$

$\forall x \neg (Fx \& Hx)$ ✓
$\exists x(Fx \& \neg Gx)*$
$\neg (Fa \& Ha)$ ✓
$Fa \& \neg Ga$

✓ $Ha \rightarrow \neg Ga$
✓ $Fa \& Ha$
Fa
Ha

Ha ✓ $\neg Ga$
Cl Ga

Fa | $\neg Ga$ ✓
Cl Ga |
          Cl

Valid.

85. ✓   ∃xFx → ∀y(Gy → Hy)
      ✓   ∃xJx → ∃xGx

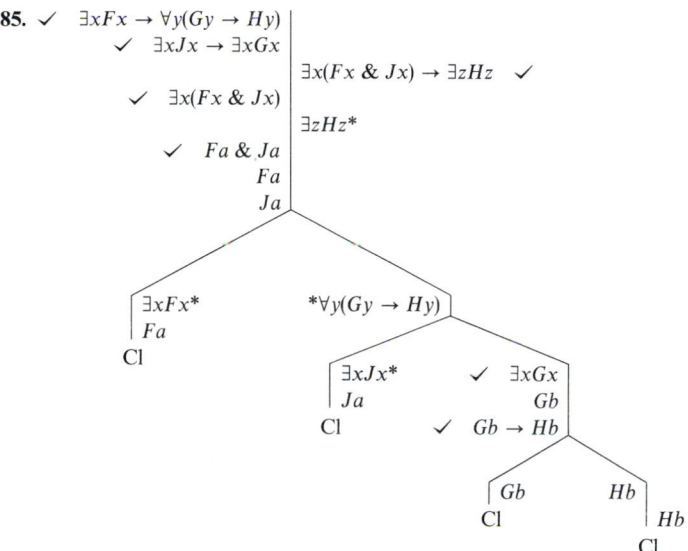

$$∃x(Fx \& Jx) → ∃zHz ✓$$

Valid.

91. *∀x((Fx & Gx) → Hx)
       ✓   Ga & ∀xFx

Valid.

97.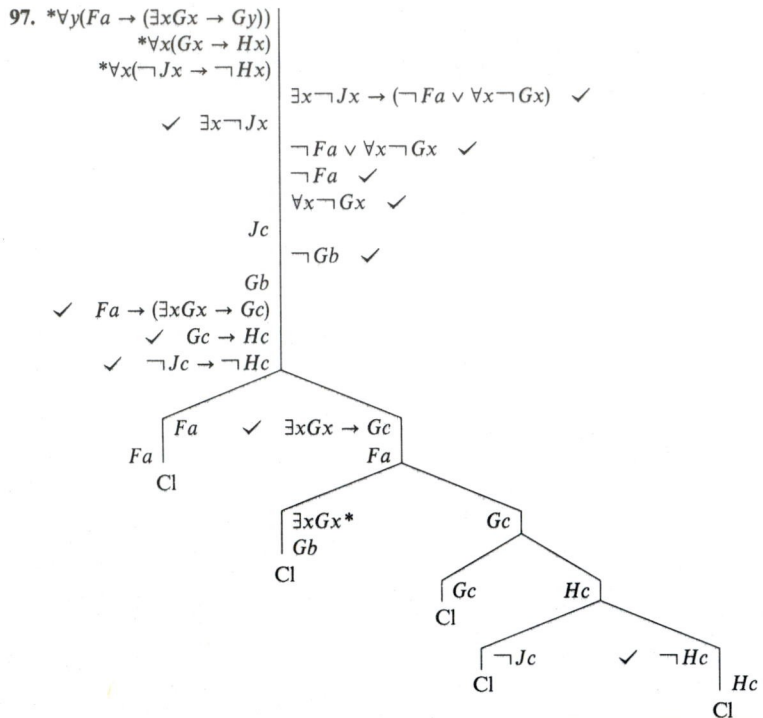

Valid.

103.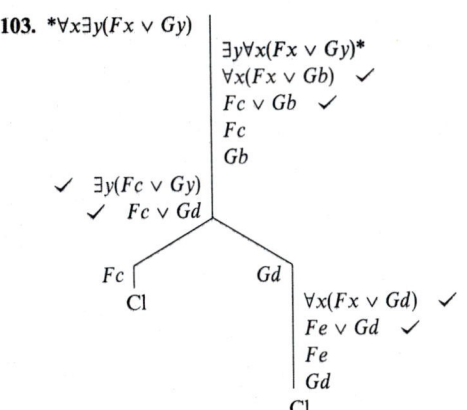

Valid.

109.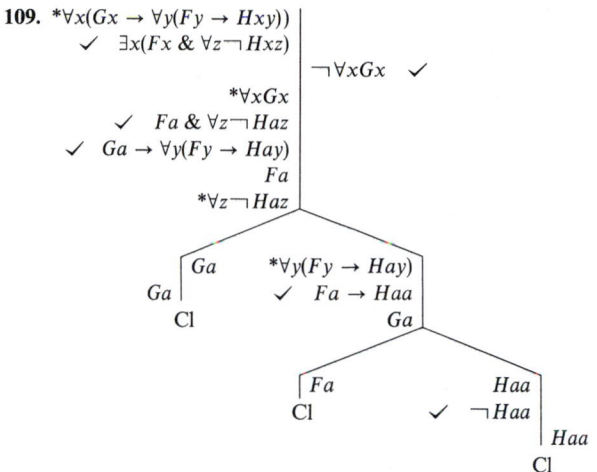

Valid.

115.

Invalid.

121.

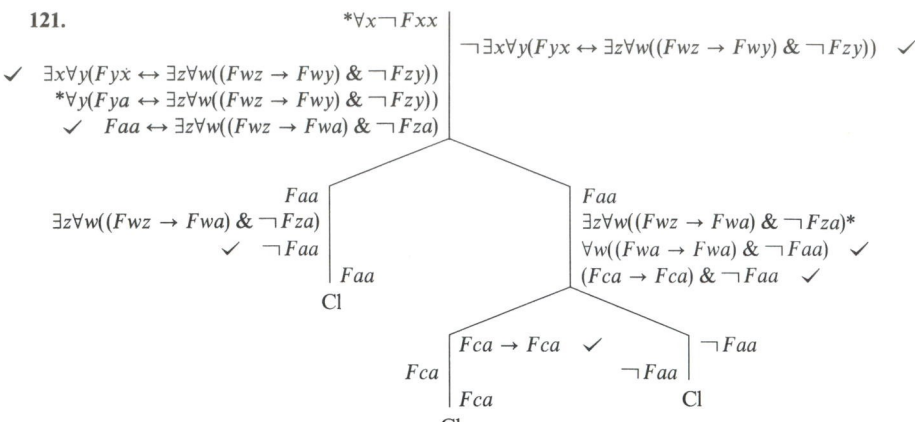

Valid.

127. ✓ $\exists x \forall y (\exists z F yz \to F yx)$
*$\forall x \exists y F xy$

$\exists x \forall y F yx$*

*$\forall y (\exists z F yz \to F ya)$

$\forall y F ya$ ✓
$F ba$

✓ $\exists y F by$
$F bd$
✓ $\exists z F bz \to F ba$

$\exists z F bz$* $F ba$
$F bd$ Cl
Cl

Valid.

Chapter 13
QUANTIFIED DEDUCTION

13.1 Deduction Rules for Quantifiers

1. 1. $\forall x Cgx$ A
2. Cgo US, 1

2. 1. $\forall x Cgx$ A
2. Cga US, 1
3. $\exists x Cgx$ EG, 2

3. 1. $\forall x Cgx$ A
2. Cgg US, 1

4. 1. $\forall x Cgx$ A
2. Cgg US, 1
3. $\exists x Cxg$ EG, 2

5. 1. $\forall x (Lx \to \neg F xi)$ A
2. $F bi$ A
3. $Lb \to \neg F bi$ US, 1
4. $\neg \neg F bi$ DN, 2
5. $\neg Lb$ MT, 3, 4

6. 1. $\forall x ((Px \& Bx) \to Cx)$ A
2. $\exists x ((Px \& Qx) \& Bx)$ A (where 'Q' symbolizes 'is a Pirate')
3. $(Pa \& Qa) \& Ba$ ES, 2
4. $Pa \& Qa$ S, 3
5. Pa S, 4
6. Ba S, 3
7. $Pa \& Ba$ C, 5, 6

8. $(Pa \& Ba) \rightarrow Ca$ US, 1
9. Ca MP, 8, 7
10. Qa S, 4
11. $Qa \& Ca$ C, 10, 9
12. $\exists x(Qx \& Cx)$ EG, 11

12.
1. $\exists x((Cx \& Kix) \& Ix)$ A
2. $\forall x((Cx \& Kix) \rightarrow Vx)$ A
3. $(Ca \& Kia) \& Ia$ ES, 1
4. $Ca \& Kia$ S, 3
5. $(Ca \& Kia) \rightarrow Va$ US, 2
6. Va MP, 5, 4
7. Kia S, 4
8. Ia S, 3
9. $Va \& Ia$ C, 6, 8
10. $\exists x(Vx \& Ix)$ EG, 9

18.
1. $\forall x \forall y(((Px \& Py) \& Cxy) \rightarrow \forall z(Cyz \rightarrow Cxz))$ A
2. $\exists x \exists y((Px \& Py) \& (Cxy \& Cyx))$ A
3. $\exists y((Pa \& Py) \& (Cay \& Cya))$ ES, 2
4. $(Pa \& Pb) \& (Cab \& Cba)$ ES, 3
5. $Pa \& Pb$ S, 4
6. $Cab \& Cba$ S, 4
7. Cab S, 6
8. $(Pa \& Pb) \& Cab$ C, 5, 7
9. $\forall y(((Pa \& Py) \& Cay) \rightarrow \forall z(Cyz \rightarrow Caz))$ US, 1
10. $((Pa \& Pb) \& Cab) \rightarrow \forall z(Cbz \rightarrow Caz)$ US, 9
11. $\forall z(Cbz \rightarrow Caz)$ MP, 10, 8
12. $Cba \rightarrow Caa$ US, 11
13. Cba S, 6
14. Caa MP, 12, 13
15. Pa S, 5
16. $Pa \& Caa$ C, 15, 14
17. $\exists x(Px \& Cxx)$ EG, 16

24.
1. $\forall x(Mx \rightarrow \neg Lx)$ A
2. $\forall x(Mx \rightarrow Sx)$ A
3. $\exists x Mx$ A
4. Ma ES, 3
5. $Ma \rightarrow \neg La$ US, 1
6. $\neg La$ MP, 5, 4
7. $Ma \rightarrow Sa$ US, 2
8. Sa MP, 7, 4
9. $Sa \& \neg La$ C, 8, 6
10. $\exists x(Sx \& \neg Lx)$ EG, 9

30.
1. $\forall x(Mx \rightarrow \neg Lx)$ A
2. $\forall x(Sx \rightarrow Mx)$ A
3. $\exists x Sx$ A
4. Sa ES, 3
5. $Sa \rightarrow Ma$ US, 2
6. Ma MP, 5, 4
7. $Ma \rightarrow \neg La$ US, 1
8. $\neg La$ MP, 7, 6
9. $Sa \& \neg La$ C, 4, 8
10. $\exists x(Sx \& \neg Lx)$ EG, 9

36.
1. $\exists x(Mx \& Lx)$ A
2. $\forall x(Sx \rightarrow \neg Mx)$ A
3. $Ma \& La$ ES, 1
4. $Sa \rightarrow \neg Ma$ US, 2
5. Ma S, 3
6. $\neg \neg Ma$ DN, 5
7. $\neg Sa$ MT, 4, 6
8. La S, 3
9. $La \& \neg Sa$ C, 8, 7
10. $\exists x(Lx \& \neg Sx)$ EG, 9

42.
1. $\forall x(Hx \rightarrow Gx)$ A
2. $\exists x(\neg Gx \& Fx)$ A
3. $\neg Ga \& Fa$ ES, 2
4. Fa S, 3
5. $\neg Ga$ S, 3
6. $Ha \rightarrow Ga$ US, 1
7. $\neg Ha$ MT, 6, 5
8. $Fa \& \neg Ha$ C, 4, 7
9. $\exists x(Fx \& \neg Hx)$ EG, 8

48.
1. $\forall x(Hx \to \neg Gx)$ — A
2. $\exists x(Gx \& Fx)$ — A
3. $Ga \& Fa$ — ES, 2
4. Fa — S, 3
5. Ga — S, 3
6. $Ha \to \neg Ga$ — US, 1
7. $\neg\neg Ga$ — DN, 5
8. $\neg Ha$ — MT, 6, 7
9. $Fa \& \neg Ha$ — C, 4, 8,
10. $\exists x(Fx \& \neg Hx)$ — EG, 9

54.
1. $\forall x(Fx \lor \neg Gx)$ — A
2. $\forall x(Fx \to Hx)$ — A
3. $\forall x(\neg Gx \to Jx)$ — A
4. $\exists x \neg Jx$ — A
5. $\neg Ja$ — ES, 4
6. $\neg Ga \to Ja$ — US, 3
7. $\neg\neg Ga$ — MT, 6, 5
8. $Fa \lor \neg Ga$ — US, 1
9 Fa — DS, 8, 7
10. $Fa \to Ha$ — US, 2
11. Ha — MP, 10, 9
12. $\exists x Hx$ — EG, 11

60.
1. $\forall x(Fx \to Gx)$ — A
2. $Fa \to Ga$ — US, 1
3. $\neg Fa \lor Ga$ — MC, 2
4. $\exists x(\neg Fx \lor Gx)$ — EG, 3

13.2 Universal Generalization

1.
1. $\forall x(Mx \to Lx)$ — A
2. $\forall x(Sx \to Mx)$ — A
3. $Sa \to Ma$ — US, 2
4. $Ma \to La$ — US, 1
5. $Sa \to La$ — HS, 3, 4
6. $\forall x(Sx \to Lx)$ — UG, 5

2.
1. $\forall x(Mx \to \neg Lx)$ — A
2. $\forall x(Sx \to Mx)$ — A
3. $Sa \to Ma$ — US, 2
4. $Ma \to \neg La$ — US, 1
5. $Sa \to \neg La$ — HS, 3, 4
6. $\forall x(Sx \to \neg Lx)$ — UG, 5

3.
1. $\forall x(Lx \to \neg Mx)$ — A
2. $\forall x(Sx \to Mx)$ — A
3. $Sa \to Ma$ — US, 2
4. $La \to \neg Ma$ — US, 1
5. $\neg\neg Ma \to \neg La$ — Tr, 4
6. $Ma \to \neg La$ — DN, 5
7. $Sa \to \neg La$ — HS, 3, 6
8. $\forall x(Sx \to \neg Lx)$ — UG, 7

4.
1. $\forall x(Lx \to Mx)$ — A
2. $\forall x(Sx \to \neg Mx)$ — A
3. $Sa \to \neg Ma$ — US, 2
4. $La \to Ma$ — US, 1
5. $\neg Ma \to \neg La$ — Tr, 4
6. $Sa \to \neg La$ — HS, 3, 5
7. $\forall x(Sx \to \neg Lx)$ — UG, 6

5.
1. $\forall x(Mx \to \neg Lx)$ — A
2. $\forall x(Sx \to Mx)$ — A
3. $Sa \to Ma$ — US, 2
4. $Ma \to \neg La$ — US, 1
5. $Sa \to \neg La$ — HS, 3, 4
6. $\neg\neg La \to \neg Sa$ — Tr, 5
7. $La \to \neg Sa$ — DN, 6
8. $\forall x(Lx \to \neg Sx)$ — UG, 7

6.
1. $\forall x(Dx \to Sx)$ — A
2. $\forall x(Ix \to \neg Sx)$ — A
3. $Da \to Sa$ — US, 1
4. $Ia \to \neg Sa$ — US, 2
5. $\neg\neg Sa \to \neg Ia$ — Tr, 4
6. $Sa \to \neg Ia$ — DN, 5
7. $Da \to \neg Ia$ — HS, 3, 6
8. $\forall x(Dx \to \neg Ix)$ — UG, 7

12.
1. $\forall x(Wx \to \neg Fx)$ — A
2. $\forall x(Px \to \neg\neg Fx)$ — A
3. $Pa \to \neg\neg Fa$ — US, 2
4. $Wa \to \neg Fa$ — US, 1
5. $\neg\neg Fa \to \neg Wa$ — Tr, 4
6. $Pa \to \neg Wa$ — HS, 3, 5
7. $\forall x(Px \to \neg Wx)$ — UG, 6

18.
1. $\forall x((Sx \& \neg Px) \to \neg Ex)$ — A
2. $\forall x((Sx \& Oxh) \to \neg Px)$ — A
3. $(Sa \& Oah) \to \neg Pa$ — US, 2
4. $(Sa \& Oah) \to Sa$ — W
5. $(Sa \& Oah) \to (Sa \& \neg Pa)$ — CC, 4, 3
6. $(Sa \& \neg Pa) \to \neg Ea$ — US, 1
7. $(Sa \& Oah) \to \neg Ea$ — HS, 5, 6
8. $\forall x((Sx \& Oxh) \to \neg Ex)$ — UG, 7

24.
1. $\forall x(Oxi \to \neg Cx)$ A
2. $\forall x(Sx \to Cx)$ A
3. $Oai \to \neg Ca$ US, 1
4. $Sa \to Ca$ US, 2
5. $\neg Ca \to \neg Sa$ Tr, 4
6. $Oai \to \neg Sa$ HS, 3, 5
7. $\forall x(Oxi \to \neg Sx)$ UG, 6

30.
1. $\forall x(\neg Nx \to \neg Mx)$ A
2. $\forall x(Lx \to Wx)$ A
3. $\forall x(Ix \to \neg Wx)$ A
4. $\forall x(Nx \to Lx)$ A
5. $Ia \to \neg Wa$ US, 3
6. $La \to Wa$ US, 2
7. $Na \to La$ US, 4
8. $Na \to Wa$ HS, 7, 6
9. $\neg Wa \to \neg Na$ Tr, 8
10. $Ia \to \neg Na$ HS, 5, 9
11. $\neg Na \to \neg Ma$ US, 1
12. $Ia \to \neg Ma$ HS, 10, 11
13. $\forall x(Ix \to \neg Mx)$ UG, 12

36.
1. $\forall x(Ixj \to \neg Rjx)$ A
2. $\forall x(\neg Lxj \to Ixj)$ A
3. $\neg Laj \to Iaj$ US, 2
4. $Iaj \to \neg Rja$ US, 1
5. $\neg Laj \to \neg Rja$ HS, 3, 4
6. $\neg\neg Rja \to \neg\neg Laj$ Tr, 5
7. $Rja \to Laj$ DN, 6
8. $\forall x(Rjx \to Lxj)$ UG, 7

42.
1. $\forall xFx \, \& \, \forall xGx$ A
2. $\forall xFx$ S, 1
3. $\forall xGx$ S, 1
4. Fa US, 2
5. Ga US, 3
6. $Fa \, \& \, Ga$ C, 4, 5
7. $\forall x(Fx \, \& \, Gx)$ UG, 6

48.
1. $\forall x(Fx \leftrightarrow (\neg Gx \vee \neg Fx))$ A
2. $Fa \leftrightarrow (\neg Ga \vee \neg Fa)$ US, 1
3. $(Fa \to (\neg Ga \vee \neg Fa)) \, \& \, ((\neg Ga \vee \neg Fa) \to Fa)$ B, 2
4. $Fa \to (\neg Ga \vee \neg Fa)$ S, 3
5. $(\neg Ga \vee \neg Fa) \to Fa$ S, 3
6. $\neg Fa \vee (\neg Ga \vee \neg Fa)$ MC, 4
7. $(\neg Ga \vee \neg Fa) \vee \neg Fa$ Cm, 6
8. $\neg Ga \vee (\neg Fa \vee \neg Fa)$ AD, 7
9. $\neg Ga \vee \neg Fa$ I, 8
10. Fa MP, 5, 9
11. $\neg\neg Fa$ DN, 10
12. $\neg Ga$ DS, 9, 11
13. $\forall x\neg Gx$ UG, 12

54.
1. $\forall x(Fx \to (Gx \vee Hx))$ A
2. $\forall x((Jx \, \& \, Fx) \to \neg Gx)$ A
3. $\forall x(\neg Fx \to \neg Jx)$ A
4. $Fa \to (Ga \vee Ha)$ US, 1
5. $(Ja \, \& \, Fa) \to \neg Ga$ US, 2
6. $\neg Fa \to \neg Ja$ US, 3
7. $\neg\neg Ja \to \neg\neg Fa$ Tr, 6
8. $Ja \to Fa$ DN, 7
9. $Ja \to Ja$ SI
10. $Ja \to (Ja \, \& \, Fa)$ CC, 8, 9
11. $Ja \to Ga$ HS, 10, 5

12. $Ja \rightarrow (Ga \lor Ha)$ HS, 8, 4
13. $\neg Ja \lor (Ga \lor Ha)$ MC, 12
14. $(\neg Ja \lor Ga) \lor Ha$ As, 13
15. $(\neg Ja \lor \neg \neg Ga) \lor Ha$ DN, 14
16. $\neg(Ja \& \neg Ga) \lor Ha$ DM, 15
17. $(Ja \& \neg Ga) \rightarrow Ha$ MC, 16
18. $Ja \rightarrow (Ja \& \neg Ga)$ CC, 9, 11
19. $Ja \rightarrow Ha$ HS, 18, 17
20. $\forall x(Jx \rightarrow Hx)$ UG, 19

60. 1. $\forall x \forall y \forall z((Fxy \& Fxz) \rightarrow Fyz)$ A
2. $\forall y \forall z((Fay \& Faz) \rightarrow Fyz)$ US, 1
3. $\forall z((Fab \& Faz) \rightarrow Fbz)$ US, 2
4. $(Fab \& Fac) \rightarrow Fbc$ US, 3
5. $(Fac \& Fab) \rightarrow Fab$ W
6. $(Fac \& Fab) \rightarrow Fac$ W
7. $(Fac \& Fab) \rightarrow (Fab \& Fac)$ CC, 5, 6
8. $(Fac \& Fab) \rightarrow Fbc$ HS, 7, 4
9. $\forall z((Fac \& Faz) \rightarrow Fzc)$ UG, 8
10. $\forall y \forall z((Fay \& Faz) \rightarrow Fzy)$ UG, 9
11. $\forall x \forall y \forall z((Fxy \& Fxz) \rightarrow Fzy)$ UG, 10

13.3 Formulas with Overlapping Quantifiers

1. 1. $\exists x \exists y Fxy$ A
2. $\exists y Fay$ ES, 1 a
3. Fab ES, 2 b
4. $\exists x Fxb$ EG, 3
5. $\exists y \exists x Fxy$ EG, 4

2. 1. $\forall x \forall y Fxy$ A
2. $\forall y Fay$ US, 1
3. Fab US, 2
4. $\forall x Fxb$ UG, 3
5. $\forall y \forall x Fxy$ UG, 4

3. 1. $\exists x \forall y Fxy$ A
2. $\forall y Fay$ ES, 1 a
3. Fab US, 2
4. $\exists x Fxb$ EG, 3
5. $\forall y \exists x Fxy$ UG, 4

4. 1. $\forall x \exists y(Fx \& Gy)$ A
2. $\exists y(Fa \& Gy)$ US, 1 a
3. $Fa \& Gb$ ES, 2 b
4. $\exists y(Fc \& Gy)$ US, 1 c
5. $Fc \& Gd$ ES, 4 d
6. Fa S, 3
7. Gd S, 5
8. $Fa \& Gd$ C, 6, 7
9. $\forall x(Fx \& Gd)$ UG, 8
10. $\exists y \forall x(Fx \& Gy)$ EG, 9

12. 1. $\forall x(\exists y Fxy \rightarrow \forall y Fyx)$ A
2. $\exists x \exists y Fxy$ A
3. $\exists y Fay$ ES, 2 a
4. $\exists y Fay \rightarrow \forall y Fya$ US, 1
5. $\forall y Fya$ MP, 4, 3
6. Fba US, 5
7. $\exists y Fby$ EG, 6
8. $\exists y Fby \rightarrow \forall y Fyb$ US, 1
9. $\forall y Fyb$ MP, 8, 7
10. Fcb US, 9
11. $\forall y Fcy$ UG, 10
12. $\forall x \forall y Fxy$ UG, 11

13.4 Quantifiers and Connectives

1.
1.	$\forall x(Lx \rightarrow Dx)$	A
2.	$La \rightarrow Da$	US, 1
3.	$(Ca \& La) \rightarrow Ca$	W
4.	$(Ca \& La) \rightarrow La$	W
5.	$(Ca \& La) \rightarrow Da$	HS, 4, 2
6.	$(Ca \& La) \rightarrow (Ca \& Da)$	CC, 3, 5
7.	$\neg(Ca \& Da) \rightarrow \neg(Ca \& La)$	Tr, 6
8.	$\neg(Ca \& \neg\neg Da) \rightarrow \neg(Ca \& \neg\neg La)$	DN, 7
9.	$(Ca \rightarrow \neg Da) \rightarrow (Ca \rightarrow \neg La)$	NC, 8
10.	$\exists x((Cx \rightarrow \neg Dx) \rightarrow (Ca \rightarrow \neg La))$	EG, 9
11.	$\forall y\exists x((Cx \rightarrow \neg Dx) \rightarrow (Cy \rightarrow \neg Ly))$	UG, 10
12.	$\forall y(\forall x(Cx \rightarrow \neg Dx) \rightarrow (Cy \rightarrow \neg Ly))$	RP→, 11
13.	$\forall x(Cx \rightarrow \neg Dx) \rightarrow \forall y(Cy \rightarrow \neg Ly)$	RP→, 12
14.	$\forall x(Cx \rightarrow \neg Dx) \rightarrow \forall x(Cx \rightarrow \neg Lx)$	VR, 13

2.
1.	$\neg\exists x(Ix \& Tx)$	A
2.	$\forall x(Sx \rightarrow Tx)$	A
3.	$\forall x(Px \leftrightarrow \neg Sx)$	A
4.	$\forall x\neg(Ix \& Tx)$	QN, 1
5.	$\neg(Ia \& Ta)$	US, 1
6.	$Sa \rightarrow Ta$	US, 2
7.	$Pa \leftrightarrow \neg Sa$	US, 3
8.	$\neg(Ia \& \neg\neg Ta)$	DN, 5
9.	$Ia \rightarrow \neg Ta$	NC, 8
10.	$\neg Ta \rightarrow \neg Sa$	Tr, 6
11.	$Ia \rightarrow \neg Sa$	HS, 9, 10
12.	$(Pa \rightarrow \neg Sa) \& (\neg Sa \rightarrow Pa)$	B, 7
13.	$\neg Sa \rightarrow Pa$	S, 12
14.	$Ia \rightarrow Pa$	HS, 11, 13
15.	$\forall x(Ix \rightarrow Px)$	UG, 14

3.
1.	$\neg\exists x((Mx \& Fx) \& \neg Bx)$	A
2.	$\forall x(Cx \rightarrow Mx)$	A
3.	$\neg\exists x(Cx \& Bx)$	A
4.	$\exists x(Fx \& Cx)$	AIP
5.	$Fa \& Ca$	ES, 1
6.	$\forall x\neg(Mx \& Fx) \& \neg Bx$	QN, 1
7.	$\forall x\neg(Cx \& Bx)$	QN, 3
8.	$Ca \rightarrow Ma$	US, 2
9.	$\neg(Ca \& Ba)$	US, 5
10.	$\neg((Ma \& Fa) \& \neg Ba)$	US, 4
11.	Ca	S, 5
12.	Ma	MP, 8, 11
13.	Fa	S, 5
14.	$\neg(Ma \& Fa) \vee \neg\neg Ba$	DM, 10
15.	$Ma \& Fa$	C, 12, 13
16.	$\neg\neg(Ma \& Fa)$	DN, 15
17.	$\neg\neg Ba$	DS, 14, 16
18.	$\neg Ca \vee \neg Ba$	DM, 9
19.	$\neg Ca$	DS, 18, 17
20.	$Ca \& \neg Ca$	C, 11, 19

(a)

4.
1.	$\forall x(Sx \to \neg Dx)$	A
2.	$\forall x(Chx \to Sx)$	A
3.	$\forall x(\neg Dx \to Bixh)$	A
4.	$Cha \to Sa$	US, 2
5.	$Sa \to \neg Da$	US, 1
6.	$Cha \to \neg Da$	HS, 4, 5
7.	$\neg Da \to Biah$	US, 3
8.	$Cha \to Biah$	HS, 6, 7
9.	$\forall x(Chx \to Bixh)$	UG, 8

5.
1.	$\neg \exists x(Gx \& \neg Rx)$	A
2.	$\forall x(\exists y(Ty \& Ixy) \to Fx)$	A
3.	$\neg \exists x(Fx \& Rx)$	A
4.	$\exists y(Ty \& Iay) \to Fa$	US, 2
5.	$\forall x \neg (Fx \& Rx)$	QN, 3
6.	$\forall x \neg (Gx \& \neg Rx)$	QN, 1
7.	$\neg (Ga \& \neg Ra)$	US, 6
8.	$Ga \to Ra$	NC, 7
9.	$\neg (Fa \& Ra)$	US, 5
10.	$\neg (Fa \& \neg \neg Ra)$	DN, 9
11.	$Fa \to \neg Ra$	NC, 10
12.	$\exists y(Ty \& Iay) \to \neg Ra$	HS, 4, 11
13.	$\neg Ra \to \neg Ga$	Tr, 8
14.	$\exists y(Ty \& Iay) \to \neg Ga$	HS, 12, 13
15.	$\forall x(\exists y(Ty \& Ixy) \to \neg Gx)$	UG, 14

6.
1.	$\forall x((Px \& \exists y(By \& Hxy)) \to Lx)$	A
2.	$\forall x((Px \& \neg \exists y(By \& Hxy)) \to \neg Fx)$	A
3.	$\forall x((Px \& Rxb) \to \neg Lx)$	A
4.	$\neg \neg \exists x((Px \& Rxb) \& Fx)$	AIP
5.	$\exists x((Px \& Rxb) \& Fx)$	DN, 4
6.	$(Pa \& Rab) \& Fa$	ES, 5
7.	$(Pa \& Rab) \to \neg La$	US, 3
8.	$Pa \& Rab$	S, 6
9.	$\neg La$	MP, 7, 8
10.	$(Pa \& \exists y(By \& Hay)) \to La$	US, 1
11.	$\neg (Pa \& \exists y(By \& Hay))$	MT, 10, 9
12.	$\neg Pa \vee \neg \exists y(By \& Hay)$	DM, 11
13.	Pa	S, 8
14.	$\neg \neg Pa$	DN, 13
15.	$\neg \exists y(By \& Hay)$	DS, 12, 14
16.	$(Pa \& \neg \exists y(By \& Hay)) \to \neg Fa$	US, 2
17.	$Pa \& \neg \exists y(By \& Hay)$	C, 13, 15
18.	$\neg Fa$	MP, 16, 17
19.	Fa	S, 6
20.	$Fa \& \neg Fa$	C, 19, 18

12.
1.	$\forall x \exists y(Fx \& Gy)$	A
2.	$\forall x(Fx \& \exists y Gy)$	RP &, 1
3.	$\forall x Fx \& \exists y Gy$	RP &, 2
4.	$\exists y(\forall x Fx \& Gy)$	RP &, 3
5.	$\exists y \forall x(Fx \& Gy)$	RP &, 4

18.
1.	$\forall x(Fx \to Gx)$	A
2.	$Fa \to Ga$	US, 1
3.	$\exists x(Fx \to Ga)$	EG, 2
4.	$\forall x Fx \to Ga$	RP$\to$, 3
5.	$\forall y(\forall x Fx \to Gy)$	UG, 4
6.	$\forall x Fx \to \forall y Gy$	RP$\to$, 5
7.	$\forall x Fx \to \forall x Gx$	VR, 6

24.
1.	$\forall x(Fx \to \neg Gx)$	A
2.	$\forall x(\neg Fx \vee \neg Gx)$	MC, 1
3.	$\forall x \neg (Fx \& Gx)$	DM, 2
4.	$\neg \exists x(Fx \& Gx)$	QN, 3

30.
1.	$\forall x(Fx \leftrightarrow Gx)$	A
2.	$Fa \leftrightarrow Ga$	US, 1
3.	$(Fa \to Ga) \& (Ga \to Fa)$	B, 2
4.	$Fa \to Ga$	S, 3
5.	$\exists x(Fa \to Gx)$	EG, 4
6.	$Fa \to \exists x Gx$	RP$\to$, 5
7.	$\forall y(Fy \to \exists x Gx)$	UG, 6
8.	$\exists y Fy \to \exists x Gx$	RP$\to$, 7

9. $\exists xFx \to \exists xGx$ VR, 8
10. $Ga \to Fa$ S, 3
11. $\exists x(Ga \to Fx)$ EG, 10
12. $Ga \to \exists xFx$ RP→, 11
13. $\forall y(Gy \to \exists xFx)$ UG, 12
14. $\exists yGy \to \exists xFx$ RP→, 13
15. $\exists xGx \to \exists xFx$ VR, 14
16. $(\exists xFx \to \exists xGx) \,\&\, (\exists xGx \to \exists xFx)$ C, 9, 15
17. $\exists xFx \leftrightarrow \exists xGx$ B, 16

36.
1. $\neg\exists x(Hxa \,\&\, \neg Gxb)$ A
2. $\forall x\neg(Fxc \,\&\, Fbx)$ A
3. $\forall x(Gex \to Fxe)$ A
4. $\neg\neg(Hea \,\&\, Fec)$ AIP
5. $Hea \,\&\, Fec$ DN, 4
6. $\forall x\neg(Hxa \,\&\, \neg Gxb)$ QN, 1
7. $\neg(Hea \,\&\, \neg Geb)$ US, 6
8. $\neg Hea \lor \neg\neg Geb$ DM, 7
9. Hea S, 5
10. $\neg\neg Hea$ DN, 9
11. $\neg\neg Geb$ DS, 8, 10
12. $\neg(Fec \,\&\, Fbe)$ US, 2
13. $\neg Fec \lor \neg Fbe$ DM, 12
14. Fec S, 5
15. $\neg\neg Fec$ DN, 14
16. $\neg Fbe$ DS, 13, 15
17. $Geb \to Fbe$ US, 3
18. $\neg Geb$ MT, 17, 16
19. $\neg Geb \,\&\, \neg\neg Geb$ C, 18, 11

42.
1. $\exists xFx \to \forall y((Fy \lor Gy) \to Hy)$ A
2. $\exists xHx$ A
3. $\neg\forall z\neg Fz$ A
4. $\exists z\neg\neg Fz$ QN, 3
5. $\neg\neg Fa$ ES, 4   ⓐ
6. Fa DN, 5
7. $\exists xFx$ EG, 6
8. $\forall y((Fy \lor Gy) \to Hy)$ MP, 1, 7
9. $(Fa \lor Ga) \to Ha$ US, 8
10. $Fa \lor Ga$ Ad, 6
11. Ha MP, 9, 10
12. $Fa \,\&\, Ha$ C, 6, 11
13. $\exists x(Fx \,\&\, Hx)$ EG, 12

48.
1. $\forall x\neg Fxx$ A
2. $\neg\neg\exists x\forall y(Fyx \leftrightarrow \exists z\forall w((Fwz \to Fwy) \,\&\, \neg Fzy))$ AIP
3. $\exists x\forall y(Fyx \leftrightarrow \exists z\forall w((Fwz \to Fwy) \,\&\, \neg Fzy))$ DN, 2
4. $\forall y(Fya \leftrightarrow \exists z\forall w((Fwz \to Fwy) \,\&\, \neg Fzy))$ ES, 3   ⓐ
5. $Faa \leftrightarrow \exists z\forall w((Fwz \to Fwa) \,\&\, \neg Fza)$ US, 4
6. $\neg Faa$ US, 1
7. $\neg\exists z\forall w((Fwz \to Fwa) \,\&\, \neg Fza)$ BE, 5, 6
8. $\forall z\exists w\neg((F\overset{\vee}{w}z \to Fwa) \,\&\, \neg Fza)$ QN², 7
9. $\exists w\neg((Fwa \to Fwa) \,\&\, \neg Faa)$ US, 8
10. $\neg((Fba \to Fba) \,\&\, \neg Faa)$ ES, 9   ⓑ
11. $Fba \to Fba$ SI
12. $(Fba \to Fba) \,\&\, \neg Faa$ C, 11, 6
13. $((Fba \to Fba) \,\&\, \neg Faa) \,\&\, \neg((Fba \to Fba) \,\&\, \neg Faa)$ C, 12, 10

Chapter 14
GENERALIZATIONS

14.3 Inductive Reliability

1. a. less—small sample
   b. more—large sample
   c. less—not much variation
   d. more—varied sample
   e. less—not much variation

2. a. more—increased sample size
   b. less—not much variation
   c. less—not much variation
   d. no effect
   e. less—counterexample to generalization

14.4 Statistical Generalizations

1. **a.** This will probably not yield a very representative sample; the sample will contain more freshmen and sophomores than the student body at large. Also, the sample is likely to be biased if many students don't return the questionnaire.
   b. Whether this will yield a representative sample depends on the university's registration procedures. If some students register in advance, or through the mail, the sample is likely to be biased. Also, the sample will be biased if many students don't return the questionnaires.
   c. Whether this will yield a representative sample depends on the university's registration procedures. If some students register in advance, or through the mail, the sample is likely to be biased. An additional source of bias is that students stand in registration lines for different lengths of time; students who want popular courses, for which they have to wait, will tend to be overrepresented.
   d. This will omit students who live off campus and thus is likely to be biased.
   e. This will produce a self-selected sample, which is very unlikely to be representative.

2. a. This sampling is not random and lacks variation through time. It covers only one shift for one week.
   b. Small variation in time, covering only one shift for one week.
   c. Small variation in time—only one week.
   d. This is good, but may overlook differences between shifts.
   e. A stratified random sample, which is excellent.

6. Problems: Few men will want to answer such a personal question; many of those who do answer are likely to lie. Those asked with their wives present are even more likely to lie. Probably no method would be very reliable.

12. Amounts of bleach may be measured by weight or volume, but that probably makes little difference here. This claim doesn't specify the other term of the comparison—"20% more bleach" than what?—but probably compares the new with the old version of the product. If it does, this claim doesn't indicate whether there is now 20% more bleach than before, per unit—per ounce, for example—or whether there is simply 20% more bleach in the container, which could result from having a bigger container. (Of course, if the product is simply bleach, there can be 20% more only by having a bigger container. Whether the claim is impressive then depends on whether the price has changed.)

18. The length of a person's life can be measured precisely. But what is the other term of the comparison? Unmarried men? Married women?

14.5 Analogies

1. a. Samaria and her idols are related to Jerusalem and her idols.
   b. They have been found, and the idols are graven images.
   c. Samaria is not Jerusalem.

2. a. False prophets are related to wolves in sheep's clothing.
  b. They appear harmless, but are extremely dangerous.
  c. Prophets are people; sheep and wolves aren't.

3. a. Men are compared to moths, mountains to tufts of wool.
  b. Men and mountains will be scattered.
  c. Men and mountains appear to be fixed and sturdy, while moths and tufts of wool don't.

4. a. The world is compared to a chariot run wild.
  b. Both are out of control, gaining speed, and dangerous.
  c. The world is bigger.

5. a. We and our lives are compared to the stuff dreams are made on; sleep is compared with death.
  b. Both dreams and lives are rounded with states of unconsciousness.
  c. Death is more permanent than sleep.

6. a. The world is compared to a stage, and people to players.
  b. People have exits and entrances, and play many parts.
  c. The world is larger; players can leave the stage and then return, but death is permanent.

12. a. This passage is ambiguous. A sinking star is compared either to this gray spirit or to knowledge.
  b. Both pass beyond the bounds of human thought or perception.
  c. The spirit and knowledge are mental, while the star is purely physical.

18. a. Seeing Yankee fans is related to waking up in a Brazilian jail.
  b. Presumably, both are shocking and very unpleasant.
  c. Yankee Stadium is in the Bronx, not Brazil; baseball is played there. No one is forced to go to Yankee Stadium or remain there for any set length of time.

24. a. Judgments are related to watches.
  b. They differ, but each person believes his own.
  c. Watches, unlike judgments, operate mechanically, can be checked against a fixed standard, and give information only about time.

30. a. High interest rates and slow growth are related to chemotherapy, the economy to a patient, inflation to cancer, and economic policymakers to physicians.
  b. High interest rates, slow growth and chemotherapy both destroy good along with bad and make the patient (or economy) sick. Policymakers and physicians try to improve the health of the patient (or economy).
  c. Physicians try to find ways of helping the patient without causing great harm; policymakers don't.

36. a. The earth is related to an egg yolk, the world to an egg, water to egg white, air to the membrane around the egg, and fire to the egg shell.
  b. The placements are similar; the earth is in the world, surrounded by water, air, and fire, as the yolk is in the egg, surrounded by white, membrane, and shell.
  c. The universe is larger than an egg.

42. a. Particles are related to idle wheels.
  b. Both enable things around them to revolve in the same direction.
  c. Particles are much smaller than idle wheels.

48. a. Light rays are related to tennis balls, or streams thereof.
  b. They travel in curved lines when struck obliquely, because of the circulating motion imparted by the strike and the resistance of the ether.
  c. Globular bodies making up light rays (that is, photons) differ significantly from tennis balls: They are much smaller and lighter, and obey laws of quantum mechanics.

Chapter 15
CAUSES

15.1 Kinds of Causes

1. a. Depends on the illness.
   b. Depends on the illness.
   c. We must assume various things about the patient's condition.
   d. Probably remote.

2. a. Depends on the illness.
   b. No.
   c. We must assume various things about the patient's condition and circumstances while recovering.
   d. Remote.

3. a. No.
   b. Possibly; depends on the poison.
   c. Perhaps something about the victim's condition, the availability of antidotes and, in general, the availability of medical assistance.
   d. Remote.

4. a. No.
   b. No.
   c. We must assume that there was no way of getting the work done on time without using the computer.
   d. Remote.

5. a. No.
   b. No.
   c. We must assume that John's presence was vital.
   d. Remote.

6. a. No.
   b. No.
   c. We must assume that neither the instructor nor other students were willing to get back on track.
   d. Remote.

12. a. Depends on whether the bread contained any other rising agents (such as eggs or baking powder).
   b. No.
   c. We must assume that the right ingredients were in the dough, that the dough rose and the bread baked at appropriate temperatures, with appropriate humidity, pressure, and so on.
   d. Proximate.

18. a. No.
   b. No.
   c. We must assume that objects capable of being destroyed were in the flood plain and couldn't be moved in time.
   d. Proximate.

24. a. No.
   b. No.
   c. We must assume various things about the perceptual systems and dispositions of the bull.
   d. Remote.

30. a. Neither necessary nor sufficient.   b. Neither.   c. Neither.
   d. Neither.   e. Neither   f. Neither
   g. Neither.   h. Neither.   i. Probably sufficient.
   The events in a and h could be counted as causing the assassin's death. For a, the context is broad; we assume that his anger made the assassin begin a course of events ending in his death. For h, we assume that his prior acts and dispositions are in the context, making the event sufficient. The events in b–g, however, are quite specific; the context doesn't supply anything that makes the outcome inevitable. It sounds very odd, for example, to say that pulling the trigger (or the gun's firing, or the loud noise, and so on) caused the assassin's death.

36. Irene's death might have resulted from an infection she acquired in the hospital; from an infection resulting from stepping on a rusty nail and failing to seek treatment; from being too weak from a prior illness to fight the infection; and so on.

15.2 Agreement and Difference

1. Agreement: All cases in which a Democrat has won the White House have agreed in having the Democrats win Texas. We can infer that a Democratic victory in Texas causes a Democratic victory across the country, if there are no other relevant elements of agreement (which, in this case, there almost certainly are).

2. Agreement: Almost all cases in which countries cut marginal tax rates agree; the cuts are followed by increased growth. Moreover, cases in which marginal tax rates are cut and currency is stabilized agree in having reduced inflation. We can infer that cutting tax rates causes increased growth and, in the presence of monetary stability, reduced inflation, if there are no other relevant elements of agreement (this is controversial in economic theory) and if we can explain the "almost".

3. This passage contains no application of Mill's methods, but it does provide fertile data for them. Derek and Eric were not among the top graduates at schools rated ten or below. They differ in this from the others; Andy and Beth were top graduates, and Andy and Claire were from top-ranked schools. Only Derek and Eric were denied tenure. The joint method of agreement and difference suggests, therefore, that not being a top graduate at a school rated ten or below causes, or is an indispensable part of the cause, of being denied tenure.

4. This passage contains no application of Mill's methods, but it does provide data for such an application. The great universities agreed in being strong in English, history, and philosophy. Those below them in stature fell short in at least one of these areas. By the joint method of agreement and difference, we may infer that having excellent English, history, and philosophy departments is causally linked to being a great university. Because one great university did not place in the top ten in philosophy, the inference is stronger for English and history than philosophy.

15.3 Residues and Concomitant Variation

1. This uses the method of concomitant variation: a decrease in speed limits has accompanied a cut in traffic fatality rates. The method allows us to infer that there is some causal link, but not its precise form. Even this inference is weak, because the sample concerns only 7 years.

2. This passage criticizes the previous one, using concomitant variation to show that increases in safety correlate with time. Presumably, as time passes, the safety of cars and roads increases. This inference is also weak; the time interval of 49 years is so large that many things could explain the drop in the fatality rate. But the passage, taken together with the previous one, also implies a criticism based on the method of agreement. The 1925–1974 case agrees with the 1975–1982 case in showing a drop in fatality rates, but there is no corresponding agreement concerning speed limits.

3. A humorous allusion to something like the method of residues. Given that the effect of a Senate is the same in both cases, what additional effects will a House have?

4. This is an argument, based on concomitant variation, that deficits do not raise interest rates. If there were such a causal link, one could expect some correlation. But there is none.

5. This argues that cutting taxes yields more revenue, based on concomitant variation.

6. This seems to rely on the method of residues. Children are often sick; a single difference, adding garlic, led to a record of uninterrupted health. So, the method indicates, the garlic must have been responsible. This argument is weak, since there are bound to be many other genetic and environmental differences between Mr. Buscaglia and other people. (Note: because this passage discusses only a single case, no other method applies.)

12. MBAs and PhDs are advanced-degree professionals and have much in common. Yet MBAs are more satisfied sexually. The method of difference implies that we should examine differences between MBAs andPhDs to find the cause, or a substantial part of the cause, of MBAs' greater satisfaction. The passage points to one such difference: MBAs have money, while PhDs have learning. Of course, there are probably many other relevant differences.

18. The method of difference suggests the inference that oxygen deprivation causes loss of reasoning ability. One might also use the method of residues to infer that oxygen in the blood is responsible for reasoning ability. Given the context of an otherwise properly functioning body, this seems reasonable.

24. The two parts of the claim are similar in form; the following deal only with the first half, about interesting things. Agreement: Examine interesting things to determine whether we care about all of them. Difference: Examine pairs consisting of an interesting thing and an otherwise similar uninteresting thing to determine whether the sole difference is that we care only about the former. Agreement and difference: Examine interesting things and otherwise similar uninteresting things to determine whether we care about all and only the former. Residue: Compare an interesting thing to something identical but uninteresting; see whether we care only about the former. Concomitant variation: See whether variations in degree of interestingness correlate with variations in degree of caring.

30. This sounds paradoxical, but could be tested. Agreement: Examine societies exhibiting mass illiteracy to determine whether everybody in them can read and write. Difference: Examine pairs consisting of a society with mass illiteracy and an otherwise similar one without it to determine whether the sole difference is that everybody can read and write only in the former. Agreement and difference: Examine societies exhibiting mass illiteracy and otherwise similar societies without it to determine whether everybody can read and write in just the former. Residue: Compare a society with mass illiteracy to a society without it but otherwise identical; see whether everybody can read and write only in the former. Concomitant variation: See whether variations in degree of mass illiteracy correlate with variations in percentage of the population that can read and write.

15.4 Causal Fallacies

1. This is a post hoc ergo propter hoc fallacy; a causal connection is alleged solely on the basis of temporal order.

2. This begins with an acceptable application of the method of concomitant variation. That method, however, allows us to infer only that there is some causal link between hemlines and stock market levels. To infer that economic activity causes fashion trends is to confuse correlation with causation.

3. This appears to be a post hoc ergo propter hoc fallacy. If eating oat bran were the only relevant change, however, the method of difference would justify an inference of causal connection.

Chapter 16
EXPLANATIONS

16.1 Explanations and Hypothetical Reasoning

1. They said we should stock up on canned goods. ∴ I went out and bought a case of beer. Covering law is implicit: Do what they say to do.

2. People in capitalist countries do not earn enough money to buy products. Soviet people can buy what they desire. ∴ Soviet shelves are empty, while shelves in capitalist countries are full. Covering law (implicit): If people can buy what they want, nothing will remain on the shelves.

3. If a man is wise, he gets rich; if he gets rich, he or his wife gets foolish. ∴ Money keeps moving around. Covering law (implicit): Money moves toward the wise and away from the foolish.

4. People were forced to be with their loved ones. ∴ There were many domestic disturbances. Covering law (implicit): People forced to be together fight.

5. See the answer to exercise 30, section 1.2. Covering law (implicit): Rent controls, restrictions on conversions, and Mafia strangleholds are attempts to suspend economic law.

6. The moon's orbit is elliptical. It departs by about five degrees from the earth's orbit around the sun. ∴ Eclipses of the sun do not occur every month. Covering laws: Laws of physics, astronomy, and geometry implying that ellipses in the same plane would lead to eclipses almost once per rotation of the moon, while ellipses in different planes will bring their objects into eclipse far more rarely.

12. Overnight, the outside temperature fell, cooling the window glass. The inside air contained water vapor, which condenses on any surface that's cold enough. ∴ The water vapor condensed when it came in contact with the cooler glass. The resulting water drops fell to the sill. ∴ The windowsills were wet. Covering laws: The temperature outside affects the temperature of window glass; water vapor condenses on any sufficiently cold surface; drops of water fall.

16.2 Scientific Theories

1. In a lunar eclipse, the earth's shadow on the moon is circular. The first parts of ships coming from over the horizon to appear are the tops. It is possible to circumnavigate the earth in ships, airplanes, and spacecraft. From space, the earth looks spherical. Satellite transmissions assume that the earth is round and occur successfully.

2. What goes up must come down. Objects whose support is withdrawn fall. The moon and various artificial satellites orbit the earth. The orbits of the other planets show the effects of the earth's gravitational attraction.

6. Hypothesis: the moon's orbit brings it, at certain times, twice as close to the earth as at other times. The fact that the moon never appears twice as big as at other times shows that this hypothesis is incorrect, given the auxiliary hypothesis that, if the moon were twice as close, it would appear twice as big.

12. Hypothesis: Caesar was ambitious. But he allowed ransoms for captives to go into the general coffers, showed compassion for the poor, and turned down a crown. These things show he was not ambitious, granted the auxiliary assumption that an ambitious person would not do all of the above.

16.3 Evaluating Explanations

1. As an explanation, there's nothing wrong with this. The child is likely to be dissatisfied, however, because his or her question is really a request for a justification, not an explanation.

2. Here, too, A really wants a justification. Even as an explanation, however, this is poor. We could take it as violating the evidence condition—as having the form, in essence, "You must because you must". Or, we could take it as a simple covering law explanation: "You must because everyone in your situation must". This is weak because it is not very powerful and receives no support from above. It invites the response, "Why must anyone in my situation do this?"

3. A's question seems ambiguous. If it means, "Why do brides wear white these days?" then B's answer is fine; in effect, B says, it's tradition. This explanation isn't very satisfying because it doesn't go very deep; why, for example, did such a tradition start? If the question means "Why have brides worn white?" then the answer violates the evidence condition.

Appendix IA
DEDUCTION-STYLE TWO

IA.2 Conjunction and Negation Rules

1.
1. $p \& q$ — A
2. q — S, 1

2.
1. $p \& (q \& r)$ — A
2. $q \& r$ — S, 1
3. r — S, 2

3.
1. $p \& \neg \neg q$ — A
2. $\neg \neg q$ — S, 1
3. q — DN, 2

4.
1. $\neg \neg p \& \neg q$ — A
2. $\neg \neg p$ — S, 1
3. p — DN, 2
4. $\neg q$ — S, 1
5. $\neg \neg \neg q$ — DN, 4
6. $\neg \neg \neg q \& p$ — C, 5, 3

5.
1. $p \& \neg q$ — A
2. $\neg r \& s$ — A
3. p — S, 1
4. s — S, 2
5. $s \& p$ — C, 4, 3

6.
1. $(p \& q) \& r$ — A
2. $p \& q$ — S, 1
3. p — S, 2
4. q — S, 2
5. r — S, 1
6. $q \& r$ — C, 4, 5
7. $p \& (q \& r)$ — C, 3, 6

IA.3 Conditional and Biconditional Rules

1.
1. $p \to q$ — A
2. p — A
3. q — MP, 1, 2

2.
1. $p \leftrightarrow q$ — A
2. p — A
3. q — MB, 1, 2

3.
1. $p \leftrightarrow q$ — A
2. q — A
3. p — MB, 1, 2

4.
1. $(p \to p) \to p$ — A
2. $[p$ — ACP
3. $p \to p$ — CP, 2-2
4. p — MP, 1, 3

5.
1. $p \leftrightarrow \neg q$ — A
2. $\neg \neg p$ — A
3. p — DN, 3
6. $\neg q$ — MB, 4, 5

6.
1. $p \to q$ — A
2. $p \& r$ — A
3. p — S, 2
4. q — MP, 1, 3
5. r — S, 2
6. $r \& q$ — C, 5, 4

12.
1. $\neg q \& (r \to p)$ — A
2. $\neg \neg r$ — A
3. $\neg q$ — S, 1
4. $r \to p$ — S, 1
5. r — DN, 2
6. p — MP, 4, 5
7. $p \& \neg q$ — C, 6, 3

18. 1. $\neg p \leftrightarrow \neg q$ A
   2. $\neg q \rightarrow \neg r$ A
   3. $\neg p \rightarrow \neg s$ A
   4. $\neg p \,\&\, t$ A
   5. $\neg p$ S,4
   6. $\neg s$ MP, 3, 5
   7. $\neg q$ MB, 1, 5
   8. $\neg r$ MP, 2, 7
   9. $\neg s \,\&\, \neg r$ C, 6, 8

24. 1. $\lceil p$ ACP
   2. $\lfloor \neg \neg p$ DN, 1
   3. $p \rightarrow \neg \neg p$ CP, 1-2
   4. $\lceil \neg \neg p$ ACP
   5. $\lfloor p$ DN, 4
   6. $\neg \neg p \rightarrow p$ CP, 4-5
   7. $p \leftrightarrow \neg \neg p$ B, 3, 6

30. p: this product will succeed; q: this product is given adequate advertizing support; r: the company will show a profit for the year; s: the Vice-President believes that another product has more potential; t: this product is great

   1. $\neg p \leftrightarrow \neg q$ A
   2. $\neg p \rightarrow \neg r$ A
   3. $\neg q \rightarrow s$ A
   4. $t \,\&\, \neg p$ A
   5. $\neg p$ S, 4
   6. $\neg q$ MB, 1, 5
   7. s MP, 3, 6
   8. $\neg r$ MP, 2, 5
   9. $s \,\&\, \neg r$ C, 7, 8

IA.4 Disjunction Rules
(from 8.4)

1. 1. p A
   2. $p \lor q$ Ad, 1

2. 1. $p \,\&\, q$ A
   2. p S, 1
   3. $p \lor q$ Ad, 2

3. 1. $p \lor q$ A
   2. $\neg q$ A
   3. p DS, 1, 2

4. 1. $\neg p \lor q$ A
   2. p A
   3. $\neg \neg p$ DN, 1, 3
   4. q DS, 1, 3

5. 1. $q \rightarrow r$ A
   2. $p \lor q$ A
   3. $p \rightarrow s$ A
   4. $\lceil \neg(r \lor s)$ AIP
   5. $\lceil r$ AIP
   6. $| r \lor s$ Ad, 5
   7. $\lfloor (r \lor s) \,\&\, \neg(r \lor s)$ C, 6, 4
   8. $\neg r$ IP, 5-7
   9. $\lceil q$ AIP
   10. $| r$ MP, 1, 9
   11. $\lfloor r \,\&\, \neg r$ C, 8, 10
   12. $\neg q$ IP, 9-11
   13. p DS, 2, 12
   14. s MP, 3, 13
   15. $r \lor s$ Ad, 14
   16. $\lfloor (r \lor s) \,\&\, \neg(r \lor s)$ C, 15, 4
   17. $\neg \neg(r \lor s)$ IP, 4-16
   18. $r \lor s$ DN, 17

6. 1. $p \lor q$ A
   2. $\neg r$ A
   3. $p \rightarrow r$ A
   4. $\lceil p$ AIP
   5. $| r$ MP, 4, 3
   6. $\lfloor r \,\&\, \neg r$ C, 2, 5
   7. $\neg p$ IP, 4-6
   8. q DS, 1, 7

12.
1.	$(p \mathbin{\&} q) \vee (r \vee s)$	A
2.	$\neg(((p \mathbin{\&} q) \vee r) \vee s)$	AIP
3.	$p \mathbin{\&} q$	AIP
4.	$(p \mathbin{\&} q) \vee r$	Ad, 3
5.	$((p \mathbin{\&} q) \vee r) \vee s$	Ad, 4
6.	$(((p \mathbin{\&} q) \vee r) \vee s) \mathbin{\&} \neg(((p \mathbin{\&} q) \vee r) \vee s)$	C, 5, 2
7.	$\neg(p \mathbin{\&} q)$	IP, 3-6
8.	$r \vee s$	DS, 1, 7
9.	r	AIP
10.	$(p \mathbin{\&} q) \vee r$	Ad, 9
11.	$((p \mathbin{\&} q) \vee r) \vee s$	Ad, 10
12.	$(((p \mathbin{\&} q) \vee r) \vee s) \mathbin{\&} \neg(((p \mathbin{\&} q) \vee r) \vee s)$	C, 2, 11
13.	$\neg r$	IP, 9-12
14.	s	DS, 8, 13
15.	$((p \mathbin{\&} q) \vee r) \vee s$	Ad, 14
16.	$(((p \mathbin{\&} q) \vee r) \vee s) \mathbin{\&} \neg(((p \mathbin{\&} q) \vee r) \vee s)$	C, 2, 15
17.	$\neg\neg(((p \mathbin{\&} q) \vee r) \vee s)$	IP, 2-16
18.	$((p \mathbin{\&} q) \vee r) \vee s$	DN, 17

18.
1.	$\neg p \vee q$	A
2.	$\neg q \vee r$	A
3.	$\neg r$	A
4.	$\neg q$	DS, 2, 3
5.	$\neg p$	DS, 1, 4

24.
1.	$p \mathbin{\&} (q \to r)$	A
2.	$q \vee \neg p$	A
3.	$(r \vee s) \to t$	A
4.	p	S, 1
5.	$\neg\neg p$	DN, 4
6.	q	DS, 2, 5
7.	$q \to r$	S, 1
8.	r	MP, 7, 6
9.	$r \vee s$	Ad, 8
10.	t	MP, 3, 9
11.	$t \vee m$	Ad, 10

30. p: someone knows where Rick was last night; q: Rick has an alibi; r: Rick is the prime suspect; s: new evidence points to someone else

1.	$\neg p$	A
2.	$q \vee r$	A
3.	$q \to p$	A
4.	q	AIP
5.	p	MP, 3, 4
6.	$p \mathbin{\&} \neg p$	C, 5, 1
7.	$\neg q$	IP, 4-6
8.	r	DS, 2, 7
9.	$s \vee r$	Ad, 8

(from 8.5)

1.
1. $r \rightarrow p$ A
2. $p \rightarrow q$ A
3. $\lceil r$ ACP
4. $\mid p$ MP, 1, 3
5. $\lfloor q$ MP, 2, 4
6. $r \rightarrow q$ CP, 3-5

2.
1. $r \rightarrow p$ A
2. $p \rightarrow q$ A
3. $\lceil \neg q$ ACP
4. $\mid \lceil r$ AIP
5. $\mid \mid p$ MP, 1, 4
6. $\mid \mid q$ MP, 2, 5
7. $\mid \lfloor q \& \neg q$ C, 6, 3
8. $\lfloor \neg r$ IP, 4-7
9. $\neg q \rightarrow \neg r$ CP, 3-8

3.
1. $r \rightarrow p$ A
2. $\neg r \rightarrow q$ A
3. $\lceil \neg p$ ACP
4. $\mid \lceil r$ AIP
5. $\mid \mid p$ MP, 1, 4
6. $\mid \lfloor p \& \neg p$ C, 5, 3
7. $\mid \neg r$ IP, 4-7
8. $\lfloor q$ MP, 2, 7
9. $\neg p \rightarrow q$ CP, 3-8

4.
1. $r \rightarrow p$ A
2. $\neg r \rightarrow q$ AP, 3-9
3. $\lceil \neg q$ ACP
4. $\mid \lceil \neg r$ AIP
5. $\mid \mid q$ MP, 2, 4
6. $\mid \lfloor q \& \neg q$ C, 5, 3
7. $\mid \neg \neg r$ IP, 4-6
8. $\mid r$ DN, 7
9. $\lfloor p$ MP, 1, 8
10. $\neg q \rightarrow p$ CP, 3-9

6.
1. $\neg r \vee \neg p$ A
2. $\lceil p$ ACP
3. $\mid \neg \neg p$ DN, 2
4. $\lfloor \neg r$ DS, 1, 3
5. $p \rightarrow \neg r$ CP, 2-4

7.
1. $r \rightarrow p$ A
2. $\lceil r$ ACP
3. $\mid p$ MP, 1, 2
4. $\lfloor r \& p$ C, 2, 3
5. $r \rightarrow (r \& p)$ CP, 2-4
6. $\lceil r \& p$ ACP
7. $\lfloor r$ S, 6
8. $(r \& p) \rightarrow r$ CP, 6-7
9. $r \leftrightarrow (r \& p)$ B, 9

8.
1. $r \leftrightarrow (r \& p)$ A
2. $\lceil r$ ACP
3. $\mid r \& p$ MB, 1, 2
4. $\lfloor p$ S, 3
5. $r \rightarrow p$ CP, 2-4

9.
1. $r \vee p$ A
2. $\neg r \& s$ A
3. $\neg r$ S, 2
4. p DS, 1, 3
5. $p \vee q$ Ad, 4

10.
1. $r \rightarrow p$ A
2. $q \rightarrow r$ A
3. $\lceil \neg(\neg q \vee p)$ AIP
4. $\mid \lceil \neg q$ AIP
5. $\mid \mid \neg q \vee p$ Ad, 4
6. $\mid \lfloor (\neg q \vee p) \& \neg(\neg q \vee p)$ C, 5, 3
7. $\mid \neg \neg q$ IP, 4-6
8. $\mid q$ DN, 7
9. $\mid r$ MP, 2, 8
10. $\mid p$ MP, 1, 9
11. $\mid \neg q \vee p$ Ad, 10
12. $\lfloor (\neg q \vee p) \& \neg(\neg q \vee p)$ C, 11, 3
13. $\neg \neg(\neg q \vee p)$ IP, 3-12
14. $\neg q \vee p$ DN, 13

11.
1. $\neg r \lor \neg q$ A
2. $r \& \neg\neg q$ AIP
3. r S, 2
4. $\neg\neg q$ S, 2
5. $\neg r$ DS, 1, 4
6. $r \& \neg r$ C, 3, 5
7. $\neg(r \& \neg\neg q)$ IP, 2-6

12.
1. $\neg(r \& \neg p) \lor \neg r$ A
2. r ACP
3. $\neg\neg r$ DN, 2
4. $\neg(r \& \neg p)$ DS, 1, 3
5. $\neg p$ AIP
6. $r \& \neg p$ C, 2, 5
7. $(r \& \neg p) \& \neg(r \& \neg p)$ C, 6, 4
8. $\neg\neg p$ IP, 5-7
9. p DN, 8
10. $r \to p$ CP, 2-9

18.
1. $(r \& \neg p) \to \neg q$ A
2. q A
3. $\neg(\neg r \lor (r \& p))$ AIP
4. $\neg r$ AIP
5. $\neg r \lor (r \& p)$ Ad, 4
6. $(\neg r \lor (r \& p)) \& \neg(\neg r \lor (r \& p))$ C, 5, 3
7. $\neg\neg r$ IP, 4-6
8. r DN, 7
9. p AIP
10. $r \& p$ C, 8, 9
11. $\neg r \lor (r \& p)$ Ad, 10
12. $(\neg r \lor (r \& p)) \& \neg(\neg r \lor (r \& p))$ C, 11, 3
13. $\neg p$ IP, 9-12
14. $r \& \neg p$ C, 8, 13
15. $\neg q$ MP, 1, 14
16. $q \& \neg q$ C, 2, 15
17. $\neg r \lor (r \& p)$ IP, 3-16

24.
1. $r \leftrightarrow p$ A
2. $\neg r$ ACP
3. p AIP
4. r MB, 1, 3
5. $r \& \neg r$ C, 4, 2
6. $\neg p$ IP, 3-5
7. $\neg r \to \neg p$ CP, 2-6
8. $\neg p$ ACP
9. r AIP
10. p MB, 1, 9
11. $p \& \neg p$ C, 10, 8
12. $\neg r$ IP, 9-11
13. $\neg p \to \neg r$ CP, 8-12
14. $\neg r \leftrightarrow \neg p$ B, 7, 13

30.

1.	$(s \,\&\, \neg q) \to \neg r$	A
2.	$(p \to \neg s) \leftrightarrow \neg r$	A
3.	r	ACP
4.	$\neg s$	AIP
5.	p	ACP
6.	$r \,\&\, \neg s$	C, 3, 4
7.	$\neg s$	S, 6
8.	$p \to \neg s$	CP, 5-7
9.	$\neg r$	MB, 2, 8
10.	$r \,\&\, \neg r$	C, 3, 9
11.	s	IP, 4-10
12.	$\neg p$	AIP
13.	p	ACP
$13\frac{1}{2}$.	$\neg s$	AIP
14.	$\neg p \,\&\, \neg p$	C, 13, 12
15.	$\neg s$	IP, $13\frac{1}{2}$-14
16.	$p \to \neg s$	CP, 13-15
17.	$\neg r$	MB, 2, 16
18.	$r \,\&\, \neg r$	C, 3, 17
19.	$\neg\neg p$	IP, 12-18
20.	p	DN, 19
21.	$\neg q$	AIP
22.	$s \,\&\, \neg q$	C, 11, 21
23.	$\neg r$	MP, 1, 22
24.	$r \,\&\, \neg r$	C, 3, 23
25.	$\neg\neg q$	IP, 21-24
26.	q	DN, 25
27.	$s \,\&\, p$	C, 11, 20
28.	$q \,\&\, (s \,\&\, p)$	C, 26, 27
29.	$r \to (q \,\&\, (s \,\&\, p))$	CP, 3-28
30.	$q \,\&\, (s \,\&\, p)$	ACP
31.	$s \,\&\, p$	S, 17
32.	$p \to \neg s$	AIP
33.	p	S, 31
34.	$\neg s$	MP, 32, 33
35.	s	S, 31
36.	$s \,\&\, \neg s$	C, 35, 34
37.	$\neg(p \to \neg s)$	IP, 32-36
38.	$\neg r$	AIP
39.	$p \to \neg s$	MB, 2, 38
40.	$(p \to \neg s) \,\&\, \neg(p \to \neg s)$	C, 39, 37
41.	$\neg\neg r$	IP, 38-40
42.	r	ON, 41
43.	$(q \,\&\, (s \,\&\, p)) \to r$	CP, 30-42
44.	$(r \to (q \,\&\, (s \,\&\, p))) \,\&\, ((q \,\&\, (s \,\&\, p)) \to r)$	C, 29, 43
45.	$r \leftrightarrow (q \,\&\, (s \,\&\, p))$	B, 44

36.

1.	$p \,\&\, \neg q$	A
2.	p	S, 1
3.	$\neg q$	S, 1
4.	$p \to q$	AIP
5.	q	MP, 4, 2
6.	$q \,\&\, \neg q$	C, 5, 3
7.	$\neg(p \to q)$	IP, 4-6

42. 1. ⌈ p & q ACP
     2. ⌊ p S, 1
     3. $(p$ & $q) \to p$ CP, 1-2

48. 1. $(p$ & $q) \vee r$ A
     2. ⌈ $\neg((q$ & $p) \vee r)$ AIP
     3. │⌈ r AIP
     4. ││ $(q$ & $p) \vee r$ Ad, 3
     5. │⌊ $((q$ & $p) \vee r)$ & $\neg((q$ & $p) \vee r)$ C, 4, 2
     6. │ $\neg r$ IP, 3-5
     7. │ p & q DS, 1, 6
     8. │ p S, 7
     9. │ q S, 7
    10. │ q & p C, 9, 8
    11. │ $(q$ & $p) \vee r$ Ad, 10
    12. ⌊ $((q$ & $p) \vee r)$ & $\neg((q$ & $p) \vee r)$ C, 11, 2
    13. $\neg\neg((q$ & $p) \vee r)$ IP, 2-12
    14. $(q$ & $p) \vee r$ DN, 13

54. p: a man can serve God; q: a man can serve Mammon; r: a man starves

     1. $\neg(p$ & $q)$ A
     2. $\neg q \to r$ A
     3. $r \to \neg p$ A
     4. ⌈ p AIP
     5. │⌈ $\neg q$ AIP
     6. ││ r MP, 2, 5
     7. ││ $\neg p$ MP, 3, 6
     8. │⌊ p & $\neg p$ C, 4, 7
     9. │ $\neg\neg q$ IP, 5-8
    10. │ q DN, 9
    11. │ p & q C, 4, 10
    12. ⌊ $(p$ & $q)$ & $\neg(p$ & $q)$ C, 11, 1
    13. $\neg p$ IP, 4-12

IA.5 Derived Rules

1. p: you are ambitious; q: you'll achieve your goals; r: life has meaning

     1. $p \to \neg q$ A
     2. $r \to p$ A
     3. ⌈ q ACP
     4. │ $\neg\neg q$ DN, 3
     5. │ $\neg p$ MT, 4, 1
     6. ⌊ $\neg r$ MT, 5, 2
     7. $q \to \neg r$ CP, 3-6

2. p: Adam comes to the party; q: Barbara comes to the party; r: Carlos will be happy

     1. $p \to q$ A
     2. $q \to p$ A
     3. ⌈ $p \to r$ ACP
     4. │⌈ q ACP
     5. ││ p MP, 4, 2
     6. │⌊ r MP, 3, 5
     7. ⌊ $q \to r$ CP, 4-6
     8. $(p \to r) \to (q \to r)$ CP, 3-7

3. *p*: interest rates will rise; *q*: Congress enacts a tax increase; *r*: the unemployment level will increase; *s*: the budget deficit will increase

1.	$p \vee q$	A
2.	$q \rightarrow p$	A
3.	$p \rightarrow r$	A
4.	$\neg r \vee s$	A
5.	$\neg s$	AIP
6.	$\neg r$	DS, 4, 5
7.	$\neg p$	MT, 6, 3
8.	$\neg q$	MT, 2, 7
9.	p	DS, 1, 8
10.	$p \;\&\; \neg p$	C, 9, 7
11.	s	IP, 5-10

4. *p*: God is omnipotent; *q*: God can do everything; *r*: God can make a stone so heavy he can't lift it

1.	$p \leftrightarrow q$	A
2.	$\neg r \rightarrow \neg q$	A
3.	$r \rightarrow \neg q$	A
4.	p	AIP
5.	q	MB, 1, 4
6.	$\neg \neg r$	MT, 2, 5
7.	$\neg \neg q$	DN, 5
8.	$\neg r$	MT, 3, 7
9.	$\neg r \;\&\; \neg \neg r$	C, 8, 6
10.	$\neg p$	IP, 4-9
11.	$\neg p \vee \neg s$	Ad, 10

5. *p*: the President pursues arms limitations talks; *q*: the President gets the foreign policy mechanism working harmoniously; *r*: the European left will acquiesce to the placement of additional nuclear weapons in Europe

1.	$p \rightarrow (q \rightarrow r)$	A
2.	$\neg r$	A
3.	$\neg p \vee (q \rightarrow r)$	MC, 1
4.	$\neg p \vee (\neg q \vee r)$	MC, 3
5.	$(\neg p \vee \neg q) \vee r$	As, 4
6.	$\neg p \vee \neg q$	DS, 2, 5
7.	$\neg q \vee \neg p$	Cm, 6

6. *p*: we introduce a new product line; *q*: we give an existing line a new advertizing image; *r*: we take risks; *s*: we may lose market share; *t*: we have to make large expenditures on advertizing

1.	$(p \vee q) \rightarrow (r \;\&\; s)$	A
2.	$\neg p \rightarrow \neg t$	A
3.	$\neg r$	ACP
4.	$\neg r \vee \neg s$	Ad, 3
5.	$\neg (r \;\&\; s)$	DM, 4
6.	$\neg (p \vee q)$	MT, 1, 5
7.	$\neg p \;\&\; \neg q$	DM, 6
8.	$\neg p$	S, 7
9.	$\neg t$	MP, 2, 8
10.	$\neg r \rightarrow \neg t$	CP, 3-9

12. p: the President retaliates against Libya with military force; q: the public will be ambivalent; r: Libya directs terrorist attacks toward Americans on American soil

1.	$p \to q$	A
2.	$r \to \neg q$	A
3.	$\lceil r$	ACP
4.	$\mid \neg q$	MP, 2, 3
5.	$\lfloor \neg p$	MT, 1, 4
6.	$r \to \neg p$	CP, 3-5
7.	$\neg r \lor \neg p$	MC, 6

18. p: Congress erects trade barriers; q: Congress grants further subsidies to American farmers; r: other countries will retaliate, s: the economy will slow down; t: Congress will find new sources of revenue

1.	$(p \And q) \to r$	A
2.	$r \to s$	A
3.	$s \to (\neg q \lor t)$	A
4.	$\neg p \to (\neg q \And \neg r)$	A
5.	$\lceil \neg(\neg q \lor t)$	AIP
6.	$\mid \neg s$	MT, 3, 5
7.	$\mid \neg r$	MT, 2, 6
8.	$\mid \neg(p \And q)$	MT, 1, 7
9.	$\mid \neg p \lor \neg q$	DM, 8
10.	$\mid \neg\neg q \And \neg t$	DM, 5
11.	$\mid \neg\neg q$	S, 10
12.	$\mid \neg p$	DS, 9, 11
13.	$\mid \neg q \And \neg r$	MP, 12, 14
14.	$\mid \neg q$	S, 13
15.	$\lfloor \neg q \And \neg\neg q$	C, 14, 11
16.	$\neg q \lor t$	IP, 5-15
17.	$t \lor \neg q$	Cm, 16

24.

1.	p	A
2.	$\neg(p \lor r)$	A
3.	$\neg p \And \neg r$	DM, 2
4.	$\neg p$	S, 3
5.	q	!, 1, 4

30.

1.	$(\neg p \to q) \lor r$	A
2.	$(\neg\neg p \lor q) \lor r$	MC, 1
3.	$(p \lor q) \lor r$	DN, 2
4.	$p \lor (q \lor r)$	As, 3
5.	$\neg p \to (q \lor r)$	MC, 4

36.

1.	$p \leftrightarrow q$	A
2.	$\lceil \neg p$	ACP
3.	$\lfloor \neg q$	MB, 1, 2
4.	$\neg p \to \neg q$	CP, 2-3
5.	$\lceil \neg q$	ACP
6.	$\lfloor \neg p$	MB, 1, 5
7.	$\neg q \to \neg p$	CP, 5-6
8.	$\neg q \leftrightarrow \neg p$	B, 7, 4

42.

1.	$p \lor q$	A
2.	$\neg q \lor r$	A
3.	$\lceil \neg p$	ACP
4.	$\mid q$	DS, 1, 3
5.	$\mid \neg\neg q$	DN, 4
6.	$\lfloor r$	DS, 2, 5
7.	$\neg p \to r$	CP, 3-6
8.	$p \lor r$	MC, 7

48. 1. $\neg s \to \neg k$ A
   2. $(s \& t) \to (p \leftrightarrow q)$ A
   3. $\neg(\neg p \lor q)$ A
   4. t ACP
   5. k AIP
   6. $\neg\neg s$ MT, 6, 1
   7. s DN, 6
   8. $s \& t$ 7, 4
   9. $p \leftrightarrow q$ MP, 8, 2
   10. $\neg\neg p \& \neg q$ DM, 3
   11. $\neg\neg p$ S, 10
   12. p DN, 11
   13. q MB, 9, 12
   14. $\neg q$ S, 10
   15. $q \& \neg q$ C, 13, 14
   16. $\neg k$ IP, 5-15
   17. $t \to \neg k$ CP, 4-16

54. 1. $p \to q$ ACP   **60.** 1. $p \lor (q \lor r)$ ACP
   2. $\neg q$ ACP   2. $(q \lor r) \lor p$ Cm, 1
   3. $\neg p$ MT, 1, 2   3. $q \lor (r \lor p)$ As, 2
   4. $\neg q \to \neg p$ CP, 2-3   4. $q \lor (p \lor r)$ Cm, 3
   5. $(p \to q) \to (\neg q \to \neg p)$ CP, 1-4   5. $(p \lor (q \lor r)) \to (q \lor (p \lor r))$ CP, 1-4

Appendix IB
ADDING QUANTIFIERS

IB.1 Deduction Rules for Quantifiers

1. 1. $\forall x Cgx$ A
   2. Cgo US, 1 (where 'o' symbolizes 'Texas')   **2.** 1. $\forall x Cgx$ A
                                                           2. Cga US, 1
                                                           3. $\exists x Cgx$ EG, 2

3. 1. $\forall x Cgx$ A   **4.** 1. $\forall x Cgx$ A   **5.** 1. $\forall x(Lx \to \neg Fxi)$ A
   2. Cgg US, 1   2. Cgg US, 1   2. Fbi A
                                   3. $\exists x Cxg$ EG, 2   3. $Lb \to \neg Fbi$ US, 1
                                                      4. $\neg\neg Fbi$ DN, 2
                                                      5. $\neg Lb$ MT, 3, 4

6. 1. $\forall x((Px \& Bx) \to Cx)$ A
   2. $\exists x((Px \& Qx) \& Bx)$ A (where 'Q' symbolizes 'is a Pirate')
   3. $(Pa \& Qa) \& Ba$ ES, 2
   4. $Pa \& Qa$ S, 3
   5. Pa S, 4
   6. Ba S, 3
   7. $Pa \& Ba$ C, 5, 6
   8. $(Pa \& Ba) \to Ca$ US, 1
   9. Ca MP, 8, 7
   10. Qa S, 4
   11. $Qa \& Ca$ C, 10, 9
   12. $\exists x(Qx \& Cx)$ EG, 11

12. 1. $\exists x((Cx \& Kix) \& Ix)$ A
   2. $\forall x((Cx \& Kix) \to Vx)$ A
   3. $(Ca \& Kia) \& Ia$ ES, 1
   4. $Ca \& Kia$ S, 3
   5. $(Ca \& Kia) \to Va$ US, 2

6. Va MP, 5, 4
7. Kia S, 4
8. Ia S, 3
9. $Va \ \& \ Ia$ C, 6, 8
10. $\exists x(Vx \ \& \ Ix)$ EG, 9

18.
1. $\forall x\forall y(((Px \ \& \ Py) \ \& \ Cxy) \to \forall z(Cyz \to Cxz))$ A
2. $\exists x\exists y((Px \ \& \ Py) \ \& \ (Cxy \ \& \ Cyx))$ A
3. $\exists y((Pa \ \& \ Py) \ \& \ (Cay \ \& \ Cya))$ ES, 2
4. $(Pa \ \& \ Pb) \ \& \ (Cab \ \& \ Cba)$ ES, 3
5. $Pa \ \& \ Pb$ S, 4
6. $Cab \ \& \ Cba$ S, 4
7. Cab S, 6
8. $(Pa \ \& \ Pb) \ \& \ Cab$ C, 5, 7
9. $\forall y(((Pa \ \& \ Py) \ \& \ Cay) \to \forall z(Cyz \to Caz))$ US, 1
10. $((Pa \ \& \ Pb) \ \& \ Cab) \to \forall z(Cbz \to Caz)$ US, 9
11. $\forall z(Cbz \to Caz)$ MP, 10, 8
12. $Cba \to Caa$ US, 11
13. Cba S, 6
14. Caa MP, 12, 13
15. Pa S, 5
16. $Pa \ \& \ Caa$ C, 15, 14
17. $\exists x(Px \ \& \ Cxx)$ EG, 16

24.
1. $\forall x(Mx \to \neg Lx)$ A
2. $\forall x(Mx \to Sx)$ A
3. $\exists xMx$ A
4. Ma ES, 3
5. $Ma \to \neg La$ US, 1
6. $\neg La$ MP, 5, 4
7. $Ma \to Sa$ US, 2
8. Sa MP, 7, 4
9. $Sa \ \& \ \neg La$ C, 8, 6
10. $\exists x(Sx \ \& \ \neg Lx)$ EG, 9

30.
1. $\forall x(Mx \to \neg Lx)$ A
2. $\forall x(Sx \to Mx)$ A
3. $\exists xSx$ A
4. Sa ES, 3
5. $Sa \to Ma$ US, 2
6. Ma MP, 5, 4
7. $Ma \to \neg La$ US, 1
8. $\neg La$ MP, 7, 6
9. $Sa \ \& \ \neg La$ C, 4, 8
10. $\exists x(Sx \ \& \ \neg Lx)$ EG, 9

36.
1. $\exists x(Mx \ \& \ Lx)$ A
2. $\forall x(Sx \to \neg Mx)$ A
3. $Ma \ \& \ La$ ES, 1
4. $Sa \to \neg Ma$ US, 2
5. Ma S, 3
6. $\neg\neg Ma$ DN, 5
7. $\neg Sa$ MT, 4, 6
8. La S, 3
9. $La \ \& \ \neg Sa$ C, 8, 7
10. $\exists x(Lx \ \& \ \neg Sx)$ EG, 9

42.
1. $\forall x(Hx \to Gx)$ A
2. $\exists x(\neg Gx \ \& \ Fx)$ A
3. $\neg Ga \ \& \ Fa$ ES, 2
4. Fa S, 3
5. $\neg Ga$ S, 3
6. $Ha \to Ga$ US, 1
7. $\neg Ha$ MT, 6, 5
8. $Fa \ \& \ \neg Ha$ C, 4, 7
9. $\exists x(Fx \ \& \ \neg Hx)$ EG, 8

48.
1. $\forall x(Hx \to \neg Gx)$ A
2. $\exists x(Gx \ \& \ Fx)$ A
3. $Ga \ \& \ Fa$ ES, 2
4. Fa S, 3
5. Ga S, 3
6. $Ha \to \neg Ga$ US, 1
7. $\neg\neg Ga$ DN, 5
8. $\neg Ha$ MT, 6, 7
9. $Fa \ \& \ \neg Ha$ C, 4, 8
10. $\exists x(Fx \ \& \ \neg Hx)$ EG, 9

54.
1.	$\forall x(Fx \lor \neg Gx)$	A
2.	$\forall x(Fx \to Hx)$	A
3.	$\forall x(\neg Gx \to Jx)$	A
4.	$\exists x \neg Jx$	A
5.	$\neg Ja$	ES, 4
6.	$\neg Ga \to Ja$	US, 3
7.	$\neg \neg Ga$	MT, 6, 5
8.	$Fa \lor \neg Ga$	US, 1
9.	Fa	DS, 8, 7
10.	$Fa \to Ha$	US, 2
11.	Ha	MP, 10, 9
12.	$\exists x Hx$	EG, 11

60.
1.	$\forall x(Fx \to Gx)$	A
2.	$Fa \to Ga$	US, 1
3.	$\neg Fa \lor Ga$	DC, 2
4.	$\exists x(\neg Fx \lor Gx)$	EG, 3

IB.2 Universal Generalization

1.
1.	$\forall x(Mx \to Lx)$	A
2.	$\forall x(Sx \to Mx)$	A
3.	$\lceil Sa$	ACP
4.	$\mid Sa \to Ma$	US, 2
5.	$\mid Ma$	MP, 4, 3
6.	$\mid Ma \to La$	US, 1
7.	$\lfloor La$	MP, 6, 5
8.	$Sa \to La$	CP, 3-7
9.	$\forall x(Sx \to Lx)$	UG, 8

2.
1.	$\forall x(Mx \to \neg Lx)$	A
2.	$\forall x(Sx \to Mx)$	A
3.	$\lceil Sa$	ACP
4.	$\mid Sa \to Ma$	US, 2
5.	$\mid Ma$	MP, 4, 3
6.	$\mid Ma \to \neg La$	US, 1
7.	$\lfloor \neg La$	MP, 6, 5
8.	$Sa \to \neg La$	CP, 3-7
9.	$\forall x(Sx \to \neg Lx)$	UG, 8

3.
1.	$\forall x(Lx \to \neg Mx)$	A
2.	$\forall x(Sx \to Mx)$	A
3.	$\lceil Sa$	ACP
4.	$\mid Sa \to Ma$	US, 2
5.	$\mid Ma$	MP, 4, 3
6.	$\mid La \to \neg Ma$	US, 1
7.	$\mid \neg \neg Ma$	DN, 5
8.	$\lfloor \neg La$	MT, 6, 7
9.	$Sa \to \neg La$	CP, 3-8
10.	$\forall x(Sx \to \neg Lx)$	UG, 9

4.
1.	$\forall x(Lx \to Mx)$	A
2.	$\forall x(Sx \to \neg Mx)$	A
3.	$\lceil Sa$	ACP
4.	$\mid Sa \to \neg Ma$	US, 2
5.	$\mid \neg Ma$	MP, 4, 3
6.	$\mid La \to Ma$	US, 1
7.	$\lfloor \neg La$	MT, 6, 5
8.	$Sa \to \neg La$	CP, 3-7
9.	$\forall x(Sx \to \neg Lx)$	UG, 8

5.
1.	$\forall x(Mx \to \neg Lx)$	A
2.	$\forall x(Sx \to Mx)$	A
3.	$\lceil La$	ACP
4.	$\mid Ma \to \neg La$	US, 1
5.	$\mid \neg \neg La$	DN, 3
6.	$\mid \neg Ma$	MT, 4, 5
7.	$\mid Sa \to Ma$	US, 2
8.	$\lfloor \neg Sa$	MT, 7, 6
9.	$La \to \neg Sa$	CP, 3-8
10.	$\forall x(Lx \to \neg Sx)$	UG, 9

6.
1.	$\forall x(Dx \to Sx)$	A
2.	$\forall x(Ix \to \neg Sx)$	A
3.	$\lceil Da$	ACP
4.	$\mid Da \to Sa$	US, 1
5.	$\mid Sa$	MP, 4, 3
6.	$\mid Ia \to \neg Sa$	US, 2
7.	$\mid \neg \neg Sa$	DN, 5
8.	$\lfloor \neg Ia$	MT, 6, 7
9.	$Da \to \neg Ia$	CP, 3-8
10.	$\forall x(Dx \to \neg Ix)$	UG, 9

12.
1.	$\forall x(Wx \to \neg Fx)$	A
2.	$\forall x(Px \to \neg \neg Fx)$	A
3.	$\lceil Pa$	ACP
4.	$\mid Pa \to \neg \neg Fa$	US, 2
5.	$\mid \neg \neg Fa$	MP, 4, 3
6.	$\mid Wa \to \neg Fa$	US, 1
7.	$\lfloor \neg Wa$	MT, 6, 5
8.	$Pa \to \neg Wa$	CP, 3-7
9.	$\forall x(Px \to \neg Wx)$	UG, 8

18.
1.	$\forall x((Sx \,\&\, \neg Px) \to \neg Ex)$	A
2.	$\forall x((Sx \,\&\, Oxh) \to \neg Px)$	A
3.	$\lceil Sa \,\&\, Oah$	ACP
4.	$\mid (Sa \,\&\, Oah) \to \neg Pa$	US, 2
5.	$\mid \neg Pa$	MP, 4, 3
6.	$\mid Sa$	S, 3
7.	$\mid Sa \,\&\, \neg Pa$	C, 6, 5
8.	$\mid (Sa \,\&\, \neg Pa) \to \neg Ea$	US, 1
9.	$\lfloor \neg Ea$	MP, 8, 7
10.	$(Sa \,\&\, Oah) \to \neg Ea$	CP, 3-9
11.	$\forall x((Sx \,\&\, Oxh) \to \neg Ex)$	UG, 10

24.
1. $\forall x(Oxi \rightarrow \neg Cx)$ A
2. $\forall x(Sx \rightarrow Cx)$ A
3. Oai ACP
4. $Oai \rightarrow \neg Ca$ US, 1
5. $\neg Ca$ MP, 4, 3
6. $Sa \rightarrow Ca$ US, 2
7. $\neg Sa$ MT, 6, 5
8. $Oai \rightarrow \neg Sa$ CP, 3-7
9. $\forall x(Oxi \rightarrow \neg Sx)$ UG, 8

30.
1. $\forall x(\neg Nx \rightarrow \neg Mx)$ A
2. $\forall x(Lx \rightarrow Wx)$ A
3. $\forall x(Ix \rightarrow \neg Wx)$ A
4. $\forall x(Nx \rightarrow Lx)$ A
5. $Ia \rightarrow \neg Wa$ US, 3
6. $La \rightarrow Wa$ US, 2
7. $Na \rightarrow La$ US, 4
8. $\neg Na \rightarrow \neg Ma$ US, 1
9. Ia ACP
10. Na AIP
11. La MP, 7, 10
12. Wa MP, 6, 11
13. $\neg Wa$ MP, 5, 9
14. $Wa \& \neg Wa$ C, 12, 13
15. $\neg Na$ IP, 10-14
16. $\neg Ma$ MP, 8, 15
17. $Ia \rightarrow \neg Ma$ CP, 9-16
18. $\forall x(Ix \rightarrow \neg Mx)$ UG, 17

36.
1. $\forall x(Ixj \rightarrow \neg Rjx)$ A
2. $\forall x(\neg Lxj \rightarrow Ixj)$ A
3. Rja ACP
4. $Iaj \rightarrow \neg Rja$ US, 1
5. $\neg \neg Rja$ DN, 3
6. $\neg Iaj$ MT, 4, 5
7. $\neg Laj \rightarrow Iaj$ US, 1
8. $\neg \neg Laj$ MT, 7, 6
9. Laj DN, 8
10. $Rja \rightarrow Laj$ CP, 3-9
11. $\forall x(Rjx \rightarrow Lxj)$ UG, 10

42.
1. $\forall xFx \& \forall xGx$ A
2. $\forall xFx$ S, 1
3. $\forall xGx$ S, 1
4. Fa US, 2
5. Ga US, 3
6. $Fa \& Ga$ C, 4, 5
7. $\forall x(Fx \& Gx)$ UG, 6

48.
1. $\forall x(Fx \leftrightarrow (\neg Gx \vee \neg Fx))$ A
2. $\neg \neg Ga$ AIP
3. Fa AIP
4. $Fa \leftrightarrow (\neg Ga \vee \neg Fa)$ US, 1
5. $\neg Ga \vee \neg Fa$ MB, 4, 3
6. $\neg Fa$ DS, 5, 2
7. $Fa \& \neg Fa$ C, 3, 6
8. $\neg Fa$ IP, 3-7
9. $Fa \leftrightarrow (\neg Ga \vee \neg Fa)$ US, 1
10. $\neg(\neg Ga \vee \neg Fa)$ MB, 9, 8
11. $\neg \neg Ga \& \neg \neg Fa$ DM, 10
12. $\neg \neg Fa$ S, 11
13. $\neg Fa \& \neg \neg Fa$ C, 8, 12
14. $\neg Ga$ IP, 2-13
15. $\forall x \neg Gx$ UG, 14

54.
1. $\forall x(Fx \to (Gx \lor Hx))$ A
2. $\forall x((Jx \& Fx) \to \neg Gx)$ A
3. $\forall x(\neg Fx \to \neg Jx)$ A
4. Ja ACP
5. $\neg Fa \to \neg Ja$ US, 3
6. $\neg\neg Ja$ DN, 4
7. $\neg\neg Fa$ MT, 5, 6
8. Fa DN, 7
9. $Ja \& Fa$ C, 4, 8
10. $(Ja \& Fa) \to \neg Ga$ US, 2
11. $\neg Ga$ MP, 10, 9
12. $Fa \to (Ga \lor Ha)$ US, 1
13. $Ga \lor Ha$ MP, 12, 8
14. Ha DS, 13, 11
15. $Ja \to Ha$ CP, 4-14
16. $\forall x(Jx \to Hx)$ UG, 15

60.
1. $\forall x \forall y \forall z((Fxy \& Fxz) \to Fyz)$ A
2. $\forall y \forall z((Fay \& Faz) \to Fyz)$ US, 1
3. $\forall z((Fab \& Faz) \to Fbz)$ US, 2
4. $(Fab \& Fac) \to Fbc$ US, 3
5. $Fac \& Fab$ ACP
6. Fab S, 5
7. Fac S, 5
8. $Fab \& Fac$ C, 6, 7
9. Fbc MP, 4, 8
10. $(Fac \& Fab) \to Fbc$ CP, 5-9
11. $\forall z((Fac \& Faz) \to Fzc)$ UG, 10
12. $\forall y \forall z((Fay \& Faz) \to Fzy)$ UG, 11
13. $\forall x \forall y \forall z((Fxy \& Fxz) \to Fzy)$ UG, 12

IB.3 Formulas with Overlapping Quantifiers

1.
1. $\exists x \exists y Fxy$ A
2. $\exists y Fay$ ES, 1   ⓐ
3. Fab ES, 2   ⓑ
4. $\exists x Fxb$ EG, 3
5. $\exists y \exists x Fxy$ EG, 4

2.
1. $\forall x \forall y Fxy$ A
2. $\forall y Fay$ US, 1
3. Fab US, 2
4. $\forall x Fxb$ UG, 3
5. $\forall y \forall x Fxy$ UG, 4

3.
1. $\exists x \forall y Fxy$ A
2. $\forall y Fay$ ES, 1   ⓐ
3. Fab US, 2
4. $\exists x Fxb$ EG, 3
5. $\forall y \exists x Fxy$ UG, 4

4.
1. $\forall x \exists y(Fx \& Gy)$ A
2. $\exists y(Fa \& Gy)$ US, 1 a
3. $Fa \& Gb$ ES, 2   ⓑ
4. $\exists y(Fc \& Gy)$ US, 1 c
5. $Fc \& Gd$ ES, 4   ⓓ
6. Fa S, 3
7. Gd S, 5
8. $Fa \& Gd$ C, 6, 7
9. $\forall x(Fx \& Gd)$ UG, 8
10. $\exists y \forall x(Fx \& Gy)$ EG, 9

12.

1.	$\forall x(\exists y Fxy \rightarrow \forall y Fyx)$	A
2.	$\exists x \exists y Fxy$	A
3.	$\exists y Fay$	ES, 2
4.	$\exists y Fay \rightarrow \forall y Fya$	US, 1
5.	$\forall y Fya$	MP, 4, 3
6.	Fba	US, 5
7.	$\exists y Fby$	EG, 6
8.	$\exists y Fby \rightarrow \forall y Fyb$	US, 1
9.	$\forall y Fyb$	MP, 8, 7
10.	Fcb	US, 9
11.	$\forall y Fcy$	UG, 10
12.	$\forall x \forall y Fxy$	UG, 11

(line 3 marked with circled *a*)

IB.4 Derived Rules for Quantifiers

1.

1.	$\forall x((Tx \ \& \ Lx) \rightarrow Dx)$	A
2.	$\forall x((Tx \ \& \ Cx) \rightarrow \neg Dx)$	ACP
3.	$Ta \ \& \ Ca$	ACP
4.	$(Ta \ \& \ Ca) \rightarrow \neg Da$	US, 2
5.	$\neg Da$	MP, 4, 3
6.	$(Ta \ \& \ La) \rightarrow Da$	US, 1
7.	$\neg(Ta \ \& \ La)$	MT, 6, 5
8.	$\neg Ta \lor \neg La$	DM, 7
9.	$Ta \rightarrow \neg La$	DC, 8
10.	Ta	S, 3
11.	$\neg La$	MP, 9, 10
12.	$(Ta \ \& \ Ca) \rightarrow \neg La$	CP, 3-11
13.	$\forall x((Tx \ \& \ Cx) \rightarrow \neg Lx)$	UG, 12
14.	$\forall x((Tx \ \& \ Cx) \rightarrow \neg Dx) \rightarrow \forall x((Tx \ \& \ Cx) \rightarrow \neg Lx)$	CP, 2-13

2.

1.	$\neg \exists x(Ix \ \& \ Tx)$	A
2.	$\forall x(Sx \rightarrow Tx)$	A
3.	$\forall x(Px \leftrightarrow \neg Sx)$	A
4.	$\forall x \neg(Ix \ \& \ Tx)$	QN, 1
5.	$\neg(Ia \ \& \ Ta)$	US, 4
6.	$Sa \rightarrow Ta$	US, 2
7.	$Pa \leftrightarrow \neg Sa$	US, 3
8.	Ia	ACP
9.	$\neg Ia \lor \neg Ta$	DM, 5
10.	$\neg \neg Ia$	DN, 8
11.	$\neg Ta$	DS, 9, 10
12.	$\neg Sa$	MT, 6, 11
13.	Pa	MB, 7, 12
14.	$Ia \rightarrow Pa$	CP, 8-13
15.	$\forall x(Ix \rightarrow Px)$	UG, 14

3.
1. $\neg\exists x((Mx \mathrel{\&} Fx) \mathrel{\&} \neg Bx)$ — A
2. $\forall x(Cx \rightarrow Mx)$ — A
3. $\neg\exists x(Cx \mathrel{\&} Bx)$ — A
4. ⌐ $\exists x(Fx \mathrel{\&} Cx)$ — AIP (a)
5. | $Fa \mathrel{\&} Ca$ — ES, 4
6. | Fa — S, 5
7. | Ca — S, 5
8. | $Ca \rightarrow Ma$ — US, 2
9. | Ma — MP, 8, 7
10. | $\forall x\neg((Mx \mathrel{\&} Fx) \mathrel{\&} \neg Bx)$ — QN, 1
11. | $\forall x\neg(Cx \mathrel{\&} Bx)$ — QN, 3
12. | $\neg(Ca \mathrel{\&} Ba)$ — US, 11
13. | $\neg((Ma \mathrel{\&} Fa) \mathrel{\&} \neg Ba)$ — US, 10
14. | $\neg(Ma \mathrel{\&} Fa) \lor \neg\neg Ba$ — DM, 13
15. | $Ma \mathrel{\&} Fa$ — C, 9, 6
16. | $\neg\neg(Ma \mathrel{\&} Fa)$ — DN, 15
17. | $\neg\neg Ba$ — DS, 14, 16
18. | Ba — DN, 17
19. | $Ca \mathrel{\&} Ba$ — C, 7, 18
20. | $(Ca \mathrel{\&} Ba) \mathrel{\&} \neg(Ca \mathrel{\&} Ba)$ — C, 19, 12
21. $\neg\exists x(Fx \mathrel{\&} Cx)$ — IP, 4-20

4.
1. $\forall x(Sx \rightarrow \neg Dx)$ — A
2. $\forall x(Chx \rightarrow Sx)$ — A
3. $\forall x(\neg Dx \rightarrow Bixh)$ — A
4. ⌐ Cha — ACP
5. | $Cha \rightarrow Sa$ — US, 2
6. | Sa — MP, 5, 4
7. | $Sa \rightarrow \neg Da$ — US, 1
8. | $\neg Da$ — MP, 7, 6
9. | $\neg Da \rightarrow Biah$ — US, 3
10. | $Biah$ — MP, 9, 8
11. $Cha \rightarrow Biah$ — CP, 4-10
12. $\forall x(Chx \rightarrow Bixh)$ — UG, 11

5.
1. $\neg\exists x(Gx \mathrel{\&} \neg Rx)$ — A
2. $\forall x(\exists y(Ty \mathrel{\&} Ixy) \rightarrow Fx)$ — A
3. $\neg\exists x(Fx \mathrel{\&} Rx)$ — A
4. ⌐ $\exists y(Ty \mathrel{\&} Iay)$ — ACP
5. | $\exists y(Ty \mathrel{\&} Iay) \rightarrow Fa$ — US, 2
6. | Fa — MP, 8, 9
7. | $\forall x\neg(Fx \mathrel{\&} Rx)$ — QN, 3
8. | $\neg(Fa \mathrel{\&} Ra)$ — US, 7
9. | $\forall x\neg(Gx \mathrel{\&} \neg Rx)$ — QN, 1
10. | $\neg(Ga \mathrel{\&} \neg Ra)$ — US, 9
11. | ⌐ Ga — AIP
12. | | ⌐ $\neg Ra$ — AIP
13. | | | $Ga \mathrel{\&} \neg Ra$ — C, 11, 12
14. | | | $(Ga \mathrel{\&} \neg Ra) \mathrel{\&} \neg(Ga \mathrel{\&} \neg Ra)$ — C, 13, 10
15. | | Ra — IP, 12-14
16. | | $Fa \mathrel{\&} Ra$ — C, 6, 15
17. | | $(Fa \mathrel{\&} Ra) \mathrel{\&} \neg(Fa \mathrel{\&} Ra)$ — C, 16, 8
18. | $\neg Ga$ — IP, 11-17
19. $\exists y(Ty \mathrel{\&} Iay) \rightarrow \neg Ga$ — CP, 4-18
20. $\forall x(\exists y(Ty \mathrel{\&} Ixy) \rightarrow \neg Gx)$ — UG, 19

6.
1. $\forall x((Px \& \exists y(By \& Hxy)) \to Lx)$ A
2. $\forall x((Px \& \neg\exists y(By \& Hxy)) \to \neg Fx)$ A
3. $\neg\exists x((Px \& Rxb) \& Lx)$ A   b
4. $\neg\neg\exists x((Px \& Rxb) \& Fx)$ AIP
5. $\exists x((Px \& Rxb) \& Fx)$ DN, 4
6. $(Pa \& Rab) \& Fa$ ES, 5   ⓐ
7. $\forall x\neg((Px \& Rxb) \& Lx)$ QN, 3
8. $\neg((Pa \& Rab) \& La)$ US, 7
9. $Pa \& Rab$ S, 6
10. $\neg(Pa \& Rab) \vee \neg La$ DM, 8
11. $\neg\neg(Pa \& Rab)$ DN, 9
12. $\neg La$ DS, 10, 11
13. $(Pa \& \exists y(By \& Hay)) \to La$ US, 1
14. $\neg(Pa \& \exists y(By \& Hay))$ MT, 13, 12
15. $\neg Pa \vee \neg\exists y(By \& Hay)$ DM, 14
16. Pa S, 9
17. $\neg\neg Pa$ DN, 16
18. $\neg\exists y(By \& Hay)$ DS, 15, 17
19. $(Pa \& \neg\exists y(By \& Hay)) \to \neg Fa$ US, 2
20. $Pa \& \neg\exists y(By \& Hay)$ C, 16, 18
21. $\neg Fa$ MP, 19, 20
22. Fa S, 6
23. $Fa \& \neg Fa$ C, 22, 21
24. $\neg\exists x((Px \& Rxb) \& Fx)$ IP, 4-23

12.
1. $\forall x\exists y(Fx \& Gy)$ A
2. $\exists y(Fa \& Gy)$ US, 1   a
3. $Fa \& Gb$ ES, 2   ⓑ
4. $\neg\exists y\forall x(Fx \& Gy)$ AIP
5. $\forall y\exists x\neg(Fx \& Gy)$ QN², 4
6. $\exists x\neg(Fx \& Gb)$ US, 5
7. $\neg(Fc \& Gb)$ ES, 6   ⓒ
8. $\neg Fc \vee \neg Gb$ DM, 7
9. Gb S, 3
10. $\neg\neg Gb$ DN, 9
11. $\neg Fc$ DS, 8, 10
12. $\exists y(Fc \& Gy)$ US, 1
13. $Fc \& Gd$ ES, 12   ⓓ
14. Fc S, 13
15. $Fc \& \neg Fc$ C, 14, 11
16. $\exists y\forall x(Fx \& Gy)$ IP, 4-15

18.
1. $\forall x(Fx \to Gx)$ A
2. $\forall xFx$ ACP
3. $Fa \to Ga$ US, 1
4. Fa US, 2
5. Ga MP, 3, 4
6. $\forall xGx$ UG, 5
7. $\forall xFx \to \forall xGx$ CP, 2-6

24.
1. $\forall x(Fx \to \neg Gx)$ A
2. $Fa \to \neg Ga$ US, 1
3. $\neg Fa \vee \neg Ga$ DC, 2
4. $\neg(Fa \& Ga)$ DM, 3
5. $\forall x\neg(Fx \& Gx)$ UG, 4
6. $\neg\exists x(Fx \& Gx)$ QN, 5

30.
1. $\forall x(Fx \leftrightarrow Gx)$ A
2. $\exists xFx$ ACP
3. Fa ES, 2   ⓐ
4. $Fa \leftrightarrow Ga$ US, 1
5. Ga MB, 4, 3
6. $\exists xGx$ EG, 5
7. $\exists xFx \to \exists xGx$ CP, 2-6
8. $\exists xGx$ ACP
9. Gb ES, 8   ⓑ
10. $Fb \leftrightarrow Gb$ US, 1
11. Fb MB, 10, 9
12. $\exists xFx$ EG, 11
13. $\exists xGx \to \exists xFx$ CP, 8-12
14. $\exists xFx \leftrightarrow \exists xGx$ B, 7, 13

36.
1.	$\neg\exists x(Hxa \;\&\; \neg Gxb)$	A
2.	$\forall x\neg(Fxc \;\&\; Fbx)$	A
3.	$\forall x(Gex \rightarrow Fxe)$	A
4.	$Hea \;\&\; Fec$	AIP
5.	$\forall x\neg(Hxa \;\&\; \neg Gxb)$	QN, 1
6.	$\neg(Hea \;\&\; \neg Geb)$	US, 5
7.	$\neg Hea \lor \neg\neg Geb$	DM, 6
8.	Hea	S, 4
9.	$\neg\neg Hea$	DN, 8
10.	$\neg\neg Geb$	DS, 7, 9
11.	$\neg(Fec \;\&\; Fbe)$	US, 2
12.	$\neg Fec \lor \neg Fbe$	DM, 11
13.	Fec	S, 4
14.	$\neg\neg Fec$	DN, 13
15.	$\neg Fbe$	DS, 12, 14
16.	$Geb \rightarrow Fbe$	US, 3
17.	$\neg Geb$	MT, 16, 15
18.	$\neg Geb \;\&\; \neg\neg Geb$	C, 17, 10
19.	$\neg(Hea \;\&\; Fec)$	IP, 4-18

42.
1.	$\exists xFx \rightarrow \forall y((Fy \lor Gy) \rightarrow Hy)$	A
2.	$\exists xHx$	A
3.	$\neg\forall z\neg Fz$	A
4.	$\exists z\neg\neg Fz$	QN, 3
5.	$\neg\neg Fa$	ES, 4 ⓐ
6.	Fa	DN, 5
7.	$\exists xFx$	EG, 6
8.	$\forall y((Fy \lor Gy) \rightarrow Hy)$	MP, 1, 7
9.	$(Fa \lor Ga) \rightarrow Ha$	US, 8
10.	$Fa \lor Ga$	Ad, 6
11.	Ha	MP, 9, 10
12.	$Fa \;\&\; Ha$	C, 6, 11
13.	$\exists x(Fx \;\&\; Hx)$	EG, 12

48.
1.	$\forall x\neg Fxx$	A
2.	$\exists x\forall y(Fyx \leftrightarrow \exists z\forall w((Fwz \rightarrow Fwy) \;\&\; \neg Fzy))$	AIP
3.	$\forall y(Fya \leftrightarrow \exists z\forall w((Fwz \rightarrow Fwy) \;\&\; \neg Fzy))$	ES, 2 ⓐ
4.	$Faa \leftrightarrow \exists z\forall w((Fwz \rightarrow Fwa) \;\&\; \neg Fza)$	US, 3
5.	$\neg Faa$	US, 1
6.	$\neg\exists z\forall w((Fwz \rightarrow Fwa) \;\&\; \neg Fza)$	MB, 4, 5
7.	$\forall z\exists w\neg((Fwz \rightarrow Fwa) \;\&\; \neg Fza)$	QN^2, 6
8.	$\exists w\neg((Fwa \rightarrow Fwa) \;\&\; \neg Faa)$	US, 7
9.	$\neg((Fba \rightarrow Fba) \;\&\; \neg Faa)$	ES, 8 ⓑ
10.	Fba	ACP
11.	$Fba \rightarrow Fba$	CP, 10-10
12.	$(Fba \rightarrow Fba) \;\&\; \neg Faa$	C, 11, 5
13.	$((Fba \rightarrow Fba) \;\&\; \neg Faa) \;\&\; \neg((Fba \rightarrow Fba) \;\&\; \neg Faa)$	C, 12, 9
14.	$\neg\exists x\forall y(Fyx \leftrightarrow \exists z\forall w((Fwz \rightarrow Fwy) \;\&\; \neg Fzy))$	IP, 2-13

Appendix IIA
DEDUCTION—STYLE THREE

IIA.2 Conjunction and Negation Rules

1.
1. p & q A
2. Show q
3. $\lceil q$ &E, 1

2.
1. p & (q & r)   A
2. Show r
3. $\lceil q$ & r &E, 1
4. $\lfloor r$ &E, 3

3.
1. p & $\neg\neg q$ A
2. Show q
3. $\lceil \neg\neg q$ &E, 1
4. $\lfloor q$ $\neg\neg$, 3

4.
1. $\neg\neg p$ & $\neg q$ A
2. Show $\neg\neg\neg q$ & p
3. $\lceil \neg\neg p$ &E, 1
4. p $\neg\neg$, 3
5. $\neg q$ &E, 1
6. $\neg\neg\neg q$ $\neg\neg$, 5
7. $\lfloor \neg\neg\neg q$ & p &I, 6, 4

5.
1. p & $\neg q$ A
2. $\neg r$ & s A
3. Show s & p
4. $\lceil p$ &E, 1
5. s &E, 2
6. $\lfloor s$ & p &I, 5, 4

6.
1. (p & q) & r A
2. Show p & (q & r)
3. $\lceil p$ & q &E, 1
4. p &E, 3
5. q &E, 3
6. r &E, 1
7. q & r &I, 5, 6
8. $\lfloor p$ & (q & r)   &I, 5, 7

IIA.3 Conditional and Biconditional Rules

1.
1. $p \rightarrow q$ A
2. p A
3. Show q
4. $\lceil q$ $\rightarrow$E, 1, 2

2.
1. $p \leftrightarrow q$ A
2. p A
3. Show q
4. $\lceil q$ $\leftrightarrow$E, 1, 2

3.
1. $p \leftrightarrow q$ A
2. q A
3. Show p
4. $\lceil p$ $\leftrightarrow$E, 1, 2

4.
1. ($p \rightarrow p$) $\rightarrow p$ A
2. Show p
3. $\lceil$ Show $p \rightarrow p$
4. $\lceil p$ ACP
5. $\lfloor p$ $\rightarrow$ E, 1, 3

5.
1. $p \leftrightarrow \neg q$ A
2. $\neg\neg p$ A
3. Show $\neg q$
4. $\lceil p$ $\neg\neg$, 2
5. $\lfloor \neg q$ $\leftrightarrow$E, 1, 4

6.
1. $p \rightarrow q$ A
2. p & r A
3. Show r & q
4. $\lceil p$ &E, 2
5. q $\rightarrow$E, 1, 4
6. r &E, 2
7. $\lfloor r$ & q &I, 5, 6

12.
1. $\neg q$ & ($r \rightarrow p$)   A
2. $\neg\neg r$ A
3. Show p & $\neg q$
4. $\lceil \neg q$ &E, 1
5. $r \rightarrow p$ &E, 1
6. r $\neg\neg$, 2
7. p $\rightarrow$ E, 5, 6
8. $\lfloor p$ & $\neg q$ &I, 7, 4

18.
1. $\neg p \leftrightarrow \neg q$ A
2. $\neg q \rightarrow \neg r$ A
3. $\neg p \rightarrow \neg s$ A
4. $\neg p$ & t A
5. Show $\neg s$ & $\neg r$
6. $\lceil \neg p$ &E, 4
7. $\neg s$ $\rightarrow$E, 3, 6
8. $\neg q$ $\leftrightarrow$E, 1, 6
9. $\neg r$ $\rightarrow$E, 2, 8
10. $\lfloor \neg s$ & $\neg r$ &I, 7, 9

24.
1. Show $p \leftrightarrow \neg\neg p$
2. $\lceil$ Show $p \rightarrow \neg\neg p$
3. $\lceil p$ ACP
4. $\lfloor \neg\neg p$ $\neg\neg$, 3
5. Show $\neg\neg p \rightarrow p$
6. $\lceil \neg\neg p$ ACP
7. $\lfloor p$ $\neg\neg$, 6
8. $\lfloor p \leftrightarrow \neg\neg p$ $\leftrightarrow$I, 2, 5

30. p: this product will succeed; q: this product is given adequate advertising support; r: the company will show a profit for the year; s: the Vice-President believes that another product has more potential; t: this product is great

1.	$\neg p \leftrightarrow \neg q$	A
2.	$\neg p \rightarrow \neg r$	A
3.	$\neg q \rightarrow s$	A
4.	$t \& \neg p$	A
5.	Show $s \& \neg r$	
6.	$\neg p$	&E, 4
7.	$\neg q$	$\leftrightarrow$E, 1, 6
8.	s	$\rightarrow$E, 3, 7
9.	$\neg r$	$\rightarrow$E, 2, 6
10.	$s \& \neg r$	&I, 8, 9

11A.4 Disjunction Rules

(from 8.4)

1.
1.	p	A
2.	Show $p \vee q$	
3.	$p \vee q$	$\vee$I, 1

2.
1.	$p \& q$	A
2.	Show $p \vee q$	
3.	p	&E, 1
4.	$p \vee q$	$\vee$I, 3

3.
1.	$p \vee q$	A
2.	$\neg q$	A
3.	Show p	
4.	Show $p \rightarrow p$	
5.	p	ACP
6.	Show $q \rightarrow p$	
7.	q	ACP
8.	Show $\neg \neg p$	
9.	$\neg p$	AIP
10.	q	R, 7
11.	$\neg q$	R, 2
12.	p	$\neg \neg$, 8
13.	p	$\vee$E, 1, 4, 6

4.
1.	$\neg p \vee q$	A
2.	p	A
3.	Show q	
4.	Show $\neg p \rightarrow q$	
5.	$\neg p$	ACP
6.	Show $\neg \neg q$	
7.	$\neg q$	AIP
8.	p	R, 2
9.	$\neg p$	R, 5
10.	q	$\neg \neg$, 6
11.	Show $q \rightarrow q$	
12.	q	ACP
13.	q	$\vee$E, 1, 4,11

5.
1.	$q \rightarrow r$	A
2.	$p \vee q$	A
3.	$p \rightarrow s$	A
4.	Show $r \vee s$	
5.	Show $p \rightarrow (r \vee s)$	
6.	p	ACP
7.	s	$\rightarrow$E, 3, 6
8.	$r \vee s$	$\vee$I, 7
9.	Show $q \rightarrow (r \vee s)$	
10.	q	ACP
11.	r	$\rightarrow$E, 1, 10
12.	$r \vee s$	$\vee$I, 11
13.	$r \vee s$	$\vee$E, 2, 5, 9

6.
1.	$p \vee q$	A
2.	$\neg r$	A
3.	$p \to r$	A
4.	Show q	
5.	Show $p \to q$	
6.	p	ACP
7.	Show $\neg \neg q$	
8.	$\neg q$	AIP
9.	r	$\to$E, 3, 6
10.	$\neg r$	R, 2
11.	q	$\neg \neg$, 7
12.	Show $q \to q$	
13.	q	ACP
14.	q	$\vee$E, 1, 5,12

12.
1.	$(p \& q) \vee (r \vee s)$	A
2.	Show $((p \& q) \vee r) \vee s$	
3.	Show $(p \& q) \to (((p \& q) \vee r) \vee s)$	
4.	$p \& q$	ACP
5.	$(p \& q) \vee r$	$\vee$I, 4
6.	$((p \& q) \vee r) \vee s$	$\vee$I, 5
7.	Show $(r \vee s) \to (((p \& q) \vee r) \vee s)$	
8.	$r \vee s$	ACP
9.	Show $r \to (((p \& q) \vee r) \vee s)$	
10.	r	ACP
11.	$(p \& q) \vee r$	$\vee$I, 10
12.	$((p \& q) \vee r) \vee s$	$\vee$I, 11
13.	Show $s \to (((p \& q) \vee r) \vee s)$	
14.	s	ACP
15.	$((p \& q) \vee r) \vee s$	$\vee$I, 14
16.	$((p \& q) \vee r) \vee s$	$\vee$E, 8, 9, 13
17.	$((p \& q) \vee r) \vee s$	$\vee$E, 1, 3, 7

18.
1.	$\neg p \vee q$	A
2.	$\neg q \vee r$	A
3.	$\neg r$	A
4.	Show $\neg p$	
5.	Show $\neg p \to \neg p$	
6.	$\neg p$	ACP
7.	Show $q \to \neg p$	
8.	q	ACP
9.	Show $\neg q \to \neg p$	
10.	$\neg q$	ACP
11.	Show $\neg p$	
12.	p	AIP
13.	q	R, 8
14.	$\neg q$	R, 10
15.	Show $r \to \neg p$	
16.	r	ACP
17.	Show $\neg p$	
18.	p	AIP
19.	r	R, 16
20.	$\neg r$	R, 3
21.	$\neg p$	$\vee$E, 2, 9, 15
22.	$\neg p$	$\vee$E, 1, 5, 7

24.
1.	$p \& (q \to r)$	A
2.	$q \vee \neg p$	A
3.	$(r \vee s) \to t$	A
4.	Show $t \vee m$	
5.	Show $q \to (t \vee m)$	
6.	q	ACP
7.	$q \to r$	&E, 1
8.	r	$\to$E, 6, 7
9.	$r \vee s$	$\vee$I, 8
10.	t	$\to$E, 3, 9
11.	$t \vee m$	$\vee$I, 10
12.	Show $\neg p \to (t \vee m)$	
13.	$\neg p$	ACP
14.	Show $\neg \neg (t \vee m)$	
15.	$\neg (t \vee m)$	AIP
16.	$\neg p$	R, 13
17.	p	&E, 1
18.	$t \vee m$	$\neg \neg$, 14
19.	$t \vee m$	$\vee$E, 12, 5, 2

30. p: someone knows where Rick was last night; q: Rick has an alibi; r: Rick is the prime suspect; s: new evidence points to someone else

1.	$\neg p$	A
2.	$q \lor r$	A
3.	$q \to p$	A
4.	Show $s \lor r$	
5.	Show $q \to (s \lor r)$	
6.	q	ACP
7.	Show $\neg\neg(s \lor r)$	
8.	$\neg(s \lor r)$	
9.	p	$\leftrightarrow$E, 3, 6
10.	$\neg p$	R, 1
11.	$s \lor r$	$\neg\neg$, 7
12.	Show $r \to (s \lor r)$	
13.	r	ACP
14.	$s \lor r$	$\lor$I, 13
15.	$s \lor r$	$\lor$E, 2, 5, 12

(from 8.5)

1.
1.	$r \to p$	A
2.	$p \to q$	A
3.	Show $r \to q$	
4.	r	ACP
5.	p	$\to$E, 1, 4
6.	q	$\to$E, 2, 5

2.
1.	$r \to p$	A
2.	$p \to q$	A
3.	Show $\neg q \to \neg r$	
4.	$\neg q$	ACP
5.	Show $\neg r$	
6.	r	AIP
7.	p	$\to$E, 1, 4
8.	q	$\to$E, 2, 5
9.	$\neg q$	R, 4

3.
1.	$r \to p$	A
2.	$\neg r \to q$	A
3.	Show $\neg p \to q$	
4.	$\neg p$	ACP
5.	Show $\neg r$	
6.	r	AIP
7.	p	$\to$E, 1, 6
8.	$\neg p$	R, 4
9.	q	$\to$E, 2, 5

4.
1.	$r \to p$	A
2.	$\neg r \to q$	A
3.	Show $\neg q \to p$	
4.	$\neg q$	ACP
5.	Show $\neg\neg r$	
6.	$\neg r$	AIP
7.	q	$\to$E, 2, 6
8.	$\neg q$	R, 4
9.	r	$\neg\neg$, 5
10.	p	$\to$E, 1, 9

6.
1.	$\neg r \lor \neg p$	A
2.	Show $p \to \neg r$	
3.	p	ACP
4.	Show $\neg r \to \neg r$	
5.	$\neg r$	ACP
6.	Show $\neg p \to \neg r$	
7.	$\neg p$	ACP
8.	Show $\neg r$	
9.	r	AIP
10.	p	R, 3
11.	$\neg p$	R, 7
12.	$\neg r$	$\lor$E, 1, 4, 6

7.
1.	$r \to p$	A
2.	Show $r \leftrightarrow (r \& p)$	
3.	Show $r \to (r \& p)$	
4.	r	ACP
5.	p	$\to$E, 1, 4
6.	$r \& p$	&I, 4, 5
7.	Show $(r \& p) \to r$	
8.	$r \& p$	ACP
9.	r	&E, 8
10.	$r \leftrightarrow (r \& p)$	$\leftrightarrow$I, 3, 7

8. 1. $r \leftrightarrow (r \& p)$ A
  2. Show $r \to p$
  3. $\lceil r$ ACP
  4. $\mid r \& p$ $\leftrightarrow$E, 1, 3
  5. $\lfloor p$ &E, 4

9. 1. $r \lor p$ A
  2. $\neg r \& s$ A
  3. Show $p \lor q$
  4. $\lceil \neg r$ &E, 2
  5. $\mid$ Show $r \to p$
  6. $\mid \lceil r$ ACP
  7. $\mid \mid$ Show $\neg \neg p$
  8. $\mid \mid \lceil \neg p$ AIP
  9. $\mid \mid \mid r$ R, 6
  10. $\mid \mid \lfloor \neg r$ R, 4
  11. $\mid \lfloor p$ $\neg \neg$, 7
  12. $\mid$ Show $p \to p$
  13. $\mid \lceil p$ ACP
  14. $\mid p$ $\lor$E, 1, 5, 12
  15. $\lfloor p \lor q$ $\lor$I, 14

10. 1. $r \to p$ A
  2. $q \to r$ A
  $2\frac{1}{2}$. Show $\neg q \lor p$
  3. $\lceil$ Show $\neg \neg (\neg q \lor p)$
  4. $\mid \lceil \neg(\neg q \lor p)$ AIP
  5. $\mid$ Show $\neg q$
  6. $\mid \lceil q$ AIP
  7. $\mid \mid r$ $\to$E, 2, 6
  8. $\mid \mid p$ $\to$E, 1, 7
  9. $\mid \mid \neg q \lor p$ $\lor$I, 8
  10. $\mid \lfloor \neg(\neg q \lor p)$ R, 4
  11. $\mid \neg q \lor p$ $\lor$I, 5
  12. $\lfloor \neg q \lor p$ $\neg \neg$, 3

11. 1. $\neg r \lor \neg q$ A
  2. Show $\neg(r \& \neg \neg q)$
  3. $\lceil r \& \neg \neg q$ AIP
  4. $\mid r$ &E, 3
  5. $\mid \neg \neg q$ &E, 3
  6. $\mid q$ $\neg \neg$, 5
  7. $\mid$ Show $\neg r \to \neg r$
  8. $\mid \lceil \neg r$ ACP
  9. $\mid$ Show $\neg q \to \neg r$
  10. $\mid \lceil \neg q$ ACP
  11. $\mid \mid$ Show $\neg r$
  12. $\mid \mid \lceil r$ AIP
  13. $\mid \mid \mid q$ R, 6
  14. $\mid \mid \lfloor \neg q$ R, 10
  15. $\lfloor \neg r$ $\lor$E, 1, 7, 9

12. 1. $\neg(r \,\&\, \neg p) \vee \neg r$ A
    2. Show $r \rightarrow p$
    3. r ACP
    4. Show $\neg r \rightarrow p$
    5. $\neg r$ ACP
    6. Show $\neg\,\neg p$
    7. $\neg p$ AIP
    8. r R, 3
    9. $\neg r$ R, 5
    10. p $\neg\,\neg$, 6
    11. Show $\neg(r \,\&\, \neg p) \rightarrow p$
    12. $\neg(r \,\&\, \neg p)$ ACP
    13. Show $\neg\,\neg p$
    14. $\neg p$ AIP
    15. $r \,\&\, \neg p$ &I, 3, 14
    16. $\neg(r \,\&\, \neg p)$ R, 12
    17. p $\neg\,\neg$, 13
    18. p $\vee$E, 1, 4, 11

18. 1. $(r \,\&\, \neg p) \rightarrow \neg q$ A
    2. q A
    3. Show $\neg r \vee (r \,\&\, p)$
    4. Show $\neg\,\neg(\neg r \vee (r \,\&\, p))$
    5. $\neg(\neg r \vee (r \,\&\, p))$ AIP
    6. Show $\neg\,\neg r$
    7. $\neg r$ AIP
    8. $\neg r \vee (r \,\&\, p)$ $\vee$I, 7
    9. $\neg(\neg r \vee (r \,\&\, p))$ R, 5
    10. r $\neg\,\neg$, 6
    11. Show $\neg p$
    12. p AIP
    13. $r \,\&\, p$ &I, 10, 12
    14. $\neg r \vee (r \,\&\, p)$ $\vee$I, 13
    15. $\neg(\neg r \vee (r \,\&\, p))$ R, 5
    16. $r \,\&\, \neg p$ &I, 10, 11
    17. $\neg q$ $\rightarrow$E, 1, 16
    18. q R, 2
    19. $\neg r \vee (r \,\&\, p)$ $\neg\,\neg$, 4

24. 1. $r \leftrightarrow p$ A
    2. Show $\neg r \leftrightarrow \neg p$
    3. Show $\neg r \rightarrow \neg p$
    4. $\neg r$ ACP
    5. Show $\neg p$
    6. p AIP
    7. r $\leftrightarrow$E, 1, 6
    8. $\neg r$ R, 4
    9. Show $\neg p \rightarrow \neg r$
    10. $\neg p$ ACP
    11. Show $\neg r$
    12. r AIP
    13. p $\leftrightarrow$E, 1, 12
    14. $\neg p$ R, 10
    15. $\neg r \leftrightarrow \neg p$ $\leftrightarrow$I, 3, 9

30.

1.	$(s \,\&\, \neg q) \to \neg r$	A
2.	$(p \to \neg s) \leftrightarrow \neg r$	A
3.	Show $r \leftrightarrow (q \,\&\, (s \,\&\, p))$	
4.	Show $r \to (q \,\&\, (s \,\&\, p))$	
5.	r	ACP
6.	Show $\neg \neg s$	
7.	$\neg s$	AIP
8.	Show $p \to \neg s$	
9.	p	ACP
10.	$\neg s$	R, 7
11.	$\neg r$	$\leftrightarrow$E, 2, 8
12.	r	R, 5
13.	s	$\neg \neg$, 6
14.	Show $\neg \neg p$	
15.	$\neg p$	AIP
16.	Show $p \to \neg s$	
17.	p	ACP
18.	$\neg p$	R, 15
19.	$\neg r$	$\leftrightarrow$E, 2, 16
20.	r	R, 5
21.	p	$\neg \neg$, 14
22.	Show $\neg \neg q$	
23.	$\neg q$	AIP
24.	$s \,\&\, \neg q$	&I, 13, 23
25.	$\neg r$	$\to$E, 1, 24
26.	r	R, 5
27.	q	$\neg \neg$, 22
28.	$s \,\&\, p$	&I, 13, 21
29.	$q \,\&\, (s \,\&\, p)$	&I, 27, 28
30.	Show $(q \,\&\, (s \,\&\, p)) \to r$	
31.	$q \,\&\, (s \,\&\, p)$	ACP
32.	$s \,\&\, p$	&E, 17
33.	Show $\neg \neg r$	
34.	$\neg r$	AIP
35.	$p \to \neg s$	$\leftrightarrow$E, 2, 35
36.	p	&E, 33
37.	$\neg s$	$\to$E, 36, 37
38.	s	&E, 33
39.	r	$\neg \neg$, 34
40.	$r \leftrightarrow (q \,\&\, (s \,\&\, p))$	$\leftrightarrow$I, 4, 30

36.

1.	$p \,\&\, \neg q$	A
2.	Show $\neg (p \to q)$	
3.	$p \to q$	AIP
4.	p	&E, 1
5.	q	$\to$E, 3, 4
6.	$\neg q$	&E, 1

42.

1.	Show $(p \,\&\, q) \to p$	
2.	$p \,\&\, q$	ACP
3.	p	&E, 2

48.

1.	$(p \,\&\, q) \lor r$	A
2.	Show $(q \,\&\, p) \lor r$	
3.	Show $(p \,\&\, q) \to ((q \,\&\, p) \lor r)$	
4.	$p \,\&\, q$	ACP
5.	p	&E, 4
6.	q	&E, 4
7.	$q \,\&\, p$	&I, 6, 5
8.	$(q \,\&\, p) \lor r$	$\lor$I, 7
9.	Show $r \to ((q \,\&\, p) \lor r)$	
10.	r	ACP
11.	$(q \,\&\, p) \lor r$	$\lor$I, 10
12.	$(q \,\&\, p) \lor r$	$\lor$E, 1, 3, 9

54. *p*: a man can serve God; *q*: a man can serve Mammon; *r*: a man starves

1.	¬(*p* & *q*)	A
2.	¬*q* → *r*	A
3.	*r* → ¬*p*	A
4.	Show ¬*p*	
5.	*p*	AIP
6.	Show ¬*q*	
7.	*q*	AIP
8.	*p* & *q*	&I, 5, 7
9.	¬(*p* & *q*)	R, 1
10.	*r*	→E, 2, 6
11.	¬*p*	→E, 3, 10

IIA.5 Derived Rules

1. *p*: you are ambitious; *q*: you'll achieve your goals; *r*: life has meaning

1.	*p* → ¬*q*	A
2.	*r* → *p*	A
3.	Show *q* → ¬*r*	
4.	*q*	ACP
5.	¬¬*q*	¬¬, 4
6.	¬*p*	→E*, 1, 5
7.	¬*r*	→E*, 2, 6

2. *p*: Adam comes to the party; *q*: Barbara comes to the party; *r*: Carlos will be happy

1.	*p* → *q*	A
2.	*q* → *p*	A
3.	Show (*p* → *r*) → (*q* → *r*)	
4.	*p* → *r*	ACP
5.	Show *q* → *r*	
6.	*q*	ACP
7.	*p*	→E, 2, 6
8.	*r*	→E, 4, 7

3. *p*: interest rates will rise; *q*: Congress enacts a tax increase; *r*: the unemployment level will increase; *s*: the budget deficit will increase

1.	*p* ∨ *q*	A
2.	*q* → *p*	A
3.	*p* → *r*	A
4.	¬*r* ∨ *s*	A
5.	Show *s*	
6.	¬*s*	AIP
7.	¬*r*	∨E*, 4, 6
8.	¬*p*	→E*, 3, 7
9.	¬*q*	→E*, 2, 8
10.	*p*	∨E*, 1, 9

4. p: God is omnipotent; q: God can do everything; r: God can make a stone so heavy he can't lift it

1.	$p \leftrightarrow q$	A
2.	$\neg r \rightarrow \neg q$	A
3.	$r \rightarrow \neg q$	A
4.	Show $\neg p \vee \neg s$	
5.	Show $\neg p$	
6.	p	AIP
7.	q	$\leftrightarrow$E, 1, 6
8.	$\neg \neg r$	$\leftrightarrow$E*, 2, 7
9.	$\neg \neg q$	$\neg \neg$, 7
10.	$\neg r$	$\rightarrow$E*, 3, 9
11.	$\neg p \vee \neg s$	$\vee$I, 5

5. p: the President pursues arms limitations talks; q: the President gets the foreign policy mechanism working harmoniously; r: the European left will acquiesce to the placement of additional nuclear weapons in Europe

1.	$p \rightarrow (q \rightarrow r)$	A
2.	$\neg r$	A
3.	Show $\neg q \vee \neg p$	
4.	$\neg p \vee (q \rightarrow r)$	$\rightarrow \vee$, 1
5.	$\neg p \vee (\neg q \vee r)$	$\rightarrow \vee$, 4
6.	$(\neg p \vee \neg q) \vee r$	$\vee$A, 5
7.	$\neg p \vee \neg q$	$\vee$E*, 2, 6

6. p: we introduce a new product line; q: we give an existing line a new advertising image; r: we take risks; s: we may lose market share; t: we have to make large expenditures on advertising

1.	$(p \vee q) \rightarrow (r \& s)$	A
2.	$\neg p \rightarrow \neg t$	A
3.	Show $\neg r \rightarrow \neg t$	
4.	$\neg r$	ACP
5.	$\neg r \vee \neg s$	$\vee$I, 4
6.	$\neg (r \& s)$	$\neg \&$, 5
7.	$\neg (p \vee q)$	$\rightarrow$E*, 1, 6
8.	$\neg p \& \neg q$	$\neg \vee$, 7
9.	$\neg p$	&E, 8
10.	$\neg t$	$\rightarrow$E, 2, 9

12. p: the President retaliates against Libya with military force; q: the public will be ambivalent; r: Libya directs terrorist attacks toward Americans on American soil

1.	$p \rightarrow q$	A
2.	$r \rightarrow \neg q$	A
3.	Show $\neg r \vee \neg p$	
4.	Show $r \rightarrow \neg p$	
5.	r	ACP
6.	$\neg q$	$\rightarrow$E, 2, 5
7.	$\neg p$	$\rightarrow$E*, 1, 6
8.	$\neg r \vee \neg p$	$\rightarrow \vee$, 4

18. p: Congress erects trade barriers; q: Congress grants further subsidies to American farmers; r: other countries will retaliate, s: the economy will slow down; t: Congress will find new sources of revenue

1.	$(p \& q) \to r$	A
2.	$r \to s$	A
3.	$s \to (\neg q \vee t)$	A
4.	$\neg p \to (\neg q \& \neg r)$	A
5.	Show $t \vee \neg q$	
6.	$\neg(t \vee \neg q)$	AIP
7.	$\neg(\neg q \vee t)$	$\vee$C, 6
8.	$\neg s$	$\to$E*, 3, 7
9.	$\neg r$	$\to$E*, 2, 8
10.	$\neg(p \& q)$	$\to$E*, 1, 9
11.	$\neg p \vee \neg q$	$\neg\&$, 10
12.	$\neg t \& \neg \neg q$	$\neg\vee$, 6
13.	$\neg \neg q$	&E, 12
14.	$\neg p$	$\vee$E*, 11, 13
15.	$\neg q \& \neg r$	$\to$E, 4, 14
16.	$\neg q$	&E, 15

24.

1.	p	A
2.	$\neg(p \vee r)$	A
3.	Show q	
4.	$\neg p \& \neg r$	$\neg\vee$, 2
5.	$\neg p$	&E, 4
6.	q	!, 1, 5

30.

1.	$(\neg p \to q) \vee r$	A
2.	Show $\neg p \to (q \vee r)$	
3.	$\neg p$	ACP
4.	$(\neg \neg p \vee q) \vee r$	$\to \vee$, 1
5.	$(p \vee q) \vee r$	$\neg\neg$, 4
6.	$p \vee (q \vee r)$	$\vee$A, 5
5.	$q \vee r$	$\vee$E*, 3, 6

36.

1.	$p \leftrightarrow q$	A
2.	Show $\neg q \leftrightarrow \neg p$	
3.	Show $\neg p \to \neg q$	
4.	$\neg p$	ACP
5.	$\neg q$	$\leftrightarrow$E*, 1, 4
6.	Show $\neg q \to \neg p$	
7.	$\neg q$	ACP
8.	$\neg p$	$\leftrightarrow$E*, 1, 7
9.	$\neg q \leftrightarrow \neg p$	$\leftrightarrow$I, 6, 3

42.

1.	$p \vee q$	A
2.	$\neg q \vee r$	A
3.	Show $p \vee r$	
4.	$\neg(p \vee r)$	AIP
5.	$\neg p \& \neg r$	$\neg\vee$
6.	$\neg p$	&E, 5
7.	q	$\vee$E*, 1, 6
8.	$\neg \neg q$	$\neg\neg$, 7
9.	r	$\vee$E*, 2, 8
10.	$\neg r$	&E, 5

48.

1.	$\neg s \to \neg k$	A
2.	$(s \& t) \to (p \leftrightarrow q)$	A
3.	$\neg(\neg p \vee q)$	A
4.	Show $t \to \neg k$	
5.	t	ACP
6.	Show $\neg k$	
7.	k	AIP
8.	$\neg \neg s$	$\to$E*, 1, 7
9.	s	$\neg\neg$, 8
10.	$s \& t$	&I, 9, 5
11.	$p \leftrightarrow q$	$\to$E, 2, 10
12.	$\neg\neg p \& \neg q$	$\neg\vee$, 3
13.	$\neg\neg p$	&E, 12
14.	p	$\neg\neg$, 13
15.	q	$\leftrightarrow$E, 11, 14
16.	$\neg q$	&E, 12

54. 1. Show $(p \to q) \to (\neg q \to \neg p)$
   2. $\quad [\; p \to q \qquad\qquad\qquad$ ACP
   3. $\quad | \;$ Show $\neg q \to \neg p$
   4. $\quad | \; [\; \neg q \qquad\qquad\qquad$ ACP
   5. $\quad | \; [\; \neg p \qquad\qquad\qquad \to$E*, 2, 4

60. 1. Show $(p \lor (q \lor r)) \to (q \lor (p \lor r))$
   2. $\quad [\; p \lor (q \lor r) \qquad\qquad$ ACP
   3. $\quad | \; (q \lor r) \lor p \qquad\qquad \lor$C, 2
   4. $\quad | \; q \lor (r \lor p) \qquad\qquad \lor$A, 3
   5. $\quad [\; q \lor (p \lor r) \qquad\qquad \lor$C, 4

Appendix IIB
ADDING QUANTIFIERS

IIB.1 Deduction Rules for Quantifiers

1. 1. $\forall x Cgx$ A
   2. Show Cgo
   3. $[\; Cgo \qquad \forall$E, 1 (where 'o' symbolizes 'Texas')

2. 1. $\forall x Cgx$ A
   2. Show $\exists x Cgx$
   3. $[\; Cga \qquad \forall$E, 1
   4. $[\; \exists x Cgx \qquad \exists$I, 3

3. 1. $\forall x Cgx$ A
   2. Show Cgg
   3. $[\; Cgg \qquad \forall$E, 1

4. 1. $\forall x Cgx$ A
   2. Show $\exists x Cxg$
   3. $[\; Cgg \qquad \forall$E, 1
   4. $[\; \exists x Cxg \qquad \exists$I, 3

5. 1. $\forall x (Lx \to \neg Fxi)$ A
   2. Fbi A
   3. Show $\neg Lb$
   4. $[\; Lb \to \neg Fbi \qquad \forall$E, 1
   5. $| \; \neg \neg Fbi \qquad\quad \neg\neg$, 2
   6. $[\; \neg Lb \qquad\qquad \to$E*, 4, 5

6. 1. $\forall x ((Px \,\&\, Bx) \to Cx)$ A
   2. $\exists x ((Px \,\&\, Qx) \,\&\, Bx)$ A (where 'Q' symbolizes 'is a Pirate')
   3. Show $\exists x (Qx \,\&\, Cx)$
   4. $[\; (Pa \,\&\, Qa) \,\&\, Ba \qquad \exists$E, 2
   5. $| \; Pa \,\&\, Qa \qquad\qquad \&$E, 4
   6. $| \; Pa \qquad\qquad\qquad \&$E, 5
   7. $| \; Ba \qquad\qquad\qquad \&$E, 4
   8. $| \; Pa \,\&\, Ba \qquad\qquad \&$I, 6, 7
   9. $| \; (Pa \,\&\, Ba) \to Ca \qquad \forall$E, 1
   10. $| \; Ca \qquad\qquad\qquad \to$E, 9, 8
   11. $| \; Qa \qquad\qquad\qquad \&$E, 5
   12. $| \; Qa \,\&\, Ca \qquad\qquad \&$I, 11, 10
   13. $[\; \exists x (Qx \,\&\, Cx) \qquad \exists$I, 12

12. 1. $\exists x ((Cx \,\&\, Kix) \,\&\, Ix)$ A
   2. $\forall x ((Cx \,\&\, Kix) \to Vx)$ A
   3. Show $\exists x (Vx \,\&\, Ix)$
   4. $[\; (Ca \,\&\, Kia) \,\&\, Ia \qquad \exists$E, 1
   5. $| \; Ca \,\&\, Kia \qquad\qquad \&$E, 4
   6. $| \; (Ca \,\&\, Kia) \to Va \qquad \forall$E, 2
   7. $| \; Va \qquad\qquad\qquad \to$E, 6, 5
   8. $| \; Kia \qquad\qquad\qquad \&$E, 5
   9. $| \; Ia \qquad\qquad\qquad \&$E, 4
   10. $| \; Va \,\&\, Ia \qquad\qquad \&$I, 7, 9
   11. $[\; \exists x (Vx \,\&\, Ix) \qquad \exists$I, 10

18.
1. $\forall x \forall y(((Px \ \& \ Py) \ \& \ Cxy) \rightarrow \forall z(Cyz \rightarrow Cxz))$ A
2. $\exists x \exists y((Px \ \& \ Py) \ \& \ (Cxy \ \& \ Cyx))$ A
3. Show $\exists x(Px \ \& \ Cxx)$
4. $\lceil \exists y((Pa \ \& \ Py) \ \& \ (Cay \ \& \ Cya))$ $\exists$E, 2
5. $(Pa \ \& \ Pb) \ \& \ (Cab \ \& \ Cba)$ $\exists$E, 4
6. $Pa \ \& \ Pb$ &E, 5
7. $Cab \ \& \ Cba$ &E, 5
8. Cab &E, 7
9. $(Pa \ \& \ Pb) \ \& \ Cab$ &I, 6, 8
10. $\forall y(((Pa \ \& \ Py) \ \& \ Cay) \rightarrow \forall z(Cyz \rightarrow Caz))$ $\forall$E, 1
11. $((Pa \ \& \ Pb) \ \& \ Cab) \rightarrow \forall z(Cbz \rightarrow Caz)$ $\forall$E, 10
12. $\forall z(Cbz \rightarrow Caz)$ $\rightarrow$E, 11, 9
13. $Cba \rightarrow Caa$ $\forall$E, 12
14. Cba &E, 7
15. Caa $\rightarrow$E, 13, 14
16. Pa &E, 6
17. $Pa \ \& \ Caa$ &I, 16, 15
18. $\lfloor \exists x(Px \ \& \ Cxx)$ $\exists$I, 17

24.
1. $\forall x(Mx \rightarrow \neg Lx)$ A
2. $\forall x(Mx \rightarrow Sx)$ A
3. $\exists x Mx$ A
4. Show $\exists x(Sx \ \& \ \neg Lx)$
5. $\lceil Ma$ $\exists$E, 3
6. $Ma \rightarrow \neg La$ $\forall$E, 1
7. $\neg La$ $\rightarrow$E, 6, 5
8. $Ma \rightarrow Sa$ $\forall$E, 2
9. Sa $\rightarrow$E, 8, 5
10. $Sa \ \& \ \neg La$ &I, 9, 7
11. $\lfloor \exists x(Sx \ \& \ \neg Lx)$ $\exists$I, 10

30.
1. $\forall x(Mx \rightarrow \neg Lx)$ A
2. $\forall x(Sx \rightarrow Mx)$ A
3. $\exists x Sx$ A
4. Show $\exists x(Sx \ \& \ \neg Lx)$
5. $\lceil Sa$ $\exists$E, 3
6. $Sa \rightarrow Ma$ $\forall$E, 2
7. Ma $\rightarrow$E, 6, 5
8. $Ma \rightarrow \neg La$ $\forall$E, 1
9. $\neg La$ $\rightarrow$E, 8, 7
10. $Sa \ \& \ \neg La$ &I, 5, 9
11. $\lfloor \exists x(Sx \ \& \ \neg Lx)$ $\exists$I, 10

36.
1. $\exists x(Mx \ \& \ Lx)$ A
2. $\forall x(Sx \rightarrow \neg Mx)$ A
3. Show $\exists x(Lx \ \& \ \neg Sx)$
4. $\lceil Ma \ \& \ La$ $\exists$E, 1
5. $Sa \rightarrow \neg Ma$ $\forall$E, 2
6. Ma &E, 4
7. $\neg \neg Ma$ $\neg \neg$, 5
8. $\neg Sa$ $\rightarrow$E*, 5, 7
9. La &E, 4
10. $La \ \& \ \neg Sa$ &I, 9, 8
11. $\lfloor \exists x(Lx \ \& \ \neg Sx)$ $\exists$I, 10

42.
1. $\forall x(Hx \rightarrow Gx)$ A
2. $\exists x(\neg Gx \ \& \ Fx)$ A
3. Show $\exists x(Fx \ \& \ \neg Hx)$
4. $\lceil \neg Ga \ \& \ Fa$ $\exists$E, 2
5. Fa &E, 4
6. $\neg Ga$ &E, 4
7. $Ha \rightarrow Ga$ $\forall$E, 1
8. $\neg Ha$ $\rightarrow$E*, 7, 6
9. $Fa \ \& \ \neg Ha$ &I, 5, 8
10. $\lfloor \exists x(Fx \ \& \ \neg Hx)$ $\exists$I, 9

48.
1. $\forall x(Hx \rightarrow \neg Gx)$ A
2. $\exists x(Gx \ \& \ Fx)$ A
3. Show $\exists x(Fx \ \& \ \neg Hx)$
4. $\lceil Ga \ \& \ Fa$ $\exists$E, 2
5. Fa &E, 4
6. Ga &E, 4
7. $Ha \rightarrow \neg Ga$ $\forall$E, 1
8. $\neg \neg Ga$ $\neg \neg$, 6
9. $\neg Ha$ $\rightarrow$E*, 7, 8
10. $Fa \ \& \ \neg Ha$ &I, 5, 9
11. $\lfloor \exists x(Fx \ \& \ \neg Hx)$ $\exists$I, 10

54.
1. $\forall x(Fx \lor \neg Gx)$ A
2. $\forall x(Fx \rightarrow Hx)$ A
3. $\forall x(\neg Gx \rightarrow Jx)$ A
4. $\exists x \neg Jx$ A
5. Show $\exists x Hx$
6. $\lceil \neg Ja$ $\exists$E, 4
7. $\neg Ga \rightarrow Ja$ $\forall$E, 3
8. $\neg \neg Ga$ $\rightarrow$E*, 7, 6
9. $Fa \lor \neg Ga$ $\forall$E, 1
10. Fa $\lor$E*, 9, 8
11. $Fa \rightarrow Ha$ $\forall$E, 2
12. Ha $\rightarrow$E, 11, 10
13. $\lfloor \exists x Hx$ $\exists$I, 12

60.
1. $\forall x(Fx \rightarrow Gx)$ A
2. Show $\exists x(\neg Fx \vee Gx)$
3. $Fa \rightarrow Ga$ $\forall$E, 1
4. $\neg Fa \vee Ga$ $\rightarrow\vee$, 3
5. $\exists x(\neg Fx \vee Gx)$ $\exists$I, 4

IIB.2 Universal Proof

1.
1. $\forall x(Mx \rightarrow Lx)$ A
2. $\forall x(Sx \rightarrow Mx)$ A
3. Show $\forall x(Sx \rightarrow Lx)$
4. Show $Sa \rightarrow La$
5. Sa ACP
6. $Sa \rightarrow Ma$ $\forall$E, 2
7. Ma $\rightarrow$E, 6, 5
8. $Ma \rightarrow La$ $\forall$E, 1
9. La $\rightarrow$E, 8, 7

2.
1. $\forall x(Mx \rightarrow \neg Lx)$ A
2. $\forall x(Sx \rightarrow Mx)$ A
3. Show $\forall x(Sx \rightarrow \neg Lx)$
4. Show $Sa \rightarrow \neg La$
5. Sa ACP
6. $Sa \rightarrow Ma$ $\forall$E, 2
7. Ma $\rightarrow$E, 6, 5
8. $Ma \rightarrow \neg La$ $\forall$E, 1
9. $\neg La$ $\rightarrow$E, 8, 7

3.
1. $\forall x(Lx \rightarrow \neg Mx)$ A
2. $\forall x(Sx \rightarrow Mx)$ A
3. Show $\forall x(Sx \rightarrow \neg Lx)$
4. Show $Sa \rightarrow \neg La$
5. Sa ACP
6. $Sa \rightarrow Ma$ $\forall$E, 2
7. Ma $\rightarrow$E, 6, 5
8. $La \rightarrow \neg Ma$ $\forall$E, 1
9. $\neg\neg Ma$ $\neg\neg$, 7
10. $\neg La$ $\rightarrow$E*, 8, 9

4.
1. $\forall x(Lx \rightarrow Mx)$ A
2. $\forall x(Sx \rightarrow \neg Mx)$ A
3. Show $\forall x(Sx \rightarrow \neg Lx)$
4. Show $Sa \rightarrow \neg La$
5. Sa ACP
6. $Sa \rightarrow \neg Ma$ $\forall$E, 2
7. $\neg Ma$ $\rightarrow$E, 6, 5
8. $La \rightarrow Ma$ $\forall$E, 1
9. $\neg La$ $\rightarrow$E*, 8, 7

5.
1. $\forall x(Mx \rightarrow \neg Lx)$ A
2. $\forall x(Sx \rightarrow Mx)$ A
3. Show $\forall x(Lx \rightarrow \neg Sx)$
4. Show $La \rightarrow Sa$
5. La ACP
6. $Ma \rightarrow \neg La$ $\forall$E, 1
7. $\neg\neg La$ $\neg\neg$, 5
8. $\neg Ma$ $\rightarrow$E*, 6, 7
9. $Sa \rightarrow Ma$ $\forall$E, 2
10. $\neg Sa$ $\rightarrow$E*, 9, 8

6.
1. $\forall x(Dx \rightarrow Sx)$ A
2. $\forall x(Ix \rightarrow \neg Sx)$ A
3. Show $\forall x(Dx \rightarrow \neg Ix)$
4. Show $Da \rightarrow \neg Ia$
5. Da ACP
6. $Da \rightarrow Sa$ $\forall$E, 1
7. Sa $\rightarrow$E, 6, 5
8. $Ia \rightarrow \neg Sa$ $\forall$E, 2
9. $\neg\neg Sa$ $\neg\neg$, 7
10. $\neg Ia$ $\rightarrow$E*, 8, 9

12.
1. $\forall x(Wx \rightarrow \neg Fx)$ A
2. $\forall x(Px \rightarrow \neg\neg Fx)$ A
3. Show $\forall x(Px \rightarrow \neg Wx)$
4. Show $Pa \rightarrow \neg Wa$
5. Pa ACP
6. $Pa \rightarrow \neg\neg Fa$ $\forall$E, 2
7. $\neg\neg Fa$ $\rightarrow$E, 6, 5
8. $Wa \rightarrow \neg Fa$ $\forall$E, 1
9. $\neg Wa$ $\rightarrow$E*, 8, 7

18.
1. $\forall x((Sx \& \neg Px) \to \neg Ex)$ A
2. $\forall x((Sx \& Oxh) \to \neg Px)$ A
3. Show $\forall x((Sx \& Oxh) \to \neg Ex)$
4. Show $(Sa \& Oah) \to \neg Ea$
5. $Sa \& Oah$ ACP
6. $(Sa \& Oah) \to \neg Pa$ $\forall$E, 2
7. $\neg Pa$ $\to$E, 6, 5
8. Sa &E, 5
9. $Sa \& \neg Pa$ &I, 8, 7
10. $(Sa \& \neg Pa) \to \neg Ea$ $\forall$E, 1
11. $\neg Ea$ $\to$E, 10, 9

24.
1. $\forall x(Oxi \to \neg Cx)$ A
2. $\forall x(Sx \to Cx)$ A
3. Show $\forall x(Oxi \to \neg Sx)$
4. Show $Oai \to \neg Sa$
5. Oai ACP
6. $Oai \to \neg Ca$ $\forall$E, 1
7. $\neg Ca$ $\to$E, 6, 5
8. $Sa \to Ca$ $\forall$E, 2
9. $\neg Sa$ $\to$E*, 8, 7

30.
1. $\forall x(\neg Nx \to \neg Mx)$ A
2. $\forall x(Lx \to Wx)$ A
3. $\forall x(Ix \to \neg Wx)$ A
4. $\forall x(Nx \to Lx)$ A
5. Show $\forall x(Ix \to \neg Mx)$
6. Show $(Ia \to \neg Ma$
7. Ia ACP
8. $Ia \to \neg Wa$ $\forall$E, 3
9. $La \to Wa$ $\forall$E, 2
10. $Na \to La$ $\forall$E, 4
11. $\neg Na \to \neg Ma$ $\forall$E, 1
12. Show $\neg Na$
13. Na AIP
14. La $\to$ E, 10, 13
15. Wa $\to$E, 9, 14
16. $\neg Wa$ $\to$E, 8, 7
17. $\neg Ma$ $\to$E, 11, 12

36.
1. $\forall x(Ixj \to \neg Rjx)$ A
2. $\forall x(\neg Lxj \to Ixj)$ A
3. Show $\forall x(Rjx \to Lxj)$
4. Show $Rja \to Laj$
5. Rja ACP
6. $Iaj \to \neg Rja$ $\forall$E, 1
7. $\neg\neg Rja$ $\neg\neg$, 5
8. $\neg Iaj$ $\to$E*, 6, 7
9. $\neg Laj \to Iaj$ $\forall$E, 1
10. $\neg\neg Laj$ $\to$E*, 9, 8
11. Laj $\neg\neg$, 10

42.
1. $\forall xFx \& \forall xGx$ A
2. Show $\forall x(Fx \& Gx)$
3. Show $Fa \& Ga$
4. $\forall xFx$ &E, 1
5. $\forall xGx$ &E, 1
6. Fa $\forall$E, 4
7. Ga $\forall$E, 5
8. $Fa \& Ga$ &I, 6, 7

48.
1. $\forall x(Fx \leftrightarrow (\neg Gx \vee \neg Fx))$ A
2. Show $\forall x\neg Gx$
3. Show $\neg Ga$
4. $\neg\neg Ga$ AIP
5. Show $\neg Fa$
6. Fa AIP
7. $Fa \leftrightarrow (\neg Ga \vee \neg Fa)$ $\forall$E, 1
8. $\neg Ga \vee \neg Fa$ $\leftrightarrow$E, 7, 6
9. $\neg Fa$ $\vee$E*, 8, 4
10. $Fa \leftrightarrow (\neg Ga \vee \neg Fa)$ $\forall$E, 1
11. $\neg(\neg Ga \vee \neg Fa)$ $\leftrightarrow$E, 10, 9
12. $\neg\neg Ga \& \neg\neg Fa$ $\neg\vee$, 11
13. $\neg\neg Fa$ &E, 12

54.
1.	$\forall x(Fx \to (Gx \lor Hx))$		A
2.	$\forall x((Jx \& Fx) \to \neg Gx)$		A
3.	$\forall x(\neg Fx \to \neg Jx)$		A
4.	Show $\forall x(Jx \to Hx)$		
5.	Show $Ja \to Ha$		
6.	Ja		ACP
7.	$\neg Fa \to \neg Ja$		$\forall$E, 3
8.	$\neg\neg Ja$		$\neg\neg$, 6
9.	$\neg\neg Fa$		$\to$E*, 7, 8
10.	Fa		$\neg\neg$, 9
11.	$Ja \& Fa$		&I, 6, 10
12.	$(Ja \& Fa) \to \neg Ga$		$\forall$E, 2
13.	$\neg Ga$		$\to$E, 12, 11
14.	$Fa \to (Ga \lor Ha)$		$\forall$E, 1
15.	$Ga \lor Ha$		$\to$E, 14, 10
16.	Ha		$\lor$E*, 15, 13

60.
1.	$\forall x\forall y\forall z((Fxy \& Fxz) \to Fyz)$	A
2.	Show $\forall x\forall y\forall z((Fxy \& Fxz) \to Fzy)$	
3.	Show $\forall y\forall z((Fay \& Faz) \to (Fzy)$	
4.	Show $\forall z(Fac \& Faz) \to Fzc)$	
5.	Show $(Fac \& Fab) \to Fbc$	
6.	$Fac \& Fab$	ACP
7.	$\forall y\forall z((Fay \& Faz) \to Fyz)$	$\forall$E, 1
8.	$\forall z((Fab \& Faz) \to Fbz)$	$\forall$E, 7
9.	$(Fab \& Fac) \to Fbc$	$\forall$E, 8
10.	Fab	&E, 6
11.	Fac	&E, 6
12.	$Fab \& Fac$	&I, 10, 11
13.	Fbc	$\to$E, 9, 12

IIB.3 Derived Rules for Quantifiers

1.
1.	$\exists x\exists yFxy$	A
2.	Show $\exists y\exists xFxy$	
3.	$\exists yFay$	$\exists$E, 1
4.	Fab	$\exists$E, 3
5.	$\exists xFxb$	$\exists$I, 4
6.	$\exists y\exists xFxy$	$\exists$I, 5

2.
1.	$\forall x\forall yFxy$	A
2.	Show $\forall y\forall xFxy$	
3.	Show $\forall xFxb$	
4.	Show Fab	
5.	$\forall yFay$	$\forall$E, 1
6.	Fab	$\forall$E, 5

3.
1.	$\exists x\forall yFxy$	A
2.	Show $\forall y\exists xFxy$	
3.	Show $\exists xFxb$	
4.	$\forall yFay$	$\exists$E, 1
5.	Fab	$\forall$E, 4
6.	$\exists xFxb$	$\exists$I, 5

4.
1.	$\forall x\exists y(Fx \& Gy)$	A
2.	Show $\exists y\forall x(Fx \& Gy)$	
3.	Show $\forall x(Fx \& Gd)$	
4.	Show $Fa \& Gd$	
5.	$\exists y(Fa \& Gy)$	$\forall$E, 1
6.	$Fa \& Gb$	$\exists$E, 5
7.	$\exists y(Fc \& Gy)$	$\forall$E, 1
8.	$Fc \& Gd$	$\exists$E, 7
9.	Fa	&E, 6
10.	Gd	&E, 8
11.	$Fa \& Gd$	&I, 9, 10
12.	$\exists y\forall x(Fx \& Gy)$	$\exists$I, 3

12.
1.	$\forall x(\exists yFxy \rightarrow \forall yFyx)$		A
2.	$\exists x\exists yFxy$		A
3.	Show $\forall x\forall yFxy$		
4.	Show $\forall yFcy$		
5.	Show Fcb		
6.	$\exists yFay$		$\exists$E, 2
7.	$\exists yFay \rightarrow \forall yFya$		$\forall$E, 1
8.	$\forall yFya$		$\rightarrow$E, 7, 6
9.	Fba		$\forall$E, 8
10.	$\exists yFby$		$\exists$I, 9
11.	$\exists yFby \rightarrow \forall yFyb$		$\forall$E, 1
12.	$\forall yFyb$		$\rightarrow$E, 11, 10
13.	Fcb		$\forall$E, 12

From 13.4

1.
1.	$\forall x((Tx \& Lx) \rightarrow Dx)$	A
2.	Show $\forall x((Tx \& Cx) \rightarrow \neg Dx) \rightarrow \forall x((Tx \& Cx) \rightarrow \neg Lx)$	
3.	$\forall x((Tx \& Cx) \rightarrow \neg Dx)$	ACP
4.	Show $\forall x((Tx \& Cx) \rightarrow \neg Lx)$	
5.	Show $(Ta \& Ca) \rightarrow \neg La$	
6.	$Ta \& Ca$	ACP
7.	$(Ta \& Ca) \rightarrow \neg Da$	$\forall$E, 3
8.	$\neg Da$	$\rightarrow$E, 7, 6
9.	$(Ta \& La) \rightarrow Da$	$\forall$E, 1
10.	$\neg(Ta \& La)$	$\rightarrow$E*, 9, 8
11.	$\neg Ta \lor \neg La$	$\neg$&, 10
12.	$Ta \rightarrow \neg La$	$\rightarrow\lor$, 11
13.	Ta	&E, 6
14.	$\neg La$	$\rightarrow$E, 12, 13

2.
1.	$\neg\exists x(Ix \& Tx)$	A
2.	$\forall x(Sx \rightarrow Tx)$	A
3.	$\forall x(Px \leftrightarrow \neg Sx)$	A
4.	Show $\forall x(Ix \rightarrow Px)$	
5.	Show $Ia \rightarrow Pa$	
6.	Ia	ACP
7.	$\forall x\neg(Ix \& Tx)$	QN, 1
8.	$\neg(Ia \& Ta)$	$\forall$E, 7
9.	$Sa \rightarrow Ta$	$\forall$E, 2
10.	$Pa \leftrightarrow \neg Sa$	$\forall$E, 3
11.	$\neg Ia \lor \neg Ta$	$\neg$&, 8
12.	$\neg\neg Ia$	$\neg\neg$, 6
13.	$\neg Ta$	$\lor$E*, 11, 12
14.	$\neg Sa$	$\rightarrow$E*, 9, 13
15.	Pa	$\leftrightarrow$E, 10, 14

3.

1.	$\neg \exists x((Mx \ \& \ Fx) \ \& \ \neg Bx)$	A
2.	$\forall x(Cx \rightarrow Mx)$	A
3.	$\neg \exists x(Cx \ \& \ Bx)$	A
4.	Show $\neg \exists x(Fx \ \& \ Cx)$	
5.	$\exists x(Fx \ \& \ Cx)$	AIP
6.	$Fa \ \& \ Ca$	$\exists$E, 5
7.	Fa	&E, 6
8.	Ca	&E, 6
9.	$Ca \rightarrow Ma$	$\forall$E, 2
10.	Ma	$\rightarrow$E, 9, 8
11.	$\forall x \neg((Mx \ \& \ Fx) \ \& \ \neg Bx)$	QN, 1
12.	$\forall x \neg(Cx \ \& \ Bx)$	QN, 3
13.	$\neg(Ca \ \& \ Ba)$	$\forall$E, 12
14.	$\neg((Ma \ \& \ Fa) \ \& \ \neg Ba)$	$\forall$E, 11
15.	$\neg(Ma \ \& \ Fa) \vee \neg \neg Ba$	$\neg$&, 14
16.	$Ma \ \& \ Fa$	&I, 10, 7
17.	$\neg \neg(Ma \ \& \ Fa)$	$\neg \neg$, 16
18.	$\neg \neg Ba$	$\vee$ E*, 15, 17
19.	Ba	$\neg \neg$, 18
20.	$Ca \ \& \ Ba$	&I, 8, 19

4.

1.	$\forall x(Sx \rightarrow \neg Dx)$	A
2.	$\forall x(Chx \rightarrow Sx)$	A
3.	$\forall x(\neg Dx \rightarrow Bixh)$	A
4.	Show $\forall x(Chx \rightarrow Bixh)$	
5.	Show $Cha \rightarrow Biah$	
6.	Cha	ACP
7.	$Cha \rightarrow Sa$	$\forall$E, 2
8.	Sa	$\rightarrow$E, 7, 6
9.	$Sa \rightarrow \neg Da$	$\forall$E, 1
10.	$\neg Da$	$\rightarrow$E, 9, 8
11.	$\neg Da \rightarrow Biah$	$\forall$E, 3
12.	$Biah$	$\rightarrow$E, 11, 10

5.

1.	$\neg \exists x(Gx \ \& \ \neg Rx)$	A
2.	$\forall x(\exists y(Ty \ \& \ Ixy) \rightarrow Fx)$	A
3.	$\neg \exists x(Fx \ \& \ Rx)$	A
4.	Show $\forall x(\exists y(Ty \ \& \ Ixy) \rightarrow \neg Gx)$	
5.	Show $\exists y(Ty \ \& \ Iay) \rightarrow \neg Ga$	
6.	$\exists y(Ty \ \& \ Iay)$	ACP
7.	$\exists y(Ty \ \& \ Iay) \rightarrow Fa$	$\forall$E, 2
8.	Fa	$\rightarrow$E, 7, 6
9.	$\forall x \neg(Fx \ \& \ Rx)$	QN, 3
10.	$\neg(Fa \ \& \ Ra)$	$\forall$E, 9
11.	$\forall x \neg(Gx \ \& \ \neg Rx)$	QN, 1
12.	$\neg(Ga \ \& \ \neg Ra)$	$\forall$E, 11
13.	Show $\neg Ga$	
14.	Ga	AIP
15.	Show Ra	
16.	$\neg Ra$	AIP
17.	$Ga \ \& \ \neg Ra$	&I, 14, 16
18.	$\neg(Ga \ \& \ \neg Ra)$	R, 12
19.	$Fa \ \& \ Ra$	&I, 8, 15
20.	$\neg(Fa \ \& \ Ra)$	R, 10

6.
1. $\forall x((Px \,\&\, \exists y(By \,\&\, Hxy)) \rightarrow Lx)$ A
2. $\forall x((Px \,\&\, \neg\exists y(By \,\&\, Hxy)) \rightarrow \neg Fx)$ A
3. $\neg\exists x((Px \,\&\, Rxb) \,\&\, Lx)$ A
4. Show $\neg\exists x((Px \,\&\, Rxb) \,\&\, Fx)$
5. $\neg\neg\exists x((Px \,\&\, Rxb) \,\&\, Fx)$ AIP
6. $\exists x((Px \,\&\, Rxb) \,\&\, Fx)$ $\neg\neg$, 5
7. $(Pa \,\&\, Rab) \,\&\, Fa$ $\exists$E, 6
8. $\forall x\neg((Px \,\&\, Rxb) \,\&\, Lx)$ QN, 3
9. $\neg((Pa \,\&\, Rab) \,\&\, La)$ $\forall$E, 8
10. $Pa \,\&\, Rab$ &E, 7
11. $\neg(Pa \,\&\, Rab) \vee \neg La$ $\neg$&, 9
12. $\neg\neg(Pa \,\&\, Rab)$ $\neg\neg$, 10
13. $\neg La$ $\vee$E*, 11, 12
14. $(Pa \,\&\, \exists y(By \,\&\, Hay)) \rightarrow La$ $\forall$E, 1
15. $\neg(Pa \,\&\, \exists y(By \,\&\, Hay))$ $\rightarrow$E*, 14, 13
16. $\neg Pa \vee \neg\exists y(By \,\&\, Hay)$ $\neg$&, 15
17. Pa &E, 10
18. $\neg\neg Pa$ $\neg\neg$, 17
19. $\neg\exists y(By \,\&\, Hay)$ $\vee$E*, 16, 18
20. $(Pa \,\&\, \neg\exists y(By \,\&\, Hay)) \rightarrow \neg Fa$ $\forall$E, 2
21. $Pa \,\&\, \neg\exists y(By \,\&\, Hay)$ &I, 17, 19
22. $\neg Fa$ $\rightarrow$E, 20, 21
23. Fa &E, 7

12.
1. $\forall x\exists y(Fx \,\&\, Gy)$ A
2. Show $\exists y\forall x(Fx \,\&\, Gy)$
3. $\neg\exists y\forall x(Fx \,\&\, Gy)$ AIP
4. $\exists y(Fa \,\&\, Gy)$ $\forall$E, 1
5. $Fa \,\&\, Gb$ $\exists$E, 4
6. $\forall y\exists x\neg(Fx \,\&\, Gy)$ QN^2, 3
7. $\exists x\neg(Fx \,\&\, Gb)$ $\forall$E, 6
8. $\neg(Fc \,\&\, Gb)$ $\exists$E, 7
9. $\neg Fc \vee \neg Gb$ $\neg$&, 8
10. Gb &E, 5
11. $\neg\neg Gb$ $\neg\neg$, 10
12. $\neg Fc$ $\vee$E*, 9, 11
13. $\exists y(Fc \,\&\, Gy)$ $\forall$E, 1
14. $Fc \,\&\, Gd$ $\exists$E, 13
15. Fc &E, 14

18.
1. $\forall x(Fx \rightarrow Gx)$ A
2. Show $\forall xFx \rightarrow \forall xGx$
3. $\forall xFx$ ACP
4. Show $\forall xGx$
5. Show Ga
6. $Fa \rightarrow Ga$ $\forall$E, 1
7. Fa $\forall$E, 3
8. Ga $\rightarrow$E, 6, 7

24.
1. $\forall x(Fx \rightarrow \neg Gx)$ A
2. Show $\neg\exists x(Fx \,\&\, Gx)$
3. Show $\forall x\neg(Fx \,\&\, Gx)$
4. Show $\neg(Fa \,\&\, Ga)$
5. $Fa \rightarrow \neg Ga$ $\forall$E, 1
6. $\neg Fa \vee \neg Ga$ $\rightarrow\vee$, 5
7. $\neg(Fa \,\&\, Ga)$ $\neg$&, 6
8. $\neg\exists x(Fx \,\&\, Gx)$ QN, 3

30.
1. $\forall x(Fx \leftrightarrow Gx)$ A
2. Show $\exists xFx \leftrightarrow \exists xGx$
3. Show $\exists xFx \rightarrow \exists xGx$
4. $\exists xFx$ ACP
5. Fa $\exists$E, 4
6. $Fa \leftrightarrow Ga$ $\forall$E, 1
7. Ga $\leftrightarrow$E, 6, 5
8. $\exists xGx$ $\exists$I, 7
9. Show $\exists xGx \rightarrow \exists xFx$
10. $\exists xGx$ ACP
11. Gb $\exists$E, 10
12. $Fb \leftrightarrow Gb$ $\forall$E, 1
13. Fb $\leftrightarrow$E, 12, 11
14. $\exists xFx$ $\exists$I, 13
15. $\exists xFx \leftrightarrow \exists xGx$ $\leftrightarrow$I, 3, 9

36.
1. $\neg\exists x(Hxa \;\&\; \neg Gxb)$ A
2. $\forall x\neg(Fxc \;\&\; Fbx)$ A
3. $\forall x(Gex \to Fxe)$ A
4. Show $\neg(Hea \;\&\; Fec)$
5. $\lceil Hea \;\&\; Fec$ AIP
6. $\mid \forall x\neg(Hxa \;\&\; \neg Gxb)$ QN, 1
7. $\mid \neg(Hea \;\&\; \neg Geb)$ $\forall$E, 6
8. $\mid \neg Hea \lor \neg\neg Geb$ $\neg\&$, 7
9. $\mid Hea$ &E, 5
10. $\mid \neg\neg Hea$ $\neg\neg$, 9
11. $\mid \neg\neg Geb$ $\lor$E*, 8, 10
12. $\mid \neg(Fec \;\&\; Fbe)$ $\forall$E, 2
13. $\mid \neg Fec \lor \neg Fbe$ $\neg\&$, 12
14. $\mid Fec$ &E, 5
15. $\mid \neg\neg Fec$ $\neg\neg$, 14
16. $\mid \neg Fbe$ $\lor$ E*, 13, 15
17. $\mid Geb \to Fbe$ $\forall$E, 3
18. $\lfloor \neg Geb$ $\to$E*, 17, 16

42.
1. $\exists xFx \to \forall y((Fy \lor Gy) \to Hy)$ A
2. $\exists xHx$ A
3. $\neg\forall z\neg Fz$ A
4. Show $\exists x(Fx \;\&\; Hx)$
5. $\lceil \exists z\neg\neg Fz$ QN, 3
6. $\mid \neg\neg Fa$ $\exists$E, 5
7. $\mid Fa$ $\neg\neg$, 6
8. $\mid \exists xFx$ $\exists$I, 7
9. $\mid \forall y((Fy \lor Gy) \to Hy)$ $\to$E, 1, 8
10. $\mid (Fa \lor Ga) \to Ha$ $\forall$E, 9
11. $\mid Fa \lor Ga$ $\lor$I, 7
12. $\mid Ha$ $\to$E, 10, 110
13. $\mid Fa \;\&\; Ha$ &I, 7, 12
14. $\lfloor \exists x(Fx \;\&\; Hx)$ $\exists$I, 13

48.
1. $\forall x\neg Fxx$ A
2. Show $\neg\exists x\forall y(Fyx \leftrightarrow \exists z\forall w((Fwz \to Fwy) \;\&\; \neg Fzy))$
3. $\lceil \exists x\forall y(Fyx \leftrightarrow \exists z\forall w((Fwz \to Fwy) \;\&\; \neg Fzy))$ AIP
4. $\mid \forall y(Fya \leftrightarrow \exists z\forall w((Fwz \to Fwy) \;\&\; \neg Fzy))$ $\exists$E, 3
5. $\mid Faa \leftrightarrow \exists z\forall w((Fwz \to Fwa) \;\&\; \neg Fza)$ $\forall$E, 4
6. $\mid \neg Faa$ $\forall$E, 1
7. $\mid \neg\exists z\forall w((Fwz \to Fwa) \;\&\; \neg Fza)$ $\leftrightarrow$E, 5, 6
8. $\mid \forall z\exists w\neg((Fwz \to Fwa) \;\&\; \neg Fza)$ QN^2, 7
9. $\mid \exists w\neg((Fwa \to Fwa) \;\&\; \neg Faa)$ $\forall$E, 8
10. $\mid \neg((Fba \to Fba) \;\&\; \neg Faa)$ $\exists$E, 9
11. $\mid$ Show $Fba \to Fba$
12. $\mid \lceil Fba$ ACP
13. $\mid \lfloor (Fba \to Fba) \;\&\; \neg Faa$ &I, 11, 6

INDEX

A, 232, 360
Absorption, 223
Accent, 99–100
Accident, 83–84
Accommodation, 43–44, 56, 63, 72
Accuracy, 405–407
Addition, 197, 204, 484, 497
Ad hominem, 46–53
 abusive, 46–48, 49, 50
 circumstantial, 46, 48–50
 tu quoque, 50–53
Adjectives and adjectival phrases, 230,
 314–16
Adverbs and adverbial modifiers, 322–24
Agreement, 431–34, 436–37
AL, 236
AL*, 276
Ambiguity, 90–95, 104–105, 109, 119,
 127–28, 427
 in grouping, 127–28
 referential, 94–95
 syntactic, 93–94, 119, 127–28
Amphiboly, 93–95
Analogy, 400, 412–17
Anselm of Canterbury, 14, 36n, 152
Antecedent, 123
Appeal to
 authority, 79–82
 common practice, 70–72
 emotion, 64–65
 fear, 72–75
 force, 72–75
 ignorance, 78–79
 the people, 65–67, 105–106
 pity, 75–76, 101
Application (of a predicate), 231, 290
Aquinas, Saint Thomas, 14, 36n, 347
Argument, 3–7, 17–18, 36n, 37–38, 49, 62, 66
 by analogy, 413–14
 and argument form validity, 133, 146, 150
 definition, 3, 36n

and explanation, 451, 464–65
 extended, 3, 5
 good, 17–19
 simple, 3, 5
 soundness, 22, 23
 standard form, 4–5
 statistical, 403
 successful, 17, 19, 38
 validity, 20–22, 24–25, 394–98
Argument form, 117, 133
 and argument validity, 133, 146, 150
 definition, 133
 validity, 135, 145, 173, 186, 208, 227
Aristotle, 2, 23, 38, 61n, 108, 138n, 152,
 205, 230, 243–46, 249–50, 253, 263,
 271, 275, 288n, 364, 368, 390
Arnauld, Antoine, 61n, 288n
Associativity, 199, 205, 210, 218, 491–92,
 500, 541, 550
Assumption, 186–88, 472, 506–507, 518
 auxiliary, 454, 461
 for conditional proof, 481–82, 530–31
 for indirect proof, 226–27, 479–80,
 526–27
 introducing, 188, 203, 226–27, 521–22
 shared in conversation, 17–19, 43–44,
 62–63, 66, 73. *See also* Common
 ground
Assumption rule, 188, 203, 475, 496, 522,
 546
Atomic
 formula, 119
 sentence, 126–27, 289–90
Audience, 6, 17–19, 62–63, 66–67
Authority, 79–82
Auxiliary assumptions, 454, 461

Bacon, Francis, 431
Begging the question, 39–41, 61n
Bernays, Paul, 225, 228n
Beth, E. W., 185n

Bias, 401, 404, 409–10
Biconditional, 124
  deduction rules, 195, 204, 209, 214, 217, 483–84, 497, 531–33
  exploitation, 214, 217, 532–33, 547
  exploitation*, 542, 548
  introduction, 531–32, 547
  rule, 195, 204, 483
  tableau rules, 168–69
Biconditional–conditional, 491–98, 540, 548
Boethius, 154
Boole, George, 138n
Bracket, 474–75, 480, 520–22, 527–28
Brahe, Tycho, 461
Branch
  closed, 156, 160, 165–66, 172–73
  definition, 155–56
  and interpretations, 160–61, 169–71
  open, 156, 160
  splitting, 156, 164–65
Burleigh, Walter, 228n

Callimachus, 138n
Carroll, Lewis, 155, 270, 274, 285, 287, 352, 368
Categorical proof, 186–87, 226, 472–73, 517
Categorical sentence form, 233–40, 294–96
  particular affirmative, 233–34, 238–39, 254–55, 295
  particular negative, 233–35, 239–40, 256
  universal affirmative, 233, 236–37, 254, 294–95
  universal negative, 233–34, 238, 254, 295–96
Causal
  explanation, 428, 451
  factor, 124, 431–34
  fallacy, 447–48
  generalization, 431
  reasoning, 425–449
Cause, 425–26
  definitions, 427–28
  proximate and remote, 428
Chrysippus, 138n, 152–53
Church, Alonzo, 340, 357n
Cicero, 44, 65, 152, 154
Clausal complementation, 322
Closed
  branch, 156, 160, 165–66, 172–73
  tableau, 156, 160, 173
Coercion, 72–75
Command, 6
Commas, 127–28, 317
Common ground, 17–19, 38–39, 43–44, 56, 62–66, 70–71, 74–75, 80, 314, 428
Common noun, 230, 291, 292, 311
Common practice, 70–72
Communication, 17, 40, 90. *See also* Common ground
Commutativity, 199, 205, 210, 218, 491–92,

  500, 540–41, 550
Complement, 247–48, 276, 288n
Completeness, 208, 358, 486, 501, 535, 551
Complex question, 43–45
Complex rule, 473, 519
Component, 114–16, 126–27
Composition, 101–102
Compound
  question, 44
  sentence, 114–16
Conclusion, 3–7, 69, 186, 417
  indicators, 7–8
Concomitant variation, 440–42, 447–48
Conditional, 123–24, 138n
  deduction rules, 193–95, 198–99, 208–216, 380–81, 387, 481–82, 529–31
  exploitation, 529–30, 547
  exploitation*, 541–42, 548
  proof, 481–82, 497, 530–31, 547
  and quantifiers, 312–14, 380–81
  tableau rules, 167–68
Conditional-disjunction, 539, 550
Condition, necessary and sufficient, 426
Confidence, 405–407
Confirmation, 454, 459–60, 467–68
Confusing the issue, 56–58
Conjunction, 122, 127, 314, 316, 318
  connectives, 122, 127
  deduction rules, 189–90, 201–203, 210, 215, 382, 387, 475–77, 491–92, 496, 522–25
  exploitation, 523–24, 546
  introduction, 524–25, 547
  reduction, 128
  rule, 190, 203, 477
  tableau rules, 162–63
Connective, 114–18, 303, 307, 324–25
  binary, 115–16
  main, 120, 161, 192
  multigrade, 121–22
  n-ary, 115
  scope, 120
  singulary, 115–16
  truth-functional, 114–17, 121, 139
  unary, 115–16
Consequent, 123
  conjunction, 191, 203
Conservative
  instance, 358, 366, 501, 506–507
  rule, 392n, 517n, 562n
Constant, 291, 298–99, 303, 306, 311, 334, 345–47, 360
Constructive dilemma, 198, 204, 211, 494, 498
Context, 6–7, 17–19, 90, 94, 105, 314, 427–28, 466
Contingent
  formulas, 135, 139, 143, 176–77
  sentences, 29–30
Contradiction, 30, 225, 479

rule, 216–17, 494, 499, 543–44, 549
Contradictories, 242–46, 250, 280–81
Contradictory
    formulas, 135, 139, 143, 176–77
    sentences, 30
Contraposition, 248, 250
Contraries, 243, 245, 250
Contrastive stress, 99–100
Control group, 436–37
Conversation, 17, 44, 46, 56, 62–63, 66, 80,
    314, 428, 466. *See also* Common
    ground
Converse, 237–40, 242, 250
Coordinate phrases, 128
Copernicus, 461, 470
Copi, Irving, 228n
Correlation, 441–42, 448
Covering law, 451–52, 466–68
C-variant, 307

Decidable property, 149
Decision procedure, 149, 155, 340
Deduction system, 186, 208, 472, 486, 501,
    518, 535, 551
Deductive validity, 20–22, 394–398
Definition, 104–109, 331–36
    analytical, 106, 108
    circular, 108, 332, 334
    clarifying, 104–105
    denotative, 106
    descriptive, 104
    goals, 104–106
    lexical, 104
    means, 106
    modern rules, 331–36
    ostensive, 106
    per genus et differentiae, 106, 108
    persuasive, 105–106
    stipulative, 104
    synonymous, 106, 108
    traditional rules, 107–109, 331, 335
Demonstrative premise, 23
DeMorgan, Augustus, 201, 228n
DeMorgan's laws, 201–203, 205, 208,
    487–88, 499, 536
Dependence, 366, 372, 506, 508–11
Dependency diagram, 373–74, 508–10
Derived rule, 208, 486, 512, 535, 557
Determiner, 231–32, 265, 289, 291, 312–14
Dialectical premise, 23
Dictionary, 126
Difference, method of, 434–37
Diodorus, 138n
Direct
    object, 322
    proof, 520
Disjunction, 122
    deduction rules, 197–203, 214–15, 379,
        386, 484–85, 491–92, 533–34
    exploitation, 534, 548

exploitation*, 543, 549
    tableau rules, 163–64
Disjunction introduction, 533–34, 547
Disjunctive syllogism, 214–17, 485, 497
Dispatch marks, 156, 342
Distribution
    of terms, 264–65, 288n
    rule, 215, 219
Division, 101–102
Dogdson, Charles, 155. *See also* Carroll,
    Lewis
Domain, 237, 292, 294, 299, 305–307, 314
Double negation, 191–92, 204, 277, 478,
    499, 525–26, 548

Effect, 425–26
Einstein, Albert, 459, 465
Eliminability, 331, 334–35
Eliminative method, 441
Emotion, 64–65
Entailment. *See* Implication
Enthymeme, 273
Enumeration
    incomplete, 82–83
    inductive, 398–400, 404
Equivalence
    in definition, 107–108
    formulas, 135, 148–49, 174–75
    and implication, 25–26, 174
    sentences, 25–26
Equivocation, 90–92
Error, margin of, 405–407
Essence, 83–84, 107–108, 335
Eubulides, 36n
Euler, Leonhard, 236, 263, 288n
Event, 425–28
Evidence, 18, 37–39, 45, 61n, 458–60, 465,
    467
Existential
    exploitation, 552–54, 560–62
    generalization, 359, 385, 502
    import, 244–47, 249–50
    introduction, 552, 560
    quantifier. *See* Quantifier, existential
    specification, 359–60, 372, 385, 391–92n,
        502–505, 516–17n
Expert, 80–82
Explanation, 428
    and argument, 451, 464–65
    causal, 428, 451
    covering law, 451–52
    dormitive virtue, 465–66
    power, 467–69
Exportation, 223
Extension, 231, 237–38, 265, 277, 288n, 290

Fallacy, 38, 43, 46, 57–58, 65, 72, 79–80,
    83–84, 100, 102
False dilemma, 82–83
Fear, 72–75

Felicitous assertion, 39–41
Figure, 264, 274
Fine, Kit, 392n, 517n, 562n
Finished tableau, 156
First-order logic, 305
Fluellenism, 83
Force, 72–75
Formation rules, 118
  AL, 236
  AL*, 276
  QL, 304
  SL, 119
Formula, 118–19
  AL, 236
  AL*, 276
  atomic, 119, 126
  contingent, 135, 139, 143, 176–77
  contradictory, 135, 139, 143, 176–77
  dead, 156
  dispatched, 156
  live, 156
  logically true, 135, 139, 143, 176–77,
    186, 208, 228
  QL, 291, 303–304
  satisfiable, 135, 139, 143, 176–77
  and sentences, 118, 126–27, 133, 144, 150
  SL, 118–19
  tautologous, 135, 139, 143, 176–77, 186,
    208, 228
  valid, 135, 139, 143, 176–77, 186, 208,
    228
Free lines, 480, 527–28
Frege, Gottlob, 224, 228, 289
Function, 115, 121, 138n
Functional completeness, 125, 201

Geach, Peter, 36n
Generalization
  causal, 431
  hasty, 401
  inductive, 399–401
  statistical, 403–10
General term, 230–32, 263, 290–92, 298
Generic formula, 341, 358, 501, 551
Generics, 232, 213
Gentzen, Gerhard, 185n, 228n
Gilbert, G. K., 424n
Grammar, 93–94, 118, 311
Grelling's paradox, 35–36
Grouping, 122–23, 126–28, 210, 491–92,
  540–41
  indicator, 118

Hasty generalization, 401
Heim, Irene, 392n, 517n, 562n
Higher-order logic, 305
Hilbert, David, 225, 228n
Hintikka, Jaakko, 185n
Homogeneity, 401, 407–10
Hunter, John, 458

Hypothesis, 23, 186–87, 414, 452–53,
  458–60, 465, 472, 519
Hypothetical
  proof, 186–88, 226, 472
  reasoning, 452–56
  syllogism, 212–13, 217

Idempotence, 210–11, 218, 225
Ignorance, 78–79
Ignoratio elenchi, 56–57
Illicit process, 267
Implication
  and equivalence, 25–26
  between formulas, 135, 147–48, 173
  between sentences, 24–25, 243, 250, 394,
    454
Incomplete enumeration, 82–83
Inconsistency, 50–53
Indirect object, 322
Indirect proof, 225–228, 479–80, 486–87,
  496, 498, 526–27, 535–36, 545–46
Induction, 394–95, 425, 452
Inductive reliability, 22, 394–398, 400–401,
  404–10, 415–17
Instance
  of formula, 341, 358, 366, 501, 551
  in induction, 399–400
Interpretation
  in AL, 256, 258
  function, 305–307
  in QL, 305
  searches for, 155, 160–61, 172–73
  in SL, 134–35, 139–41
  and tableau branches, 160–61, 169–73,
    344
Intersective adjective, 315
Intransitive verb, 322
Invertible rule, 192, 195, 198–99, 202,
  204–205, 218–19, 386–88, 478–79, 526
Issue, 18, 45–46, 56–58, 90, 466–67

Jaskowski, Stanislaw, 228n
Jesuits of Coimbra, 288n
Junge, Joachim, 390

Kamp, Hans, 392n, 517n, 562n
Karttunen, Lauri, 61n
Kepler, Johannes, 468–69
Kilwardby, Robert, 228n

Law, 451–52, 459
Leaves, 155–56
Leibniz, Gottfried, 354
Lemma, 473
Lesniewski, Stanislaw, 331
Lewis, David, 61n
Lightman, Alan P., 424n
Live formula, 156
Logical truth, 29, 30, 135, 139, 143,
  175–77, 186, 208, 228

Lukasiewicz, Jan, 224

Main
  column, 139, 142
  connective, 120, 142, 161
Major
  premise, 263
  term, 263
Margin of error, 405–407
Material
  conditional, 198–99, 205, 490, 500
  equivalence, 223
Meaning, 90–111
Mendel, Gregor, 462
Metalanguage, 118–19
Metaphor, 413
Middle term, 263
Mill, John Stuart, 91, 394, 424n, 425,
  431–32, 434, 449n
Mill's methods, 425, 431–42, 447–48
  agreement, 431–34
  agreement and difference, 436–37
  concomitant variation, 440–42, 447–48
  difference, 434–36
  residues, 440
Minor
  premise, 263
  term, 263
Misapplication, 63–65, 75, 78, 83–84
Miscommunication, 90
Model. *See* Interpretation
Modeling, 415
Modus both-ends, 483–84, 493, 497, 498
Modus ponens, 187, 193–94, 204, 211, 214,
  474, 481, 483, 497, 529
Modus tollens, 211, 214, 216, 492–93, 498,
  541
Mood, 264, 274
Motive, 49–50
Multigrade connective, 121

Name, 231, 290–91, 311
Natural
  deduction system, 186, 208, 472, 486,
  501, 518, 535, 551
  language, 3
Necessary condition, 107, 426
Negated
  biconditional, 209, 218
  conditional, 208–209, 218
Negation, 115–16, 121–22, 276–77, 280
  deduction rules, 191–93, 201–203,
  208–209, 211, 213, 477–78, 487–89,
  525–27
  exploitation/introduction. *See* Double
  negation
  quantifier, 377–78, 386, 513–14, 516,
  558–61
  tableau rules, 161–62
Negation-biconditional, 538, 549

Negation-conditional, 538, 549
Negation-conjunction, 536, 549
Negation-disjunction, 537, 549
Negative result, 460–62
Newton, Isaac, 459, 462 465, 468–70
Noncontradiction, 202
Noncreativity, 331, 335
Nonintersective adjective, 315–16, 322
Noun phrases, 230–32, 290, 311, 318

Object language, 118–19
Obligation, 69–71
Observed instance, 399–400
Obversion, 248–50
Ockham's razor, 469
Ockham, William of, 32, 228n, 391n, 469,
  516n, 561n
Only, 233, 314
Opposition, square of, 243–50
Other things being equal, 63–65, 70–71,
  74–75

Paradox, 34–36
Parentheses, 118–19, 124, 127–28, 141–42,
  189, 303–305
Participle, 230
Particular
  affirmative sentence, 233–34, 238–39, 295
  negative sentence, 233–35, 239–40
Passage, rules of, 376–82, 386–87
Peirce, Charles Sanders, 289, 487, 536
People, appeal to the, 65–67, 105–6
Persuasion, 7, 17, 19, 49, 51, 72, 105–6
Peter of Spain, 288n
Philo of Megara, 138n
Plato, 64
Polish notation, 124–25
Poll, 403–404, 406, 408–10
Polyadic predicate, 298, 322, 356
Population, 401, 407–10
Port Royal Logic, 38, 262, 288n
Post hoc, ergo propter hoc, 447
Post, Emil L., 154n
Power, 467–69
Practical reasoning, 69–70
Predicate logic, 230
Predicates, 230–32, 247–48, 253, 276, 291,
  298, 303, 306, 311, 322, 332–33
Premise, 3–5, 36n
  additional, 396–97
  demonstrative, 23
  dialectical, 23
  indicators, 7–8
  relation to conclusion, 7, 17–21, 37–38,
  62, 394–95, 417, 465
Prepositional phrases, 318–323
Presupposition, 39–40, 43, 61n, 63, 99–100
Primitives, 332
Probability, 22, 397–398, 415
Pronouns, 94–95, 231

Proof, 186, 472, 474, 480, 518
 by cases, 198, 534
 categorical, 186–87, 226, 472–73, 518
 conditional, 481–82, 497, 530–31, 547
 direct, 520, 545
 hypothetical, 186–88, 226, 472–75, 518
 indirect, 225–28, 479–80, 486–87, 496,
  498, 526–27, 535–36, 545–46
 strategies, 219–20, 473, 495–96, 544–45
 subordinate and superordinate, 473, 519
 universal, 556–57
Proper names, 231, 290–91, 311
Protoformula, 303, 376–77
Pseudo-Scot, 228n, 288n
Ptolemy, 461–62, 470
Putnam, Hilary, 471n

QL, 303–304
Quality, 233, 265
Quantifier, 289, 292–93, 298–99, 303, 376
 deduction rules, 358–62, 501–16, 552–62
 existential, 289, 312–24, 341–42
 negation, 377–78, 386, 513–14, 516,
  558–61
 scope, 301, 304, 313
 semantics, 307, 314
 tableau rules, 341–44
 universal, 289, 293–94, 312–14, 343–44
Quantity, 233, 265
Question, 6, 43–45
Quine, Willard van Orman, 391n, 516n,
  561n

Random sample, 408
Range of quantifiers, 292, 294, 299, 305,
  314
Red herring, 57–58
Reductio ad absurdum, 226. See *also*
  Indirect proof
Referential ambiguity, 94–95
Reflexive relation, 349
Reiteration, 528–29, 547
Relation, 349
Relative clauses, 316–18
Relevance
 condition, 19, 37–38, 46, 49–52, 56, 64,
  90
 in induction, 415–16, 433–34, 466–67
Reliability, 19–20, 49–50, 80, 394–398,
  400–401, 404–10, 415–17, 431–442,
  465, 467
 deductive vs. inductive, 20–21, 394–398
Replacement, 192, 478–79, 526
Representative sample, 401, 404
Residues, 440
Response rate, 409
Root, 155–56
Rule, 63–64
Rule of inference, 186–87, 472, 518
 absorption, 223

addition, 197, 204, 484, 497
associativity, 199, 205, 210, 218, 491–92,
  500, 541, 550
assumption, 188, 203, 475, 496, 522, 546
biconditional, 195, 204, 209, 214, 483–84,
  497, 531–33
biconditional-conditional, 491, 498, 540,
  548
biconditional exploitation, 214, 217,
  532–33, 547
biconditional exploitation*, 542, 548
biconditional introduction, 531–32, 547
commutativity, 199, 205, 210, 218,
  491–92, 500, 540–41, 550
complex, 473, 519
conditional, 193–95, 198–99, 208–209,
  211–13, 215–16, 380–81, 387, 481–82,
  529–31
conditional-disjunction, 539, 550
conditional exploitation, 529–30, 547
conditional exploitation*, 541–42, 548
conjunction (connective), 189–90,
  201–203, 210, 215, 382, 387, 475–77,
  491–92, 496, 522–25
conjunction exploitation, 523–24, 546
conjunction introduction, 524–25, 547
conjunction (rule), 190, 203, 477
consequent conjunction, 191, 203
conservative, 392n, 517n, 562n
constructive dilemma, 198, 204, 211, 494,
  498
contradiction, 216–17, 494, 499, 543–44,
  549
DeMorgan's laws, 201–203, 205, 208,
  487–88, 499, 536
derived, 208, 486, 512, 535, 557
disjunction, 197–203, 214–15, 379, 386,
  484–85, 491–92, 533–34
disjunction exploitation, 534, 548
disjunction exploitation*, 543, 549
disjunction introduction, 533–34, 547
disjunctive syllogism, 214–17, 485, 497
distribution, 215, 219
double negation, 191–92, 204, 478, 499,
  525–26, 548
existential exploitation, 552–54, 560,
  561–62n
existential generalization, 359, 385, 502
existential introduction, 552, 560
existential quantifier, 359–60, 372, 502–5,
  516, 552–54, 560
existential specification, 359–60, 372,
  385, 391–92n, 502–5, 516–17n
exportation, 223
hypothetical syllogism, 212–13, 217
idempotence, 210–11, 218, 225
introduction and exploitation, 473, 501
  519, 551
invertible, 192, 195, 198–99, 202, 204–
  205, 218–19, 386–88, 478–79, 526

material conditional, 198–99, 205, 490, 500
material equivalence, 223
modus both-ends, 483–84, 493, 497–498
modus ponens, 187, 193–94, 204, 211, 214, 474, 481, 483, 497, 529
modus tollens, 211, 214–16, 492–93, 498, 541
negated biconditional, 209, 218, 489–90, 500
negated conditional, 208–209, 218, 488–89, 499
negation, 191–93, 201–203, 208–209, 211, 213, 477–78, 487–89, 525–27
negation-biconditional, 538, 549
negation-conditional, 538, 549
negation-conjunction, 536, 549
negation-disjunction, 537, 549
negation exploitation/introduction. *See* Double negation
quantifier negation, 377–78, 386, 513–14, 516, 558–61
reiteration, 528–29, 547
rules of passage, 376–82, 386–87
self-implication, 194, 204
simple, 473, 519
simplification, 188–89, 203, 475–76, 496
thinning, 215
transposition, 213, 218
truth-preserving, 391n, 517n, 562n
universal exploitation, 555, 560
universal generalization, 366, 386, 391–92n, 506–11, 516–17n
universal quantifier, 361–62, 366, 505–11, 516, 555, 561–62
universal specification, 361–62, 385, 505
variable rewrite, 382–83, 388, 512–13, 516, 558, 561
weakening, 215–17
Rules for syllogistic validity, 263–67, 271
Russell, Bertrand, 35, 36n, 225, 400

Sample, 401, 404
  biased vs. representative, 401, 404
  random, 408
  self-selected, 409–10
  size, 401, 404–407
  stratified random, 408
  variation, 401, 408–10
Satisfaction, 231, 290
Schemata, 119, 138n
Science, 450
Scientific
  law, 451–52, 459–60
  theory, 413–14, 458–62
Scope
  connective, 120
  quantifier, 304, 313
Scotus, John Duns, 228n
Self-implication, 194, 204

Semantics, 118, 155. *See also* Interpretation
  AL*, 277
  QL, 305–308
  SL, 119
Semantic tableau, 155–85, 340–57
  closed, 156, 160, 173
  finished, 156
  nonterminating, 340, 347, 350
  open, 156, 160
  policies, 164–66, 344–47
  quantified, 340–57
Semantic tableau rules
  biconditional, 168–69
  conditional, 167–68
  conjunction, 162–63
  disjunction, 163–64
  negation, 161–62
  quantifiers, 341–44
Sentence, 4, 6, 114–15
  atomic, 126–27, 289–90
  categorical, 231–34
  component, 114–16, 126–27
  composition, 290–91
  compound, 114–16
  connective, 114–17, 120–21, 127
  construction, 93–94, 119
  context-dependence, 6–7
  contingent, 29–30
  contradictory, 30
  and formulas, 126, 144, 150
  letter, 118–19, 139, 303, 306
  logically true, 29–30
  logical properties, 29–30
  satisfiable, 30
  tautologous, 29–30
  truth value, 6, 114–15
  valid, 29–30
Sentential logic, 114, 289–90
Sextus Empiricus, 5, 126, 128, 134, 152
Show line, 519–22, 527–28
Similarity. *See* Analogy
Similar situations, 52, 76
Simile, 413
Simple rule, 473, 519
Simplicity, 467, 469–70
Simplification, 188–89, 203, 475–76, 496
SL, 117–19, 303
Slanted language, 66–67, 105–106
Smullyan, Raymond, 36n, 185n, 449n
Sorites, 287
Soundness
  argument, 22–23
  deduction system, 208, 358, 391–92n, 486, 501, 516–17n, 535, 551, 561–62n
Splitting, 156, 344
Square of opposition, 243–50
Stalnaker, Robert, 61n
Standard form
  argument, 4–5
  syllogism, 263–64

Statistical generalization, 403–10
Steamrolling. *See* Common practice
Stoics, 138n, 154, 228n
Stratified random sample, 408
Straw man, 58
Stress, 99–100
Subaltern, 243
Subcontraries, 243, 245, 250
Subformula, 119, 141–42, 478–79
Subject, 232, 298–99, 325
Subordinate proof, 473, 519
Substitution, 303
Sufficient condition, 107, 426
Superficiality, 78–79
Syllogism
    categorical, 62, 205, 212–15, 230, 253–60,
      263–70, 276–84, 289, 296
    disjunctive, 214–17, 485, 497
    hypothetical, 212–13, 217
Symbolization, 117, 125–30, 133
    QL, 311–326
    SL, 125–30, 133
Symmetric relation, 349
Synonymous definition, 106, 108
Syntactic ambiguity, 93–94
Syntax, 118–19
    AL, 236
    AL*, 276
    QL, 303–304
    SL, 118–19

Tableau. *See* Semantic tableau
Tautology, 29–30, 135, 139, 143, 175–76,
    186, 208, 228
Telescoping, 128
Temporary dispatch mark, 342
Theophrastus, 205, 364, 368
Theorem, 186, 227, 473
Thinning, 215
Threat, 72–75
Tip, 155–56
Transitive relation, 349
Transitive verb, 322, 333
Transposition, 213, 218
Tree, 119, 142, 155–56, 160
Trunk, 156
Truth, 6, 19–23, 39–40, 115, 157, 306–307,
    467
    function, 115, 121, 139, 201
    table, 136, 139–55, 160
    value, 114–15, 121, 160–61, 243–44

Truth-preserving rule, 391–92n, 516–17n,
    561–62n
Tu quoque, 50–53

Undecidability, 340
Universal
    affirmative sentence, 232–33, 294–95
    exploitation, 555, 560
    generalization, 366, 386, 391–92n,
      506–11, 516–17n
    negative sentence, 232–34, 238, 295–96
    proof, 556–557, 561
    quantifier. *See* Quantifier, universal
    specification, 361–62, 385, 505
Universe of discourse, 237, 299, 305, 314
Unless, 124

Vagueness, 104–105
Validity, deductive
    argument, 20–22, 24–25, 394–398
    argument and argument form, 117, 133,
      149–50
    argument form, 117, 133, 135, 145–47,
      173, 186, 208, 227
    formula, 135, 175–76, 186, 208, 228
    sentence, 29–30
    sentence and formula, 144, 150
Validity, rules for syllogistic, 263–67, 271
Value (of variable), 292, 314
Variable, 292–94, 303, 314
    rewrite, 382–83, 388, 512–13, 516, 558,
      561
Variation
    direct vs. inverse, 442
    in population or sample, 401, 407–10
Venn diagrams, 236–240, 244–45, 253–60,
    276–84
Venn, John, 236, 263, 288n
Verb phrases, 230–32, 290–91, 311, 322
Verbs, 230, 322, 333
Voltaire, 8

Weakening, 215–17
Weakness of will, 51–53
Whately, William, 61n
Whitehead, Alfred North, 225
William of Ockham, 32, 228n, 391n, 469,
    516n, 561n
William of Sherwood, 36n
Wittgenstein, Ludwig, 154n, 401

Zeno of Citium, 138n

DERIVED RULES

RULES APPLYING ONLY TO ENTIRE FORMULAS

Modus Tollens (MT)

n. $\mathcal{A} \to \mathcal{B}$

m. $\underline{\neg \mathcal{B}}$

p. $\neg \mathcal{A}$ MT, n, m

Disjunctive Syllogism (DS)

n. $\mathcal{A} \vee \mathcal{B}$

m. $\underline{\neg \mathcal{A}}$ (or $\neg \mathcal{B}$)

p. $\mathcal{B}$ (or $\mathcal{A}$)   DS, n, m

Hypothetical Syllogism (HS)

n. $\mathcal{A} \to \mathcal{B}$

m. $\underline{\mathcal{B} \to \mathcal{C}}$

p. $\mathcal{A} \to \mathcal{C}$ HS, n, m

Biconditional Exploitation (BE)

n. $\mathcal{A} \leftrightarrow \mathcal{B}$

m. $\underline{\mathcal{A}}$ (or $\mathcal{B}$)

p. $\mathcal{B}$ (or $\mathcal{A}$)   BE, n, m

n. $\mathcal{A} \leftrightarrow \mathcal{B}$

m. $\underline{\neg \mathcal{A}}$ (or $\neg \mathcal{B}$)

p. $\neg \mathcal{B}$ (or $\neg \mathcal{A}$)   BE, n, m

Weakening (W)

n. $(\mathcal{A} \,\&\, \mathcal{B}) \to \mathcal{A}$ (or $(\mathcal{A} \,\&\, \mathcal{B}) \to \mathcal{B}$)   W

m. $\mathcal{A} \to (\mathcal{A} \vee \mathcal{B})$ (or $\mathcal{B} \to (\mathcal{A} \vee \mathcal{B})$)   W

Contradiction (!)

n. $\mathcal{A}$

m. $\underline{\neg \mathcal{A}}$

p. $\mathcal{B}$!, n, m

INVERTIBLE RULES

Negated Conditional (NC)

n. $\underline{\underline{\neg(\mathcal{A} \to \mathcal{B})}}$ NC, m

m. $\mathcal{A} \,\&\, \neg \mathcal{B}$ NC, n

Negated Biconditional (NB)

n. $\underline{\underline{\neg(\mathcal{A} \leftrightarrow \mathcal{B})}}$ NB, m

m. $\neg \mathcal{A} \leftrightarrow \mathcal{B}$ (or $\mathcal{A} \leftrightarrow \neg \mathcal{B}$)   NB, n

Commutativity of Conjunction (Cm)

n. $\underline{\underline{\mathcal{A} \,\&\, \mathcal{B}}}$ Cm, m

m. $\mathcal{B} \,\&\, \mathcal{A}$ Cm, n

Associativity of Conjunction (As)

n. $\underline{\underline{(\mathcal{A} \,\&\, \mathcal{B}) \,\&\, \mathcal{C}}}$ As, m

m. $\mathcal{A} \,\&\, (\mathcal{B} \,\&\, \mathcal{C})$ As, n

Idempotence (I)

n. $\underline{\underline{\mathcal{A} \vee \mathcal{A}}}$ I, m

m. $\mathcal{A}$ I, n

Transposition (Tr)

n. $\underline{\underline{\mathcal{A} \to \mathcal{B}}}$ Tr, m

m. $\neg \mathcal{B} \to \neg \mathcal{A}$ Tr, n

Distribution (D)

n. $\underline{\underline{\mathcal{A} \,\&\, (\mathcal{B} \vee \mathcal{C})}}$ D, m

m. $(\mathcal{A} \,\&\, \mathcal{B}) \vee (\mathcal{A} \,\&\, \mathcal{C})$ D, n

n. $\underline{\underline{\mathcal{A} \vee (\mathcal{B} \,\&\, \mathcal{C})}}$ D, m

m. $(\mathcal{A} \vee \mathcal{B}) \,\&\, (\mathcal{A} \vee \mathcal{C})$ D, n